ANIMALS INTO ART

TITLES OF RELATED INTEREST

ANIMALS INTO ART

Edited by Howard Morphy

Department of Ethnology and Prehistory, University of Oxford

London
UNWIN HYMAN
Boston   Sydney   Wellington

Published by the Academic Division of
Unwin Hyman Ltd
15/17 Broadwick Street, London W1V 1FP, UK

Unwin Hyman Inc.,
8 Winchester Place, Winchester, Mass. 01890, USA

Allen & Unwin (Australia) Ltd,
8 Napier Street, North Sydney, NSW 2060, Australia

Allen & Unwin (New Zealand) Ltd in association with the
Port Nicholson Press Ltd
Compusales Building, 75 Ghuznee Street, Wellington 1, New Zealand

First published in 1989

British Library Cataloguing in Publication Data

Animals into art.—(One world archaeology).
1. Visual arts, to ca 499. Special subjects
Animals 2. Man. Relationships with
animals
I. Morphy, Howard II. Series
704.9'432'0901
ISBN 0–04–445030–3

Library of Congress Cataloging in Publication Data

Animals into art / edited by Howard Morphy.
    p.   cm.—(One world archaeology; 7)
Includes bibliographies and index.
ISBN 0–04–445030–3 (alk. paper)
1. Rock paintings—Congresses. 2. Animals in art—Congresses.
3. Petroglyphs—Congresses. 4. Art, Prehistoric—Congresses.
5. Art, Primitive—Congresses. I. Morphy, Howard. II. Series.
GN799.P4A55 1988
709'.01'1—dc19   88–14061
CIP

Typeset in 11 on 12 point Bembo
and printed in Great Britain by Butler & Tanner Ltd, Frome and London

List of contributors

Jose Berenguer, Museo Chileno de Arte Precolombino, Santiago, Chile.

Jean Clottes, Direction des Antiquités Préhistoriques de Midi-Pyrénées, Foix, France.

Iain Davidson, Department of Archaeology and Palaeoanthropology, University of New England, Armidale, NSW, Australia.

Whitney Davis, Department of Art History, Northwestern University, Evanston, USA.

Jeannine Drouin, Institut National des Langues et Civilisations Orientales, Paris, France.

Josephine Flood, Australian Heritage Commission, Canberra, ACT, Australia.

Ivan P. Haskovec, Australian National Parks and Wildlife Service, Jabiru, NT, Australia.

W. Fred Kinsey, III, North Museum, Franklin and Marshall College, Lancaster, USA.

Anne Legast, Independent Researcher, Geneva, Switzerland.

Michel Lorblanchet, Centre National de la Recherche Scientifique, Lot, France.

Sudha Malaiya, Department of Ancient Indian History, Culture and Archaeology, Sagar University, MP, India.

Jose Luis Martinez, Museo Chileno de Arte Precolombino, Santiago, Chile.

Brian Molyneaux, Department of Archaeology, University of Southampton, UK.

Howard Morphy, Department of Ethnology and Prehistory, Pitt Rivers Museum, University of Oxford, UK.

Osaga Odak, Institute of African Studies, University of Nairobi, Kenya.

Nancy H. Olsen, Intercultural Studies Division, De Anza College, Cupertino, California, USA.

Polly Schaafsma, Museum of New Mexico, Santa Fe, USA.

Marianne Cardale Schrimpff, Independent Researcher, Bogotá, Colombia.

Hilary Sullivan, Australian National Parks and Wildlife Service, Jabiru, NT, Australia.

Paul S. C. Tacon, Department of Prehistory and Anthropology, Australian National University, Canberra, ACT, Australia.

Luke Taylor, Australian Institute of Aboriginal Studies, Canberra, ACT, Australia.

Deborah B. Waite, Department of Art, University of Hawaii at Manoa, Honolulu, Hawaii.

Anne-Catherine Welté, Independent Researcher, Toulouse, France.

Foreword

This book is one of a major series of more than 20 volumes resulting from the World Archaeological Congress held in Southampton, England, in September 1986. The series reflects the enormous academic impact of the Congress, which was attended by 850 people from more than 70 countries, and attracted many additional contributions from others who were unable to attend in person.

The *One World Archaeology* series is the result of a determined and highly successful attempt to bring together for the first time not only archaeologists and anthropologists from many different parts of the world, as well as academics from a host of contingent disciplines, but also non-academics from a wide range of cultural backgrounds, who could lend their own expertise to the discussions at the Congress. Many of the latter, accustomed to being treated as the 'subjects' of archaeological and anthropological observation, had never before been admitted as equal participants in the discussion of their own (cultural) past or present, with their own particularly vital contribution to make towards global, cross-cultural understanding.

The Congress therefore really addressed world archaeology in its widest sense. Central to a world archaeological approach is the investigation not only of how people lived in the past but also of how, and why, changes took place resulting in the forms of society and culture which exist today. Contrary to popular belief, and the archaeology of some 20 years ago, world archaeology is much more than the mere recording of specific historical events, embracing as it does the study of social and cultural change in its entirety. All the books in the *One World Archaeology* series are the result of meetings and discussions which took place within a context that encouraged a feeling of self-criticism and humility in the participants about their own interpretations and concepts of the past. Many participants experienced a new self-awareness, as well as a degree of awe about past and present human endeavours, all of which is reflected in this unique series.

The Congress was organized around major themes. Several of these themes were based on the discussion of full-length papers which had been circulated some months previously to all who had indicated a special interest in them. Other sessions, including some dealing with areas of specialization defined by period or geographical region, were based on oral addresses, or a combination of precirculated papers and lectures. In all cases, the entire sessions were recorded on cassette, and all contributors were presented with the recordings of the discussion of their papers. A major part of the thinking behind the Congress was that a meeting of many hundreds of participants that did not leave behind a published record of its academic discussions would be little more than an exercise in tourism.

Thus, from the very beginning of the detailed planning for the World Archaeological Congress in 1982, the intention was to produce post-Congress books containing a selection only of the contributions, revised in the light of discussions during the sessions themselves as well as during subsequent consultations with the

academic editors appointed for each book. From the outset, contributors to the
Congress knew that if their papers were selected for publication, they would have
only a few months to revise them according to editorial specifications, and that they
would become authors in an important academic volume scheduled to appear within
a reasonable period following the Southampton meeting.

The publication of the series reflects the intense planning which took place before
the Congress. Not only were all contributors aware of the subsequent production
schedules, but also session organizers were already planning their books before and
during the Congress. The editors were entitled to commission additional chapters
for their books when they felt that there were significant gaps in the coverage of a
topic during the Congress, or where discussion at the Congress indicated a need for
additional contributions.

One of the main themes of the Congress was devoted to 'Cultural Attitudes
to Animals, including Birds, Fish and Invertebrates'. The theme was based on
discussion of precirculated full-length papers, covering four and a half days, and
was under the overall control of Tim Ingold, Senior Lecturer in the Department
of Social Anthropology, University of Manchester, and Mark Maltby, Research
Fellow in the Faunal Remains Unit of the Department of Archaeology, University
of Southampton. The choice of this topic for a major theme arose from a desire to
explore, from an interdisciplinary perspective, the many facets of the varying relationships that have developed between humans and animals, as these are reflected
by the historical diversity of cultural traditions.

Discussions during the Congress were grouped around four main headings,
each of which has led to the publication of a book. The first, organized by Tim
Ingold, was concerned with 'What is an Animal?', leading to the book of the same
title. The second subtheme, on 'The Appropriation, Domination and Exploitation
of Animals', lasted for over a day and a half and was under the control of Juliet
Clutton-Brock, editor of the volume *The walking larder: patterns of domestication,
pastoralism, and predation.* A day was devoted to discussion of the 'Semantics of
Animal Symbolism' and the co-ordinator, Roy Willis, is also the editor of the
resulting book on *Signifying animals: human meaning in the natural world.* Howard
Morphy was in charge of the fourth subtheme on 'Learning from Art about the
Cultural Relationships between Humans and Animals', and has edited this volume.

The overall theme took as its starting point the assumption that there is no *one*
human attitude consistently maintained towards a particular species of animal, and
that similar human sentiments have been attached to a huge variety of different animals at different times and in different places. It set out to investigate the similarities
and differences in practices and beliefs connected with animals, including birds, fish,
and invertebrates, across both time and space.

Prior to this century, in the West, animal behaviour was usually portrayed and
interpreted in terms of a contrast with human behaviour. Darwin was not alone in
his frequent adoption of an anthropocentric perspective in formulating questions and
in presenting hypotheses and interpretations. It has often been claimed that people
of non-Western cultures generally view animals quite differently. Another aim of
the Congress theme was to explore such contrasts and to suggest some of the factors underlying both anthropomorphic and anthropocentric perceptions of animals

which are currently prevalent at least in Western society.

Ecological, psychological, cultural, and utilitarian considerations are all involved in peoples' attitudes to, and treatment of, other species. These factors were considered not only from a wide, interdisciplinary point of view but also, as befits a world archaeological context, especially in an historical perspective, giving due emphasis to their changes over time.

For example, in the West when those of us who live in towns and cities think of dogs and cats we usually think of them as companions, although dogs are also, in other contexts, considered essential for herding, guarding, and hunting other animals. In ancient Egypt, cats were often shown in artwork as pets, but they were possibly also used to hunt and catch birds. In many present-day cultures across the world people think of quite different animals, such as cattle and pigs, as friends or companions. On the other hand, the hyaena is normally considered by the layman today to be wild and untrainable, yet an ancient Egyptian representation appears to show one being handled. Once we move beyond the normal level of trying to ascertain from any excavation simply what animals were eaten or used for transportation, we are bound to look again at the nature of the relationships and interactions between human groups and the animals in their environments. Another aim of this theme, therefore, was to investigate how different people think, and thought, about different classes of animals, to discover the principles of classification involved, and to show how these principles constituted logical systems of belief and action. The presence of so many Congress participants from the so-called Third and Fourth Worlds made it possible to embrace a truly cross-cultural perspective on these issues.

One point of interest lies in the investigation, on a worldwide basis, of the reasons why particular animals have been domesticated by humans – whether for food, such as meat or milk, or for other reasons, such as for ritual purposes.

Contributors to the theme on 'Cultural Attitudes to Animals' adopted a variety of perspectives for looking at the complex ways in which past and present humans have interrelated with beings they classify as animals. Some of these perspectives were predominantly economic and ecological, others were symbolic, concerned with the classification of both the physical and the social environment, and still others were primarily philosophical or theological. All these different perspectives are required for a full interpretation of the artworks of the past, which in their representations of humans and animals reveal some of the foci and inspirations of cultural attitudes to animals.

In focusing on the nature of the varying relationships that can develop between humans and animals, one is led inevitably to the question: what actually is an animal or a human? By asking such a question, archaeologists and others are forced to become aware of their own individual and cultural preconceptions, and to pay attention to a set of problems concerning attitudes.

The main themes in *Animals into art* are discussed in detail in its editorial introduction (pp. 1–17). My aim in what follows is to examine a few of the points which have struck me personally as being of particular note or fascination.

In this book Howard Morphy and his contributors explore the way that the animal world features in the works of art of a variety of cultures of different dates and in different parts of the world. Originally, the plan was to have almost a day's discussion at the Congress on the different ways of interpreting zoomorphic representations in art; a further lengthy period discussing the way that inferences can be made from visual images about the ways the people who created and used the art thought about the relations between humans and animals; and a separate three days of verbal presentations on the cultural contexts of rock art, particularly the relationships between the rock art and other facets of that culture's activities. During the Congress all these topics, based both on precirculated papers and lectures, were grouped together under different titles, as agreed by the editor, his co-organizer Mark Maltby, and myself. Discussion lasted for one and a half days. The first session dealt with 'The Identification of Symbols and Concepts of Humans and Animals in Palaeolithic and Post-Palaeolithic Art', followed by a discussion which focused on 'The Palaeolithic Picture'. The next main meeting was on 'Interpreting Human and Animal Representations in Ethnographic and Historic Art', and the subsequent one considered 'Ethnographic and other Interpretations of Human and Animal Representations in Prehistoric Art'. The final discussion session focused on 'Temporal and Regional Variations in the Significance of Animals in Art'.

Several of the subjects of this book, not surprisingly, also receive some consideration in the other three books that derive from this Congress theme. Other topics such as the questions of style and meaning also cross-cut many of the other Congress themes. How style should be defined and interpreted and how, and in what sense, material culture objects have 'meanings' are central questions in the interpretation of symbolism and material culture in general (and see *The meanings of things*, edited by I. Hodder and *Who needs the past?*, edited by R. Layton) as well as being related to power and control in several complex societies (and see *Domination and resistance*, edited by D. Miller, M. J. Rowlands & C. Tilley).

One of the fascinations of the beginning chapters of *Animals into art* is the realization of how difficult it is to isolate the real style of a past society from the styles of their later decoders, and how the assumptions of what constitutes an animal or a human (and therefore its representation) may condition much of such subsequent decipherments. In the case of Palaeolithic art it is still not entirely clear whether some 'humans' and 'animals' were ambiguous representations of two discrete entities (as assumed in some recent interpretations of the art), or whether they simply share certain stylistic features and conventions (such as the dorsal lines of their backs). Nor is it clear whether these particular representations were in fact separate and distinct from representations of a category which can indeed be called 'animal', which is itself distinct and intentionally 'animal'. When read in connection with *What is an animal?* (edited by T. Ingold) and *Signifying animals* (edited by R. Willis), the enormity of the problems confronting those attempting to 'read' the 'message(s)' of this chronologically remote Ice Age art become strikingly evident.

Many of the current interpretations of this art still rely on rather dubious observations about the localization of particular images, combined with the subjective 'reading' of postures and placements in terms of such things as 'rearing up to fight', and so on.

To be unaware of the complexities of concepts such as style and perception (and see *The meanings of things*, edited by I. Hodder), or to assume that relationships between animal and human are always, solely or predominantly, economically based (and see *The walking larder*, edited by J. Clutton-Brock), is to risk using the evidence of the art forms of another society, past or present, in unwarranted ways which may build up misleading pictures of past activities of hunting methods or other subsistence techniques (and see *Hunters of the recent past*, edited by L. B. Davis & B. O. K. Reeves). It is certainly true that almost all art forms reveal that the 'animal' subjects selected for representation are neither the full 'natural' repertoire available for depiction, nor appear in the same proportions as the actual proportions that existed in the environment, as revealed by the archaeologists from animal bones, or can be assumed (in the case of 'insects', etc.) to have existed 'in the wild'. But, of course, many chapters in this book (and see *Signifying animals*, edited by R. Willis) reveal clearly that what is conceived of as 'the wild' is a conceptual category, not a 'reality of nature'. Frequently certain animal species appear to have become metaphors – expressed in complex symbolism and by a variety of stylistic conventions – for relationships between the supernatural and the human. Several of the chapters in this book reveal that the human/animal distinction itself is not a hard and fast one; humans and animals may often be components or parts of the same thing, but in different guises – often they 'are' all the ancestors. In other cases they may be conceptually linked by features which would not normally occur to those from a different culture, such as the fact that humans and bonito both have red blood and both are controlled by the same supernatural spirits.

Amongst the most important messages from all the chapters in *Animals into art* which deal with ethnohistory or contemporary art forms are those concerning the complexity of the relationships and meanings which are expressed through art, and the variety of such expressions which often coexist within what we would traditionally identify as only one single art form. There is little to suggest that a simple system of binary opposition, or even binary complementarity, would be an adequate approach to these art forms, or that depictions related to 'sympathetic magic' or to the recording of 'historical episodes' are the only concerns of any particular society's form of art. In many cases such differential stylistic usage is linked to the nature of the art as one intended for restricted use as opposed to one intended for open discussion.

Some 20 years ago many people were shocked when it was first pointed out (Ucko & Rosenfeld 1967) that Palaeolithic cave art was at least as much an art of 'signs' as an art of 'animals'. This has now been accepted as self-evidently so. This book will be equally revolutionary in showing that non-representational (or non-figurative) depictions may be at least as significant and important as representational (or figurative) ones. *Animals into art* demonstrates that the 'geometric design' can be full of meanings; meanings of subtlety and complexity often particularly well suited to metaphysical conceptualization as well as matters of personal and social identity (and see *Who needs the past?*, edited by R. Layton). Such non-representational (or non-figurative) styles (sometimes schematic depictions which have an iconic basis, but often (in Australia, East Africa, etc.) non-representational items or motifs) have a multivalency of meanings and significance. In some cases, non-figurative styles, like figurative ones, may conform to 'regional styles' which presumably reflect some aspects of past historical and group tradition (and see *The meanings of things*, edited by I. Hodder), but often they are contemporary with other artistic styles in use within the same culture. This book thus gives a new impetus to the consideration of questions about so-called 'beginnings of art'. Would such 'beginnings' have been designed to communicate through the figurative or representational, or would they rather have started from the non-figurative or non-representational, only reaching iconicity as the result of lengthy and hesitating development from the non-representational? Whatever the answer, this book also casts doubt on the current simple distinction between representational and non-representational, since most art styles include features which cannot be seen in the normal course of events, whether by an X-ray style, or by the incorporation of distinctive features of an animal, such as fangs. It is also of interest that the features depicted in this way are often not those which Europeans would recognize as being the distinctive features of the animal concerned.

As will be seen, much in *Animals into art* reveals new information about Australian Aboriginal art forms and stylistic conventions. Some of this new information will have immense consequences in the interpretation of other art forms. For example, whereas archaeologists have often assumed that the different use of perspective ('twisted', 'semi', 'three-quarter', 'profile') may be equated with different cultural traditions (ethnicity) or chronological stages in development, the same Aboriginal rock art tradition employs different perspective conventions for different animals (e.g. turtles/snakes/lizards as opposed to land mammals/birds as opposed to bats/mythical beings/humans, and so on). Also, much archaeological literature assumes that retouching of depictions is carried out to activate the assumed powers of sympathetic magic – in Aboriginal Australia, such retouching of a depiction may be carried out if the fishing or hunting activity has not been successful!

Another of the important revelations of *Animals into art* concerns the complex nature of concepts of change in art. In some societies art is conceived of as unchanging (deriving from the spirits/ancestors), despite evidence which shows that in fact its styles (and sometimes content) have indeed been modified over time. In the case of the elephants in Saharan rock art it appears that the art depictions must have been reinterpreted, and reinterpreted in major ways, to suit the changing cultural traditions of the societies concerned in their evaluation. Such reinterpretation does not necessarily argue against a presumption that human attitudes to particularly demanding animals may always have something in common (and see Midgley, Ch. 3, in *What is an animal?*, edited by T. Ingold). In the past it has often been tempting to assume that where one finds constancy of image, so one can assume continuity of meaning. In reality, however, the evidence of rock art – which remains in the place where it was first created – must be subject to continual reinterpretation by its 'viewers' and 'users'. Often, it may be presumed, such changes in conceptualization, or cognitive systems, are also accompanied by changes in actions.

It is obvious that much recent work has concentrated on attempts to read the significance of artworks as if they were texts of some kind (and see *The meanings of things*, edited by I. Hodder). For Palaeolithic and many other past arts there are, of course, no clues to be gained from other contemporary sources (beyond those of environment, ecology, and demography). In the case of the Solomon Islands, however, it is the known mythologies of the culture which give the clues to the choice of motifs employed in the art, as opposed to what might be predicted from a mere reflection of the physical environment. It is again the evidence of mythology, this time derived from ethnohistorical sources in Chile, which allows a brilliant re-reading of the structure, and therefore the significance, of the rock art – removing it from the simple levels of assumed 'sympathetic magic' and the recording of narrative, to the complex interplay of symbols of darkness and light, mythological characters and actions, and even rituals of animal breeding (and see *The walking larder*, edited by J. Clutton-Brock).

Animals into art is therefore extraordinarily strong in its development of sophisticated discussion of methodology and the formulation of research strategies and methods appropriate for different art complexes. It should therefore become a classic work whose influence is bound to spread to the study of many other art forms from other parts of the world. In addition, it contains up-to-date analytical reviews of Palaeolithic cave art which are both overdue and, in their critical approach to this Ice Age art, exceptional within the traditions of French and Spanish scholarship which dominate this field of art enquiry. It is also particularly strong in its consideration of the arts of the Americas, art forms which are rarely brought together with the arts of other parts of the world, either within one volume or in the exploration of common problems and questions. The chapters dealing with Australian Aboriginal art are also unique for the same reasons and, in addition, they represent a body of young scholarship working on this art complex which has not been published in this way before, even within Australia. Finally, but by no means least, this book reiterates the centrality of the human–animal discrimination in the conceptualization, by any society, of the world around it. For archaeologists to attempt to enter into the worlds of such distinctions demands an interdisciplinary and eclectic approach to works of art.

P. J. Ucko
Southampton

Reference

Ucko, P. J. & A. Rosenfeld 1967. *Palaeolithic cave art*. London: Weidenfeld & Nicolson.

Contents

INTERPRETING THE SYSTEM

List of colour plates

Preface

This book is the product of a subtheme of the 1986 World Archaeological Congress titled 'Learning from Art about the Cultural Relationships between Humans and Animals' that I organized jointly with Mark Maltby, building on earlier work by Meg Conkey and David Lewis-Williams. Most of the chapters in this book are derived from papers given at the Congress revised in the light of the themes that are outlined in the Introduction. Paul Tacon and Josephine Flood prepared papers for the Congress but circumstances prevented them from attending. Subsequently Flood wrote an entirely new contribution for this book, as did Osaga Odak. Whitney Davis's chapter was commissioned specifically for this book.

I would like to acknowledge the help of a number of people in organizing the Congress sessions and preparing this volume. First and foremost Mark Maltby, my co-organizer, and Paul Crake, Caroline Jones, and other staff of the World Archaeo-logical Congress at Southampton who enabled the sessions to go so smoothly. Iain Davidson, Knut Helskog, Ian Keen, and Michel Lorblanchet helped by chairing sessions. Whitney Davis, who was to have chaired one of the sessions but was unable to attend the Congress at the last minute, provided helpful written comments on the section he was to chair. Peter Ucko helped in the planning of the subtheme but was especially helpful in the editing of this book. He performed the role of series editor in an ideal way by helping with the really difficult problems. I also benefited greatly from the editorial skills of Frances Morphy whose work in checking the translations from French and Spanish was invaluable.

Howard Morphy
Oxford

Introduction

HOWARD MORPHY

Perhaps in keeping with a common Western attitude to art as being non-utilitarian, prehistorians and anthropologists with some notable exceptions have until recently neglected art as a source of data about other cultures. This may have been because on the surface art promised so much yet appeared from a limited investigation to yield so little. Art, some prehistorians felt, must, more readily than most other sources of archaeological data, provide access to past systems of thought, values, and perception, to qualitative aspects of peoples' lives. Something as ephemeral as an attitude to an animal is surely more likely to adhere to a painting on a rock wall than to remain in the eroded and dispersed debris of a prehistoric meal? Yet the gap between prehistoric painting and cultural concept seemed to be almost too great to cross and to many eyes the promise of art remained unfulfilled. The neglect of art may have been a consequence of this lack of interpretative progress or it may have been a cause.

The reasons for the neglect of art, indeed, are still not well understood; on the other hand the reasons for the limitations of many early analyses are well known, yet ironically in some respects they amount to one and the same thing. The analyses of prehistoric art were held up for two main reasons. First, they often failed to incorporate art in an integrated way with other archaeological data and failed to subject it to analogous methods of analysis (Ucko & Rosenfeld 1967, Lewis-Williams 1983). Secondly, prehistorians in particular of the Palaeolithic failed to realize the complex ways in which art could be integrated within the social and cultural fabric of hunting and gathering societies. As Ucko & Rosenfeld (1967) have shown, a more sophisticated analytic approach coincided with changes in attitude to contemporary indigenous societies and the realization of the complexities of their conceptual systems. Perhaps less explicably, ethnographic analyses also failed because studies of art and material culture were separated from the main stream of anthropological research and lay in a methodologically and theoretically sterile backwater (Ucko 1970, Forge 1973a, Dark 1978). Non-European art, increasingly admired for its looks, remained for a long time neglected as a source of information.

Periodically people have argued that its good looks are in part to blame for its predicament, or rather that the tight corset of 'art' that constrains the way it is viewed has caused much of the problem (cf. Firth 1973, p. v). Researchers have tried to solve the problem by changing the name; by switching from 'art object', to 'image' or 'representation' or 'information system' on the grounds that these are more neutral, less value-laden terms. Yet the replacement terms do not really help the situation. They are often more narrow in their definition than 'art' itself which, because of all the argument over what it is (for discussions see Dark 1978, Layton 1981), can have the advantage of being broadly conceived, whereas 'representation' (cf. Davis 1986), for example, may apply to only one aspect of an object. Indeed, the other problem of past approaches to the analysis of art is that there was a failure to realize the enormous complexity of the data, and that for any society's art there was unlikely to be a unitary explanation or interpretation except at the most general level. And when it comes to looking at a corpus so vast in distribution and time as European Palaeolithic art then Occam's razor has no place in the initial sorting-out of data. The probability that we are dealing with many different systems, each of which may have a multiplicity of functions and determinations must be accepted almost before productive work can begin (cf. Ucko & Rosenfeld 1967, p. 7; see also Davidson, this volume, Ch. 21). So we probably have no better word than 'art' as a rag-bag kind of label as long as we realize that the bag can contain many different kinds of clothes as well as some things that aren't even clothes at all, and if we want to use any of the contents of the bag we must sort them out first to find what kinds of things they are. If any of us have a more precise definition of art than the intuitive agreement that a set of objects might belong in the same rag-bag, then *after* the sorting is the time to throw out objects that do not fit and to re-label them as something more appropriate. On a more positive note, and one that perhaps anticipates such a narrower definition, the label 'art' is a useful reminder that the aesthetic/expressive qualities of objects may be relevant to understanding their form and the motives behind their production; for the reason they are in the same rag-bag is often that people think that they have been made to be looked at. Even if this is part of the definition adopted, it is important to remember that they were not made to be looked at by us. The most general questions to be asked are: what did the people who made or commissioned the objects see, and how did they understand the images? As Davis phrases it in Chapter 7, 'our task is to reconstruct that local common knowledge about images', to reconstruct the context for looking at, and the knowledge required to interpret, the messages, if messages there be.

The theme of this book is the ways in which people have represented animals in their art, an apparently simple theme with complex implications. The complexity lies in the fact that representation is always more than a question of the way in which the natural form of the animal is reduced to artistic impression. People are not so much representing a nature that is 'out there' as encoding it, and codes involve culture. It would be nice if animal art was a window to a world inhabited by another culture that we could simply step through. Nice, but we wouldn't learn as much – for the window is distorted by the intricate pattern of the glass of culture, and in learning how to see through this we learn the structure of the cultural system that produces the images. Encoding the meaning 'horse' in a geometric sign, in a highly schematic figure, or in a detailed and elaborated figurative representation involves encoding the meaning within quite different systems, with different conditions of interpretation, the potential for producing different messages, and with different aesthetic effects. A geometric system where there is a relatively arbitrary relation between signifier and signified, form and content, requires an interpreter who is already familiar with the code for the meaning to be grasped, whereas an iconic image, one based on look-alike criteria, may be interpreted at some level by some-one who has never seen the image before (for detailed consideration of these issues, see Munn 1973, H. Morphy 1977a, 1980). The way an animal is represented tells us something about how the animal is conceived and understood, for example through the parts that are selected to represent it or the contexts in which it is included. But equally important is the fact that the particular encoding systems employed may tell us something about the society using them – for systems of representing and encoding are forms of cultural knowledge embedded in institutional contexts. In an ethnographic context the properties of the code may provide us with information on the interpretability of a system and how it helps to maintain a system of restricted knowledge, or how it designates particular roles or statuses. In prehistoric contexts it may enable us to identify the duration of a particular institutional complex or identify contexts in which restricted codes might have been used.

Art to archaeologists is not simply a source of information about other aspects of society, 'a window to another world', but a source of information in itself. 'What kind of system is this?' and 'What does the art mean?' are two central interdependent questions that arise from this perspective (cf. Llamazares 1987, p. 80). However, while the first question must always have a positive answer the second question need not. While I suspect that the concept of meaning in a semiotic sense is relevant to many systems intuitively defined as art, it may not be relevant in all cases. It is possible that certain lines are present on a wall simply because people enjoyed running their fingers across the soft surface, and often it must be the case that a pattern is present because it is pleasing to the eye or because it is conventionally present. The classic answer to the anthropologist's question 'Why do you do x?' is often said to be 'We do it because we always do it'. In the case of art, the answer 'We paint because the ancestors painted it' has to be taken into account even if it is not accepted as a sufficient explanation for the presence of a motif.

Chapters of this book are arranged in sections according to stages they represent in the process of interpreting art, interpretation not being a synonym for meaning but a wider concept that centres on explaining the form of the art in relation to its use in a given cultural context. In an archaeological context, interpretation requires the development of hypotheses about its date, its use, and about the structure and institutions of the culture that produces it.

The five sections of the book are concerned with:

(a) identifying the images or components of the art, determining what the images are and locating them in time and space;
(b) determining how the image represents, i.e. how it encodes meaning;
(c) examining the relationships between images and considering the question of composition;
(d) finding out what the images and components mean;
(e) interpreting the images and compositions as part of a wider cultural system.

Although conceptually distinct phases of an analysis, these are not independent of one another nor are they temporally distinct: it may be necessary to model the system and know how meaning is encoded before the image can be firmly identified. Interpretation is the last stage conceptually, because to begin with an interpretation would be to begin with preconceptions, and because an interpretation must be an interpretation of something and not an imposition. Moreover, the image, because of its material form, must have logical priority even if the image incorporated in the analysis is inevitably an abstraction (see Lewis-Williams & Loubser 1986, for a relevant methodological discussion).

Identification

I am using identification as a shorthand for the initial stages in the process of preparing the data, the images, the 'art', for interpretation, though as Clottes (Ch. 1) shows, it is an initial stage that requires analytic and methodological rigour and which must be continually open to the possibility of revision. The elements of the system must be identified, the motifs must be segregated, and the elements must be organized into sets according to time and space so that hypotheses can be tested against known orders and distributions. But those orders and distributions and the identifications upon which they are based are not absolute and may often have to be changed. Identification is a positive statement that something is an element of such and such a status, or that it represents a particular meaning; in some ways it is a state of mind and has the epistemological status of 'a hard fact about this object' – though it is a hard fact that is the product of an analytic process that involves concepts such as representation and system of meaning. Identification requires filling-in the label with all the kind of information that is going to be needed to locate or relocate the image as part of a social process: who made it, which group they belonged to, what it is, and when it was made. The problem of identification increases with time and distance from the data, and what is routine information in an ethnographic context becomes in many prehistoric contexts hypothetical. More often than not, the final answer is simply 'we do not know'.

In studies of prehistoric rock art, the identification of the individual artist is related to the more general problem of the dating of the art, in particular the identification of contemporaneous images. This topic of individual identification is one that was once considered of importance, and is now again being seen as one of great relevance in areas such as the development of style and the relationship between artist and society. Clottes (Ch. 1) hints at examples of sets of paintings where an individual's hand could have been at work in the Upper Palaeolithic but the problems of establishing identity in such a context are enormous. In a body of rock art much closer to us in time, Haskovec & Sullivan (Ch. 2) have succeeded in establishing the corpus of work by Najombolmi, an Australian Aboriginal artist from western Arnhem Land, who died in the 1960s. Almost shockingly, their work is unique in Australia but should inspire further studies which try to break the anonymity of rock art in Australia and elsewhere where such studies are possible. Pushing individual identity back beyond living memory obviously requires different techniques, based on morphological-stylistic analysis as well as on attempts to establish the hand of an artist through analysing the pigments and fixatives used. It may (often) seem to be an impossible task but it is certainly made easier if a reasonable model exists for the relationship between individual product and the artistic corpus as a whole for a particular period of time. Haskovec & Sullivan's work provides the basis for the development of such a model in western Arnhem Land.

In much prehistoric art, however, the initial problem lies not so much in identifying the artists as in identifying the motifs, or as Clottes phrases it 'distinguishing the subjects of the art'. Clottes provides some excellent examples of how experts over the years have misidentified representations through inaccurate recording of what was engraved on the rock surface, through failure to correctly interpret Palaeolithic conventions, through a lack of knowledge of Ice-Age fauna, and so on. Mistakes are to be expected, the 'don't knows', the representation which the particular analyst failed to identify to his or her own satisfaction, should be a welcome category. Though, as Lorblanchet shows (Ch. 4), ambiguous or intermediate figures may be very productive of analytic insight and should not be neglected. Cutting them out of an analysis may cause as much of a distortion as does interpreting them too easily and unambiguously. The problems occur when tentative or ambiguous interpretations slip into the category of definite identifications, achieve the status of 'hard fact' and as such enter the statistical mill. The lesson to be learnt from Clottes' chapter (Ch. 1) is the inevitability of subjectivity in the interpretative process, and the originality of the contribution is in showing how contemporaries' mistakes can be used as a method of exploring the possible creative processes of Palaeolithic artists, of posing questions of the data.

The problem of identification is particularly apparent in the case of composite figures, representations that are made up of parts of different animals organized together as a whole. Cardale Schrimpff, Chapter 3, takes us on a journey of exploration through Ilama art of Colombia in an attempt to trace out the contours of one such polymorphic figure which she refers to as the 'Fabulous Beast'. The problem for the analyst in such a case is that there is no external model for the object, the artists are not representing some extinct creature that once existed in the world but a creature of the imagination that may have come into being through the art. The parts may be recognizable but how do we know they belong to the same whole, how do we know where one fabulous beast ends and another begins? The problem is compounded by the fact that different cultures select different features of animals when representing them in art. Schrimpff shows convincingly an ambiguity between representations of bat and feline in Ilama art that reflects the choice of elements used to represent the respective species – a choice that may or may not reflect similarities in the way the species are conceived, or their position in a system of symbolism. The Fabulous Beast dramatizes the fact that we are dealing with mental representations of animals, not the animals themselves, and measures taken from the outside world can, as Clottes argues (cf. Ucko 1989), only be a component of an analysis and never the sole criterion of identification. Composite animals can have a cultural reality that may be more revealing than representations of known species because they create sets of species that cross-cut our categories and force us to ask questions about the relationships between those creatures in the cultures concerned.

Theoretically, the questions of identification should be much easier to resolve in an ethnographic context where questions can be asked of the artist and the intended audience. But many problems of identification are likely to remain. In some cases this may be simply because people do not want to reveal information about their art. However, very often it is because the initial simple stage of identification is elusive (see Forge 1979). People may use visual systems without being conscious of how the parts operate and, in an analogous way to the case with language, the analyst has to abstract the components and the system through elicitation and analysis. Even if the elements of the system can be readily identified, they may have no verbalizable meaning, or there may be a series of alternative interpretations. These qualifications apply centrally to geometric or arbitrary systems, but they can also apply to figurative art where frequently identification proves to be no easy matter (cf. Macintosh 1977). And even if identification is established and consistent, it is necessary to go beyond mere attribution to establish the basis of identification, for this will provide insight into the way the tradition is transmitted from generation to generation, how the art is produced.

Representation

The concept of representation is integral to the process of identification. By representation I mean the process by which meaning is encoded in art, in simpler language, how art 'means'. This inevitably involves the consideration of some pragmatic factors, such as how the art was intended to be seen and who the intended audience was − for representation involves interpretation and the knowledge and position of the interpreter.

The concept of a representational system is so important for the simple reason that the way in which meaning is encoded affects the meaning of the element. Indeed, one can go further than that and argue that it affects the kind of meaning it is possible for an element to have and how it interacts or combines with other elements of the same or different systems. To choose a simple example, in an iconic system, one in which the relationship between form and content is based on formal resemblance, an O may represent a ball or an orange. In an arbitrary system, e.g. a map of the London underground, it can be used to represent a place and/or a station, something which it does not look like except under the conventions of the particular system. It is clearly important to establish what kind of system an element belongs to in order to begin to interpret its meaning (for an extended discussion see Morphy 1980).

Lorblanchet (Ch. 4) and Clottes (Ch. 1) both show how figurative and geometric elements have existed side by side throughout the entire span of Palaeolithic art. In the case of some geometric signs it is enormously difficult to determine whether to assign them a figurative or arbitrary status. Some geometric elements may well have been schematic forms of figurative elements and readily interpretable by Palaeolithic people on that basis, others may have had their origins in a long process of schematization but have operated as arbitrary signs, while others still may have originated as arbitrary elements. Ultimately the interpretation of the status of such signs depends on the reconstruction of plausible systems of which they are a part.

There has been a tendency in studies of prehistoric art to push interpretation of geometric elements in an iconic direction wherever possible. This is understandable in a way, as the interpretation of arbitrary systems in prehistoric contexts must seem a daunting task. Odak (Ch. 6) provides an interesting example from Kenyan rock art where the temptation was defeated by chronology. If taken together, the geometric elements on a rock wall could be interpreted as a representation of the solar system, but in fact they consisted of components from a number of distinct time-phases. Odak also provides an interesting example of a case where the boundary between iconic and non-iconic systems breaks down (the representation of cattle brands in rock art). The rock art is iconic if the cattle brands are taken as the referent but perhaps both are best seen as a manifestation of the same arbitrary system. Morphy (Ch. 5) provides an analogous example from Yolngu art, where paintings often contain representations of sacred objects, but the sacred objects themselves are part of an arbitrary system.

More than one system of representation may in fact be current at the same time. Morphy (Ch. 5) gives an example from northern Australia where two distinct systems of representation are used, one geometric, the other figurative. The two may be used separately or they can be used in conjunction to encode meaning. The two systems have quite different potential for encoding meaning and require different conditions of interpretation. Yolngu paintings are part of a system of restricted knowledge and the geometric art can only be interpreted by those who have been provided with the key. In contrast, the figurative system can be at least minimally interpreted by anyone who recognizes the form of the object as it is represented.

Within the respective categories of iconic figurative and non-iconic geometric there is enormous variation in the ways in which things are represented, or meanings are encoded. There also exist representational systems that do not fit easily into either category. The non-iconic : iconic continuum is most useful when applied to artistic systems in which there is an encoding of meanings, in which the form of the art is influenced by the relationship between signifiers and signifieds. There are going to be other cases in which such a semiologically based continuum is going to be less useful, Chilkat blankets (cf. Holm 1965, p. 9) and Abelam flat-paintings, for example. In the case of Abelam paintings, Forge (1970, 1973b) argues that the system is a closed one without direct external referents. Consistent with this, the painting process is not guided by the objective of encoding certain meanings, rather what is important is that a whole series of elements, collectively and individually charged with sentiments associated with ritual, secrecy, and power, are manipulated to make effective communication, the impact very definitely enhanced by aesthetic effect (Forge 1973b, p. 177). All this simply reinforces the point made earlier that the initial stages of analysis must involve determining the kind of system we are dealing with.

Lorblanchet's review of Palaeolithic human figures (Ch. 4) shows enormous diversity in the way the human form has been represented, varying from 'realistic' portrait-like figures through increasingly schematic forms to almost minimalist signs whose iconic origins only emerged as a result of detailed analysis (cf. Rosenfeld 1973). As Lorblanchet notes, more than one of these systems may have been employed at the same time and it is likely that they were used with different properties (see F. Morphy 1977 for an example of how in northwest coast American Indian art 'realistic' and 'symbolic' representations occupy quite different functional contexts).

Lorblanchet's chapter also reminds us that in analysing representational systems we must always take into account aesthetic factors as possible motivations. Indeed, when considering combined human–animal representations or multiple ambiguous figures, it is often difficult to decide whether the forms have 'risen out of a game with shapes or out of deep symbolism expressing a relationship between man and animal'.

One of the main points of George Kubler's book *The shape of time* (1962) was to stress the relative autonomy of form in art, form as a resource with a trajectory of its own that intersects with human uses of it but also has an independent existence. While I think one can go too far in cutting form loose from function, the idea of form as a resource is an appealing one. It is one of the ideas developed by Davis in Chapter 7. His other argument is a sceptical one, taken from Wittgenstein, that we can never know how another person intended an object to be seen. Davis's argument is a necessary corrective to the tendency to over-interpretation in analysing prehistoric art, in particular the tendency to come down too easily with a firm identification. However, much of human life is based on the presupposition that we share meanings with others, that we are able to interpret their actions and the objects they produce in the way they intended. The aim of identification in prehistoric art must be to push that possibility back in time, always wary of the fact that the cognitive overlap we share with others may diminish with time and space. In a sense, the reconstruction of representational systems by developing models of how art-forms encode meaning, how they may have been interpreted, is a way of crossing that cognitive divide.

Composition

The next stage after identification and representation is to consider composition: the way in which elements and/or representations are combined together or organized into a whole. The whole is something we can imagine people interpreting or creating. However, in rock art it may have been (and in some cases may still be) an evolving or developing whole that may have been, in effect, subject to changes in composition over time, as new groups responded to, and incorporated, existing images. The concept of composition employed here is a broad one and includes such things as the distribution of, relationship between, and frequency of, elements (cf. Lewis-Williams & Loubser 1986). It is designed to get away from a definition of composition which sees it in some ways equivalent to 'scene' which is liable to be arbitrary and culture-bound. Halverson (1987), for example, writes that in contrast to the Palaeolithic 'when we come to Mesolithic rock paintings, composition is perfectly evident and for the most part immediately intelligible as scenes depicting ordinary activities of hunting, warfare, etc. – supporting the evolution in art from free images to composition'. Halverson is confusing a particular type of composition, familiar in Western European art, with the more general concept of composition.

In determining what is part of the same composition one must consider the representational systems employed as, in order to know how elements relate to one another, one must first know how they encode meaning and how they may contribute to the meaning of other elements. Composition is an analytic concept, and the same element may be the component of different compositions in space and time.

Molyneaux (Ch. 8) provides an excellent example, from Micmac art from eastern

Canada, of the way in which images may be reinterpreted over time, and how they may be altered in part to incorporate them within new compositions. He shows how this may be a guide to conceptual changes in society and to what is important in the world-view of a particular culture. Detailed recording and analysis of Palaeolithic representations have revealed similar cases of the modification of figures over time, and open the road to further interpretative possibilities. Both Clottes (Ch. 1) and Lorblanchet (Ch. 4) provide examples of the modification of representations that may reflect reinterpretation of them.

Although scenes of the type Halverson (1987) is looking for, in which a set of images are connected in an apparent event or sequence of action, are extremely rare in Palaeolithic art, many other possible composition types exist. One of these, 'confronted animals', is the subject of Welté's chapter (Ch. 9). The compositional theme referred to consists of two animals (sometimes more) of the same species standing at the same level and in similar attitudes 'opposing' one another, either adjoining or separated by a small space. Although infrequent, such compositions are widespread in Palaeolithic art and clearly invite explanation. It is, of course, possible that 'confronted animals' is a false category consisting of a series of different cases with nothing in common. On the other hand, bearing in mind my remarks about the relative autonomy of form, Welté shows convincingly that it is an aesthetic idea (or, as she refers to it, 'an architectural construction') of long history. The analysis of associations between species and the distribution of such associations in Palaeolithic art is clearly a productive line of enquiry, but one that is likely to provide no short-term answers. Another profitable approach, that has almost become obligatory, is the statistical analysis of frequency rates of species within corpuses of rock art – a method that, as Lewis-Williams' (1981, 1983) studies of South African rock art have shown, is best carried out as part of a broader research strategy.

Studies of frequencies are compositional studies in the broader sense that they are concerned with establishing the pattern of choices made by artists as to what to place where. Once the pattern is established then the aim is to explain it. The method of explanation is obvious and consists of relating the frequency pattern to other aspects of the archaeological record and to the environment, and developing hypotheses to explain the relationship: seeing, for example, if the frequencies reflected the actual frequency of occurrence of the creatures in the environment or their relative importance as hunted food. Tacon's study of the motifs used in western Arnhem Land (Ch. 10) shows how frequency studies can provide useful hypotheses about the interpretation of the art. Ultimately such hypotheses must be tested back against detailed aspects of the form of the art and the structure of particular compositions: the more tight the fit between hypothesis and data, the greater likelihood of the interpretation being correct, even if it is unlikely to be finally proved. Tacon is fortunate enough to be able to relate his findings to quite detailed ethnographic accounts from the same region and is able to use as informants artists still painting in the same tradition. In this case the pattern, at least of the more recent paintings, can be related to details of the ethnographic record. Ultimately, a fine-grained graph of frequency changes over time will be helpful in pushing the ethnographic record back and altering its contours to attempt to make it pass through what, in effect, becomes a rock-art filter. Olsen has in fact pursued such an approach in her analysis (Ch. 20) of the relationship between contemporary Pueblo and prehistoric Anasazi art of the south-western United States.

Berenguer & Martinez (Ch. 19) provide a detailed analysis of composition from a different perspective. In their analysis of the art of Taira on the Upper Loa River in Chile, they are concerned not so much with overall frequencies of motifs as with the organization and distribution of motifs within a panel. They show how the composition of a panel of rock-art as a whole can convey a meaning that is separate from the sum of its parts. This is partly because in the Taira case the relative positions of representations in a panel may be significant, the upper part of the panel being associated with increase and abundance and the lower half being associated with creation. They also provide an explanation in the particular case of superpositioning, a compositional feature of rock art that is as elusive of explanation as it is widespread in occurrence. In Taira they argue convincingly that superpositioning may be a means of representing, and perhaps attempting to create through ritual, an abundance of animals. They also see it as a device for creating an illusion of perspective.

Meaning

Meaning is a broad concept and I have already discussed many of the issues that concern it in one sense or another. In this section I am more concerned with meaning of art in the sense of why a particular motif is used in a given context, with meaning as it merges with symbol and metaphor rather than referential sign – we know now that the figure represents a horse, the question is 'Why a horse?' Meaning in this sense is very much part of the process of interpretation. Of course that does not mean that we have left form behind, because any hypotheses will have to be tested against the particular form of the horse, the way it is encoded.

We are moving into an area which may appear impossibly difficult, in particular to the sceptical eye of Davis's chapter (Ch. 7). In prehistoric contexts the method followed must be that outlined earlier for interpreting frequencies – a laborious task of seeking patterns in the data, trying to correlate art with context, site use with the changing seasons; continually developing and testing hypotheses against what hopefully becomes a more detailed archaeological record. As the art becomes better recorded and more known, the possibilities of breakthroughs in small corners emerge. But again I must stress that the search for all-embracing unitary explanations is likely to be a red herring. The grand schemes such as that developed by Leroi-Gourhan (1964), that subordinate the art of millenniums to a single system of meaning, while stimulating in the context of their time, are likely to be replaced by a myriad of smaller fits between limited hypotheses and restricted sets of data.

The shift away from simple theories of the meaning of ethnographic and prehistoric art towards complex ones has recently increased the importance of ethnographic data in the analysis of art. People even refer to an ethnographic approach to the analysis of art. What, one is tempted to ask, would an ethnographic approach to contemporary Yolngu art have in common with an ethnographic approach to

Upper Palaeolithic art? Ethnography enters the analysis of art in at least four different ways, or rather there are four distinct kinds of relationships between ethnography and art. First, there is ethnographically produced art, art produced by living people whose production, use, and knowledge of the art can be observed and questioned. Secondly, there is art on the boundaries of ethnography, art that can be reached if the ethnography is stretched a little. Examples of this include cases where present practice and production can be shown to exist in continuity with a past record, where information exists for the latter part of the production of a vast corpus of art, much of which is prehistoric. Much Australian rock-art fits into this category. Then there is a related category where art intersects with early, partial, inadequate ethnography, where the fit between the two has to be reconstructed and where the art may be as helpful in interpreting the ethnography as the ethnography the art. Many of the arts of Fourth World peoples whose societies were disrupted early by colonialization fit this category. And, finally, there are the cases where the connection between ethnography and the art is broken, where the art ceased to be produced before the ethnographic recorder arrived and where a connection cannot be firmly established. Clearly, to an extent, the divisions between these groups are arbitrary and internally they are diverse, but they reflect important differences in the role that ethnography can play in different studies. At the one extreme ethnography is part of the data to be analysed; at the other, ethnography provides a resource for analogy and for hypothesis testing and generation (see, for example, Ucko 1969, Orme 1981, Layton 1987).

Schaafsma (Ch. 11) in her analysis of the rock-art of the southwest of the United States, and Legast (Ch. 12) in her analysis of Tairona art from Colombia, both deal with cases in which the connection is based on a hypothesis of cultural continuity. The similarities in their analyses extend beyond that, however, for they both attempt to pursue the meaning of representations, associated with, in the one case, a single species, the roadrunner, and in the other, a single type of animal, the bat. They do so by relating characteristics of the species to the form in which they are represented in art and then relating them to aspects of the regional ethnography.

In Chapter 13, Flood's ethnographic connection is not much closer. She considers the art of the Koolburra region of north Queensland, and her aim is to explain the occurrence of two types of zoomorphs at certain sites within the region. She does so by relating the pattern and form of the art to what can be argued to be fairly general features of ethnographically known Aboriginal societies, in effect associating the art with a particular cultural structure.

Kinsey's study of Susquehannock animal art from south central Pennsylvania (Ch. 14), like Tacon's, Flood's, and Olsen's studies, is based on analysis of the frequency of occurrence of motifs. The art in this case is known from excavated objects and the ethnographic record is very slender indeed. The basis for Kinsey's interpretation rests on the relationship between the animals represented in the art and the seasonal factors in Susquehannock life.

In Waite's case (Ch. 15), both the ethnographic record and the surviving body of art are more substantial. Waite does not focus on how the animals are represented in Solomon Island art but on a content analysis – considering why the particular species were selected out of the environment. She compares the art of the East and West

Solomon Islands and argues that the differences can only be explained in terms of cultural differences – in particular the different symbolic value attached to particular animals in the respective areas. She shows how the crocodile in the one case is the structural equivalent of the shark in the other.

The chapter by Drouin (Ch. 16) presents a quite different hermeneutic exercise, in that she tries to trace continuities in a motif across time and across cultural boundaries in the art and myth of North Africa. She connects the existence of a Tuareg oral tradition about elephants, a species which no longer lives in their region, with representations of elephants in rock art done by prehistoric populations who subsequently moved out of the region. She has the ethnographic accounts and the rock art, and disavows any genetic connection between them, yet argues convincingly for the transmission and transformation of a theme over time, a theme whose continuity may have been ensured by the permanence of motifs in the regional rock-art.

Finally in this section, Malaiya (Ch. 17) also attempts an interpretation across a great span of time, but in this case arguing that continuities in Indian cultural traditions may provide avenues to the interpretation of rock art. In her suggestive chapter she shows how by using ethnographic information on Indian 'tribal' dance it is possible to identify certain dance forms and dance movements represented in rock paintings from the Mesolithic onwards. The case may be an exceptional one, but one that may provide a crucial avenue for the reconstruction of the cultural history of the Indian subcontinent. Interpretation of representations of dance is made easier in India with the long history of formal instruction in dance: India is almost a dance-literate culture. But with the development of ethnochoreology in countries such as Australia, it may soon be possible to attempt such interpretation elsewhere. Odak's identification of contemporary cattle brands in Kenyan rock art (Ch. 6) is in certain respects analogous.

Interpreting the system

In interpreting the system we have both reached the final goal of the analysis and returned again to its beginning for, as we have seen, interpretation was involved at every stage of the process and modelling the system may well change the interpretation of components and affect the identification of elements. Such qualifications apply in the case of ethnographic art, but they apply even more so in the case of prehistoric art. In the case of archaeological analysis, pragmatic factors, such as the social context in which a system of representation operates, often have to be inferred from the art itself, together with any other contextual material available (relating, for example, to site use). In an ethnographic context, pragmatic factors can be used independently to inform the analyst about the art and the social context of its interpretation. In archaeological interpretation there is nearly always a double movement: from data to interpretation, and back again. For example, in an archaeological case one might advance the hypothesis that X system of encoded meaning is widely interpretable (i.e. many people should be able to interpret it or say what it means), and that therefore contexts in which it occurs may be open ones. Such a hypothesis requires confirmation from other sources of data which must eventually be fed back into the original interpretation of the art being widely interpretable (the latter can perhaps be said to be the guiding or leading interpretation!). Ethnographically, the fact that art is widely interpretable may be used to explain the contexts of its occurrence.

The chapters in the final section of the book all share in common the attempt to place art in the context of a wider socio-cultural system, using the art to contribute to a more general archaeological or anthropological analysis of the society concerned. Taylor's analysis of Kunwinjku X-ray art (Ch. 18) from northern Australia complements the studies by Tacon (Ch. 10) and Haskovec & Sullivan (Ch. 2). Taylor focuses on the contemporary painting tradition of western Arnhem Land that exists in direct continuity with the rock-art traditions of Kakadu. He shows how X-ray art is the product of a system of representation that operates at a metaphysical level to symbolize the relationship between different dimensions of existence from physical to spiritual to ancestral forms. At a more concrete level, he shows how the art encodes the relationships between ancestral beings and the land, and how certain compositions, in particular the theme of the divided body, provide a root metaphor that can be employed to show the relationships between human groups at different levels of organization. Taylor provides another example of a society in which a number of different representational systems are used which encode meanings in different ways. He shows how the artistic system plays a role in structuring the system of knowledge and, ultimately, in the process of social reproduction.

Berenguer & Martinez (Ch. 19) likewise see the art that they have analysed as having had a role in the social reproduction of the Indian societies of the Upper Loa River. Using ethnographic data from both contemporary and early post-colonization Indian societies, they show how rock art and oral myths are products of the same underlying system of meaning, and how what they refer to as 'the same axis of signification' is present in both. Rock art does not consist of representations of oral myths but refers to the same subjects independently: oral 'myths' and painted 'myths' are both the product of the encoding of meanings, of categories and oppositions which exist independent of any one medium. Although in this case accounts of oral myths provided a way into the interpretation of the rock art, there is no reason why similar conclusions could not have been deduced independently, to be subsequently confirmed by myths. Indeed, once the process of interpretation had been initiated the analysis of the rock art began to throw further light on the oral versions of the myth. The other important feature of Berenguer & Martinez' analysis is that they show the way in which the context of a painting may be part of its meaning. The art of Taira is part of a semiotic system which includes natural as well as cultural signifiers, part of the semantic load being carried by topographical features of the landscape, by springs and high canyon walls.

Olsen's chapter (Ch. 20) condenses the results of a remarkably bold and ambitious enterprise. Her concern is with cultural continuity in the Pueblo region of the southwestern United States. She uses an analysis of the distribution of motifs according to context of occurrence drawn from Zuni and Hopi ethnography, and relates this to a distributional study of motifs in prehistoric Anasazi sites. She is able to show convincingly the relationship between the two populations, and uses the ethnographic data to help reconstruct aspects of the social structure of the Anasazi.

Beyond that she argues that the structure of the artistic system itself could have been a contributing factor to cultural continuity in the region.

Similarly, in Chapter 21 Davidson aims to establish the place of (a particular category of) art within a regional system. His subject is the plaquette art of the Spanish Upper Palaeolithic. Davidson reconstructs the context in which the art could have operated, arguing that plaquettes had a key place in a system of knowledge associated with political and territorial organization. He has provided an excellent example of the kind of interpretative hypothesis that can be fed back into an analysis of the art itself to see whether it provides any insights into it, and whether, in turn, the art provides any supporting evidence for the grand hypothesis. Davidson considers factors such as the distribution of the art, its material composition and quantity, but does not consider its form. An obvious next stage of the analysis would be a morphological analysis of the art, to see if the system of representation employed can be identified, and to see whether the art is likely to articulate with a system of restricted information as Davidson suggests. Increasingly detailed ethnographic examples of art operating as part of a system of restricted information are known (e.g. H. Morphy 1977b) and could provide the basis for analogy, in conjunction with a detailed morphological analysis to show the structure of the system.

Conclusion

In this introduction I have presented only one of the possible readings of the chapters in this book, although I hope it is one that is helpful in setting readers off on a voyage of discovery on their own. Obviously such a rich harvest can be used for many purposes, in particular in finding out about the cultures that produced the art and how they differed among themselves in the way they used animals in their art and the ways in which they represented them. For animals in art do not provide a window to the world but a selection from the world, a selection that tells us as much about human societies and human concerns as about the animals themselves. When animals are transformed into art they often become reflections on the human condition, adjuncts of human thought. But there are two-way processes involved in the relationships between men and animals, art and reality, for in using animals for certain purposes and encoding them in particular ways people inevitably affect the concept of an animal that they have.

Some connotations of animals may seem to the members of a particular society to be fixed and inevitable, almost human universals: in Western Europe, the strength, ferocity, and lethal nature of the crocodile, shark, and jaguar for example. But even in such cases the value of the animal, and how they are seen in relation to each other, may vary enormously, from respect and awe, for example, to loathing and disgust. In fact, however, in many cases the connotation that a particular animal has is culture-specific, not obvious at all, and there will be enormous cross-cultural variation. The analogy between the jaguar and the bat that Legast (Ch. 12) argues for in Tairona art is just such an example (see also Cardale Schrimpff, Ch. 3). Art may be an excellent means of finding out how an animal is perceived by analysing the attributes through which it is portrayed. Drouin (Ch. 16), for example, argues that the way in which elephants are represented in Saharan art, albeit in different media, is a sign of increased domination of man over the animal.

Art has the potential both to differentiate between species and to show what they have in common. The X-ray art analysed by Tacon (Ch. 10) and Taylor (Ch. 18) shows common structures and organs lying beneath the surface of most species, enabling people to draw analogies between human and animal lives, natural and cultural processes. The symbolism of the art alludes to things they share in common, growth and decay, life and death, linking man and animal firmly together within the same spiritual universe.

Haskovec & Sullivan, writing in Chapter 2 about the same body of art, show how what the artist chooses not to represent may be equally important information as what he chooses to depict. They refer to the body of art produced by one man at a time of rapid social change and they argue, following Chaloupka (1982), that Najombolmi's selection of certain content from his environment, and his rejection of others, may have been a statement of his opposition to European society.

In Chapter 5 Morphy argues that the system of representation used to represent a particular content may be related in part to the nature of the content itself. For example, some aspects of the concept of a Yolngu ancestral being may be more appropriately captured by the non-iconic system of geometric representations than they would be by figurative representations: for example, their transformational nature and their existence outside normal time. This may, in part, explain the predominance of geometric designs in the sacred art of Aboriginal Australia, though it must be borne in mind that there are many exceptions, of which Flood (Ch. 13) and Taylor (Ch. 18) both provide examples. How gods or spiritual forces should be represented has been part of the dialectic of many religious systems.

Art also provides a means of looking for long-term cognitive changes or developments in human evolution. In Chapter 4 Lorblanchet alludes to the possible role of animal representations in the development of human consciousness and in differentiating humans from animals. In Chapter 7 Davis considers the question of the creation of the first figurative representation. Although he is more concerned with the impossibility of positively identifying such a first image, rather than arguing that there necessarily was such an object, the general topic of the evolution of figurative representations is becoming increasingly important. Such general problems may appear at the opposite end of the interpretative pole from the detailed attempts to reconstruct the fit between art and society that concern most of the authors in this book. Yet although such grand tasks may be approached as an independent field of enquiry, they have to be tested against detailed models of the ways in which art was used by people at the time, and of the variety of relationships possible between iconic and non-iconic systems. For it seems unlikely that the development of a capacity to represent accurately in figurative form the features of animals was something that emerged independent of the uses to which representations were put by human societies. 'Representation for representation's sake' seems as improbable as 'speech for speech's sake' or 'agriculture for agriculture's sake'. It is only by reconstructing the purposes to which image-making was put, and the varieties of

systems of representation that may have existed, and placing them in the context
of human biological evolution that we will be able to reconstruct the origins of
figurative representation.

Overall, this book shows that it is possible to use art as a means of extending
our knowledge of past cultures and our insights into present ones. Although we
are never going to be able to excavate verbal accounts of the mythology that may
have been associated with some prehistoric art, the analyses suggest that we are in
many cases going to be able to push the interpretation of the art much further than
pessimists have thought. Even in the hardest cases, where there is no historical or
ethnographic data that can be firmly connected with the art, some avenues are open
to uncover much of what now goes under the rubric of 'the meaning of art'. We may
be able to identify the representational systems employed, we may be able to develop
models of the relative value of animal symbols (and of the spatial organization of
animal representations), and we may be able to develop persuasive models of the
possible function and significance of composite representations. And all this should
be attempted as part of general anthropological and archaeological research.

Acknowledgements

I would like to acknowledge the constructive criticisms and editorial hands of Peter
Ucko and Frances Morphy in writing this introduction, and Catherine Hart for preparing the manuscript.

References

Chaloupka, G. 1982. *Burrunguy, Nourlangie Rock*. Darwin: Northart.
Dark, P. J. C. 1978. What is art for anthropologists? In *Art in society*, M. Greenhalgh & V.
    Megaw (eds), 31–50. London: Duckworth.
Davis, W. 1986. The origins of image making. *Current Anthropology*, **27**, 193–215.
Firth, R. 1973. Preface. In *Primitive art and society*, J. A. W. Forge (ed.), v–viii. London:
    Oxford University Press.
Forge, J. A. W. 1970. Learning to see in New Guinea. In *Socialisation: the approach from social
    anthropology*, P. Mayer (ed.), 269–91. ASA monograph 8. London: Tavistock.
Forge, J. A. W. 1973a. Introduction. In *Primitive art and society*, J. A. W. Forge (ed.),
    xii–xxii. London: Oxford University Press.
Forge, J. A. W. 1973b. Style and meaning in Sepik art. In *Primitive art and society*, J. A. W.
    Forge (ed.), 169–92. London: Oxford University Press.
Forge, J. A. W. 1979. The problem of meaning in art. In *Exploring the visual arts of Oceania*,
    S. M. Mead (ed.), 278–86. Honolulu: University of Hawaii Press.
Halverson, J. 1987. Art for art's sake in the Palaeolithic. *Current Anthropology* **28**, 63–89.
Holm, B. 1965. *North west coast Indian art*. Seattle: University of Washington Press.
Kubler, G. 1962. *The shape of time*. New Haven: Yale University Press.
Layton, R. 1981. *The anthropology of art*. London: Granada.
Layton, R. 1987. The use of ethnographic parallels in interpreting Upper Palaeolithic rock
    art. In *Comparative anthropology*, L. Holy (ed.), 210–38. Oxford: Basil Blackwell.
Leroi-Gourhan, A. 1964. *Les religions de la prehistoire*. Paris: Presses Universitaires de France.

Lewis-Williams, D. 1981. *Believing and seeing: symbolic meanings in southern San rock paintings.* London: Academic Press.

Lewis-Williams, D. 1983. Introductory essay. *South African Archaeological Society, Goodwin Series* **4**, 3–13.

Lewis-Williams, D. & J. H. N. Loubser 1986. Deceptive appearances: a critique of Southern African rock art studies. *Advances in World Archaeology* **5**, 253–89.

Llamazares, A. M. 1987. Comment on Halverson's 'Art for art's sake in the Paleolithic'. *Current Anthropology* **28**, 80.

Macintosh, N. W. G. 1977. Beswick Creek cave two decades later: a reappraisal. In *Form in indigenous art*, P. J. Ucko (ed.), 191–7. Canberra: Australian Institute of Aboriginal Studies.

Morphy, F. 1977. The social significance of schematisation in North-west Coast American Indian art. In *Form in indigenous art*, P. J. Ucko (ed.), 73–6. Canberra: Australian Institute of Aboriginal Studies.

Morphy, H. 1977a. Schematisation, meaning and communication in *toas*. In *Form in indigenous art*, P. J. Ucko (ed.), 77–89. Canberra: Australian Institute of Aboriginal Studies.

Morphy, H. 1977b. *Too many meanings*. Unpublished PhD thesis, Australian National University, Canberra.

Morphy, H. 1980. What circles look like. *Canberra Anthropology* **3**, 17–36.

Munn, N. M. 1973. *Warlbiri iconography*. Ithaca: Cornell University Press.

Orme, B. 1981. *Anthropology for archaeologists*. London: Duckworth.

Rosenfeld, A. 1973. Profile figures, schematisation of the human figure in the Magdalenian culture of Europe. In *Form in indigenous art*, P. J. Ucko (ed.), 90–109. Canberra: Australian Institute of Aboriginal Studies.

Ucko, P. J. 1969. Ethnography and archaeological interpretation of funerary remains. *World Archaeology* **1**, 262–80.

Ucko, P. J. 1970. Penis sheaths: a comparative study. *Proceedings of the Royal Anthropological Institute for 1969*, 27–68.

Ucko, P. J. 1989. Subjectivity and the recording of Palaeolithic cave art. In Gonzales Morales, M. R. (ed.). Un Siglo después de Santuola, Santander: Diputación Regional de Cantabria y Universidad de Cantabria.

Ucko, P. J. & A. Rosenfeld 1967. *Palaeolithic cave art*. London: Weidenfeld & Nicolson.

A QUESTION OF IDENTITY

1 *The identification of human and animal figures in European Palaeolithic art*

JEAN CLOTTES
(translated by Meg Conkey)★

The civilizations of the Paleolithic have left tens of thousands of graphic representations on cave walls and on a very diverse range of objects. Prehistorians have classified these representations as animals, humans, and signs. The study of the art has traditionally involved the description of its iconography, its technique, and its dating, the determination of styles, and – over the past 30 years – the study of the relationships among the animal depictions, the relationships between the figures and the topography of the cave for the wall art, or even the syntax of the art as a whole, including signs and humans.

Many attempts have been made to derive all sorts of information from the identification of Palaeolithic pictures, for example, about the climate and, by extension, about the chronology. Breuil attributed the art of Levantine Spain to the Upper Palaeolithic based on his identification of cold-loving or extinct species, such as the rhinoceros, the reindeer, or the saiga antelope (Beltrán 1984, p. 355). More recently, Gonzalez-Echegaray (1974) has postulated that the animal associations in various specific caves could be taken as an accurate reflection of the faunal assemblages of the period, and thus could provide insights into the ecosystems, as well as a way to date the art of the cave to a cold or warm period. Other inferences have been made about seasonality; for example, the characteristic depictions of male salmon, with its hook-like lower jaw, indicate the spawning season, which is late autumn. Or again, according to Schmid (1984), the animals drawn on the walls at Niaux would be animals in their winter coats. Still others have tried to make inferences about domestication, which may be evidenced by certain horse depictions (Piette 1906, Bahn 1978).

Furthermore, a relatively recent phenomenon in this area of study has taken on more and more importance: the use of statistics. Most contemporary monographs include tables, numerical comparisons, and calculations of percentages. This kind of research can be very fruitful, but everyone knows that statistical results are only as valid as the elements on which they are based. Rosenfeld has noted that 'the question of the correct identification of animal species in [Australian] Aboriginal art is only rarely discussed in the literature. . .although the listing of frequencies of motifs in

★ State University of New York, Binghamton.

1

rock art has become almost common practice in analyses of Aboriginal art' (1984, p. 400). One cannot go quite as far in criticizing studies of European Palaeolithic art since numerous authors, especially during the past 20 years, have broached the subject; and moreover *all* of them, when re-analysing a decorated cave or in more general studies, have challenged various interpretations made by their predecessors. Researchers are well aware that a problem exists at the level of the identification of animal and human depictions. The questions one must pose, and this is the goal of this chapter, are simply to know to what extent the existing statistics and inventories are objective and reliable, and how we can develop an increased objectivity.

The fact that we are trying to answer these questions does not mean that we are examining the works of our predecessors merely in order to reveal their possible errors. Rather, we are using their very studies and discussions to consider how prehistorians initially interpret these images, how they assign a label to them and classify them. And we do this in order to gain insights into the complex processes that led Palaeolithic peoples to create their works of art.

The identification of human and animal representations is, epistemologically speaking, a crucial stage in the process of research into Palaeolithic art and one that conditions many subsequent stages and developments. Because the scope of this topic is so vast, yet one that must be approached from a holistic perspective, we must of necessity approach it in the most general terms, without narrowing it down to a single art form, period or region, but using relevant illustrative examples. Nonetheless, we are fully aware that the differences between the portable and wall art sometimes pose quite different problems, and that these vary according to the different periods or geography, or even from one cave to another.

The realization of animal and human depictions

Logically, this should be the last part of my chapter, because to approach this topic at the beginning supposes, to a certain extent, that the problem has been resolved. The prehistoric artists are obviously no longer available to explain to us how they proceeded or what it is that they had wished to represent. Of course, we can try to retrace the process of their creations only through knowledge acquired by methods whose merits must be evaluated *post hoc*. We must begin with the works themselves as they have come down to us and as we reasonably think they once were, before going on to assess modern interpretations.

Motivations

If there is one point on which specialists agree, it is the recognition that prehistoric art is not unmotivated: it responds to religious preoccupations, it is the expression of, or in support of, myths. It does not really matter whether it is the result of simple magical activities repeated over millenniums, as was thought and often written by Bégouën and Breuil, or whether it is (more probably) much more complex and organized; and whether it translates one or more mythologies about which we can have only the most general idea. In all cases, the basic principle implies the idea of communication, of intelligibility. This art must have been understood by the peoples of the time, even if the comprehension was limited to a small group, over a brief period of time, and over a narrow geographic zone. These are all problems worthy of discussion, but which are not strictly relevant here. Leroi-Gourhan said: 'The meaning of the figures, even the most abstract ones, always remained clear from beginning to end for those who used them' (1965, p. 60). The knowledge that we have about contemporary primitive arts fully supports this assertion.

That the big-game hunters of the Upper Palaeolithic chose to use the animals of their environment as terms of their discourse should not be surprising. Their repertoire can certainly be qualified as 'a bestiary, that is, a conventional assemblage of fauna based on definite socio-religious traditions' (Leroi-Gourhan 1981–2, p. 478). This bestiary could theoretically have been quickly reduced to hyper-stylized depictions and could have lost its natural characteristics without ceasing to have been intelligible to those who used the images, had they been a small group of initiates. But we know that naturalism and schematism coexisted throughout these 15 000–20 000 years (Lorblanchet 1977), and that they are indissolubly associated, even during the peak of naturalistic art in the Middle and Late Magdalenian.

The natural models

The animals engraved or painted on the walls of the caves, like those represented in portable art, result from a complex process, which we will summarily review, since it conditions our attempts at interpretation. The natural models, the choices of the artists, the conventions, the raw and supporting materials, and many other factors intervene.

The Palaeolithic artists 'projected onto the rock. . .an inner vision of an animal' (Breuil, in Pales 1969, p. 33). This vision was formed from daily contact with a fauna of a variety and richness that has not been witnessed in these same latitudes for a long, long time. With an acuity that can be found among some living indigenous peoples, the particularly sharp eye of the hunter enabled him to recognize the different species, the sex, the age, and the behaviours of the animals around him. The dead game and the various butchering practices also contributed to his precise knowledge of anatomical details and to the construction of mental images.

The artist was able to draw at will from this infinite stock of images. Certain examples tend to show that at times the animals were represented in a natural state, in a very direct way, such as they would have appeared at the moment when the artwork was realized. This is Vialou's thesis about the deer depicted on the walls at Lascaux, whose antler racks are far from being stereotyped but give an accurate image of the deer according to their age during the different seasons (1984, p. 214). Bosinski has gone even further with the portable art from Gönnersdorf, where the individualized and very naturalistic depictions of mammoths were found in an area of the site that was occupied in winter, whereas the engraved images of birds were found in the part of the site occupied in summer. This led him to consider that the animals depicted here are those that were living in the surroundings at the time of their being engraved (1984, p. 320).

The shared conventions of Palaeolithic art can produce an appearance of uni-formity across representations, but underlying this is a great diversity in the art such that one can find everything and its opposite. The Palaeolithic artists elabo-rated representations from their 'bank of images' in different ways, for example the animals are sometimes sexed, but more frequently they are not, and in order to distinguish the sexes one must look to the secondary sexual characteristics, which are often present, but not always (Baffier 1984). And yet, on the other hand, although they viewed animals in a natural state, in situations and in action, grazing, running, fleeing, etc., they almost systematically represented them fixed (in place), in 'a state of no animation' (Leroi-Gourhan 1973–4, p. 390). But we also know of a good number of animated subjects, whose behaviour evinces a more precise action, such as the bison on the ceiling of Altamira, the leaping salmon on the *bâton* from Lortet, the celebrated fawns with birds from Mas d'Azil, Bédeilhac, and Arudy, etc. Leroi-Gourhan (1984, p. 87) even classified the different types of animal behav-iour depicted in Palaeolithic art under four principal rubrics (aggressive, sexual, cynegetic, anecdotal).

The hunter ceaselessly observed the animals in his environment, and – as Poplin has so aptly shown (1984, p. 234) – must have automatically identified them from a distance, thanks to the characteristic profile of their silhouette. When the artist wished to create an animal form, the details that came to him naturally were those that had allowed him to recognize the animal, and are those that are the most likely ones to enable an interpreter to identify the schema. This most likely explains why the animals are almost always represented in profile, since that is how they were most recognizable.

From the raw image in nature one comes to the graphic convention. This trans-formation is best illustrated by the way in which feet are represented, often depicted from the front (90° twisted perspective). A number of complementary hypotheses have been put forward to explain this: it could have been a convention adopted to facilitate contemporary identification of species (Rousseau 1984b, p. 243); it could have been derived from observations of slain animals (Vialou 1984, p. 214); or it could have been based on animal tracks (Guthrie 1984, p. 58).

However a mental image was formed, its being made concrete on rock, bone, or antler brings into play a double process – whether conscious or not – of remembering (calling an image to mind) and of teaching (leading others to both seeing and understanding).

Artistic and conventional reduction

The transformation of a natural scene into a mental image, and thence into a concrete rendering on a wall or portable medium, has the inevitable consequence, inherent in all of art, of stylization and reduction (Ucko & Rosenfeld 1966, p. 48), if only because an infinite amount of raw information is condensed into a necessarily limited set of lines or forms (Layton 1977, p. 42, Lorblanchet 1977). It is here that the choice of the artist intervenes, in the form of his aims and also of the conventions of his time and place. It is these that determine the degree of realism or rather, of naturalism, of the work.

Leroi-Gourhan (1970–1) defined various stages of the 'figurative state'; he distinguished the *geometric figurative*, where we can still identify the subject – although it tends towards abstraction – from the *synthetic figurative*, 'in which identifying details. . .are pushed more towards the abstract than other parts of the body' (p. 352), and the *analytical figurative*, which is marked 'by the search for a certain optical reality' (id.), and which roughly corresponds to (his) Style IV. This approach seems more concrete than that of Luquet (1926), whose *visual realism* was artificially separated from *intellectual realism*[1] since, aside maybe from the case of reproductions with a model at hand, which does not concern us here, the restored images are always mental images and thus come from an intellectual realism. The *schematic* of Luquet corresponds more or less to the *synthetic figurative*, and the *stylization* corresponds in part to the *geometric figurative*, or even to the *pure geometric* of Leroi-Gourhan.

These useful attempts at classification are fundamentally based on a double principle: that the Palaeolithic artists chose elements of a very widely identifiable bestiary as the terms of their mythogram;[2] and that they did not have our preoccupations with a zoological exactitude (Rousseau 1984a, p. 163, Ucko 1989), so that their criteria for identification were not necessarily identical to ours (Capitan *et al.* 1924, p. 157, Ucko 1977, p. 16).

Numerous authors (see most recently Leroi-Gourhan 1979–80, p. 513, Sieveking 1984, Ucko 1989) have insisted on the consequences of this and have shown that the representations of the animals – far from being faithful portraits – were highly standardized and frequently strayed from visual realism, even though they remained identifiable. Two conventional processes, among others, were often used by the artists:

(a) that which Leroi-Gourhan calls abbreviation, and which Delporte (1984) calls 'synecdoche', where the depiction of one part (for example a cervico-dorsal line, or the rack of a cervid) can stand for the entire animal; and

(b) on the other hand, an exaggeration, sometimes beyond the bounds of anatomical probability, of certain morphologically distinctive traits of a species (for example, the massiveness of the forequarters of a bison; the long horns of the male ibex; the antler rack of certain cervids; the long neck of hinds and of horses, etc.).

The representation of anatomical details that are usually invisible given the viewpoint or angle selected for depiction is a process which is also connected with the previous convention because its intent is to display some characteristics or features to which the artist attaches a particular importance.

It is clear that the existence of these procedures, which are widely attested to, is not going to be without problems (see below) when the modern researcher tries to make fine distinctions. Other conventions also overburden our possibilities for interpretation. For example, there is the absence of scale: in some cases extreme differences in size do not affect identification – in the case of the variable horses at the Salon Noir at Niaux the species identification is clear. But distinctions can become quite delicate among animals that are morphologically differentiated primarily by differences in size (cave or brown bear, fox or wolf, etc.).

Certain conventions more or less openly distance the representations from anatomical reality. Thus Rousseau, for example, reports that 'with very rare exceptions' the shoulder-line of horses is single (1984a, p. 187). In parietal art, however, they are more often multiple. The explanation for this may be that horses of the Upper Palaeolithic were different, that the artists deliberately chose to represent anomalies, or, more likely, that it was just a matter of convention.

Conventions and style can go much further still and supplant specific features, as often happens – for very different reasons – in modern art. This can be seen in the hyper-stylized figures of the final Magdalenian of the type found at Gönnersdorf or Gare de Couze, or even in some Dolni Vestonice objects, such as the *bâton à seins* ('*bâton* with breasts') (Delporte 1979, pp. 270–1).

Finally, in some instances, the artists deliberately chose to depict composite animals; in other words, they combined attributes of different species: for example, the fish engraved on an antler from Morsodou (Dordogne) that borrows details from several different forms of fish (Breuil & Saint-Périer 1927, p. 38); or the La Marche quadruped with a horse's head on a bovine body (see Pales & Tassin de Saint-Péreuse 1981, Pl. 85); or the fantasy animals that have no equivalents in nature. These representations are sufficient in number and of a graphic quality that allows us to exclude the hypothesis that they were mistakes: at Pergouset, Lorblanchet (1984b, p. 506) noted that engravings become progressively more and more fantastic as one goes farther into the cave, even though they are probably done by the same hand as the detailed realistic drawings at the entrance.

Even more numerous, because they are in almost every decorated cave and in all the assemblages of portable art (especially on the engraved plaquettes), are the indeterminate animals, that is animals which do not have specific characteristics that are recognizable to us. Even in a cave where naturalistic figures are quite dominant, such as at Les Trois Frères, there are indeterminate animals in proximity to the most beautiful representations. Vialou, who has made a careful study of the occurrence of these representations, finds that they are associated with a particular topographical position (at the beginning of sets of wall panels) and with the theme of bison (1981, p. 377). He thus concludes that they are intentionally vague images (ibid., p. 1031).

We are not justified in believing that these indeterminate figures had less importance for the Palaeolithic peoples than the more naturalistic representations, no matter what meaning they held (great ancestors, mythological spirits, or any other explanation that one could imagine from the bias of our ethnological knowledge).

With regard to the more or less poorly characterized depictions, it is appropriate to recall that the humans benefit, if one can say that, from a treatment that differs from that of the animals. Although realistic human representations exist (La Marche; La Magdeleine), most of them are more imprecise and less defined than the majority of animals. The rare realistic humans attest that this is not the result of an incapacity to represent men and women except as caricatures and clumsily, as Luquet claimed. Rather, the artists followed certain conventions for image-making from which they did not often stray.

In many cases, we see that 'the convention dominates the representation' (Leroi-

Gourhan 1965, p. 153), which does not make it any easier for us when we set about the task of identifying depictions.

But other parameters equally enter into play.

The personal equation

When facing the animals superbly painted, drawn, or engraved at Lascaux, Niaux, and Les Trois Frères; when facing the clay bison at Le Tuc d'Audoubert that are so magnificently set in place; or when looking at certain works of portable art, one easily refers to them as masterpieces, which implies an artistic knowledge and aim, and an aesthetic that goes beyond the simple reproduction of animal images intended to be the basis for a message. For the message alone it would have been enough for them to have been immediately intelligible. The elements of the mythogram certainly do not necessitate the reproduction of the nuances of the fur, nor that the artist would add such other details that demand our admiration but which seem superfluous in the elaboration of a symbol. The Palaeolithic bestiary, despite all its conventions, is far from being stereotyped, and in many cases such as these the competence and creative enjoyment of the artist may be a significant factor that, although difficult to quantify, must be allowed for.

In contrast, we know many poorly done, unskilful works, and almost shapeless scribblings, in which there may be vague animal silhouettes. In the wall art, Leroi-Gourhan has drawn our attention to the 'panels with incomplete outlines' next to the major works, where realism was not necessary or where one imagines the less gifted individuals were expressing themselves (1965, p. 126). In the portable art, there is a very similar phenomenon with the engraved plaquettes: both perfectly proportioned animals and ones with rough and awkward lines can regularly be found at the same sites. This phenomenon was recognized very early and has been variously interpreted: as 'schools' or 'workshops', as at Limeuil, with masters and students (Capitan & Bouyssonie 1924, p. 39), or even as the works of 'more or less experienced and informed copiers' who, by distorting the works that they copied from, could misrepresent them to the point of becoming simple ornamental motifs or signs (Breuil 1905).

Even if these hypotheses seem simplistic, the fact remains that these clumsy lines exist, in which the lack of experience and the heavy-handedness are striking, and which can cause errors in interpretation. In a good many cases, it is not easy to decide which of the indeterminate animals result from the lack of skill of the artist and which represent a deliberate attempt at an indeterminate form.

Certain anatomical errors recur throughout the art, as Pales has shown in the case of horses, which are always drawn too long, and in the inaccurate position of the canines of carnivores (Pales & Tassin de Saint-Péreuse 1981). But other errors are sometimes those of a particular artist: thus, at Les Combarelles, equid Number 27 was initially determined by Breuil to be a donkey because of its long ears, but then Novel (1984) noted that in this cave a further number of horses had been depicted with ears disproportionately long. There thus exist real idiosyncracies that we must be aware of, if only because they are otherwise likely to mislead us.

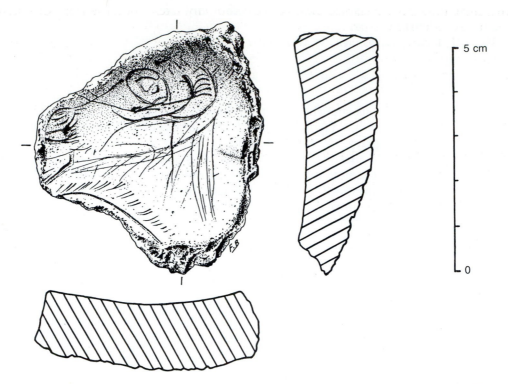

Figure 1.1 Fragment of a stalagmite from Enlène (Montesquieu-Avantès, Ariège). Two interpretations are possible: according to which one is chosen, it could either be a completely naturalistic figure, or one in which the constraints of the raw material support have distorted the position of the horn. In the first case, because of the position of the horn, it would depict an ovibos; in the second instance, one could argue that the Magdalenian artist had wanted to represent a bison but that there was not enough room to engrave the horn in the normal anatomical position. (Drawing by F. Briois, from the excavations of R. Bégouën, J. Clottes, J.-P. Giraud, & F. Rouzaud.)

The supports and their constraints

The form or the relief of the supporting medium often determined the choice of subject (such as fish being abundant on perforated *bâtons* and spear-throwers, and innumerable examples in wall art: the bird at Altxerri, the deer head in the demi-cupola of the Salon Noir at Niaux, etc.). Sometimes they constrain the way in which a representation is produced, influencing the posture of the human or animal, or the attributes which are included. This can be a cause of possible confusion (Fig. 1.1). Leroi-Gourhan provides a striking example of the problem, citing a sculpted reindeer antler from Laugerie Basse (1965, p. 62, Fig. 51). 'This figure is an example of the difficulties in the identification of subjects: if it is a case of a fragment of a spear-thrower, and the posture was necessitated by the form of the object, then the animal could have been a feline, or even a young ruminant; but if the form translates an accurate animal posture, it can only be a bear.' (op. cit.) This animal should therefore logically be classed among the 'indeterminates'[3] because it is not possible for us, in its present state, to decide between the two possibilities.

Palaeolithic art has been produced on cave walls of great scale with more or less tortuous relief. The artists exploited the shapes of the surfaces masterfully, often using the fissures and the accidents of erosion and calcification to advantage, as in the eye of the bison engraved on the ground at Niaux. If this instance, and many others, cannot be challenged, there are nevertheless numerous more ambiguous examples, where taking the natural lines or reliefs into account (or refusing to) fundamentally changes the interpretation of the figure (see, for example, the head of a bison at Hornos de la Peña, built up by Breuil in an arbitrary way out of several natural fissures; in Ucko 1989).

In conclusion, the visual images of Palaeolithic artists were transformed by successive steps, as a result of very diverse phenomena, into a great corpus of materials, which were intelligible at a given moment, perhaps quite a brief one, for a human group, which was perhaps not very large. A great many factors influenced their production; some of these we may perceive, but in general we are not in control of the images. Consequently, ever since the conception and production of the images, the causes of confusion and error have increased and continue to increase with the passage of time (cf. Macintosh 1977).

The proof of time

The art forms that have survived into the present have undergone numerous alterations or depredations, which have often diminished or transformed them.

Already in the Upper Palaeolithic, some painted or engraved panels in the decorated caves were renewed, and some plaques and plaquettes (cf. La Marche, Enlène) were renovated with new representations. These may have been in conjunction with existing works (as compositions) or added to by chance; this is not our immediate concern. What matters here is that the entanglements that result from these renovations often render the figures barely intelligible to us today. Even when they are studied under the best of conditions, that bring out all of the details, there will always remain a number of outlines or traces for which several readings are possible according to the particular lines chosen. The nature of the reading in such cases, what species it is, what details of the body are included, or what degree of animation is shown, can vary according to the choices of the interpreter (see, for example, the plaquette no. 122, Pl. XXIX, from Limeuil, in Capitan & Bouyssonie 1924).

In addition, the materials used for portable art have rarely survived intact. The perforated *bâtons*, the spear-throwers, and the engraved bones are often broken, and we have only partial depictions which, because of their incomplete nature, allow for different interpretations (see the polemics over the 'woman-with-reindeer' from Laugerie-Basse, in Lhote 1968). This is most often the case with the plaquettes, in that several authors have proposed that they were purposefully desecrated, broken, and their fragments dispersed (Capitan & Bouyssonie 1924, p. 40, Saint-Périer 1930, p. 81, Bégouën *et al.* 1982a, p. 54). It is not rare to find that they were damaged or reused as elements in pavements, in floors and hearths, or as lamps.

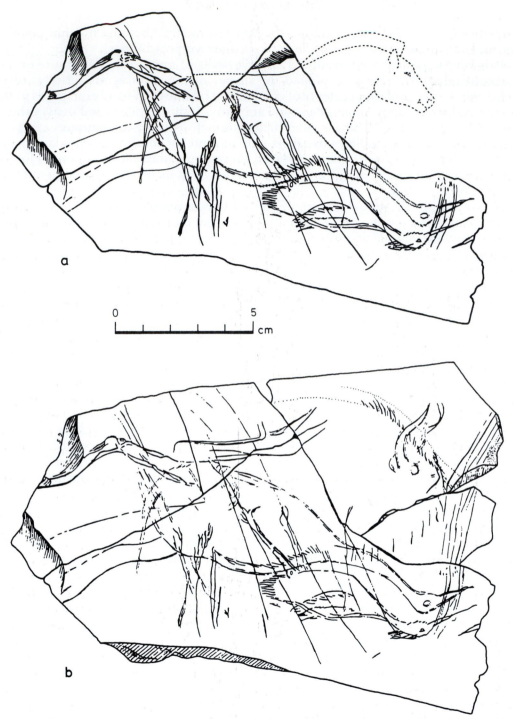

Figure 1.2 Plaquette from Labastide (Hautes-Pyrénées): (a) at the time of its discovery, showing a figure interpreted as a horse (after Simonnet 1947); (b) after the discovery of missing fragments it became clear that the horse, in fact, was a bison (Simonnet *et al.* 1984).

After being decorated, one engraved stone from Enlène was used as a wedge, at the bottom of the cave, and flakes were struck from it, ruining the engravings (Bégouën & Clottes 1979b).

The identification of incomplete subjects is risky, as two examples will demonstrate. Simonnet published a convincing interpretation of some imagery from the cave of Labastide (Hautes-Pyrénées) that he believed represented the hindquarters of a horse (Simonnet 1947, p. 60). But some years later he discovered the missing pieces and realized that it was now, in fact, unquestionably a bison (Simonnet *et al.* 1984, p. 29). Furthermore, 'that which had been taken to be the hollow of the back of the horse when drawn was, in fact, one of the feet, folded back, of a large bird' (ibid., p. 28). This also illustrates the problems of superimposed figures (Fig. 1.2).

The second example is taken from the human representations on a large plaquette from Enlène (Ariège) (Fig. 1.3). The first fragment, discovered 50 years ago, was described and published by Bégouën (1939, pp. 292-3) as a copulating couple, with a gracile subject (the man) and a more bulky person (the woman) (no doubt because large stomachs were considered distinctively female). Bégouën (and Bouyssonie who did the tracing), adopting this perspective, interpreted certain lines attributed to the 'man' as a penis sheath. The Abbé Breuil, on the other hand, provided his own drawing of the plaquette (Fig. 1.3b) in which he, in effect, reinterpreted it, perceiving only a single individual – 'an obese human figure, probably female' (Bégouën & Breuil 1958, p. 106). Breuil's interpretation was implicitly accepted by numerous authors (Graziosi 1960, Pl. 883e, Leroi-Gourhan 1965, p. 370, Ucko & Rosenfeld 1972, p. 174, Clottes 1976, Fig. 8 no. 5). Subsequently, Pales and Tassin de Saint-Péreuse studied the plaquette in great detail and came up with several possible interpretations, one of which has proved to be correct (1976, Figs 37c & d). The incorrect hypothesis they put forward, albeit with question marks, was that the delicate figure was male and the pot-bellied subject female; the correct interpretation is the reverse.

We were able to resolve the controversy when we discovered the fragments that completed the plaquette. We discovered that there were indeed two overlapping figures, contrary to what Breuil and his successors had accepted. However, if as seems likely the two figures are engaged in coitus, it is the female who is the gracile figure and the man who is the larger one. The so-called penis sheath (which had been contested by some authors) turns out to be the extension of the belt of the gracile subject. In other words, everybody, myself included, who had interpreted the plaquette was proved to be seriously mistaken, sometimes because of preconceived ideas, always because of the fragmentary nature of the evidence (Bégouën *et al.* 1982b).

Despite its monumentality, wall art in many caves has also been subject to the vicissitudes of time from such factors as calcification, running water, currents of air, etc. Thus, at Erberua (Pyrénées-Atlantiques) many of the paintings are washed out or diffused, with smudgy and indistinct shapes, so that only half of the figures can be identified (Larribau & Prudhomme 1984, p. 279).

Degradation originating from human action is unfortunately more frequent. At the International Colloquium on Parietal Art in Périgueux (1984), Ucko presented a paper that developed this theme, particularly with regard to the cave of Hornos de la Peña: he showed how modern visits to the cave, rubbing against the cave

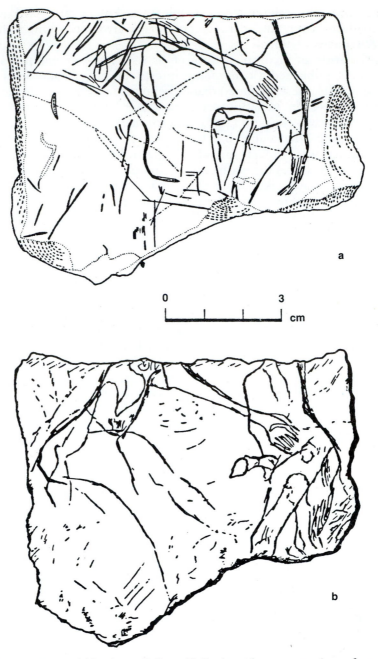

Figure 1.3 Pebble from Enlène (Ariège) with an engraving of an ithyphallic man and an indeterminate human, holding out its hand above the penis of the opposite figure: (a) drawing by C. Servelle; (b) by H. Breuil. In version (b) the human on the left has become a female, with prominent buttocks and a breast.

walls, and graffiti often made it impossible to interpret many lines, much less to put forth hypotheses, since it was impossible to differentiate in some cases between modern inscriptions, Palaeolithic engravings, or even natural cracks in the wall (Ucko 1989).

The deciphering of figures

We can now turn to the question of deciphering the Palaeolithic messages, which, as we have shown, may have been inaccessible at the very beginning in some cases, and which have become harder to interpret through the actions of both nature and humans. They can be deciphered, to varying degrees, but each step presents its own obstacles.

Degrees of identification

The three main categories of Palaeolithic representation as traditionally defined – humans, animals, signs – are not always as distinct as one might like (Ucko 1989). Prehistoric artists did, on occasion, pursue ambiguity and play with shapes (Leroi-Gourhan 1965, p. 96), so that in certain border-line cases, basic distinctions between animal–human, animal–sign, or human–sign are difficult to establish.

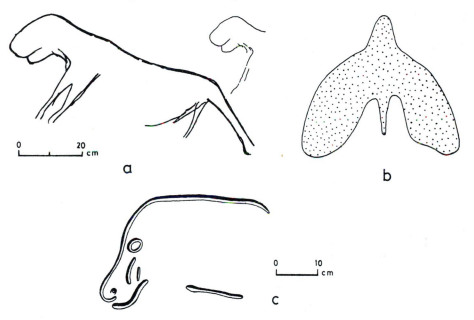

Figure 1.4 Examples of indeterminate figures that have been interpreted in various ways. (a) Indeterminate animal from Rouffignac (Dordogne) interpreted as an anthropomorph (after Barrière 1982, Fig. 454–5); (b) a painting from Le Portel (Ariège) (after Breuil & Jeannel 1955), interpreted variously as a bird in flight, a connected sign, a bird-like sign, and a domed hut; (c) head from Commarque (Dordogne) (after Delluc & Delluc 1981), interpreted as that of a bear or of an animal-like human.

At Commarque, for example, a head that was identified by Breuil as a bear's (Fig. 1.4c) is more likely to be a human profile made in an animal style according to Delluc & Delluc (1984, p. 121). In a reverse process, an anthropomorphic head with animal-like attributes identified by Leroi-Gourhan at Fond-de-Gaume was interpreted by Roussot (1984a, p. 133) as the head of a feline or of a bear. Examples of this type are legion.

Human depictions, or those supposed to be such, have often been prejudged without really probing the criteria for identification, and the interpretations have been biased, either by anthropocentrism, by theories of hunting-magic, or by ethnographic parallels (on this subject, see Ucko & Rosenfeld 1972, Pales & Tassin de Saint-Péreuse 1976, Delporte 1979). For example, Baffier has recently queried why the 'bison-sorcerer' from Les Trois Frères should be considered a sorcerer although it has only animal attributes: 'this identification is certainly due to the semi-vertical position of the animal and to the "human" articulation of the back leg' (1984, p. 144). There has also been an obvious tendency to place indeterminate figures among the anthropomorphs, not on their intrinsic merits but simply because they do not resemble any single possible animal (Fig. 1.4a). This is what motivated, among others, Capitan *et al.* at Les Combarelles (1924, pp. 191–6, cited in Ucko & Rosenfeld 1972, p. 204) or – more recently – Barrière at Rouffignac (1982, p. 147).

Distinguishing between humans and signs rarely poses such fundamental problems, although examples do exist, such as at Eglises d'Ussat (Ariège) where a small red silhouette was interpreted by Breuil as a schematic human, while Beltrán (1969) and then Vialou (1981, p. 848) took it to form part of a tectiform (but see Clottes & Rouzaud 1984, p. 431). In re-analysis, it is not always easy to identify the different isolated anatomical elements, real or imaginary: some realistic vulvas have indeed been painted, engraved, or modelled in various caves, but all the incomplete circles are not necessarily vulvas (Roucadour, Pech-Merle), and even fewer of the simple geometric figures – such as squares, circles, or triangles – can be interpreted as vulvas. Whether or not these are signs of a feminine type, as they are according to Leroi-Gourhan's theory, is another problem, since one moves then from the realm of identification to that of interpretation, which is quite a different matter. What differentiates realistic vulvas from 'feminine' signs is, in fact, quite illusory and subjective. To an extent it could be the same for other body parts (positive hands, phallus, arms, heads, etc.).

The difficulties can be of the same order when distinguishing between animals and signs. Sometimes the specialists come out with interpretations that are very different from each other. In the principal gallery at Le Portel, there is a large red depiction (Fig. 1.4b), which Leroi-Gourhan classed as a connected sign (*en accolade*) 1965, p. 268), whereas Breuil had seen it as a domed hut (Breuil & Jeannel 1955, Pl. V). To Beltrán the picture was a possible vulva and to Vézian a bird in flight (Beltrán *et al.* 1966, p. 81). Most recently it has been more prudently qualified by Dauvois and Vézian (1984, p. 834) as a bird-like sign. The case is even more difficult when dealing with lines that could either be independent signs or attributes of animals (such as lines that could represent breathing or blowing out, wounds, or details of fur – See Fig. 1.5a–c). We know, for example, that the lines on the shoulders of horses and the flattened 'M' on the bodies of horses from the Middle Magdalenian are stylistic conventions that represent real anatomical characters. Barandiarán (1972, p. 370) interprets in the same way some zig-zags engraved on bison and on reindeer at Les Trois Frères and Altxerri, and suggests that they could be interpreted as nuances of the fur or animal hair; yet for the three bison that he refers to (op. cit. Fig. 29) the fur coat is expressly indicated by a series of short marks, as on the great majority of animal figures at Les Trois Frères. Were there, in this case, two distinct conventions for indicating the fur of the same animal? This is not impossible, but it is more likely that this broken line should be considered as a sign, like the one that obliquely divides the body of a horse engraved on a pebble from Enlène (Bégouën & Clottes 1979b) and which, because of its position, cannot be accounted for as an anatomical detail (Fig. 1.5d).

To be able to identify animals, however, implies that we must first be able to identify the species (in the familiar and not the zoological sense of the word) to which they belong. Roussot (1984c) has discussed the major obstacles that prehistorians encounter when trying to do this, and has proposed that the study of Palaeolithic bestiary should rest on precise zoological inventories. He argues that for such inventories to be agreed on they must be based on zoological systematics (classes, orders, families, genera, species, eventually using the intermediary categories of 'super' or 'sub') and that such classifications should aim at generating a 'type-list of depicted animals' (ibid., p. 114), comparable to those used for lithic industries (see also Roussot 1985).

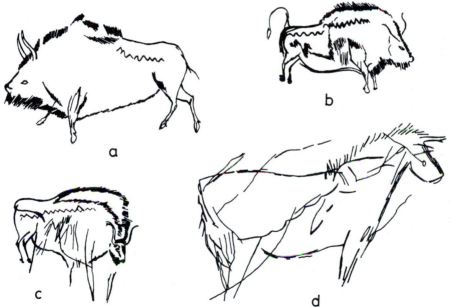

Figure 1.5 (a)–(c) Engraved bisons from Les Trois Frères (Ariège) (drawing by H. Breuil, cited in Barandiarán 1972: Fig. 29). The zigzag line is interpreted as a conventional representation of its fur. This is not very probable, given that fur is usually represented in this cave, and even in the case of these figures, by a series of short hatch marks. (d) Engraved horse on a pebble from Enlène (Ariège), with the same sign in a broken line, but done very obliquely (drawing by C. Servelle). Various scales are used here.

At the same colloquium that Roussot presented these ideas, Ucko (1989) strongly criticized such an approach because of the existence of so many indeterminate animals and because an approach which is exclusively zoological appears to assume that Palaeolithic artists were concerned with clearly indicating the species and sub-species. If they were not, he asked, should the study of Palaeolithic art really be concerned with such problems?

In fact, these two authors are taking different perspectives and their positions are much less incompatible than it appears. Certainly, the difficulties of identification are great, as are the dangers of approaches that are too refined. Obviously, Palaeolithic artists were hardly concerned with the zoological classifications that modern specialists have defined: so, for example, there are numerous representations of fish, reptiles, and birds that cannot be identified more precisely than at the level of zoological class. However, there is no reason to suppose that their referent was any less clear to the authors or their symbolic value inferior to those which can be identified at the level of their order (e.g. carnivores), their family (cervids, equids), their species (horse, bison, aurochs), or even their sub-species (hemione). This unquestionable absence of taxonomic hierarchy in the Palaeolithic representations should not lead us to use a less precise vocabulary nor prevent us from better defining the images that we encounter. Zoological classification is not an end in itself, but a means, which allows us to speak in the same language. An analogous situation exists in the case of lithic typology. Palaeolithic peoples did not oblige us by creating a lithic or bone typology. They did, however, make tools that fit into the categories of endscrapers, burins, and other tool types. The usefulness of this typological approach is not vitiated by the fact that within their lithic industries we find a number of ambiguous objects for which the specialists have had to create a category called 'miscellaneous'.

It is sometimes possible to go even further than the identification of class, species, or even sub-species, and to distinguish the sex, and, more rarely, the age. The problems posed by the identification of sex have been discussed in detail both for the human depictions (Ucko & Rosenfeld 1972, Pales & Tassin de Saint-Péreuse 1976, Rosenfeld 1977, Delporte 1979) and for those of animals (Ucko & Rosenfeld 1966, Bandi 1968, 1972, Baffier 1984). We can simply note that when prehistorians have tried to distinguish sex the obstacles they have encountered as a result have led to a certain lack of methodological logic. For example, certain representations of deer are almost always classed as hinds because of their long necks and lack of antlers, despite the fact that they could also represent stags which have lost their antlers after the rut (Ucko & Rosenfeld 1966, p. 205). Interestingly enough, in the faunal inventories other species are usually not listed separately on the basis of sex (for example, in the case of stallions and mares, bulls and cows, or male and female ibex), even though secondary sexual characteristics and, more rarely, primary ones quite often make them identifiable by specialists (e.g. Leroi-Gourhan 1965, p. 121, Baffier 1984, p. 153). The fact that they can be identified now suggests that they would have been even more readily identifiable to Palaeolithic people who probably attached as much symbolic value to a stallion or a bull as to a deer.

Attributing the age to a Palaeolithic depiction of an animal is very difficult indeed, because Palaeolithic stylistic conventions could be misleading, and, in addition, most representations lack scale. The absence of young animals in Palaeolithic art has often been noted. Barrière, on the basis of the length of the horns of ibex, concluded that five of the ibex at Rouffignac were animals of at least 15 years of age (1982, p. 154). He would be correct if we could assume that the Magdalenian artist wished to make a faithful and realistic portrait; but, in fact, we have no way of knowing this. Also, it is not impossible that the horns were rendered out of all proportion and that it could be a case of a stylistic exaggeration, such as those identified elsewhere (e.g. the antlers on deer at Lascaux or one of the ibex at Les Trois Frères), with the intent of accentuating the sexual differences among the ibex.

The inherent difficulty of adopting an objective approach can be illustrated by two examples. The first concerns evidence for the domestication of the horse in the Palaeolithic. The possibility of this was initially propounded by Piette at the beginning of this century, based on certain works of art, and although the idea was refuted by Cartailhac it has been recently taken up again by Bahn (1978). Since then, however, Schmid's work with representations of the horse (1984, p. 160) has shown that the very morphology of the head results in a number of lines that would be followed by a bridle if one were used. To interpret these lines as a bridle, she argues, would be far from certain and would involve subjective judgements.

Secondly, fish are often depicted with a horizontal dividing line along their backs. This line has been interpreted in various ways:

(a) as the skeleton, or backbone, which would imply that the whole body had been depicted as if transparent (similar to the 'X-ray' art of Australian Aborigines, see Ch. 18, this volume);[4]

(b) as a groove separating the two parts of the body to show their different pigmentation; and even

(c) as the depiction of a realistic anatomical characteristic of salmonids (Breuil, cited by Chollot-Varagnac 1980, p. 476).

In fact, such a lateral line is the sensory organ of a fish, giving it information about vibrations and obstacles in the water (Bégouën & Clottes 1979a, p. 11). Its regular depiction by the Magdalenians, who definitely stressed it, probably demonstrates their practical knowledge of its fundamental role in the defensive system of fish.

In the two cases mentioned above, while absolute certainty can never be reached (after all, it is not impossible that the lateral line could *also* represent the backbone of the fish, as in the well-known sole from Lespugue), precise identification requires a zoological background. It is just the same, *a fortiori* for the interpretation of animal postures, which Leroi-Gourhan has called 'animation', and which comprises the highest degree in his scale of figurative determinations. In recent years there have often been calls for a mandatory collaboration between zoologists, ethologists, and prehistorians; this was the only aim of the colloquium at Sigriswill in 1979 (see also Bandi 1968, Barandiarán 1972, Novel 1984, Roussot 1984c). Such collaboration should promote the reintegration of much Palaeolithic iconography within a more ecologically informed framework, following the terms of Leroi-Gourhan (1980–1, p. 455), whereas formerly the evidence was too often interpreted very simplistically. An example of the consequences of such an approach is that the famous 'browsing reindeer' from Thayngen can now be seen as a male at the time of the rut.

Such a collaboration, however, is far from being an infallible panacea; even if it often leads to the avoidance of gross errors, it still may only offer a set of alternative interpretations. For a long time, the bison at Altamira had been described as sleeping, wounded, or dying animals. The hypothesis that has prevailed since Leroi-Gourhan, and that is still prevailing (Guthrie 1984, p. 48, Rousseau 1984a, p. 181), is that these bison are males rolling in the dust after they have urinated to mark their territory. However, at about the same time as these hypotheses were developed, a prehistorian-ethologist had noted that one of the bison could be a female (Bandi 1968, p. 17), and an eminent faunal specialist, Count Vojkffy (who had previously corrected the error about the reindeer at Thayngen), suggested that it was clearly a case of females giving birth (calving) (Giedion 1964, p. 193). In other words, with these divergent opinions, we are again encountering the subjectivity that more or less strongly permeates all attempts at identification. This leads us to examine the identification process itself, that is, the way in which researchers make their decisions, and to try to define and classify the problems that they encounter, some of which we have already mentioned.

The process of identification

Two principal, but not exclusive, attitudes influence this process, depending on whether we examine the intrinsic or extrinsic characteristics of the subjects to be identified. In addition, there exist instinctive tendencies, common to all researchers, that condition the process.

What are taken to be the intrinsic characteristics of humans and animals, that is the distinctive features of their shape and posture from which we form our mental images of them, vary from one individual to another according to their cultures. The mental images we hold today must almost by definition differ from those held by the artist-hunters of the Palaeolithic. When faced with the figure of an animal that is more or less naturalistic and coincides well with our own image of the animal, we react immediately and exclaim: 'it is a bison, or a horse, or an ibex. . .'. Depending upon the experience and background of the particular individual, this image as it is seen results from observations of living animals (in nature or, in most cases, from the bias of television, film, or photography), from professional understanding of anatomy or osteology in the case of palaeontologists, or even from experience with Palaeolithic art itself. It is evident that this will vary considerably from a prehistorian who specializes in Palaeolithic art, to an ethologist, a palaeontologist, a hunter, or an amateur, and will depend also upon the personality and experience of each person.

The initial interpretation of an image is thus almost an instinctive one that is of relative value according to who made the judgement. It is at this level that the argument from authority can come into play. For example, the opinion of the Abbé Breuil could be used in support of certain identifications because of his incomparable experience of Palaeolithic art. However, this argument from authority has only superficial validity as even the best specialist is subject to errors of interpretation.

In numerous cases, though, Palaeolithic depictions are fortunately instantly recognizable. Intuitive identification, as a sort of short-cut that skips stages of analysis, has even been confirmed in some instances by subsequent discoveries. For example, the hyper-stylized female silhouettes, such as those at Lalinde, were not recognized as such at first. It was 20 years before they were recognized as representations of women, and then identification was on a fairly intuitive basis since there were no figures known that could bridge the gap between them and more realistic representations. Later on, the discovery of figures with breasts, that were unquestionably female, confirmed the original identification (Pales & Tassin de Saint-Péreuse 1976, p. 101). But, along with some successes of this kind, there are a good number of intuitive identifications that have fallen short.

It is thus necessary, above all in the doubtful cases, to apply the most objective methods to give a solid basis to the identifications made. Reference to works on zoology or prehistoric art, and consultation with a variety of experts does not change the process of identification discussed above. The process still concerns the creation of mental images, but the more evidence that is marshalled the more possibilities are opened up and the greater the chances are of avoiding mistakes.

Another possible method is to set up a quadrilateral frame for the image or to use a comparative set of anatomical measures that, as Pales (1969, p. 104) cautiously noted, are not panaceas but can be useful. He was able to show that all but one of the felines depicted were inscribed within certain limits, which indicates that 'the prehistoric engravers had followed a canon for the anatomy of felines' (ibid., p. 61). As a consequence, he was able to come to the conclusion that the one exception – the 'lion with the mane' at Les Combarelles, whose specific identification had never been challenged – was the result either of a gross error by the engraver, or, more likely, of 'an error of reading and zoological identification' (ibid., p. 62), and that it should be eliminated from the list of quaternary felines. This reinterpretation had wider implications, as Koby had presumed, based on this figure, that there were two sub-species of lion during the Pleistocene, one with a mane and the other without (ibid.).

The literature provides us with numerous examples of another type of justification for an identification that has a much less rigorous methodological basis. In this case the interpreter begins with an unarguably life-like depiction and, going through a succession of approximations, ends up attributing particular animal characteristics to representations that have little relationship to the animal concerned. The best example of this can be found in the work of Breuil & Saint-Périer (1927) with fish, where everything that was spindle-shaped ('fusiform'), all double markings in rows, and many other signs were identified as fish. It is true that they used some circumspection in their language (see p. 164) but not enough for us to accept a faulty methodology that could lead anywhere provided general-enough criteria of resemblance are used. In the same way, some undulating or even straight lines have been interpreted as serpents (why not as worms (Ucko 1989), eels, or water ?), and branching signs have been likened to phalli (Giedion 1964, pp. 149, 153).

This process is only methodologically admissible in two cases:

(a) when one can move from a naturalistic depiction to another that is less clear, when they are both on the same object (such as the caprids on an antler from Massat, Fig. 1.6), or from the same site (see the argument below); and

(b) when the author proposes an interpretation that is by definition hypothetical and does not give a definitive identification to the figure, which is then

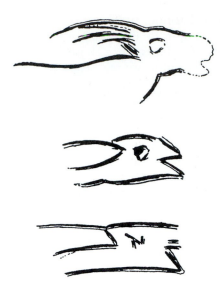

Figure 1.6 Three engravings of caprids on the same reindeer antler from Massat (Ariège). The first is naturalistic and the others much less so. Their identification is acceptable due to the association of all three on the same piece. (Drawing by H. Breuil 1905.)

finally classified among the 'indeterminates' or among the signs. In this way Leroi-Gourhan had every right to interpret claviforms as feminine signs, but he would not have been justified to classify them as human images.

In particular, in the case of the parietal art, certain identifications may be determined not on the basis of mental images alone but on certain criteria that are extrinsic to the representations themselves. For example, when the distinction between bears as *Ursus arctos* or *Ursus spelaeus* cannot be made directly from the drawings alone (Bandi 1968, p. 94), identification rests largely on the controversial question of whether or not the species survived into the Magdalenian (Ucko & Rosenfeld 1966, p. 94). In the first place, therefore, it becomes a palaeontological problem. The same is true for other species that have become extinct (e.g. types of rhinoceros), or are absent from the faunal remains found in the sites thar de Cougnac (cf. Roussot 1984d)).

The archaeological context, whether pictorial or topographic, has frequently been used, rightly or wrongly, to support identifications. If one motif exists which is sufficiently explicit to serve as a reference, the repetition of the same theme in the same locality has rightly been taken as support for the same identification: at Le Portel (Ariège) there is a human silhouette that is painted in conjunction with a stalagmite in such a way that it evokes an erect phallus. This figure has thus been interpreted as masculine although the stalagmite in the image could have been a coincidence. Several metres along the same wall is another human representation also painted in red and drawn around a concretion that is in the correct place to represent the penis. The presence of two such figures supports the identifications of both as masculine (Fig. 1.7). The same can be said for Gönnersdorf where there are many schematic figures that, outside of their context, would be classified as

Figure 1.7 Ithyphallic men from Le Portel (Ariège). These red depictions are located just a few metres from each other and each uses a fortuitous stalagmitic formation for the penis. Their identical conception as well as their proximity supports this interpretation. (Drawings by M. Dauvois.)

non-figurative but which, in comparison with the numerous unquestionably female silhouettes, can also be accepted as female outlines (Rosenfeld 1977, p. 98).

On the other hand, identification of sexual distinctions based on the topographic position of certain figures in the caves has been quite justly denounced by Ucko & Rosenfeld (1972, p. 194). For the same reasons, Novel (1984) has criticized Leroi-Gourhan who thought he saw bears among the very dubious figures at Bernifal, Reverdit, and Cap-Blanc, because of their marginal or remote topographical location. In another instance, an engraved piece of portable art from the Abri Murat (Lot) was interpreted by Lemozi and his followers (Giedion 1964, p. 369, Fig. 333) as a man following a woman when, although two humans are certainly represented, there is nothing at all to indicate their sex.

In fact, almost each time that two humans are represented near to each other, interpreters have postulated couples of opposite sex, despite the absence of distinctive characteristics (cf. the two heads named 'Adam and Eve' at Rouffignac). This has had some surprising results, such as with the second person on an engraved bone from Isturitz, which had been interpreted as a man pursuing a woman ('amorous pursuit') until Leroi-Gourhan noted correctly that 'the man' was really another woman, with a part of the breast visible.

These examples illustrate certain a priori assumptions and presuppositions that are often the origin of amazing interpretations; thus, even Vialou (1981, p. 873) has classed two fantasy animals at Le Tuc d'Audoubert as humans because, he says, 'from a symbolic approach, they can be compared to humans, although, from a strictly figurative point of view, they can be connected to the animal figures' (ibid., p. 888). Following this, he then includes them in the inventory of human figures (ibid., p. 885) and, as such, in the percentages that he establishes (ibid., p. 911). Clearly, they should have been placed in the category of 'fantasy animals' or at most among the 'indeterminates'.

The examples cited are not just a few isolated cases, but they represent attitudes and temptations which are widespread and to which most, if not all, researchers have succumbed at least on occasion, namely:

(a) the tendency to deny that the depictions may be unintelligible; and
(b) the propensity to extract more from the evidence than it can support.

Lorblanchet (1984a, p. 44) has described the first of these phenomena well: 'Facing a confusion of digital lines or engravings, the mind instinctively seeks. . .forms and motifs. Right away it refuses the unintelligible. This could lead the prehistorian to misleading interpretations', such as those of Lemozi, that he cites, for the great ceiling of Pech-Merle where Lemozi believed he discerned bizarre animals. The temptation to over-interpret, to read meanings uncritically into a mass of lines, is something that the prehistorian must be cautious of. Positive identifications are particularly dangerous when applied to natural forms or to traces that are of doubtful authenticity. Such identifications once proposed are often accepted lightly into the secondary literature and become accepted through usage. At Cap-Blanc, for example, Roussot (1984b, p. 161) cites two 'little sculpted bison', discovered by Hours and noted also by Leroi-Gourhan which, he points out, do not really exist and result from a risky interpretation derived from 'a series of scalings and other surface alterations' (ibid., p. 160). In the same cave, an engraved hand that was identified by Blanc, reproduced by Graziosi, and accepted by Verbrugge, turns out to be only a grouping of natural little hollows (ibid., p. 161). Similarly, Dams & Dams (1979) published numerous red depictions (bison, caprids, signs, humans) from the cave of Mayrière Supérieure (Tarn-&-Garonne) which are, in fact, natural phenomena (Clottes *et al.* 1981).

Even skilled specialists can be taken in by the projection of their mental images. Beltrán *et al.* published (1973, p. 138) what they believed to be a possible anthropomorph in the panel of the deer in the Salon Noir at Niaux. In 1985 another prehistorian intended to publish the same figure and compare it with the sorcerer of Les Trois Frères. However, I was able to dissuade him from doing so by making him acquainted with a photograph from the Musée de l'Homme on which the anthropomorph can clearly be seen to be the result of alterations suffered over the years by an earlier graffiti. This photograph (Fig. 1.8), first published by Cartailhac and Breuil in 1908 (p. 20, Fig. 5), shows the figure to be the beginning of the name 'Gustave', which was much more legible in the early years of this century than it subsequently became.[5]

Another great problem with Palaeolithic art studies is the tendency to push identification to extreme lengths. It is not only the unfortunate attempts by various authors, including Bourdelle, to establish sub-species of Palaeolithic horses on the basis of Palaeolithic depictions which are so worrying. Even Bosinski followed a similar approach with regard to the representations of mammoths at Gönnersdorf. He pointed out that most of them did not have tusks although they were otherwise quite naturalistic. The depiction of tusks would not have posed any technical problem and he argued that it was hard to imagine that the artists just would not have drawn any tusks if tusks were there. Following on from this he proposed the hypothesis that certain mammoths in the Rhine valley, at the end of the Bölling, did not have tusks because they belonged to a late type of biologically regressive mammoths (Bosinski 1984, p. 301). Although this hypothesis has some merits, it is countered by the fact that some of the mammoths *are* represented with their tusks and that two fragments of tusks of a normal size were found in the excavations. From the evidence it would be just as plausible or more so to propose that in the eyes of the Magdalenians the mammoth would be adequately characterized by its trunk and the curve of its spine. A similar type of reasoning to that employed by Bosinski, though in this case motivated by the absence of hair in certain representations, led to the mammoths at Pindal and Cougnac being identified as smooth-skinned elephants, specifically *Elephas antiquus*.

Subjectivity, after all, is inherent in the process of identification. The animals with large stomachs, for example, could be pregnant females (the traditional hypothesis from the viewpoint of fertility and hunting magic); conversely, they could be animals that have swollen up in spring after eating too much wet grass (a more ethological and modern hypothesis); or the large stomach could even have been a 'stylistic and chronological characteristic' (Delporte 1984, p. 117).

Interpretation of postures, as we have seen, is very risky. It is made more so by the consistent absence of a base or ground line. In the wall art we tend to take the orientation of the figures in relation to the natural ground, which may

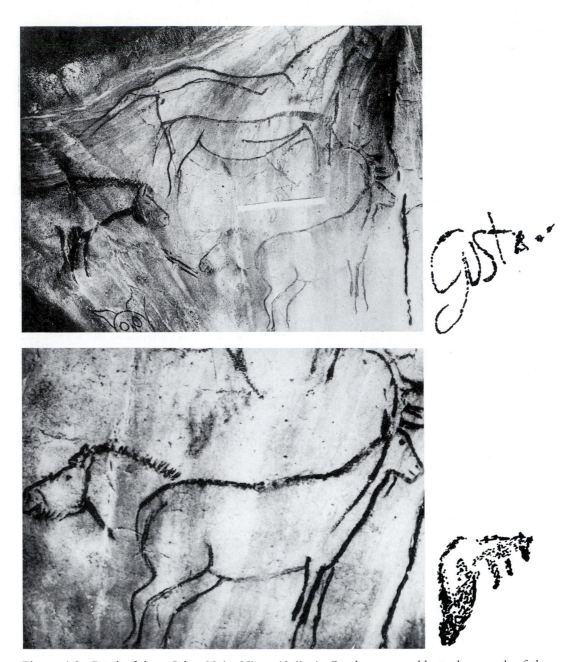

Figure 1.8 Panel of deer, Salon Noir, Niaux (Ariège). On the upper, oldest, photograph of the drawing (from the Musée de l'Homme), the word 'GUSTA' is clearly visible between the deer and the horse, under the white band that represents the scale. On the lower, most recent, photograph (from the archives of the Direction des Antiquités Préhistoriques), the signature is blurred and resembles a curved anthropomorph, with the legs connected, the head represented, and the two arms hanging down. The two lateral drawings show these two versions and are drawn to scale.

be irrelevant in the case of the numerous animals that are represented vertical or at an angle. The problem is further heightened for portable art, as Pales has shown when he speaks of 'arbitrary verticality' (Pales & Tassin de Saint-Péreuse 1976, p. 77 *et seq.*). Pales himself, however, succumbed to what he criticized when he represented, for example, the sorcerer of Les Trois Frères almost on four feet, although its position is more or less on an angle, depending on the exact position from which one observes it in the Sanctuary.[6] We have no way of knowing if the Magdalenians, in this case, preferred one way of vision from another.

Inventories and tracings

Taking into account everything that has been said above, it is not surprising that the identification of the same subject has sometimes been very different according to various authors. At Covalanas, for example, Ripoll-Perello (1984, p. 274) cites an animal as a reindeer although del Rio *et al.* saw it as a bovid, while it was identified as a deer by Leroi-Gourhan and an auroch by Barandiarán (1984, p. 274).

Such differences of opinion become translated into inventories, all the more when the authors concerned do not discuss the details of the evidence (on this subject, cf. Novel 1984, Roussot 1984d). Even in the case of caves which have been seriously studied only recently, we still find some strange variations. At Marsoulas, in the account of Méroc *et al.* (1947) are listed 21 bison, 11 horses, 1 bovid, 2 ibex, 2 hinds, 1 deer, 16 humans. In the more complete version by Plenier (1971) are found 32 bison, 32 horses, 1 bovid, 3 ibex, 1 hind, 1 deer, 17 humans, 1 chamois, 1 fantasy animal, as well as 1 feline, 1 woman, 1 chamois, 1 bird, and 1 vulva cited as questionable identifications. These last figures do not feature at all in the inventory of Vialou (1981, p. 506), even though it is based on Plenier's work. Vialou cites 30 bison, 26 horses, 2 ibex, 12 humanoids, 5 indeterminate animals, 9 indeterminate motifs, and 26 indeterminate groupings. In the latter case, increased rigour has led to a considerably reduced species inventory and to a high proportion of indeterminate figures.

The same comments can be made for Le Portel, where Beltrán *et al.* (1966, p. 175 *et seq.*) enumerate 33 horses, 27 bison, 7 cervids (of which one is considered doubtful), 3 bovines (of which one is doubtful), 3 caprids, 1 salmonid, 1 owl, 6 humans. According to Vialou (1981), there are 26 horses, 23 bison, 4 cervids, 1 ibex, 1 salmonid, 1 owl, 5 humans, and 8 indeterminate animals. According to Dauvois & Vézian (1984, p. 382), however, there are 30 bison, 31 horses, 8 complete or partial cervids (antler racks), plus 1 hind, 2 bovines, 3 ibex, 1 salmonid, 1 owl, 4 humans, 1 indeterminate.

The differences between these inventories are considerable, and the proportions of humans, or of certain species of animals, vary greatly. In such cases, the problem arises as to which data to adopt for synthetic reviews. What are the criteria for making a choice? Usually it is impossible to verify the inventories for practical reasons and, when that is the case, should one prefer the most recent study? Or the researcher that one judges to be the most rigorous? Or does one accept the results that appear to be the most convincing, i.e. those that coincide

Figure 1.9 Feline from the Chapel of the Lion in the cave of Les Trois Frères (Ariège). In the detailed photograph on the right hand side, note the human forearm, with the elbow well marked, which is extended towards the tail of the animal (photo by R. Bégouën). Note the difference from the drawing by H. Breuil, who had interpreted this arm as a second tail.

with one's own ideas? In these circumstances one is forced to make a choice that is inevitably subjective, this time at a second level of subjectivity.[7]

The figures included in inventories are often distorted by a very widespread phenomenon. Often in their analyses people move cautiously towards a hypothetical identification of a subject. They may apply all sorts of subtle qualifications and cautions to their interpretation of doubtful representations. But in the end they include them without qualification in the totals and percentages of the various species included in the inventories, in effect validating the identification.[8]

Since the work of Leroi-Gourhan, statistics are commonly used in the study of Palaeolithic art and it is likely they will be used more and more (Roussot 1984d). These methods, with their apparent rigour, are also very reductive, with raw counts and percentages that do not allow for any reservations and subtle nuances. In the light of the above discussion, such statistics must, inevitably, often present a very biased view of reality.

Tracings are not always consistent or faithful and some comparisons with the originals are often necessary (Pales 1969), p. 34 *et seq.*, Ucko 1989). Even those that have been done by the most skilful and celebrated dicipherers when in their prime may sometimes be erroneous. For example, Abbé Breuil at Les Trois Frères, where his recordings in general are models of perception and precision, gave an extra tail to a feline engraved in the Chapel of the Lion, although, as R. Bégouën first noted, this pseudo-appendage was an isolated human arm, extended towards the true tail of the animal (Fig. 1.9).

The tracings that are the basis for so many studies of Palaeolithic art are never neutral nor perfectly objective. They always bear the full imprint of their author who can distort important details in the identification of the subject. Thus, Pales has demonstrated how Abbé Breuil transformed an ibex at Niaux into an alpine ibex by giving its horn a curvature that was a little bit too perfect (and without a terminal straightening), whereas the Magdalenian artist had in fact depicted a typical Pyrenean ibex (Pales & Tassin de Saint-Péreuse 1981, p. 139, and see Ucko & Layton 1984 for similar over-precision of details at Hornos de la Peña).

Sometimes the drawing of a figure may be influenced by an erroneous interpretation of what it represents. The tracing may be unconsciously influenced to produce the desired result. Again, in this case we are concerned with the projection of a mental image, but in a tracing the effect is to materially distort the transcription of the subject and thus to cause a doubling of error. The drawings of Dams & Dams at Mayrière Supérieure (1979) are striking examples (see Clottes *et al.* 1981), as is the drawing of a plaquette from Enlène by Bouyssonie who represented a bison (Fig. 1.10) because he had already pre-identified it as such; the engraving, in fact, was certainly not that of a bison, but could be better interpreted as one or two birds (Bégouën 1939, p. 304, Fig. 13). Had he conceived of this latter interpretation, Bouyssonie's rendering would most probably have been different.

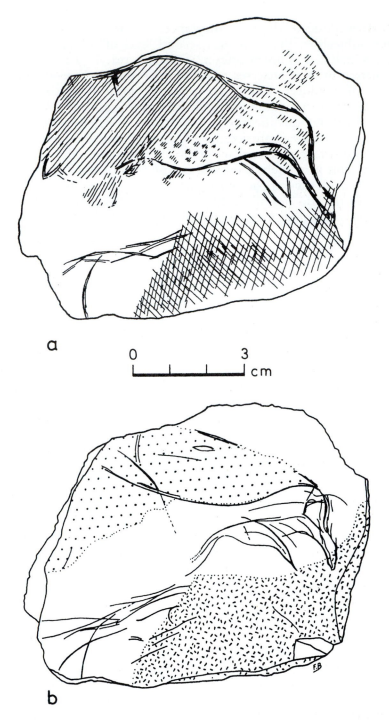

a

0   3

cm

b

Figure 1.10 Limestone with an engraving of a probable bird, from the cave of Enlène (Ariège), interpreted by L. Bégouën (1939 p. 305, Fig. 13) and by J. Bouyssonie as a bison and copied as such (a). The drawing by F. Briois (b) clearly shows the influence of this interpretation and how it warped the first rendering of the figure.

Conclusion

We have now reviewed numerous examples on the long process from the conception of the works to their modern identification in order to evaluate, if only approximately, the validity of such identifications. This exercise has been no more than suggestive and schematic: to verify, image by image, the copies and attributions of all Palaeolithic wall and portable art would be useful but would take several research teams many years.

The main results of this review suggest that:

(a) all the old inventories – that is, those done prior to the past 20 or 25 years (as well as a certain number of the more recent ones)[9] – must be looked at again critically, using explicit and and very much stricter criteria to avoid merely substituting our own subjectivity for that of our predecessors.

(b) Nevertheless, progress is evident over the past two decades. The role of zoology and ethology is generally recognized now and both disciplines have been shown to be very useful. Copies are more precise than ever before, and they take account of numerous factors that had been overlooked previously. Following, among others, the works of P. Ucko and A. Rosenfeld, and L. Pales and H. Delporte for mobiliary art, a new generation of researchers is proceeding to study the human and animal representations and their identifications with a severity and an objectivity that had not been seen before. Evidence of this can be seen in the justifiable increase in the number of figures classified as 'indeterminates'.

(c) At the same time, these unquestionable methodological improvements, encouraging as they are, must not be allowed to hide the reality, that in this field of inquiry *subjectivity is inevitable* (Ucko 1989), since it intervenes, as we have seen, at all stages in the process and no one can be free from it.

There is considerable danger in simply ending with this conclusion and then giving up! Such a conclusion has indeed sometimes been advocated with regard to recording work: each tracing would constitute a personal study, fundamentally subjective. In this way, subjectivity would be assumed, one would sign one's drawing, and it would then be a study of such-and-such a bison by Miss X, with the implicit admission that the study of the same animal by Mr Y would be notably different. It seems preferable, however, to try instead, as far as possible, to minimize the personal factor; for example, working in a team which is undertaking copying work in the field allows one to take note of the criticisms of others, and thus try to get as close as possible to the Palaeolithic original (Clottes 1980, p. 90). This is not to say that we can ever eliminate all subjectivity, because this is illusory, but rather that we should limit it as much as possible. There is indeed no miraculous cure, but we can minimize subjectivity by increased rigour. We need to at least check, if not completely reverse, our natural tendency to push identifications as far as we can. By so doing, we would undoubtedly remain on this side of prehistoric reality and our assertions would be better founded. It is better to err on the side of caution, i.e. it is better to avoid any interpretation of certain representations rather than to make errors that will be adopted later and then confirmed through usage (and see Ucko & Rosenfeld 1972, Rosenfeld 1977, p. 107).

The aim of this chapter has been to call for this effort and to contribute to it by drawing attention to a certain number of traps that are, in theory, well known, but into which we all fall time and time again.

The identification of human and animal figures of the European Upper Palaeolithic will never become an exact science. It will continue to exist in a dim arena, one of imprecision and of mystery. The role of specialists is neither to minimize the problems inherent in the subject, nor to despair about them, and certainly not to resign themselves to them, but rather to define them as clearly as possible and to study the ways in which they can be reduced.[10] It is only thus that – as Leroi-Gourhan has said (1973–4, p. 388) – one can try to 'establish the objective content of the message. . .before, perhaps, specifying its meaning'.

Acknowledgements

I would like to thank my friend Professor P. J. Ucko, who asked me to tackle this subject for the World Archaeological Congress at Southampton. I also extend my deep thanks to R. Bégouën and M. Garcia who provided me with data and information, as well as to C. Servelle for practical assistance, and, above all, to my friends and colleagues Dr M. Conkey, who offered to take on the very heavy job of translating this bulky paper and who did it with such ability, and Dr H. Morphy to whom fell the job of editing it, which also proved no mean task.

Notes

1 According to Luquet, *visual realism* corresponds to what the eye perceives: it is a sort of photographic image. *Intellectual realism*, on the other hand, is the image that the artist has in mind, which can include details that are invisible naturally or because of the chosen angle for depiction, but which are of importance to the artist (or, inversely, images which omit details judged by the artist to be of no interest).

2 According to Leroi-Gourhan, the mythogram 'is a statement of symbols which are situated in, and animated by, verbal discourse, and its symbolic significance dies out at the same time as the oral tradition' (1973–4, p. 383).

3 This is, in fact, the way it is classified in the CID Breuil (Centre d'Information et de Documentation) of the Musée des Antiquités Nationales, where it is referred to as 'animal, carnivore? rodent? (. . .)' (Delporte & Mons 1982–3, p. 9). Leroi-Gourhan, however, captions the figure 'Sculpture on a reindeer antler representing a carnivore, probably a bear'. Later on in the same text (1965, p. 63) he refers to it simply as 'a bear on a reindeer antler' without any qualification. The decision appears to have been made and it is likely that the representation is counted as a bear in the final summary counts (Leroi-Gourhan 1965, p. 438, Fig. 754).

4 X-ray art was almost never used in the European Palaeolithic, except perhaps for the digestive tract of a fish at Lortet (Breuil & Saint-Périer 1927, p. 21, Barandiarán 1972, p. 348, Fig. 1).

5 Another lesson which must be learnt from this error is the absolute necessity of recording and referring to modern alterations noted at the time of one's own study, so that those who follow should not fall into this sort of error.

6 As noted by R. Bégouën, if one looks at the sorcerer while standing in the centre of the chamber, one effectively views it in a very stooped position, almost on all fours. However, if one views it from much closer – that is, immediately below it – from where the engravings in the Sanctuary are most visible, it appears to be inclined forwards, with its back forming an angle with the ground. In relation to the vertical axis, the sorcerer is again in an inclined position but no longer on all fours.

7 If most errors derive from adventurous identifications, the reverse is also possible. Thus, Vialou eliminated the mammoth associated with the owls in the cave of Les Trois Frères, because, he said, 'it is hardly possible to decide what the adjacent curved line is. Direct scrutiny and the copy made by Breuil is not convincing for the existence of a partial mammoth silhouette superimposed on the second owl; this incurvate line is indeterminate and in part composed of the bird' (1981, p. 292). Re-examination of these figures *in situ* on 17 July 1985 with R. Bégouën and H.-G. Bandi, confirms the nature and the existence of these two animals. The engraved lines of the owl on the right and of the mammoth were made with two different tools, and the traces of these on the wall can be differentiated and easily followed. There is a clear mammoth's head, with its characteristic profile, a very clear oval eye (not depicted in the recording made by Breuil (Bégouën & Breuil 1958, Figs 16 & 17) which thus led Vialou to make his error), and a trunk, which is quite distinct from the body of the owl. In general, of course, extreme rigour is preferable to being lax; a lack of information is much less harmful to research than faulty information.

8 This shifting methodology is almost a general one. It has become so general that we can find it in most recent inventories including ones done by excellent researchers. In his study of Labastide, Omnès (1982) produces a number of daring interpretations, for example the interpretations of numbers 160 and 161 as respectively an anthropomorph and a horse (see ibid., p. 125, Fig. 132). Even in cases where he shows doubts, as with figures number 93, 97, and 134 which he identifies 'without great certainty' as wild boar (ibid., p. 137), he includes them without qualification in his cumulative table (ibid., p. 137). The same process can be seen to have happened at Mas d'Azil. Leroi-Gourhan (1965, p. 311) identified a painted head as a horse. Later Alteirac and Vialou saw it more as a feline though they qualified their interpretation by writing that 'no argument can be advanced with assurance' (1980, p. 64). However, when they cite it further on in the text (pp. 71–3) the head has become that of a feline without qualification and has, in fact, been accepted into that category along the way.

9 For example, the inventories by A. Glory for birds, and by L.-R. Nougier for numerous animal species, were recently criticized by Novel (1984) and Roussot (1984d) respectively. Re-recording is also necessary for Omnès's work at Labastide (1982) where close checking by R. Bégouën, R. Simonnet, and myself has shown that Omnès's mistakes are at two levels:

(a) On some very corroded rock faces, he has unconsciously picked and chosen cracks or small cupulas or flaking, with no trace of engraving, either to create or complete a non-existent figure by imagining engraved lines or adding to existing ones, or to give more precision to an indeterminate shape.

(b) Some very vague lines, or unintelligible representations, have had meanings ascribed to them which are, to say the least, doubtful. For example, no. 5 (Fig. 16, p. 64), no. 8 (Fig. 20, p. 65), nos 26 and 27 (Fig. 34, p. 74) do not exist; no. 15 (Fig. 15, p. 63) is an indeterminate head and not a horse's; no. 29 (Fig. 37,

p. 75) is extremely dubious, as is no. 30 (Fig. 37, p. 75) which is called a bear; the interpretation of no. 39 (Fig. 44, p. 79) as a human head is far-fetched.

These errors must be the result of working alone and allowing full play to 'mental images', without the critical eye of a colleague to check and possibly refute what one imagines one sees, especially in the case of a difficult cave such as Labastide.

10   On the other hand, there are some practical steps that can be taken even if they would not solve all of our problems. We have drawn attention to the importance of mental images in the process of identification. In order to broaden their scope and to make comparative evidence more widely available it would be useful for prehistorians, palaeontologists and zoologists to get together to produce an atlas of the animals of the Upper Palaeolithic. This would include photographs of surviving species (bison, horses, reindeer/caribou, deer, etc.), detailed descriptions of their morphology (criteria for determining the species, sex, and seasonal variations) and of their characteristic postures and attitudes. The atlas should also include reproductions of Palaeolithic drawings to illustrate principal conventions used by the artists. At present this information has to be sought from a multitude of different sources. The works of Pales on the felines (1969) and on horses and bovids (Pales & Tassin de Saint-Péreuse 1981) included in monographs on La Marche are exemplars of this approach.

In addition to the naturalistic representations, we are left with a number of doubtful or ambiguous figures and it would be desirable if an agreed system of classification could be developed for these. This is a necessary condition for the application of statistics and the use of computers. Computer inventories and storage are already under way for the portable art, notably the Centre d'Information et de Documentation (CID Breuil) at the Musée des Antiquités Nationales at Saint-Germain-en-Laye (Delporte & Mons 1982–3). An open list of types has been established which can serve as a basis of discussion and consideration of its extension to wall art.

Work on ambiguous and doubtful figures could benefit from a series of seminars with some attempt to reach a consensus. Some interesting work on the subject has already been done. Working on human figures, Pales & Tassin de Saint-Péreuse (1976) distinguish between realistic humans (subdivided into males, females, and those of indeterminate sex), the humanoids, and the composite beings. The latter are questionable in this context, for it could be argued that as they combine human and animal in the one image they should belong to a category that is quite separate from both humans and animals. Otherwise there is always going to be a problem with anthropocentrism (the problem of the 'sorcerers'). In the case of animals we can distinguish between composite animals (ones that combine the characteristics of different species), the fantasy animals, and the indeterminate animals. Other categories that may be developed include different anatomical parts or indeterminate heads. This last term, which applies to cases where it is impossible to separate animal from human features, is preferable to employing the too-specific label 'mask'.

References

Alteirac, A. & D. Vialou 1980. La grotte du Mas d'Azil: le réseau orné inférieur. *Préhistoire Ariégeoise, Bulletin de la Société Préhistorique de l'Ariège* **XXVII**, 59–72.

Baffier, D. 1984. Les caractères sexuels secondaires des mammifères dans l'art pariétal paléolithique franco-cantabrique. In *La contribution de la zoologie et de l'éthologie à l'interprétation de l'art des peuples chasseurs préhistoriques*, M. G. Bandi et al., 143–54. Fribourg: Editions Universitaire.

Bahn, P.-G. 1978. The 'unacceptable face' of the West European Upper Palaeolithic. *Antiquity* **LII**, 183–92.

Bandi, H.G. 1968. *Art quaternaire et zoologie*. Simposio de arte rupestre, Barcelona 1966, 13–19.

Bandi, H.-G. 1972. *Quelques réflexions sur la nouvelle hypothèse de A. Leroi-Gourhan concernant la signification de l'art quaternaire*. Santander Symposium 1970, 309–19.

Barandiarán, I. 1972. *Algunas convenciones de representación en las figuras animales del arte paleolítico*. Santander Symposium 1970, 345–81.

Barrière, C. 1982. *L'art pariétal de Rouffignac*. Paris: Picard.

Bégouën, H. & H. Breuil 1958. *Les Cavernes du Volp. Trois-Frères – Tuc d'Audoubert*. Travaux de l'Institut de Paléontologie Humaine. Paris: Arts et Métiers Graphiques.

Bégouën, L. 1939. Pierres gravées et peintes de l'époque magdalénienne. *Mélanges Bégouën*, 289–305. Toulouse: Editions du Museum.

Bégouën, R. & J. Clottes 1979a. Le bâton au saumon d'Enlène (Montesquieu-Avantès, Ariège). *Préhistoire Ariégeoise, Bulletin de la Société Préhistorique de l'Ariège* **XXXIV**, 5–13.

Bégouën, R. & J. Clottes 1979b. Galet gravé de la Caverne d'Enlène à Montesquieu-Avantès (Ariège). *Caesaraugusta*, **49–50**, 57–64. Zaragoza.

Bégouën, R., F. Briois, J. Clottes & C. Servelle 1982a. Art mobilier sur support lithique du Tuc d'Audoubert à Montesquieu-Avantès (Ariège). *Préhistoire Ariégeoise, Bulletin de la Société Préhistorique de l'Ariège* **XXXVII**, 15–60.

Bégouën, R., J. Clottes, J.-P. Giraud & F. Rouzaud 1982b. Plaquette gravée d'Enlène, Montesquieu-Avantès (Ariège). *Bulletin de la Société Préhistorique Française* **79**(4), 103–9.

Beltrán, A. 1969. *La Cueva de Ussat-les-Eglises, y tres nuevos abrigos con pinturas de la Edad de Bronce*. Zaragoza, Monografías arqueològicas, no. 5.

Beltrán, A. 1984. Les animaux de l'art rupestre des chasseurs du Levant espagnol. In *La contribution de la zoologie et l'éthologie à l'interprétation de l'art des peuples chasseurs préhistoriques*, H. G. Bandi et al. (eds), 353–69. Fribourg: Editions Universitaire.

Beltrán, A., R. Gailli & R. Robert 1973. *La Cueva de Niaux*. Zaragoza, Monografías arqueològicas, no. 16.

Beltrán, A., R. Robert & J. Vézian 1966. *La Cueva de Le Portel*. Zaragoza, Monografías arqueològicas, no. 1.

Bosinski, G. 1984. The mammoth engravings of the Magdalenian site Gönnersdorf (Rhineland, Germany). In *La contribution de la zoologie et de l'éthologie à l'interprétation de l'art des peuples chasseurs préhistoriques*, H. G. Bandi et al. (eds), 295–322. Fribourg: Editions Universitaire.

Breuil, H. 1905. La dégénérescence des figures d'animaux en motifs ornementaux à l'époque du Renne. *Comptes-rendus de l'Académie des Inscriptions et Belles-Lettres*, 105–20.

Breuil, H. & R. Jeannel 1955. La grotte ornée du Portel à Loubens (Ariège). *L'Anthropologie* **59**, 197–204.

Breuil, H. & R. de Saint-Périer 1927. *Les poissons, les batraciens et les reptiles dans l'art quaternaire*. Archives de l'Institut de Paléontologie Humaine Memoir. 2. Paris: Masson.

Capitan, L. & Abbé J. Bouyssonie 1924. *Un atelier d'art préhistorique. Limeuil. Son gisement à gravures sur pierres de l'Age du Renne*. Paris: E. Nourry.

Capitan, L., H. Breuil & D. Peyrony 1924. *Les Combarelles aux Eyzies (Dordogne)*. Archives de l'Institut de Paléontologie Humaine. Paris: Masson.

Cartailhac, E. & H. Breuil 1908. Les peintures et gravures murales des cavernes pyrénéennes. III: Niaux (Ariège). *L'Anthropologie* **19**, 15–46.

Chollot-Varagnac, M. 1980. *Les origines du graphisme symbolique. Essai d'analyse des écritures primitives en Préhistoire*. Paris: Fondation Singer-Polignac.

Clottes, J. 1976. Les civilisations du Paléolithique supérieur dans les Pyrénées. *La Préhistoire Française* **I** (2), 1214–31.

Clottes, J. 1980. Eléments sur l'art rupestre paléolithique en France. *Préhistoire Ariégeoise, Bulletin de la Société Préhistorique de l'Ariège* **XXXV**, 79–110.

Clottes, J., M. Garcia, R. Guicharnaud, J. Lautier, M. Lorblanchet, F. Rouzaud, A. Vialou & D. Vialou 1981. Vrais et faux bisons de Mayrière supérieure (Bruniquel, T. et G.): problèmes d'observation et de méthode. *Bulletin de la Société Préhistorique Française* **78**(3), 71–4.

Clottes, J. & R. Rouzaud 1984. Grotte des Eglises. *L'Art des Cavernes. Atlas des grottes ornées paléolithiques françaises*, 428–32. Paris, Ministère de la Culture: Imprimerie Nationale.

Dams, L. & M. Dams 1979. La grotte de Mayrière supérieure à Bruniquel (Tarn-et-Garonne). *Bulletin de la Société Royale Belge d'Anthropologie et de Préhistoire* **90**, 85–98.

Dauvois, M. & J. Vézian 1984. Grotte du Portel. *L'Art des Cavernes. Atlas des grottes ornées paléolithiques françaises*. Paris, Ministère de la Culture: Imprimerie Nationale, 381–8.

Delluc, B. & G. Delluc 1981. La grotte ornée de Comarque à Sireuil (Dordogne). *Gallia Préhistoire* **24**(1), 1–97.

Delluc, B. & G. Delluc 1984. Grotte de Comarque. *L'Art des Cavernes. Atlas des grottes ornées paléolithiques françaises*. Paris, Ministère de la Culture: Imprimerie Nationale, 119–22.

Delporte, H. 1979. *L'image de la femme dans l'art préhistorique*. Paris: Picard.

Delporte, H. 1984. L'art mobilier et ses rapports avec la faune paléolithique. In *La contribution de la zoologie et de l'éthologie à l'interprétation de l'art des peuples chasseurs préhistoriques*, H. G. Bandi *et al.* (eds). Fribourg: Editions Universitaire.

Delporte, H. & L. Mons 1982–3. Une operation informatisée au Musée des Antiquités Nationales: le Centre d'Information et de Documentation (CID). *Henri Breuil Antiquités Nationales* **14–15**, 7–11.

Giedion, S. 1964. *L'éternel présent. La naissance de l'art*. Bruxelles: Editions de la Connaissance.

Gonzalez-Echegaray, J. 1974. *Pinturas y grabados de Las Chimeneas (Puente Viesgo, Santander)*. Monografías de Arte rupestre, Arte paleolítico 2, Barcelona.

Graziosi, P. 1960. *Palaeolighic art*. London: Faber & Faber.

Guthrie, R.-D. 1984. Ethnological observations from Palaeolithic art. In *La contribution de la zoologie et de l'éthologie à l'interprétation de l'art des peuples chasseurs préhistoriques*, H. G. Bandi *et al.* (eds.), 35–74. Fribourg: Editions Universitaire.

Larribau, J.-D. & S. Prudhomme 1984. Grotte d'Erberua. *L'Art des Cavernes. Atlas des grottes ornées paléolithiques françaises*, 275–9. Paris, Ministère de la Culture: Imprimerie Nationale.

Layton, R. 1977. Naturalism and cultural relativity in art. In *Form in indigenous art*, P. Ucko (ed.), 33–43. London: Duckworth.

Leroi-Gourhan, A. 1965. *Préhistoire de l'art occidental*. Paris: Mazenod.

Leroi-Gourhan, A. 1970–1. Résumé des cours de 1970–1971. *Annuaire du Collège de France* **71**, 343–53.

Leroi-Gourhan, A. 1973–4. Résumé des cours de 1973–1974. *Annuaire du Collège de France* **74**, 381–90.

Leroi-Gourhan, A. 1979–80. Résumé des cours et travaux. *Annuaire du Collège de France* **80**, 513–20.

Leroi-Gourhan, A. 1980–1. Résumé des cours et travaux. *Annuaire du Collège de France* **81**, 453–67.

Leroi-Gourhan, A. 1981–2. Résumé des cours et travaux. *Annuaire du Collège de France* **82**, 477–94.

Leroi-Gourhan, A. 1984. Le réalisme de comportement dans l'art paléolithique d'Europe de l'Ouest. In *La contribution de la zoologie et de l'éthologie à l'interprétation de l'art des peuples chasseurs préhistoriques*, H. G. Bandi *et al.* (eds), 75–90. Fribourg: Editions Universitaire.

Lhote, H. 1968. La plaquette dite de 'La Femme au Renne' de Laugerie-Basse et son interprétation zoologique. In *Simposio de arte rupestre, Barcelona 1966*, E. Ripoll–Perello (ed.), 79–97. Barcelona.

Lorblanchet, M. 1977. From naturalism to abstraction in European prehistoric art. In *Form in indigenous art*, P. J. Ucko (ed.), 44–56. London: Duckworth.

Lorblanchet, M. 1984a. Les relevés d'art préhistorique. *L'Art des Cavernes. Atlas des grottes ornées paléolithiques françaises*, 41–51. Paris, Ministère de la Culture: Imprimerie Nationale.

Lorblanchet, M. 1984b. Grotte de Pergouset. *L'Art des Cavernes. Atlas des grottes ornées paléolithiques françaises*, 504–6. Paris, Ministère de la Culture: Imprimerie Nationale.

Luquet, G.-H. 1926. *L'art et la religion des hommes fossiles*. Paris: Masson.

Macintosh, N. W. G. 1977. Beswick Creek cave two decades later: a reappraisal. In *Form in indigenous art*, P. J. Ucko (ed.), 191–7. London: Duckworth.

Méroc, L., L. Michaut & M. Ollé 1947. La grotte de Marsoulas (Haute-Garonne). *Bulletin de la Société d'Histoire Naturelle de Toulouse*, no. 82, 284–320.

Novel, P. 1984. *Les animaux rares dans l'art pariétal aquitain*. Mémoire de Maîtrise, Université de Lyon, Vol. 2.

Omnès, J. 1982. *La grotte ornée de Labastide (Hautes-Pyrénées)*. Lourdes.

Pales, L. 1969. *Les gravures de la Marche. I. – Félins et Ours*. Publications de l'Institut de Préhistoire de l'Université de Bordeaux, Mém. no. 7. Avec la collaboration de M. Tassin de Saint-Péreuse.

Pales, L. & M. Tassin de Saint-Péreuse 1976. *Les gravures de la Marche. II. – Les Humains*. Paris: Ophrys.

Pales, L. & M. Tassin de Saint-Péreuse 1981. *Les gravures de la Marche. III. – Equidés et Bovidés*. Paris: Ophrys.

Piette, E. 1906. Le chevêtre et la semi-domestication des animaux aux temps pléistocènes. *L'Anthropologie* **XVII**, 129–76.

Plenier, A. 1971. *L'art de la grotte de Marsoulas*. Institut d'Art Préhistorique, Mém. no. 1, Toulouse.

Poplin, F. 1984. Sur le profil dorso-lombaire des bisons dans la nature et dans l'art paléolithique. In *La contribution de la zoologie et de l'éthologie à l'interprétation de l'art des peuples chasseurs préhistoriques*, H. G. Bandi *et al.* (eds), 217–42. Fribourg: Editions Universitaire.

Ripoll-Perello, E. 1984. Notes sur certaines représentations d'animaux dans l'art paléolithique de la péninsule ibérique. In *La contribution de la zoologie et de l'éthologie à l'interprétation de l'art des peuples chasseurs préhistoriques*, H. G. Bandi *et al.* (eds), 263–82. Fribourg: Editions Universitaire.

Rosenfeld, A. 1977. Profile figures: schematisation of the human figure in the Magdalenian culture of Europe. In *Form in indigenous art*, P. J. Ucko (ed.), 90–109. London: Duckworth.

Rosenfeld, A. 1984. The identification of animal representations in the art of the Laura region, North Queensland (Australia). In *La contribution de la zoologie et de l'éthologie à l'interprétation de l'art des peuples chasseurs préhistoriques*, H. G. Bandi *et al.* (eds) 399–422.

Rousseau, M. 1984a. Les pelages dans l'iconographie paléolithique. In *La contribution de la zoologie et de l'éthologie à l'interprétation de l'art des peuples chasseurs préhistoriques* H. G. Bandi *et al.* (eds), 161–97.

Rousseau, M. 1984b. Torsions conventionnelles et flexions naturelles dans l'art animalier paléolithique et au-delà. In *La contribution de la zoologie et de l'éthologie à l'interprétation de l'art des peuples chasseurs préhistoriques* H. G. Bandi *et al.* (eds), 243–9.

Roussot, A. 1984a. Grotte de Font-de-Gaume. *L'Art des Cavernes. Atlas des grottes ornées paléolithiques françaises*, 129–34. Paris, Ministère de la Culture: Imprimerie Nationale.

Roussot, A. 1984b. Abri du Cap Blanc. *L'Art des Cavernes. Atlas des grottes ornées paléolithiques françaises*, 157–63. Paris, Ministère de la Culture: Imprimerie Nationale.

Roussot, A. 1984c. *Inventaire et analyse du bestiaire paléolithique.* Colloque International d'Art pariétal paléolithique, Périgueux 1984, 111–14.

Roussot, A. 1984d. Approche statistique du bestiaire figuré dans l'art pariétal. *L'Anthropologie* **88**(4), 485-98.

Saint-Périer, R. de 1930. *La grotte d'Isturitz. I, le Magdalénien de la Salle Saint-Martin.* Archives de l'IIPH, Vol. 7. Paris: Masson.

Schmid, E. 1984. Some anatomical observations on palaeolithic depictions of horses. In *La contribution de la zoologie et de l'éthologie à l'interprétation de l'art des peuples chasseurs préhistoriques*, H. G. Bandi *et al.* (eds), 155–60. Fribourg: Editions Universitaire.

Sieveking, A. 1984. Palaeolithic art and animal behaviour. In *La contribution de la zoologie et de l'éthologie à l'interprétation de l'art des peuples chasseurs préhistoriques*, H. G. Bandi *et al.* (eds), 91–109. Fribourg: Editions Universitaire.

Simonnet, G. 1947. Une nouvelle plaquette de pierre gravée magdalénienne de la grotte de Labastide, commune de Labastide (Hautes-Pyrénées). *Bulletin de la Société Préhistorique Française* **XLIV**, 55–64.

Simonnet, G., L. Simonnet & R. Simonnet 1984. Quelques beaux objets d'art venant de nos recherches dans la grotte ornée de Labastide (Hautes-Pyrénées). Approche naturaliste. *Bulletin de la Société Méridionale de Spéléologie et de Préhistoire* **XXIV**, 25–36.

Ucko, P. J. 1977. Introduction. In *Form in indigenous art*, P. J. Ucko (ed.), 11–18. London: Duckworth.

Ucko, P. J. 1989. La subjectivité et le recensement de l'art paléolithique. In *Un siglo después de Santuola*, M. R. Gonzales Morales (ed.). Santander: Disputación Regional de Cantabria y Universidad de Cantabria.

Ucko, P. J. & A. Rosenfeld 1966. *L'art paléolithique.* L'univers des Connaissances. Paris: Hachette.

Ucko, P. J. & A. Rosenfeld 1972. *Anthropomorphic representations in Palaeolithic art.* Santander Symposium 1970, 149–211.

Vialou, D. 1981. *L'art pariétal en Ariège magdalénienne.* Museum d'Histoire Naturelle, Laboratoire de Paléontologie Humaine et de Préhistoire, Mém. no. 13, Paris.

Vialou, D. 1984. Le cervidés de Lascaux. In *La contribution de la zoologie et de l'éthologie à l'interprétation de l'art des peuples chasseurs préhistoriques*, H. G. Bandi *et al.* (eds), 199–216. Fribourg: Editions Universitaire.

2 Reflections and rejections of an Aboriginal artist

IVAN P. HASKOVEC
& HILARY SULLIVAN

Introduction

The rock art of Kakadu National Park (Fig. 2.1) is one of the most significant bodies of art in the world.[1] Most studies so far have been carried out at a macro level, concentrating on its complexity, density, continuity, and age. Initially most workers concerned themselves with establishing a chronological framework for the development of the many styles that had been identified within the region (Mountford 1956, Brandl 1973, Chaloupka 1977, Lewis 1983). There is clear evidence that Aboriginal people were living in the region at least 25 000 years ago (Schrire 1982) and recent work has suggested that they may have been there from much earlier (Jones 1985). Chaloupka has argued that the art spans the entire period of human occupation, and that the earliest art dates from the Pleistocene age some 30 000 years ago. Painting on rock has continued to the present and this chapter deals only with paintings produced this century. Our fieldwork suggests that there are 5000–6000 art sites in the Park, of which perhaps 2000 have been recorded.

This chapter focuses on the works produced by Najombolmi, a painter responsible for some of the most beautiful paintings of the Alligator Rivers Region. He is among a small group of artists whose works can be individually identified by contemporary Aborigines. It had been known for a long time that Najombolmi had painted the so-called 'Main Gallery' at Anbangbang and the Blue Paintings nearby. During the course of our fieldwork we became aware that paintings at many other sites could be identified as his work.

In following up this discovery we had a number of aims in mind. We were provided with the possibility of documenting the geographical extent of one artist's work. This would enable us to relate a single artist's work to the rock-art corpus as a whole. We could then address the question of the extent to which the apparent homogeneity of a body of art could be explained as the result of the work of a small number of very prolific artists rather than as a result of a large number of painters working within narrow stylistic parameters. We were also interested in constructing an ethnographic model of a contact period artist, his art, his perceptions of the times and his reaction to them, as well as examining the way in which rock art reflected the changing social conditions of the times. Finally, the fact that Aboriginal people were interested in taking

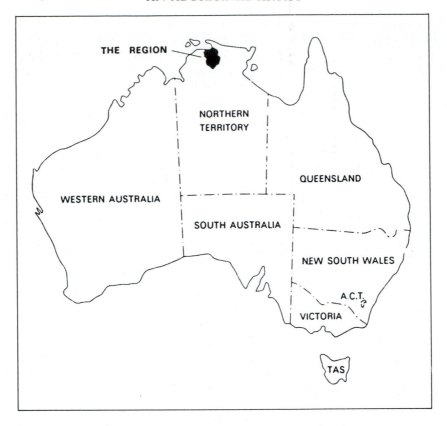

Figure 2.1   The location of Kakadu National Park.

part in the project gave us the opportunity to record Aboriginal perceptions and interpretations of the paintings.

The life history of Najombolmi

The recent social history of the region to which Najombolmi belonged is complex. The Aborigines had seasonal contact with Macassan trepangers from South Sulawesi for at least the past 300 years (Macknight 1976). From the early 1800s onwards a number of small British settlements were set up along the coast, for trade and defence. The closest settlement to Kakadu, Port Essington, lasted from 1838 to 1846. In 1845 the explorer Ludwig Leichardt crossed the region on his journey from Queensland to Port Essington, and encountered large numbers of friendly Aboriginal people on the flood plains (Leichardt 1847). Buffalo introduced from Asia were becoming widespread by the 1880s.

From the 1880s onwards, European settlers were attracted into the region by the discovery of gold at Pine Creek (to the south) and in order to shoot the buffalo.

Their enterprises were small in scale and depended on Aboriginal labour. Introduced diseases and violent conflict with the Europeans caused a severe reduction in the size of the Aboriginal population. New towns that grew up on the periphery also had an effect by attracting people away from the region (Levitus 1982).

European interest in the region intensified after World War II with the discovery of uranium in 1953, and the subsequent mining developments. Much of the Kakadu National Park region became Aboriginal land in 1978 under the provisions of the Aboriginal Landrights Act (NT).

Najombolmi was born around 1895 in the southern escarpment country of what is now Kakadu National Park. Local people identify his semi-moiety as Narwagite, his mother being a Djawan woman from the south and his father of the Bardmardi clan from Balawaurru, Deaf Adder Creek. He inherited his father's clan land, and 'belonged to Deaf Adder'. A clan, or *gunmugugur*, is a patrilineal local descent group, who are the primary owners of land. There are 19 such clans in the study area, each owning a clan estate of some 1000 km^2 (ANPWS 1980).

There is little information about Najombolmi's childhood and adolescence. He appears to have grown up in his clan's land and surrounding lands, living a traditional lifestyle. However, as buffalo shooters, mining prospectors, missionaries, etc. were already well established in the area at the turn of the century, it is likely that he at least knew of Europeans even if he had no direct contact with them.

In adulthood, Najombolmi is described as a tall powerful man, a good bushman, and a successful hunter. He was well versed in the techniques of traditional weapon manufacture. He was renowned for his hunting skills with these weapons. George Namingum described one incident in which he killed a buffalo with a spear. He was also a very skilled fisherman.

His skill with the spear also extended to disputes with other people. He is remembered as a particularly jealous man who was involved in a lot of disputes over women. He was a prodigious traveller and walked extensively throughout what is now Kakadu National Park. He passed through all the stages of ceremonial life and is described as a fully initiated man. He was also involved in the Bulla ceremonies of his mother's country. He spoke both the Djawan and Gundjeibmi languages.

After World War I he became more involved with Europeans through working in buffalo camps on the South Alligator floodplains and further west. The hunting of buffalo for hides and horns continued in the region from the 1880s until the 1950s, when it collapsed with the introduction of synthetic materials.

Life in the buffalo camps was a combination of excitement, danger, and hard work. European buffalo shooters made their way to the floodplains as soon as these were accessible after the wet season. They would come prepared with tobacco, flour, tea, sugar, mosquito nets, and other goods with which to buy the services of Aboriginal workers for the duration of the dry season. Work in these camps was rough and dangerous. Buffalo were shot at close range from horseback. A team of skinners would follow behind, while Aboriginal women would salt and dry the skins. When the season was over, the Europeans would return to Darwin after paying off their workers in kind. Aboriginal people were then at liberty to pursue their traditional activities in the wet season, returning to their country (Levitus 1982, pp. 13–21). Najombolmi had two wives who accompanied him to the buffalo camps. He did not have any children.

While working for the buffalo shooters, Najombolmi began to live with groups of Aboriginal people employed as labourers and guides at the newly established tourist safari camps (Nourlangie Camp and Muirella Park) which began to operate in the area. These businesses flew in people from southern Australia and overseas to spend a week or two fishing, hunting buffalo and crocodile, and viewing rock art.

Fred Hunter (a European who worked at both Nourlangie and Muirella Park) remembers him at this time as 'the old man of the mob, a real decent old bloke'. He received some stores from the safari camp, such as tobacco, sugar, flour, and tea, in return for occasionally supplying fish. His renown as a fisherman, particularly skilled in spearing barramundi, resulted in him being called 'Barramundi Charlie' by Europeans.

As an old man, in the 1960s, Najombolmi lived with communities of Aboriginal people at local cattle stations. He died at Mudginberry Station (now part of Stage II of Kakadu National Park) in 1967, probably in his seventies.

Methodology

Although Najombolmi had been dead for some 20 years, when we carried out this study recollections of him and his paintings were quite widespread among the Aboriginal community. We worked in the field with four main people during this study, Nipper Gabirrigi, George Namingum, Jacky Namandali, and Fred Hunter. Nipper Gabirrigi and George Namingum are half-brothers of Najombolmi, aged between 60 and 70. They belong to Najombolmi's clan and provided direct evidence of his activities from the 1930s onwards, as well as stories of earlier exploits. Jacky Namandali is a younger man who was Najombolmi's companion during his later years in the 1950s and 1960s. And, finally, Fred Hunter was the manager of the Muirella Park safari camp where Najombolmi worked towards the end of his life. In addition, we talked to many other Aborigines who had lived in the area during Najombolmi's lifetime.

We identified sites of art painted by Najombolmi in three ways. First, there were sites that could be directly identified by people who had actually witnessed Najombolmi doing the painting. Secondly, possible Najombolmi sites were identified by us and then people were taken to the sites to confirm the identification. Thirdly, people were shown photographs of sites which, for a variety of reasons, it was impossible to take them to. Obviously, these three methods of identification vary in the level of accuracy achieved, the first being the most accurate, the last the least.

People were quite definite in their attributions, except in cases where sites were in poor condition and details of painting were not visible. In some cases other artists were identified for particular paintings. People were asked in each case a number of questions, such as when the paintings were done, who was present, the reason for the paintings, and how long the party stayed at the site. Often details were missing, as up to 50 years had passed since the painting of some sites and people no longer remembered the exact circumstances of the event. Nonetheless, in such cases visits to the sites were likely to trigger stories about Najombolmi's life, his hunting successes, and times spent at the buffalo camps.

Recollections of the artist

From the safari camps Najombolmi made frequent trips to the bush, to camp, hunt, and paint. Often he would go in the company of another prolific painter, Old Nym Djimurrgurr. Fred Hunter recalls that 'he used to camp all along the Nourlangie escarpment. He used to like that country better than any other, good hunting, plenty of fish there. It was his country – he used to look after the paintings at Nourlangie Rock, used to touch them up.'

Jacky Namandali, who was also employed at Nourlangie Camp, recalls times when a group of Aboriginal people, including himself and Najombolmi, used to return to the bush for 'a holiday' during the wet and early dry seasons. These groups of people travelled through and around the escarpment, living a fairly traditional lifestyle for a few months at a time.

Few of the informants could recall the exact circumstances in which individual paintings were done. One thing that became clear, however, was that most of the people who accompanied Najombolmi did almost no painting during those trips, apart from the occasional hand stencil. They did not consider themselves artists and were not interested in painting. It would appear, therefore, that the majority of the paintings were done by skilled individuals such as Najombolmi.

People usually explained that Najombolmi's artistic output was due to his love of painting. His subjects, particularly animals, were painted to record a successful hunting or fishing expedition. Jacky Namandali recalled one incident in which fish were painted as part of an 'increase ceremony' in which various chants, rituals, and paintings were performed to ensure a plentiful supply of fish in local waterways. His propensity for painting women was usually said to reflect his personal interest in them.

It was during his time at the safari camps that Najombolmi repainted two famous sites in Kakadu National Park, the Blue Paintings and the so-called Main Gallery at Nourlangie. The Blue Paintings site contains traditional X-ray subjects but painted in blue pigment, the origin of which is thought to be washing blue. There is a considerable controversy among the Aborigines over this incident. Some deny that he painted with blue at all, believing this to be a slight on his name. One informant said:

> Charlie did first paintings in white, yellow and red and then someone went over it in blue. Charlie wouldn't do that, you can't blame him, there's no blue in this country, we got *delek* (white) *calbar* (yellow) *cawbulam* (dark yellow) *kuwadjbe* (red) *maawarr* (dark red). That's all, no other, no blue.

However, other informants who lived at the time with the painter claim that Najombolmi first painted the rock shelter in traditional colours and then he repainted it in blue at the request of Frank Muir, the owner of Muirella Park safari camp.

At this time (1964) Najombolmi also repainted the so-called Main Gallery at Anbangbang. Originally, this consisted of a scene of two men and their wives, and was photographed by David Attenborough in 1962. Najombolmi repainted this scene and added the creation heroes Namargon, Bargini, and Namondjolk. Chaloupka has re-created this event as follows:

In 1964, only a year before his death, he camped for the last time in this shelter. By then he had witnessed the impact of European contact on Aboriginal sociocultural systems elsewhere in the Northern Territory, and now he saw changes happening within his own region. Bridges began to span the rivers, which were the actual barriers in the past, and each year an increasing number of outsiders were intruding onto his land. He thought of the people who once used to live here, and of the Dreaming. In his swag he carried ochres which he had collected on his travels. He took them out, prepared the pigments and painted the people back into the shelter. There are two family groups, men standing amidst their wives, some of whom he depicted with milk in their breasts, as if he really wished them to be alive, to procreate and to people the land again. He built a platform and from this he painted the mythic beings, Namargon, the Lightning Man and his wife Bargini, and Namondjolk, a malignant spirit. This painted wall is unique, the last work of a great artist. (Chaloupka 1982, p. 22)

The sites

Forty-six sites were identified as places where Najombolmi painted, and 604 individual paintings were identified as his work (Fig. 2.2). Najombolmi's paintings are found over an area of 1800 km² in the Mayali language area, within and outside his clan lands. In terms of recent Aboriginal social organization, the sites are located within the Gundjeibmi/Mayali language area (see Figs 2.3 & 2.4). The clan territories in this area include Bardmardi, Warramal, Rol, Djamgolor, Wardjag and Mirrar Gundjeibmi (Fox 1977, p. 278).

The distribution of art sites coincides in most cases with occupation sites. The sites are located usually at or slightly above the bottom of a scree slope, where there are large boulders (some hundreds of square metres in size) beneath which are suitable living areas. Only exceptionally is a site located higher on a scree slope, at the base of the cliff face or above the scree slope.

The occupational deposits at the art sites vary from a few scattered pieces of lithic material on the surface to a deposit measuring at least 240 cm in depth. The occupation of some sites, such as Nawlabila, was continuous from at least 25 000 years ago (Kamminga & Allen 1973, Jones 1985).

The sequence of superimposition of paintings at some sites suggests that

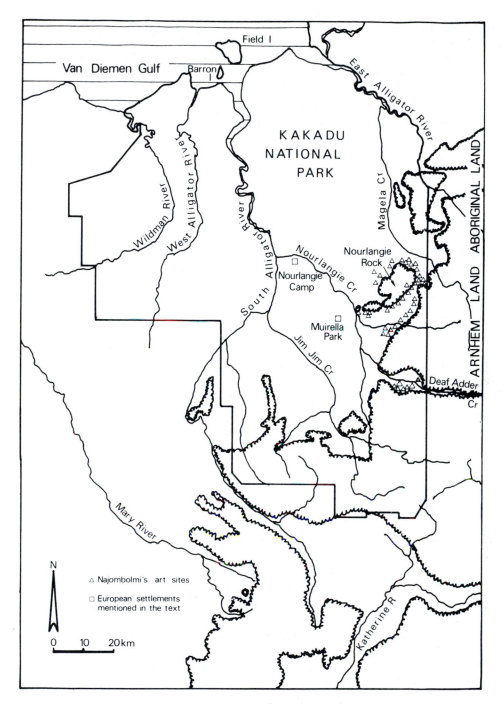

Figure 2.2 Distribution of sites.

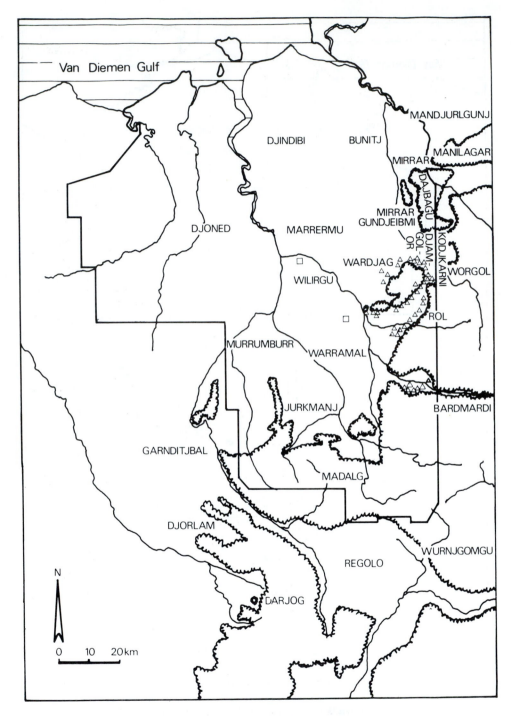

Figure 2.3 Aboriginal clan territories.

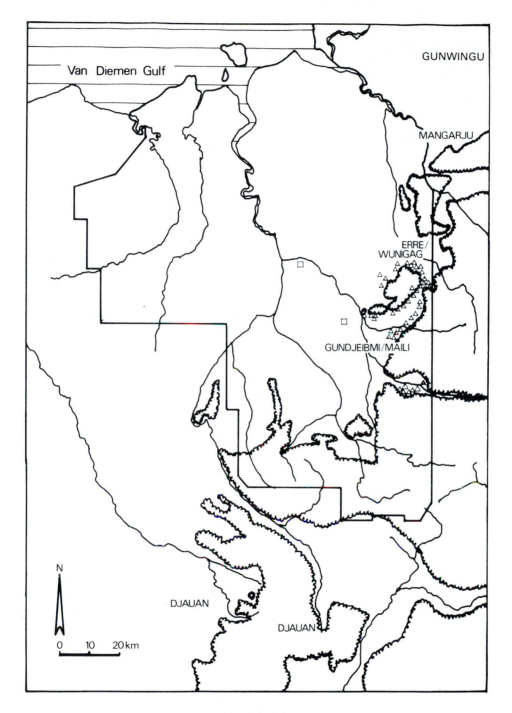

Figure 2.4 Aboriginal language areas.

Najombolmi's paintings were the last (sometimes second or third last) in the long chain of painting incidents. The long history of occupation at most of the sites suggests that Najombolmi and his group followed traditional routes and camping cycles, if perhaps in an abbreviated form in his later years when he was working for Europeans.

The art of Najombolmi

Najombolmi's paintings are in the style that Chaloupka (1983b) refers to as 'decorative X-ray'. Chaloupka defines decorative X-ray in relation to what he identifies as the preceding style, 'descriptive X-ray'. Of descriptive X-ray he writes:

> The artist depicted the internal features of a subject within its external form. Thus the animals were portrayed not only in their dominant recognisable aspect, generally in profile, but also with their internal organs and bone structure. The human body in this style is usually portrayed with a schematised skeletal form. (Chaloupka 1983b, p. 13)

Decorative X-ray is then described as follows:

> . . .some artists lost interest in the anatomical details of internal organs and subdivided the animal's body for purely decorative purposes. However, the descriptive form of X-ray continued to be used along with that of the decorative expression. (Chaloupka 1983b, p. 14)

Decorative X-ray art usually consists of large polychrome paintings. The lines used in the paintings vary from hair-line to quite thick in width (1–1.5 cm). Paintings generally have a thick outline with internal divisions, the ground being painted in another colour. The subjects are predominantly fish, people, and wallabies. While animals are shown in profile, people are usually shown *en face*. The inner structure of organs is sometimes shown together with further abstract patterning. The degree of elaboration varies from a simple silhouette outline of the subject, to a painting with a complex design infilled with cross-hatched lines.

A characteristic of the X-ray style is the static, rigid impression of the subject – the paintings appear to represent categories of subject rather than interaction and movement between them. These characteristics seem to apply even in the case of a man hunting or a copulating couple.

Characteristics of the art

Subjects

We recorded 42 separate categories of subjects. This includes categories such as 'fish unidentified' or 'animal unidentified', which, if positively identified, would undoubtedly enlarge the number of categories. The subjects fall into six large groups. These are: fish (35.6 per cent), people (32 per cent), animals (11.5 per cent), material culture (10.7 per cent), plants (4.5 per cent), and mythological (4 per cent). The range of subjects shows an intimate knowledge of the environment. The pig-nosed turtle (*warradjan*) portrayed at the Blue Paintings site was not known by European scientists to live in Australia until the early 1970s. Indeed, its depiction at this site encouraged scientists to begin to search for it in local waterways.

It is interesting to note that while Najombolmi's rendering of subjects remains largely within the X-ray tradition, the relative proportions of subjects he chose to represent diverges. In comparison with X-ray art as a whole, Najombolmi's art is heavily biased towards paintings of human figures, in particular of human females. Few other sites examined to date show a comparable concentration on the human form. Recent analysis by Tacon (1987, p. 1) supports the observation (see Ch. 10, this volume). In his analysis of 3224 X-ray paintings from 316 sites, Tacon found that, in the descriptive and decorative art, fish formed 60.17 per cent of representations whereas human figures made 11.9 per cent. In comparison, in Najombolmi's case, fish, though still the largest category, comprise only 35.6 per cent of subjects whereas people form 32 per cent. The number of human representations is almost three times that in Tacon's sample. In a few cases Najombolmi atypically represents the faces of the human figures in profile, and in some cases the difficulty he found in painting the face in profile is obvious.

Colour

The colours used by Najombolmi in his paintings were: at least two different shades of red, white, black, yellow, and green. The white, black, red, and yellow pigments are readily obtained at a number of locations within the area. The brilliance of the colours used by Najombolmi is striking and it may be that he was particularly selective about the quality of pigments he used. However, it may be that the brilliance is due to the fact that his paintings are relatively recent and have not had time to fade.

In addition to monochrome paintings, colours were used in 16 different combinations. The most frequent combination of colours is red and white (45.36 per cent), followed by red and yellow (17.55 per cent). White and yellow were used on their own quite frequently (17.07 per cent and 5.63 per cent, respectively). The usual technique was to paint the subject matter in white and then outline the form and the decorative segments in red.

The size of subjects

Unlike earlier styles (excluding the large naturalistic period) the decorative X-ray artists, including Najombolmi, painted relatively large figures. The mean size of paintings is 75.61 cm. This measurement is based on the maximum dimensions of the painting. There does not immediately appear to be any correlation between the mean sizes of the painted subjects and real mean sizes. The only realistic size is that of barramundi, 74.93 cm in paintings, against 72.5 cm in reality. All other species of fish painted by Najombolmi are depicted longer than life when compared with specimens measured by the Office of the Supervising Scientist (K. Bishop pers. comm.).

In contrast, the size of people is smaller in paintings than in reality. One may, with tongue in cheek, explain the size of fish as – all fisherman are the same – but the smaller size of people may be seen as derived from cultural practice. The possibility of a 'natural painting size' cannot be excluded – that is, a size which is dictated by a tradition. A comparison of Najombolmi's work with other artists in decorative X-ray tradition favours this explanation as the most feasible. The 'natural painting size' leads to pictures of between 30 cm and 90 cm maximum dimensions. Within these limits sizes may vary according to real-life sizes, importance, or some other convention.

Composition

Composition is an aspect of Najombolmi's work which is both obvious and elusive. Rock art is not a framed picture. The beginning and end of 'a painting' can be hard to define. For the purposes of this chapter composition is defined as those subjects (two or more) which, by their position in relation to each other and/or by their similar colour and use of similar stylistic elements, appear to have been painted, at one point in time, as a scene. Identifying compositions by this definition is extremely subjective. However, the groups of subjects identified below as compositions are those that almost everyone, both Aborigines and Europeans, recognized as 'going together'. The reasons for this association were based primarily, as far as one could tell, on the three elements outlined above. Whatever the cause, these associations were consistently identified.

Narrative scenes, such as a man hunting a macropod, are particularly easy to identify as compositions. These are, however, relatively rare in Najombolmi's work. The most common form of composition in his work is groupings of humans or animals in various poses. Many of these compositions are repeated several times at sites many kilometres apart in almost identical form.

The most striking and unusual of Najombolmi's compositions are those featuring relatively large numbers of humans, some mythological figures, anthropomorphs, and other animals. There are such compositions stretching over 40 m² of rock surface at three sites (see Fig. 2.5, Colour Section 1). The overall similarity between these sites is remarkable.

In these compositions, women outnumber men by at least 2 : 1 while one site has no human males at all. Mythological creatures in the form of Namargon (Lightning Man) and creation heroes are present at one site, five birds at another, and the macropod and snake at the third. Several aspects of the depiction of humans are repeated throughout, and women in particular are often painted with interlocking arms. Pairs of females are the most common form of human composition (see Fig. 2.6, Colour Section 1). There is no example of three females together and one example of two males together. In contrast to the horizontal lines of humans in the large compositions, most of the pairs of females are, in fact, reclining and are often positioned one on top of another. This may be due to the fact that the rock surfaces used in such cases were usually longer than they were high, and the fact that humans were the largest subjects painted. However, the possibility that the women were painted as if sleeping or relaxing cannot be discounted.

Najombolmi's compositions of male and female human subjects appear to fall into three categories:

(a)   maternal scenes of a larger female figure lying above a smaller male figure with the arms of the female surrounding the male in the protective pose;
(b)   sexual relationships between male and female;
(c)   domestic scenes of a male and female with typical tools used in hunting and gathering.

The emphasis in these scenes is very much of the male hunter, in contrast to the female emphasis of most of his other paintings. A comparison of the two paintings in this category show that they are almost identical with a few minor variations (see Fig. 2.7, Colour Section 1).

Males also feature in one other type of composition – hunting scenes. These are not common in Najombolmi's art and occur at only two sites. They are more common in the larger body of X-ray art, and the typical scene is of a very small male hunter with spear-thrower raised and the spear piercing a very large macropod. There is a contact version of this theme, executed in wax, with a male hunter with knife and gun in pursuit of a buffalo. (Abstract designs and human and animal figures formed by pressing beeswax onto the rock surface are found throughout the study area, but are not common.)

Groupings of fish were the most common form of Najombolmi's animal composition. These may be fish of the same species but, just as often, groups of fish of different species (see Figs. 2.8 & 2.9, Colour Section 1). Fish in compositions, numbering from two to six are either in a horizontal-line configuration or in a box-like formation stacked one on top of the other. The other most commonly associated animals are groups of flying foxes.

A remarkable feature of Najombolmi's compositions is their constancy. The different types of composition are repeated at sites spread over a large area. In some cases almost identical representations occur at widely separated sites. Certain characteristics of the way in which Najombolmi organized compositions seem to be unique to him rather than common features of the general body of recent X-ray art. The way in which human figures are linked together within compositions is one example. The use of interlocking arms and the depicting of human beings in a protective stance towards other human beings is particularly interesting, demonstrating the relationship between the people in the paintings and, at least subjectively, conveying strong emotional connotations. Although not as obvious as hunting scenes, the groups of humans in Najombolmi's paintings do convey the impression of indeed being painted as narrative scenes. Animals (fish) lack this characteristic and give the impression of being mere listings of animals.

The characteristics of Najombolmi's art that we have been discussing are, we believe, part of the normal range of variation that can occur within the X-ray art tradition. They reflect the flexibility of the X-ray art tradition that allows for considerable variation within a homogeneous whole.

It would appear that the capacity of the X-ray tradition to allow variation was much greater than the previous art styles of the region. Styles such as the Dynamic Figure style are composed of a very limited range of subject, motif, and colour combinations. Variations within these elements would indeed change the style obviously and dramatically. Within the X-ray tradition, however, made up as it is of a great many more elements initially, much more flexibility is possible without going outside the boundaries of the style. Najombolmi's choice of subjects, colours, and poses are aspects which are certainly different, possibly new, but can be contained within the X-ray tradition.

His compositions, however, appear to us to be quite a significant innovation within the X-ray tradition, where the expression of relationships between subjects are not emphasized, and certainly not in the ostentatious way they are by Najombolmi.

One artist's contribution

The body of data we have gathered enables us to begin asking questions about an individual artist's contribution to the body of rock art generally. There is no doubt that Najombolmi's contribution was outstanding. He was responsible for at least 604 individual paintings at no less than 46 sites. It is difficult to give a precise measure of the quantitative significance of this relative to the recent rock art as a whole, since the regional survey is as yet incomplete. Nevertheless, it is clear that he was the major individual contributor to the rock art during the past 100 years. As Najombolmi's party had to provide food and shelter for themselves on their trips through the bush, it is not unreasonable to suggest that painting on this scale was possible prior to European contact. Although Najombolmi's paintings are spread over an area of 1800 km^2, the area is well within the documented traditional seasonal range of an individual living within this region (Chaloupka 1980).

One question to consider is what it cost the society in time and effort to support such a prolific artist. We have been fortunate to witness the execution of recent rock paintings in Kakadu National Park. The actual paintings themselves took very little time:

One bichrome turtle	50 min
One bichrome fish	30 min
One monochrome human female	15 min

Prior to the painting, the party, with the aid of a Toyota, spent seven hours collecting pigments and fixatives.

In a more traditional setting, pigments, brushes, fixatives, etc. were readily available in the normal course of hunting and gathering activities. Other necessary objects, such as dilly bags to carry the items or grinding stones to prepare the ochre, were also part of the general technology used in everyday activities.

It is likely that occasionally a long journey may have been necessary to

Figure 2.5 Large composition by Najombolmi, from Kakadu National Park, Australia

Figure 2.6 Two female figures by Najombolmi, from Kakadu National Park, Australia

Figure 2.7 Domestic scene by Najombolmi, from Kakadu National Park, Australia

Figure 2.8 Group of fish by Najombolmi, from Kakadu National Park, Australia

Figure 2.9 Group of fish by Najombolmi, from Kakadu National Park, Australia

obtain ochre of a particular quality, either spiritual or physical, and possible that other goods such as flaking stone or bamboo may have been exchanged for it (Gabirrigi pers. comm.). Generally, however, it can be said that it was probably no great economic burden to have a prolific artist within one's group. Indeed, Najombolmi is as famous among his contemporaries for his hunting skills as for his artistic endeavours.

Painting took relatively little time and did not involve elaborate physical preparations, although the process of creativity must vary a great deal between individual artists. Moreover, the perception of painters and painting in Aboriginal society may be very different from that in recent European society. An Aboriginal painter is not seen as a person with unusual gifts but as a man who paints often and with some skill. The artist's role in increase ceremonies and in educating the young may in fact place him securely within the economic sphere.

Art as a social indicator

As prehistorians, we were interested in looking at Najombolmi's art and seeing how accurately it reflected his lifestyle and the social conditions of the time. Comparing our knowledge of Najombolmi's life history with his artistic output, it can be seen that while the art reflects aspects of his traditional lifestyle well, it does not reflect the substantial contacts Najombolmi had with Europeans. In fact, his extensive contact with Europeans is not represented at all, apart from one portrayal of a goat, a buffalo hunter, and the use of European pigments in the Blue Paintings. It is possible that this absence of the European world in Najombolmi's art is deliberate. Following Chaloupka's argument that the repainting of the Anbangbang site was an attempt to recreate the traditional Aboriginal world, it is possible that Najombolmi deliberately excluded the European experience from his art as an act of rejection.

Alternatively, it could be argued that conceptual constraints, semantic in their nature, did not allow the creation of images of non-Aboriginal origin. If this is the case, then these constraints must have been specific to Najombolmi as contact themes are very common in the art of the Alligator Rivers Region. A great many Macassan and European objects were painted on rock following the first contacts with these outside visitors. This trend continued through to recent times when aeroplanes and the written English language have been incorporated into the art.

Najombolmi's emphasis on traditional subjects in his art is also very interesting. Whatever the cause of Najombolmi's selection of subject matter, it is clear that the individual Aboriginal artist's subjects do not necessarily reflect his everyday lifestyle and experience.

The fact that the buffalo industry and other European endeavours were carried out on a seasonal basis and away from the rock country may have facilitated the demarcation of traditional and European experience. It may be that the temporal and spatial oppositions between dry season, floodplain, Europeans, and no art on the one hand, and wet season, rock country, no Europeans, and art on the other are significant in this process.

Table 2.1   Art sites painted by Najombolmi.

Gunmugugur	Number of sites	Percentage
Bardmardi	8	17.4
Warramal	3	6.5
Rol	12	26.1
Wardjag	3	6.5
Mirarr Gundjeibmi	3	6.5
Djamgolor	17	37.0
Total	46	100

Another question to consider is how Najombolmi's paintings related to indigenous cultural boundaries. Figure 2.3 shows the position of the patrilineal clans (*gunmugugur*) of the region, as determined by the Fox (1977, p. 278) inquiry. It should be noted that these boundaries were very fluid and their nature is not well defined by a line on a map. In particular, it should be noted that while the *gunmugugur* is the primary land-owning unit of the region, the social, economic, and religious activities of individuals went well beyond clan boundaries.

The art sites painted by Najombolmi are distributed across the territories of six *gunmugugur* as indicated in Table 2.1 (see also Fig. 2.3).In fact, the majority of the art sites fall outside Najombolmi's Bardmardi clan territory, which contains only 17.4 per cent of sites. However, the estates further to the north, which contain the majority of painting sites, were within the annual range of members of the Bardmardi clan. Moreover, apart from economic and social ties involving neighbouring clans and clan estates, people also had spiritual and ceremonial responsibilities for the land and sites of their neighbours. Chaloupka (1983a, p. 104) argues that the Bardmardi clanspeople had special responsibility for the Warramal estate. This relationship was expressed in phrases such as 'we were the biggest countrymen, walking up and down all the time', 'they are drinking our water', and 'we are of one river'. Chaloupka also notes that Najombolmi's paintings in the Warramal estate are evidence of this connection. However, despite this close connection between the Bardmardi and Warramal clans, only 6.5 per cent of Najombolmi's sites are located in Warramal territory. The majority of sites are in the neighbouring Rol and Djamgolor estates.

Although the area of distribution of Najombolmi's paintings may reflect a pattern that was established in pre-contact times, the proportion of sites in each clan territory may have been influenced by the effects of colonization. The distribution of sites can, in part, be explained by their proximity to the European settlements at Nourlangie Camp and Muirella Park, where Najombolmi spent the most prolific part of his artistic life. As Najombolmi's social centre of gravity moved from Deaf Adder Gorge to the latter two places, so too did the centre of his artistic output. It is this that may explain the higher density of sites in the northern clan estates. Thus, while the subject matter of Najombolmi's paintings does not directly reflect European contact, the particular distribution of his art may well do.

Conclusion

The most important issue considered in this chapter is 'Who and what makes up a body of art?' Previously, in approaching a body of art such as that at Kakadu there has been a tendency to divide the art into groups relative to each other in a chronological sequence. Each style identified tends to be viewed as an anonymous conglomeration of paintings. Indeed, Aboriginal people of the region share this latter view in the case of the older monochrome art, which they explain as the work of spirit people and which is of very little relevance to the human sphere.

In this chapter we have shown how perhaps quite a small number of individuals may be responsible for a large proportion of a particular body of art. Art is not necessarily produced by individuals who slavishly follow normative values but by individuals who, through their innovative action, are effective in stylistic change. Najombolmi's development of the 'grand composition' is an example of this process. Perhaps, in general, much more attention should be given to the impact of individuals on what is perceived as an 'art style'. For example, in considering the Palaeolithic art sites of southern France, which are relatively few in number and located close together, a model that emphasizes the individual contribution may be more appropriate than one that treats the rock art as a broad-scale social phenomenon.

Acknowledgements

We would like to thank the Gagudju Association and the Australian National Parks and Wildlife Service for supporting this research financially.

We would particularly like to thank Nipper Gabirrigi, George Namingum, Jimmy and Sarah Wok Wok, Toby Gangale, Jacky Namandali, David Gannari, and Fred Hunter for all the information they gave to us. In the field we were assisted by Jimmy Ahtoy, Queenie Brennan, Daisy Balmarig, Shirley Madalk, Fred Nagawali, and Peter Rotumah.

John Clegg and Sharon Sullivan provided useful comments on previous drafts of the paper.

Note

1   This chapter is based on a study carried out in Kakadu National Park in the Northern Territory of Australia (Fig. 2.1). Kakadu is Aboriginal land that has been leased back by the traditional owners to the Commonwealth of Australia to be run as a National Park. The study was jointly supported by the Australian Parks and Wildlife Service and the Gagudju Association, which represents the traditional owners.

The Kakadu region has a seasonal climate, characterized by a rainy tropical monsoon season from November to April and dry conditions through the remainder of the year. The Park area contains a variety of environments, ranging from coastal beach and mangrove communities, through extensive saline and freshwater floodplains and diverse woodland communities, to a major sandstone escarpment and plateau that extends the length of the Park. Our study centred on the rocky country (Fox 1977, ANPWS 1980).

References

ANPWS 1980. Kakadu National Park plan of management, Commonwealth of Australia.

Brandl, E. 1973. *Australian Aboriginal paintings in western and central Arnhem Land: temporal sequences and elements of style in Cadell River and Deaf Adder Creek art.* Canberra: Australian Institute of Aboriginal Studies.

Chaloupka, G. 1977. Aspects of the chronology and schematisation of the prehistoric sites on the Arnhem Land Plateau. In *Form in indigenous art: schematisation in the art of Aboriginal Australia and prehistoric Europe*, P. J. Ucko (ed.), 243–59. Canberra: Australian Institute of Aboriginal Studies.

Chaloupka, G. 1980. Bardmardi year of seasons. Unpublished paper, Northern Territory Museum, Darwin.

Chaloupka, G. 1982. *Burrunguy, Nourlangie Rock.* Darwin: Northart.

Chaloupka, G. 1983a. Back to my country, Namarrkanga. Unpublished report to Australian National Parks and Wildlife Service.

Chaloupka, G. 1983b. Kakadu rock art, its cultural, historic and prehistorical significance. In *The rock art sites of Kakadu National Park. Some preliminary research findings for their conservation and management*, D. Gillespie (ed.), 1–35. ANPWS Publication 10, Canberra: Australian National Parks and Wildlife Service.

Fox, R. W. 1977. *Ranger uranium environmental inquiry.* Canberra: Australian Government Publishing Service.

Jones, R. (ed.) 1985. *Archaeological research in Kakadu National Park.* ANPWS Special Publication 13, Canberra: Australian National Parks and Wildlife Service.

Kamminga, J. & H. Allen 1973. Alligator Rivers environmental fact-finding study. Canberra: Australian Government Publishing Service.

Leichardt, L. 1847. *Journal of an overland expedition in Australia from Moreton Bay to Port Essington.* London: T. W. Boone.

Levitus, R. 1982. Everybody bin all day wórk. Unpublished report to Australian National Parks and Wildlife Service.

Lewis, D. 1983. *Art, archaeology and material culture in Arnhem Land.* Unpublished BA hons. thesis. Australian National University, Canberra.

Macknight, C. C. 1976. *The voyage to Marege, Macassan trepangers in Northern Australia.* Melbourne: Melbourne University Press.

Mountford, C. P. 1956. *Art, myth and symbolism.* Melbourne: Melbourne University Press.

Schrire, C. 1982. *The Alligator Rivers: prehistory and ecology in western Arnhem Land.* Terra Australis 7, Department of Prehistory, Research School of Pacific Studies. Canberra: Australian National University.

Tacon, P. S. 1987. A preliminary summary of certain trends evident in X-ray rock paintings of western Arnhem Land, northern Australia. *Anlar*, January.

Tacon, P. S. 1989. Art and the essence of being: symbolic and economic aspects of fish among the peoples of western Arnhem Land, Australia. In *Animals into art*, H. Morphy (ed.), Ch. 10. London: Unwin Hyman.

3 The snake and the Fabulous Beast: themes from the pottery of the Ilama culture

MARIANNE CARDALE SCHRIMPFF

Introduction

Those of us who have not forgotten the fairy stories of our childhood will recall a world where birds and beasts were believed to converse in languages no less rich than those used by humans. In this world each animal species had a king, and individuals might be helped by humans, often repaying this aid in times of acute need. At the same time, many of these beasts could take human shape while humans were frequently turned into animals by sorcerers or through their own powers. It was a world in which relationships between human beings and the other animals were much more intimate, and where the concept of a hard and fast division between the two had not yet arisen.

These attitudes were common at a time when the population was largely rural, when those who lived in towns remained heavily dependent on the countryside, a countryside in which extensive tracts of forest and marsh provided habitats for numerous wild animals whose appearance, and many of whose habits, were known at first hand.

The Amerindians today, or until very recently, have been able to enjoy a style of life that was in many ways similar. As they scoured forest, mountain, and plain on hunting expeditions or in search of raw materials, they had ample opportunity of becoming closely acquainted with the animals that lived around them. It is hardly surprising that these animals became interwoven in the Indians' beliefs and attitudes to life, and were considered as neighbours, occupying their territory on an equal plane with the humans living in the same area.

In a study of the Kogi Indians who inhabit the slopes of the snow-capped Sierra Nevada de Santa Marta in northern Colombia, Reichel-Dolmatoff (1949–51, p. 261) has summarized this group's attitude as follows:

> For the Kogi there is no strict dividing line between man and beast. The animals are considered essentially as beings endowed with all the characteristics of man excepting only his outward appearance. The Kogi believe that the animals talk, think, have 'souls' and live an ordered life just as humans do. . .The animals are neither friends nor enemies of man but simply beings who live apart and who man should treat with the same caution, the same respect and perhaps

the same fear with which he would treat any neighbouring human family
in his own society.

The Ilama potters

This intimate knowledge of the beasts that shared their territory is displayed by the
Ilama potters, a study of whose wares forms the body of this chapter. The Ilama
culture flourished during the first millennium BC in the mountains and forests of
a small part of the Colombian Western Cordillera centred on the Calima area (Fig.
3.1). It is the earliest known of a sequence of three Formative and post-Formative
cultures in the region. Most of the Ilama sites known so far (Herrera *et al.* 1984, p.
381 *et seq.*, Bray *et al.* 1985, Salgado 1986) have been found at altitudes of between 1200
and 1500 metres, where there is a benign, subtropical climate with mean annual
temperatures of around 18–20 °C. The Ilama farmers grew maize and beans on the
fertile volcanic-ash soils, and, probably, a wide range of other subtropical crops.

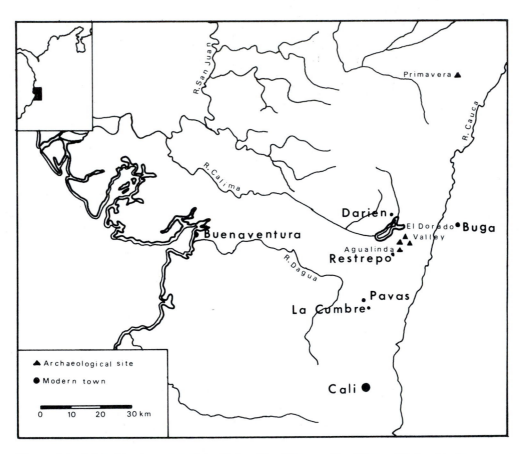

Figure 3.1 Map showing part of the Colombian Western Cordillera. All the sites known so
far have been found within the small rectangle.

Figure 3.2 Toad of the *Bufo* genus; red slip with traces of black, white fill in spots; height 15 cm, private collection.

Since the soils are acid and the rainfall relatively high, little of the Ilama material culture has been preserved, so that for examples of these people's representative art we are almost entirely dependent on pottery. Vessels in the shapes of different kinds of birds, mammals, and reptiles are relatively common in Ilama graves. Most of the species still occur locally (Legast n.d.). In some cases, such as the toad of the *Bufo* genus illustrated in Figure 3.2, the creature is portrayed with a wealth and accuracy of detail which includes the pores of the skin and the glands for secreting fluid. Figures are far from standardized, however, and individual potters will emphasize different features of the same animal or depict the same features in different ways, as with the armadillos illustrated in Figure 3.3, variations which perhaps hold some significance which we cannot now decipher. In the case of some of these animals, the problem of identification is made harder by the large numbers of different species that inhabit the northern Andes.

These Ilama animals are usually depicted alone, occasionally in groups (lizards and frogs, for instance, around the mouth of a bowl), but always in a basically naturalistic way. Much less common are vessels with representations in a totally distinct category where elements drawn from a number of different animal species are combined to form a composite creature. Three categories of composite creatures

Figure 3.3 Armadillos: (a) height 12.5 cm, MO CC9; (Museo del Oro, Bogotá); (b) height 17 cm, Bright collection; (c) height 14 cm, private collection.

have been recognized so far in Ilama pottery (Table 3.1),[1] but by far the most frequent is the one we have called the 'Fabulous Beast'.

Table 3.1 The distribution of animal, human, and composite motifs according to vessel form (FB: Fabulous Beast; CB: composite beast).

Vessel form		Modelled motif					
		Naturalistic		Composite			
	zoom	anthr	FB	CBa	CBb	Total	%
Spouted	200	56	7	7	5	275	2.5
Tubular			1			1	
Jars							
stemmed a			4			4	100
stemmed b		3	2			5	40
other	13	4				17	
Beakers							
'snake pots'		17				17	100
related		3				3	
Canasteros:							
fan		8				8	
smooth crest		16	9			25	56
spiked crest		11	5			16	31
long hair		13				13	
other	2	3	3			8	37
Toby jugs		23	6			29	20
Patones		8	10			18	55
Cups	3		1?			4	
Whistles	5	16				21	
Pipes	1					1	
Lime pots?	2		1			3	
Bowls	2					2	
Total	228	162	69	7	5	471	15

The snake and the Fabulous Beast on Ilama pottery

Figure 3.4 gives an idea of the complexity of this creature, made up of elements drawn from as many as seven different species (Table 3.2). Besides being composite, the Beast is also polymorphic, with the degree of prominence given to the different elements varying between one example and another. At one end of the continuum the impression is of a massive, four-legged animal, while at the other we appear to be looking at human figures with some zoomorphic features.

In the following pages I first attempt to identify the different species which make up the Fabulous Beast and then describe the various categories into which the representations of this creature fall. It will be seen that within this composite, polymorphic concept, the snake has rather a special role. The snake is the most constant and explicit component (Table 3.2) though it should not necessarily be assumed that it is the most important element. It is also unusual in that the entire animal is shown.

Figure 3.4 The Fabulous Beast: (a), (b) height 24 cm, private collection; (c) height 21 cm, private collection.

Table 3.2 Components of the Fabulous Beast.

Form: Collection	Snake	Bat	Feline	Toad	Tortoise	Bird	Human
Spouted							
1. MO CC4492	×	×	×		×		
2. BP C1023	×	?	×			×	
3. Land	×	?	×				
4. Private	×	?	×	×	×		
5. Private	×	?	×				
6. Private	×	?	×				
7. Private	×	×	×			×	
Tubular							
1. MO CC1975	?	×					?
Jars							
stemmed a							
1. MO CC4518	×	×					?
2. MO CC4520	×	?	?				?
3. MO CC5627	×	?	?				?
4. Private	×	?	?				?
stemmed b							
1. Private	×						×
2. Private	×						?
Beakers							
'snake pots'							
1. Arango C.	×	×	?				?
2. MM C1028	×	×	?				?
3. BP C11893	×	×	?				?
4. BP C12664	×	×	?				?
5. BP C11895	×	×	?				?
6. MO CC1970	×	×	?				?
7. MO CC3185	×	×	?				?
8. MO CC1972	×	×	?				?
9. MO CC1973	×	×	?				?
10. MO CC4522	×	×	?				?
11. Private	×	×	?				?
12. Private	×	×	?				?
13. MO CC4523	×	×	?				?
14. BP C11892	×	×	?				?
15. Private	×	×	?				?
16. MO CC792	×	×	?				?
17. UV 1868	×	×	?				?
's.p.' related							
1. MO CC4525	×			×			
2. Private	×	?					
3. BP C3712	×	?	?				
Canasteros							
smooth crested							
1. MO CC72	×						×
2. Private	×						×
3. Private	×						×
4. MO CC71	×						×
5. Arango C.	×						×

(continued overleaf)

(Table 3.2 continued.)

Form: Collection	Snake	Bat	Feline	Toad	Tortoise	Bird	Human
6. MO CC394	×						×
7. BP C10770	×	?	?				×
8. MO CC4536	×	?	?				×
9. MO CC4534	×	?	?	×			×
spiked crest							
1. MO CC6299	?	×					×
2. Private	?	×					×
3. Private	?	×					×
4. Private	×	×					×
5. Cuenca		×					×
atypical							
1. Private	×	×					×
'Toby jugs'							
1. Private	×						×
2. BP C1031	×	?					×
3. Cuenca	×	?					×
4. MM C9172	?	?		?			×
5. Private	?	?		?			×
6. Cuenca		×					×
Patones							
1. MO CC5625	S	?					×
2. Private	S	?					×
3. Private	S	?					×
4. Private	S	?					×
5. Private	×, S						×
6. Private	×	?					×
7. MO CC5622	×	?					×
8. Private	×	?					×
9. Private	×	×					×
10. Private	×						×
Cups							
1. MO CC1968	×			×			
Lime pots?							
1. MO CC1974	×	×					?

Note: MO = Museo del Oro, Bogotá; BP = Museo Arqueológico del Banco Popular, Bogotá; MM = Museo La Merced, Cali; UV = Universidad del Valle, Cali.

As we shall see later, other species tend to be represented by special features, such as characteristic dentition or their way of carrying the tail. Finally, the snake is unique in the way it is used as a substitute, or kenning, for parts of the beast.[2] In Figure 3.4 the creature's legs and feet, though rendered as snakes, are still clearly the legs of a quadruped; the tail, though a snake's head, is no less the curling tail of a (?) feline.

A creature as polymorphic as the Fabulous Beast is not always easy to recognize, and far from easy to study coherently. One possibility would be to group the representations according to themes – the Beast in its toad aspect, or the theme of

Table 3.3 Position of the snake in its role as an element of the Fabulous Beast.

Vessel	Hair/crest	Limbs	Body	Tail	Belt	Fillet	Brows	Ears	Nose	Tongue	Necklace
Spouted											
1.		×	×	×							
2.	×	×	×	×							
3.	×	?	×	?							
4.		×	×								
5.			×	×							
6.		×	×								
7.	×	×	×	×							
Tubular											
1.		?									
Jars stemmed a											
1.	×										
2.	×					×					
3.	×										×
4.	×										
stemmed b											
1.											×
2.						×					
Beakers 's.p.'											
1.		×	×			×					
2.		×	×			×					
3.		×	×			×					
4.		×	×			×					
5.		?	×			×					
6.		×	×			×					
7.		×	×			×	×				
8.		×	×			×	×		×		
9.		×	×				×	×	×		
10.		×					×				
11.		?	×			×	×		×		
12.		×				×	×	×	×		
13.		×	×			×				×	
14.		×	?			×				×	
15.		×	×			×			×	×	
16.		×				×					
17.		×				×					
related											
1.											
2.	×	×				?	?		?		
3.		×	?			?					
Canasteros smooth cr.											
1.	×										?
2.		×				×					
3.	×	×	×			×					

(continued overleaf)

(*Table 3.3 continued*)

Vessel	Hair/crest	Limbs	Body	Tail	Belt	Fillet	Brows	Ears	Nose	Tongue	Necklace
4.	×	×	×		×						
5.	×	×	×		×			head			×
6.		×									×
7.	×	S	S		×					×	
8.		S	S					×			
9.	×	S									
spiked cr.											
1.	?										
2.	?										
3.	?										
4.	?	×									
5.	?										
atypical											
1.		×									
'Toby jugs'											
1.						×					
2.		S	S								
3.		S	S			×					
4.		S?	S?								
5.		S									
6.											
Patones											
1.		(S)			S						
2.		S	S		S?						
3.		S			S?						
4.		S	S								
5.		(S)	×		×	×					?
6.					?		×	×	?		
7.		×				S					
8.		(S)					×	×	?		×
9.		S	S		?	×		×		×	
10.		S								×	
Cups											
1.		×									

the protruding tongue = penis = snake. However, since there is a fairly strong link between a particular representation of the Fabulous Beast and the type of vessel it is found on (Tables 3.2 & 3.3), I have decided to classify them according to shape. It seems reasonable to suggest that the vessels were made for use, though we can only speculate as to whether this was daily or ritual. A classification according to shape has the additional advantage that it allows particular aspects of the Fabulous Beast to be linked potentially to particular needs, occasions, or ceremonies.

In contrast to the numerous vessels with relatively naturalistic representations of birds, monkeys, and a variety of other creatures (Legast n.d.), naturalistic representations of snakes shown alone appear to be rare. Only two were seen in a total of nearly 500 vessels examined. One of these (a double-spouted vessel with a bridge handle) came from the Agualinda cemetery, near Restrepo (Bray *et al.* 1983, p. 29), and the second is an outstandingly fine jar in the Museum für Völkerkunde, Berlin (VA 65233), illustrated by Fischer (n.d., Fig. 102). In both cases the snake is curled around the pot.

A third fairly naturalistic representation is found on a cup (Fig. 3.5), where a very toothy snake pursues a frog around the rim. The teeth are an unusual, almost unique feature in Ilama snakes but may merely be emphasizing the role of this example as a predator, rather than indicating a different species.

Two further vessels (Museo Arqueológico del Banco Popular, Bogotá (BP) C1023 and an example in a private collection) actually show snakes devouring their prey. In each case they are swallowing a bird, starting at the head (Fig. 3.4). However, in both cases the snake's head and neck is at the same time the curling tail of a four-footed beast. We are meeting, for the first time, the snake as a kenning, used as a replacement for part of another animal, in short in its role as a component of the Fabulous Beast. In the Banco Popular example (Fig. 3.4a) the snake's head is shared by two snake bodies which meander round the vessel, and which also have heads at the other extreme. What is more, the bird being swallowed is, at the same time, the tail of another snake whose two heads form the main animal's head-dress.

Both the examples just mentioned belong to a group of double-spouted and bridge-handled vessels[3] which show a composite, fabulous beast whose attributes include a prominent, toothy jaw, round 'doughnut' eyes, and a rather strange, turned-up nose. On this group of vessels the beast is a quadruped with a tail, traits which, as we shall see, place it firmly at the zoomorphic end of a continuum in which

Figure 3.5 Snake pursuing a frog; black with red slip now showing through; height 14 cm, MO CC4537.

anthropomorphic traits become increasingly dominant. In all the vessels in this shape-category the quadrupeds are accompanied by snakes which wreathe their way round the sides of the vessel and usually form the fabulous creature's limbs. In three of the seven cases known to the writer, snakes form the creatures' 'hair' or crest, but in a further two the head-dress is another reptile – a tortoise, or perhaps a turtle.

Identifying the animals in the Fabulous Beast

Exactly which other animals contribute elements to the Fabulous Beast is far from easy to determine, and the identifications made here and in Table 3.2 can only be tentative. The prominent, toothy jaw, the curling tail, and the four, squarely-planted legs might suggest that we are dealing with a 'fabulized' version of the felines modelled on some other double-spouted vessels (Herrera *et al*. 1984, Fig. 6,F). The resemblance seems sufficiently close to justify the identification of a feline element in this category of vessels and, by analogy, to suspect it on other vessels where the curling tail and firmly planted feet are not shown. However, the head of the Fabulous Beast, while far from standardized, clearly incorporates elements which are not feline. One of these elements is almost certainly the bat.

Bats, too, have prominent teeth with fangs, as well as round eyes and, in some species belonging to the Phyllostomidae family, a leaf-shaped membrane that stands up vertically from the nose. The triangle shown immediately above the jaws of a beast in the Gold Museum (Museo del Oro, Bogotá (MO) CC4492), and in the example illustrated in Figure 3.4b, is identical to that used to denote the nose-leaf in the Tairona bat figures (Legast & Cadena 1986, Fig. 2, and Ch. 12, this volume). The Phyllostomidae or New World leaf-nosed bats, form an enormous family with as many as 50 genera and 140 species, many of which are found in Colombia. The different species vary widely in their food habits and physical appearance (Hill & Smith 1984, p. 204), so much so that the wealth of variety in the latter can be quite bewildering. However, the specialized dentition on some of the Fabulous Beast heads to be described later is characteristic of the vampire bat (Grzimek 1975, Vol. XI, p. 94). In Table 3.2 the bat element is considered to be identifiable wherever the nose-leaf or specialized dentition is shown and, where these are absent, whenever the head bears a close general resemblance to examples with these features. Although the Ilama potters were perfectly capable of depicting bat bodies (e.g. Legast & Cadena 1986, Fig. 6, and see Ch. 12, this volume), only the head seems to have been used as a component of the Fabulous Beast.

In the group of double-spouted vessels, a toad, or perhaps a frog, is recognizable in only one example (in a private collection). The outline of the toad is incised at the back of the vessel and its modelled head forms the Fabulous Beast's knob-like tail. Toads appear to be a less important, or at least, a less commonly represented, component of the Fabulous Beast. They are included in Table 3.2 either when the animal is sufficiently complete to be recognizable, or when the characteristic pores of its skin are represented by circular impressions (Fig. 3.2). These impressions can be distinguished from those used to designate fur by the slightly smaller size and closer spacing of the latter.

Other elements may also be present in the representations of the Fabulous Beast

– it is possible that we should be looking for isolated features of the tortoise mingled in with the other elements that form this composite creature. Our eyes undoubtedly see but a sadly impoverished version of what to the Ilama must have been precise and meaningful representations.

As we examine other categories of Ilama vessel shapes, we will find that although the Fabulous Beast appears on a number of them, the degree of resemblance to the Beast portrayed in the first group described varies very considerably. The same beast as that portrayed on the double-spouted vessels, or something that appears to be closely related to it, is immediately recognizable on a long, tubular vessel in the Gold Museum (MO CC1975) – the only example of this shape seen so far. In this specimen, the nose is markedly bat-like while both the head-dress and the sinuous way the limbs are depicted are suggestive of snakes. However, the creature's posture appears to be anthropomorphic.

Anthropomorphic elements in the Fabulous Beast

Anthropomorphic elements are also important in the next group of vessels.[4] These elements are most easily recognizable in both the posture of the creature represented and in its 'hair'. In one example, human sexual organs (male) are also shown. Known so far from four examples, this group is composed of relatively large jars with stems, and with the upper part of the vessel, immediately below the neck, modelled in the shape of two large animal heads, one on either side of the vessel (Fig. 3.6). Like the Fabulous Beasts already described, the creature has a prominent, toothy jaw and round eyes. Again like the other Fabulous Beasts, the features vary in detail,

Figure 3.6 Two-headed Fabulous Beast with hair or head-dress of stylized snakes: traces of black on faces, especially eyes; height 21.5 cm, MO CC4518.

being sometimes more suggestive of a feline while in other examples, such as the one illustrated here, the bat elements predominate. The nose-leaf is clearly shown, as are the teeth with an extra pair of fangs at the rear of the jaw, characteristic of the dentition of the vampire bat.

The creature's hair or head-dress is composed of two-headed snakes, shown

Figure 3.7 Anthropomorphic jar with a single foot. Note the swelling that possibly indicates goitre, and the snake necklace. Height 19 cm, private collection.

with a greater or lesser degree of stylization and with the heads forming a sort of crested fillet round the animal's brow, more reminiscent of a human hair-style than of an animal's fur or crest. Besides the snake 'hair', one example (MO CC4520) has a fillet on its brow in the form of another two-headed snake: this is probably a different species since it is shown with a series of short horizontal bars on either side of a central stripe that runs its whole length. On another of the Gold Museum examples (MO CC5627), a modelled necklace or collar with incised cross-hatching is also suggestive of a snake.

A second, very different, group of vessels, which usually depict human figures (e.g. MO CC5619 illustrated in Bray 1978, p. 551), is included here since these vessels belong basically to the same shape category. A human head modelled on the upper part of the jars, immediately below the neck, is of a toothy individual with a pronounced swelling below the chin that appears to indicate goitre. This is the only group of Ilama vessels with this feature. The stem of the vessel represents the human trunk and feet. On four of the five examples it is left plain, but on the fifth it ends in a single large foot (Fig. 3.7). This individual has two additional swellings on his body and 'wears' a two-headed snake around his neck. A second example (also in a private collection) wears a snake fillet on his brow. No other elements of the Fabulous Beast complex are recognizable.

Much more closely related to the Fabulous Beast jars are a group of beakers[5] with a similar composite head, this time in a slightly simplified and cruder form. These beakers are relatively common in Ilama graves and are often rather roughly made, factors which suggest that they may have been produced in fairly large quantities. This form is also one of the easiest to copy, and there are few collections which do not include a 'reproduction' or two, either of these beakers or of other modelled vessels.[6] After some judicious sifting, the sample so far consists of 17 examples.

Once again we are faced with the difficulty of distinguishing possible feline elements from those that probably represent bats. Although incontrovertibly diagnostic bat features such as the nose-leaf are absent, a number of traits – such as the fact that the large, round eyes are also quite markedly protuberant, and that the head has a high, rather than a sloping, profile – suggest the bat.

On these beakers, the Fabulous Beast has so many snakes among its components that the vessels are known locally as 'snake pots' (Fig. 3.8). Since the beaker walls are vertical, no hair is shown but instead there is a snake fillet composed generally of a pair of two-headed serpents running just below the rim (Fig. 3.8d). As on the jars, the beast is in a human squatting position with snakes as legs. Additional two-headed snakes (between one and three) lie horizontally along the sides of the vessels, possibly indicating stylized ribs.

Six of the examples have snake 'eyebrows' with the serpent heads forming or symbolizing, at one extreme, ears and, at the other, uniting as the nose of the Fabulous Beast (Fig. 3.8d). While this could be interpreted as an anthropomorphizing element, there is a zone over the eyes with special markings on many of the Fabulous Beasts shown on the double-spouted vessels already described. Since on these vessels it is represented by clustered depressions or spots which, in Ilama convention, usually signify fur, it may well be that some sort of distinctive pelage is meant, such as, for instance, the light stripe found on some New World fruit bats

Figure 3.8 'Snake pots': (a), (b) remains of black; height 12 cm, MO CC1970; (c) height 8 cm, MO CC1973; (d) note snake eyebrows with heads as ears and nose, height 8 cm, private collection.

of the genus *Artibeus* (another member of the Phyllostomidae family; Grzimek 1975, Vol. XI, Pl. V, no. 4).

Yet another snake kenning is found on a vessel in the Museo del Banco Popular (BP C11895). In this case two little snake tabs 'hang down' from the fillet on the Beast's brow, with the snakes' heads doubling as the Beast's eyes. A curious theme, which recurs in association with the Fabulous Beast on a number of other shape categories, is found on three vessels. These have snake-like appendages running from the jaw to the genital area. In the Banco Popular example the appendage appears to protrude from between the Beast's lips (a tongue?), and the cross-hatching, indicating snake scales, together with the three characteristic cross-bars are clearly shown. The two final examples in the sample are simplified versions. In no. 16 (Table 3.2), the face is reduced to eyes and a small, toothless mouth, while no. 17 has no face at all.

In this same shape category one more vessel must be mentioned (MO CC 4525) for the prominence it gives to the toad element. The whole of the lower part of the vessel is rather naturalistically modelled in the shape of a toad, whose clearly represented poison glands allow us to identify it as belonging to the genus *Bufo*. In fact it is so naturalistic that at first sight there seems no reason to classify it in the Fabulous Beast category. However, a closer look reveals that it, too, has a snake fillet around the rim.

So far in this survey of the Fabulous Beast we have been moving from what appears to be a purely zoomorphic context (the double-spouted and bridge-handled vessels) to representations where zoomorphic aspects are combined with some human attributes suggested by details such as posture and head-dress. The final context to be considered is basically an anthropomorphic one, in which vessel shapes closely associated with human figures sometimes display features associated with the Fabulous Beast, particularly snakes, and very occasionally have the Fabulous Beast's head on a largely human body.

Most of the examples known are on the *canasteros* or 'basket bearers' as they are called colloquially. These are the local version of a kind of vessel widely distributed in Andean and coastal Ecuador and southern Colombia, in which a human figure appears to be carrying a large receptacle – a pot or perhaps a basket – on his back. In some cases (e.g. Lathrap *et al.* 1975, Fig. 60) the strap or tump line supporting the container is clearly indicated, and in most cases the 'burden bearer' is shown resting, either squatting or seated.

In Calima this vessel is in fact an anthropomorphized beaker, and its basic shape is clearly related to that of the 'snake pots'. In size, the two groups of vessels are also similar, for while very large *canasteros* measuring as much as 40 cm in height are found, the majority are between 9 and 11 cm. Bray *et al.* (1985, pp. 7–9) have divided the *canasteros* into four groups, based on their head-dresses, and found that the use of a certain type of head-dress tended to be accompanied by a number of other specific details.

Although the sample size has increased considerably since 1985 (more than 70 *canasteros* have now been studied), it is interesting to note that of the four categories defined in this way, neither snakes nor other elements of the Fabulous Beast appear to be associated with more than two of them. So far, no examples have been found associated either with those *canasteros* wearing tall, fan-shaped crests (Bray *et al*. 1985, Figs 14 & 15) or with those with long, straight hair hanging over their shoulders (Bray *et al*. 1985, Fig. 16). On the other hand, the Fabulous Beast is clearly associated with both the 'basket bearers' with smooth crests and those with spiked crests.

In the first category, no fewer than nine out of a total of 25 examples have features clearly identifiable as components of the Fabulous Beast.[7] The most usual component is the snake which frequently forms the 'basket bearer's' head-dress. In most cases (e.g. Bray *et al*. 1985, Fig. 13a), the smooth crests are probably natural-istic representations of a hair-style in which the hair is perhaps shaved over the ears and piled on top of the head, with several divisions or partings running from the forehead to the back of the crown. However, when these smooth crests and partings are transformed into serpents (Fig. 3.9b), they become identical to the head-dress worn by the Fabulous Beast on the stemmed jars.

The serpent element varies widely in its intensity. Serpent crests are found on seven of the nine zoomorphic vessels in this category (one of the two exceptions was modelled without a head), but whereas in some examples (two) the rest of the features are all anthropomorphic, on others (five examples) twisted snakes form the limbs. A particularly fine example in a private collection has a head-dress composed of four snakes and a snake fillet on the brow (Fig. 3.9a). The limbs are two-headed snakes, each coiled round in a knot, the heads forming, respectively, the figure's shoulders, hands, knees, and feet. A curious example in the Gold Museum (MO CC71) has two human heads, each with a similar head-dress and fillet; an open mouth, in which incisions on the lips double as teeth; and a more abstract version of the knotted, snakey limbs, with the reptile heads protruding as a series of steps. Three more snakes run vertically down the front of the figure. In addition to the usual horizontal bands, the snakes also have a diagonal line running from one head to the other. A peak of 'snakeyness' is reached in the example illustrated in Figure 3.9b, where even the creature's head and genitals are rendered as snake heads.

A final group is formed of examples with the head of a monstrous animal below the snake crest. Although no two of the heads are exactly alike, most can be paralleled with other representations of the Fabulous Beast. Other features, such as the genitals and the creatures' squatting position, remain unmistakably human. It is striking that in this group limbs are no longer represented as snakes but are shown as covered in snake skin. Cross-hatching on the body of two examples suggests a similar covering, perhaps a snake-skin garment.

A particularly fine example of this category (Fig. 3.10a) has the hair or head-dress composed of five snakes. A fillet around the brow is, at the same time, a snake whose two heads form the creature's ears. The characteristic horizontal bars and the cross-hatching used to represent snake scales are just visible on a modelled appendage protruding from the creature's mouth. Although the other extreme of this appendage ends, or is held, in the hands, it is highly reminiscent of the jaw-to-genital appendages already described for the snake pots. The rear of the vessel is very worn but traces of another round-eyed, toothy head are still visible (Fig. 3.10b). This animal, which shares the limbs of the main creature, appears to be shown in a crouching position, although when the vessel is viewed from the front, the position of the limbs of the main animal remain unmistakably human.

Figure 3.9 (a) *Canastero* with snake head-dress, fillet, and limbs; height 11 cm, private collection; (b) *Canastero* in which even the main figure is a snake; height 16 cm, private collection; (c) *Canastero* which appears to have a snake head-dress with snake-skin markings on the limbs, and toad markings on the head (the small circular depressions are characteristic of toad skin); height 12 cm, MO CC4534.

Figure 3.10 The Fabulous Beast on *canasteros*. (a), (b) Two views of a vessel in the Banco Popular Museum (BP C10770). This *canastero* is unusual in having a second head at the back of the vessel. The head belongs to a crouching creature which shares its legs with the main figure. Height 11 cm. (c) Note the triangular incision on the nose, indicating the nose-leaf of a bat, as well as the extra fangs, visible in the partly open mouth, and characteristic of the vampire. The highly developed ears shown flat at the side of the figure are another bat feature. Height 11.5 cm, MO CC6299.

Another vessel in this group has the same prominent, toothy jaw but the eyes are elongated like those on human figures (Fig. 3.9c). The cross-hatched band running across the centre of the head and ending at the creature's nose is almost certainly a stylized snake, like some of those on the Fabulous Beasts on the double-spouted and bridge-handled vessels. Although ending in hands and feet and in an anthropomorphic position when viewed from the front, the limbs are curiously sinuous, as though suggesting snakes, an impression reinforced by the cross-hatching on the arms. Circular impressions on the head introduce a further element: these impressions probably represent the pores on the skin of a toad (cf. Fig. 3.2), reinforcing the suggestion that in some contexts this creature, or aspects of it, also appears to be a component of the Fabulous Beast.

In the second category of *canasteros* associated with the Fabulous Beast, the defining head-dress is in any case closely related, if not identical, to that worn by this composite creature in other contexts. It is possible that, even when the face of the *canastero* is human and no other attributes of the Fabulous Beast are shown, we should in fact consider the head-dress as a direct reference to this creature.

This spiked-crested category of *canasteros*[8] is markedly different from the smooth-crested group, starting with the fact that the snake element, so common in the former, is here hardly ever explicit. Snake heads (though without the characteristic cross-hatching) are depicted on the limbs of one example only and on what appears to be a related figure with an atypical head-dress, published by Bray. Snakes may also be implied by the strip of cross-hatching that forms the central part of the head-dress on most of the figures (cf. Fig. 3.4).

The monstrous head is set on an entirely anthropomorphic body (Fig. 3.10c) on which (with the exceptions mentioned above) even the fingers and toes are clearly shown. Geometric designs on the chest and stomach clearly represent body paint or tattooing of the sort found on other anthropomorphic figures (Bray *et al.* 1985, Figs 13c, 15, 16), rather than animal pelage, plumage, etc. (e.g. Herrera *et al.* 1984, Fig. 6, B & H).

The figures form a much more homogeneous group than those of the smooth-crested category, so much so that three of the examples in the sample are virtually identical both in body markings and in facial features. In these the bat element is very clear, with a well-marked triangular nose-leaf and large, round eyes. The bared teeth are visible in a heavy, prominent jaw, and in the Gold Museum example (Fig. 3.10c) we find once more the extra pair of fangs characteristic of the vampire bat (*Desmodus rotundus*). Curiously enough, the highly developed ears shown flat at the side of the head are much more like those found on another species, the hairy-legged vampire (*Diphylla ecaudata*; Grzimek 1975, Vol. XI, Pl. VI, p. 136), than the sharply pointed, front-facing ears of *Desmodus rotundus*. Additional lines near the eyes and double triangles above them may, perhaps, represent distinctive markings such as those postulated for the snake 'eyebrows' on the beakers.

Two other categories of vessel fall into the 'anthropomorphic' category of representations of the Fabulous Beast. In both categories the figure is usually human and is closely related iconographically to the *canastero* (Bray *et al.* 1985, p. 8). Both categories, the 'toby jugs'[9] and the *patones*[10] (a Spanish term referring to the exaggerated size of the feet), are based on the jar. The representations of the

Fabulous Beast vary considerably within a range comparable to that described for the *canasteros* (see Tables 3.2 & 3.3). The 'toby jugs' are relatively low, round-bodied jars (Fig. 3.11) on which are modelled human figures (usually, if not always, male); representations of the Fabulous Beast are relatively scarce (six out of 29 examples).

In the *patones* the basic jar shape is subordinated to that of the figure (Fig. 3.12); the Fabulous Beast, and particularly the snake element, is far more common (ten out of 18 examples). In almost all cases, the hands are exceptionally large and carefully depicted with long fingers (sometimes as many as six), even when the arms are shown as, or covered in, snake skin. Another special feature is what appears to be a rather thick, snake-skin belt worn round the hips (Fig. 3.12b).

When this group of vessels is considered as a whole, we find that not only on the two *patones* but also on the 'toby jugs' and *canasteros*, the mouths of the human figures are unnaturally protruding, much more so than on other categories of human figures. Occasionally, as in the case of a 'toby jug' from the La Merced farm, vereda El Porvenir, the jaw is emphasized to a point where it appears more animal than human. In her discussion of some Tairona figures from northern Colombia, Legast (1987, p. 88) has suggested that a certain kind of tubular nose-ornament worn by the Tairona may have been used to push up the nose in such a way as to make it resemble a nose-leaf, giving the wearer a bat-like appearance. While in the case of the Tairona, numerous nose-ornaments of this sort have been found in graves and house foundations, there is no concrete evidence of this kind in the Ilama material culture. The mouths do, however, give the impression that some sort of lip-plate may have been worn to push the lips not up but out, in the process giving the wearer an appearance that brings him closer, perhaps, to that of the Fabulous Beast with its protruding jaws.

Figure 3.11 'Toby jug' with snake fillet from Hacienda La Iberia, grave 5 (Restrepo, Valle); height 16.5 cm, private collection.

Figure 3.12 *Patones*: (a) red with traces of black – note the snake 'arms' with the snake heads doubling as human fingers; height 17.5 cm, MO CC5622; (b) appears to be wearing a broad, and rather thick, snake-skin belt around his hips; height 13.0 cm, MO CC5625.

One final piece (MO CC1968) reinforces my argument as to the connection between snake and toad. It consists of a cup with snakes curling along the rim, borne on the back of a scaley quadruped (Legast n.d., Fig. 92). This beast has been identified by Legast as a crocodile, although she points out that a number of features, such as the short snout, are not characteristic. Nor, of course, are teeth such as this creature has, characteristic of a toad. On the other hand, the shape of the eyes and body and the position of the legs are extremely toad-like. However, at the same time the sinuous hind legs have the horizontal bars that we have seen to be characteristic of Ilama snakes.

Interpretation

In dealing with the art of a people who existed over 2000 years ago, we cannot, of course, ever hope to know exactly what significance a particular representation would have had for them. All we can do is to examine the beliefs and attitudes of surviving indigenous groups today and, where we can, extend our knowledge a little further back in time through information recorded by earlier travellers and the Spanish chroniclers. This information, while it cannot be applied in a direct sense to the beliefs of a people so long dead, can at least give us an idea of the climate of thought in which these beliefs and the art they reflect may have flourished.

It can, of course, be objected that there is no universal pattern of thought found among the enormous numbers of Amerindian groups inhabiting north-western South America and that if there were, they would undoubtedly be different to those that were extant 2 ½ millenniums ago. However, in spite of considerable, and sometimes irreconcilable, differences in detail, a number of themes are found spread over large areas of north-western South America. One of these is the 'master of animals' found both among the Cuna of north-western Colombia and the Tukano, living well over 1000 km to the south-east (Reichel-Dolmatoff 1968, p. 103, Diaz Granados *et al.* 1974, pp. 208–9). The shaman–jaguar theme is even more widespread (e.g. Reichel-Dolmatoff 1975, Ch. 3; for this and other widely diffused myths, see also Roe 1982). Other themes or representations, notably the figure with certain highly specific traits found on the 'Darien' pendants, appear to have a considerable time-depth (Falchetti 1979).

The Fabulous Beast has three salient features. One is that it is composite, with elements drawn, as we have seen, from as many as seven different creatures: snake, bat, feline, toad, tortoise, bird (as prey), and human. The second salient feature is the Beast's polymorphism, with the emphasis first on one element and then on another. Thirdly, the snake is almost always present and is used more as a kenning than as an element in the composite whole. In this attempt to form an idea of the climate of thought reflected in the Fabulous Beast, I first consider each of its components, making a brief survey of the animal in question in the archaeological record and then examining some of the beliefs surrounding that animal as recorded in the present century and in the historic period. I then look in a more general way at Amerindian thought processes with regard to myth and animals.

The snake

Snakes, represented mainly in pottery or in gold, are found in a number of prehispanic cultures in Colombia. Nearest geographically to the Ilama culture are the large vessels from Tierradentro with snake-like figures climbing up the sides (Reichel-Dolmatoff 1965, Pl. 12). However, the available radio-carbon dates (Chaves & Puerta 1980, p. 20), which place these vessels in the second half of the 1st millennium AD, suggest that they are very much later than the Ilama examples.

Moving north, we find that snakes are particularly frequent in the material culture of the Tairona, where they were modelled both in pottery (Bray 1978, p. 325) and in gold (Legast 1987, pp. 57–61). These Indians, who inhabited the northern part of the Sierra Nevada de Santa Marta at the time of the Spanish Conquest, are considered to be the direct ancestors of the Kogi Indians, whose attitude to animals we have already quoted; it is interesting to discover that the snake is one of three animals which hold a particularly strong symbolic significance for the Kogi today. Together with the jaguar and the toad, the snake plays an outstanding role in myth and tradition, and holds a fundamental position in religious belief (Reichel-Dolmatoff 1949–50, p. 265). Snakes not only should not be killed, they cannot be killed since they are immortal; by sloughing their skins they become rejuvenated

(Reichel-Dolmatoff 1949–50, p. 269). They are closely associated with ponds and lakes, particularly those of the remote *paramo* region near the mountain peaks; according to Preuss (1926–7, p. 185) small snakes were the children of the 'bad' lakes, drained by Hiuika to provide agricultural land for the Kogi. Another myth, recorded by Reichel-Dolmatoff, relates how, after having sexual intercourse with a serpent, a woman gave birth to innumerable snakes. Snakes are at the same time a fertility symbol and a symbol of death. Both in the heavens as a constellation, and as a concept, they are the antithesis of the jaguar: while the latter is an expression of positive energy, the snake symbolizes the death of this energy.

Among the objects left to posterity by the Muisca Indians of the central part of the eastern Cordillera are small gold snakes and pottery cups with serpents twining around their rims (e.g. Broadbent 1974, Pl. 253a & b, Bray 1978, Figs 342 & 343). Something of the significance the snake held for these people is recorded by the early Spanish chroniclers. While the Muisca believed that the world was created by the god Chiminigagua, the human race stemmed from the goddess Bachue who rose from Lake Iguaque, high in the cloud-covered mountains, leading a boy by the hand. On attaining manhood, the boy became her husband; after producing numerous progeny, they returned to Lake Iguaque and taking the form of serpents, disappeared beneath its waters (Simon 1981, Vol. 3, p. 368). This, continues the chronicler, is why water, streams, rivers, and particularly lakes were held in special veneration by the Muisca.

While we should beware of reading too much into the snakes on Muisca representational art, this myth seems to indicate that here, too, the snake was associated symbolically with fertility and death.

In a single chapter we cannot pretend to cover all those periods and areas in prehispanic Colombia where the snake is found. Due to conservation factors the record is undoubtedly far from complete. A reminder of this is provided by the Tukano Indians of the Vaupes River in the Colombian north-west Amazon. For the Tukano, snakes of a number of species are of enormous importance in their myth and belief system but are almost unrepresented in those items of their material culture that would be preserved in the archaeological record. In the past, objects such as the posts of the long-houses were decorated with coloured designs – often the snakes that the Indians would see twisting round the same posts during their *yage* trances (Reichel-Dolmatoff 1975, p. 178).

Our understanding of the role played by the snake in Ilama thought-systems might be clearer if we could identify the species of snake represented. While it is possible that the Ilama potters were depicting the snake as an abstract concept, it seems more likely that they were thinking in terms of actual species, and possibly of more than one. Contemporary Indians such as the Tukanoan-speaking groups have beliefs and attitudes that are specific to particular snake species. Reichel-Dolmatoff notes (1975, pp. 138–9) that for these Indians 'there are two entirely different categories of snakes, which can never be confused' – the anacondas and other water-dwelling snakes on the one hand, and the land-dwelling snakes on the other.

For the Barasana (one of the Tukanoan-speaking groups), the anaconda is an ancestor that swam up the rivers from the east and populated Tukanoan territory by vomiting the first people from the river onto dry land. At the same time, the anaconda is *yage* (*Banisteriopsis* sp.), the hallucinogen taken at certain ceremonies which 'enters their bodies and establishes an umbilical connection with the past' (Hugh-Jones 1979, p. 216 *passim*). Surrounding these themes is a complex network of ancillary symbolism and analogy. For instance, the anaconda can represent sexual intercourse (vomiting ancestors = ejaculation). At the same time it stands for the order of emergence and ranking of the different sibs, the highest ranking ones living at the mouths of the rivers and the lowest at the headwaters, reflecting the anaconda's up-river journey. The way the musical instruments are laid out in certain Yurupary ceremonies reconstructs the anaconda's body, and anaconda imagery appears to permeate, to a greater or lesser degree, almost all aspects of Barasana life.

In the course of this survey we have come across a number of snakes with special features – the snake with a prominent row of teeth (Fig. 3.5); a Fabulous Beast on a double-spouted and bridge-handled vessel (not illustrated) on whose head-dress two of the usual barred snakes flank one with lozenge-shaped markings; and, on a similar vessel, a snake with lines and spots (Fig. 3.4c). Two more spotted snakes are found on the head of a *canastero* (BP C10524). The snake on the vessel in the Berlin Museum (VA 65233) has diagonal bars.

However, these snakes are the exception. The vast majority have bodies on which incised cross-hatching gives a remarkably true-to-life impression of scales, and very characteristic plain bands at certain intervals which cross the snake's body at right angles. These bands are usually in groups of three and most snakes have three groups, one at each end (just behind the heads) and one in the centre; longer snakes may, however, have more. These kinds of markings immediately bring to mind the bands on some species of coral snake, such as *Micrurus frontalis*. There are some 20 different species and sub-species of coral snake in Colombia (Dunn 1944, p. 210), and it is one of the commonest in the Calima region today. While the coral snake is extremely poisonous, it seldom attacks man, perhaps partly because its mouth is small and it has no mechanism which allows it to open sufficiently wide to bite anything much larger than a finger or toe. Like some of the snakes we have seen on the Ilama pottery, it generally eats small creatures such as frogs, lizards, birds, and insects. A noteworthy feature, and one that may well have struck the Ilama people, is that it also eats other snakes. It lives a semi-subterranean existence among shrubs and stones and, like many of the other creatures modelled by the Ilama potters, is particularly active at dusk. On the other hand, the snake represented may not be a poisonous species after all, since the false coral snake (*Erythrolamprus* sp.) also has horizontal bars across its body, round eyes, and a rather rounded head, which would agree well with the Ilama snakes. For the present, any identification of the Ilama snakes must remain tentative.

It is a striking fact that nearly all the snakes associated with the Fabulous Beast have heads at both ends of their bodies, a reflection, perhaps, of the Ilama artists' taste for symmetry, combined with the fact that in some species of snake it is not always immediately easy to distinguish head from tail. Two-headed snakes are, however, occasionally born in nature (Grzimek 1974, Vol. VI, p. 422). They do not usually live long in the wild but in captivity have been kept alive for periods of several years. The two heads usually act independently from one another and one may even try to snatch the prey from the jaws of the other, an act that could hardly have failed to impress a possible Ilama observer.

The bat

The next most important element seems to be the bat. This creature, although sometimes difficult to recognize, is not uncommon in archaeological material in Colombia (Legast & Cadena 1986). Besides the Ilama material considered here, it is also found on the goldwork of the so-called Tolima style, in Tumaco pottery figures, and on at least one of the San Agustin statues. Legast & Cadena recognize three different families: Phyllostomidae, Molossidae, and Mormoopidae. The bat is particularly common in gold and pottery items made by the Tairona, and forms the subject of a special study by Legast in his book. Elizabeth Benson, in her study of bats in South American iconography (n.d.), emphasizes the very human characteristics of many bats. They have 'hands' with thumbs and can hold food between their forearms. They are one of the few mammals that suckles their young from two breast nipples. Thanks to their system of echo location, they are also extremely successful nocturnal hunters and it does not take very much imagination to see the bat as a sort of flying super-human.

Many of the bats found on Colombian archaeological items are part human. The Tairona figures often consist of a human body and limbs with a bat head, or even a human figure wearing a nose-ornament that gives it a bat-like appearance.

Apart from the Kogi beliefs about the bat, summarized by Legast, according to which this animal is malignant, associated with misfortune, darkness, and death, references to this creature are rather scarce in the Colombian ethnographic literature.

The jaguar

The jaguar, on the other hand, might almost be described as one of the commonest animals in ethnographic literature, so much so that whole books or large sections of books have been devoted to it (Reichel-Dolmatoff 1975, Roe 1982). One of the most oft-repeated themes associated with the jaguar is its association with people – the jaguar that can turn into a handsome man, the shaman that, with the help of hallucinogenic drugs or a jaguar-skin cloak, assumes the form and powers of the feline. In the archaeological record this man–jaguar, or feline monster, association is best known from the stone statues of San Agustin where it appears to be one of the most dominant motifs (Reichel-Dolmatoff 1972, Ch. 6).

The toad

Where sufficient detail is shown, figures of toads can be distinguished from frogs by features such as their heavy back legs and their rough skin. Examples in stone are known from San Agustin (Reichel-Dolmatoff 1972, p. 109). In the Calima area, representations of toads alone are fairly rare in the Ilama period; however, double-spouted vessels modelled in the shape of large toads of the *Bufo* genus – complete with warty skin and poison glands – are highly characteristic of the following Yotoco period. Toads, or possibly frogs, occur frequently in late period goldwork of the middle Cauca valley (Perez de Barradas 1965, p. 306, Plazas & Falchetti 1983, p. 23). Frogs and toads are common, both in stone and in metal, in the Tairona culture (Legast 1987, pp. 63–73) and we have already mentioned the importance of this animal, together with the snake and the jaguar, for the Kogi (Reichel-Dolmatoff 1949–51, Vol. II, pp. 28,86,262). Both here and among a number of Amazonian Indian groups, the toad stands for the female sexual organ, often with aggressive and adulterous connotations (Reichel-Dolmatoff 1981, p. 22 (for the Desana), Roe 1982, pp. 152–7).

The turtle

Although the turtle is found occasionally in both the archaeological and the ethnographic record, numerically it is considerably less important than the other animals described.

The bird

The bird occurs seldom on the Fabulous Beast (two examples) and then not so much as an element as an extension of the snake in the form of its prey. Unless the number of Fabulous Beasts with bird features increases, it would seem unwise to include birds as a characteristic component.

During the course of this survey one cannot fail to be struck by the many parallels with Tairona composite creatures. Over and over again the bat, the snake, and the feline are found associated with each other and with human figures. The serpent, moreover, is two-headed. These associations are even more striking when we consider that they appear to be absent on archaeological remains from other parts of the country. While the Ilama and the Tairona are much too far removed from each other, both in space and in time, for us to be able to draw any conclusion at present, the parallels are too marked to be easily forgotten.

Conclusions – reconstructing a climate of thought

In this chapter I have gone through the various kinds of pottery vessels on which the Fabulous Beast occurs, and have described the different forms the Fabulous Beast takes on each. I have then tried to form some idea of what these representations may have signified for the Ilama people. Since the Ilama culture vanished some 2000 years ago, I cannot use direct ethnographic parallels but have attempted to reconstruct a climate of thought, which, widespread today, almost certainly has roots deep in time.

'Ancestral Beings are transformative. Many, but not all Ancestral Beings change shape themselves, in particular moving between a human and animal form. . .The Ancestral Beings are highly complex concepts that cannot be said to have a single image. . .'. Although Morphy (1986, p. 1) is describing the Yolngu, an Australian Aboriginal people, these words could well be applied to the Fabulous Beast.

Moving nearer to the territory of this creature, we recall that we have already met a number of creatures that change between a human and an animal form – the Muisca mythical ancestor Bachue, who turned into a snake, the anaconda ancestor-snake, the were-jaguar. The ethnographic literature abounds with beings which, in the course of a myth, take on the form of first one animal and then another. For instance, a Barasana myth, recorded by Hugh-Jones (1979, pp. 295–6), records how Yeba, the first man, looks for a wife. Using a length of thorny, creeping palm, he catches a fish-woman who turns first into an anaconda, then into a boa constrictor, then into a woman, and finally into the cunauaru frog.

Not only do these changes take place, but steps must be taken to prevent them happening too often, in which case the situation would get out of hand. Among the Tunebo Indians of the eastern Andes 'chanted myth links the past to the present and the future' (Osborn 1986). If not performed, it is conceivable that things will get 'out of place', and animals, plants, and trees return to their former states as people, or vice versa.

If we can project the belief in shape transformation back 2000 years and more, it seems possible that the Fabulous Beast might be a transformative creature with an important role in Ilama myth. It could also be argued that at one end of the representational continuum we are looking at the Beast, while at the other, we see the shaman as the Beast – either directly transformed or representing the creature by wearing his attributes, such as a mask and a snake's skin.

We stated earlier that the large number of different shapes, each with a rather different range of varieties of representations of the Fabulous Beast, might be significant. We find that the only entirely 'animal' representations are on the double-spouted vessels which, from their shape, were almost certainly used for holding liquid. The other forms are mainly jars or beakers, shapes that are suited to drinking from.

Further than this we can only speculate. However, given the fact that the Beast may well represent a polymorphic ancestor that played an important role in Ilama myth, and taking into account the importance attributed by many Indian groups to ceremonies at which myth is chanted, it seems not unreasonable to suggest that these vessels may have been made for use in these ceremonies. On these occasions the taking of hallucinogens plays an essential part. Could these rather special vessels have been used for serving and drinking a hallucinogenic potion?

Acknowledgements

The material for this study has been collected jointly with Warwick Bray of the Institute of Archaeology, London University, and with Leonor Herrera of the Instituto Colombiano de Antropologia in Bogotá, as part of the research carried out by the Calima project. This project is largely financed by the Pro-Calima Foundation with headquarters in Switzerland. Research focused specifically on the Ilama culture was supported through a contract with the Fundación de Investigaciones Arqueológicas Nacionales of the Banco de la República in Colombia, and a monograph on the Ilama culture is in preparation. Anne Legast has been an untiring help in identifying the animals represented. This chapter has also benefited from comments by Ann Osborn.

Notes

1   One of these composite beasts is relatively standardized and consists of a double-spouted vessel with an animal head at one extreme and a bird head doubling as a tail at the other (Herrera *et al.* 1984, Fig. 6G). The second is a rather doll-like anthropomorphic figure wearing a fan-shaped head-dress and displaying a number of zoomorphic features, such as round eyes and prominent teeth (e.g. Museo La Merced, Cali C10698, illustrated by Barney-Cabrera 1977, p. 307, bottom left). Both categories are known from a very limited number of examples (six of each), and their relation to the Fabulous Beast is at present unclear.

2   Used in the sense that Rowe (1967, pp. 78–9) employs the term in his analysis of Chavin art.

3   Spouted vessel no. 5 (see Tables 3.2 & 3.3) is said to have been found in an Ilama cemetery near Aguamona, in the Municipio of Restrepo. The only example I have not been able to study at first hand is that in the Land collection (no. 3 in Tables 3.2 & 3.3) published by Nicholson & Cordy-Collins (1979, p. 185), who label it 'Quimbaya'.

4   According to informants in Restrepo, MO CC4518 is very similar to one found on the hacienda La Suiza, in the El Dorado valley. MO CC4520 was almost certainly a jar originally, but has been sawn off below the head. The fourth example, seen in a private collection in Restrepo, was said to have been found in the Aguamona region.

5   The following 'snake pots' have provenances: no. 11 (private collection) is said to have come from Puente Tierra; no. 15 was found at La Florida farm, near Darien. It was in a typical Ilama grave together with a plain Ilama jar and a double-spouted and handled vessel in the shape of an owl. Of the Gold Museum vessels, four (nos CC 1970, 1972, 1973, and 3185) are simply catalogued as from 'Restrepo, Valle', while a fifth has a confusing catalogue entry. This states that it came from the hacienda La Suiza in the El Dorado valley, and was found with certain gold items. However, other items in the Museum's collection (CC 789–91) are also catalogued as having been found with the same gold items, although these other items apparently came from Madronal.

6   The enormously successful industry in fake Ilama pottery which has developed over the last few years makes it increasingly difficult to study the iconography of this culture. The 'replicas' vary considerably in quality but the best are very elaborate and can be difficult to distinguish from original pieces, particularly in photographs. They are often smeared with mud when first offered for sale, and in many cases have been intentionally broken so that repairs are visible.

7   Smooth-crested *canasteros* nos 1 and 4 (MOCC72 and 71) (see Tables 3.2 & 3.3) are registered in the catalogue as coming from the vereda Calimita, near Restrepo. According to the same document, they were found with the gold items nos 7512–7527 (see also Dussan de Reichel 1965–6). Number 2 is illustrated in Barney-Cabrera (1977, p. 315), no. 5 by Arango Cano (1979, Pl. 32). Number 6 is catalogued as from the El Dorado valley.

8   The spiked head-dress *canastero* no. 3 (see Tables 3.2 & 3.3) is illustrated by Arango Cano (1979, Pl. 33).

9   'Toby jug' no. 1 was excavated at the hacienda La Iberia in an Ilama cemetery, grave no. 5, together with a plain jar. Number 5 was seen in a private collection in Restrepo. It comes from the La Merced farm, vereda El Porvenir, and was found in the same grave as the *paton* no. 5.

10 *Paton* no. 2 is illustrated in Arango Cano (1979, Fig. 36), and no. 4 by Barney-Cabrera (1977, p. 305). Number 5 was found with the 'toby jug' no. 5 (see above). Number 9 was seen in a private collection in Restrepo and comes from the Los Tambores farm, vereda San Salvador. It was found in the same grave as a *canastero* of the long-haired type, very similar to that illustrated by Labbé (1986, Fig. 45).

References

Arango Cano, J. 1979. *Cerámica Precolombina*. Bogotá: Plaza and Janes.

Barney-Cabrera, E. 1977. Calima, El Dorado Prehispanico; expresiones del Arte Calima. In *Historia del Arte Colombiano*, Vol. II, Ricardo Martin (ed.), 269–320.

Benson, E. n.d. Bats in South American iconogaphy. Anthropology Department, Cornell University.

Bray, W. 1978. *The gold of El Dorado*. Exhibition catalogue. Times Newspapers Ltd., London.

Bray, W., L. Herrera & M. Cardale Schrimpff 1981. Preliminary report on the 1980 field season. *Pro Calima* **II**. Solothur.

Bray, W., L. Herrera & M. Cardale Schrimpff 1983. Preliminary report on the 1981 field season in Calima. *Pro Calima* **III**, 2–30, Basel.

Bray, W., L. Herrera & M. Cardale Schrimpff 1985. Preliminary report on the 1982 field season in Calima. *Pro Calima* **IV**, Basel.

Broadbent, S. 1974. Kunst in Kolumbien, 259–75. *Propylaen Kunstgeschichte*. Berlin: Propylaen Verlag.

Chaves, A. & M. Puerta 1980. *Entierros primarios de Tierradentro*. Fundación de Investigaciones Arqueológicas Nacionales, Banco de la República, Bogotá.

Diaz Granados, A., L. Herrera & M. Cardale Schrimpff 1974. Mitología Cuna: los Kalu. *Revista Colombiana de Antropología* **XVII**, 203–47.

Dunn, E. R. 1944. Los generos de anfibios y reptiles en Colombia III, Tercera Parte: Reptiles: orden de las serpientes. *Caldasia* **III** (12), 155–224.

Dussan de Reichel, A. 1965–6. Contribuciones al estudio de la Cultura Calima en Colombia. *Revista del Museo Nacional* **XXXIV**, 61–7.

Falchetti, A. M. 1979. Colgantes 'Darien'. Relaciones entre areas orfebres del occidente Colombiano y Centro–américa. *Boletín del Museo del Oro*, Banco de la República, Bogotá, Vol. II, 1–55.

Fisher, M. 1984. *Typologie der Calima-Temprano-Keramik, Kolumbien*. Unpublished MA thesis, Freien Universität, Berlin.

Grzimek, B. 1975. *Le monde animal*. 13 vols. Zurich: Stauffacher.

Herrera, L., M. Cardale Schrimpff & W. Bray 1984. El hombre y su medio ambiente en Calima (altos ríos Calima y Grande, Cordillera Occidental). *Revista Colombiana de Antropología*, **XXIV** (1982–3), 381–424.

Hill, J. E. & D. Smith 1984. *Bats: a natural history*. London: British Museum (Natural History).

Hugh-Jones, S. 1979. *The Palm and the Pleiades. Initiation and cosmology in northwestern Amazonia*. Cambridge: Cambridge University Press.

Labbé, A. J. 1986. *Colombia before Columbus. The people, culture and ceramic art of prehispanic Colombia. Rizzoli: New York. In Association with the Bowers Museum, Santa Ana, California*.

Lathrap, D., D. Collier & H. Chandra 1975. *Ancient Ecuador. Culture, clay and creativity, 3,000–300 BC*. Field Museum of Natural History, Chicago; Museos del Banco Central del Ecuador, Quito-Guayaquil.

Legast, A. n.d. *La fauna en el material arqueólogico Calima*. Manuscript presented to the Fundación de Investigaciones Arqueológicas Nacionales, Banco de la República, Bogotá.

Legast, A. 1987. *El animal en el mundo mítico Tairona*. Fundación de Investigaciones Arqueólogicas Nacionales, Banco de la República, Bogotá.

Legast, A. 1989. The bat in Tairona art: an under-recognized species. In *Animals into art*, H. Morphy (ed.), Ch. 12. London: Unwin Hyman.

Legast, A. & A. Cadena 1986. El murciélago en el material arqueólogico Colombiano. *Boletín de la Fundación de Investigaciones Arqueológicas Nacionales*, Banco de la República, Bogotá.

Morphy, H. 1986. On representing ancestral beings. In *Cultural attitudes to animals, including birds, fish and invertebrates*. World Archaeological Congress, Vol. 3 (mimeo).

Nicholson, H. B. & A. Cordy-Collins 1979. *Pre-Columbian Art from the Land Collection*. Californian Academy of Sciences and L. K. Land.

Osborn, A. 1986. Eat and be eaten: animals in U'wa (Tunebo) oral tradition. In *Cultural attitudes to animals including birds, fish and invertebrates*, Vol. 2. (Mimeo) World Archaeological Congress.

Perdomo, L. R. de 1979. *Manual de la arqueológia Colombiana*. Bogotá.

Perez de Barradas, J. 1965. *Orfebrería prehispanica de Colombia: Estilos Quimbaya y otros*. 2 Vols. Madrid: Museo del Oro, Bogotá.

Plazas, C. & A. Falchetti 1983. Tradición metalúrgica del suroccidente Colombiano. *Boletín del Museo del Oro*. Banco de la República, no. 14, 1–32.

Preuss, K. T. 1926–7. Forschungsreise zu den Kagaba. 2 Vols. Wien.

Reichel-Dolmatoff, G. 1949–51. Los Kogi. Una tribu de la Sierra Nevada, en Colombia. *Revista del Instituto Etnológico Nacional*. Vol. IV, parts 1 and 2. Bogotá.

Reichel-Dolmatoff, G. 1965. *Colombia. Ancient peoples and places*. London: Thames &Hudson.

Reichel-Dolmatoff, G. 1968. *Desana. Simbolismo de los Indios Tukano del Vaupés*. Universidad de los Andes, Departamento de Antropología, Bogotá.

Reichel-Dolmatoff, G. 1972. *San Agustin. A Culture of Colombia*. London: Thames &Hudson.

Reichel-Dolmatoff, G. 1975. *The shaman and the jaguar. A study of narcotic drugs among the Indians of Colombia*. Temple University Press, Pennsylvania.

Reichel-Dolmatoff, G. 1981. Things of beauty replete with meaning – metals and crystals in Colombian Indian cosmology. In *Sweat of the Sun, tears of the Moon: gold and emerald Treasures of Colombia*. D. Halle Seligman, (ed.). Los Angeles: Natural History Museum of Los Angeles County.

Roe, P. G. 1982. *The cosmic zygote: cosmology in the Amazon Basin*. New Brunswick: Rutgers University Press.

Rowe, J. H. 1967. Form and meaning in Chavin art. In *Peruvian archaeology. Selected readings*, J. H. Rowe & D. Menzel (eds). Palo Alto, California: Peek Publications.

Salgado, H. 1986. Investigaciones arqueológicas en el curso medio del río Calima, Cordillera Occidental, Calima. *Boletín de Arqueología*, Fundación de Investigaciones Arqueológicas, Banco de la República, Vol. I, no. 2, 3–15. Bogotá.

Simon, F. P. 1981. *Noticias historiales de tierra firme en las Indias Occidentales*. 6 vols. Biblioteca Banco Popular, Bogotá, Vols 103–8.

REPRESENTATIONS

4 *From man to animal and sign in Palaeolithic art*

MICHEL LORBLANCHET

Methodological considerations

When we call a representation realistic, we often push the implications to an extreme in trying to assign species and even subspecies to the depiction. By assigning the identification of horse, human, deer, or doe to a parietal representation we often risk stopping the search for its real significance, for we appear to find an intellectual satisfaction by the simple act of identification.

When we come across a motif which resists all attempts at identification, whether animal or sign, we call it 'indeterminate'. To invent such a category itself risks giving the impression of spurious exactitude, for, in this case, the whole complex of representations appear to have been assigned to meaningful categories. In the study of Palaeolithic art the category of 'indeterminate' risks becoming a bottomless holdall which may be stuffed beyond measure with configurations of every kind. In 1972, out of the 474 anthropomorphs which are reported in the literature, Ucko & Rosenfeld retained only 324, and in 1976 Pales & Tassin de Saint-Péreuse counted only 302 (to which can be added the 108 human figures of La Marche) (Pales & Tassin de Saint-Péreuse 1976, p. 142). One wonders what has become of some 150–70 motifs which have been eliminated; have they all fallen into the discard-heap of the 'indeterminate'?

At the beginning of their study, Ucko & Rosenfeld (1972, p. 156) provide a 'minimal definition' of what they describe as an anthropomorph:

> Man's distinctive features include: sexual hair in the shape of a triangle on the female, as on no other species; beard, breasts, position of penis, hands and feet as also on several monkeys and apes; flat face as also on owls; eyes placed on the front of the face, as also on other primates, carnivorous animals and predatory birds. Man has relatively long hind legs and bipedal gait (the latter on occasion also shown by bears), collar-bone and shoulders, and the potential for holding the arms in various unique positions, some of which are shared by monkeys and apes but by no other animals.

As examples of animals who least resemble the human form one would cite fish, who normally have neither limbs or neck, and quadrupeds, such as horses. However, horses may be shown rearing with the hind legs positioned in a vertical axis. In this vertical position the haunches are drawn together, the front legs hang down alongside the body, the neck is slightly shortened and the head tends to become rounded. And at Bruniquel a rearing, or simply 'leaping', horse that has been sculpted onto the shaft of a reindeer antler spear-thrower shows the ease with which an animal can be transformed into an elongated being with a silhouette that comes close to that of man.

Just as the upright position is not exclusive to humans, many human figures are not entirely vertical; a large number of those known are bent forwards. Animals in Palaeolithic wall art are frequently tilted and sometimes shown in a vertical plane, as if floating in a way which allows and encourages flexibility. The variety of the curves of bodies, also their orientations (sometimes even upside-down), the restricted nature of bodies, or sometimes their elongation, demonstrates their adaptation to the shape of the cave wall but also the freedom allowed to artists to play with shapes, culminating in the crossing over of the boundaries between living species and allowing the artist, in graphic terms, to move from one creature to another.

This everlasting freedom of Palaeolithic art is an embarrassment to prehistorians. They seek to understand the meaning of the inversion of such and such an animal; they make suppositions: 'Was it wounded', or 'Dying?'; 'In the act of rolling in the dust?', or 'Of giving birth?'; 'What does such and such an engraving which is neither wholly man nor wholly animal represent?' Any resistance to interpretation causes them to redouble their efforts to be precise; makes them more rigid in their systems of classification so that they attempt to constrain the moving world, constantly comparing these shapes with a vanished reality instead of first of all making comparisons between the shapes themselves.

A short time after the publication of Ucko & Rosenfeld's study, Pales in his turn described human Palaeolithic configurations but he did not give any preliminary definition. Throughout his work he merely specified their anatomical characteristics in a very searching analysis (Pales & Tassin de Saint-Péreuse 1976).

It is noted that Ucko & Rosenfeld explained the reasons which led them to exclude about 30 figures from their 'anthropomorphs' category, but they dismissed a total of 150. For 120 of them we know of no precise reason. Pales for his part gives no detailed reason whatsoever for his choice, while he rejects wholesale more than 170.

Most certainly, it is essential to put forward sound criteria for selection but is it enough? Are there not just as many inherent difficulties in applying these criteria to figures in general and to each one in particular? If we make up our minds that a human representation ought to show this and that feature, will all prehistorians then agree that such a figure actually does show these features and that it conforms to proposed definitions?

All inventories are a matter of personal choice. It must be significant that three such eminent writers, whose intense studies forcefully denounce the lack of precision and the subjectivity of most of the works on the subject of Palaeolithic art, should reach no agreement about the exact number of Palaeolithic human figures.

The number of subjects eliminated by Ucko, Rosenfeld, and Pales underscores the risks of imbalance in our classification. If the category of 'indeterminate' begins to reach 20–30 per cent of the Quaternary figurations, it is evident that this would

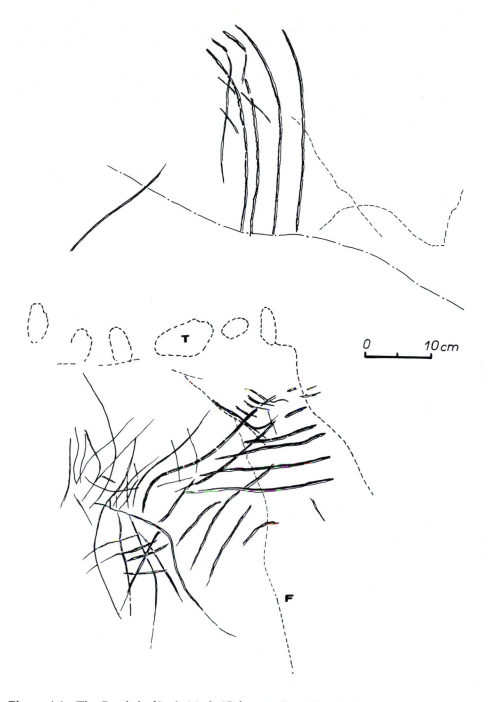

Figure 4.1 The Combel of Pech-Merle (Cabrerets, Lot, France). Bear scratches interpreted as an anthropomorph by Lemozi (1952) and others. F=fissure, T=hole. (Lorblanchet's recording.)

represent an important loss of information. In the typological breakdown of stone tools, for example, there are 92 recognized types, and no more than between 1 and 3 per cent of pieces are generally placed in the category of 'various'.

The notion of the 'indeterminate' is embarrassing for two further reasons: it implies a pejorative connotation; the unidentified figures are those motifs with which no one can cope, they are cast off, the waste from the analytical process; set down at the end of the list even though this much too vague term describes a variety of configurations, some of which despite, or even because of, the difficulties in reading them may be extremely important in the interpretation of prehistoric art. One might find grouped together in this 'indeterminate' category the female/bison figures at Pech-Merle, the 'masks' from Altamira, and certain networks of lines at Gouy or at Combarelles, where silhouettes of animals or humans have been guessed at.

By contrast, such a notion gives exaggerated importance to the figurations which may qualify as 'determinate' or identifiable, as though all identifications were beyond question and as though the boundaries between the categories were well defined and therefore indisputable.

There is, therefore, the risk that our statistics will not hold good except for the most realistic representations, those which are the easiest to interpret, without knowing whether they were of equal importance in the eyes of Palaeolithic man. Too often our methods and our classifications tend to favour realism, a point of view which is without doubt, erroneous.

Obviously, one welcomes attempts to establish a more objective basis for the identification of figures. The critical point of view taken up by Ucko, Rosenfeld, Pales, and Clottes (see Ch. 1, this volume) marks a step forward in our subject. They force us to look closely again at the 'indeterminate' group and, indeed, a systematic verification of old tracings resolves some of the inaccuracies and removes many disputes about the distinction between human and animal figures. For example, the so-called 'anthropomorphs' of the Combel of Pech-Merle reported by Lemozi (1952) and others does not stand up to such a scrutiny because it is made up of an assemblage of bear claw marks, of which some are scored in an oddly, almost horizontal, plane, as may also be seen on other wall surfaces (see Fig. 4.1). Likewise, the anthropomorph of Panel VIII (Fig. 4.2) at Cougnac in which Meroc, Mazet, and other authors like Laming-Emperaire (1962, p. 287) saw a 'wounded bird-man' in the process of falling 'head first', is no more than a group of badly preserved lines in different colours (bistre, red, and black). The light reflected from the rock, the overlying calcite layers, and the heterogeneous state of preservation create a deceptive amalgamation to which photographers further add the finishing touches by the use of shadow.

However, despite the removal of incorrect or inaccurate renditions, this does not provide a solution to all the problems. The remaining large number of so-called 'indeterminate' representations puts clearly into perspective the fact that our difficulties in interpretation and classification arise, above all, out of the material itself and not exclusively from our methods of study. For the most recent approaches have not enabled a sharp distinction between human and animal figures to be made, because such a distinction is an illusion. On the contrary, it has isolated

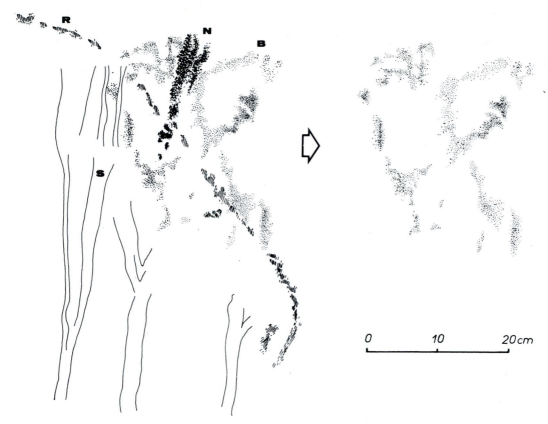

Figure 4.2 Cougnac (Lot) Panel VIII. Light-brown marks interpreted as a 'wounded diving bird-man' by several authors. B=light brown, N=black, S=stalagmite flow, R=back of red mammoth. (Lorblanchet's recordings.)

an important group of figures which are difficult to classify and which, through the very imprecision of their nature, may be of the greatest interest to research.

It was this fundamental question which was posed by Ucko & Rosenfeld, 'Is there a legitimate basis for permitting a distinction between anthropomorphs, animals and signs?' (Ucko & Rosenfeld 1972, p. 162). We must answer 'no', because art from its very beginning, that is since the Palaeolithic, has always played with shapes which themselves have had changing and variable meaning.

Horses, bison, ibex, and other animals, humans and signs are only the visible stitches in a continuous graphic fabric whose unity must be respected. Between 'poles' made up of the most classifiable motifs are many indeterminate ones, as well as innumerable traces without structure allowing the creators of the forms to move freely all along the fabric.

Metamorphosis as a function of art was evident right from its beginning. If the Magdalenians had had bicycles in advance of Picasso they would have taken them to pieces and changed them into cattle.

From line to animal

Grappling in his thesis with the engraved surfaces in the 'Salon des Petits Rennes' and other equally rich sectors of the cave of Trois Frères, Vialou makes us aware of the limitations of our classificatory categories. There, where Breuil tentatively suggested 'I think I can identify' and then declared 'I refuse to push any further the attempt to decipher this difficult complex (of engravings)' (Bégouën & Breuil 1958, pp. 21–2), Vialou continued to search for 'a structure', fully recognizing 'that there exists alongside the structured and organised representations, groups and elements of which the figurative or symbolic character completely escapes comprehension'. He adds:

> There is all the same a spatial and graphical reality, even less trivial because it is juxtaposed and superimposed on recognisable representations; as such they are 'graphic units'. In order not to introduce a sequential organization of meaning, we refused to be marooned among the assemblages of elements capable of being subjected to morphological description. This would have risks in relation to Palaeolithic reasoning, as clearly attested by the structured representations. In consequence, we define an assemblage as a 'grouping of lines' or 'painted markings' rather than breaking them into '20 incised short lines, more or less rectilinear in shape; scattered over and around bison x or near an angular sign x'. (Vialou 1981, p. 200)

According to what Vialou has said, therefore, it appears that 'assemblages' may be either small or large. However, demarcation of particular 'groupings' is often as arbitrary as is the counting of each individual component part.

After having extrapolated from a surface the more or less complete motifs which are recognizable, there remains an irreducible entanglement of marks, which it would be tempting to describe as 'remnants' or 'subsidiary' lines, as has often been done – a cut-off point which can only be very artificial. Vialou's concept of a 'graphic base' is also debatable, for if the components described as organized are sometimes superimposed on these marks, very often too the interlacing of all these graphics, 'structured' or not, is such that one perceives a purpose. The figurative components extricate themselves from a formless 'magma', from such a web of lines is born a hoof, such curving lines give birth to a nameless muzzle, a wavering line of a backbone, an eye conceals itself, and the space is vibrant with awakening life (Fig. 4.3).

If more than half of the evidence of parietal art consists of marks, lines, undiagnostic parts of animals, or only partially recognizable parts of animals, one begins to wonder not only whether it is possible to distinguish between animal and human figures as Ucko & Rosenfeld attempted to do, but whether it is possible even to separate structured drawings from disorganized non-figurative marks.

Anatomical animal segments, floating around the entanglements of engravings or finger drawings, illustrate the tendency of Palaeolithic shapes towards that quality of 'disassociation' emphasized by Leroi-Gourhan (1984a, pp. 234–40). This phenomenon is of two-fold significance: the representation of isolated parts of the anatomy, such as outline drawings of hoofs or any other part of the body, or

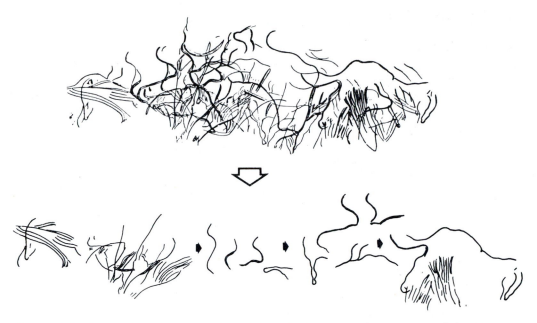

Figure 4.3   Where does the animal begin? Detail of a maze of engravings of the 'Aurignacian passage' of the Trois Frères cave (after Breuil's recording). In the entanglement of lines a few curves, legs, horns, then an almost complete drawing of a bison emerge.

'abbreviated' drawings which 'search for the minimum of lines absolutely necessary to ensure identification of the animal' (Leroi-Gourhan 1984a, p. 64).

In the former case, for which we have already given several examples, the parts which are represented appear chosen at random, it is almost an outline simply left unfinished; whereas in the latter case the parts have been chosen to typify and summarize the whole animal – the section replaces a complete representation by the process of synecdoche.

In certain caves and in particular geographical areas, the tendency towards separation of constituent parts of the motif (which applies to animals just as much as to humans and geometric shapes) is more marked than elsewhere.

The Pyrenean area offers some good examples: there are the isolated stags' antlers at Le Portel, the cervico-dorsal line of a bison in the Reseau R. Clastres, and the back of the horse in the Salon Noir at Niaux. But it is, above all, in Quercy that Palaeolithic artists evolved their conception of abbreviation. Forty per cent of the animal figurations in Cougnac are reduced to a set of horns, a mane, or the outline of the back (Fig. 4.4) and it is more or less the same at Pech-Merle. These partial motifs, these kinds of 'spare parts', always freely accessible to the mind of the Palaeolithic symbol-maker combine, like the components of a jigsaw puzzle, to make up transitional animal figurations weaving multiple threads between the species depicted. Sometimes the components belonging to difference species are so intimately mixed together that the emerging shape is non-specific – ambiguous – this is notably the case with a motif at Le Portel suggesting both elk and horse

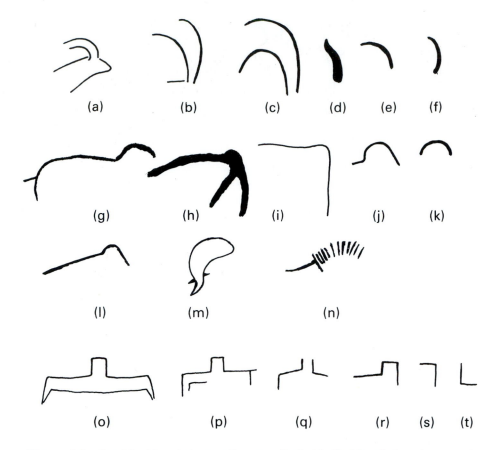

Figure 4.4 Graphic abbreviations at Cougnac (Lot): (a)–(f) abbreviations (segments) of ibex; (g)–(k) mammoth; (l) animal; (m) Megaceros antler; (n) horse; (o)–(t) abbreviations of 'aviforme signs' (bird-like signs). Note the similarity between (j) and (r).

without being either one or the other (Fig. 4.5). In other instances the grouping is so heterogeneous that identification is impossible. The resultant animal is defined as 'imaginary' or as 'monstrous': there is a feline and a rhinoceros quality to the unicorn at Lascaux, and something feline and bovine about the strange engravings in the Tuc d'Audoubert. The 'antelopes' in the Combel at Pech-Merle (Fig. 4.6) are the result of an amalgamation of animals common in the Quercy bestiary: the female *megaceros* with pronounced shoulder (c,d,e), the short-horned young or female caprid (b), the horse reduced to the line of its mane (a), and the *megaceros* tail (f,g,h). These figures therefore demonstrate an interesting synthesis of the Quercy style in handling animals, confirming the multiple relationships established elsewhere between the three most important decorative groups in the region of Pech-Merle, Cougnac, and Roucadour.

There has been a tendency to use the words 'imaginary' and 'composite' almost indiscriminately to refer to these mixed animal images. It may be more useful to

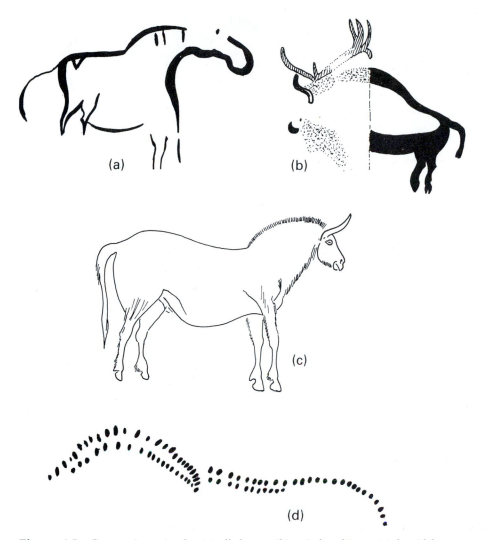

Figure 4.5 Composite animals: (a) elk-horse; (b) reindeer-bison; (c) bovid-horse; (d) dotted outline of a horse back. (a)(b)(d) from Le Portel; (c) from Les Combarelles (Breuil's recording).

apply the terms to somewhat different sets of images: 'imaginary' applying to those images which, despite being apparently well-integrated representations, are not readily identifiable either as a whole or as a sum of their parts; and 'composite' applying to images which appear to consist of a set of loosely connected body parts of a number of identifiable animals.

Composite figures may be executed all at once or they may result from the re-use of a pre-existing figure through correction, addition, or superimposition. Examples of the first type occur at Trois Frères in the case of part-deer, part-bird figures and composite bear-wolf and bear-bison figures (Bégouën & Breuil 1958,

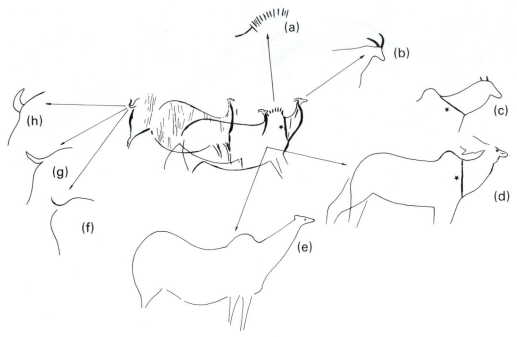

Figure 4.6 The 'antelopes' in the Combel at Pech-Merle are the result of an amalgamation of animals: (a) horse from Cougnac; (b) caprid from Cougnac; (c), (d) Megaceros from Cougnac (note the line across the neck); (e) Megaceros from Roucadour; (f,g,h) Megaceros tails from Roucadour.

p. 77, Fig. 80). The fish at Pindal identified by Leroi-Gourhan (1971, p. 483, Fig. 804) as 'a trout disguised as a Tuna fish' may be another example. An example of the second type is provided at Roc de Sers by the replacement of the low-relief head of a bison by that of a wild boar (Delporte 1984). Slightly less clear examples are provided by the ambiguous engraving of a horse with possible bovine features at Les Combarelles (Fig. 4.5c) (Capitan *et al.* 1924, p. 74), and the bison at Le Portel that overlies a red-deer antler. These hybrid figures are not numerous but they are proof that in Quaternary iconography the boundaries between species are far from inseparable and, in the case of the altered figures, are a concrete manifestation of the dynamism of the art.

In some cases the mode of representation lends itself to ambiguity. The low relief at Roc de Sers where the head was changed from bison to wild boar is a case in point. Animals at the site all have the same body conformation, for example the same sag in the back and the same short legs. In order to typify the species it is enough to accentuate one or two features and create the appropriate head. So in the case of the bison/wild boar it is hard to say if it represents a change from one to the other or a cross between the two.

The fact that the same component could be shared by a variety of different figurations facilitated, in some cases, the easy transition from one animal shape to another. The famous 'Agnus Dei' at Pair non Pair is an example of this. From a horse and an ibex facing in opposite directions, the engraver succeeded in making a horse with a long neck turning its head.

Leroi–Gourhan demonstrated that the construction of figures throughout Palaeolithic art is based on the cervico-dorsal line (Leroi–Gourhan 1971, p. 477). It is this common denominator of all Palaeolithic representations that permitted the instantaneous transition from one animal shape to another. In fact, however, this situation is more complex than this for, in each cave, artists had at their disposal a set of precise conventions and a series of graphic segments or motifs which could be used within local conventions. The way in which each artist put together these components enabled him to stamp his personal mark on his creation, within, of course, the overall Palaeolithic stylistic conventions. Thus, for example, the animal figurations at Ebbou in the Ardèche (Fig. 4.7) are variations on a single, highly

Figure 4.7 Construction of animal figurations at Ebbou (Ardèche).

standardized model, with chest rising vertically up to a straight neck, and with legs in the shape of an X, to which it was sufficient to add a few specific additions such as horns, antlers, or tail in order to obtain at will the representation of a horse, a bull, a deer, or an ibex. At Ebbou, unlike many other caves, the uniformity of the process – except for two figures – suggests that all the engravings (except for those two) were made by the same hand.

From animal to sign

In 1905 Breuil convincingly demonstrated the processes of schematization of zoomorphic motifs. He showed how a drawing of a deer, the head of a caprid, a horse, or a bovid led to a variety of different signs; how a line of horses gave birth to a broken line, etc. However, his interpretation of such schematization is wholly unacceptable today. He considered that art achieved its highest form when it copied nature, and degenerated as it distanced itself from nature (1905, p. 120). This obsession with realism is nonetheless interesting because it has permeated all 20th-century work on Palaeolithic art, which continues to focus attention on anatomical realism to the detriment of analysis of stylistic conventions.

From 1958 onwards Leroi-Gourhan maintained that 'signs are the symbols of male and female sexual characteristics' using as his basis the schematization of certain realistic motifs. However, from amongst the many evolutionary schema suggested explicitly by Breuil or implicitly contained in his view of schematization, Leroi-Gourhan (1984b, p. 64) retained only those which appeared to support his sexual theory; that a horse, a 'masculine' symbol, should be able to give birth to an oval shape, a 'female' symbol, was unacceptable to him.

However, Leroi-Gourhan also recognized that 'complete figures through progressive abbreviation, are reduced to an ideogram' (1984b, p. 66) and he compared the double, parallel, or convergent lines on surfaces of the axial gallery or the apse at Lascaux with the decorations on the lamp and the assegais in the same cave, and other Magdalenian sites. He again followed the method suggested by Breuil and traced their origins from either complete or partial schematic representations of deer, or from simplifications of 'footprints of herbivores' (Leroi-Gourhan 1979, p. 360, Fig. 374).

The transition of animal figures into signs is shown in various ways: some highly schematized animal figures drawn in outline are so similar to signs that they are sometimes confused with them.

There are two examples from Quercy: in the Cave of the Merveilles (Rocamadour, Lot) a black marking with three branches (Fig. 4.8a) is juxtaposed with a horse in the same colour (Lorblanchet 1970). This black marking was convincingly interpreted by Peyrony as a schematic deer turned to the right (Peyrony 1926), but described by Leroi-Gourhan as a 'scutiform sign with an appendage' or as a 'coupled sign' whose central setting would allow one to place the cave 'among those sanctuaries presenting a constant layout'. Leroi-Gourhan even makes a mistake in the shape of the drawing, showing it as a closed rectangle (Leroi-Gourhan 1958, p. 320, Fig. 10 centre).

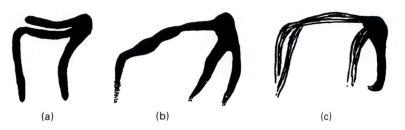

(a)   (b)   (c)

Figure 4.8 Animal signs (linear schematization): (a) cervid from the Merveilles (Rocamadour, Lot); (b) mammoth from Panel VIII at Cougnac; (c) mammoth from La Baume Latrone (Gard). (a) & (b), Lorblanchet's recordings; (c) after Dr Drouot.

The second example is provided by Panel VIII at Cougnac: immediately below a human figure pierced by lines is a linear motif in red (Fig. 4.8b), first interpreted as 'a large enigmatic sign in the shape of an inverted red-deer antler' (Meroc & Mazet 1956), and then as a 'three branch sign' (Leroi-Gourhan 1971, p. 267). However, there is no reason to think that it is not a simplified mammoth, whose style recalls that of the cervid of Merveilles and other mammoth drawings from Baume Latrone (Fig. 4.8c). The graphic style of these two motifs in Quercy puts them in a position of being at the turning point between animal figurations and signs. Their close association with realistic motifs shows once again the synchronization between realism and schematization.

Some animal silhouettes are made up of dots, like the pointillist bison at Marsoulas or the 'outline of the back of the horse' from the Camarin at Le Portel, which makes up a double line of dots (Fig. 4.5d). Likewise, a dot implies a line and a line suggests contours. At Lascaux, Pech-Merle, Covalanas, La Pasiega, etc. many animal representations are made up of dots, more or less continuous, executed either by a blowing process or with the fingers.

Dots, signs, and different painting techniques weave multiple links between signs and animals.

From animal to human

In the case of Trois Frères, three figures were formed (Bégouën & Breuil 1958, p. 51) by the simple juxtaposition of figurative segments which may be readily identified as belonging to humans as well as to various animal species. Some bore male human sexual organs and human legs drawn in minute detail, even down to the feet with the big toe marked separately. The stress laid on the limbs, the feet, and knee joint undoubtedly expresses a desire to characterize the human elements of the figures, man being defined in these cases by the lower half of the body, including the penis.

The parts of the anatomy judged as being characteristic of the human being in our own era were not, according to the evidence, the same for Palaeolithic man. During the reindeer age man was not defined by his head and facial features.

The association of human components with elements belonging to bison and deer may be placed in the context of the abundance of reindeer and bison in the sanctuary. Besides, many of the beings represented here are ambiguous. Reindeer and bison are here interwoven and superimposed, mixed up, so that many figures appear to have a double meaning, and to be at the same time both reindeer and bison. A complete animal in front of the 'sorcerer' with the musical bow likewise brings together, as we have seen, the appearance of reindeer and that of bison; and, in the niche of the 'Dieu Cornu', horns have been added to the reindeer to change it into a bison (Bégouën & Breuil 1958, p. 51).

Vialou comments on this panel: 'The structuring of the entanglements of lines and superimpositions of figures is not initially apparent, however it becomes obvious when the figures carrying a dual role on the right side are carefully considered: a reindeer and bison split up and superimposed as if some zoological ambiguity had made them one on the wall surface' (Vialou 1986, p. 14).

In Trois Frères this 'magma', to use Breuil's expression, of animals which are often symbolically polyvalent, as though set in a gestating world, contained three creatures half-way between man and animal. In the same chamber there is also the famous 'Dieu Cornu' which apparently also contains polyvalent elements of several different animals as well as human characteristics. The whole complex can be interpreted as a scene of the creation of the animated world.

At Gabillou a 'sorcerer' with human body and limbs and bison's head appears to occupy a special position at the end of the cave, from where it 'rules' over a long procession of animals along both sides of the cave, a procession which contains two further anthropomorphs with bovid heads (Gaussen 1964, p. 32).

Many of the parietal figures reveal links between the animals and human worlds. There are, for example, the bird-headed men discovered at Altamira and Lascaux. Some writers have also assigned some of the figures at Pech-Merle and Cougnac to this category: they have round heads drawn out sideways with a beak – those at Altamira lift their arms in the air and have hands drawn in detail. Two show erect penises. The legs are either sketchily portrayed or not at all. In one case the feet take on the shape of those of a bear with paws.

If at Lascaux and Altamira some figures really do have birds' heads, the humans at Cougnac and Pech-Merle, contrary to the statements of Lemozi (1961) and Meroc & Mazet (1956), have simply one side of the face with a slight point like a muzzle rather than in the shape of a bird's beak. 'The archer' at Pech-Merle has no tail either; the curving line on the right-hand side being simply the outer edge of the second leg.

Ucko & Rosenfeld have strongly criticized Laming-Emperaire's identification of a 'bird-man' theme (Laming-Emperaire 1962, p. 287). In discussing the interpretation of human figures from Addaura, some of which seem to show a beak, these authors correctly comment: 'many of the alleged representations with bird beaks are very difficult to read (as for example at Altamira). It is moreover difficult to distinguish precisely between a head with a beak and a head with a prominent nose or a face with a snout'. Besides, it is even more important to note that bird-headed anthropomorphs do not belong exclusively to the Palaeolithic: they are to be met in many post-Palaeolithic cultures (Ucko & Rosenfeld 1972).

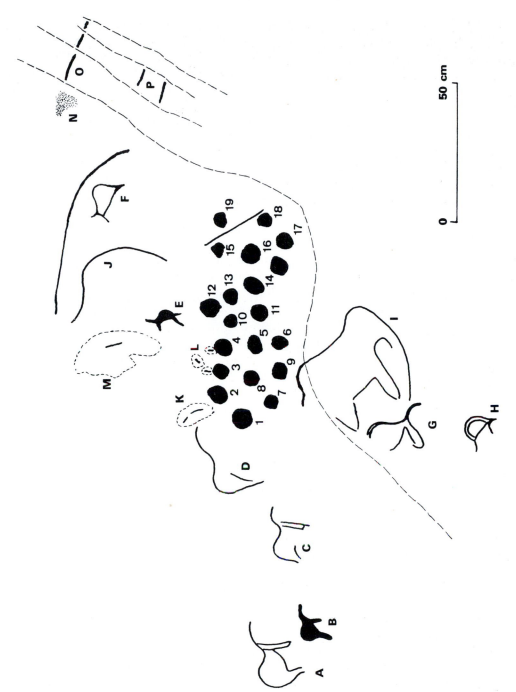

Figure 4.9 The panel of the bison–women at Pech–Merle.

The identification of the anthropomorphs at Cougnac and Pech-Merle, whose 'stumps of arms' have even been interpreted as wings, cannot be accepted, all the more because their elongated heads do not make them bird figures. Even while accepting the justifiable criticisms of Ucko & Rosenfeld and rejecting Laming-Emperaire's hypothesis, which went so far as to assert that these 'bird men are in every case represented in a difficult location' (Laming-Emperaire 1962), one cannot deny that one figure at Lascaux, and several at Altamira, show such a pronounced lengthening of the face and such a striking similarity to birds that it must have been intentional. Is that just a graphical convention? There is a strong possibility that the conventional lengthening of the face was, in certain cases, pushed deliberately to such extremes that the likeness to a bird had, in fact, been intentionally sought by the artist (for whatever reason).

The bison-headed men at Trois Frères and Gabillou, the owl- and deer-headed men in the same cave in Ariège, the bird-headed men at Altamira and Lascaux, to which we can add other examples from mobile art (the 'diablotins' from Teyjat, etc.), are infrequent representations. But they are of crucial importance because they show the close connection between man and animal. They testify to the temptation to make the human shape like an animal during the Palaeolithic, or

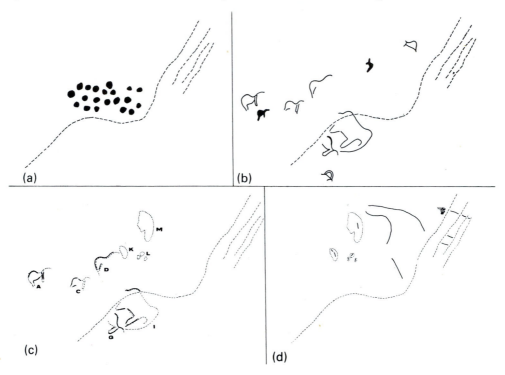

Figure 4.10   The four phases of the realization of the panel of the women-bison at Pech-Merle: (a) red dots (first painting period of Pech-Merle); (b) women-bison and mammoth in brown-red (second painting period of Pech-Merle);   (c) scratches and renovation of women-bison with a dark-brown pigment; (d) black marks ((c) & (d) belong to the second painting period of Pech-Merle). (Lorblanchet's recording.)

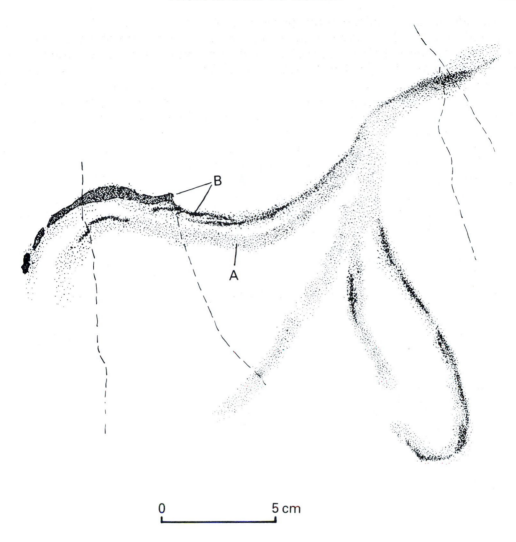

0   5 cm

Figure 4.11 Woman-bison (Pech-Merle), G in Fig 4.9. A and B are different shades of red ochre. showing the figure has been repainted (Lorblanchet's recording.)

rather *since* the Palaeolithic. This dominance of the animal in the human world is expressed in a simple combination of human and animal characteristics, the various anatomical pieces remaining perfectly distinguishable and identifiable.

Since, as we have seen, there are composite figures, there are also some ambiguous representations which it is possible to interpret at one and the same time as animals and humans on account of the *complete integration* of the characteristics of both species. In this case the separate anatomical precision is no longer detectable.

New analysis of the panel of 'bison-women' (Fig. 4.9) at Pech-Merle shows that the group of 21 red dots were made by blowing pigment onto the surface, and

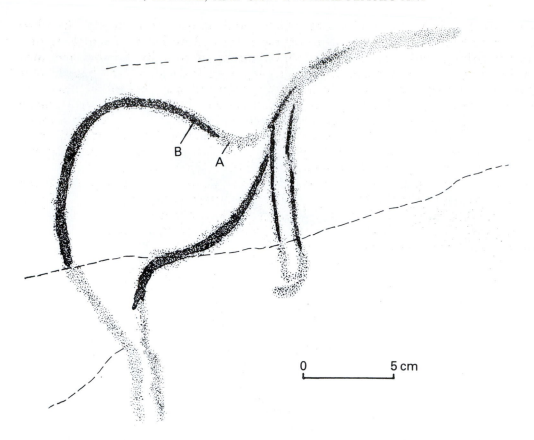

Figure 4.12 Woman-bison (Pech-Merle), A in Fig. 4.9. A and B are different shades of red ochre. (Lorblanchet's recording.)

reveals details of the eight motifs described as 'women-bison' by Leroi-Gourhan (1971, p. 264) (Fig. 4.9 A–H), as well as a red mammoth (I), three scraped areas (K–M), a curved black line (J), three black lines (O–P), and a diffused black stain (N). Analysis of the superimpositions, of the arrangements of the components, and the shades of pigment reveals four successive phases in the development of this panel (Fig. 4.10).

These details show that the red-brown colouring of the women-bison and the mammoth are the same, and that the representations therefore belong to a group. This links them to the finger-traced female figures on the ceiling, which are also associated with mammoths. The small 'women-bison', which are also placed on a small ceiling, appear in these ways to be related to the large ones, and in both cases the motifs indeed represent stylized women. The new tracings (Figs 4.11–4.14) show that the lines representing the breasts form a closed shape and not the back legs of any animal. However, their assimilation into an animal shape remains possible, as is suggested, above all, by the central motif (Fig. 4.15), which shows no single typically female characteristic but is reduced to the line of the back and one limb, either of which could be part of an animal. If it had been an isolated motif, it would never have been identified as a female figure. Does it belong with the 'bison' as was thought in turn by Lemozi and then Leroi-Gourhan, or to a horse as was the opposing suggestion by Lhote (1968)? There is no possible answer to this question. Some 12 years before the discovery of the paintings at Pech-Merle, Luquet had shown the integration of a female body with that of a bison by comparing the outline of a large-bellied woman on the reindeer plaque from Laugerie Basse with the outline of the body of a bison from Altamira (Luquet 1910, p. 4, Fig. 24). To some extent, this drawing prefigured some aspects of Leroi-Gourhan's theory (Fig. 4.16).

Leroi-Gourhan suggested (1984b, p. 56) that a masculine figure engraved at the end of the cave of Pergouset (Bouzies, Lot) has 'a bison's tail' by way of a head, and he saw in this a repetition of the *femmes-bisons* theme at Pech-Merle. In fact the Pergouset man has no head and cannot be considered as a confirmation of the Pech-Merle *femmes-bisons* theme.

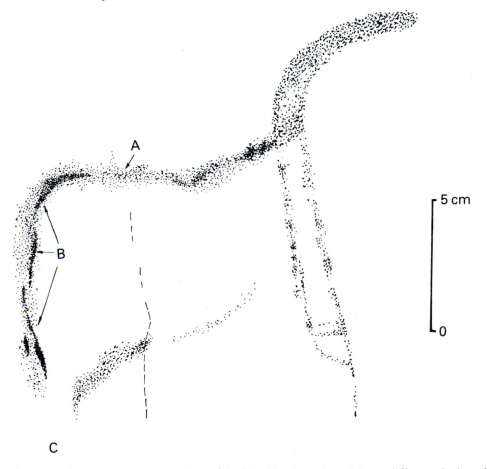

Figure 4.13 Woman-bison (Pech-Merle), C in Fig. 4.9. A and B are different shades of red ochre. (Lorblanchet's recording.)

0   5 cm

Figure 4.14 Woman-bison (Pech-Merle), E in Fig. 4.9. A and B are different shades of red ochre, D are modern finger-prints. (Lorblanchet's recording.)

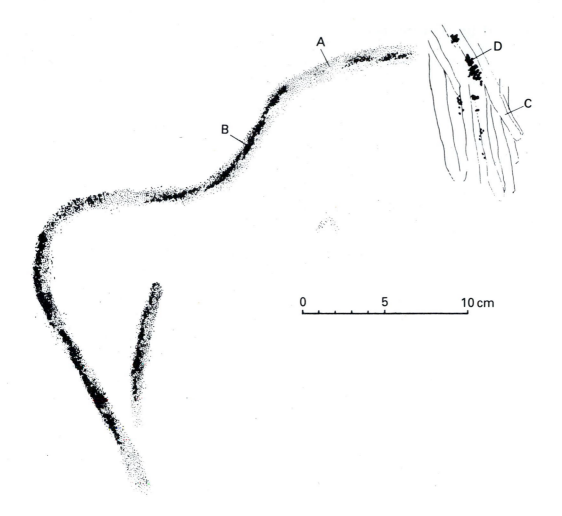

Figure 4.15 Woman-bison (Pech-Merle), D in Fig. 4.9. All the women-bison first drawn in red-brown (A) were renovated with a dark-brown pigment (B). (D) is a recent mark left by a tourist. (Lorblanchet's recordings.)

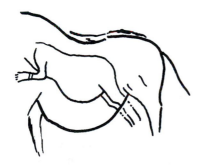

Figure 4.16 Superimposition of the outline of a bison from Altamira and of the 'Femme au Renne' from Laugerie-Basse shelter (Dordogne). (Luquet's drawing 1910.)

The real human figures

Unambiguously human representations are not numerous in Palaeolithic parietal art, but they do occur. The most typical human figures are the profiles with well-proportioned features from the caves of St Cirq and Sous Grand Lac in the Dordogne (Delluc & Delluc 1971, Roussot 1980). Other representations consist only of segments of the body, for example the headless male figure from Laussel and the famous reclining 'Venuses' from La Madeleine.

These few parietal representations suffice to show that Palaeolithic artists were capable of depicting the human form at its most characteristic and its furthest removed from the animal. But this 'realistic' style should not make us forget their extremely conventional nature: the figures are often in profile with lower limbs slightly bent and the trunk leaning forward, arms often horizontal or raised, hands and feet missing, heads frequently scarcely indicated, and the sexual organs, where present, accentuated.

Many human silhouettes are not as explicit as this, and are reduced to elongated shapes provided with a rounded mass in place of a head. This is true of the Los Casares figures and the small figures on several engraved bone pieces from Eyzies, Gourdan, and La Vache. These are of the same subject matter as the simple fusiform sketches of which only the general outlines recall the human body, some of which in mobile art are apparently carrying a baton or assegai.

The majority of human figures are incomplete; the parts of the body most often depicted, in parietal as well as in mobile art, being the head, trunk, sexual organs, and hands.

The head, although occasionally depicted full-face, is most commonly shown in profile and may show two characteristics; either they are 'ghostly', which is to say they lack facial features except sometimes the eyes; or alternatively they are 'caricatures' (such as at Marsoulas), in which the facial features are so strongly emphasized that they are reduced to geometric motifs.

A score of ghostly human figures are known from the caves of Combarelles, Cougnac, Marsoulas, Le Portel, and Trois Frères; and, in the mobile art, at least one on a bone baton from the Magdalenian shelter of Cambous (Lot) (Fig. 4.17h). The faces of these 'ghosts' are in some way portions of the complete fusiform silhouettes already described, which also had a general appearance of 'ghostliness'. Despite their lack of detail, there is no doubt that they are representations of human beings, as is revealed by a head from Cougnac (Fig. 4.17e) which is completed by an interrupted line indicating the arms and the body, while the legs are suggested by stalagmite flows. A further confirmation of the human nature of these 'ghost' heads is a curious engraving at Combarelles, interpreted by Capitan *et al.* (1924, p. 22, Fig. 6) as a 'man-mammoth' and restored to its true nature by Delluc & Delluc who discovered two engraved hands at the ends of the curves, showing that what were previously interpreted as 'elephant tusks' were, indeed, arms (Delluc & Delluc 1985, pp. 22 & 58, Figs 17 & 84).

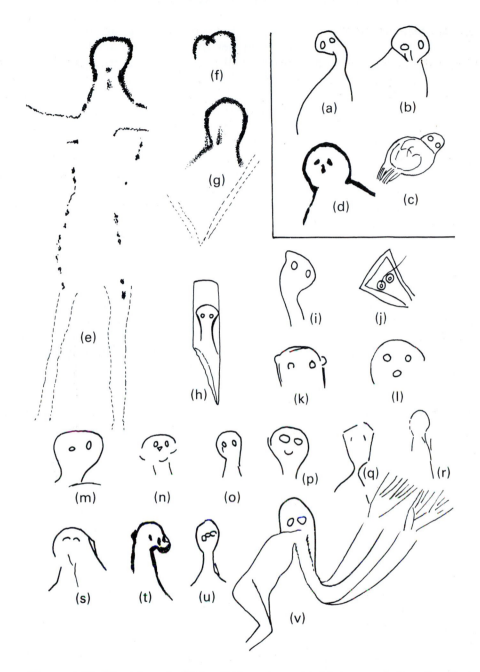

Figure 4.17 The 'ghosts' of Palaeolithic rock art: (a)–(c) snow owls from Les Trois Frères ((a) is a young owl); (d) *idem* Le Portel; (e)–(g) Cougnac (Lot); (h) Les Cambous shelter (Cabrerets, Lot); (i)–(l) Les Trois Frères; (m)–(s) Marsoulas; (t) Le Portel; (u), (v) Les Combarelles.

Several prehistorians have noted that these figures are all in some sense ambiguous: like the majority of human images they maintain a relationship with the animal world and they can equally well be interpreted as snowy owls or humans (e.g. Le Portel and Trois Frères). The perfunctory engraving of a young snowy owl between two adult birds in this latter cave is exactly the same as all the 'ghosts' (Fig. 4.17a). Perhaps we have here a new contribution to the suggested assimilation of bird and man.

Heads shown in profile are very much more numerous than 'ghosts', with facial features always highly accentuated, even caricatured, but not turned into geometric shapes. They are most usually elongated into a snout or made really grotesque. The bestialization of the human face during Palaeolithic times has greatly puzzled prehistorians, some of whom, such as Piette, saw from the outset monkeys rather than men in such crude drawings.

These grotesque drawings gave rise to three main hypotheses:

(a)   Human beings were represented wearing animal masks (e.g. Cartailhac & Breuil 1906).

(b)   The drawings reflected the clumsiness of the Palaeolithic artists or their conceptual limitations. Luquet thought that 'the men were only animals standing up straight' and that Palaeolithic artists would have unconsciously transposed to man the schema which to them was familiar from the animal world (Luquet 1910, p. 409). Deonna (1914), on the other hand, assigned the 'confusion' between human and animal to technical inadequacies, stating that '. . . a lack of precision without distinction lends the same features to both man and animals until the hand of the artist is sufficiently certain to know how to render the delicate subtleties of draftsmanship and modelling so that they differentiate between human and animal features and give to each their specific characteristics.'

(c)   There was a taboo on human representation (e.g. Nougier 1966, p. 111).

Since then the debate has continued, with Pales & Tassin de Saint Péreuse claiming that the *personae* in Palaeolithic art could have been 'knowingly made bestial or masked' (1976, p. 93), and Leroi-Gourhan stating that 'the truth is perhaps not far distant from Luquet's hypothesis' (1971, p. 91). Leroi-Gourhan's view was that these representations afforded useful connections between man and animals within the context of his theories about sexual symbolism. The muzzle- or snout-shaped human faces were masculine and the artists had therefore wished to show the equal value of man and horse, affirming the maleness of the horse (Leroi-Gourhan 1971, p. 96).

On the other hand, Ucko & Rosenfeld ascribe the different treatments given to human and animal figures in the Palaeolithic simply to the 'variety of artistic models and stylistic conventions and the diversity of subjects portrayed'. More-over, they reject the idea of there being any taboo on the human figure during the Palaeolithic (1972, p. 203).

Incomplete human figures are often reduced to just a trunk, that is to say, the middle parts of the body, the chest, pelvis, and thighs. This is notably the case with the low-relief women at Angles sur Anglin and the unsexed 'wounded' person at Cougnac. The abbreviation to just a trunk emphasizes the tendency to ignore the head and feet which is found in many human representations. The complete absence of the head and the accentuation of the sexual organs proceeds from the same tendency, which in the end reduces the individual to a sexual part.

The isolated vulva figures which may sometimes be very debated (such as that from Bedeilhac) but which are often schematic (such as those on the Aurignacian blocks in Périgord, or the cave walls at Gouy, Pergouset, or Combarelles) are quite common in parietal art, and isolated phallus representations are exceptional (Laussel, Le Mas d'Azil).

The reduction of human figures to a hand (15 positive and 400 negative) is the only direct and intentional mark which Palaeolithic man has left revealing the exact shape of one part of his anatomy.

From human to sign

The splitting of the human motif into separate components – head, sexual organs, trunk, or hand – and the careless treatment of the head or its bestialization are accompanied by a continual tendency towards schematization, which, through progressive simplification of the human outline, takes it into the world of signs.

Leroi-Gourhan's suggested development from the realistic portrayals of vulva, phallus, or the entire female body to signs has been discussed by several writers, in particular Ucko & Rosenfeld (1967, pp. 215–20) who stressed the often 'obscure' nature of these descendants. Despite these criticisms, Leroi-Gourhan's suggestion expresses one of the characteristic features of Palaeolithic art: its taste for abstraction and for playing on shapes. The simplification of the profile of the female silhouette, with its prominent buttocks ending up as a straight Pyrenean claviform, is an attractive idea, which if not entirely demonstrated, yet remains very plausible.

According to Rosenfeld (1977) there are at least three diachronic processes in the schematization of the female figure, stemming from three different realistic models, each being a slight variation on a single ideal. These three processes (that is the descendants of Pech-Merle, Gönnersdorf, and Gebel Fisilah) end up with the same ultimate schema: a vertical shape with lateral excrescence. Even though this graphic expression comes close to the claviforms, it remains distinguishable from them, thanks to the typological links which connect it with its point of departure. The leap to sign is never achieved (Rosenfeld 1977). On the other hand, Pales & Tassin de Saint-Péreuse argue for a simple schematization process applied to the human form throughout all Upper Palaeolithic cultures (1976, p. 103).

In the case of vulva-shaped signs, the situation is if anything less clear and, indeed, the signs are doubtless multiply determined. The Delluc's study (1985), for example, shows the possible relationships between vulva shapes and horse hoofprint signs, the schematization of the vulva into a deeply scooped-out circle resulting in an ambiguous motif which was probably loaded with multiple meanings concerning the relationship between the worlds of men and animals.

It may be that certain techniques lend themselves to creating ambiguities in the relationship between figures by playing on the relationship between techniques and content. Breuil (1905) had already noticed this with regard to grid signs and pectiniforms which he derived from hand prints, and the painted schematic hands at Santian are just as much forked and branching signs as they are hands. In several caves in Quercy, at Cougnac, Pech-Merle, and Les Fieux the transition of hand images to dots and animal outlines is imperceptible (Fig. 4.18). Thus the large black and red dots, both single and in series, the dotted black outlines of the horses at Pech-Merle, the large bison at Marcenac, and some of the mammoths at Cougnac, as well as the negative hands, were all made by the same method: the paint was blown onto the cave wall. This blowing technique shows the continuity between all these representations, and it may itself have had an exceptional symbolic value, since it was the breath of man and the expression of the very depths of his being, which directly created the animals and signs on the cave wall.

Another less direct Palaeolithic technique for depiction was finger tracings which, in the caves of Quercy, made use of paint or clay (Lorblanchet 1984); then on to oblong dots which are padded finger impression marks in twos and threes; then to round dotted impressions made with finger tips; and finally on to round dots, as on the deer at Pech-Merle, reminiscent of the 'dotted' outlines of the Pyrenean Cantabrian animals (Fig. 4.18f–k).

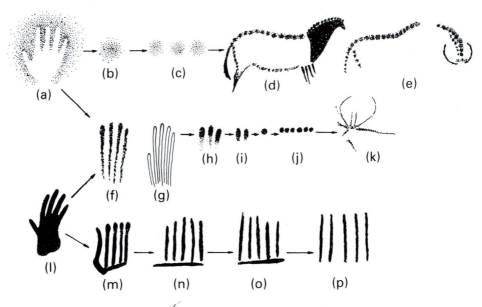

Figure 4.18 From hand prints to signs and animals. (a)–(d) Pech-Merle; (e) Marcenac (Lot); (f) hands from Pech-Merle (g) Cougnac; (h)–(j) Cougnac and Les Fieux (Lot); (k) Pech-Merle; (l) Altamira; (m)–(n) Marsoulas; (n)–(p) Altamira.

Views on chronology

In order to clarify the relationships which Palaeolithic human and animal figurations sustain, it is useful to place them within a chronological context.

The first human representations are the segmented motifs of vulvas and phalli, highly simplified and reduced to geometric signs and hand imprints which are the immediate and faithful reproduction of a part of the anatomy.

At the same time as these were on the increase, there also developed the Perigordian figurines and some of the low reliefs presenting the first complete human shapes. Both being schematic and conventional images, they transmit the concept of man rather than any realism. In the same sense, the Venus of Lespugue is a surrealist grouping of geometric solids. There are, nevertheless, at this period two notable exceptions: the Dolni Vestonice head and the hooded head from Brassempouy, which is, as Delporte asserts, 'The first human portrait' and one of the rare portraits from prehistory (Delporte 1980).

On the one hand, therefore, there appear to be very old assemblages at Gargas, Pair non Pair, and Roucadour, which are rich in animal engravings and where there are no representations of humans; and, on the other hand, new sanctuaries such as Trois Frères, Marsoulas, Combarelles, where the presence of man is regularly attested, both in a great variety of complete drawings and in the small figures jotted in the network of engravings intimately associated with bison and horses.

On account of their proximity on the same panels, as well as through the juxtaposition of both human and animal attributes as exhibited by some fantastic figures, man and animal become confused.

The Magdalenian possesses the only true individual Palaeolithic 'portraits'. The Magdalenian III engravings on stone plaques from La Marche contain more than 80 human faces which, with their beards, their straight hair, long or short, tidy or dishevelled, with their noses, hooked, snub, straight or pointed, their prominent or receding chins, make up a veritable 'ancestral gallery' (see Pales & Tassin de Saint Péreuse 1976). Almost all are in profile.

One full-face portrait portrays a bearded old man in an extraordinarily life-like way (Fig. 4.19). Even the wrinkles on his cheeks and forehead are indicated (Airvaux & Pradel 1984) in a way that rivals the Brassempouy heads, or statuette no. 15 from Dolni Vestonice (Delporte 1979).

From then onwards the Upper Magdalenian is characterized by the almost exclusive dominance of figurines or schematic female silhouettes (including some of the Lalinde, Gönnesdorf and Gare de Couze type) on cave walls of Les Combarelles, Carriot (Lot) (Lorblanchet & Welté 1987), and, above all, Fronsac (currently being studied by Delluc & Delluc).

There are three main lines to the evolutionary development reviewed above:

(a) The continuance of the process of simplification of the human figure during the Upper Palaeolithic, from the Aurignacian vulvas to the Mezzine and Gönnersdorf women;

Figure 4.19 Engraved human faces from La Marche (Lussac-les-Chateaux, Indre, France). (a)–(h) after Pales; (i) after Airvaux & Pradel.

(b) the presence of half-human, half-animal figures and bestialized human profiles, reflecting a close liaison between man and animal;

(c) the sporadic appearance of real human faces and the existence of true portraits at one site (the shelter of La Marche).

Relationship between humans and animals during the Upper Palaeolithic

It is imperative, first of all, to accept the fact that Upper Palaeolithic artists were perfectly capable of conveying a precise and doubtless faithful image of themselves. The faces and the disturbingly life-like humanity of the Dolni Vestonice and Brassempouy heads, the men engraved on the cave walls of St Cirq and Sous Grand Lac, and the series of portraits from La Marche affirm this continued capability of the first artists, who occasionally showed that they could succeed as well in their handling of the human as of the animal figure. These documents cover a very long period of time from around 26 000–12 000 BC, that is to say, from the beginnings up to the climax of Palaeolithic art. They seem to bring a dissenting voice to the hypotheses of Luquet and Deonna who postulated the innate clumsiness of man, who had still not attained the mental capacity to assure complete mastery of draughtmanship. The perfection of these works confirms the opposite.

Nevertheless, it appears amazing that there are so few human figures which may be counted as 'fully realistic'. But even these small numbers are sufficient to destroy the hypotheses about the inborn incapacity of man at self-portrayal, unless 98 per cent of the artists are assumed to have been incapable of such an accomplishment and that there were a very small number of upstart masters. Or maybe the same artists were sometimes outstandingly skilled at realistic portrayals and sometimes, indeed more frequently, were schematic and conventionalized animal painters. The same sites, even the same levels, occasionally yield figures of different styles. Delporte concluded his study of the Dolni Vestonice works by discovering 'the co-existence of very realistic and stylised shapes' (1979, p. 144).

La Marche makes a sharp break with Quaternary iconography. Its impressive portraits are not a matter of isolated object but of an important series, and there is no truly bestialized profile amongst them. The significance of these drawings must have been radically different to that of all other Magdalenian human figures.

Paradoxically, at approximately the same moment – during the Middle Magdalenian, there developed the animalization of the human shape, spilling over into the most characteristic hybrid figures, combining the attributes of men and animals. Almost all of these motifs date from the end of the Solutrean and, above all, from the Magdalenian.

How can this pattern be explained? One interesting hypothesis was put forward by Giedion (1965) in which he argued that early man was in his own conception subordinate to animals, and saw his physical shape as inferior. According to Giedion this explains the composite man – animal figures, and it could also explain why, in contrast to Spanish Levantine art, there is a complete absence of hunting scenes in which man can be said to dominate.

The only juxtapositions of man with animal in Palaeolithic art are those of Villars and at Roc de Sers, where Leroi-Gourhan (1971) detected a 'theme of man fleeing before a bovid'. In fact, the pose of the man and animal at Villars in equivocal. Some people have jokingly seen in the man at Villars the figure of 'bull-fighter', which would change the whole meaning.

Representations of wounded animals or animals seeming to 'spit blood' are not at all unusual: the bison in the pit shaft at Lascaux, losing its guts with its belly pierced through by an assegai could be thought to embody the existence and the strength of man, but, in fact, the small human motif which accompanies the bison does not appear to be in the least triumphant.

Virel (1965) argued that the paintings of the Ice Age belonged to a stage in man's psychological development in which he identified with animals. He wrote:

> Without doubt hunting initially had a utilitarian object but eating is also in the mythical sphere a means of appropriating the powers of that which is eaten. And the single act of killing already reveals an identification with an animal. In order to come near to the beast and kill it, man disguised himself in a head of an animal of the hunted species either with the complete poll of hair or more simply with its horns or antlers. Apart from hunting, man's transition into the hide of a sacred animal was equivalent to dissolving the personality of the individual in that of the group. (Virel 1965, p. 147)

He continued, 'Primitive man and his animal prey have only a single moment when the arrow gives concrete form to the bond which unites them, outside both space and time, just as the drawing of an animal struck by an arrow conveys the primeval integration of two lives, without having to call upon any magical motive as is too often supposed' (ibid., p. 191). In representing animals, man began a process of 'personal identification' or 'individuation', whereby eventually he began to differentiate himself from animals and began to develop a concept of self through projecting himself on to cave walls in human form in contradistinction to animal.

In the process of 'personal identification' the cave plays a vital part:

> Man cannot become autonomous without liberating himself from the surroundings of the material world, without remaking for himself the real world. His hand redraws the image of the world, then thought is separated from the body and projects itself to a world beyond it, where it builds up this body again. It is the dawn of abstract thought because the abstract idea like a void is in opposition to the concrete world. For this man must internalize the three-dimensional hollows of the cave, and thereby reproduce his own double in the depths of the earth. (Virel 1965, p. 50)

For Virel, negative hand prints are the evidence for self-projection by which 'man becomes aware of a part of himself'. Virel interprets the composite cave beings as 'a projection separating the ambivalence of man and animals' (ibid., p. 148).

One of the problems with this theory is that Virel sets this conceptual conquest of nature through separation of man from animals, at the threshold of history. Yet human figures appear throughout the Palaeolithic and, indeed, the Dolni Vestonice XV face, dated to 26 000 BC, may antedate all other animal representations. If the theory is right, that art was part of the process of self-conceptualization, then the occurrence of alternating phases of realism and conventionalism and the early occurrence of human figures suggests that the process may have begun much earlier than Virel suggested, and that it was one that continually went back on itself. Is the record of Palaeolithic art composed of a few gleams of human light in the vast animal darkness?

There are, however, other quite different hypotheses that may explain the pattern of representation, and in particular the infrequency of human representations, just as well.

Ucko & Rosenfeld (1972, p. 199) interpret 'the society of obvious humans . . . as a reflection of the activities which were taking place in the decorated caves in which humans themselves were present as the "actors" and therefore required no parietal depiction'. This attractive explanation stresses the theatrical aspect of much of the body of Palaeolithic art and representations. It again focuses attention on the need for in-depth examinations of the archaeological contexts of the art (footprints, etc.).

The above interpretation does not exclude other explanations, such as that the schematization of Palaeolithic human figures, their division into separate parts, the frequently undifferentiated character of asexual outlines, the animal maskings, or the complete reduction to 'animal', express a voluntary denial of the human shape rather than a conceptual incapacity by man to free himself from that of the animal. Such a denial of representing the human form could, indeed, have been the case because of the presence of actual humans in the caves.

Whatever the reason(s), the first representations of man were usually anonymous. Everything combines to depersonalize them: the individual disguises himself behind the ever-present animal and within its schematic form. To ignore the head or to bestialize it are two equally effective ways of avoiding the human embodiment; all these images are 'anti-portraits'. The artists seem to have avoided the snare of individual personality, as though to represent the individual would be beneath the artist, as though it were not possible to reduce an art focused on the universal forces of creation to the level of the particular or the anecdotal. In representing a generalized man, it was necessary to avoid involuntarily giving it features which might have brought to mind particular members of the group. Similarly, the bison on the cave wall must have been intended as the universal bison, the conceptual 'bison', and not a particular large bull, either fat or lean, with his summer coat, his different horns, his old wound, who haunts this or that area of the plateau at any particular moment in the year.

Conclusions

This chapter has highlighted the graphic continuity of Palaeolithic art. Dot, outline, and profile were the successive stages in a journey along which, in every sense, the first artists travelled continuously. Little by little the path bends in on itself, changing itself into partial outlines, into fragments of an animal body, then into the curve of the back, and in the end the representation asserts itself as a more or less complete animal outline.

The fragmentary parts of animals join together as fantastic intermediate animals with the attributes of different species. The complete animal is caught only for a brief instant in this graphic form, a form which is soon outmoded.

These animal parts come together with parts of humans and join with them to give birth to men–animals. To begin with, humans are no more than a sexual organ, a hand, or a body. Gradually it is built up, an outline emerges but facial features are only parsimoniously revealed over thousands of years of evolution.

Segmentation and reduction to geometric stages are a constant phenomenon in the representations of animals and humans. The world of signs and shapes derived from reality communicate with one another. In his exploration of the world, the Palaeolithic artist went beyond likeness. He found the essence of form.

There is, then, an obvious difference between our present-day care for definition, for clear precise distinctions, and that which is revealed by Palaeolithic art: a kind of cosmic placenta, a primeval magma, where all creatures, living and imaginary, merge into formal games which are often much more than a 'graphic play on words', since they express in symbolic terms the eternal bonds which unite all creatures and, since they demonstrated it from the very beginning, the varied creative trends of the human mind.

Our classifications will always be powerless to grasp such complexity which we are inevitably condemned to cut into arbitrary sections. In order to translate the 'inexpressible' subtlety of the Palaeolithic graphic forms, we must avoid vague descriptions like 'indeterminate' and we must increase our categories sufficiently to cover as much as possible of the full range of graphic form.

Figure 4.20 proposes a circular system of classification, highlighting the links which exist between different kinds of Palaeolithic representations and the transitional forms which exist. The central form in this systematic format, which is also the point of origin, is comprised of unstructured strokes or lines, either entwined or isolated. One variation includes finger tracings or 'macaronis' and the other includes 'marks' which may be diffuse or accidentally structured, in the style of 'spots', 'stains', and 'smears' (Lorblanchet 1974, Delluc & Delluc 1983). From these traces develop the 'animal', which may be either zoomorphic or undifferentiated, segmented, complete and characterized (e.g. horse, bovid, coprid, cervid, etc.), or composite (masters, hybrids). The path from the 'animal' to the 'human' is marked by the 'animal–human' or the 'anthropozoomorph' with bestialized head (or mask, or composite representations such as the 'Dieu Cornu' of Trois Frères). The 'human', or anthropomorph, includes simple or undifferentiated humans with simple silhouettes and with only a single human characteristic; parts of humans (headless bodies, heads, sex, or hand); 'real' humans, which include sexless representations, men, and women; and schematic humans, including caricatures, 'ghosts', and female representations such as those of Lalinde. On the route to 'signs' are the 'human signs', with characteristics visibly derived either from human parts or from the whole human body. 'Geometric signs' include all those derived from basic motifs: circles, ovals, triangles, quadrilaterals, dots, strokes. The 'animal sign' is intermediate between the 'animal' and the 'sign' and derives a geometric stylization of either a complete animal or of a part of an animal. This derivation is usually accomplished by means of dotted lines which lead perfectly on to the world of 'signs'.

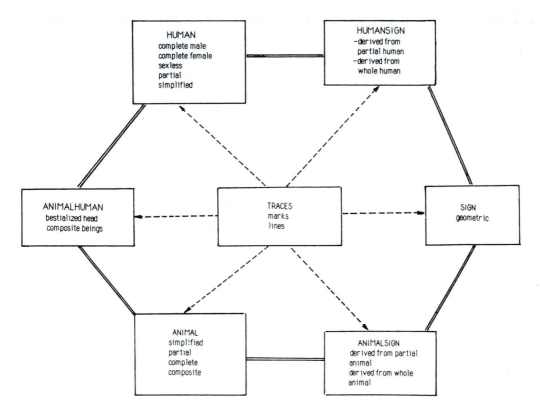

Figure 4.20   The different types of representations in Palaeolithic rock art and their relationships.

Acknowledgements

I thank Mrs Ann Eastham, Marianne Dumartheray, and especially Professor P. J. Ucko for the translations of my text into English. The original text being too long, the translation made by Ann Eastham was then substantially shortened and modified by P. J. Ucko.

References

Airvaux, J. & L. Pradel 1984. Gravure d'une tête humaine de face dans le magdalénien III de la Marche-Cne de Lussac-Les-Chateaux, Vienne. *Bullé mensuel Société Préhistorique Française* **81** 212–15.

Bégouën, H. & H. Breuil 1958. *Les cavernes du Volp, Trois Frères, Tuc d'Audoubert à Montesquieu-Avantès (Ariège)*. Paris: Arts et Métiers Graphiques.

Breuil, H. 1905. La dégénérescence des figures d'animaux en motifs ornementaux à l'époque du renne. *Comptes rendus des séances de l'Académie des Inscriptions et Belles Lettres* janvier–février, 105–20.

Capitan, L., H. Breuil & D. Peyrony 1924. *Les Combarelles aux Eyzies (Dordogne)*. Archives de l'Institut de Paléontologie Humaine. Paris: Masson.

Cartailhac, E. & H. Breuil 1906. *La caverne d'Altamira à Santillane près Santander (Espagne)*. Imprimerie de Monaco.

Clottes J. 1989. The identification of human and animal figures in European Palaeolithic Art. In *Animals into art*, H. Morphy (ed.), ch. 1. London: Unwin Hyman.

Delluc, B. & G. Delluc 1971. La grotte ornée de Sous Grand Lac (Dordogne). *Gallia Préhistoire* **14** (2), 245–52.

Delluc, B. & G. Delluc 1978. Les manifestations graphiques aurignaciennes sur support rocheux des environs des Eyzies (Dordogne). *Gallia Préhistoire* **21**(1–2), 213–438.

Delluc, B. & G. Delluc 1983. Les grottes ornées de Domme (Dordogne); La Martine, le Pigeonnier, et Le Mammouth. *Gallia Préhistoire* **26**(1), 7–80.

Delluc, B. & G. Delluc 1985. De l'empreinte au signe. *Histoire et Archéologie, Traces et Messages de la Préhistoire* **90**, 56–62.

Delporte, H. 1979. *L'image de la femme dans l'art préhistorique*. Paris: Picard.

Delporte, H. 1980. *Brassempouy – La grotte du Pape – Station préhistorique*. Landes: Association Culturelle de Contis.

Delporte, H. 1984. L'abri du Roc de Sers (Charente). In *L'Art des Cavernes*, 578–82. Paris, Ministère de la Culture: Imprimerie Nationale.

Deonna, W. 1914. Les masques quaternaires. *L'Anthropologie* **25**, 107–13.

Gaussen, J. 1964. *La grotte ornée du Gabillou*. Publication de l'Institut de Préhistoire de l'Université de Bordeaux, no. 3.

Giedion, S. 1965. *L'éternel présent, la naissance de l'art*. Bruxelles: Editions de la Connaissance.

Laming-Emperaire, A. 1962. *La signification de l'art rupestre paléolithique. Méthodes et applications*. Paris: Picard.

Lemozi, A. 1952. Le Combel du Pech-Merle, commune de Cabrerets (Lot) et ses nouvelles galeries. *Bulletin de la Société Préhistorique française* **XLIX**, 320–6.

Lemozi, A. 1961. Le grand abri sous roche solutréen du bourg de Cabrerets. *Bulletin de la Société des Etudes* **LXXXII**, 100–6.

Leroi-Gourhan, A. 1958. La fonction des signes dans les sanctuaires paléolithiques. *Bulletin de la Société préhistorique française* **55** (56), 307–21.

Leroi-Gourhan, A. 1971. *Préhistoire de l'art occidental*, 2nd edn. Paris: Mazenod.

Leroi-Gourhan, A. 1979. Les animaux et les signes. In *Lascaux inconnu*, A. Leroi-Gourhan & J. Allain (eds), 343–66. Paris: CNRS.

Leroi-Gourhan, A. 1984a. *Arte y graphismo en la Europa prehistorica*. Madrid: Collegio Universitario Ediciones Istmo.

Leroi-Gourhan, A. 1984b. *Introduction à l'art pariétal paléolithique*. Coll. Empreinte de l'Homme. Milan: Jaca Book.

Lhote, H. 1968. A propos de l'identité de la femme et du bison selon les théories récentes de l'art préhistorique. In *Simposio de arte rupestre, Barcelona 1966*, E. Ripoll-Perello (ed.), 99–108. Barcelona.

Lorblanchet, M. 1970. La grotte des Merveilles à Rocamadour et ses peintures préhistoriques. *Bull. Soc. des Etudes du Lot* **CXI** (4).

Lorblanchet, M. 1974. *L'art préhistorique du Quercy : La grotte des Escabasses-Thémines, Lot*. Morlaas: PGP.

Lorblanchet, M. & A. Welté 1987. *Les figurations féminines schématiques du Magdalénien supérieur du Quercy*. Actes du Congrès des fédérations des Sociétés savantes de Languedoc-Pyrénées-Gascogne-Souillac-Bull. Soc. des Etudes du Lot, no. 3, 3–57.

Luquet, G. 1910. Sur les caractères des figures humaines dans l'art paléolithique. *L'Anthropologie* **21** 409–23.

Meroc, L. & J. Mazet 1956. *Cougnac*. Stuttgart: Kolhammer.

Nougier, L. R. 1966. *L'art préhistorique*. Paris: PUF.

Pales, L. & M. Tassin de Saint-Péreuse 1976. *Les gravures de La Marche: Les humains*. Paris: Ophrys.

Peyrony, D. 1926. Les peintures murales de la caverne des Merveilles à Rocamadour (Lot). *L'Anthropologie* **XXXVI**, 401–7.

Rosenfeld, A. 1977. Profile figures : a schematisation of the human figure in the Magdalenian culture of Europe. In *Form in indigenous art*, P. J. Ucko (ed.), 90–109. London: Duckworth.

Roussot, A. 1980. Un portrait millénaire. In *Membres de la Société historique et archéologique du Périgord – Cent portraits périgourdins*, 16–17. Périgueux: Société Historique et Archéologique du Périgord.

Ucko, P. J. & A. Rosenfeld 1967. *L'art paléolithique*. Paris: Hachette.

Ucko, P. J. & A. Rosenfeld 1972. *Anthropomorphic representations in Palaeolithic art*. Simposio International de Arte rupestre Santander.

Vialou, D. 1981. *L'art pariétal en Ariège magdalénienne*. Museum National d'Histoire Naturelle. Laboratoire de Paléontologie Humaine et de Préhistoire, Mémoire no. 13, Paris.

Vialou, D. 1986. *L'Art des grottes en Ariège magdalénienne*. Paris: CNRS.

Virel, A. 1965. *Histoire de notre image*. Geneva: Mont Blanc.

5 On representing Ancestral Beings

HOWARD MORPHY

Introduction

The Yolngu are an Aboriginal people who live in eastern Arnhem Land, a coastal region of northern Australia.[1] Until the 1940s the Yolngu were hunters and gatherers leading a semi-nomadic life in a rich natural environment. More recently, as a consequence of European colonization, Yolngu life has been in many respects transformed, with people spending much of the year in larger settlements that are, to a considerable extent, integrated within the political and economic life of the wider Australian society. However, the Yolngu still retain considerable cultural and political autonomy, and many Yolngu continue to practise a predominantly hunter–gatherer way of life. Indeed, in the past decade, with the increasing return of people to their traditional lands to live in small 'outstation' communities and the granting of land rights under Australian law, a new impetus has been given to the maintenance and development of a distinctively Yolngu way of life. To the outsider, nowhere do continuities with the past seem stronger than in the case of the rich and varied artistic life of contemporary Yolngu.

From the Yolngu perspective, art mediates between the Ancestral Past, or Dreaming, when the form of the land was created by the actions of mythical Ancestral Beings, and the present. Art is an extension of the Ancestral Past into the present and one of the main ways in which ideas or information about the Ancestral Past is transmitted from one human generation to the next. The Ancestral Past is never directly experienced, in that no human beings living today were present when the Ancestral events took place. Rather, an understanding of the Ancestral Past is developed through representations and encodings in art and ceremony. Such understandings may be converted by the imagination into feelings of participation in the Ancestral Past, when stimulated by certain events or induced by periods of reflection. In this chapter, however, I am not so much concerned with these inner states as with the nature of the information transmitted, with the ways in which Ancestral Beings are represented in the art and the kinds of images and understanding of the Ancestral Past that it is possible for the individual to develop.

Some general characteristics of Ancestral Beings

Before considering the ways in which Ancestral Beings are encoded in paintings, it will be helpful to consider some general characteristics of Ancestral Beings and the Ancestral Past to see the kind of characteristics and properties that might be portrayed in the art.

The Ancestral Past (*wangarr*) is a complex concept precisely because it is both cut off from the present yet at the same time interpenetrates it.[2] The Ancestral Past existed before human beings, yet extends into the present. Some myths refer to a time before human beings existed, when Ancestral Beings journeyed across the Earth and through their actions created the form of the landscape. They dug in the ground and wells were formed, they stuck their digging sticks in the ground and trees grew up, they bled and great deposits of red ochre were formed. Some Ancestral Beings were able to transform themselves as well, from human to animal form, from animate to inanimate object, and back again. Some Ancestral Beings had forms that were not unlike creatures living today, though differing in their scale and capacities. They had the form of animals such as crocodiles and sharks, albeit crocodiles and sharks that could talk, travel underground, and transform parts of their bodies into features of the landscape. Other Ancestral Beings had forms that, though connected to existing objects, seem at first to be further removed from everyday reality. They may be said to be inanimate objects such as rocks or mangrove trees, but as rocks they could move, talk, think, and behave just like an animate being. Indeed, in some cases it is hard to conceive of the Ancestral Beings having any comprehensible unitary form, because either we consider it intrinsically a part of something else, as in the case of the Cough Ancestor, or we consider it to be a complex phenomenon of many parts rather than a unitary being, as in the case of the Flood Ancestor. In short, almost anything can be the focal form for a Yolngu Ancestral Being. The image of an Ancestral Being is constructed out of properties of the object, animal, or abstract concept concerned, though not absolutely constrained by it.

At all times, Ancestral Beings interacted with things that are today part of the real world: they caught fish or hunted wallaby, lit fires, and threw spears. While creating the real world, they were at the same time part of it. Later on in the creative period Ancestral Beings interacted with human beings; they gave birth to them, gave them language, and instituted correct social and religious practices for them to follow. The subsequent occupation of the land by human groups was conditional on them performing the ceremonies and passing on the sacred law that commemorated the Ancestral creativity. The Ancestral Beings who interacted most with the founding human ancestors of the respective clans tended to be the most human in form and characteristics. They are often presented as intermediaries between human beings and those Ancestral Beings with more fantastic and imaginary attributes. However, although it is tempting to divide the Ancestral past into temporal zones, it would be misleading, since the events seldom follow sequentially as in ordinary time, and often seem out of phase with one another. Indeed, from a certain perspective Ancestral events have not really ended. They continue to be created again anew through the performance of ceremonies. The Ancestral Beings continue to intervene in everyday life through the process of spirit conception and through the transference of spiritual power from one generation to the next, and in many respects the Ancestral Past is better conceived as a dimension of the present, rather than as a period distant in time (see Morphy 1984, Ch. 2).

Systems of representation

Yolngu art employs two very different systems of representation or ways of encoding meaning, and the majority of paintings involve a combination of both systems. One system is iconic and figurative, the other system is non-iconic and geometric.[3] The iconic system represents objects by producing an image that is intended to look like the object concerned, while the non-iconic system operates in a more abstract way by encoding meanings in particular combinations of geometric motifs. The questions thus arise as to whether we can see the possible form of Ancestral Beings in figurative representations, and in what ways, if any, the geometric art functions to build up or create images of Ancestral Beings. Do the Yolngu use the figurative system to portray the Ancestor in the act of transformation, and, if not, in what ways are the transformational properties of Ancestral Beings encoded in paintings?

Paintings as self-representations

Before trying to answer these questions, it must be noted that paintings are not simply representations of Ancestral Beings, but are themselves creations of, and manifestations of, the Ancestral Past. Paintings are said by Yolngu to be Ancestral in origin and simply handed on from one generation to the next, though we shall see that exactly what this means is somewhat problematical.

The Yolngu paintings that I am primarily concerned with are ones that can be referred to as *mardayin miny'tji* or 'sacred paintings'. Paintings of this category form the majority of paintings that Yolngu produce, though paint is used with purely decorative intent on everyday material culture objects, and today some paintings which are not derived from the 'sacred' category are produced for sale. Indeed, I later refer to one of the latter types of painting, that is paintings which, although not 'sacred paintings', represent mythical events that are traditionally presented in the form of 'camp stories' or moral fables.

Mardayin miny'tji are Ancestral (*mardayin, wangarr*) in two senses: first, they are designs which were created by Ancestral actions and handed on to the ancestors of the human social groups who today own them; and, secondly, they encode meanings about the Ancestral past, about the 'Dreamtime' events and the resulting creation of the landscape. The same component of a painting may perform both functions. For example, one design element in Gumatj clan paintings is a pattern of linked diamonds.[4] According to myth, the design originated when it was burnt into an Ancestral clap stick as a bush fire passed through a ceremonial ground. The design was then reproduced on the chests of the Ancestral Beings as they subsequently danced on the ground. The design thus originated in Ancestral times and when it is produced today reproduces the Ancestral events – it is a form from the Ancestral Past that is continually recreated. Yet the design is at the same time a sign of the event, and refers to the fire and the origin of the design. Particular details of the design can encode more specific meanings, especially when it is produced in an elaborated form. The diamonds may be infilled in different colours (in red, white, yellow, and black) and these in turn may refer to different aspects of the fire (to flames, ash, smoke, and burnt wood). The diamond design is likely to be only one component of a *mardayin miny'tji*, and other components will encode or refer to other details of the same mythic event. The same fire that burnt the clap stick was spread by a quail who flew with burning sticks in its beak, and elsewhere the fire forced a bandicoot to hide in a hollow log while the flames swept by. The episodes may be represented either by a figurative representation of the quail or bandicoot, or by a geometric element that, in the context of the particular painting, encodes an associated meaning.[5] The bandicoot in the hollow log may, for example, be represented by a rectangular figure with a diamond pattern on it. It is not just the diamond pattern that is said by Yolngu to be an Ancestral form, but the whole painting, including figurative representations or signs that elaborate on its meaning. The whole painting will be said to have been handed on to the founding ancestors of the owning groups by one of the Ancestral Beings associated with the land. The Ancestor may be a different one from the one involved in the origin of the design (see Morphy 1977a, Ch. 4). In the example given, one Ancestral Being or set of Ancestral Beings may have been involved with the events that resulted in the origin of the diamond design, and another Ancestral Being in contact with those events may have handed the design, in the form of a body painting, on to the first human group occupying the land. The painting is thus of Ancestral origin and designation. However, one must add a note of qualification to this discussion. What the Yolngu mean when they say a painting is of Ancestral origin is not that every element of the form of the painting is as it was in the Ancestral Past, rather they mean that every part of the painting is produced by an Ancestral template which prescribes the possible content of the painting and which contains elements such as the diamond design which originated through Ancestral action. In a sense they could mean nothing else, for the paintings are what the Ancestral Past is measured by, rather than vice versa – the designs are both part of the events of the past and a record of those events, they are essentially reflexive images that refer to their own creation and which create their own value.[6]

The encoding of Ancestral Beings: figurative representations

Most often, when an Ancestral Being is represented in figurative form, it is represented in a single unambiguous form only – the form by which it is usually characterized. If it is usually referred to as a goanna, then it will be represented as a goanna (Fig. 5.1); if it is thought of as primarily human in form, then it will be represented by a human figure. Transformational aspects of the Ancestor are usually *not* represented figuratively. There are no part-snake/part-emu/part-crocodile representations as there are, for example, in western Arnhem Land (*Kunwinjku*) art.[7] However, in myth and song many Ancestral Beings are referred to as existing

Figure 5.1   A painting by Roy Dardanga Marika of the ancestral goanna at Yalangbara. (Photograph courtesy of Australian National University.)

in different states, in particular in the form of an animal, a human, a feature of the environment, and a sacred object (cf. Munn 1965). These different manifestations of the Ancestral Being may all be represented figuratively (though rarely in the case of a natural feature). Representations which combine features of two or more states occur very rarely.[8]

An Ancestral Being may be represented in the same painting as a fish and a human being, but is unlikely to be represented by a composite figure that is part human and part fish. In the case of Ancestral Beings of fantastic form, such as trees that move and stones that talk, then such aspects of their form are never represented figuratively.

Similar considerations apply to transformational acts – there are no figurative reproductions of the landscape undergoing transformation. The acts that resulted in the transformations are sometimes represented, but they are represented as if they were acts in the natural world. For example, an Ancestral Being in human form may be represented digging a well in the ground with a digging stick. Eventually, the well concerned was transformed into a lake and the digging stick became a tree, but these transformations are not represented. Similarly, representations of Ancestral Beings in animal form focus on the animal as a natural species rather than as a transforming agent and, indeed, represent it in a passive mode. For example, the Crocodile Ancestor is usually represented from above, stretched out, and is said to be lying on the river bank or basking in the water. The goanna in Dhuwa moiety paintings is shown in a similar mode, and is said to be lying on the sand dunes in the sun. On the whole, the animal manifestations are not incorporated into scenes which relate to their land-transforming actions, they are simply rather static portraits of the animal concerned.

In most *mardayin* paintings the figurative content is limited to one or two representations of animals or objects, the remainder of the painting consisting of geometric elements. However, in some categories of paintings humans and animals are represented organized into scenes that refer to events or stories. These paintings are generally referred to as 'hunting stories', and they relate to public phases of ceremonies, to almost secular myths, and to the content of public songs (Fig. 5.2).

Scenes involving figurative representations

For heuristic purposes I have defined three distinct types of scenes that are represented in Yolngu art.[9] Although not exhaustive, these types cover the majority of paintings in which figurative representations are organized into scenes.

Scene type 1 People taking part in a ceremony. These typically show people taking part in a ceremony by dancing or acting at a ceremonial ground, manufacturing ceremonial objects, or performing various parts of a mortuary ritual. Occasionally, paintings containing such scenes may also represent spiritual or mythical aspects of the respective ceremony. A painting of a mortuary ritual may represent, in one of its sections, a scene from the land of the dead, in which figures are shown acting as spirits in the afterworld. The precise interpretation of a particular scene of a ritual is often impossible without the artist's guidance. Even if the scene is clearly of a mortuary

Figure 5.2 A painting by Wuyulwuy of the Marrakulu clan who died in 1974. The painting represents a female Ancestral Being hunting a kangaroo through the forests of eastern Arnhem Land. At one level the designs represent rocks in country. (Photograph courtesy of Australian National University.)

ritual, the artist could have intended it to be a mortuary ritual performed by human beings or a mortuary ritual performed in the Ancestral Past. In a society in which the present shades into the Ancestral Past, interpretation is never going to be simple.

Scene type 2 Episodic representations of myths. Since the late 1950s, Yolngu at Yirrkala have produced paintings which illustrate in segments a series of episodes of myths. In particular, these paintings were developed by artists of three clans: Mawalang of the Rirratjingu clan, Munggurrawuy of the Gumatj clan, and Narritjin of the Manggalili clan. Perhaps the best known of these are Mawalang's paintings of the Djan'kawu mythology and Narritjin's paintings of the Djert (eagle) and Bamapama (trickster) stories.[10] Narritjin's paintings represent semi-secular myths, which concern events which are not located in the Ancestral Past but which involved transformational events and have locational referents. Figure 5.3 illustrates a painting of the Bamapama story. It is in paintings of this type that figurative representations of the act of transformation sometimes occur. In the case of the Djert paintings, for example, which refer to a myth in which an angry child was gradually transformed into a sea eagle during a temper tantrum, part-human part-bird figures are sometimes produced. Djert and Bamapama are moral tales told to children as examples of the consequences of breaching moral norms or behaving badly – they are also very much a form of entertainment.

Scene type 3 Hunting and manufacturing scenes. These are the most common scenes represented figuratively. They consist of people hunting a wallaby with spears (see Fig. 5.2), people in a boat harpooning dugong, or people manufacturing a rope for hunting turtle. Again depending on context, the scene may refer to a mythic event or represent human beings going about their lives. As Ancestral Beings frequently carried out the same everyday actions as living people, a hunting scene quite often has a mythological referent. Dharlwangu clan paintings often show people fishing at a fish trap.[11] In this case the fish trap was an Ancestral creation at Gaarngarn in Dharlwangu country, resulting from an Ancestral transformation, and the fish trap is manifest today as a rocky bar across the river. The figurative representations usually give no clue as to the Ancestral significance of the events depicted and do not show the transformations that occurred. They portray the Ancestral Beings as if they were ordinary people taking part in everyday activities.

The encoding of Ancestral Beings in the geometric art

How then are Ancestral Beings, in particular the fantastic and transformational aspects of them, encoded in paintings if they are not represented figuratively? The answers to this question are multiple and have already partly been given: where they are represented in paintings they are present indirectly in the relationships between sets of paintings, they are alluded to in the content of the paintings, and they are encoded in the geometric art. The characteristic of each of those means of representation is that they are indirect, and the message is dependent on knowledge of the code and even on foreknowledge of what is encoded – meaning is not (if it ever is) internal to the painting.

a

b

e

f

g

d

c

As we have argued already in the case of diamond designs, geometric patterns are themselves often thought to be transformations of the Ancestral Beings. To take another example, the design of the Manggalili clan represents marks left by the ebb and flow of the tide on the body of an Ancestral Being as he lay dead on the beach, cast up by the sea. The design painted as the background in a sacred painting refers to and recreates that transforming event in which the design was etched into the Ancestor's body. Yet the meaning of the design, and hence the concept of the Ancestral Being, is filled out by its connection to myth and song and through the metaphors contained within them. Although here is not the place to explore Yolngu symbolism, the image of the tide mark in the sand is a key symbol to the Yolngu of the ephemeral nature of people – for the marks wash away with every subsequent tide.[12] The tide itself is the great cleanser of the beach, washing debris out to sea. The particular clan design and the myth of the body on the beach is associated with mortuary rituals and with the removal of pollution associated with death. The concept of the Ancestral Being consists partly of the core metaphors associated with them. The transitory patterns of the sand on the beach transformed into permanent form on the body of the Ancestral Being provide the focal point for metaphors about the impermanence of life.

Frequently, sacred paintings have no obvious figurative component and various aspects of the Ancestral Being concerned are encoded in different geometric elements. A characteristic of the geometric art is that it is multivalent and the same element may encode a number of different meanings. Figure 5.4 is of a painting by Dula Ngurruwutthun of the Munyuku clan. The painting represents the Wild Honey Ancestor at an inland place of paperbark lagoons. The diamond pattern has some relationship with the Gumatj pattern discussed earlier, since it, too, is associated with fire. In this case, however, fire is an attribute of the Wild Honey Ancestor rather than the core Ancestral Being of the painting. At one level of interpretation the diamonds represent the cells of the hive, the cross-hatching signifies different components of the hive, the grubs, the honey, the pollen, and the bees; the cross-bars that bisect some of the diamonds represent small sticks that are found in the hive; while the dots within the circles represent the bees swarming from the entrance of the hive.

Figure 5.3 A painting by Narritjin Maymuru of the Manggalili clan who died in 1982. The painting represents the story of Bamapama, a trickster Ancestral Being. Bamapama (see Warner 1958, p. 545 *et seq.* Groger-Wurm 1973, p. 124), was sent to collect young men for a ceremony. He went to a nearby settlement (a), but asked for young girls instead of boys. He challenged them to a race, saying that only the fastest one would be selected for the ceremony (b). One girl, his classificatory sister, raced ahead of the rest, and eventually she and Bamapama were alone. They rested to fish at a lake, and Bamapama sent her to collect firewood. While she was away, he inserted a fish bone in his foot, and on her return said that they would have to camp the night because he was lame. They built a hut with a fire in the centre (c). In the night he threw stones onto the roof, and frightened her by saying that the sound was made by a sorcerer. She moved over to his side, whereupon he raped her, killing her with his large penis. He hid her body in a bark container and returned to her camp (a). When the people found out what had happened, they started to beat him (a). He became wild, and began to spear dogs (e) and vegetable food (d), that is, things that people do not normally spear. After a while, everything began to change. All the people turned into the animal species that were totems to their clan (f) and (g), and returned to their own clan territories. Finally, a great flood came and covered the area where the events took place. (Photograph: Australian National University.)

Figure 5.4 A painting by Dula Ngurruwutthun of the Munyuku clan representing the Wild Honey Ancester at Mandjawuy. (Photograph courtesy of Australian National University.)

At another level, elements of the design signify attributes of the fires lit by hunters who collected the wild honey: the white cross-hatching is the smoke, the red is sparks, and the white dots ash. At another level still, the diamond pattern represents the sparkling fresh water as it flows beside the flowering paperbark trees, the trees in which the honey is found. The other components of the painting have associated meanings: the two lateral figures representing the trunks of paperbark trees, and the central figure representing the hive and its entrance. These all have an iconic aspect in that they represent similarly shaped ceremonial objects. However, as the objects themselves are largely non-iconic representations of Ancestral Beings, the iconicity is arguable. Indeed, it is misunderstanding the nature of the Wild Honey Ancestor to think of it as being able to be represented figuratively. For the Ancestor is an abstract concept that consists of all those things associated with wild honey: the hive, the bees, the trees and flowers, the floodwaters, and the season. All of those things in turn have components – the tree has branches, roots, leaves, bark, and so on, the hive has cells, honey, bees, grubs, and pollen – and all of the components have their own connotations. Many of them are taken up in songs about the Wild Honey Ancestor, others are the product of individual experience and depend on the subject's relationship to the Ancestral Being.[13] But from another perspective, the Wild Honey Ancestor is an entity rather than an amorphous complex of associated traits, for it has a name and a journey, and places that it has created, and manifestations in the form of paintings, sacred objects, and transformations of the landscape. Figurative representations could encode its components by representing the bees, trees, flowers, hunters, and so on separately but it seems that the multivalency of the geometric art creates the possibility of an individual grasping it as a whole. And as a collectively acknowledged manifestation of the Ancestor it does, of course, represent itself.

This same potentiality of the geometric art for multivalency enables paintings to encode transformational aspects of Ancestral Beings and Ancestral events. Elsewhere I have argued that it is productive to think that there is a template underlying each set of Yolngu sacred paintings, which in effect generates their surface form (Morphy 1977a). The template consists of a set of positions which exist in a fixed relationship one with another, at each of which a series of meanings is encoded. Depending on which of the respective set of meanings is focused on, the surface picture changes. A hypothetical example should clarify what I mean.[14] A particular template has two loci, (a) and (b). At locus (a) the meanings well, lake, and vagina are encoded. At locus (b) the meanings digging stick, river, and penis are encoded. There are clearly a number of possible pictures that combinations of those sequences could generate. Three of them would be a river flowing into a lake, a digging stick being used to dig a well, and a penis going into a vagina. The three stories may all be interconnected as events in the same mythic sequence:

A Kangaroo Ancestor was digging a well with a digging stick. When he finished, a female wallaby bent down to drink the fresh water, and the kangaroo seized his opportunity to have sexual intercourse with her. The semen flowed out of her body and into the waterhole. Today a river flows into the lake at that place and the kangaroo's penis was transformed into a digging stick which can be seen as a great log beside the lake.

Now, as well as generating a whole series of pictures depicting the various events, the template could be represented by a single multivalent design as shown in Figure 5.5. In this design the meanings at locus (a) are represented by the circle and the meanings at locus (b) are represented by a straight line, to produce a familiar component of Yolngu clan designs. In this way, the transformational events are encoded in a single motif without being directly represented. The geometric motif gives priority to no one meaning but allows all to be active. This is precisely how Ancestral transformations are encoded in Yolngu paintings, by marking the positions where they occur rather than by directly represting them.

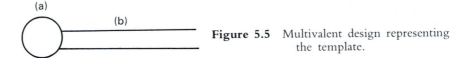

Figure 5.5 Multivalent design representing the template.

Discussion: the nature of the Being

How do we explain the way in which Ancestral Beings are represented in Yolngu art, in particular the lack of figurative representation of transformational events and of the fantastic aspects of their beings? I think that the answer involves two issues: the nature of the Beings themselves and the system of knowledge of which they are a part. The first I have largely dealt with already.

Yolngu Ancestral Beings are highly complex concepts that cannot be said to have a single image. When they are represented by a single image then that image is misleading, often deliberately so. As I argued in the case of the Wild Honey Ancestor, the Ancestor consists of that whole complex of things to do with wild honey. Yolngu do not have a single image of it but acquire an emergent and, in part, connotative understanding of it over time.[15] The geometric design as a manifestation of the Ancestral Being is structured to encode those developing understandings.

Moreover, Ancestral Beings are really inseparable from the concept of totemism and the process of myth. They are not discrete separable objects with defined boundaries, but just as they transform the world they are, in turn, in a constant state of transformation. Representations of Ancestral Beings involve the whole way in which objects of the environment are used by the Yolngu as components of a semiotic system. The Wild Honey Ancestor gains its meaning through the connotations of its parts and through the symbolism, actively created, of fire, water, and honey (of red, white, and yellow), and also through its associations with particular clans and countries. Over time it can absorb some more components or leave some behind, it can follow new routes across the land, transforming itself anew into the landscape and becoming the emblem of new groups. Images of the Ancestral Beings must be continually changing as the system is used over time. But the geometric art can remain the same while the concept changes, because of the distance between form and content and because of its multivalency (see Morphy 1980). Its detailed meaning can change while it remains a fixed image associated with the Ancestor, a timeless manifestation. Even in cases where the Ancestor is associated with a characteristic human or animal form, the Ancestor cannot be fully represented by a single fixed image. The Crocodile Ancestor is a case in point. The crocodile in paintings is frequently presented figuratively with a background pattern of diamonds, representing fire. In myth the crocodile grew out of fire. He was sleeping in his bark hut when it was set fire to by his wife, the blue-tongued lizard. The crocodile fled, with the burning bark from the hut torturing his body, and dived into the sea to cool off, leaving the fire burning beneath the waves. The serrated back of the crocodile is the ragged bark burnt into his skin, and the pattern of the scales is the product of blistering. But what was the form of the crocodile during these events, what was his shape before they occurred, and how does the fire burn beneath the waves? The crocodile in the painting is a sign for the Crocodile Ancestor, not a representation of it.

Coming into being

Yolngu art is incorporated in a system of revelatory knowledge in which one learns more and more about the connections between things as one goes through the system. It is not so much that aspects of Ancestral Beings are secret, though indeed some are, as the fact that they are presented in parts spread over a long period of time. One part will be presented in one ceremony, another in a later one; one aspect will be represented in a dance, a different one in a painting, and so on. At whatever stage one first encounters an Ancestral Being, one encounters a part not a whole, the whole only emerges later. Thus, the Ancestral transformations from one state to another are separated out in time and space. The myth is never enacted as a whole, the connections are made retrospectively, the transformations are not supposed to be seen but to be revealed. The geometric art integrates well within this system. It gives priority to no one transformation, to no one meaning, it enables all the parts to be encoded in a concealed way and their connections to be subsequently revealed. In other words, the template is a template for transformation. If we return to our example of the circle and line (Fig. 5.5) we will be able to see how this works.[16]

A person may get to know 'Kangaroo Lake' by walking around it as a child. He is shown the lake and the stream that flows into it which is called 'digging-stick creek'. Later when he is shown the circle and line design on the painting he is told it represents the lake with the stream flowing into it. On a subsequent occasion in a ceremony, a dancer acting the Kangaroo Ancestor digs a circle in the ground with his digging stick and marks a line leading into that circle. The connection is made, the lake is called Kangaroo Lake because it was created by the kangaroo digging a well that was subsequently transformed into a lake. But some things still puzzle the child about the lake. Why is the water cloudy white and why do women avoid bathing in it? Later he hears about a further transformation and the true origin of the lake's water, created from the sperm of the Ancestral Kangaroo as it flowed into the water hole. It is then he is told of a second name of the lake, 'wallaby vulva'.

In this way a series of transformations get encoded in the form of a single design, which cumulatively encodes Ancestral events.

Conclusion

Figurative representations in Yolngu art are not intended to represent the mythical form of the Ancestral Beings – they are signs of the natural objects that are incorporated into totemic discourse; organized in scenes, they represent events in the ordinary world, hunting and gathering, and taking part in ceremonies. The only transformational images (humans changing into animals and so on) concern fantastic events associated with 'actual' human beings in 'fables' and moral tales – paintings with such images are recent innovations. On the whole, transformations are encoded in the geometric art enabling individuals to develop their own concepts of the Ancestral events, enabling the images to be psychologically satisfying and to maintain their power – they are condensation symbols which, although they allude to the form of the Ancestral Beings and refer to a time of transformation when everything was possible, do so without directly presenting the event in a phantasmagorical way. However, all is not freedom. At the same time the geometric art – the sacred paintings – consists of relatively fixed forms, belief in their Ancestral origins is collective, meanings are encoded in them in a structured and systematic way, and interpretation of them is constrained by their incorporation in a hierarchical system of knowledge. In Giddens's terms (1979) they are the ideal medium for structuration, they are socially transmitted forms associated with collective ideas about a particular Ancestral Being acted out in ritual and acquired in everyday life, yet they also allow individual perceptions and understandings of the object to vary within limits and with respect to individual experience. The collective design does not give the lie to that experience but absorbs it, and may even transmit it while maintaining the illusion of continuity. Subtle shifts of form, meaning, and ownership go unnoticed in a timeless universe with no recorded history.

Notes

1   The Yolngu are sometimes referred to in the anthropological literature as the Murngin, Lloyd Warner's name for them (1958). Warner's book is still the best general account available.
2   For a more detailed discussion of Yolngu religion see Morphy (1984). Berndt (1983) has also written on the ways Ancestral Beings are represented in Yolngu art.
3   To an extent, this distinction follows Munn's distinction (1966) between continuous and discontinuous meaning systems. For a theoretical discussion of the concept of iconicity in Yolngu art and a critical consideration of Munn's distinction see Morphy (1980).
4   For a detailed discussion of Yolngu clan designs see Morphy (1977a, 1988).
5   For a fuller account of this myth and paintings associated with it see Groger-Wurm (1973, pp. 82–6) and Berndt (1964, Pl. 35).
6   My perspective here is influenced by Stanner (1963) and Munn (1965).
7   See Taylor (1984) for a discussion of the way transformations are represented in Kunwinjku art.
8   An exception to this is that sacred objects themselves may have components that represent iconically an animal form of the Ancestral Being concerned. Such objects represented in painting thus combine elements of the sacred object and, through it, the animal concerned.

9 The best source of illustrations of Yolngu paintings is Groger-Wurm (1973), which provides many examples of different scene types.

10 Perhaps the most famous of Mawalang's Djan'kawu series is that of the Djan'kawu giving birth, which is in the collections of the Art Gallery of New South Wales (see Berndt 1964, Pl. 25). Paintings by all three artists are well represented in Groger-Wurm (op. cit.).

11 See Groger-Wurm (op. cit., Pl. 100).

12 For a more detailed discussion of the symbolism involved see Morphy (1977b).

13 Frances Morphy suggested when reading this chapter that part of the problem may be created by the use of the phrase Ancestral Being as a translation of the word *wangarr*. It results in the reader seeing the *wangarr* in too concrete terms. In using the phrase I am following the convention adopted by most Australian anthropologists in translating words like *wangarr, altjeringa* (Aranda), and *djugurba* (Warlbiri). Probably, it is desirable in a case like this to break with tradition by simply using the Aboriginal word!

14 Though hypothetical, this example is close to an actual example discussed in Morphy (1977a, Section III).

15 Donald Thomson had this insight into Yolngu art but never published it. In his field notes on a paddle painted at Trial Bay on 11 June 1942 by Djimbarryun, the father of Dula Ngurruwutthun who painted the wild honey design, Thomson wrote 'The whole [design] represents not so much an actual barrakalla or paperbark tree as a symbolic representation or material personification (words fail me, − rationalisation, projection) of the natives' ideas of this tree in mythology but coloured by their personal living experience of life.'

16 Munn (1973) provides an excellent account of socialization into meaning in the case of Warlbiri art.

References

Berndt, R. M. (ed.) 1964. *Australian Aboriginal art.* Sydney: Ure Smith.

Berndt, R. M. 1983. Images of god in Aboriginal Australia. *Visible Religion* **II**, 14–39.

Giddens, A. 1979. *Central problems in social theory: action, structure and contradiction in social analysis.* London: Macmillan.

Groger-Wurm, H. 1973. *Australian Aboriginal bark paintings and their mythological interpretations.* Vol. 1: Eastern Arnhem Land. Canberra: Australian Institute of Aboriginal Studies.

Morphy, H. 1977a. *Too many meanings.* Unpublished PhD thesis, Australian National University, Canberra.

Morphy, H. 1977b. Yingapungapu: bark painting as sand sculpture. In *Form in indigenous art,* P. J. Ucko (ed.), 205–9. Canberra: Australian Institute of Aboriginal Studies.

Morphy, H. 1980. What circles look like. *Canberra Anthropology* **3**, 17–36.

Morphy, H. 1984. *Journey to the crocodiles nest.* Canberra: Australian Institute of Aboriginal Studies.

Morphy. H. 1988. Maintaining cosmic unity: ideology and the reproduction of Yolngu clans. In *Politics, power and ideology in hunting and gathering societies.* J. Woodburn, T. Ingold & D. Riches (eds), 141–63. London: Berg.

Munn, N. M. 1965. The transformation of subjects into objects in Warlbiri and Pitjantjanjara myth. In *Australian Aboriginal anthropology,* R. M. Berndt (ed.). Nedlands: University of Western Australia Press.

Munn, N. M. 1966. Visual categories: an approach to the study of representational systems. *American Anthropologist* **68**,: 936–50.

Munn, N. M. 1973. *Warlbiri iconography*. Ithaca: Cornell University Press.

Stanner, W. E. H. 1963. *On Aboriginal religion*. Oceania monograph no. 11. Sydney: University of Sydney.

Taylor, L. 1984. Dreaming transformations in Kunwinjku bark paintings. Paper delivered at the Australian Institute of Aboriginal Studies Biennial Conference, *Aboriginal arts in contemporary Australia*, Canberra.

Warner, W. L. 1958. *A black civilisation*. Chicago: Harper & Row.

6 *Figurative and schematic rock art of Kenya: animal representation and tentative interpretation*

OSAGA ODAK

Introduction

Kenyan rock art is basically geometric, although there are a few sites with figurative representational art. However, any panel containing figurative art invariably also contains additional abstract signs. This means that any efforts towards interpreting the art must involve analysis of the spatial and temporal relationship between figurative and schematic art within one and the same panel. A similar strategy includes comparison of the art in sites within one area with those in others. Comparison has to involve detailed distributional analysis of patterns and motifs within panels at a particular site and also a comparison of differences between sites within a region. This chapter focuses on the figurative art of Kenya and the relationship between it and schematic art within a panel or across groups of sites, so as to show how animals are represented and to provide tentative interpretations of some schematic art.

Typology of schematic art

Kenya does not have many sites with figurative art. So far there are about 60 rock art sites known in the country, of which only six (i.e. 10 per cent) have animals and humans in addition to abstract symbols in each panel of a site. Most of the geometric–schematic figures within each panel are in some way linked to animals or humans.

Among the many geometric art sites found are those with cup- or peck-marks, alone or with additional types of figures. Cup-marks range from fairly small to large holes. Generally, they occur within the range of from 2 mm to 4 cm in diameter. Although we have little direct evidence about them, it is known from ethnography that they were put to different uses by different ethnic groups. They are arranged differently in different sites or sections of sites and are associated with different functions. Certain arrangements or patterns (see Figs 6.1 & 6.2) suggest that some cup-marks were used as games (Townshend 1979). In other cases it seems probable that they would be used for 'grinding or pounding of wild fruits or other vegetable

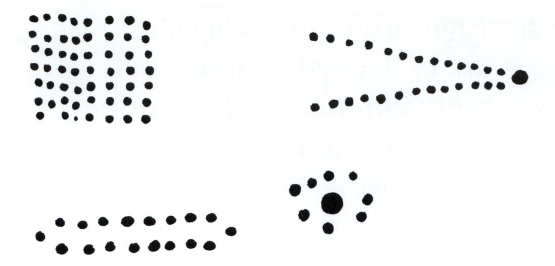

Figure 6.1 Major patterns in Gusii cup-marks.

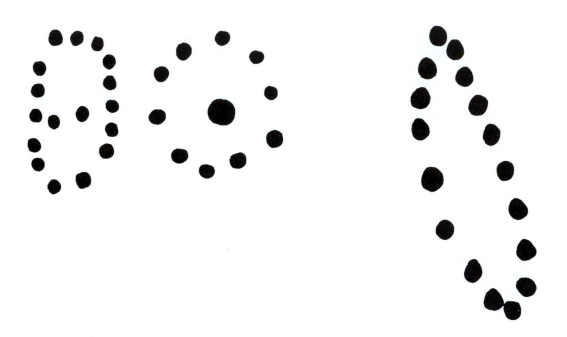

Figure 6.2 Patterns of Kebaroti (Kuria) petroglyphs.

matter' (Soper 1966, p. 155). Soper cites Cooke as having suggested that Zimbabwean cup-marks were probably used for 'pulverising quartz for flux used in iron-smelting or grog for pot making'. Fosbrooke (1954) suggested that the Tanzanian Ugweno (Pare Hills) cup-marks were used for 'shattering small lumps of iron ore. . . used as currency in the local market'. But the different types and sizes of Kenyan cup-marks, like the differences in their patterns of arrangement, suggest that there are yet other uses to which they were put and which have yet to be discovered.

Linear designs

This is another group of schematic art found in Kenya. Although this group is usually found along with figurative art, there are sites where they are found alone. Examples include the Gisambai sites (Wagevella and Matsingulu) (Figs 6.3 & 6.4). It is possible that they served as some form of communication medium probably associated with writing (Odak 1986, pp. 16–23).

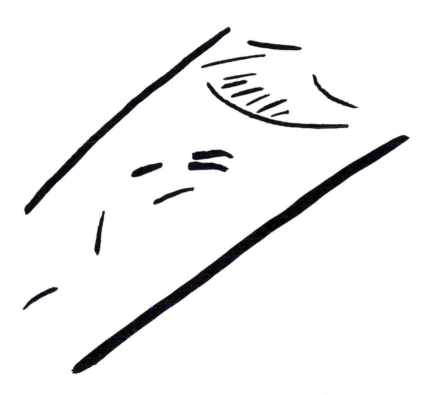

Figure 6.3 Engravings at Matsingulu site, Kakamega District (tracings from a photograph).

Figure 6.4   Engravings at Wagevella site,
Kakemega District (tracings from a photograph).

Dots and dotted motifs

These are numerous tiny signs found together as clusters which sometimes make up patterns. They can form squares, rectangles, circles, or some other patterns. Dots are found in sites whose painted surfaces include figurative art (e.g. Kakapeli pictographs), or are used in the form of pecking as a technique to bring out an animal or human figure on rock surfaces (e.g. at Juma Min Aboy site near Mandera in North Eastern Province of Kenya, or with the anthropomorphs at Fock's farm site). Several clusters of dots (or peckings which make up particular motifs) are also found in Goti Chaki site (see Fig. 6.5) which has no figurative art.

Circular designs

These are circles and related figures which abound in several sites with schematic and figurative art. They are normally found in the forms of single and/or concentric circles; in the forms of arcs, or concentric arcs, or as concentric circles with one or more incomplete concentrics. The circles are sometimes found attached to certain linear figures which together constitute one motif. Circular designs can be found, for instance, in concentric, crossed, radiated,[1] arc-like, ovular, incomplete ovular,

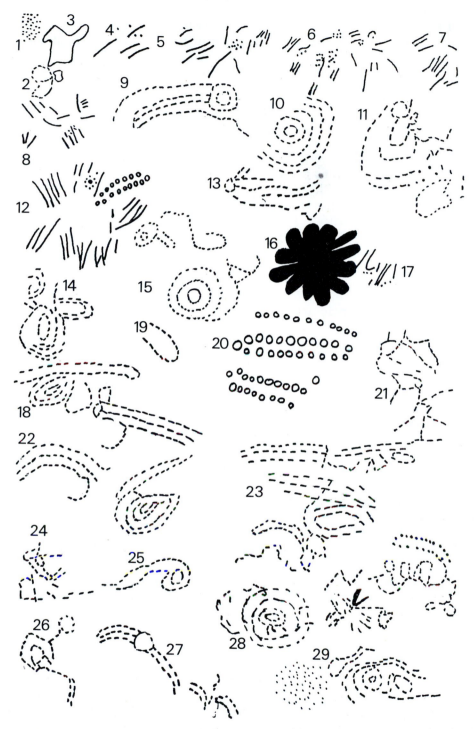

Figure 6.5 Motifs at part of a Gusii site (Goti Chaki) (free-hand sketch).

or spiral forms. This design tradition is very popular in both figurative and schematic rock art in Kenya. Sites where they occur together with animal and human representations are Kakapeli, Chemasari and Kimothon.

Modified circular designs

These are individual figures or compositions shaped in circular form. Oval and oval-related designs are frequently employed – both of which are sometimes profusely rayed, radiated, or spoked (internally[2] or externally, or both) in a gear-like structure.[3] The internal radiations, or spokes, involve criss-crossings of various forms. External radiations, on the other hand, involve gearing patterns. Some of these designs are shield-like in structure. In some sites there are angular figures attached to radiations, which make up oval-shaped figures. Most sites in the Western Highlands of Rift Valley are characterized by these types of motifs, with the exception of the Tapsagoi and Chepkit sites in Ndalat Hills where this type of art is associated with zoomorphs and, at times, anthropomorphs. The sites belonging to this tradition are almost exclusively schematic.

Figurative and schematic art

The proportions of figurative representations at a site vary on a regional basis. In some sites (e.g. Itone on Lake Victoria) only abstract signs are depicted. In others (e.g. Kakapeli) there are animal and human figures along with abstract signs. In yet others only humans and animals are represented with little or no addition of abstract signs (e.g. Kimothon). The relationship between figurative and schematic representations include: isolated abstract figures executed next to, or touching, animal figures (e.g. in Chemasari); isolated abstract figures executed next to, or touching, a human figure; two or more separate abstract figures executed close to, or actually touching, each other; and one or more domestic animals, next to, or in some ways linked with, one or more wild animals and/or humans.

There are instances where only human and animal figures are represented in a particular relationship (e.g. in proximity with each other, etc.). The nature of the relationship between figurative and schematic representations takes the form of superpositionings, or isolation of individual figures or groups from other similar figures. There may be either direct linkage between figures or separation of them by a wide gap. Both are found in sites where both figurative and schematic representations exist within the same panel. For example, at Kimothon (where both wild and domestic animals are drawn) there are pictures of oxen, bulls, and cows. However, there are only a few schematic figures which are superimposed on, and sometimes drawn under, an animal or a human figure. A notable example at Kimothon is a concentric circle drawn in red under a bull.

At Chemasari, another Mount Elgon area site in the Luucho Hills (Odak 1980), there are three cows facing right, drawn parallel to each other and facing in the same direction (i.e. east). The uppermost cow is superimposed upon a group of red concentric circles, which are also superimposed on an unidentifiable figure. The middle cow is embossed on a red motif. Directly under the fore and hind limbs of the middle cow are two white, but less discernible, schematic figures. The lowest cow, which has a white circle drawn over it and under its belly, is a partially rayed white circle. Four human figures are drawn within the same panel. These include an adult male and an adult female, each holding a 'girl' and a 'boy' who in turn are holding each other. They are positioned to the left of the middle cow.

In other parts of the Chemasari shelter wall are depictions of artefacts (Odak 1980). At the Kakapeli site (Odak 1977a) one panel shows an anthropomorph, a red vertical figure and a 'head' formed of concentric and single circles. Some of the circles are profusely rayed. There is a highly stylized animal figure and also concentric circles next to each other, as well as another rayed circle drawn over the animal figure. From another animal figure's belly extends a white loop.

The second panel at Kakapeli (see Fig. 6.6) contains two brown and yellow(ish) cows (nos 1 & 2) which are positioned next to each other. To their top right is a cow proportionally drawn in black (no. 3). Below the two cows is a wild animal (no. 4) which is superimposed on a schematic figure which itself was drawn over a white shield-like motif. To the left (facing the shelter) is an arrow-head shaped figure (no. 5). There is a red circle which is part of a long, meandering line on top of which is drawn the wild animal (no. 4), one of whose horns is crossed by the same line to form a loop. On top of the loop is a shield-like motif. Lower down are three separate but closely drawn circles (no. 7). The third panel of the shelter wall contains several schematic figures and zoomorphs, one of which is in white and resembles a tortoise (no. 1a). It was drawn on top of a crossed circle (no. 2a). Below it is an oval shield-like figure (no. 3a) crossed by two lines which also cross each other at right angles. Touching the tortoise motif and the crossed circle are gazelle-like polychrome animals in white and brown (nos 4a & 5a). Extending from the latter's tail is a white 'spiral' (no. 6a) which appears to be a separate motif upon which the gazelle-like figure was superimposed. Lower down from the animal, and drawn in red and white, is a fat pig-like zoomorph (no. 7a) to whose large belly are connected several schematic figures (no. 8a) and which appears to be 'eating grass' (no. 9). The grass is represented by a series of parallel vertical lines, each of which ends in a dot. To the right of these lines is a heart-like motif (no. 10).

Representation

In painting, most animals are drawn on top of abstract figures. This can be seen at Kakapeli, Chemasari, and Kimothon sites. Certain abstract signs touch sections of the animal figures. Humans, however, are isolated from other figures and are not linked to any schematic figures, except where one such motif is drawn on top of an anthropomorph. At Kimothon there is a drawing of a squatting human holding an arrow-like motif (Wright 1961), but the arrow does not seem to be aimed at any particular animal or human symbol.

Concentric circles, which are found in abundance in other sites, are almost absent at Kakapeli, although there are depictions of animals, humans, and artefacts. This is also the case at the Chemasari site. A few single circles are found at Kimothon. Most figures at Kakapeli represent either objects from nature, artefacts, or parts

Figure 6.6 Paintings at Kakapeli (part of Panel 2 and the whole of Panel 3).

of the human body. Animals are generally represented in white at Chemasari, where they are usually drawn over schematic figures. Superimposition of animals over schematic figures also exists at Kimothon, where there are schematic designs and artefacts which have no discernible relationship with other signs. This is also the case at Chemasari where such artefacts are drawn independent of both humans and animals.

At Kakapeli an apparent wild animal figure is painted over schematic figures. This is an instance of a connection between schematic figure and wild animal. There is also a direct relationship between the domestic animals themselves, although one cow stands alone at the top right-hand of the panel.

Wild animals are also superimposed upon schematic figures which, in turn, are superimposed upon other schematic figures.

Surima Water Hole site contains motifs, some of which stand by themselves and others which are directly related to other figures. Most of the engraved animals at this site are isolated individuals (Fig. 6.7). There are, however, also representations showing activity between wild animals and humans.

Among the wild animals are elephants, rhinoceroses, giraffes, ostriches, buffaloes, and gazelles. The camel is typical of the engraved domestic animals. Anthropomorphs are usually close to zoomorphs but without any direct linkage (or 'joining string').

Many of the exclusively geometric–schematic sites may, of course, also include reference to animals or the part of systems of symbolism that involve animals. In many cases the interpretation of such sites is elusive. In some cases, for example that of Namoratunga (see Fig. 6.10), we do have information that links the geometric designs directly to animal referents, since the designs represent cattle branding (Lynch & Robbins 1977, Lynch & Donahue 1980). The schematic rock art sites at Lukenya Hill in eastern Kenya, Leshuta Ol-pul in Entonyoosoita Hills in Narok District (Gramly 1975, Pl. II), and Samburu sites at Lodung'okwe (Odak 1981) are also connected with cattle.

Problems of origins and interpretation

Some of the schematic art mentioned above is known to have been executed by recent or modern local peoples of the areas. However, it is difficult to attribute any of the early Kenyan rock art to any particular group of modern or past peoples. The paintings in the Mount Elgon area have several superimpositions which are double (one on top of another) or multiple. However, at Kabaragutwa (Fig. 6.8) there is one fresh dotted motif in white from which the early brown dots are easily distinguishable. This clearly shows some continuity over time in the tradition of painting groups of dots. Similar conclusions can be drawn with reference to cup-marks. At Kebaroti sites several of the cup-marks within the same cluster of a panel are more heavily patinated than in other sections of the panels (e.g. Ng'oina and Kebaroti II sites). These differences in patination are an apparent indication that two or more different time periods were involved. Furthermore, the differences in patterns of cup-mark arrangements at different sites imply execution by more than one group,

Figure 6.7 Engravings at Surima Water Hole, northern Kenya (after Adamson 1966).

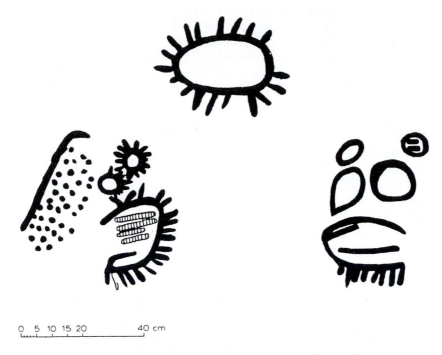

0 5 10 15 20   40 cm

Figure 6.8 Some of the paintings at Kabaragutwa (from Odak 1977b).

probably at different times. On the other hand, the engravings at Wagevella and Matsingulu in western Kenya appear to belong to one general tradition and show more or less equal degrees of patination. It is, therefore, probable that the engravings were made by the same people, although not by the Maragoli people, resident nowadays around the site's location, who deny any knowledge of the art. Their execution could have extended over a long period of time.

The paintings at Kipkul Kul site (Odak 1986) have almost equal degrees of freshness and were, therefore, probably done by the same people at the same time. The likelihood of this is reinforced by the small numbers of figures at the site. The interrelationship between dating and interpretation is highlighted by the Goti Chaki site which belongs to the Gusii tradition of petroglyphs. At the level of interpretation the site as a whole provides an impression of the sky with several planets, stars, and other heavenly bodies arranged in particular patterns. However, if one is to interpret it as a whole, one has to take into account that the engravings were produced by different people at different times. Based on the analysis of the styles of the engravings and the degree of patination, it is possible to say that the large cup-marks, flower figures, 'flying objects', and certain other figures were executed earlier than the tiny 'holes', scratches, and dots. Although it is possible that at some time the representations became a representation of the universe, it would be invalid to conclude that this theme motivated the original representations.

From the way in which animals are represented in Kenyan rock art and the observable socio-cultural realities of the local people, there is no doubt that different styles of rock art exist in different parts of the country that could relate to ethnic differences. This can be seen, for example, by examining the different degrees of stylization in which animals and humans are represented in different parts of the country. Based on this variable alone one can distinguish three main styles.

The first is the extreme stylization of animals: here the trunk is represented by a horizontal line which ends in a dot for the head and four vertical lines extending from these horizontal lines to depict the legs (Fig. 6.9). In this style humans are represented with a long vertical line representing the trunk which ends in a dot for the head. From the vertical trunk at the upper side of the figure extend two lines on opposite sides, to represent arms, and two more at the lower end to represent legs (Fig. 6.10). This style is found among the pastoralist Samburu, especially in rock shelters recently used as meat feasting sites. It is also found at Kangetet and Fock's Farm (Soper 1968).

Secondly, animals may be stylized with emphasis on one part of the body only. Here it is possible to recognize the species of animal represented. This style is found mainly in the Mount Elgon area (e.g. at Kimothon).

Thirdly, there is a form of petroglyph stylization where humans have the four limbs, plus one long line extending from between the legs which appears to represent a giant penis (Fig. 6.11).

These three methods of stylization were used as a medium of representing animals and humans in Kenyan figurative art, and the occurrence of such representations at different sites within particular regions should permit the delineation of distribution areas of one particular style. However, since one style can be found modified in different sites within an area, the whole area is, in fact, represented by one overall set of styles, which is itself evidence of one common ideology. The local variations manifested at individual sites may signify local modifications of that ideology. From the above it would follow that an intensive study of the manner of figurative representation should permit the delineation of sub-styles within the stick-figure genre.

Similarly, recurrent combinations of attributes within one general locality can lead to the delineation of a particular regional style. Thus, in an area such as Mount Elgon we would expect stylistic attributes, such as the distinctive representation of animals and humans; and the representation of humans in particular relations with animals which themselves are represented in certain ways. For example, the northern Kenyan style, as represented at Surima Water Hole site, includes such attributes as engraving in pecking technique, the separate representation of animal limbs (as opposed to their being joined together as in the Mount Elgon style), the proportions of the limbs to the body, minimal stylization, and emphasis on those parts of an animal which characterize the particular species.

Each area style probably indicates one cultural group, or groups of related peoples, sharing several elements of culture since 'style is a conscious statement of group solidarity or identity' and can be used not only as a measure of social interaction but also of (social) boundaries (Franklin 1986, p. 121).

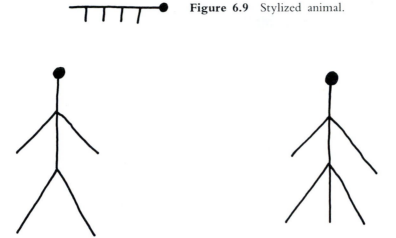

Figure 6.9 Stylized animal.

Figure 6.10 Stylized human.

Figure 6.11 Petroglyph stylization of human.

Tentative interpretation

The problem of authorship of Kenyan rock art is directly linked to issues of interpretation. The first major question to arise is why whoever executed the art did so. This question, which is related to interpretation, can be answered by trying to examine the way in which animals are represented in figurative art (Fig. 6.12).

Examination of this issue with respect to Kenyan rock art reveals that, in certain sites in the country, cattle and other animals are represented with horns drawn with considerable detail and in a frontal position. Sexually distinguishing features of the animal are exaggerated; for example, teats are depicted as prominent. Limbs are, within the Mount Elgon area, shown close together, and are short in proportion to body size. But the reverse is the case at Surima Water Hole. The Mount Elgon style emphasizes posture rather than movement, and cattle are drawn generally in attentive posture. The exception to this are the two cows at Kakapeli, which are drawn as if running away from the viewer. There is also a mole-like animal figure at the same site, which is shown as if escaping from a large pig-like creature. Both of these are shown as if in movement.

These stylistic factors may have interpretative significance. The exaggeration of horns and sexually distinguishing features could be related to a certain cult, probably the cult of horns and procreation – the latter based on representation of prominent teats, horns, and the emphasis on certain parts of the animal body. It is possible that these factors had certain ideological implications which may, or may not, be related to such a cult. On the other hand, depicting the limbs shorter than normal could easily indicate lack of interest in those aspects of animal bodies which did not have much prominence in the cult. However, other features of the animal

Figure 6.12 How animals are represented in Kenyan rock art.

representations, such as those at Surima Water Hole, may simply reflect a regional style based on local tradition.

Schematic paintings at Lukenya Hill site have been interpreted as relating to cattle brands (Gramly 1975, Figs 8,9). Similar paintings occur in the Narok District. Gramly (1975, p. 117) cites Merker's (1904) and Hobley's (1910) works which show that the cattle-brand figures of the Maasai and Kamba peoples are similar to the schematic paintings in Lukenya and Loita Hills. Although cattle branding is known to be practised by several Kenyan groups, such as the Kalenjin-speaking peoples, the Agikuyu, the Akamba, and the Maa-speaking peoples, Gramly (ibid.) concludes that 'drawing cattle brands on the walls of rock shelters appears to be confined to the regions formerly inhabited by the Maa-speaking pastoralists or presently occupied by them'. In this case, the rock shelters on whose walls such schematic art symbols appear are associated with the meat-eating feasts of the warriors.

The engravings at Namoratunga site in northern Kenya include motifs similar to those of Lukenya Hill. Research at this site has shown strong association between the symbols and Turkana people's cattle-brand systems. This is shown by the fact that the Turkana can recognize a large number of Namoratunga designs (Fig. 6.13) as symbols which they use as brands for livestock. Also, the Turkana employ a large number of designs similar to the ones at Namoratunga and, indeed, recognize many of the designs, although there is no evidence that they are the people who engraved the marks at Namoratunga site. However, if the designs were thus utilized by the then Namoratunga residents in similar manner, the art can provide insights into their social organization. It was observed that a Turkana bull was branded with several of the designs found at the site (Lynch & Robbins 1977, p. 539). Most of these schematic symbols were recognized by the Turkana as brands which had individual names. Many of the signs commonly branded on the cattle, camels, and donkeys, and other livestock in the area, are found in the rock art. Ethnographically, the signs are marks of ownership. Among the Turkana, men inherit symbols through the male line and the symbols serve to delineate lineages (Gulliver 1955). But not all animals owned by an individual receive the same signs, since the same clan owns several different designs. Many Turkana individuals possessing quite different brands but belonging to the same clan will identify their brands by a common clan name.

Archaeological excavation at Namoratunga shows that only the graves of the males are decorated with symbols, thus suggesting the relationship between males and inheritance. An animal may bear a number of different brands. The Maasai and the Pokot share a significant number of these symbols and they utilize them in similar manners. Thus Lynch & Robbins (op. cit.) discovered that the Pokot near Panyao shared at least 14 per cent of Turkana brands. A new brand could be obtained as the result of a cattle raid in which the opponent was killed and his cattle taken. This is one of the ways in which similar brands came to be used by different groups. Shared brands strongly suggests common origin or historical relationship.

Conclusions

The different ways in which animals are represented in Kenyan rock art, and the way in which humans are depicted, can provide clues to interpretation. But there

Figure 6.13 Some motifs from Namoratunga site.

are serious problems when we try to interpret figurative and schematic art which appears together within the same panel. First, one has to contend with the depiction of animals in particular relationships with each other; secondly, the animal figures may have some special relationship with the schematic art of the same period. Thirdly, there is the possibility of a meaningful relationship between animals, humans, and schematic figures of the same time period. Finally, there is the actual nature of the temporal relationship between schematic figures and figurative art as manifested in superimpositions. The relationship between colours and the local availability of raw material for such colours must also be considered.

The interpretation of schematic art poses even further problems. We have seen that certain cup-marks had particular significance (e.g. as games). Other signs may also have functioned as means of communication, e.g. the Gisambai petroglyphs, and those designs representing cattle brands. It is also possible that the manner in which figures are represented on a rock-shelter panel, and the degree of complexity of particular motifs in schematic representations, reflect aspects of the cognitive structures of the societies that produced them. However, we are still very far from being able to confidently interpret the relationship between figurative and schematic art in Kenyan rock art.

Notes

1 'Radiated' or 'rayed' as used here is synonymous to 'sun-figure' which means a circle or circles from whose circumference extend lines (e.g. Fig. 6.14a or b). This is also synonymous to externally radiated (or rayed) circles.
2 Internally radiated circle or oval, as used here, means a circle from whose internal circumference lines extend (e.g. Fig. 6.14c).
3 Circles with gear-like structure, as used here, means a situation where two or more circles with rays join together (e.g. Fig. 6.14d).

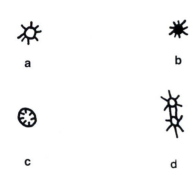

a

b

c

d

Figure 6.14 Circular designs in Kenyan schematic art.

References

Adamson, J. 1966. Rock engravings near Lake Rudolf. *Journal of the East African and Ugandan Natural History Society* **XIX** (1) 70–1.

Fosbrooke, H. A. 1954. Further light on rock engravings in Northern Tanganyika. *Man* **LIV**, 157.

Franklin, N. R. 1986. Stochastic vs emblemic: an archaeologically useful method for the analysis of style in Australian rock art. *Rock art research* **3**, (2) 121–40.

Gramly, R. M. 1975. Meat feasting sites and cattle brands: patterns of rock shelter utilisation in East Africa. *Azania* **X**, 107–21.

Gulliver, P. H. 1955. *The family herds*. London: Routledge & Kegan Paul.

Hobley, C. W. 1910. *Ethnology of the A-Kamba and other East African tribes*. Cambridge: Cambridge University Press.

Lynch, M. & J. Donahue 1980. Statistical analysis of two rock art sites in northwest Kenya. *Journal of Field Archaeology* **7**.

Lynch, M. & L. N. Robbins 1977. Animal brands and interpretation of rock art in East Africa. *Current Anthropology* **18**, 538–9.

Merker, M. 1904. *Die Maasai*. Berlin: Dietrich Reimer.

Odak, O. 1977a. Kakapeli and other rock paintings in the Western Highlands of Rift Valley. *Azania* **XII**, 187–92.

Odak, O. 1977b. *Some pictographs in the western highlands of Kenya (and other related rock art sites in the Country)*. Seminar paper no. 77, Institute of African Studies, University of Nairobi.

Odak, O. 1980. Preliminary report of field work in West Kenya. *Nyame Akuma* **16**.

Odak, O. 1981. *Archaeological method and ethnographic analogy: evidence from a pastoral society in Kenya*. Proceedings of 8th Pan-African Congress, Nairobi. *Tilimiap*. (Kenyatta, 1984).

Odak, O. 1986. Interpretation of West Kenya schematic rock art. In *Cultural attitudes to animals, including birds, fish and invertebrates*. World Archaeological Congress, vol. 2 (mimeo).

Soper, R. C. 1966. Cup-marks and grinding grooves. *Azania* **I**, 155.

Soper, R. C. 1968. Petroglyphs in Northern Kenya. *Azania* **III**, 189–91.

Townshend, P. 1979. Mankala in Eastern and Southern Africa: a distributional analysis. *Azania* **XIV**, 108–38.

Wright, R. 1961. Painted rock shelters on Mount Elgon. *Proceedings of the Prehistoric Society* **XXVII**, 28–34.

7 Finding symbols in history

WHITNEY DAVIS

Some notoriously demanding passages of Wittgenstein's *Philosophical investigations* (1968) raise a sceptical puzzle that any theories or histories of human symbol-making will ignore at their peril. Stated in one of its strongest forms (and not worrying about Wittgenstein's own exact sense), it is this: although some overt behaviour may represent (e.g. denote or depict) something to you and me, having a conventional 'meaning' for us in a 'language' we share, there is no guarantee that, and no final test to determine whether, that same overt behaviour – as we could ever perceive and study it – 'means' the same thing, or anything at all, to someone else. For example, you and I might represent something by the way in which we blink our eyes and grunt; however, someone else is *just* blinking and grunting. Or, to take Kripke's example (1982, pp. 8–9), by writing the mark/sign '+' you and I 'mean' the addition function or 'plus', but for someone else the same sign '+' actually means something else, say, 'quus' – a function in which x quus $y = x$ plus y, if x, y are less than 57, but otherwise (always) = 5. Obviously, you and I could not even tell that our 'rule' for using '+' diverges from his in any (qu)adding of integers less than 57; we do not detect that his (or our?) rule is 'bent' (Blackburn 1984). We can imagine other, perhaps even more extreme, examples in which *no possible test we could ever make* would ever settle the possibility that our practices diverge or, more profoundly, that one of us actually lacks 'practice' altogether (see Davis n.d.).

In this chapter I cannot explore all the implications of the sceptical puzzle (see Kripke 1982) for art history and the anthropology or archaeology of symbols. For my purposes, I simply assert that no empirical or experimental scrutiny of a behaviour (like grunting) or a morphology (like a mark) 'on the ground' or 'in front of our noses', as it were, can definitively establish that it is a sign (symbol, representation) and/or what its referent might be for its producer. Because it *looks like* a picture does not mean it *is*; because it *seems* to depict my dog does not mean it *does*. We need to know something *further* about it. I will interweave a specific form of the sceptical puzzle, applicable to visual depictions as considered by art historians, with a specific kind of answer or avoidance manoeuvre. However, I hope it will be obvious that my strategy, suitably rewritten, could be made fully general; it can be phrased for *any* symbols.

Twenty-five thousand or more years ago, for the first time someone entered the cave of Gargas, a small self-contained cavern at an elevation close to 700 m, near the present-day village of Aventignan in the French Pyrenees. Within 50 m of the entrance, the cave became fairly dark, and at 100 m, making a turn to the left, completely so; our visitor lighted his way with oil or fat burning in a stone lamp. Fortunately, the cave was smooth and dry, though from time to time animals had inhabited it. The sharp-clawed cave bear had even scratched on its walls. Although our visitor may have known other caves in the region, we do not know what purposes animated his first visit to Gargas. But one of his actions – and, of course, perhaps one of his purposes – was to draw, or, more precisely, to make marks (Leroi-Gourhan 1967, pp. 307–8, Barrière 1976, 1984).

Oozing from hidden fissures, water carrying fine silts of calcium carbonate had deposited panels of moist *Montmilch* on many surfaces of the cave. With his fingers together, our visitor gouged straight and curving traces, or, with one finger only, traced somewhat more complicated zigzags and swirls (Barrière 1976). We cannot say exactly how long this activity was kept up – perhaps for generations (the fundamental general study is Bednarik 1986). Finally, someone traced a simple line in the minimal form of a bison's forequarters – its horns, head, and muzzle (e.g. Barrière 1976, Vol. I, p. 151, for such images). Later, the whole outline was drawn, including details of eyes, fetlocks, and hooves, and incised with a sharp stone on the harder surfaces of the cave walls. Horses, reindeer, various species of antelope, and other animals were depicted with increasing differentiation, detail, and modulation, and in individually recognizable styles. At least for this people in this part of the world, about 20 000 BC, image-making had been born.

It is the ring of inevitability in this narrative I wish to subvert – or, more exactly, its sufficiency in helping us to understand what it could be for image-making *to be* born. For although I accept that some narrative of the crystallization of symbolic technologies and conventions underwrites the history of all arts, and by some is regarded *as* the history of art, the status of these 'first' images in traditions is puzzling.

I must make the obvious reminder that the cave of Gargas is not *the* origin of image-making. It is being used here as *one example* of how image-making originates. Images were certainly made elsewhere and perhaps earlier, like the simple but seemingly unmistakable depictions of animals on portable limestone blocks from rock shelters in the Perigord, the earliest dated to about 30 000 BC (Delluc & Delluc 1978), or other animal figures painted on stone from the Apollo XI Cave in Namibia, dated at the earliest to about 24 000 BC (Lewis-Williams 1983, Figs 42–3; Willcox 1984, pp. 231–7). We cannot know whether images were made by earlier hominids in a perishable medium, like bark painting or sand drawing. In the preserved media, *Homo sapiens neanderthalensis* produced non-figurative graphics (e.g. Marshack 1976), and on the present view, image-making is associated with the technologically 'modern' Upper Palaeolithic culture of *H. sapiens sapiens*. In fact, *sapiens sapiens* has often been defined as just that creature which makes images and uses other complex symbol systems (Preziosi 1982, Davis 1986). But for our purposes, the whole question of the absolutely 'first' image in chronological terms is a red herring.

Although they were broadly related to and descended from earlier Upper Palaeolithic people, there is no direct evidence that the people of Gargas had learned about earlier images. (However, they did make other *kinds* of images; the wall engravings are in part 'dated' by a tendentious association with one figure on incised plaquettes found in the cave.) Theoretically, a feral child or a Robinson Crusoe, completely cut off from society or tradition, or both, could make images (Davis n.d.); theoretically, image-making inaugurates time and time again in history. Though Gargas is a useful example, the same general puzzles arise for *any* real inaugural image-making, whenever and wherever we find it archaeologically.

For an inaugural image, our problem is not external – the problem of identifying its stylistic affiliations or formal sources – but, rather, internal. Since he had never seen one before, how did the first image-maker *know* how to make an image? By hypothesis, no one had told him what they are or how they can be used.

Now in our initial narrative, the visitor to the cave simply began tracing lines resembling the silhouettes of bison, horses, and other creatures. But this description fails to come to grips with two issues. First, as a projection of a three-dimensional object, a two-dimensional visual display is *ambiguous*. According to any standard of projective fidelity, it can correctly represent any number of different real objects (Hagen 1986). What, then, accounts for the particular judgement that, for example, a square depicts a cube and not some other kind of six-sided object? (This is the kind of question the sceptical puzzle would dramatize.) Secondly, that a visual display happens to *resemble* some real object does not guarantee it *depicts* that object. (The sceptical puzzle also worries this point.) Shadows and mirror 'images' resemble the objects which produce them, but are not necessarily representations of those objects. All kinds of patterns, like Leonardo's mottled wall, resemble various objects fortuitously. (On the vexed question of resemblance-in-representation, see variously Manns 1971, Goodman 1972, Ch. 1, Tversky & Gati 1978.) How is it, then, that the simple curves in the cave of Gargas, resembling animal profiles (as well as resembling many other things), were also apparently taken to *stand for* just those aspects of animals? How is it, in other words, that we could recognize them as images?

The obvious answer to both questions is that the marks in Gargas, whatever they may look like to us, were (or were not) *produced as* depictions of particular objects. However, this answer provokes a vicious regress. It seems to imply that the image-maker already knows *what an image is* and *how to produce it*. Where was this knowledge acquired? Unqualified, this 'conventionalist' answer cannot apply to the *first* image-maker (see Davis 1987, and for a potential solution to the paradoxes and regresses of conventionalism, Lewis 1967).

Let us look more carefully at what was happening in Gargas. Non-depictional tracing – the 'digital flutings' and scribbles made with one or more fingers in the soft *Montmilch* – accumulated on the walls, covering long panels. The tracing has internal rhythms of its own. Although a good deal more should be said about it, for our purposes some fraction of it results in marks which can be *seen as* certain objects – like panels of digital tracing thought by some observers to contain animal forms (e.g. Barrière 1976, Vol. I, p. 136, Pls 23, 35, 39). Similar complex and suggestive marking can be found in other archaeological contexts, for instance, among the incised blocks of the Perigord (Delluc & Delluc 1978, 1985), and, of course, in the scribbling of simians (e.g. Schiller 1951, Morris 1961, Smith 1973; see generally Davis 1986, 1987). That such marks in some contexts *can* be mistaken for real things derives directly from the fact that the perceptual system sometimes arrives at mistaken interpretations of the information it picks up in reflected light (Gibson 1979, Marr 1982); although it is in itself a complex phenomenon, for our purposes we can take 'seeing-as' to be an 'automatic' (autonomic) operation of the visual system responding to perceptual ambiguity (Wilkerson 1973a, Wollheim 1980, pp. 205–26, Budd 1986).

Like any psychological event, if it has no overt manifestations, seeing-as is inaccessible to direct observation. Whether it occurred ten seconds or 10 000 years ago, it is, as it were, 'outside' history – that is, the material evidence of overt human behaviour as it is preserved in a fragmentary way in the archaeological record of actions performed and things made. Although it took place *in* history, seeing-as often has no history.

Recall now that just because someone momentarily sees a mark as an object is not enough for it to *depict* that object. In the flickering semi-darkness, our visitor to the cave may have momentarily mistaken some of the marks – whether made by him or anyone else – as animal forms, but they were not necessarily thereby *representations* of animals.

Still, if he looked again, our visitor could at least learn that what he took to be something else is just and only a mark, morphologically indiscernible as it might be from any of the marks he (or anyone else) had been making all along, for whatever purpose or lack of purpose. In this, he would already learn that he can make the mark not just and only *as a mark* but also as a mark which can be seen *as an object*. If and when he re-makes that or that kind of mark *for* seeing-as – knowing it is just a mark but interested in its object-resembling properties – then he is making an image (see in detail Davis n.d.) Mark becomes remark. And in so far as this marking and remarking is a kind of making and remaking, it has a history: we can find it archaeologically.

We will never know, then, whether many of the tracings in Gargas were ever seen as objects. Their recognizability *to us* as images (or not) is – as the sceptical puzzle reminds us – no evidence one way or another; *our* seeing-as may have nothing to do with someone else's. Furthermore, we do not even know why the *marks*, seen-as or not, were being made in the first place – perhaps, as Barrière (1976) and many others have supposed, merely as 'spontaneous graffitomania' (see Bednarik 1986).

But for some tracings, we *can* observe the continual *replication* of an object-resembling mark. At Gargas, drawn vertically, a double S-curve can be seen as the curving horns, forehead and muzzle, and neck of a bison. Drawn horizontally, the same curve can be seen as the horns, humped back, and rising tail or descending hindquarters (e.g. Barrière 1976, Vol. I, Fig. 43, nos 10, 11). Gargas exhibits a good deal of replication and variation of this particular form. The curves are repeated in the whole or in part of their length to give two horns; two curves are placed at angles to each other to produce a half- or two-thirds-complete outline; the final flips of each curve can be neatly fitted or superimposed; fingerholes establish an eye; a few strokes create legs or tail; the whole contour may be finished off by a second horizontal (ventral) curve below the first (dorsal) one (Davis 1987, Fig. 10). *As marks*, these elaborations are indiscernible from what had already appeared in (hypothetically) non-depictional or even non-semantic tracing. We can infer that they were, in fact, being made *for* seeing-as, i.e. as images, because in replication the object-resembling properties were preserved in the transition from surface to surface or the translation from one tool and medium to another. (Similarly, we could infer they were being made as 'notations' if other kinds of properties, like the discreteness and disjunction of 'characters', were held constant in use and re-use, in replication; see Marshack 1977, 1984.) But, to reiterate, the very first mark in this and the other replicatory sequences was not made as an image but only as a mark.

Although this analysis solves the logical paradox of regress, it has potentially troublesome implications. Because of the possibility of ambiguity, fortuitous resemblance, and the variability of seeing-as, no amount of study of the visual properties of a mark can definitively tell us whether it is an image, and precisely what it is an image of. Despite the apparently bizarre consequences of this result (surely we just *know* that the Sistine Chapel paintings are images – otherwise what in the world could they be doing up there?), *an interpreter must know the whole chain of replication and variation of all the properties of the mark right back to the initial moment of seeing-as in his or in someone else's 'psychological' experience*. For depiction, this claim is a close (but not exact) parallel for so-called 'causal' or 'historical' theories of the reference of proper names and natural kind terms (Putnam 1975, Schwartz 1977, Evans 1979, Kripke 1980, Devitt 1982); in the successful production and perception of symbolic reference, an interpreter does not so much have a correct and complete 'description for' or 'belief about' a sign (Russell 1956 is the *locus classicus*) as a more or less hazy understanding of its *history* of first application ('baptism'), transmission, and change. If I may hideously oversimplify (see David n.d.), he does not so much *decipher* as *excavate* a language. The point, of course, applies to someone within *or* outside a particular community of language-users or sign-makers.

Now sometimes we can study this whole closed cycle of production, from 'baptism' on, in an experimental setting – with simians in a laboratory, infants in a playpen, or draughtsmen in a workshop. Most important, we can observe ourselves at work: *we* can see our *own* images (notations, etc.) for what they are images (notations) of, irrespective of someone else's ability to pick this up. Otherwise, however, it will be difficult to identify the sequence and structure of the relevant chains of replication.

For one thing, each variant in a chain is necessarily separated from preceding and following variants by some span of space or lag of time. An interpreter's archaeological survey of sign production has to be extremely comprehensive to pick them all up. For another, some properties of the morphology are reproduced in succeeding variants, often becoming inextricably incorporated (drawn over or built into the latest variant), while others, *not* reproduced, are abandoned or destroyed. We are left archaeologically with a complex morphology, presenting itself as a single unitary 'artefact', which is simultaneously a selection and palimpsest of many variations – and the garbage of the studio contains a good deal of what we would like to know.

It is the task of so-called 'archaeopsychology' or 'palaeosemiotics' to sort out these relations: archaeopsychology becomes *the interpretation of both dimensions of the artefact–sign, and especially of the interrelation or identity of artefactuality and representationality, on the basis of formal theories about this interrelation and pursuing direct or indirect evidence for it in well-defined cultural and historical contexts*. Although it is obvious that this task requires rigorously formulated and, in some manner or other, empirically or theoretically defensible theories about both representation (e.g. semiosis; interpretation; reference) and artefactuality (e.g. morphology; style; sequence and distribution), it will be enormously complex; admitting both evolutionary and cultural-relativistic premises, perhaps no fully general assertions will be possible.

At any rate, at Gargas and in other unusual art historical or archaeological cases, we can sometimes circumvent the immediate difficulties. Because the palaeolithic engraver was removing matter from a surface rather than adding to it, he could not easily change or erase his work; it tends to accumulate in one place. We can, therefore, watch a chain of replications forming as a palimpsest with an internal 'stratigraphy' all the way back to the initial variation of a non-depictional trace. For instance, in the deepest chamber of Gargas, the 'Panel of the Great Bull' (Barrière 1976, Vol. II, Pl. 56, etc.) exhibits many complete and incomplete animal forms super-imposed on one another. Individual lines are re-used to establish new images. Several images can share a single line. (We would not predict such morphologies if superim-position were 'random', i.e. with the later engraver taking no account of the work of the earlier.) A number of more complete forms can be resolved, but some seem to be arrested in replicatory development – an elk with a subtly modulated contour; horses with forehead or muzzle apparently attempted twice, or redrawn by a later artist; two bison; a heavily worked ibex with outline deeply scraped and interior filled in, with three 'versions' of its head; and the Great Bull himself, created partly by a carved line and partly by a much finer incised line, perhaps preliminary to heavier cutting (see Davis n.d., Ch. 1, Sect. 8, for 'chains of replication' in Aurignacian and pre-Magdalenian portable and parietal graphics).

Replication is simply the sequential production of similar artefacts substitutable for one another in some specific context of use (Davis n.d.). The general notion of a chain of replications, somewhat parallel to linguistic philosophers' concept of a 'history of reference' (Kripke 1980, p. 95) or 'designation chain' (Devitt 1982), goes by various names already in art history and archaeology. For example, Kubler (1962) called it a 'form class', descending from a 'prime object', an artefact with no formal antecedents. It is perhaps equivalent to what some art historians mean by style, a set of similarities among artefacts explained by their common historical descent (Davis 1988), although style encompasses artefacts which do not represent (reference neces-sarily has a style, but not vice versa) (Davis n.d., Ch. 2). A variety of sophisticated formal, comparative, and statistical methods are required to understand these chains, classes, or sets (e.g. Sneath & Sokal 1973, Clarke 1978, Hennig 1979).

Often we assume, circularly, that some property of a visual display does or should signify something, perhaps because similar-looking properties in other displays do. We make up a psychological event – a perceptual episode, a belief or intention or rule – to account for it. But as the possibility of ambiguity and of fortuitous resemblance entails, we cannot know in advance *which* property of the display was seen as some-thing else and what this something exactly was. On my analysis, depiction occurs *within* a chain of replications. Therefore the interpretation of any image is *necessarily* historical: it requires that the interpreter should know how the mark/sign was pro-duced and how its various properties were seen/interpreted. Surely, in a sense this is good news for art history: it provides us with a strictly logical justification for the very existence of art history itself.

However, there is bad news built in here: the epistemic conditions for inter-pretability are extremely strict, and the evidence generally poor. *Without* full archaeological knowledge of its history, the interpreter cannot be certain what a mark signifies. More worrying still, the initial moment of seeing-as itself, investing the whole chain with that particular significance, as a psychological event is actually inaccessible to direct archaeological investigation. It can only be reconstructed infer-entially as that perceptual episode (whether or not it is *our* episode or recognizable to us) which would best explain the whole package of formal and contextual properties of the chain.

Emile Durkheim (1938, p. 104) wrote 'every time a social phenomenon is directly explained by a psychological phenomenon, we may be sure the explanation is false' – and, indeed, there has been a tendency in modern anthropology to see 'rules' or 'codes' of interpretation as somehow suprapsychological, in 'the culture' or some other reified supra-individual entity. Without worrying about the metapsychological questions, in ordinary social situations people do readily infer or learn the relevant archaeological knowledge about making marks – just as they learn how the words of a language have been and are to be used. Images are labelled; their properties are pointed out; particular denotations and connotations are socially discussed. Supposedly this knowledge becomes conventional or institutional. The social group takes it for granted that certain properties of a visual display are to be interpreted in a certain way; 'rules' and 'codes', as it were, come to replace actual historical understanding and investigation. As art historians, our task is simply to reconstruct that local common knowledge about images. One strand in the so-called social history of art – although not explicitly Durkheimian – has set out to do just that (although with literally hundreds of versions, the *locus classicus* is still Baxandall 1972).

I have been using the example of a palaeolithic cave in part to suggest that if conventional knowledge about images and the archaeology of their production is vastly removed from us, then our interpretative task is just that much harder and the results that much less complete. Despite intriguing speculation (e.g. Leroi-Gourhan 1967, Conkey 1983), we really have no idea exactly in what sense the cave drawings and paintings represented aspects of their makers' world. The images of folk, 'outsider', or 'eccentric' artists, of other cultural marginals, or of the mad are similarly detached, in varying degrees, from conventional routines of interpretation; their significance is equally hard to reconstruct (I do not claim, of course, that their significance is *like* that of prehistoric art). But these are platitudes, pointing only to the practical limitations of art historical or other 'archaeological' evidence. In so far as such images *are* images at all, they are part of a chain of replications; in theory, they have *some* history establishing *some* signification. But I have been making a stronger claim. With a first image, wherever and whenever we find it, there *is* no pre-existing history of replication to anchor it, no history of interpretation in which it is deciphered. It is, as it were, a novel remark in an unknown language. (Although I will not develop the point, it seems to me that all accounts of images in a 'tradition', which in a way postpone the 'diachronic' problem of origins for a 'synchronic' or 'structural' analysis, are exposed to the sceptical puzzle and concomitant difficulties of conventionalism; recent art historical writing – e.g. Sauerländer 1983, Clark 1985 – problematizes the notion of 'tradition' or 'art history'.)

Palaeolithic images on portable blocks or cave walls may be the first images in some absolute chronological sense, but this is inessential to the argument. Through-out history, chains of replication are continuously inaugurated in novel episodes of 'seeing-as'. Many of these chains are firmly embedded in existing practices, guided by rules like those in the modern West for perspective projection. These are undoubted realities of social life – about the power of institutions – to be explained in a variety of ways. But there is no *logical* restriction on when and where seeing-as will take place – no restrictions on the mark or which object-resembling properties can be replicated, or even, of course, on how resemblance itself is judged. Wherever and whenever people make marks, or work matter in any way, a visual form may take on, inaugurally, semantic significance of any kind.

Let us put together our results. Art historians often assume that images are readily recognizable as such, somehow in advance of art historical research *on* and interpretation *of* them. However, *it is a kind of art history – the archaeology of replication – which establishes them as images in the first place*. To understand what an image signifies, an interpreter must know exactly in what way the properties of a visual display were produced for seeing-as. Because of the possibility of ambiguity and of fortuitous resemblance, no amount of inspecting the display itself, 'empirically' recording its 'attributes', can possibly provide this information. The interpreter must have what I called 'archaeological' knowledge about the replication of seeing-as. Such knowledge is often co-ordinated conventionally and passed on institutionally, although this is hardly even a reliable generality and there are no promises about how easy it will be to reconstruct any part of the history. It might be enough to determine that the physical properties and context of the artefact (its apparent morphology, distribution, mode of manufacture, deposition, or preservation, etc.) are most compellingly and comprehensively explained by supposing that it is a sign and/or a sign with such-and-such a representational value. Of course, without even knowing the precise meaning of the sign, we can still make useful, pointed statements, or collect information, about the 'archaeological' place of apparently representational activity in a society – e.g. about its chronology, frequency, distribution, socio-economic or other behavioural correlates, and so forth. But however it is codified by its users or reconstructed by us, knowledge about images is anchored inaugurally in a psychological event 'outside history', the moment of taking a mark for something in the world, forever inaccessible to us archaeologically.

I do not feel threatened by this result and hope for an archaeology vigorously embracing, rather than avoiding, it. By phrasing the problems of art history or an anthropology of symbols as I have done here, I am merely questioning a conception of art history as a fully *empirical* enterprise – the usual positivism awkwardly accompanying a final mysticism. We can certainly gather the facts about the making of marks, and image-making is something people do with the marks they have made; the more empirical precision about both, the better. But when mark first becomes image, when a mark remarks, there is no fact of the matter to be located archaeologically.

What kind of history or archaeology is it that could never dig up and display its central event? It is, I think, a history which necessarily offers not only the facts about its objects but also *a theory about itself* – a systematic organizing hypothesis, like those of Darwin or Freud, about how the present inherits its form from the past and why the past is, or is not, coherent. On my account, symbolic meaning is a particular function of how the present inherits its forms – it is a form of the archaeological coherence of making. 'Seeing-as' and 'replication' might remind us in various ways of mutation and selection, or trauma and repetition. My own hunch is that this hypothesis, whatever its final form, will arise for art history from the study of perception and visual cognition, and for other sign systems from the study of other cognitive domains. Be that as it may, symbols without history are a puzzle only when history is without theory.

Acknowledgements

This chapter was provoked in part by my reading as Chair (unfortunately, *in absentia*) of papers in the session 'Ethnographic and other interpretations of human and animal representation in prehistoric art' at the World Archaeological Congress, 1986. The text was delivered in a somewhat different version as a paper for the symposium 'Art without history' at the Annual Meeting of the College Art Association, Boston, February 1987, along with a related paper by P. J. Ucko (1987). I thank Ucko for intensive discussion of many points.

References

Barrière, C. 1976. *L'art pariétal paléolithique de la grotte de Gargas*. BAR Supplementary Volume 14 (2 Vols). Oxford: British Archaeological Reports.

Barrière, C. 1984. Gargas. In *L'art des cavernes: Atlas des grottes ornées paléolithiques françaises*, A. Leroi-Gourhan (ed.), 514–22. Paris: Imprimerie Nationale/Ministère de la Culture.

Baxandall, 1972. *Painting and experience in fifteenth century Italy*. Oxford: Oxford University Press.

Bednarik, R. J. 1986. Parietal finger markings in Europe and Australia. *Rock Art Research* **3**, 30–61.

Blackburn, S. 1984. *Spreading the word: groundings in the philosophy of language*. Oxford: Clarendon.

Budd, M. 1986. Wittgenstein on seeing aspects. *Mind* **96**, 1–17.

Clark, T. J. 1985. *The painting of modern life: Paris in the art of Manet and his followers*. New York: Knopf.

Clarke, D. 1978. *Analytical archaeology*, 2nd edn. New York: Columbia University Press.

Conkey, M. W. 1983. On the origins of palaeolithic art: a review and some critical thoughts. In *The Mousterian legacy: human biocultural change in the Upper Pleistocene*, E. Trinkaus (ed.), 201–27 BAR International Series 164. Oxford: British Archaeological Reports.

Davis, W. 1986. The origins of image making. *Current Anthropology* **27**, 193–215.

Davis, W. 1987. Replication and depiction in palaeolithic art. *Representations* **19**, 109–44.

Davis, W. 1988. Style and history in art history. In *The uses of style in archaeology*, M. W. Conkey & C. Halstorf (eds), in press. Cambridge: Cambridge University Press.

Davis, W. n.d. *Seeing through culture: the possibility of the history of art*, in press.

Delluc, B. & G. Delluc 1978. Les manifestations graphiques aurignaciennes sur support rocheux des environs des Eyzies (Dordogne). *Gallia Préhistoire* **21**, 213–438.

Delluc, B. & G. Delluc 1985. De l'empreinte au signe. *Dossiers de l'archéologie* **90**, 56–62.

Devitt, M. 1982. *Designation*. New York: Columbia University Press.

Durkheim, E. 1938. *The rules of sociological method*. Chicago: University of Chicago Press.

Evans, G. 1979. *Varieties of reference*. Oxford: Clarendon.

Gibson, J. J. 1979. *The ecological theory of perception*. Boston: Houghton Mifflin.

Goodman, N. 1972. *Languages of art: an approach to the theory of symbols*, 2nd edn. Indianapolis: Bobbs–Merrill.

Hagen, M. 1986. *Varieties of realism*. Cambridge: Cambridge University Press.

Hennig, W. 1979. *Phylogenetic systematics*, (trans. D. D. Davis & R. Zangerl). Urbana, Ill.: University of Illinois Press.

Kripke, S. 1980. *Naming and necessity*, 2nd edn. Cambridge, Mass.: Harvard University Press.

Kripke, S. 1982. *Wittgenstein on rules and private language*. Cambridge, Mass.: Harvard University Press.

Kubler, G. 1962. *The shape of time: remarks on the history of things*. New Haven, Conn.: Yale University Press.

Leroi-Gourhan, A. 1967. *Treasures of prehistoric art*, (trans. N. Guterman). New York: Abrams.

Lewis, D. 1967. *Convention: a philosophical study*. Cambridge, Mass.: Harvard University Press.

Lewis-Williams, J. D. 1983. *The rock art of southern Africa*. Cambridge: Cambridge University Press.

Manns, J. W. 1971. Representation, relativism, and resemblance. *Journal of Aesthetics and Art Criticism* **11**, 281–7.

Marr, D. 1982. *Vision: a computational investigation into the human representation and processing of visual information*. San Francisco/New York: Freeman.

Marshack, A. 1976. Some implications of the Palaeolithic symbolic evidence for the origin of language. *Current Anthropology* **17**, 274–82.

Marshack, A. 1977. The meander as a system: the analysis and recognition of iconographic units in Upper Palaeolithic compositions. In *Form in indigenous art*, P. J. Ucko (ed.), 286–317. Canberra: Australian Institute of Aboriginal Studies.

Marshack, A. 1984. Concepts théoriques conduisant à de nouvelles méthodes analytiques, de nouveaux procédés de recherche et catégories de données. *L'Anthropologie* **88**, 85–100.

Morris, D. 1961. *The biology of art: a study of the picture-making behaviour of the great apes and its relationship to human art*. New York: Knopf.

Preziosi, D. 1982. Constru(ct)ing the origins of art. *Art Journal* **42**, 320–5.

Putnam, H. 1975. The meaning of 'meaning'. In *Mind, language, and reality: philosophical papers II*. Cambridge: Cambridge University Press.

Russell, B. 1956. *Logic and knowledge*, R. C. Marsh (ed.). London: Allen & Unwin.

Sauerländer, W. 1983. From stilus to style: reflections on the fate of a notion. *Art History* **6**, 253–70.

Schiller, P. 1951. Figural preferences in the drawings of a chimpanzee. *Journal of Comparative and Physiological Psychology* **44**, 101–11.

Schwartz, S. (ed.) 1977. *Naming, necessity, and natural kinds*. Ithaca, New York: Cornell University Press.

Smith, D. A. 1973. Systematic study of chimpanzee drawing. *Journal of Comparative and Physiological Psychology* **82**, 406–14.

Sneath, P. H. A. & R. R. Sokal 1973. *Principles of numerical taxonomy*, 2nd edn. San Francisco: Freeman.

Tversky, A. & I. Gati 1978. Studies of similarity. In *Cognition and categorization*, E. Rosch & B. Lloyd (eds), 79–98. Hillsdale, NJ: Erlbaum.

Ucko, P. J. 1987. Débuts illusoires dans l'étude de la tradition artistique. *Préhistoire Ariégoise* **XLIII**, 15–81.

Wilkerson, T. E. 1973a. Representation, illusion and aspects. *British Journal of Aesthetics* **18**, 45–58.

Wilkerson, T. E. 1973b. Seeing-as. *Mind* **82**, 481–96.

Willcox, A. 1984. *The rock art of Africa*. New York: Holmes & Meier.

Wittgenstein, L. 1968. *Philosophical investigations*, (trans. G. E. M. Anscombe), 3rd edn. Oxford: Basil Blackwell.

Wollheim, R. 1980. *Art and its objects*, 2nd edn. Cambridge: Cambridge University Press.

COMPOSITIONS: FREQUENCIES AND SCENES

8 Concepts of humans and animals in post-contact Micmac rock art

BRIAN MOLYNEAUX

Took up an Indian carrying a load of eels to market. Talked to him about his soul's salvation. Bought a dozen eels and had one fried for dinner.★

Animal metaphors in hunting and gathering cultures

Placing oneself, other humans and other animals in a coherent world is a cultural rather than a biological problem. For outside the constraints of Western taxonomy the lives of animals and humans converge, in oral and literary texts, the visual arts, dance and ritual – indeed, in virtually all forms of metaphorical communication.

If humans and animals are often metaphorical equals, however, their working relationship is much more problematic – animals are also a primary source of food. Among many groups the violation of this conceptual fellowship by killing requires some form of compensation: the hunting process may have specific rules of conduct and the processing, distribution, consumption, or disposal of the animal remains may be attended by ritual in an attempt to maintain the necessary equanimity among the species. This intellectual dilemma may be behind the extensive mythology and ritual in the boreal regions of the Northern Hemisphere concerning the bear (e.g. Hallowell 1926). The tension between the metaphorical bear 'person' and bear as food is probably enhanced by the fact that the skinned carcass of a bear looks even more human.

From this kind of evidence, it appears that the role and status of animals among hunting and gathering peoples will be somewhat ambiguous, ranging between the demands of ideology and subsistence, and relative to the place of the individual observer or participant in a social group. An attempt to understand concepts of humans and animals in a specific society, then, must consider the way that humans and animals enter each other's worlds in specific cultural contexts. And as every description of humans and animals will be modified by the context of events in which it exists, this understanding will not be a definition of some 'original' aboriginal state of human and animal being. As time passes, new interpretative events are derived from the material remnants of older ones, whether objects, texts, or images.

★ Journal of Silas Rand, a Methodist missionary, at Little Baddeck, Nova Scotia, 29 August 1866.

So at all times received information will exist as a contemporary interpretation of progressively denser and more distant remnants of the past.

The difficulty of looking for conceptual evidence about past worlds is illustrated by the conflicting ideas surrounding the degree of change in Algonkian-speaking hunting and gathering cultures in north-eastern North America after the coming of Europeans. Although the facts of the uprooting and destruction of aboriginal cultures are clear, the effect of the destruction on the cultural life of the native peoples is not. Did the replacement of a prehistoric way of life by an alien and disjunctive system result in the breakdown of conceptual continuity with the past? Or was what remained of aboriginal ideology – however diminished – still capable of being a carrier of tradition? As it was the fur trade that struck directly at the heart of aboriginal hunting and gathering cultures, changes in the cultural relationship of humans and animals may reveal the extent of more fundamental conceptual change.

Historical concepts of human and animal history

The kind of metaphorical status accorded to animals by hunting and gathering groups, emphasized by the use of ritual compensation to resolve the ideological conflict between fellowship and predation, has greatly influenced European concepts of the state of prehistoric life. The way in which these values were expressed in native rhetoric and in literary transcriptions of myths and legends from the 17th century onwards provoked an idealistic concept of the New World hunter–gatherer as a 'noble savage' in harmony with nature. This view, most clearly developed in 19th-century romanticist readings of the 18th-century social utopianism of Jean Jacques Rousseau, provided a foundation for a still persistent view that native people were 'natural' conservationists who had a traditional culture with 'an ecologically sound concept of Nature' (Martin 1978, p. 19).

Certainly, these ideas were supported by the range of ecological resources available in some regions. For example, the Micmac, an Algonkian-speaking people who inhabit the eastern maritime region of Canada from Nova Scotia to the Gaspé Peninsula, were a relatively small population distributed over a large area rich in food resources. Moose were plentiful in the marshy lowlands and caribou in the uplands of the interior forests; beaver, fish, and eels were taken from lakes and rivers; and coastal regions had extensive shellfish, fish, and sea-mammal resources. This situation led Denys (1908, p. 419) to observe in 1672 that:

> the hunting by the Indians in old times was easy for them. They killed animals only in proportion as they had need of them. When they were tired of eating one sort, they killed some of another. If they did not wish longer to eat meat, they caught some fish.

As a result of this melange of philosophical and literary traditions and eyewitness accounts of daily life, then, many observers regarded prehistoric native North American peoples as having achieved a state of balance with the natural world.

It was equally clear that as the influence of European culture increased the aboriginal community of humans and animals was disrupted and began to decline rapidly.

Along with the other north-eastern native peoples, the Micmac were faced with an economic and ideological assault, exacerbated by the diseases that had arrived before the permanent occupation of the country by Europeans (Martin 1978, p. 51). The development of the fur trade and the introduction of Christianity at the beginning of the 17th century began a process of erosion of traditional cultural values that was greatly accelerated by the flood of English settlers that began in Nova Scotia with the founding of Halifax in 1749. For at least one animal species the change was striking indeed: by the beginning of the 20th century, the caribou had been hunted to extinction.

The general picture of the post-contact history of native people was of a spiritual dystopia in which degraded and demoralized survivors presided over the last remnants of their culture, their once harmonious relationship with animals ended (cf. Martin 1978, p. 155). The severity of the change was obvious if one looked back to an utopian past, when ritual and taboo gave 'order and meaning to their universe' (ibid., p. 145).

A more optimistic view of the fur-trade period exists, however. In the midst of the devastation one can see the struggles of native people as creative responses to extraordinary stress. Drawn into the competition of the fur trade, for example, the Micmac attempted to become middlemen for the French and, in the effort, fought wars with their linguistic cousins to the west and south, the Maliseet and Abnaki (Salisbury 1982). This tradition of native entrepreneurship may even have been in place before the beginning of the 17th century in the Gulf of Maine (Borque & Whitehead 1986). In the face of English colonialism, the Micmac stoically maintained the French (Roman Catholic) faith, largely as a means of maintaining independence within the new, much more aggressive, regime (Upton 1979). And in the midst of poverty and disease in the 19th century, 'these same people were producing tea cosies in multi-hued quillwork, lavish beadwork and delicate moosehair embroidery for their European patrons' use' (Whitehead 1987) even as they were in what Whitehead calls, 'the most wretched period of their history' (Whitehead 1987).

These conflicting accounts of Micmac history leave us with a conundrum. In one view, the Micmac have been driven from their 'natural' historical path in harmony with nature during 500 years of post-contact life. In the other, the Micmac people make a more positive and pragmatic response to the ideological and economic pressures of European cultures. Is it possible to examine this question, as Martin attempts to do, 'from the Indian side of the issue' (Martin 1978, p. 154)?

The use of rock art as an ethnohistoric source

Any attempt to learn more about the 'original' prehistoric Micmac world from the archaeological record is vexed by the fact that such small, mobile groups of individuals with flexible social boundaries and networks of largely interpersonal relationships do not usually leave much material evidence. Even the Micmac pattern of ecological exploitation in prehistory is poorly known. For example, Nash (1977) could not obtain an appropriately clear faunal sample with which to refute Hoffman's

(1955) contentious view that extensive hunting of land mammals by the Micmac was a fur-trade phenomenon.

But this problem of interpretation is not necessarily one that more records or artefacts will resolve. It might be argued that post-contact history could best be seen through the first-hand experiences of native people. The problem is that not only are the documents of the past like artefacts, removed from the context of their time, but native impressions and experiences were seen only through the records of missionaries, travellers, or anthropologists. As recorders or witnesses of isolated cultural events, these observers then had to generalize their experiences in order to obtain a coherent picture.

One place that the native point of view still resides, however, is in the domain of art. Discovering that point of view is, of course, fraught with dangers: as its language is visual rather than verbal, a work of art becomes a contemporary text as soon as it is analysed. A significant advantage of art as an information source, however, is that one may view and interpret the works of an artist directly, rather than through the eyes of a later observer or intermediary.

The largest body of representational art in the north-east is a group of petroglyph sites situated on slate rocks along the shores of several lakes in Queens County, south-central Nova Scotia. The images extend back to the 18th century, and probably earlier, providing an artistic view of the Micmac post-contact experience. The fixed position of rock art within a fluid cultural landscape makes it potentially sensitive to changes in the patterns of group occupation or adaptation within a region. If differences in the form, subject, or location of images are shown to reflect changes in conceptual orientation, rock art may reflect the wider socio-economic and ideological changes in the lives of cultural groups. It might be possible, then, to use rock art in the analysis of the problem of Micmac cultural history and continuity during the last several hundred years of acculturative pressure.

Cheska (1981) has developed an interpretation of the post-contact history of Micmac culture which accords with Martin's model (1978) of conceptual decline. She has taken the Micmac rock art of Kejimkujik Lake, Nova Scotia to document changes in the Micmacs' concept of self in relation to nature, dividing it into three phases corresponding roughly to the 18th, 19th, and 20th centuries: 'identification of self with nature (respect). . .identification of self over nature (control); and. . .iden-tification of self on nature (abuse)' (Cheska 1981, p. 82). In order to determine whether or not this view of the Micmac is reasonable, I first examine the intellectual transformation of Micmac life in the early years of the European invasion and then consider to what extent this process is reflected in the way native artists pictured themselves and the animals they observed or hunted. The aim is to gain further insight into how the Micmac adapted to the stresses of conceptual change – and to what extent these changes took them further from their aboriginal past.

Micmac hunter–gatherers and animals: an ethnohistorical perspective

To provide a background for analysing the rock art, I first discuss from an ethnohistorical basis the conceptual changes in Micmac world-view that have occurred over the post-contact era.

The traditional relationship between the eastern Algonkian peoples and animals was defined by hunting. Strictly, in terms of the hunting process, animals were living things procured for food. In the cultural experience of hunting, however, procurement was seen through a filter of socially prescribed behaviour, wherein animals and hunters exercised a compact that was supported and (ideally) sustained by ritual. And so animals were both a subsistence and a metaphorical resource.

However, the worlds of hunting and ritual were not as closely integrated as is sometimes made out; the animal as symbol and the animal as food may have been conceptually separable. This distinction emerges from the duality of cultural life itself: although individuals face day-to-day existence within a socially-given ideological frame of reference, the contingencies of that life require the pragmatic application of spiritual beliefs. The result is an ambiguity in the human–animal relationship, a condition that may be seen in the early historical records of native beliefs.

One may conclude from these sources that animals were not frozen in the present, simply objects which could be manipulated in a suitably socialized hunting process. On the contrary, animals had a past history, referring to a time when people and animals were integrated to the extent that in some beliefs they could transform from one state to another at will. But this time of integration was always in the past except to the shaman, who affirmed what the metaphorical language alluded to by maintaining the ability to transform into an animal or, at least, summon animal helpers for curative purposes or hunting magic. As Biard (Thwaites 1959b, pp. 131–3) relates about the Micmac shaman in 1611, 'they say that the Magic of the Pilotoys [shamans] often calls forth spirits and optical illusions to those who believe them, showing snakes and other beasts which go in and out of the mouth while they are talking; and several other magical deeds of the same kind.'

The leaving of the spiritual present and past in the hands of the shaman may be seen as a tacit acceptance of a world beyond the constraints of ordinary experience, even of dreams, that was largely inaccessible to ordinary people and, in some respects, to shamans. Indeed, when Chief Arguimaut, a Micmac shaman, told the Abbé Maillard c. 1750 that Micmac people discarded all food bones in a ritual way because the ancestors had told them to do so, he declared that 'None of the medicine men, not even I, the foremost one (since I held the office before I was bathed in holy water), could give any other reasons for these practices to our young people. . .' (Maillard 1863, pp. 304–5). Is it possible, then, that what Martin (1978) interprets in the protohistoric period as evidence of an internal spiritual malaise among native people – a condition critical to his thesis that they became disaffected with the spiritual community of animals (1978, p. 155) – was simply an ambivalence towards the spiritual past? The ideological problem of the hunting of animals may have been a conflict between the act of procuring food and the exercising of a social responsibility. Although it may have been necessary to give the sacred past its due, however, it is equally possible that the individual hunter was most concerned with the more immediate problem of tracking and killing his prey.

If a more ambivalent attitude to the natural world existed, the ideological transition to the acceptance of European trade goods would not have been difficult. As is suggested for other native peoples in the north-east, the Micmac may have treated some glass beads, copper kettles, and other goods as magical objects (e.g. Denys 1908, pp. 439–41), but certainly by the time of the Jesuit missions in Nova Scotia the utility of European goods was accepted and, as Borque & Whitehead (1986) point out, taken advantage of. A Micmac burial dated to the late 16th century, for example, included 22 copper cooking pots, axes, a saw, fishhooks, adzes, caulkers, daggers, spear heads, swords, awls, a wine cork, a ceramic apothecary jar, trade beads, and wool blankets (Harper 1956, 1957; cited in Whitehead 1987). And as Biard observed (Thwaites 1959b, p. 77), 'they are also quite willing to make use of our hats, shoes, caps, woolens and shirts, and of our linen to clean their infants, for we trade them all these commodities for their furs.'

With the beginnings of a market economy already in place early in the 17th century (Borque & Whitehead 1986), what followed was perhaps inevitable. Micmac people wanted European goods because of their utility; and they were able to adapt their traditional hunting skills, enhanced by the efficiency of European weapons, to the increased demand for furs. By narrowing the hunting pattern to fur-bearing animals and altering the seasonal round, however, the Micmac began to experience food shortages which could only be removed through further trade. Consequently, they were drawn into a state of dependency in a market economy at the expense of their traditional way of life.

At the same time the teachings of Christian missionaries held that the world was not a community of humans and animals, but a divinely ordered hierarchy in which animals were created to serve humankind – thereby providing a resolution to the ideological problem surrounding the unbraided hunting of animals. This Jesuit teaching was part of an aggressive campaign to discredit shamans and remove all traces of aboriginal beliefs and religious practices. By effectively dissolving the concept of animal society through Christian teachings, priests replaced shamans as the primary mediators with the spirit world.

The most significant result was that the missionaries democratized the access to hunting magic through the efficacy of prayer. For example, Membertou, the Micmac chief who was 'converted' to Christianity in 1610, was impressed with the fact that after prayers for food he was successful in obtaining smelt the next day and herring and moose on others (Thwaites 1959a, p. 167). In the old days the *buoin* (shaman) had control; now hunters could achieve success directly, by appeals to the Christian god.

In terms of economy and ideology, then, what had been, at least metaphorically, an equitable relationship between humans and animals changed. The status of animals as persons was firmly consigned to the past – with the notable exception of the snakes and serpents that were part of the Christian iconography of the devil. With this loss of metaphorical depth, contemporary animals became more clearly isolated as an economic resource and, as a result, native people gained the ideological sanction for a relentless antisocial exploitation of their fellow creatures.

The Micmac once regarded animals as a complex of social participant and prey; in adapting to the ideological and economic pressures of the fur trade, however, the Micmac began to see animals not as subjects, but as objects and, ultimately, as products. By the same process, the world became human-centred, with an emphasis on economic and religious individuality. This socio–economic transformation, then, was also a conceptual one: as humans became increasingly particularized, animals lost their individuality and became part of the natural resources of the physical world.

The Micmac petroglyphs of McGowan Lake

Attempts to outline the native expression of the post-contact conceptual transformation in rock art, as Cheska has done (1981), are hampered by the fact that whereas the images on Kejimkujik Lake represent a wide variety of objects and events in Micmac life, they cannot be ordered chronologically.

The difficulty is the softness of the slate. The weathering process, involving seasonal inundation, freezing and thawing cycles, and wave and ice wash, has created a highly polished surface which can be cut with any reasonably hard object. Because of the ease of carving, most of the incisions are mere scratches; and because of the inexorable weathering, they become virtually invisible to the naked eye once the powdery abrasion in the grooves washes away – in as little as 25 years. Only in the raking light of sunrise and sunset, or of a torch, do they reappear. But in this state, the detail necessary to distinguish sequences of superimposed images has been worn away.

In 1983, however, the draining of a hydroelectric reservoir on nearby McGowan Lake exposed one site that had been flooded periodically by timber dams since the late 19th century and completely by the construction of the hydroelectric dam in the 1940s (Molyneaux 1984b). Unlike other petroglyph sites in the region, this small rock was situated on a sheltered bend in a river where the soft slate surface was protected from the abrasive action of waves and ice. As a result, the succession of superimposed petroglyphs has been preserved. An examination of one palimpsest (Fig. 8.1) with three separable strata, along with associations to unstratified petroglyphs on other parts of the site, has yielded a relative chronology of images that give us some insight into the conceptual world of the Micmac carver.[1]

The earliest stratum (Fig. 8.2) includes an outlined human figure, faceless and armless, clothed in an hour-glass-shaped garment, and a two-masted, gaff-rigged sailing vessel with a high afterdeck. Although these petroglyphs appear stylistically unrelated, similar forms are combined nearby in an image consisting of two human figures standing on the deck of a similarly gaff-rigged vessel (see Fig. 8.6). Like the solitary figure, these are armless and faceless (one appears to have a nose); and, in addition, each has an arc-shaped form over the head that appears to be a head-covering. The outlines of the figures and vessel are carved in a cross-hatched style typical of Micmac carving.

Figure 8.1 McGowan Lake: a palimpsest with three separable strata.

Although detail in the three figures is sketchy, the few identifiable features allow for a tentative distinction between them. The hour-glass shape and swellings on the inside of each leg of the solitary figure suggest the traditional costume of a Micmac man: a robe or blanket, thrown over the shoulders and drawn in at the waist, and leggings. The lack of headwear is consistent with early descriptions of Micmac costume but contrasts with the convention throughout the historic period when European hats were worn. Because they lack these features, the other two figures appear more European: the arcs above their heads suggest hats or haloes; and the legs are enlarged above, but not below, the knee.

A clue to the relative date of this group may be found in the hull design and rigging of the two vessels (see Molyneaux 1986). By the late 17th century, the fore-castle had been largely eliminated and the large castle on the afterdeck was reduced, leaving a poop which was level with the upper deck. These designs persisted until the development of the full upper deck in the late 18th century (Taillemite 1967,

Figure 8.2 McGowan Lake: the earliest stratum of the palimpsest, including an outlined human figure and a sailing vessel.

Chapman 1968). It appears, then, that the hull design of the petroglyph vessels is characteristic of the late 17th to early 18th century. The gaff-rigging, however, appears anachronistic: square sails were exclusively used on ocean-going vessels until the development of fore-and-aft-rigged schooners in the 19th century. Prior to this period, however, gaff-rigging was used by the Dutch and English for small coastal vessels, beginning in the 17th century, and in North America as early as the beginning of the 18th century (Greenhill 1951, p. 25, Dickason 1986). If these carvings represent a type of late-17th-century coastal vessel with a high poop, or simply a high transom if the manned vessel is a smaller craft, the human figures may then be interpreted as wearing a style of dress consistent with a European military man of the period: a broad-brimmed hat cocked on one side, a great-coat or an overcoat, gathered slightly at the waist and flaring to about knee level, and boots with broad tops (e.g. Leloir 1951, p.52). Of course, the figures may have been rendered in an exaggerated scale to emphasize their significance; and if one then interprets the circles around the heads as haloes (e.g. Robertson 1973), the scene may be related to a Micmac tradition that among the first Europeans who arrived on a strange, floating island was a man in a white robe who brought them Christianity (Rand 1894, p. 225). In any event, however, these petroglyphs appear to reflect a time relatively early in the post-contact period.

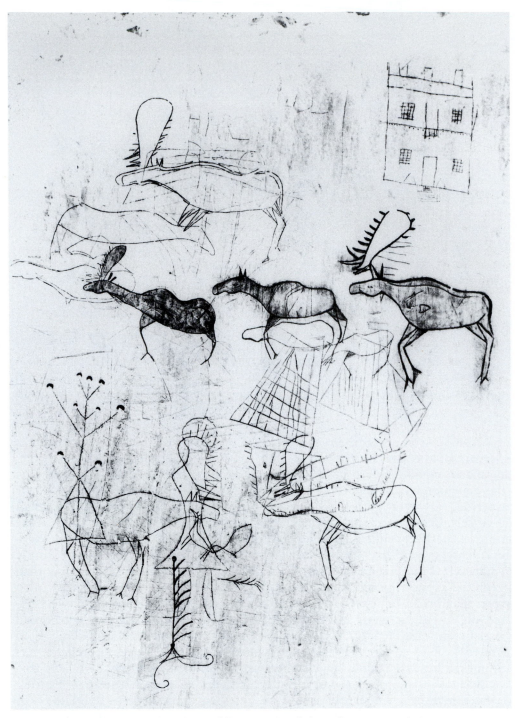

Figure 8.3 McGowan Lake: the middle stratum of the palimpsest, including several groups of moose arranged in ranks.

Figure 8.4   McGowan Lake: the upper stratum of the palimpsest, a Micmac man, woman, and child.

The second stratum consists of a pattern of moose arranged in three ranks (Fig. 8.3). In the top rank is a single bull moose; below this, three moose walk in single file – a cow between two bulls; and in the lowest rank two bulls face one another. This arrangement appears to be a realistic portrayal of seasonally specific behaviour: the normally solitary animals gather temporarily in the autumn to mate, with the bulls fighting during the rut. These petroglyphs cannot be dated further by content, but the style and organization of the animals do correspond generally to images painted by related Algonkian-speaking peoples in the Canadian Shield region of central Canada. Although this latter rock art is similarly undated, it reflects essentially aboriginal rather than post-contact concerns and has been generally regarded, therefore, as a traditional form of expression (Dewdney & Kidd 1967). Indeed, it is known that the Micmac were making images of cervids (moose, caribou, or deer) in 1606, when Lescarbot (1907–11) saw one painted on the sail of a shallop manned by Micmacs.

The last carver to work here (other than two local settlers who left their initials just prior to the final flooding of the site in the 1940s) created images of a number of people over the surface (Fig. 8.1). The main group consists of a man, woman, and child (Fig. 8.4). The man wears the typical Micmac 19th-century dress of a coat gathered at the waist and a top hat; and the woman wears a bonnet, a bead necklace, and a long dress with ribbon appliqué decoration. In addition, she brandishes a cross in one hand and a frond in the other. Among the other figures is a woman on horse-back, riding side-saddle (Fig. 8.5). The carver created the horse from the cow moose in the middle rank of the earlier group; he simply added a large tail and reins.

The clearest indication that the human figure petroglyphs of the upper stratum were incised relatively later than the rest is the clothing and accessories of the

Figure 8.5 McGowan Lake: the upper stratum of the palimpsest, a Micmac woman riding side-saddle on a horse (the cow moose of the middle stratum).

woman. By the appliqué designs on her European-style dress, she is Micmac; but instead of a peaked cap she wears a bonnet, and in her hand she carries the cross of the Roman Catholic Church.

The combined evidence suggests that the first images may have been carved sometime in the late 17th to early 18th century, during the French colonial period. Given a period of time for the earlier petroglyphs to patinate so that subsequent carvers would overlook them (considerably more than 50 years – nearby graffiti lightly scratched into the rock in the early 1940s is still unpatinated), it is likely that the animals were incised at some time during the period of English colonization, from the early 18th to the early 19th century. The last carver worked at the site prior to 1888, when all these images were recorded by a pioneering rock-art researcher, George Creed (see Robertson 1973).

Conceptual change in the McGowan Lake petroglyphs

These few images tend to support the conceptual pattern of increasing specificity in the concept of humans as suggested by the ethnohistoric record. The change may be interpreted in terms of the way the objects and events are depicted.

In the 17th–18th-century group, the 'Micmac' figure is defined solely by its costume. Any expressiveness has been eliminated by a severe economy of means; and the lack of arms and facial details make the image completely static and generalized. The nearby 'European' figures are similarly generalized, although they are depicted on a sailing vessel (Fig. 8.6). This lack of detail is particularly unusual, given the ease of carving and the abundant space enclosed by the figures.

In comparison, the animals of the 18th–19th-century group have a more specific reference. The moose are arranged in a way that reveals both sexual dimorphism and seasonality; the images are true to life, as if observed by a hunter.

The last group, probably carved in the mid- to late 19th century, seems almost autobiographical, for the man in the family group gestures at the viewer. Indeed, he may be the carver himself. As he transformed the cow moose into a horse, he may also have been responsible for the alteration of two other moose, located on another part of the site, which were carved in the same style as those in the middle stratum (Fig. 8.7). Here, the artist created a hunting scene around the animals by adding the figure of a Micmac man, with a smoking pipe in his mouth, gesturing or pointing an object at the moose while two dogs attack them.

The conceptual difference is most clearly suggested by the changes in the specificity of human and animal depictions. Whereas the first carver portrayed humans in general terms, and the second carver depicted the animals in their own world, without humans, the last carver appropriates the animals as features of scenes or events of human, and probably personal, significance. As the relative dating suggests a separation between the latter two strata as being that between the height of the fur trade in the 18th century and the mid-19th-century decline, the difference may be interpreted as a reflection of the transformation from the social being of the traditional society to the 19th-century individualist. In these different worlds, visual images were put to different use: static, probably symbolic, representations

Figure 8.6 McGowan Lake: a gaff-rigged sailing vessel with two human figures on board.

Figure 8.7 McGowan Lake: a moose-hunting scene, created around an earlier pair of moose similar to those in the middle stratum of the palimpsest.

gave way to more visually complex depictions of human participants and animals in scenes of documentary precision.

An application of the McGowan Lake chronology to the petroglyphs of Kejimkujik Lake

This tentative scheme of conceptual change may be applied to the much more extensive and well-known petroglyph sites of nearby Kejimkujik Lake (Myers 1972, Creed 1887–8 in Robertson 1973, Molyneaux 1981, 1984a). The main problem at the Kejimkujik sites is that no chronological separation of superimposed images is possible, due to the weathering of the slate, so that, with the exception of petroglyphs having inscribed dates, it has been necessary to determine the chronology by subject matter. However, when the human and animal petroglyphs are examined according to the degree of historical specificity, as suggested by the conceptual criteria outlined above, two separate groups may be detected.

Corresponding to the mid- to late-19th-century carvings at McGowan Lake are a large number of Micmac images of animals, humans and hunting scenes, most inscribed with dates and names in English or Micmac script. The year 1877 had some obvious significance for the Micmac. It is found 16 times on various sites on Kejimkujik Lake, most often in association with typical images or events of post-contact Micmac culture. Among these are a porpoise-hunting scene in which the names of the two hunters are written in Micmac script below the canoe (Fig. 8.8). Other 1877 petroglyphs include a lynx, two men in ceremonial clothing wearing Glengarry hats, a man smoking a pipe, and two associated with European sailing vessels. In a photograph taken at a St Ann's day celebration at Shubenacadie in 1893, nine of the young men are wearing Glengarry-style hats and chest badges similar to those rendered in the dated petroglyphs (see Whitehead 1980, p. 27). On the basis of this evidence it is possible that the creation of these images was inspired by a St Ann's day festival – a focus of Micmac cultural pride that may also have inspired the last carver at McGowan Lake.

Among undated petroglyphs, a scene consisting of two human figures and a schooner has a similar documentary content (Fig. 8.9). The male carrying the sabre or cutlass is wearing a finely detailed tail-coat or coatee, complete with a row of buttons and what may be a military tricorn or a shako, enhanced with plumes (see Molyneaux 1986). The costume is consistent with British regimental wear of the 18th and 19th centuries – and if the headwear is a shako, the image would necessarily date after its introduction into the British army in 1800 (Lawson 1967, Barnes n.d., p. 118).

Figure 8.8 Kejimkujik Lake: a porpoise-hunting scene, including Micmac script and the date 1877.

Figure 8.9 Kejimkujik Lake: two human figures, one of which wears European (British) military clothing.

A second group of petroglyphs scattered over the several sites on Kejimkujik Lake have an emphasis similar to the subjects of the earlier strata (17th–18th, 18th–19th centuries), and hence, the period of traditional aboriginal expression, at McGowan Lake. Human subjects lack the historical reference and documentary content of the previous group – indeed, the most common image is the peaked cap, a hat worn by Micmac women on formal occasions (Fig. 8.10). In addition, a number of the human figures have elaborately decorated headwear and may be participating in a procession

Figure 8.10 George Lake: a group of human figures, elaborately costumed; a peaked cap and a decorated top hat.

or dance (Fig. 8.10). As clothing was designed, manufactured, and decorated by women (Whitehead 1980), it is likely that the majority of these petroglyphs were also carved by women. The decorative details reflect a Micmac woman's creative interests in the same way as the image of a moose reflects the interest of a hunter. The several moose incised here conform generally to the McGowan Lake style of animals rendered in profile, sometimes with a ground line or with a spatial reference conveyed by relative position.

Viewed as a whole, these human subjects tend to portray specific objects and events in Micmac life, such as ceremonial occasions and ceremonial clothing, but the artists have emphasized the design of the garments and caps rather than the wearers – in most instances, in fact, the wearers are omitted. It is tempting, therefore, to place these images in association with the 18th–19th-century group in the McGowan Lake chronology, where the interest is focused on the generalized depiction of humans and on the hunted (the animal subjects) rather than the hunter.

This provenance is supported by our knowledge of the relation between the seasonal round of the Micmac and that of the lake itself. For most of the year the lake floods the rocks, and in winter they become iced-in and snow-covered. Only in the drier months of July and August are they fully exposed; and even then, if the summer is wet, the lowest surfaces may remain submerged. Most petroglyphs, then, were carved during the summer. Some of these were, no doubt, the work of summer travellers, for Kejimkujik Lake is barely 30 miles from either the eastern, Atlantic coast and the Bay of Fundy to the west. However, it was not simply during the summer, but during a period of summer settlement that the Micmac probably made most of the petroglyphs. It is then that women, especially, would have had the opportunity or the time to create the profusion of peaked caps, decorative designs, ceremonial costumes, and family scenes that are scattered over the sites. To judge from ethnohistoric sources, the Micmac lived most of the year by the sea and would have travelled inland to the Kejimkujik area to harvest eels and to hunt moose and caribou in the fall and winter. As English settlement began to spread along the coast after the mid–18th century, however, the moose and caribou were depleted and the Micmac were driven away from their traditional coastal camping grounds and forced inland for a greater proportion of the year (cf. Martin 1978, Upton 1979, Whitehead 1987). Indeed, Joseph Howe was able to report to the Colonial Government in 1842 that several families had set up permanent residence by the shore of Kejimkujik Lake (Howe 1842). It was during the English colonial period, then, that for reasons beyond their control, Micmac people most frequently saw the lake at its lowest ebb and carved on the exposed slate outcrops.

Conclusion

The Micmac rock art of McGowan and Kejimkujik Lakes does not provide a large, well-established, or representative chronology of Micmac life through the post-contact period, but it does show a glimpse of this world from the point of view of a few men and women who lived there. The identification of three different groups of petroglyphs, according to the way that humans and animals are depicted, and their position in a relative chronology appear to reflect the increasing specificity of humans and the personalization of events that is suggested by ethnohistoric accounts.

The earliest petroglyphs, preserved by their submergence in McGowan Lake, possibly date as early as the late 17th century; but they are inadequately supported elsewhere. However, if this group is combined with the images of game animals, humans and peaked caps, which also appear to depict objects and events which are culturally, rather than individually specific, the extent of the conceptual break represented by the last Micmac petroglyphs, those of the late 19th century, may be appreciated.

The personalizing and individualizing of events in the later petroglyphs was certainly influenced by the gradual increasing of at least elementary literacy among some Micmac in the 19th century; and this new-found ability to define both persons and events and fix them in time may have been decisive in the final break with the traditional community of humans and animals. People had less need to refer to the metaphorical past: they could now write their own personal histories.

The autobiographical sense of the later historical period is outlined by Keyser (1979) in a study of warfare patterns in petroglyphs incised on sandstone in the Milk River region of southern Alberta. Keyser suggests that 'in contrast to the Prehistoric period emphasis on vision-quest experiences as the primary conferrent of status, a Historical period warrior's status was determined not by the spirit helper itself, but rather by what deeds he accomplished' (1979, p. 47).

The need to emphasize individual rather than social power and status gradually increases among the Micmac through the post-contact period. In an attempt to counter the steady decline of collective cultural traditions, the Micmac replaced the metaphorical relationship with animals with new economic and ideological values. Indeed, what appears to be conveyed in the scene of a Micmac man and his family is not a celebration of the abuse of nature (Cheska 1981) or the conquest of animals (Martin 1978), but an optimism that is simply focused on more individual concerns. The fact that this Micmac carver transformed a moose into a horse suggests that he was conceptually a man of the 19th century – it was a time when animals were no longer culturally significant outside their use as food, as 'tools', or as commodities. The metaphorical animals, although still preserved in oral traditions and some lingering religious beliefs outside the Roman Catholic orthodoxy, were now fixed in the past.

It would be wrong, then, to presume in the decline of a socially equitable relationship between Micmacs and animals that the new conceptual state was degraded as Martin (1978, p. 155) and Cheska (1981, p. 62) have suggested or, indeed, that continuity with the aboriginal past was broken. As shown by the many other petroglyphs of colonial settlements, wigwam villages, churches, altar-pieces, sailing ships, and other aspects of 18th- and 19th-century life, the Micmac were observers and, from their side of the issue, participants in the changing world. As so many ethnohistoric sources reveal, they adapted new technologies to their own use with ease. And, judging by their aggressive attempts to monopolize trade with the French, they could have worked well within the new economic order – if, at any time during the post-contact period, the colonial governments had made any genuine attempt to allow the Micmac to have equal access to the economic resources of the thriving mercantile economy. Instead, they were compelled to retreat to their traditional winter hunting grounds, such as Kejimkujik Lake, and were encouraged to take up agriculture in the infertile forests. Here they were forced to maintain a hunting relationship with animals that had lived out their cultural life, through economic and ideological forces beyond their control. Indeed, the last Micmac hunters of Kejimkujik worked as guides at the hunting lodges that replaced the Micmac settlements, leading whites to the last of the moose in the early 20th century.

This is perhaps the final irony of the post-contact changes in the Micmacs' concepts of animals and themselves. The Micmac took power over animals in the complex world of the fur trade; but when the trade and the animals were gone, they were prevented from using their considerable human resources to develop an equitable relationship with the European world that had taken the animals' economic and metaphorical place.

Acknowledgements

I wish to acknowledge the following institutions, that provided the financial support that made my research in Nova Scotia possible: Parks Canada, Atlantic Region, for the study of the petroglyphs in Kejimkujik National Park; the Nova Scotia Museum, for the study of the McGowan Lake petroglyphs; and the Royal Ontario Museum, for providing research space and logistical support. The Acadia University archives generously provided access to the Silas Rand diaries. This chapter was read by Ruth Holmes Whitehead, Nova Scotia Museum, who provided useful critical comments and, most significantly, contributed, in her usual unselfish way, some of her own hard-won research and unpublished manuscripts to the cause.

Note

1   The petroglyphs, fine scratches and deeper knife cuts in slate, were enhanced for recording – traced with a water-soluble white poster paint, using very fine sable brushes, under ×4 binocular magnification. As part of the recording, the enhanced images were photographed as colour transparencies, using a photomacrographic lens. The representations in this chapter are reversed prints of the colour transparencies of the enhanced petroglyphs, rather than second-generation drawings or tracings. Consequently, petroglyphs and rock surface features extraneous to the arguments presented here are necessarily included in the site record.

References

Barnes, R. M. n.d. *A history of the regiments and uniforms of the British Army*. London: Seeley Service.

Borque, B. J. & R. H. Whitehead 1986. Tarrentines and the introduction of European trade goods in the Gulf of Maine. In *Origins and adoption of innovation*, World Archaeological Congress, Vol. 1 (Mimeo).

Chapman, F. 1968 (first published 1768). *Architectura Navalis Mercatoria*. London: Adlard Coles.

Cheska, A. T. 1981. The Micmac Indian petroglyphs: Evidence of self/nature concept changes. *The Nova Scotia Historical Review* **1**, 54–66.

Denys, N. 1908. *The description and natural history of the coasts of North America (Acadia)*, (trans. W. F. Ganong). Toronto: The Champlain Society.

Dewdney, S. & K. E. Kidd 1967. *Indian rock paintings of the Great Lakes Region*, 2nd edn. Toronto: University of Toronto Press.

Dickason, O. 1986. La 'guerre navale' des Micmacs contre les Britanniques, 1713–1763. In *Les Micmacs et la Mer*, C. A. Martijn (ed.), 233–48. Montréal: Recherches Amerindiennes au Québec.

Greenhill, B. 1951. *The merchant schooners*. Newton Abbot: David & Charles.

Hallowell, A. 1926. Bear ceremonialism in the Northern Hemisphere. *American Anthropologist* **28**, 1–175.

Harper, J. R. 1956. Portland Point: preliminary report of the 1955 excavation. Appendix One. *Historical Studies* no. 9. St. John: New Brunswick Museum.

Harper, J. R. 1957. Two seventeenth-century copper-kettle burials. *Anthropologica* **4**, 11–36.

Hoffman, B. 1955. *Historical ethnography of the Micmac of the sixteenth and seventeenth centuries*. Unpublished doctoral dissertation in Anthropology, University of California, Berkeley.

Howe, J. 1842. An account of the visit of Joseph Howe to the Micmac people settled at Fairy Lake. *Journal of Assembly*, 1844, Paper no. 50, 123–5.

Keyser, J. 1979. The Plains Indian war complex and the rock art of Writing-on-Stone, Alberta, Canada. *Journal of Field Archaeology* **6**, 41–8.

Lawson, C. C. P. 1967. *A history of the uniforms of the British Army*, Vol. 5. London: Kaye & Ward.

Leloir, M. 1951. *Dictionnaire du Costume*. Paris: Librairie Grund.

Lescarbot, M. 1907–11 The history of New France. 3 vols. Toronto: The Champlain Society.

Maillard, Abbé A. 1863. Lettre à Madame de Drucourt. In *Les Soirées Canadiennes*. Québec: Brousseau Frères. (Trans. by M. A. Hamelin, Nova Scotia Museum, for Whitehead 1988).

Martin, C. 1978. *Keepers of the game*. London: University of California Press.

Molyneaux, B. 1981. *The Kejimkujik petroglyphs: a resource manual*. Ms. Report. Parks Canada, Halifax.

Molyneaux, B. 1984a. *The Micmac petroglyphs of Kejimkujik National Park*. Ms. Report. Parks Canada, Halifax.

Molyneaux B. 1984b. *The McGowan Lake petroglyphs site*. Ms. Report. Nova Scotia Museum, Halifax.

Molyneaux, B. 1986. Images de la mer dans l'art rupestre des Micmacs. In *Les Micmacs et la Mer*, C. A. Martijn (ed.), 49–63. Montreal: Recherches Amerindiennes au Québec.

Myers, H. B. 1972. *Report on the recording and mapping of petroglyphs located at Fairy Bay, Kejimkujik National Park*. Halifax: Parks Canada.

Nash, R. J. 1977. *Prehistory and cultural ecology – Cape Breton Island, Nova Scotia*. National Museum of Man, Mercury Series, Canadian Ethnology Service Paper no. 40, 131–56.

Rand, S. 1894. *Legends of the Micmacs*. New York: Longmans Green.

Robertson, M. 1973. *Rock drawings of the Micmac Indians*. Halifax: Nova Scotia Museum.

Salisbury, N. 1982. *Manitou and providence*. Oxford: Oxford University Press.

Taillemite, E. 1967. The golden age. In *The great age of sail*, J. Jobe (ed.), 139–52. London: Patrick Stephens.

Thwaites, R. G. 1959a. *Jesuit relations and related documents*, Vol. I. New York: Pageant Press.

Thwaites, R. G. 1959b. *Jesuit relations and allied documents*, Vol. III. New York: Pageant Press.

Upton, L. F. S. 1979. *Micmacs and colonists*. Vancouver: University of British Columbia Press.

Whitehead, R. H. 1980. *Eliteley*. Halifax: Nova Scotia Museum.

Whitehead, R. H. 1987. I have lived here since the world began. In *The spirit sings: artistic traditions of Canada's first peoples*, 17–49. Toronto: McClelland & Stewart and the Glenbow Museum.

9 *An approach to the theme of confronted animals in French Palaeolithic art*[1]

ANNE-CATHERINE WELTÉ

The representation of confronted animals constitutes an association with a very precise intention, a particular type of intraspecific link with a geometrical organization. The association consists of two animals (sometimes more) of the same species,[2] of the same size and conformation, and represented in the same attitude (either static or dynamic) on the same plane. The foreheads of the animals are either adjacent (to such an extent that their heads may even merge into one another) or very close (the space between them not being wide enough for another individual of the same size to fit in between). This space is either left empty or filled by a central element, animal or non-animal.

The fact that two animals are facing each other is not a sufficient reason in itself to say that they are really confronted. The link between the two must conform to certain precise criteria (such as same species, same size, a similarity in the technical stylistic characteristics, and contemporaneity). Moreover, as far as possible, their attitude (whether it is static or dynamic) must reveal the link between them ('passive' or 'active' confrontation).

Using these criteria, we can define such an association which is very common in protohistoric times (in the Near East, in Greece, and even in Precolumbian America) as well as in historic times (where it often appears on Coptic, Persian, and Scandinavian fabrics; Mesopotamian ceramics; Roman sculptures; Chinese bronzes; heraldic art; etc.). This type of association is, therefore, part of a set of geometric graphic expressions (the frieze would be another example). This chapter is concerned with the motif of the confronted animals as it occurs in Palaeolithic art.

The term 'confronted' was used very early to describe animals represented in prehistoric caves and mobile art. Breuil used it when referring to horse heads engraved on a perforated baton from Mas d'Azil (Breuil 1909); when referring to reindeer heads embossed on a perforated baton at La Madeleine; and to reindeer, bison, and aurochs at the cave of Font-de-Gaume (Capitan *et al.* 1910). The mammoths engraved on a perforated baton at Laugerie-Haute were also described as being 'confronted' (Peyrony & Peyrony 1938).

The same term was used to describe the wolves at La Vache (Malvesin–Fabre *et al.* 1951), as well as the ibexes and saïga antelopes discovered in the same cave (Fig. 9.1) and the various mammoths at Rouffignac (Fig. 9.2) (Nougier & Robert 1956, 1958, 1965). Leroi-Gourhan (1965) also used the same term to describe the ibexes of

Figure 9.1   Antelopes/saïgas on rib-bone, La Vache (Ariège). Drawings and photograph by R. Robert, Nougier & Robert 1958.)

the axial 'diverticule' at Lascaux, those of the Cartailhac gallery at Niaux, and some anthropomorphous figures at Font-de-Gaume and Rouffignac.

Several of these compositions of confronted figures have been known for a considerable time, but it was only with the pioneering work of Laming-Emperaire (1962) and Leroi-Gourhan (1958a, b, c, 1965) that the intentional significance of this type of association was underlined.

In order to list the Palaeolithic manifestations of confronted animals, it is necessary to review the evidence in the light of the following methodological and analytic criteria:

(a)   It is always difficult to compare mobile and parietal art, as the former is but a 'fragmental art' (Delporte 1984b) which rarely appears 'in its original situation'. Moreover, the surfaces available are much larger for cave art than for mobile art, and this may have affected the number and disposition of the animals represented. The method of counting the confronted animals as a simple subject-matter theme (Leroi-Gourhan 1965) enables us to overcome most of these problems.

(b)   Sometimes this particular theme is clearly recognizable when it is represented alone or nearly alone, isolated on a wall or on an object – as with the mammoths of the 'Gallery of Two Mammoths' at Rouffignac (Barrière 1982), or the horses at Le Mas d'Azil, and with the headless ibexes represented on a spear-thrower at Enlène (Zervos 1959). In these cases, premeditation is clear. More frequently, however, the walls or objects are overcrowded with all sorts

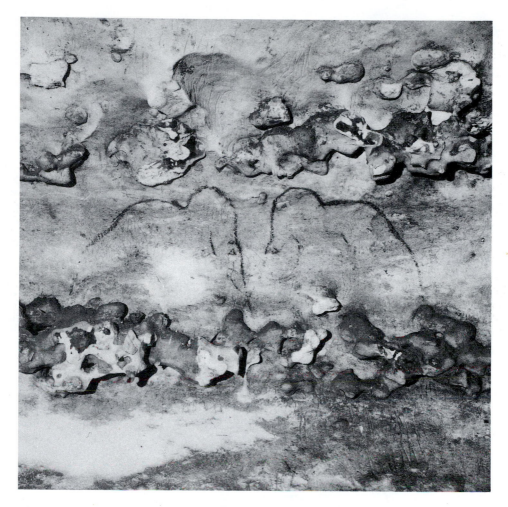

Figure 9.2 Mammoths in the 'Galley of Two Mammoths', Rouffignac (Dordogne). (Photograph by R. Robert.)

of representations, and certain animals may therefore appear to be confronted without really being so. It is then that a thorough analysis becomes necessary to determine the stages of execution of the palimpsest, and eventually to find a co-ordinating link which could help isolate the theme from a confused environment, as has been shown to be possible in the case of the Sanctuary of Trois Frères (Fig 9.3) (Vialou 1981) and on the stones at La Marche (Pales & Tassin de Saint Péreuse 1969).

(c)   Some cases of fortuitous confrontation may also be due to the radial or circular arrangement of motifs on ceilings (the cows on the ceiling of the axial 'diverticule' at Lascaux, Bataille 1955), or to the various orientations of animals within a group (the bears at La Vache, Breuil *et al.* 1956), or else to an opposition between animals of different species (the association between them

Figure 9.3 Bison 21–3 and 33–4 in the Sanctuary, Trois Frères (Ariège). (Bégouën & Breuil 1958, Vialou 1981.)

may be intentional, but as they belong to different species, we cannot securely discern an intentional confrontation). In these cases the representation will be described as 'face-to-face' (Welté 1976, 1982).

The number of cases of definitely confronting animals is less than 100 of which 56 cases[3, 4] are parietal and 29 mobile. A total of 204 animals are represented. Although these figures are very low, and one must be very careful when drawing conclusions from them, they do show that a greater proportion of them occurs in cave art.

The confrontation theme has existed in parietal and mobile art from the Perigordian period onwards, but early examples are very rare: two in the Perigordian period and three in the Solutrean period (Table 9.1). During the Magdalenian, however, we find 51 cases in cave art and 28 in mobile art (see Table 9.1). The theme occurs between the Loire valley, the Rhône valley, the Atlantic Ocean, and the Spanish border, and its distribution is very irregular (see Table 9.1).[5, 6]

(a) *Charentes–Périgord* appears to be the most important area for both mobile and parietal examples, although examples are more frequent in cave art, in a ratio of 4 : 1. Also it is the only area in which examples (parietal and mobile) occur throughout nearly all periods.

(b) In the *Pyrenees* the theme is equally represented in mobile and parietal art, but only in the Magdalenian period.[3]

(c) Elsewhere, the theme appears intermittently, in Solutrean cave art at Oulen (Fig. 9.4) (Combier *et al.* 1958, Combier 1984a) and in Magdalenian mobile

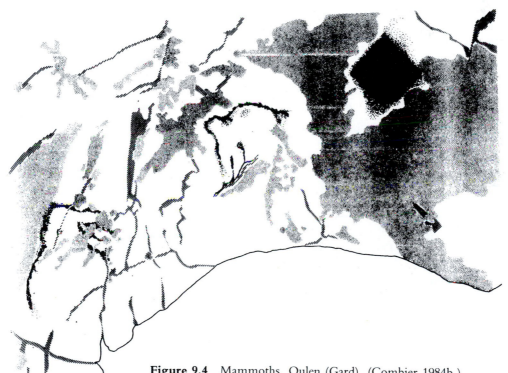

Figure 9.4 Mammoths, Oulen (Gard). (Combier 1984b.)

Table 9.1 Chronological and geographical distribution of the theme of 'confronted animals' in France.

		Cave art			Mobile art		
Zone	Perigordian	Solutrean	Magdalenian	Perigordian	Solutrean	Magdalenian	Total
Charentes, Périgord	1	2	43	1		11	58
Pyrenees			8			11	19+1 (see note 3)
Quercy						5	5
Mediterranean France		1					1
North and East France						1	1
Total	1	3	52	1		28	84+1 (see note 3)
Total per type of art		55 (+1) (see note 3)			29		85

Table 9.2 The bestiary of individual cases of 'confronted animals'.

		Cave art			Mobile art		
Species	Perigordian	Solutrean	Magdalenian	Perigordian	Solutrean	Magdalenian	Total
Antelope						2	2
Batrachians						2	2
Bisons			37				37
Bovidae	2	2	7				11
Canidae						2	2
Capridae		2	6			10	18
Cervidae			8			11	19
Elephantinae		2	47	2		2	53
Equidae			25			14	39
Felidae			3				3
Birds						4	4+2 (see note 3)
Salmonidae						2	2
Suidae						8	8
Indeterminate						2	2
Total	2	6	133	2		59	202
General Total		141 (+2) (see note 3)			61		204

art at Fontalès (Darasse 1954, 1955, 1959, Welté[7]), Sainte-Eulalie (Lorblanchet 1973), and La Marche (Pales & Tassin de Saint-Péreuse 1969). This is all the more curious since the artists created other compositions of a geometric construction, such as the fish-shaped designs (on bone pieces from Abri Murat and Thorigné-en-Charnie) and signs (Cuzoul-des-Brasconies), and the perforated baton of Gazel cave at Sallèles – Cabardès). They also drew other geometric designs, such as ibexes engraved in a head-to-tail posture (on a bone at La Salpétrière) and horses (represented back-to-back at Pech-Merle de Cabrerets and at Mayenne-Sciences).

Table 9.3 The bestiary of themes of 'confronted animals' (Leroi-Gourhan 1965).

Species	Cave art			Mobile art			Total
	Perigordian	Solutrean	Magdalenian	Perigordian	Solutrean	Magdalenian	
Antelope						1	1
Batrachians						1	1
Bisons			16				16
Bovidae	1	1	2				4
Canidae						1	1
Capridae		1	3			5	9
Cervidae			5			5	10
Elephantinae		1	12	1		1	15
Equidae			12			6	18
Felidae			1				1
Birds						2	2+1 (see note 3)
Salmonidae						1	1
Suidae						2	2
Indeterminate						1	1
Total	1	3	51	1		26	82
General Total		55 (+1) (see note 3)			27		83

Only 14 caves have confronting parietal animals (whereas ten times as many cave-art sites are known in the area studied). Some of them show one or two examples while others – Font-de-Gaume, Combarelles, and Lascaux (Fig. 9.5), in the Périgord, and, above all, Rouffignac (see Fig. 9.2) – have more.

Only 14 sites have produced such works on mobile art. In Périgord, confronted animals have so far been found in four places, although an old inventory (Saint-Perier 1965) listed a total of 72 sites in that area 'with sculptures and engravings', and the number has grown since then.

In just a few sites this theme is found on both mobile and parietal work: six examples from the complex of Trois Frères (see Fig. 9.3), Tuc d'Audoubert and Enlène[4] (Bégouën 1926, Bégouën & Breuil 1958, Bégouën & Clottes 1984) and five examples from Niaux (Fig. 9.6) and La Vache (see Fig. 9.1) (if these two caves were indeed inhabited by the same group of people in the Late Magdalenian, as suggested by Nougier 1973).

Confronted animals

The bestiary

In both the Perigordian and the Solutrean, the theme is found only amongst Bovidae and Capridae in cave art, and Elephantinae in both forms of art. In the Magdalenian, the theme becomes more diversified and is found among seven species in the cave art, and ten in the mobile art: four species are common to both forms of art, and if one counts the animals (Table 9.2), they appear either in equal proportions (Capridae, Cervidae) or in reversed proportions (Elephantinae, Equidae). It is inter-

Figure 9.5   Large bulls in the 'Rotunda', Lascaux (Dordogne). (Photograpy N. Augoulat, Centre National de Préhistoire.)

esting to compare the bestiary with the statistics published by Leroi-Gourhan 1965 (Table 9.3, which counts not the animals but the species). In parietal art mammoths become numerous; the relative proportions of horses and the 'bison–aurochs' group are reversed. In mobile art, there are so few examples of confronted animals that their relative proportions cannot be considered significant.

Where statistical inventories are available, the species most represented confronting each other at any given site generally correspond (logically enough) to the species most commonly represented in the cave or mobile art of that site (mammoths at Rouffignac and Oulen; bison at Font-de-Gaume, Niaux (see Fig. 9.6), Trois Frères (see Fig. 9.3), and Le Portel; horses at Gabillou (Gaussen 1964), Lascaux, Combarelles, and Fontalès (Fig 9.7); reindeer at La Madeleine; and ibexes at La Vache (Fig. 9.8)), but it is important to note the cases where the species is otherwise represented infrequently (Felidae, birds, Salmonidae) and those in which rare species are involved (batrachians, Canidae, Suidae).

The numbers opposed

Following the present statistics, in the majority of cases (70), confrontation is represented by two animals confronting one another. Nevertheless, in 15 cases this minimum is exceeded, the numbers involved reaching three, four, five, six, and even ten. In such cases we can speak of a frieze of confronted animals (all of them being placed front-to-front, or side-by-side, in such a way that no other animal of the same size could be placed between them).

The most frequent arrangements, of one animal confronted by two or three, can be found in both mobile and parietal art, whereas two confronted by two, three or four, or even four confronted by six (frieze of '11 mammoths' at Rouffignac, deciphered by Barrière (1982)) only exist in parietal art. It is interesting to note how the friezes of confronted animals are distributed: in the Magdalenian period, they only appear in cave art in the Dordogne at Rouffignac, Font-de-Gaume, and Lascaux; in mobile art, they only appear at Fontalès, as far as we know.

Morphological homogeneity

The theme is not really affected by the slight differences in morphological homogeneity which can be observed.

Figure 9.6   Two bison in the 'Salon Noir', Panel VI, Niaux (Ariège.) (Photograph by N. Aujoulat, Centre National de Préhistoire.)

Figure 9.7   Horses 8–9 in the 'Galerie Principal', Les Combarelles aux Eyzies (Dordogne). (Captain *et al*. 1924.)

Figure 9.8   Ibexes on antler, La Vache (Ariège). (Drawings and photograph by R. Robert, Nougier & Robert 1958.)

(a) Complete animals are found confronting bodiless heads (bisons of Panel VI 'Salon Noir' at Niaux (see Fig. 9.6) (Beltrán *et al*. 1973, Clottes 1984) or batrachians[8] at Fontalès), or else confronting necks and heads (horse 109 at Combarelles (Capitan *et al*. 1924), Capridae at Fontalès).

(b) Sexual dimorphism, as shown by the Capridae at Fontalès, Cervidae at Combarelles (nos. 56–7), (Baffier 1979, Barrière 1981) and the bison at Le Portel (Beltrán *et al*. 1966), or intraspecific variability (some of the mammoths at Rouffignac) no doubt account for the known examples of differences in size between confronting animals.

Attitudes

In 24 cases of confronted animals in cave art, and in 29 cases in mobile art, the attitude or posture of the animals could be described as dynamic. This remains a difficult matter to determine in other cases because the animals are often too incomplete (e.g. the horses at Sainte Eulalie (Fig. 9.9), engraved on reindeer bones, and the horses at Lortet (Merlet 1980)), or do not show any elements which allow us to apply such a concept as dynamism with certainty.

Be that as it may, dynamic attitudes, on present evidence, seem to be proportionally a little more frequent in confronted postures in mobile art than in cave art, but it is not clear whether this has to do with the theme itself or with the form of art.

Techniques

Techniques are extremely varied, their diversity apparently being limited only by the properties of each art form (mobile or parietal). In parietal art, confrontation is expressed in sculptures in relief (ibexes at Roc-de-Sers (Delporte 1984a)), in polydigital tracings (mammoths 220–1 at Rouffignac (Barrière 1982)), in engraving (mammoths of the 'Découverte' at Rouffignac), in black-coloured drawing (bison at

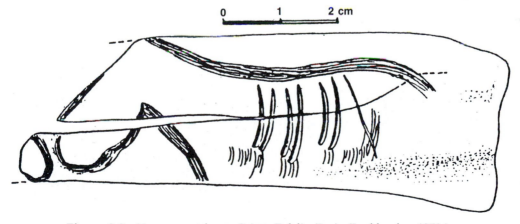

Figure 9.9 Horses on a bone, Sainte-Eulalie (Lot). (Lorblanchet 1973.)

Niaux (see Fig. 9.6) and certain bison and mammoths at Rouffignac (see Fig. 9.2)), in red painting (mammoths at Oulen (see Fig. 9.4)), or painting combined with engraving (bison at Le Portel and Font-de-Gaume). Very rarely, a difference in colouring among the figures confronted can be observed (Capridae in the axial diverticule at Lascaux, reindeer at Font-de-Gaume, bison on the 'Pillar' at Rouffignac).

Where confrontation on mobile art is concerned, with the exception of modelling or finger-shaping on plaquettes, all technical possibilities are used, often in combination: sculpture in relief (ibexes of Enlène), *champlevé* (with fine engravings in the case of the mammoths of Laugerie-Haute and the ibexes of Le Mas d'Azil (Fig. 9.10) (Clottes *et al.* 1981)), a partly cut-out and carved outline (horses at Le Mas d'Azil), a more or less fine engraving (at Fontalès and La Madeleine (Capitan & Peyrony 1928)).

The techniques common to both parietal and mobile art are therefore sculpture and the varied types of engraving, often used together.

Organization in space

Location on a base

Cave art   When the Palaeolithic entrances of caves are known, confronted animals can be found both in the first part of the cave, with or very near the first representations, and in the inner part of the cave. Sometimes they appear in both parts (Lascaux, Rouffignac, Trois Frères).

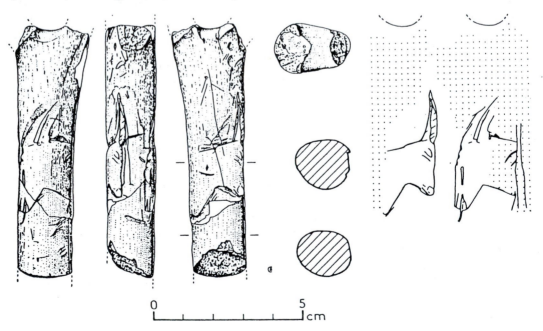

Figure 9.10   Ibexes on a perforated baton, Mas d'Azil (Clottes *et al.* 1981).

Mobile art   Confronted animals appear most frequently on *objets d'usage* (Leroi-Gourhan 1965), 'tools' (one lance-head, one spoon, two spear-throwers, four polishers, seven perforated batons), and on only five bone plaquettes and two flat stones.

Context

Confronted animals are found in several contexts:

(a)   isolated in the centre of a wall (e.g. the mammoths of the 'Gallery of Two Mammoths' at Rouffignac (see Fig. 9.2)) or on a mobile base (Cervidae at La Madeleine);

(b)   represented in a lateral position together with many other representations (bison at Niaux (see Fig. 9.6), reindeer at Fontalès);

(c)   integrated in an elaborate geometric composition of a three-part structure – for example, the bison at Le Portel; horses 109, 110, 112 at Combarelles; the birds at Teyjat (Alcade del Rio *et al.* 1912) or in a triangular situation (bison of the 'Pillar' at Rouffignac);

(d)   incorporated within a palimpsest (Cervidae at Lascaux, bison at Trois Frères (see Fig. 9.3), mammoths at La Marche).

Although there is a tendency for the confronted animal composition to be oriented along the longitudinal axis of any long-shaped bases (e.g. perforated batons, polishers, foreshafts, spoons, and wall panels), there are examples where it cuts across the surface along the shorter axis (ibexes and horses on the perforated batons at Le Mas d'Azil (see Fig. 9.10), bison of the 'Pillar' at Rouffignac). The shape of the base on which the composition occurs acts as a constraint only in the case of friezes, which of necessity require room to expand in length.

There seems to be a particular case of topographical association in cave art since we find confronted animals near some *bouches-d'ombre* (Nougier 1964): at Lascaux (at least once), at Rouffignac (seven times), and maybe at Niaux. There is nothing similar in mobile art.

The space in between[9]

In both forms of art, the confronted animals are generally adjoining or are very near one another.

In 28 out of the 29 cases known in mobile art, and in 51 cases out of the 54 in cave art, there is either no space between the figures or the space is less than half their average individual length. When there is space, it is either empty or filled with a 'central' element (in one mobile and 12 parietal examples), not necessarily borrowed from the animal world but contemporaneous with the animals that it separates.

Correlations with surrounding representations

The central element

A small animal belonging to the same species as the protagonists (for example a young one) may be the central motif as with the frieze of five mammoths at Rouffignac and the owls at Trois Frères (Fig. 9.11) (Bégouën & Breuil 1958, Bégouën & Clottes 1984) (unless the representation is an anthropomorph of the 'ghost-like' type (Lorblanchet 1986) or an undefined sign (Clottes & Bégouën 1986)).

Elements having nothing to do with the confronted animals may also be the central motif: it may be part of a different animal (such as the horses between bison 19 and 20 at Font-de-Gaume; the undefined animal between reindeer 55–6 at Combarelles), an anthropomorphic being (between bison 19 and 20 at Font-de-Gaume, deciphered by Barrière 1969; Equidae 109 at Combarelles, deciphered by Breuil), a rocky edge or a vertical unevenness of the wall (bison of the 'Pillar' and mammoths in the 'Panel of the Patriarch' at Rouffignac, Equidae at Lascaux), or an enigmatic design (ibexes at La Vache and Lascaux (Fig. 9.12)).

The question is whether or not these central elements have any special relationship with the confronted animals. The case of the ibexes at Lascaux is very interesting, for a quadrangular, lined sign stands between the confronted animals of the *Diverticule Axial*. Similar signs are superimposed or placed side-by-side with ibexes 398–9 of the *Abside*, with the frieze of seven ibexes, and with those in Panel VIII (295–9). At Lascaux, this kind of ornament could be connected more with the species than with the graphical arrangement.

The presence of an anthropomorph, or that of a rock edge between the confronted animals, remains enigmatic. One cannot but think of the protohistoric developments of the theme where the median element is a symbol of life and fecundity (*arbor vitae*–mountain–pillar–sky axis–great goddess and her attendant. . .). In the present state of our investigation, nothing enables us to conclude that the prehistoric central ornament prefigures what in protohistory becomes a central element (some interpretations are controversial, Roussot 1984).

Figure 9.11 Owls in the 'Tréfonds', Trois Frères (Ariège). (Bégouën & Breuil 1958.)

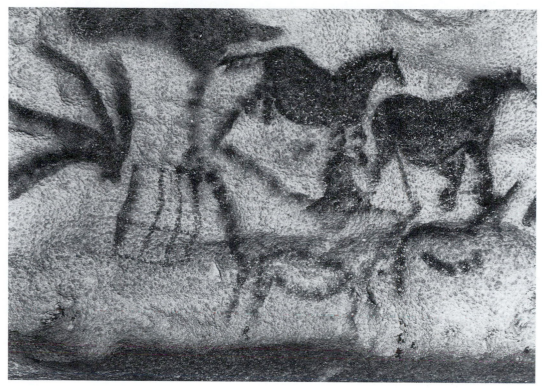

Figure 9.12 Ibexes in the 'Diverticule Axial', Lascaux (Dordogne). (Photograph by N. Aujoulat, Centre National de Préhistoire).

The mammoth–bison correlation

A smaller bison is overlapped with confronted mammoths engraved on a perforated baton at Laugerie-Haute (Perigordian) and at Rouffignac (Magdalenian). Is it intentional? In mobile art there are very few mammoths and a fair number of bison (one mammoth and five bison on perforated batons, eight mammoths and 52 bison on all mobile pieces), according to Leroi-Gourhan's statistical tables (1965). Consequently their appearance together is quite exceptional, and may be intentional.

At Rouffignac, 150 mammoths make up more than 66 per cent of all the animals represented, and so they are most likely to be found in connection with other species (including confronted animals). But out of the ten cases of confronted mammoths a bison appears only twice (superimposed at 'La Grande Fosse', and as an ornament in the 'Panel of the Patriarch'), and out of the five cases of confronted bison two have a superimposed mammoth and two have a mammoth represented very near (although together with other species). At Font-de-Gaume where the panels are very intricate, there are three cases of confronted bison overlapping mammoths, or overlapped by them.

There does, therefore, seem to be a connection between confronted mammoths and bison, or between confronted bison and mammoths. But, considering the overall frequency of bison and mammoths on cave walls, either superimposed or side-by-side (at least in Charentes Périgord), it is an open question whether this connection depends more on the species represented than on the figuration of the design itself.

An approach to 'motivation'

Naturalism of the postures

The majority of the animals represented as confronted are social, that is to say, they live normally in flocks, in families, or in shoals (La Faune 1975). Their postures, for which we have ethological information, or a basis for inferring it, seem to refer to various types of behaviour.

'Fighting' or 'combat'   The realism of some scenes is remarkable. In the case of the ibexes at Roc-de-Sers, one of them is rising up on its hindlegs in order to be in a better position to fall upon its antagonist, which, in turn is leaning on its forelegs. The wolves at La Vache are characterized by their steady look, upright ears, open mouths, with their noses pointed at one another. The bison at Trois Frères (see Fig. 9.3) are also poised for a fight – with their tails slightly up, backs arched, and muscles contracted – as are the mammoths at Laugerie-Haute, which are presented joined at the base of their trunks (as present-day elephants do when fighting) (Kingdon 1979).

The fights that we are considering appear to be ritual struggles in which looks, postures, and movements are 'more expressive than aggressive' (Ruffie 1986). There are rarely fights to the death, which are prevented by submission postures, except with saïgas. Such encounters of intimidation may take place between younger animals, first to compare strength (Capridae), then before sexual maturity to determine each other's rank – their position being overturned or put in question by a principle of 'dynamic hierarchization' (e.g. in Capridae, Canidae, Elephantinae). They may also take place between adults, to defend their territory, for access to food (e.g. in Antilopinae, Bovidae, Canidae, Felidae), to take females (e.g. in Antelopinae, Bovidae, Canidae, Cervidae, Equidae, Salmonidae, Suidae, mammoths), or as a substitution reaction (a discharge of aggressiveness after a collective threat, an intense emotion).

Sexual parade   Palaeolithic art contains scenes of animals apparently smelling each other (e.g. bison, Cervidae, Equidae, Suidae, mammoths), as well as some which show the heads of the protagonists leaning towards each other (e.g. Capridae, Cervidae, Equidae, birds).

Other actions which appear in art include: galloping (e.g. Bovidae, Cervidae, Equidae, Felidae), stamping on the ground (e.g. Equidae), moving of the head (e.g. Equidae: head nodding, or drooping to drink, holding high to feel the wind), moving of the trunk (e.g. mammoths), 'emissions', and leaping (e.g. batrachians: at the moment just before re-contacting the ground).

Even an apparently static attitude is often a prelude to a quicker motion. For example, before charging, or between two assaults, males eye each other from head to foot. And, in the case of ungulate couples, the female standing still is a prelude to acceptance (e.g. Capridae at Fontalès, Cervidae at Combarelles).

On the basis of this review, it is probable that many representations of confronted animals were part of figurative narration and could have had an anecdotal meaning.

Ornamental composition

The theme of confrontation is also an architectural construction. The balanced distribution of the volumes of the bodies, the curves of the horns, antlers, and tusks are in themselves decorative elements. There is a real harmony and equilibrium sometimes underlined by devices such as the disposition of mammoth tusks in the 'Gallery of Two Mammoths' at Rouffignac, and in the alternating striped and smooth bodies of the confronting Cervidae on the spoon from Fontalès. It is also sometimes underlined by means of a pyramidal composition, with a smaller animal of the same species situated in the middle. This concern for symmetry between two individuals or two groups, or the elaborate geometric composition of the three-part structures seems to reflect a striving for ornamental rhythm.

Influence of location and situation

Confronted representations in cave art occur equally on vast accessible surfaces and in those deep and inaccessible places that Leroi-Gourhan considered may have been used as a temple and a sanctuary (Leroi-Gourhan 1984). In mobile art, on the contrary, they appear more on 'useful' objects (e.g. perforated batons, spear-throwers, 'polishers', foreshafts, spoons) than on plaquettes. It remains to be determined whether the motivations were the same. Equally, the importance of the location of the theme, whether central or lateral, whether isolated or buried among other designs, is still not known. Surrounding animals and signs, and particularly the central element, may have had a profound significance.

Symbolic meaning

Speaking of the designs on pebbles at the Abri de Rochedane, Thevenin (1982, 1983) claims that a strict choice of one type of base and decoration means that the design has a symbolic significance. Is it also the case here? We have already underlined the small number of confronted animals represented (85 cases) and the small number of animals concerned (204). The comparative number of confronted animals in each site enables us to distinguish three groups:[10]

(a)   Rouffignac, where confronted animals form 21.68 per cent of all the animals represented;
(b)   some sites like Font-de-Gaume, Combarelles, Fontalès, and Oulen, where they represent between 8 and 15 per cent;
(c)   other sites where they make up less than 4 per cent.

These results suggest that the theme may well have had a strong symbolic meaning for the artists of Rouffignac, and less so for the artists of the sites belonging to the second group; their motivations seem to have been quite different from those of the artists of the third group where the theme only appears occasionally.

Conclusion

In general, the theme of confronted representation can be seen to have developed over several thousand years in France. We can observe the continued existence of this graphic theme and the development of variations in its expression that undoubtedly reflect complex underlying conceptual patterns which may have varied from place to place and time to time.

Acknowledgements

The author is grateful to N. Aujoulat, L. R. Nougier, and R. Robert for the photographs that they have provided.

Notes

1 This chapter does not aim to deal with all the cave and mobile art in the Upper Palaeolithic in France, but only with some aspects related to this particular and important theme (Welté 1970, 1975, 1976, 1982). The work on which it is based is ongoing, and is constantly being revised as new discoveries are reported, new analyses completed, and new determinations made.

2 For the sake of convenience, the term *species* will be used to refer to all animals belonging to the same zoological family. We must also note that humans (e.g. at Rouffignac, Enlène, La Marche, Gönnersdorf, etc.), as well as stylized figurations (fish-shapes) and signs, may also be found in a confronting association.

3 The confronted owls of the 'Galérie du Tréfonds' in Trois Frères, have not been included in the tables because their date is uncertain: they therefore only appear in the 'general totals'. Their chronological attribution is not determined: they are 'Magdalenian additions' according to Leroi-Gourhan (1965). They might date back to the Perigordian period, since in that gallery are found engravings – of a different style from those of the Sanctuary – that are commonly thought to belong to the Perigordian age (Bégouën & Breuil 1958, Clottes & Bégouën 1986).

4 In 1952, Breuil had reported confronting reindeer at the cave of Marsoulas, but these were not confirmed by Plenier (1971). We must also note that the confronted Bovidae engraved on Block C of the frieze at Roc de Sers (Charente) were destroyed by prehistoric people themselves: the initial block has probably been 'broken and hammered' (Delporte 1984a).

5 For the sake of convenience, we adopt the geographical division used by Leroi-Gourhan (1965), and we take the sites of the Aveyron Valley (Fontalès) as situated in Quercy.

6 It is interesting to note that the theme of confronted animals is also found outside France. In Spain it is found in both forms of art (parietal at Castillo and Pindal, and mobile at Cueto de la Mina and La Paloma (Oviedo)). It is also found in Czechoslovakia (at Pekarna).

7 A study of these objects from the Abri de Fontalès is to be found in my doctoral thesis (Doctorat d'Etat). This work is supervised by Prof. A. Thevenin. Further close study of these figures often enables precise conclusions on certain important points.

8 It is very difficult to identify securely the designs on this foreshaft. Darasse (1959) now considers them to be anthropomorphic, whereas he had previously thought they were batrachians. For various reasons, and particularly on morphological grounds, I adopt this second hypothesis.

9 The lengths given of the confronted animals and of the space (*I*) between them are only approximate and they, therefore, give information only about the average (not absolute) size of *I* in proportion to the average length of the figures present.

10 For each site, the figures in the inventory adopted are those published in the *Atlas des grottes ornées paléolithiques françaises* (1984) or in various specialized recent works.

References

Alcade del Rio, H., H. Breuil & L. Sierra 1912. *Les cavernes de la région cantabrique (Espagne)*. Monaco: Imprimerie Chêne.

Baffier, D. 1979. Les caractères sexuels secondaires des mammifères dans l'art pariétal paléolithique franco-cantabrique. In *La contribution de la zoologie et de l'éthologie à l'interprétation de l'art des peuples chasseurs préhistoriques*, H. G. Bandi, W. Huber, M. R. Sauter & B. Sitter (eds), 143–54. Fribourg: Editions Universitaires.

Barrière, C. 1969. Une scène anthropomorphique à Fond-de-Gaume. *Bulletin de la Société Préhistorique de l'Ariège* **XXIV**, 39–53.

Barrière, C. 1981. La grotte des Combarelles: relevés de la paroi droite. *Travaux de l'Institut d'Art préhistorique* **XXIII**, 13–96.

Barrière, C. 1982. *L'art pariétal de Rouffignac*. Paris: Picard.

Bataille, G. 1955. *La peinture préhistorique: Lascaux ou la naissance de l'art*. Lausanne: Skira.

Bégouën, H. 1926. L'art mobilier de la caverne du Tuc d'Audoubert. *Ipek (Jahrbuch für Präehistorische und Ethnographische Kunst)*, 219–28.

Bégouën, H. & H. Breuil 1958. *Les Cavernes du Volp. Trois-Frères, Tuc d'Audoubert, à Montesquieu-Avantès (Ariège)*. Paris: Arts et Métiers graphiques.

Bégouën, R. & J. Clottes 1984. La grotte des Trois-Frères. In *l'Art des cavernes. Atlas des Grottes ornées paléolithiques françaises*, 400–9. Paris, Ministère de la Culture: Imprimerie Nationale.

Beltrán, A., R. Robert & J. Vezian 1966. *La cueva de Le Portel*. Zaragoza, Universidad de Zaragoza.

Beltrán, A., R. Gailli & R. Robert 1973. *La cueva de Niaux*. Zaragoza, Universidad de Zaragoza.

Breuil, H. 1909. L'évolution de l'Art quaternaire et les travaux d'Edouard Piette. *Revue Archéologique* **XIII**, 378–411.

Breuil, H. 1952. *Quatre cents siècles d'art pariétal*. Montignac: Centre d'Etudes et de Documentation Préhistoriques.

Breuil, H., L. R. Nougier & R. Robert 1956. Le lissoir aux Ours, de la grotte de la Vache à Alliat et l'ours dans l'art franco-cantabrique occidental. *Bulletin de la Société préhistorique de l'Ariège* **XI**, 15–78.

Capitan, L., H. Breuil & D. Peyrony 1910. *La caverne de Font-de-Gaume aux Eyzies (Dordogne)*. Monaco: Imprimerie Chêne.

Capitan, L., H. Breuil & D. Peyrony 1924. *Les Combarelles aux Eyzies (Dordogne)*. Paris: Masson.

Capitan, L. & D. Peyrony 1928. *La Madeleine: son gisement, son industrie, ses oeuvres d'art*. Paris: Librairie Noury.

Clottes, J. 1984. La grotte de Niaux. In *L'art des cavernes. Atlas des grottes ornées paléolithiques françaises*, 416–23. Paris, Ministère de la Culture: Imprimerie Nationale.

Clottes, J. & R. Bégouën 1986. Nouveau regard sur la grotte des Trois Frères. In *Cultural attitudes towards animals including birds, fish and invertebrates*. World Archaeological Congress, vol. 3 (mimeo).

Clottes, J., A. Alteirac & C. Servelle 1981. Oeuvres d'art mobilier magdaléniennes des anciennes collections du Mas d'Azil. *Bulletin de la Société Préhistorique de l'Ariège* **XXXVI**, 37–76.

Combier, J. 1984a. La Grotte Chabot. In *L'Art des cavernes. Atlas des grottes ornées paléolithiques françaises*, 317–22. Paris, Ministère de la Culture: Imprimerie Nationale.

Combier, J. 1984b La grotte d'Oulen. In *L'Art des cavernes. Atlas des grottes ornées paléolithiques françaises*. 327–32. Paris, Ministère de la Culture: Imprimerie Nationale.

Combier, J., E. Drouot & P. Huchard 1958. Les grottes solutréennes à gravure pariétales du canyon inférieur de l'Ardèche. *Mémoires de la Société Préhistorique Française* **V**, 61–117.

Darasse, P. 1954. Notes sur l'abri de Fontalès, près Saint-Antonin (Magdalénien supérieur). *Actes de Xème Congrès de la Fédération des Sociétés académiques et savantes*, Montauban, 47–64.

Darasse, P. 1955. Deux oeuvres d'art magdaléniennes de l'abri de Fontalès, près Saint-Antonin (Tarn-et-Garonne). *Bulletin de la Société Préhistorique Française* **LII**, 715–18.

Darasse, P. 1959. Une curieuse gravure de Fontalès. *Bulletin de la Société des Amis du Vieux Saint-Antonin* **XXIII**, 21–5.

Deffarge, R., P. Laurent & D. de Sonneville-Bordes 1975. Art mobilier de Magdalénien supérieur de l'abri Morin à Pessac-sur-Dordogne (Gironde). *Gallia-Préhistoire* **XVIII**, pp 1–64.

Delporte, H. 1984a. L'abri du Roc-de-Sers. In *L'art des cavernes. Atlas des grottes ornées paléolithiques françaises*, 578–82. Paris, Ministère de la Culture: Imprimerie Nationale.

Delporte, H. 1984b. *Rapport entre l'art mobilier et l'art pariétal*. Colloque international d'art pariétal paléolithique, Périgueux-Le Thot, 1–32.

Gaussen, J. 1964. *La grotte ornée de Gabillou*. Bordeaux: Imprimerie Delmas.

Kingdon, J. 1979. *East African mammals IIIB*. London: Academic Press.

La Faune 1975. *Eurasie, Amérique du Nord*, Vols IV–VI. Paris: La Grange Batelière.

Laming-Emperaire, A. 1962. *La signification de l'art rupestre paléolithique*. Paris: Picard.

Leroi-Gourhan, A. 1958a. La fonction des signes dans les santuaires paléolithiques. *Bulletin de la Société Préhistorique Française* **LV**, 307–21.

Leroi-Gourhan, A. 1958b. Répartition et groupement des animaux dans l'art pariétal paléolithique. *Bulletin de la Société Préhistorique Française* **LV**, 515–28.

Leroi-Gourhan, A. 1958c. La symbolique des grands signes dans l'art pariétal paléolithiqus. *Bulletin de la Société Préhistorique Française* **LV**, 384–98.

Leroi-Gourhan, A. 1965. *Préhistoire de l'art occidental*. Paris: Mazenod.

Leroi-Gourhan, A. 1984. *Introduction à l'art pariétal paléolithique*. Milan: Jaca Book.

Lorblanchet, M. 1973. La Grotte de Sainte-Eulalie à Espagnac. *Gallia-Préhistoire* **XVI**, 3–62 233–325.

Lorblanchet, M. 1986. De l'Homme aux animaux et aux signes dans les arts Paléolithique et Australien. In *Cultural attitudes towards animals including birds, fish and invertebrates*. World Archaeological Congress, Vol. 3 (mimeo).

Malvesin-Fabre, G., L. R. Nougier & R. Robert 1951. Engins de chasse et de pêche de Magdalénien de la grotte de la Vache (Ariège). *Bulletin de la Société Préhistorique de l'Ariège* **VI**, 13–30.

Merlet, J. C. 1980. Quatre oeuvres d'art mobilier magdalénien provenant de Lortet (Hautes-Pyrénées). *Bulletin de la Société Préhistorique de l'Ariège* **XXXV**, 115–23.

Nougier, L. R. 1964. *La Préhistoire. Essai de Paléosociologie religieuse*. Paris: Bloud et Gay.

Nougier, L. R. 1973. L'évolution esthétique de l'art mobilier du Magdalénien final des Pyrénées (Essai d'une évolution graphique). *Travaux de l'Institut d'Art Préhistorique* **XV**, 295–320.

Nougier, L. R. & R. Robert. 1956. Rouffignac en Périgord, la Grotte aux Mammouths. *La Nature*, no. 3258, 377–80.

Nougier, L. R. & R. Robert 1958. Le lissoir aux Saïgas de la grotte de la Vache à Alliat et l'antilope saïga dans l'art franco-cantabrique. *Bulletin de la Société Préhistorique de l'Ariège* **XIII**, 13–28.

Nougier, L. R. & R. Robert 1965. Bouquetins affrontés dans l'art mobilier Magdalénien de la grotte de la Vache (Alliat). In *Miscellanea en Homenaje al Abbate H. Breuil*, 197–203. Barcelona: Instituto de Preistoria y Archeologia.

Pales, L. & M. Tassin de Saint-Péreuse 1969. *Les Gravures de la Marche: I - Les félins et les ours*. Bordeaux: Delmas.

Peyrony, D. & E. Peyrony 1938. *Laugerie-Haute près des Eyzies (Dordogne)*. Paris: Masson.

Plenier, A. 1971. *L'art de la grotte de Marsoulas*. Toulouse: Institut d'Art Préhistorique.

Roussot, A. 1984. La grotte de Font-de-Gaume. In *L'Art des cavernes. Atlas des grottes ornées paléolithiques françaises*. 129–34. Paris, Ministère de la Culture: Imprimerie Nationale.

Ruffie, J. 1986. *Le sexe et la mort*. Paris: Odile Jacob, Le Seuil.

Saint-Périer, R. de. 1965. Inventaire de l'art mobilier paléolithique en Périgord. *Bulletin de la Société Historique et Archéologique du Périgord*, special edition, 139–59.

Thevenin, A. 1982. *Rochedane, l'Azilien, l'Epipaléolithique de l'Est de la France et les civilisations épipaléolithiques de l'Europe Occidentale*. Strasbourg: Université des Sciences Humaines de Strasbourg.

Thevenin, A. 1983. Les galets gravés et peints de l'abri de Rochedane (Doubs) et le problème de l'art azilien. *Gallia–Préhistoire* **XXVI**, 139–88.

Vialou, A. 1981. *L'Art pariétal en Ariège magdalénienne*. Paris: Museum National d'Histoire Naturelle, Laboratoire de Paléontologie humaine et de Préhistoire.

Welté, A. C. 1970. *Etude du thème de l'affrontement dans l'art préhistorique*. Thesis, Faculté des Lettres et Sciences Humaines de Toulouse.

Welté, A. C. 1975. L'affrontement dans l'art préhistorique (première partie). *Travaux de l'Institut d'Art Préhistorique* **XVII**, 207–306.

Welté A. C. 1976. L'affrontement dans l'art préhistorique (seconde partie). *Travaux de l'Institut d'Art Préhistorique* **XVIII**, 187–330.

Welté A. C. 1982. *L'affrontement animal dans l'art mobilier préhistorique*. Paper presented to the Seminaire de Préhistoire et d'Archéologie, Ecole des Hautes Etudes en Sciences Sociales, Antenne du Toulouse.

Zervos, C. 1959. *L'art de l'époque du Renne en France*. Paris: Editions Cahiers d'art.

10 *Art and the essence of being: symbolic and economic aspects of fish among the peoples of western Arnhem Land, Australia*

PAUL S. C. TACON

Introduction

In the various languages spoken across Arnhem Land in the Northern Territory of Australia there is no separate term for 'art' as we know it. Paintings on rock or bark, carved wooden sculptures, woven mats and baskets, decorated musical instruments, and other forms of creative expression are not divorced from their cultural or natural environments. They are very much extensions of their environment and are related to the many facets of human experience encountered and embellished by their creators. Art objects, therefore, not only record events or reflect the aesthetic preferences of the people that produced them but also express aspects of economics, philosophy, social relations, cosmology, and world-view. Art may even be regarded as a branch of metaphysics in the sense that it serves to explain aspects of being in both the past and the present of traditional Arnhem Landers, and acts as a link between these two temporal states.

Visual expression is also closely related to myth and ritual, the three appearing 'to be completely interlocked and interdependent' (Forge 1971, p. 293). This does not mean that one of these systems is more powerful or pervasive than the others, however, for 'it seems rather as if they were all three different ways of expressing aspects of the same thing in words, in action, and visually, none of them being complete without the other, and none of them being the entire expression on its own' (Forge 1971, p. 293). Consequently, by studying forms of artistic expression various cultural relationships between man and environment may be elucidated.

Of the many cultural relationships expressed visually in Arnhem Land, that of the relationship between man and animal is one of the most complex as it may be both literal and symbolic. This is particularly true of recent rock and bark paintings where the same image may have various levels of meaning and both prosaic and abstract associations. Morphy (1977, 1984, Ch. 5, this volume) has discussed this idea in depth for the Yolngu of eastern Arnhem Land, focusing on recent bark paintings in particular. Taylor (1982, p. 198, Ch. 18, this volume) has demonstrated the existence of a similar phenomenon among the Kunwinjku of western Arnhem Land, again in terms of recent bark paintings but paintings stylistically different from those studied by Morphy. In each area both 'inside' and 'outside' meanings were shown to be inherent in the art. Further west, my own ongoing study has revealed that there are multiple meanings bound up in the recent rock art of the Kakadu and related peoples. These groups left thousands of painted images behind in rock shelters and on rock walls, including numerous complex depictions of animals stylistically related to the bark paintings studied by Taylor. Many of these animals figure prominently in their mythic and oral traditions as well, and attached to them are a variety of symbolic meanings and associations.

The rock art of Kakadu

Archaeological investigations have revealed that ochre crayons have been used in the Kakadu National Park area (see Figs 2.1–2.3) for at least 18 000 years (Jones 1985, pp. 218–19). This region contains one of the most concentrated and varied bodies of rock painting in the world, and the earliest forms have been ascribed to a Pleistocene period of at least 15 000 years BP (see Brandl 1973, Chaloupka 1984, 1985). The subject matter of these early depictions indicates that they were produced under environmental and cultural conditions quite different from those now or recently present. Aborigines argue that these early paintings were produced by *mimi* spirits and that it was these spirits and their paintings that their ancestors encountered when they first moved into the area in the distant, Dreamtime past.

The more recent, Holocene paintings of Kakadu differ from their Pleistocene counterparts dramatically. They differ in terms of form, style and subject matter, the range of rock art produced over a similar period of time, and a tendency towards greater stylistic regionalism (Lewis 1983, Tacon 1986b). One of the more prominent forms of rock painting to develop has been labelled 'X-ray' art by Europeans because both internal and external features of subjects are portrayed, and it is this form of art that Aborigines identify with most closely. The most recent X-ray rock paintings were produced in the early 1960s by the Aboriginal artist Najombolmi (see Haskovec & Sullivan, Ch. 2, this volume), and many of the paintings found throughout the region were produced by cousins, brothers, fathers, uncles, or grandfathers of Aboriginal elders living in Kakadu today. The X-ray tradition continues on barks, and many early bark-painters may also have painted in rock shelters (Taylor 1982, Tacon 1986a).

X-ray images illustrate internal anatomical features, such as the backbone, long bones, body cavities, internal organs, the digestive tract, and even soft tissue, but they were not the only form of art to be produced in the recent period of Kakadu prehistory. Various forms of human stick-figures were also produced, and many of them are arranged in hunting or warfare scenes or pictorial compositions. Along with these, many non-X-ray paintings of humans, animals, and mythological beings were produced as well. Most are identical in form to X-ray paintings except for their lack of internal detail. Instead, they are infilled with solid, stroked, or hatched areas of pigment and are usually monochromatic rather than polychromatic. They are found in the same, or nearby, shelters as X-ray paintings and are often associated with them. In this sense it is important to understand 'X-ray' as a motif applied to some paintings and not to confuse it as a style, as many have done in the past. Aborigines recognize that X-ray paintings are a part of a wider system of representation, and point out that X-ray images represent creatures in a different state of being from the creatures depicted without internal details. A variety of stencils, geometric line drawings, and beeswax compositions were also produced and these, too, appear to have been functionally different from X-ray paintings.

Numerically, the X-ray paintings of the greater Kakadu National Park area outnumber non-X-ray solid and stroke infill paintings of the same period. As well, differences between depictions of humans and depictions of animals are most distinct in X-ray art, whereas they are only slight in non-X-ray art. Because of this, and for other pragmatic reasons, further discussion will focus primarily on X-ray art forms. All of the relationships between man and animal illustrated by the art may not, therefore, be discussed, but some of the more important ones will be examined.

Recent X-ray paintings of humans and animals

Between 1985 and 1987, 3224 X-ray rock-paintings were recorded at 316 art sites. Of these, 2979 were ascribed to a recent period of less than 3000 years BP on the basis of subject matter, form, style, and superimpositioning, and they were found at a total of 231 rock-shelter sites (see Tacon 1986a, 1986b). Some regional and temporal variation was detected but, generally, these paintings are lifesize or slightly smaller, have four or more X-ray features, and are bichromes or polychromes. Earlier forms of X-ray paintings are 3–4 times smaller, detail only one or two internal features, and are usually monochromatic red.

The predominant colours in recent X-ray paintings are red, white, and yellow, but black, purple, blue, pink, and cream were used on occasion. The most common X-ray feature is that of the backbone, found on 96.4 per cent of all recent representations. Some aspect of the digestive tract is almost as frequent. A large range of internal features were illustrated and these were elaborated with a combination of solid, stroked, hatched, dashed, stippled, dotted, lozenged, or, occasionally, cross-hatched infill.

The most common subject in the art is that of fish. Fish comprise over 62 per cent of the sample – 1864 of the 2979 paintings. Various species of X-ray fish were found at over 75 per cent of all recent X-ray art sites, and fish in general seem to have been a most important or popular subject to paint. Human subjects make up a further 11.92 per cent of the sample, or 355 paintings; macropods comprise 4.16 per cent, or 124 individuals; turtles form 3.46 per cent (103 images); snakes form 3.05 per cent (91); and paintings of goannas and other lizards make up a further 2.69 per cent (80). Another 33 subjects, including mythological beings, were identified with the help of Aboriginal consultants, but all make up less than 2.5 per cent of the sample each.

There are distinct differences between the way in which human beings and animals are portrayed in X-ray detail. Human subjects with X-ray features consistently lack illustrations of organs, fat, muscle, or flesh. The backbone, ribs, long bones, and body cavities are common but soft tissue is not. Often long bones are intimated by thin lines through the centre of limbs, and the backbone is only occasionally segmented. This is true of mythical beings as well and, on the whole, human and mythical representations are more alike in terms of X-ray detail than are humans and fish or animal subjects. Fish and other animal paintings often have segmented backbones, detailed, skilfully drawn long bones, and a variety of organs, cavities, and soft tissue. They generally contain many more X-ray features than do human subjects and these often appear more naturalistic and detailed. As well, more colours were used in individual paintings to define these features. This clearly illustrates that a distinction between man and animal was made in terms of the inner structure at a symbolic, representational level, even though, as hunters who dealt with death frequently, the artists were aware that the differences were only slight at the literal level.

One possible explanation for part of this was provided by a couple of Aboriginal elders who explained that traditionally there was a belief that evil 'Namorodo' spirits would cause death by eating the guts, heart, or other organs of humans, and that these spirits would often appear in the sky in the form of shooting stars at night, or eagles and similar birds by day. If one were to portray these internal features in paintings of humans on rock shelter walls, one might arouse these spirits and attract them to the camp (Tacon 1986a, see also Chaloupka et al. 1985, p. 88, Hill 1951, p. 380).

Other differences between human and animal forms are also apparent, and these are found in both X-ray and non-X-ray paintings. The most obvious is that of perspective which also varies between species of animal. Fish and crocodiles, for instance, were both painted in profile or in a combination of overhead and profile perspectives. Turtles, snakes, and goanna/lizards were all painted from the overhead perspective. Land mammals and birds were painted in profile. Humans, mythical beings, and flying foxes (bats) were usually painted in the obverse or frontal view, although all three were occasionally painted in profile. Humans and mythical beings were also sometimes painted in contorted, twisted perspective, especially if a concept of evil was intended to be conveyed, as in a Namande spirit or sorcerized human.

Little sexual differentiation is apparent in paintings of animals, except for a few macropod paintings where sex is indicated by way of a female pouch or obvious sexual organs. X-ray and non-X-ray paintings of human figures, on the other hand, show extreme sexual dimorphism with exaggerated sexual organs in males and full, prominent breasts in females. Breasts and male genitalia were usually detailed in profile on figures painted in obverse perspective. Human females predominate over human males in X-ray art. Almost two-thirds of the representations are female, while less than one-third are male. Female subjects are particularly prevalent in the centre of the Kakadu region, where they comprise 73.5 per cent of the total human subject matter sample for that area. Human stick-figures contemporary with X-ray paintings, on the other hand, are predominantly male or lack distinguishing sexual characteristics, and many were positioned in more dynamic poses and in scenes indicative of male activities, such as hunting or warfare.

Many recent human X-ray figures have complex lozenge-shaped patterns on their chests and limbs. The designs are similar to body painting designs reported by early ethnographers, such as Spencer (1914, p. 151, Fig. 47), and are said to represent the backbone of the kangaroo. These designs are rarely found on animal paintings but occasionally are found on some paintings of fish. Most are found on X-ray paintings of female humans, but, in ritual, comparable designs are only worn by men. This appears paradoxical but many myths record how men's rituals originally belonged to ancestral women. These rituals were given to men or stolen by them so that now only men may practise them. The paintings of women with these designs may relate to this time in the past (Luke Taylor pers. comm. 1986). They also emphasize the integration of art, myth, and ritual in this area.

Superficially, human and animal paintings in recent X-ray rock art appear quite similar. A closer examination, however, has revealed significant differences which allude to conceptual differences within the minds of the artists who portrayed them. The lack of soft tissue and organs in humans, as well as their abstractly portrayed skeletal structure, contrasts remarkably with the detailed anatomy prevalent in animal paintings. This suggests definite natural/cultural distinctions. It also suggests that attention to detail in animal paintings was more important than in humans. Some of the differences may be related to specific beliefs, as was suggested above. Others seem to be related to wider cultural patterns and processes, as a closer examination of the symbolic associations attached to some of these anatomical features reveals. This is particularly true of some of the features portrayed in paintings of fish, the most common X-ray subject. As well, fish themselves are powerful in a metaphoric sense and are associated with aspects of the universe that are culturally important to the various peoples of the region.

Fish and economics

The incidence of fish in X-ray art is greatest in the northern end of Kakadu National Park, where fish comprise 76 per cent of all recent X-ray paintings. In the central and southern regions of the Park they make up between 40 and 45 per cent of the totals. Since the northern end of Kakadu is close to the sea and the mouths of tidal rivers, one would expect that fish would figure prominently in the environment of the artists of that area, and that this would be reflected in their art. What is surprising is that fish are also found in such high numbers in the art located deep in the interior, along the escarpment. Their popularity may be indicative of an increase in importance, as earlier art forms and styles of the region contain many fewer fish representations (Chaloupka 1984, Tacon 1986b).

Between 3000 and 1400 years ago there were changes in the landscape of Kakadu, with the establishment of freshwater wetlands and swamps, and a reduction in the amount of mangrove, saline swamps (Hope et al. 1985, Jones 1985, p. 293). These changes greatly increased the food resources, including fish, available to Aboriginal populations, and the archaeological evidence shows a dramatic increase in population density at both dry-season, swamp-edge camps and wet-season, rock shelters (Jones 1985, p. 293, Jones & Johnson 1985, p. 183). Recent rock-art studies indicate that most X-ray paintings are likely to date to this freshwater period (see Lewis 1983, Tacon 1986b).

With the increase in population, there would also have been an increase in concern for a large, stable food supply and for human control over it, whether this be spiritual, actual, or both. Some of the paintings may have played a role in the process, and the preoccupation with fish may indicate the important role they undertook as an easily available staple food resource. Many early studies of Arnhem Land rock art focused on animal art as food and concluded that the paintings were related to hunting magic or the regeneration of species (Mountford 1956, Arndt 1962, Elkin 1964, p. 15, Edwards 1979, pp. 101–2, McCarthy 1979, p. 66). The former seems unlikely as fish are relatively easy to catch and numerous techniques were used by men, women, and children to quickly gather them. Large macropods, alternatively, take a great deal of knowledge and skill to successfully stalk and kill, so one would expect few fish and many macropods in the art if the paintings were related to hunting magic. On the other hand, if large quantities of fish were consumed and were continually in demand, then any human contribution toward their regeneration and maintenance would be both psychologically and physically adaptive. The paintings may also be related to observations of seasonal fluctuations in fish populations in the water drainage systems of the region (Supervising Scientist 1983, 1984) if a regenerative function is accepted for them.

Discussions with several Aboriginal elders revealed that paintings of fish or other animals were usually done after the catch (Tacon 1986a). It was explained that often when someone returned to a shelter with fauna, someone else would suggest that its likeness be painted on the shelter wall or ceiling. When this was done the artist would sometimes refer to the actual species brought back as a model, but the final painted product always conformed to the stylistic conventions of the group. Only one elder remarked that occasionally, if someone failed to catch a fish or animal when hunting, he would return and retouch a painting of the same species on the shelter wall, usually adding fine lines or other infill (Tacon 1986a, George Chaloupka, pers. comm. 1987). Most elders, however, were insistent that painting was done after hunting and not before, and that usually only food-animals were painted. They also remarked that only good things were painted in shelters where people were living, and that fish were a very good subject to paint.

During the Alligator Rivers Fact–finding Study a total of 43 native fish species were recorded in the region. Ten of these have high food value (Fox *et al.* 1977, p. 53). In X-ray rock art the silver barramundi (*Lates calcarifer*), saratoga (*Scleropages jardini*), fork-tail catfish (*Hexanematichthys leptaspis*), eel-tail catfish (various *Neosilurus* spp.), and mullet (*Liza dussumieri* and *Liza diadema*) are the most frequent species portrayed, but at least 12 species are sometimes illustrated (see Figs 10.1–10.7, Colour Section 2). Their distinguishing features are easily discernible and were shown to me by Aboriginal elders. All of the above have tremendous food value but four are also carnivorous. All but the mullet spawn in the wet season when water temperatures are higher (Lake 1971) and many migrate at the beginning of the wet season when water levels rise.

Both the fork-tail catfish and the saratoga are buccal incubators (Lake 1971, p. 47). In the catfish it is the male who incubates the eggs in his mouth, while it is the female among saratoga. This unique mode of reproduction is similar to that attributed to Rainbow Snakes in the Dreamtime. Many myths record how a male

Rainbow Snake gave birth to mythical ancestors, species of animals, or features of the landscape through disgorgement. As well, young initiates are considered to be reborn into the tribe in this manner. Whether these ideas are related to observations of the above two species of fish is debatable, but it may have added to their importance in the art, myth, belief system, and diet of traditional Arnhem Landers.

The silver barramundi also has an unequalled reproductive cycle. Barramundi usually reach maturity in freshwater rivers or billabongs and move downstream to spawn in saltwater estuaries, often with the assistance of floodwaters (Lake 1971, p. 31) (see Fig. 10.8, Colour Section 2). Then they migrate back 'up to the freshwater reaches before the wet season flow subsides' (Fox *et al.* 1977, p. 53). The silver barramundi is 'an hermaphrodite, changing from male to female at roughly two years of age' (Vaughan 1982, p. 59). Males are long and slim, while sexually inverted aged females are fat and bulky, sometimes reaching weights of over 50 kg (Lake 1971, p. 31). Aborigines recognized this, and in the Gundjeibmi and Kunwinjku languages there are separate terms for immature, developed male, and sexually inverted aged female specimens (Gillespie 1982, p. 18). In the Dreamtime, species of animal could change form, change from or into human beings, and change sex. Some bisexual beings are portrayed in recent X-ray and non-X-ray art, and, generally, images with a combination of animal and human, or male and female, traits are considered to be powerful, special, and related to the supernatural (or Dreamtime) realm (see Elkin *et al.* 1950, Proskouriakoff 1971, p. 134, Harner 1982, p. 76). The observation of this phenomenon in the barramundi may have made this fish particularly notable as a being with both economic and symbolic status. Both the barramundi and the fork-tail catfish figure prominently in Mardayin and other ceremonies, and it is said that a barramundi created the East Alligator River (Aboriginal Arts Board 1979, p. 137).

Fish as a symbol

Fish are very good to eat in western Arnhem Land but in the past they may also have been good to think (see Lévi-Strauss 1964, Vinnicombe 1976, Conkey 1982, pp. 118–19, for the importance of this concept and distinction among indigenous peoples elsewhere). Fish as a symbol in the oral and mythic literature of the peoples throughout Armhem Land is powerful and pervasive. The symbolic associations are finite, however, and generally focus around water, clan wells, spirit children, growth, reproduction, reincarnation, and states of ultimate transition or transformation, such as death, birth, or rebirth. The exact link between fish symbolism in oral literature and fish symbolism in rock art is only now emerging, and current research involves extensive discussions with Aboriginal elders on the topic. These discussions and early ethnographic literature from the area have thrown much light on the relationship.

In the early 1900s Spencer recorded many myths and beliefs among the Kakadu. In one passage he mentions that the Kakadu were very frightened of a large perch-like fish, presumably barramundi (the giant perch), that lived deep in water-holes. A bone from this fish could bring death if placed in a person, and only old men could catch and eat it. Women and younger men would only be able to eat it if it was ritually made fit for consumption and had its neck broken (Spencer 1928, pp. 762–3).

In a later passage, Spencer relates beliefs about powerful Rainbow Snake beings and Rainbow Snake (Numereji) men and how they are continually associated with fish and fishing. The myth he recorded concludes with a fishing net used to catch catfish turning itself into a Rainbow Snake which then becomes the Numereji, or Rainbow Snake, of the northern division of the Kakadu. It was said to reside in a nearby river and men were afraid to approach its home for fear of being dragged into the water and swallowed (ibid., pp. 782–7).

In a third passage, Spencer explains various soul conceptions among the Kakadu, and often these revolve around fish and bones of the dead. There was a strong belief in reincarnation among the Kakadu and usually this involved a transformation of the Yalmuru, or original spirit part of each individual. Often the transformed part of the soul would be placed in a fish or some other food and then would be driven into a fishing net. This was how one of Spencer's informants claimed to have been handled by his original Yalmuru before conception and birth (ibid. pp. 815–18). The cycle of spiritual existence for these people was lengthy but always definite. It rotated from a physical human body to a spiritual form identified with the former's bones, to a rejuvenated duplicate placed in a fish or some other food form, to a new physical human form, and so forth.

In the latter two myths there is an equivalence of human soul and fish. In the first the fear of being swallowed by the transformed net/Rainbow Serpent among the Kakadu is comparable to the original action of the net catching or swallowing fish. Rainbow Snakes are said to devour human bodies and souls while nets devour or entrap fish. Humans may be released from Rainbow Snakes alive through action, and so may fish from nets. This myth, however, emphasizes the destructive power of nature, and metaphorically equates the human soul with fish. In the last myth the creationary aspects of nature are emphasized but, again, the human soul appears as a fish for part of its birth/rebirth journey.

Among the Dalabon, at the far south-eastern end of the X-ray art region, a similar belief is still prevalent. The Dalabon believe child-spirits live in water and occasionally reveal their presence over water as rainbows. It is these that enter women in order that women become pregnant (See Fig. 10.9, Colour Section 2) and the child-spirits are reincarnated (Maddock 1978b, p. 113). The Dalabon also believe in two spirit selves that separate at death; one is associated with fish and the other has a skeletal appearance and is associated with stick figures at rock art sites. The latter wanders in the bush unable to enter into women again unless it is transformed and given *bolung* or 'rainbow' power. 'This returns it to the water-dwelling child-spirit phase of existence and is ritually effectuated' (ibid., p. 113).

In the Dalabon belief system there are several different levels of Rainbow Serpent power, or *bolung*. 'Bolung' may be used as a name, attribute, or 'cycle of existence posited by Aborigines' (ibid., p. 103). For the Dalabon, *bolung* is also very much a part of spirit-children, 'the incarnation of which is necessary if there are to be people' (Maddock 1978a, p. 18). Both spirit-children and fish emanate from the same place – water-holes – and this connection with water may well be one of the keys to understanding the symbolism. As well, when a child is born water is also released from the womb, reinforcing the association between child-spirit, water, and life.

A similar belief system is said to be held by Djawan-, Maiali-, Rembarnga-, and Kunwinjku-speakers. As well, throughout the entire Kakadu–Maiali–Djawan–Dalabon–Rembarnga–Kunwinjku area recent human stick–figures are frequently associated with X-ray art, and fish are the dominant X-ray subject. Many painted shelters or places in the rocks nearby are said to have housed the bones of the dead, and some still do. Most sites are near permanent sources of water, often considered to be ancestral clan wells. All of these patterns appear in spiritual reincarnation myths and it would seem that the art is part of a larger symbolic system.

Elsewhere in Arnhem Land these patterns of relationship are reinforced through song (Berndt 1952) and everyday conversation. Among the Kunwinjku of central Arnhem Land and their neighbours to the east, for instance, fish are such a potent symbol of fertility, sexual relations, rebirth, and so forth that coitus is often described as a women 'netting a fish' in everyday speech (Berndt 1952, p. 24, Luke Taylor pers. comm. 1986). In this statement there is reference to the similarity between using a net to catch fish and legs to catch penises. Penises and fish are symbolically linked through the similar actions of legs and nets, but they are also linked at a deeper level in terms of beliefs about the sources of human life. The penis is considered to be the biological source of human life while a small fish-like spirit-child is the spiritual. Therefore, in order for a woman to become pregnant it is necessary for her vagina to catch or 'net' both (see Fig. 10.10, Colour Section 2).

In eastern Arnhem Land similar beliefs are held and this general symbolic pattern appears to be characteristic of most of the peoples in the Northern Territory's Top End. Warner (1969), for instance, argues that 'the most important unifying concept in the whole of clan ideology is that of the sacred water hole in which reposes the spiritual unity of clan life' among the Murngin (ibid., p. 19). He also points out that 'when a child is born it comes from this well as a spirit. In the well it has the appearance of a very small fish' (ibid., p. 21) (see Fig. 10.11, Colour Section 2).

The fish as a symbol of spiritual transformation is used not only for birth but also for death. Among the Yolngu, for instance, a coffin and the body within it is often interpreted as a fish, and a 'fish is one of the most basic symbols of birth and death in Yolngu culture' (Morphy 1984, p. 88).

> A major image that occurs frequently in Yolngu burial ceremonies is of a fish breaking out of a fish trap, bursting through a dam, or dragging a harpoonist through the water – in short, of fish struggling for freedom from containment and the threat of death . . . The meaning of the coffin as a fish, is connected with a more positive image of death, of the soul breaking away on its journey and perhaps with the idea of regeneration of souls (Morphy 1984, pp. 88–9).

The symbolic relationship between fish, water, spirit-child, dead people, and bones of the dead can be found in other accounts of the Kakadu (Spencer 1914, pp. 326, 345–6) and among other Australian tribes (see Roheim 1925, pp. 194–6). As well, the belief that the human soul or spirit-child is like a little fish swimming through the water is widespread across all of Northern Australia and throughout Arnhem Land, and a belief in reincarnation was widespread throughout traditional Aboriginal Australia (Mathews 1906, Mountford 1981). Whether there was a similar connection and inside meaning to X-ray fish and other animals of the painted rock shelters of western Arnhem Land is an important matter to discern. If, for example, fish became significant in this symbolic sense, the addition of the X-ray motif to the paintings may have been fundamental. Many ethnographers have described how the Kakadu and other tribes of the area conceived of the soul or life-essence as residing in the skeleton or organs of the body (Spencer 1914, Basedow 1925, p. 204, Lockwood 1962, p. 202, Tacon 1985). Thus, in depicting internal features, the spirit of a creature or human would be suggested as well as the physical form. Fish painted in this manner would be more powerful and complete and more illustrative of transformational processes intrinsic to the belief system.

In this sense, bones in paintings and bones of the dead can be considered to be symbolic of the transformation from life to death. After life, physically only the bones are left. After death a transformation has to be effected 'by the appropriate ceremony or ceremonies' to move the spirit (Maddock 1978b, p. 114). The digestive tract, another frequent X-ray component in the paintings, may also be symbolic of transformation. Food enters the system and is transformed into faecal matter. Initiates are swallowed by Rainbow Snakes and are regurgitated, transformed into men (see Hiatt 1975 for an expanded explanation). Most animals portrayed in the art are food animals which, in reality, are transformed by the human digestive system in order to sustain human life.

Food animals are a good subject to paint according to Aboriginal people, but fish, in particular, are good not only because of some of the above-mentioned properties and associations but also because of an additional property that they exhibit extremely well. This feature is based in their physiology and is something that has great metaphoric potential in terms of explaining abstract concepts about life and the Aboriginal universe. It is also a characteristic that is shared by the most powerful beings in both the natural and supernatural worlds, namely, snakes and Rainbow Serpents. Finally, it is a property that is ideally suited to be expressed in visual art, for it is that of colour.

The importance of colour was emphasized by several Aboriginal elders on a number of occasions. It was explained that X-ray paintings were of fish or animals that were alive, while solid or stroke infill paintings were of dead or cooked species and that the colour had been roasted out of them. In X-ray art, fine bands of hatching or cross-hatching in and around organs or bones of the body were said to represent the being's flesh and colour and were what gave you 'feeling' or Dreamtime essence (Tacon 1986a). All living creatures exhibit colour in their skins or flesh but at death the colour quickly fades. This phenomenon is more pronounced in cold-blooded beings, such as fish or reptiles, where marked changes in skin and scale colour are easily detected soon after death. In fish and many species of snake the scales often appear to radiate the colours of the rainbow when the creatures are living, but shortly after death they fade to a dull grey. As a consequence, the presence of colour, especially of rainbow colours, has become associated with life and things that are alive while its absence is associated with death. In order for a being to be alive it must have some aspect of 'rainbowness' or colour within it (Tacon 1986a). In order for Aboriginal spirits to be 'recycled' and returned to the water-dwelling child-spirit phase they must be given *bolung* or 'rainbow' power (Maddock 1978b, p. 113). In order for initiates to be reborn into the clan as men they must be transformed by the Rainbow Serpent (Spencer 1914, 1928, Berndt & Berndt 1970). And, finally, in order for the life-giving rains to alleviate the drought and heat of the dry season there must be storms and rainbows in the sky. Rainbows and the quality of 'rainbowness' have thus become associated with the creative and destructive forces of nature and a rainbow is a powerful symbol of this abstract concept.

Rainbowness is also associated with ancestral power or 'Dreamtime essence' and it is this that adds life to creatures and potency to paintings. In eastern Arnhem Land this is termed *bir'yun* or 'brilliance' and may be described as the brilliance one would experience from a flash of light (Morphy 1986, p. 14). In paintings this is conveyed by the visual effect that finely cross-hatched lines have on the viewer. The lines add a shimmering effect to the art that seems to make objects radiate. Morphy has examined this in detail and states that 'this brightness is one of the things that endows the painting with Ancestral power' (ibid., p. 14). Thus it can be seen that in both eastern and western Arnhem Land light is associated with ancestral power and with life, or the driving force of life, but in the west it is refracted light and the brilliant colours that are produced that are emphasized while in the east it is more often white light. This may account for some of the differences in their systems of visual art but the underlying principles are the same.

In the natural world of western Arnhem Land, of those animals which exhibit the rainbow colour in their skin, snakes are the most powerful and threatening species to mankind. They can be considered both a food and an enemy, and in this sense have both constructive and destructive attributes. In the mythology and general belief system of the area they have come to symbolize the fine line between life and death, and in their most powerful form, as Rainbow Serpents, are said to be responsible for great acts of creation, destruction, or transformation.

Fish, on the other hand, generally have more positive associations. They exhibit rainbowness in their skin but do not cause the destruction that snakes bring about. Rather than taking human life, they sustain it. Fish live in water, a place where spirit-children and Rainbow Snakes also reside. Aboriginal elders consistently describe child-spirits as resembling small fish (Tacon 1986a). Water is associated with life and growth and so, too, are fish. To think of fish is to think of something good, and, on one level, fish have become symbolic of both human life and life in general. George Namingum, an elder of the Bardmardi clan, emphasized this when telling about how his mother had died. When she was ill he said that he 'wanted to take her to Djuwarr where she could sit in the clear sand, eat fish and become strong again' (Chaloupka *et al.* 1985, p. 132).

Other elders related many more stories involving fish, and generally they all put fish in a positive light. It was explained that most of the paintings of fish in rock shelters were food and not spirit-children or Dreamtime fish *per se* but that they could be used to tell stories or beliefs about these beings as well. X-ray paintings always had the most potential for story-telling or illustrating aspects of traditional belief or practice, and many meanings could be found in given works or sets of paintings at particular sites. Much of this had to do with the nature of these art forms and the very fact that several levels or aspects of particular creatures were illustrated in one work of art; that is, the external surface, the internal structure, and the life-force that unites the internal with the external and keeps the being operational. Some people

Figure 10.1   Recent X-ray barramundi (*Lates calcarifer*) painted in the early 1900s, Bala-uru, Deaf Adder Gorge, Australia.

Figure 10.2   Two recent X-ray saratoga (*Scleropages jardini*), near Hawk Dreaming, Australia.

Figure 10.3 Recent X-ray fork-tail catfish (*Hexanematichthys leptaspis*) painted by 'Old Nym' in the 1950s, Nangaloar, Nourlangie Rock, Australia.

Figure 10.4 Recent X-ray eel-tail catfish (*Neosilurus* sp.) from a shelter at the base of the escarpment across from the Mount Brockman massif, Australia.

Figure 10.5 Recent X-ray boney bream/herring (*Nematolosa erebi*), Ubirr, Australia.

Figure 10.6 Recent X-ray archer fish (*Toxotes chatareus*) shooting a jet of water at a spider, Ubirr, Australia.

Figure 10.7 Two recent X-ray mullets (*Liza dussumieri*) with broken necks, Injuluk, Oenpelli, Australia. Note the numerous layers of superimpositions and the fine-hatched infill.

Figure 10.8 Low-lying shelter with a row of recent X-ray fish said to be migrating downstream with the first wet season rains, Djuwarr, Deaf Adder Gorge, Australia.

Figure 10.9 Recent X-ray human figures, eel-tail catfish, and other paintings by Najombolmi, from a shelter at the base of the escarpment across from the Mount Brockman massif, Australia. The rectangular areas with dotted infill on the women's torsos are said to illustrate that they are pregnant, while the dotted infill in the breasts indicates that they are lactating.

Figure 10.10 Close-up of recent X-ray couple engaged in intercourse, Upper Waterfall Creek, south of Kakadu National Park, Australia. Note the spirit-child stick-figure crawling up the woman's right leg.

Figure 10.11   A typical permanent water–hole at the base of the escarpment near dozens of painted rock shelters, Djuwarr, Deaf Adder Gorge, Australia. It is water–holes such as these that are home to multitudes of fish, spirit-children, and other creatures.

Figure 10.12 Close-up of recent X-ray barramundi with an eel-tail catfish in its stomach, Ubirr, Australia.

within the traditional society would have had access to many levels of meaning while others would only have been privileged to a few generalized ones. In this sense it is important to understand the paintings as visual expressions of belief and metaphysics that do not have rigid, fixed meanings or interpretations. Fish, because of their positive associations with food and rainbowness are ideally suited to express some of the things most important to the culture. They are, indeed, good to think about and to have about on the walls of one's shelter or in the environment as a whole.

Of course, the contemporary ideas and interpretations outlined above may differ from the ideas and intentions of the original artists 20, 50, 100, or 1000 years ago, but because they are so basic and fundamental to the belief system of the region it is likely that they vary only slightly. Even if they do differ greatly they are not invalid but, instead, illustrate the importance rock paintings have acquired for the Aboriginal elders who still care for and manage them today. As Bill Neidjie of the Bunitj clan explained at the Ubirr rock paintings (see Fig. 10.12, Colour Section 2):

> This one now, history, history book; good for you. This make a man sit up. Give you feeling, better. Think about it. You think about this one. . . if you miss all this story well bad luck; you can't help 'em any more. Telling story more better, good for us (Neidjie 1986 in Tacon 1986a: Cassette Tape 08, Side A, recorded at Ubirr on 24 October 1986).

Conclusions

The recent rock art of western Arnhem Land is both aesthically powerful and symbolically complex. A full understanding of its relatedness to other aspects of culture and its inherent meaning is only beginning to be realized. What has emerged so far, however, is that the art was not produced in isolation, in a vacuum or merely for art's sake. On the contrary, it is illustrative of ideas basic to the belief system of the society responsible for its production and is intimately related to and interlocked with myth and ritual. Complex cultural relationships are exhibited in its symbolic structure and these shed light on the belief system as a whole. What this has revealed in terms of the relationship between man and animal in this part of the world is that animals, and fish in particular, were not always considered mere fodder. Food animals may be the essence of 'being' physically, but for the people of western Arnhem Land they also were spiritually.

Acknowledgements

Most research today cannot be conducted in isolation. Many people have contributed help, advice, support, and resources, and I wish to express my great appreciation to all who have participated. In particular, I would like to thank Andrée Rosenfeld (Australian National University, Canberra), Howard Morphy (Pitt Rivers Museum, Oxford) and George Chaloupka (Northern Territory Museums and Art Galleries, Darwin) for constructive criticism, generous help, and diligent supervision. I would also like to single out all of the Aboriginal people of Kakadu National Park without whom this research would not have been possible. They very patiently and generously showed me their paintings and explained their significance. David Canari, Toby Gangali, Nipper Kapirigi, George Namingum, Big Bill Neidjie, and McGuiness McGee are especially thanked.

The research was supported by grants from the Australian Institute of Aboriginal Studies and the Faculty of Arts, Australian National University. It was conducted between 17 June and 22 November 1985, and between 24 April 1986 and 29 January 1987, after approval from the Gagadju Association and the Australian National Parks and Wildlife Service.

References

Aboriginal Arts Board 1979. *Oenpelli bark painting*. Sydney: Ure Smith.

Arndt, W. 1962. The Nagorkun–Narlinji cult. *Oceania* **32** (4), 298–320.

Basedow, H. 1925. *The Australian Aboriginal*. Adelaide: F. W. Preece & Sons.

Berndt, R. M. 1952. *Djanggawul: an Aboriginal religious cult of North-Eastern Arnhem Land*. London: Routledge & Kegan Paul.

Berndt, R. M. & C. H. Berndt 1970. *Man, land and myth*. Sydney: Ure Smith.

Brandl, E. 1973. *Australian Aboriginal paintings in Western and Central Arnhem Land: temporal sequences and elements of style in Cadell River and Deaf Adder Creek art*. Canberra: Australian Institute of Aboriginal Studies.

Chaloupka, G. 1984. *From palaeoart to casual paintings: the chronological sequence of Arnhem Land Plateau rock art*. Darwin: Northern Territory Museum of Arts and Sciences.

Chaloupka, G. 1985. Chronological sequence of Arnhem Land Plateau rock art. In *Archaeological research in Kakadu National Park*, R. Jones (ed.), 269–80. Canberra: Australian National Parks and Wildlife Service Special Publication 13.

Chaloupka, G., N. Kapirigi, B. Nayidji & G. Namingum 1985. *Cultural survey of Balawurru, Deaf Adder Creek, Amarrkananga, Cannon Hill and the Northern Corridor: a report to the Australian National Parks and Wildlife Service*. Darwin: Museum and Art Galleries Board of the Northern Territory limited edition manuscript.

Conkey, M. W. 1982. Boundedness in art and society. In *Symbolic and structural archaeology*, I. Hodder (ed.), 115–28. Cambridge: Cambridge University Press.

Edwards, R. 1979. *Australian Aboriginal art: the art of the Alligator Rivers region, Northern Territory*. Canberra: Australian Institute of Aboriginal Studies.

Elkin, A. P. 1964. Art and life. In *Australian Aboriginal art*, R. M. Berndt (ed.), 11–19. New York: Macmillan.

Elkin, A. P., R. M. Berndt & C. H. Berndt 1950. *Art in Arnhem Land*. Melbourne: Chesire.

Forge, A. 1971. Art and environment in the Sepik. In *Art and aesthetics in primitive societies*, C. F. Jopling (ed.), 290–314. New York: E. P. Dutton.

Fox, R. W., G. G. Kelleher & C. B. Kerr 1977. *Ranger uranium environmental inquiry*, 2nd rep. Canberra: Australian Government Publishing Service.

Gillespie, D. 1982. The artist as scientist. In *Aboriginal art at the top*, P. Cooke & J. Altman (eds), 17–20. Maningrida: Maningrida Arts and Crafts.

Harner, M. 1982. *The way of the shaman*. Toronto: Bantam Books.

Haskovec, I. P. & H. Sullivan 1989. Reflections and rejections of an Aboriginal artist. In *Animals into art*, H. Morphy (ed.), ch. 2. London: Unwin Hyman.

Hiatt, L. R. 1975. Swallowing and regurgitation in Australian myth and rite. In *Australian Aboriginal mythology*, L. R. Hiatt, (ed.), 143–62. Canberra: Australian Institute of Aboriginal Studies.

Hill, E. 1951. *The Territory: a sprawling saga of Australia's tropic north*. London: Angus & Robertson.

Hope, G., P. J. Hughes & J. Russell-Smith 1985. Geomorphological fieldwork and the evolution of the landscape of Kakadu National Park. In *Archaeological research in Kakadu National Park*, R. Jones (ed), 229–40. Canberra: Australian National Parks and Wildlife Service Special Publication 13.

Jones, R. 1985. Archaeological conclusions. In *Archaeological research in Kakadu National Park*, R. Jones (ed.), 291–8. Canberra: Australian National Parks and Wildlife Service Special Publication 13.

Jones, R. & I. Johnson 1985. Deaf Adder Gorge: Lindner site, Nauwalabila 1. In *Archaeological research in Kakadu National Park*, R. Jones (ed.), 165–227. Canberra: Australian National Parks and Wildlife Service Special Publication 13.

Lake J. S. 1971. *Freshwater fishes and rivers of Australia*. Melbourne: Thomas Nelson.

Lévi-Strauss, C. 1964. *Le cru et le cuit*. Paris: Librairie Plon.

Lewis, D. 1983. *Art, archaeology and material culture in Arnhem Land*. Unpublished BA honours thesis, Australian National University, Canberra.

Lockwood, D. 1962. *I, the Aboriginal*. Adelaide: Rigby.

McCarthy, F. D. 1979. *Australian Aboriginal rock art*. Sydney: The Australian Museum.

Maddock K. 1978a. Introduction. In *The Rainbow Serpent*, I. A. Buchler & K. Maddock (eds), 1–21. The Hague: Mouton.

Maddock, K. 1978b. Metaphysics in a mythical view of the world. In *The Rainbow Serpent*, I. A. Buchler & K. Maddock (eds), 99–118. The Hague: Mouton.

Mathews, R. H. 1906. Notes on some native tribes of Australia. *Journal and Proceedings of the Royal Society of New South Wales* **40**, 95–129.

Morphy, H. 1977. *'Too many meanings'; an analysis of the artistic system of the Yolngu of North East Arnhem Land*. Unpublished PhD thesis, Australian National University, Canberra.

Morphy, H. 1984. *Journey to the crocodile's nest*. Canberra: Australian Institute of Aboriginal Studies.

Morphy, H. 1986. *From dull to brilliant – the aesthetics of spiritual power among the Yolngu*. Unpublished manuscript (forthcoming *Man*, March 1989).

Morphy, H. 1989. On representing ancestral beings. In *Animals into art*, H. Morphy (ed.), ch. 5. London: Unwin Hyman

Mountford, C. 1956. *Art, myth and symbolism. Records of the American–Australian Scientific Expedition to Arnhem Land*, Vol. 1. Melbourne: Melbourne University Press.

Mountford, C. 1981. *Aboriginal conception beliefs*. Melbourne: Hyland House.

Proskouriakoff, T. 1971. Studies on Middle American art. In *Anthropology and art*, C. M. Otten (ed.), 129–37. Garden City, NY: Natural History Press.

Roheim, G. 1925. *Australian totemism: a psycho-analytic study in anthropology*. London: George Allen & Unwin.

Spencer, W. B. 1914. *The native tribes of the Northern Territory of Australia*. London: Macmillan.

Spencer, W. B. 1928. *Wanderings in wild Australia*, Vol. II, 736–858. London: Macmillan.

Supervising Scientist for the Alligator Rivers Region 1983. *Annual report 1982–83*. Canberra: Australian Government Publishing Service.

Supervising Scientist for the Alligator Rivers Region 1984. *Alligator Rivers Research Institute research report 1983–84*. Canberra: Australian Government Publishing Service.

Tacon, P. S. C. 1985. Field journals and notebooks: field research in Kakadu National Park, 17 June–22 November 1985. Department of Prehistory and Anthropology, Australian National University, Canberra.

Tacon P. S. C. 1986a. Field journals, tapes, and notebooks: field research in Kakadu National Park and Arnhem Land, 24 April 1986–29 January 1987. Department of Prehistory and Anthropology, Australian National University, Canberra.

Tacon P. S. C. 1986b. *Food for thought: a report on the 1985 archaeological and ethnographic investigations into the 'X-ray' concept in the art and culture of Western Arnhem Land, Australia.* Canberra: Australian National University limited edition manuscript.

Taylor, L. 1982. Bark paintings in Western Arnhem Land. In *Aboriginal art at the top*, P. Cooke & J. Altman (eds), 24–5. Maningrida: Maningrida Arts and Crafts.

Taylor, L. 1987. *'The same but different': social reproduction and innovation in the art of the Kunwinjku of Western Arnhem Land.* Unpublished PhD thesis, Australian National University, Canberra.

Taylor, L. 1989. Seeing the 'inside': Kunwinjku paintings and the symbol of the divided body. In *Animals into art*, H. Morphy (ed.), ch. 18. London: Unwin Hyman.

Vaughan, H. 1982. *The Australian fisherman's companion.* Sydney: Landsdowne Press.

Vinnicombe, P. 1976. *People of the Eland: rock paintings of the Drakensberg Bushmen as a reflection of their life and thought.* Pietermaritzburg: University of Natal Press.

Warner, W. L. 1969. *A black civilization.* Chicago: Harper & Row.

THE MEANINGS OF
THE MOTIFS

11 *Supper or symbol: roadrunner tracks in southwest art and ritual*

POLLY SCHAAFSMA

Introduction – rock art and hunting magic

For quite some time now (Heizer & Baumhoff 1962, Von Werlhof 1965, Meighan 1966, 1969, Grant *et al*. 1968, Heizer & Hester 1974, Grant 1974, Thomas 1976, Brewer 1978, King 1978) rock art interpretation has been influenced by a general trend in archaeological studies which is concerned with the study of human ecology and adaptive strategies. Some exponents of this trend feel that if it can be shown that rock art is part of an adaptive strategy, i.e. 'hunting magic', then the study of rock art is justifiable (Heizer & Hester 1974). Further, it provides information regarding diet, procurement practices, and seasonality (Rector 1981), and it takes on a significance beyond that of simply being one component of a 'thin veneer' of cultural traits embracing religion and ideology (Madsen 1979).

'Hunting magic' as an explanation for rock art, however, is fraught with problems. It is often misunderstood as merely being related to physiological necessities, a means of ensuring an adequate supper. As such, 'hunting magic' becomes a 'sort of applied pseudo-science that deals with cause-and-effect relations' (Kroeber 1948, p. 308), an early view espoused by Frazer (1890). This type of interpretation is descriptive and literal, and imbued with our own pragmatic cultural biases. Recent statements with reference to some Baja California petroglyphs: 'Thus the insect motif at the site may reflect the portrayal of a subsistence practice. The depiction of snakes is also probable in view of their use as food' (King 1978, p. 163), are good examples of a simplistic interpretation based on food procurement and one which dispenses with any other possible interpretations that these figures may have had.

Even if rock art may be related to hunting ritual, ethnographic evidence, such as that presented by Reichel-Dolmatoff (1967) for the Tukano paintings in the Amazon, indicates that the function of this art work is far more complex than a mere 'hunting magic' label implies. The function and meaning of such work are specific to particular cultural systems and certainly must be understood outside of our own cultural matrix. In the Tukano example, the paintings are made to communicate requests to the supernaturals and are part of a ritual involving a shamanic maintenance of biotic equilibrium through a balance of energy and fertility.

Rock art imagery often relates to the mythological structure of the authoring group, and imagery, including animals of prey, whether or not hunting ritual is connected with the art, may have important symbolic values. The recognition of this dimension of rock art content is not new, and a number of scholars have questioned previously offered hunting magic explanations for the content and function of rock art sites. Lewis-Williams (1981), for example, made an in-depth study of the eland as a symbolic figure as opposed to a game animal in southern San rock paintings of South Africa. Rector & Ritter (1978) and Rector (1981), on the basis of equivalent percentages of fish and turtle figures present in littoral and inland rock art sites in Baja California, have called into question food procuration as the motive behind the depictions of these animals. Nissen (1982), who supports the hunting magic function for Great Basin sites, does suggest that bighorn sheep may have had symbolic significance beyond their use as a food source. The symbolic potential of these figures is also discussed by Hedges (1983). Whitley (1982), while not discounting the possibility that rock art in the Coso Range may have been associated with sheep hunting, suggests that the idea of a hunting cult may be an oversimplification of the prehistoric situation, and proposes symbolic interpretations for the sheep, based on the etiological mythology of the western Shoshone. He proposes that the sheep symbolized generalized concepts of male success in hunting and sexual activities, and that they are not documents of a hunting cult and associated rituals.

Roadrunner tracks in southwestern petroglyphs

In the American Southwest, roadrunner tracks appear in Jornada-style petroglyphs in southern New Mexico and in the historically related but later Pueblo rock art to the north. In the Jornada region petroglyphs of the tracks of these plentiful birds are often associated with those of carnivores, particularly those of the mountain lion. It is well known that carnivores, and mountain lions in particular, have a variety of Pueblo ritual powers, not the least of which are their roles as patrons of the hunt. Although no one thinks of the roadrunner as a major game bird, lacking more information and given the current emphasis on adaptive strategies in American archaeology, the prolific representations of these tracks and their association with carnivore prints might well suggest the possibility that this rock art imagery reflects a prehistoric hunting practice. (And why not, after all – the much smaller robin was regularly consumed, for example, in Taos Pueblo.) As we shall see, however, a perusal of the ethnographic literature suggests otherwise.

As a graphic image, the roadrunner track is best known from its appearance in the rock art of the Jornada style, where it is one of the less spectacular but more frequently occurring elements. The Jornada style of the lower desert of southern New Mexico and adjacent parts of Texas and Chihuahua is the product of Mogollon peoples living in the region between roughly AD 1050 and 1400 (Fig. 11.1, Schaafsma 1980, pp. 196–242). Like the Anasazi to the north, these people were farmers living in Pueblo-style villages, making pottery and growing corn, beans, and squash as an important part of their subsistence. Their graphic art, which has been preserved through the centuries in the form of rock art and in the Mimbres ceramic tradition, is some of the richest in iconography and most sophisticated in form in southwestern prehistory. Rock-art elements include mask designs, some of which are highly

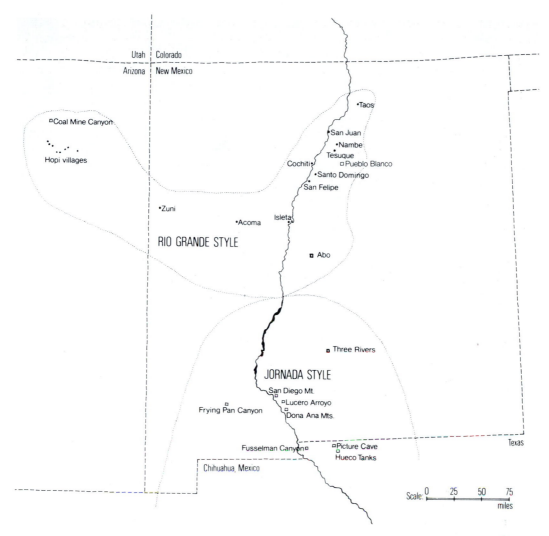

Figure 11.1 Map showing the distribution of Jornada and Rio Grande rock art styles, contemporary Pueblo villages, and rock art sites in which roadrunner tracks have been documented.

abstract, stylized as well as naturalistic anthropomorphic figures, animals of all kinds, mythical or composite creatures, burden baskets, corn, cloud terraces, and as well, human, animal, and bird tracks. It was this art, along with its underlying ideology that set the stage for future developments among Pueblo peoples to the north, who in the 14th century adopted the style and iconographic complex, and who continued the tradition into the historic present. Modification of the Jornada style and its contents occurred once it was in Pueblo hands, and with these changes it became the Rio Grande style (Schaafsma 1980, pp. 254–9). The roadrunner track also occurs in the rock art of the Rio Grande style, but it is comparatively rare. The ethnographic record, however, has numerous references to its reproduction in other media and use in ritual contexts.

Figure 11.2 Roadrunner tracks in a sandy *arroyo* bottom.

The actual track of the roadrunner, *Geococcyx californianus*, along with that of other members of the cuckoo family, as well as of woodpeckers and some owls, is zygodactylous; that is, two toes point forward and two point backward. As a result, the direction of travel of such birds as indicated by their tracks is ambiguous. Among them it is the ground-dwelling roadrunner, also known as the 'chaparral cock' that most often leaves his track, and in sandy desert *arroyos* where it is commonly observed, the roadrunner's trail of X-shaped tracks (Fig. 11.2) can be followed for considerable distances.

In its most distinctive form, the petroglyph replica of the track is a pecked 'X' a few inches tall, the ends of which are curved in toward each other (Figs. 11.3–11.6). Davis (1978) mentions in his discussion of those at Hueco Tanks, Texas, that not all are incurved. A simple 'X', however, is such a basic element that unless it appears in a context within which a track identity may be inferred, this interpretation is risky.

From a sample of nine Jornada-style sites, over 30 examples have been documented (Table 11.1). Among these, ten are shown in clear association with a carnivore track which can usually be further identified as feline, probably that of a mountain lion. Long, curved claws are usually depicted with the track. Although they are absent in the actual footprint, they are represented because of their conceptual importance in relationship to this animal. Claws may take the form of whorls

Figure 11.3 Roadrunner track and carnivore track as petroglyphs, San Diego Mountain.

Figure 11.4 Roadrunner track petroglyphs juxtaposed with face (a) and a carnivore track (b), San Diego Mountain.

Table 11.1 Sample of Jornada-style and Rio Grande-style sites in which the × element, or roadrunner track, occurs. All examples of the track may not have been documented from each site. The large number of occurrences of the roadrunner track with that of carnivores is apparently a purposeful association.

Site	Number of recorded tracks	Association
Jornada style		
Dona Ana Mountains	1	bear or human tracks (Fig. 11.5b)
Frying Pan Canyon	1 (identity questionable)	none (Fig. 11.5e)
Fusselman Canyon	6	4 with carnivore tracks, 1 with serpent, 1 alone (Green 1967b)
Hueco Tanks 15-c	12	on horizontal boulder surface with carnivore, bird (turkey?), and possible bear tracks; circle with cross; line-dots series; and other small figures (Davis 1978, pp. 88–9)
Lucero Arroyo	1	none (Fig. 11.5d)
Picture Cave	4	3 with carnivore tracks (Sutherland 1976, Fig. 17), 1 with outline mask (Davis 1978)
San Diego Mt., Site 1	2	each with carnivore track (Figs. 11.3 & 11.5a)
San Diego Mt., Site 2	2	1 with carnivore track (Fig. 11.4b), 1 with outline mask (Fig. 11.4a)
Three Rivers	3	1 near circle-dot design (Fig. 11.5c), 1 as feet of bird (Fig. 11.7), 1 (questionable) as design on outline mask
Rio Grande style		
Abo	1	none (Fig. 11.6)
Coal Mine	1	?
Pueblo Blanco	2	near bear track and mask

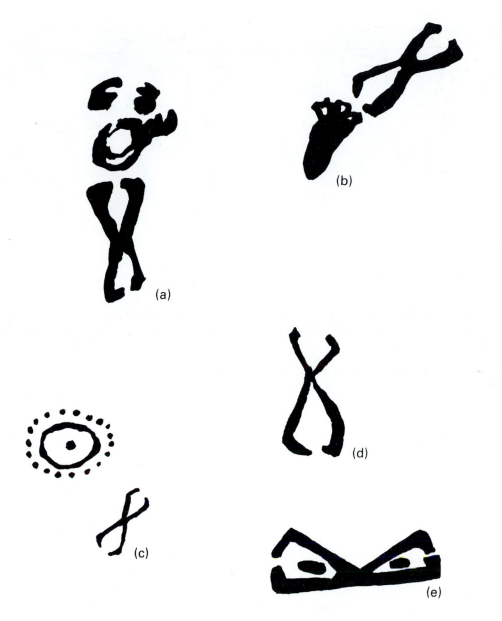

Figure 11.5 Jornada-style petroglyph roadrunner tracks from (a) San Diego Mountain, (b) the Dona Ana Mountains, (c) Three Rivers, (d) Lucero Arroyo, and (e) Frying Pan Canyon.

Figure 11.6 Pueblo petroglyph roadrunner track, Abo.

around a circular pat (see Smith 1952, pp. 203–4 and compare Figs 41b & 43a, Dutton 1963, p. 77, Fig. 86, Hibben 1975, Figs. 47 & 48). Sometimes, as at Fusselman Canyon in the Franklin Mountains near El Paso, Texas, as many as three X s occur with a single carnivore track. Twelve roadrunner tracks at Hueco Tanks, Site 15-c, are shown with two carnivore tracks along with other small figures (Table 11.l) (Davis 1978, p. 99, Fig. 3).

The importance of the association of the incurved X and the carnivore track is further emphasized by their appearance together as designs on artefacts. Green (1967a) notes that these elements are engraved on arrowshaft smoothers from El Paso Phase habitation sites east of El Paso. Roadrunner tracks also occur alone on other smoothers and on a paint palette from this region. Further, incurved incised X s decorate shell beads and shell trumpets (Medio Period artefacts from Casas Grandes, Chihuahua (Di Peso *et al.* 1974, p. 404, Figs 504–6)). On one of the trumpets, two roadrunner tracks flank a carnivore track. Revised Medio Period dates fall between AD 1150 and 1300 (LeBlanc 1980, p. 800, Fig. 1). The occurrences at Casas Grandes in northern Chihuahua are consistent with the close cultural affiliations postulated between this site and neighbouring areas in southern New Mexico and Texas (LeBlanc 1980, p. 802, Schaafsma 1980, pp. 241–2).

The roadrunner track appears only occasionally in Rio Grande-style petroglyphs (AD 1350–present), but it is retained in a variety of contexts and media in contemporary Pueblo ritual and ideology.

Figure 11.7 Petroglyph of a roadrunner with distinctive topknot, long beak, and foot depicted.

The ethnographic significance of the roadrunner track

The mere presence of the roadrunner track in prehistoric rock art was strongly indicative that the roadrunner and/or its track had religious significance in the prehistoric southwest. The tracks of animals are not a general feature of Pueblo art. Rather a selected few are chosen for graphic depiction because of the special roles the animals in question played in religious ideology and ritual. The whole animal may be signified by a track, although in certain cases the track (or paw in the case of bears) is imbued with specific ritual powers. Thus, the ethnographic record was examined in order to determine what special significance roadrunner and/or roadrunner tracks might have in Pueblo ideology today. Because of the continuity in style and subject matter between modern Pueblo religious iconography, the Rio Grande rock-art style, and its predecessor, the Jornada style, any current meanings could help explain the past.

When Don Talayesva of Hopi identified the incurved X petroglyph from Coal Mine Canyon as a roadrunner track (Dan Murphy pers. comm. 1981), he also added that the roadrunner is a liar. Thus, he opened the door to some of the roadrunner's more esoteric meanings. Investigation of the ethnographic literature reveals a complex of ideas and concepts surrounding this bird, and particularly its unusual track, that is consistent with Talayesva's statement.

Birds function in major roles in Pueblo ritual and ceremony. Birds (and animals in general) are viewed by the Pueblos as man's extended kin and agents of nature. The Zuni perspective on the use of birds and animals in ceremonial contexts, as outlined by Young (1985, p. 18), undoubtedly holds for other Pueblos as well. At Zuni all inhabitants of this world are arranged along a continuum from 'raw' to 'finished'. A being's degree of 'rawness' indicates his closeness to the world of myth, and the degree of this affiliation with the mythic realm and the events that transpired therein gives him a concomitant degree of power. Access to power enables one to make changes in this physical world. Man, the most 'finished' of all beings, has the least power of all, and therefore he must draw upon the power of others who can mediate between him and the supernaturals (Young 1982, p. 138). Mediation can be effected by graphically representing the mediator in a variety of contexts and forms, including perhaps rock art (Young 1985, p. 18), and in the case of birds, by the use of their feathers in rituals.

Among all Pueblos, specific powers are assigned to different species on the basis of careful observations. These observations are not made for the purpose of describing order in nature in the manner of a naturalist, but instead are made in order to understand each bird's, animal's, or insect's salient features, strengths, and magical properties, which can then be utilized in various ways for the benefit of man (Tyler 1979).

Wright (1977, p. 91) has suggested that the use of birds by the Hopi surpasses that of any other North American tribe. At Hopi, as at other Pueblos, feathers are used on altars, shrines, prayer sticks, *kachinas*, deities, and men as ceremonial participants, and each kind of feather has its own particular significance. Birds' roles are extremely varied and numerous, and birds are endowed with a vast number of characteristics and powers, often grounded in narrative poetry and myth. In ritual a single bird, or the feathers of the same, may embody several different attributes, depending upon the context.

It follows that representations of birds proliferate in Pueblo art. Fewkes stressed this in his study of Sikyatki pottery designs (1898, pp. 682–98). In Rio Grande-style rock art and in Pueblo *kiva* murals after AD 1325, birds are particularly prominent. In both of the latter contexts their meanings are to be sought in their esoteric significance and ceremonial roles.

Whereas in many cases the representation of an animal or bird track may be an abbreviated statement for the whole creature, and as well, an attempt to secure its supernatural aid, investigation shows that in Pueblo ritual the roadrunner track itself as well as the bird alone are both items of importance. The occurrences of the roadrunner track and the roadrunner in Pueblo ceremonies have been summarized by Tyler (1979).

The roadrunner and its tracks appear in a Zuni mythic account of the activities of the Ahaiyute, the warrior twins. The tale, which underlies the Scalp Ceremony, illustrates how the tracks function, and it establishes other affiliations of this bird. As is commonly the case, the myth in question as told to various ethnologists has several versions. In a detailed account related by Benedict (1935, pp. 62–8) from the myth 'The Ahaiyute destroy the monsters' there is a tale of the pursuit of the Ahaiyute by the ghost of a Navajo girl with whom they had made love and then killed. As the ghost chased them, they fled to the village and tried unsuccessfully to take refuge in various society rooms. Finally, at the Knife Society room they hit her and took her to the west where they scalped her with a stone knife:

> They laid her down on her back, and they said, 'Lie there and count the stars.' She could not trouble them any more. They took up the scalp, and they returned to the room of the Knife Society. They laid the scalp on the roof.
>
> The headman had made a broad meal road from the ladder to the altar. When the Ahaiyute came down the ladder, he said to them, 'Look hard at this road of cornmeal. Perhaps something has happened to it.' They looked and there were the tracks of Chaparral cock. Younger Brother said, 'It was coming in.' Elder Brother said, 'It was going out.' They looked, and there was the chaparral cock. Younger Brother took it in his arms, and he said, 'My, it's pretty.' Elder Brother stroked its feathers. He said, 'It is pretty.' He stretched out the wing feathers separately and then the tail feathers. Nobody could tell how the chaparral cock came to be behind the altar. The headman said, 'Count the feathers.' They counted and Younger Brother said, 'There are twelve.' The headman said, 'So many days will there be (in the scalp dance).' The Ahaiyute did not know what he was saying. He said, 'It is your wife. She has become the chaparral cock. Hang her scalp up from the roof.' (Benedict 1935, p. 68)

One of the versions of the tale as recorded by Parsons (1924, pp. 28–9) illustrates a relationship between the Scalp Ceremony and the Ant Society. In a footnote Parsons points out that the Knife Order at Zuni (see Benedict's version above) is a division of the Ant Society. The story goes as follows:

> Long ago when the two little boys (the war gods, *ahayuta achi*) were going around fighting, they found a Navajo girl. They had intercourse with her, they then killed her or said they had killed her, laying her on her face. She came to life, the two boys ran away. They sought to hide with the societies (*tikyawe*), but nobody would take them in until they came to the Ant people. They went in and said, 'Where can we hide?' 'We are not going to hide you,' said the Ant people, 'Sit down there.' The Navajo girl came to the top of the house and called, 'Where are my husbands?' 'Come in, they are in here!' She advanced one step and ran back, she advanced two steps and ran back, she advanced three steps and ran back, she advanced four steps and there was but a half step to enter when they said, 'Go and kill your wife.' They got up and ran after her and killed her outside. They laid her face up, her eyes open to the stars. They knew she would not come to life again. They said to her, 'Count the stars.' She did not speak, so they knew she was dead. They went in, and the Ant people asked what they had done. 'We did what you told us to do, we killed her, we laid her with her face to the sky, as you said.' The Ant people said, 'Now, look at the altar (*teshkwi*). What do you see?' They saw the tracks of the Chaparral Cock. Older Brother said, 'It looks as if it came in.' 'No,' said Younger Brother, 'It is going out.' They said these things four times. 'Look around at the back of the altar,' said the Ant people. There they found Chaparral Cock. 'How many feathers are on it?' 'There are twelve feathers.' 'That will be your count when you kill Navajo, that will be your *teshkwi* (taboo time). . .'

In still another version also recorded by Parsons (1924, pp. 29–33), the Ahaiyute have the help of Bear, White Bear, Mountain Lion, and Achiyalatopa (Knife Wing) who lent them their knives for the scalping.

This myth fixes the relationship between the roadrunner and the Scalp Ceremony, and by extension this bird's association with war. It illustrates the directional ambiguity of the roadrunner's tracks, and it makes explicit the relationship between the number of feathers in the bird's tail and the number of days of taboo necessary after killing an enemy. In a footnote by Ladd in Dutton (1963, p. 82) he states that the 12 feathers in the tail determine that the Scalp Ceremony originally was intended to last 12 days. Also, the bringing together of the roadrunner and the Ant Society seems to be more than coincidental. Both the ants and roadrunner have roles to play in either the destruction of, or creation of, confusion with regard to trails: while ants destroy Zuni footprints so they cannot be found by the enemy, the roadrunner in war conveys messages and the enemy cannot tell from which direction he came (Stevenson 1904, p. 582).

It follows that during the Scalp Ceremony the roadrunner is symbolized by its track in various ways. The scalp kickers wear crossed roadrunner feathers in the toes of their left moccasin and wear similar but larger feathers in their hair on the left side of their head. Knowledge and courage are said to come from these feathers, the roadrunner being the 'keeper of courage' (Stevenson 1904, p. 584, Parsons 1924, p. 37). Further, within the pottery drum used during the ceremony are two crossed roadrunner feathers and two crossed pieces of yucca (Parsons 1924, p. 38). Finally, from the Ant altar, an excavation also representing the Shi'papolima and which is flanked by meal mounds symbolic of the war gods' home, is a meal road crossed at right angles by shorter lines of meal. Where these lines intersect, crossed pieces of yucca representing roadrunner tracks to the altar are placed. Passage up the meal road marked in this way by the participants secures their safety from the enemy. Parsons suggests that this is a dramatization of the myth itself (1924, pp. 36–7).

The symbolic use of the roadrunner track in Pueblo ceremony is not restricted to Zuni, but it is used by other villages in other ceremonies, often for the similar purpose of confusing some undesirable entity. In the eastern Pueblos, altar and other ritual roads may have crossed pieces of yucca blades similar to those just described, placed to indicate stepping spots. These yucca crosses are said to represent roadrunner tracks which, because of their non-directional character, preclude pursuit by witches (Parsons 1929, p. 253, 1939, p. 362). The Tewa Pueblos of Tesuque and San Juan are mentioned specifically in this context. From the latter village Parsons illustrates altars made at the installation of the Winter Man and a Kossa (clown) altar, both of which have roadrunner tracks on meal roads (Parsons 1929, Pls 16, 17). She also has a sketch of the altar at the installation of Winter Chief at Tesuque. Here two roads of meal and pollen are marked with crossed yucca, and in addition, the track is painted on the wall of the room (1929, p. 228, Fig. 13).

At Nambe, Jemez, and Cochiti the track is used in funeral and in other services for the dead, both to confuse evil spirits which might plague the soul of the deceased and to keep the dead from following the living. At Nambe during funerals, the left sole and palm of the participants are marked with the tracks to keep the dead from following and harming them (Parsons 1939, p. 859). Also on All Souls' Day, family members who bring food to the dead, who have returned to the village at this time, similarly mark their left palm and sole with charcoal (Parsons 1929, p. 237). In a ceremony following burial at Jemez a wooden effigy of the departed placed within a circle drawn on the floor, is protected by roadrunner tracks (Reagan 1917, p. 41). Similarly, at Cochiti the tracks are used to protect the soul of the deceased from witches and evil spirits. The X s or tracks are scratched in a circle on the floor to form a protective barrier around an ear of blue corn in which the soul of the dead is said to reside (Bandelier, in Lange 1959, p. 416). In a diagram of a Cochiti altar for the dead (Dumarest 1919, pp. 167–70) the meal road is under the protection of turkey, snake, eagle, bear, and the roadrunner, all of whom have their tracks represented on both sides. Also described are funerary bowls in which offerings for the dead are placed and on which roadrunner tracks occur as part of their decoration (Dumarest 1919).

Similarly, at Isleta Pueblo a cross is marked on a circle drawn around the grave in order to protect the dead from witches, and a cross is made on the door after chasing away the deceased in the funeral ceremony (Parsons 1932, p. 249). Parsons does not say what the significance of this cross is, but it is likely to be a roadrunner track, judging from the other examples in which the track is used as protection both for and from the dead.

The relationship between roadrunners and their tracks, war, and scalps, which in turn are closely associated with rain (Bunzel 1932, p. 676, Parsons 1939, Parmentier 1979, pp. 610–11) probably explains why the use of roadrunner feathers at Zuni is restricted to the rain priests (Ladd 1963). That the feather may guard against witchcraft (Wright 1977, p. 97) is a power undoubtedly derived from the power of the track, but other attributes appear to be independent. The roadrunner as a source of courage and knowledge was mentioned earlier in connection with the Zuni Scalp Ceremony in which the use of the feathers (arranged to imitate the shape of the track) conveyed those qualities to the wearer. Strength and speed are significant character-istics of the bird itself, and roadrunner feathers are often used when those attributes are desired. Particularly important is their use in prayer plumes at Hopi during the winter solstice ceremonies when strength and speed are needed by the sun to offset the malevolent powers to which the sun is subjected at this point (Fewkes 1897, pp. 271–2). The Hopi also tie roadrunner feathers to their horses' tails for speed and tirelessness, and the Hopis themselves may eat roadrunners to attain these desirable qualities (Stephen 1936, p. 950).

As a symbol of strength, the roadrunner has a role in curing ceremonies. The director of the Shu'maakwe Society at Zuni, for example, which treats rheumatic troubles and convulsions, must be from the Roadrunner Clan as dictated by the folk-loric origins of this fraternity (Stevenson 1904, pp. 410–11). It has been suggested that the Shu'maakwe Society, directed as it is by a Roadrunner Clan member, is in charge of these particular diseases because of the straight, strong, and swift qualities of this bird (Tyler 1979, p. 263).

To summarize, the roadrunner, both because of its special attributes as a bird, as well as the particular zygodactylous character of its track, plays a role in several aspects of Pueblo ritual and ceremony. Strength, courage, knowledge, and speed were just mentioned in connection with winter solstice rites, curing, and the Scalp Ceremony which is intimately tied to war. The track may sometimes be used as a symbol for these things, but generally it is important because of its power to confuse. As a track pointing in both directions, it creates deception which is useful in war and in funeral ritual as well as in cases where it is necessary to guard against witchcraft.

The track is not described as a petroglyph or rock painting in these ethnographic contexts, but it is represented in various other ways: as crossed feathers on persons or in pottery drums, crossed yucca blades on altar roads, as body markings, as a design scratched into the ground, and as decoration on funerary bowls. Finally, it has been described as a painted element on the wall in the room of the Winter Chief. It remains to be asked what the ethnographic data tell us about the roadrunner track as an element appearing in the context of prehistoric rock art.

Discussion

From its presence in the rock art, it is apparent that the roadrunner track which is so important in Pueblo ritual today has had a role to play in Pueblo and Mogollon ideology for over 800 years. One may assume from the complex meanings and usages of the track, as well as from the significance of the bird itself in the present ethnographic context, that the track in the prehistoric record is a symbol rich in esoteric significance. It is not a document of an observed natural phenomenon, nor does it have economic implications.

That the prehistoric symbol has meanings exactly equivalent to those in modern usage is hard to demonstrate, as meanings tend to shift while symbols remain constant (Spier discussed this phenomenon between Plains tribes). While clues about its prehistoric meaning are scanty, the association of the roadrunner with carnivore tracks suggests that the roadrunner's various relationships to war may not have changed substantially through time. The petroglyphs may have served as shorthand records of myths and ceremonies similar to those just described. Along with other carnivores, such as the bobcat and wolf, the mountain lion is not only a patron of the hunt as discussed at the beginning of this chapter, but he is a patron of both war and medicine societies as well. The mountain lion along with other predators often acts as a guardian and protector. The roadrunner's attributes of courage and strength as ritualized by the Pueblos are also consistent with these affiliations, and we have seen that the roadrunner in Pueblo religion is linked in various ways to all of these functions. On the other hand, hunting magic does not have a place in his symbolic repertoire.

Roadrunner clans are, or have been, present recently in a number of villages including Keresan San Felipe, Santo Domingo, and Acoma, as well as at Zuni. Although it could be argued that some of the prehistoric representations may have been clan symbols, their frequent juxtaposition with carnivore tracks signifies its broader symbolic meanings and functions.

In conclusion, the example of the roadrunner track, for which we are fortunate in having ample documentation of its use and meaning in Pueblo rituals, illustrates the potentially complex significance of any one figure found painted or inscribed on rocks. The study shows how background information on the symbolic significance of even one element can radically alter interpretation. Even when ethnographic data are not available, caution should be exercised in ascribing hunting magic interpretations to rock art.

The study of anthropology is more than a study of adaptive mechanisms (Flannery 1982). Graphic imagery of prehistoric societies is a record of past ideological behaviour and a statement of symbolic systems which shaped members' responses to the world. Methods for dealing with rock art data in terms of ideology have recently been outlined by Hudson & Lee (1981). As the example of the roadrunner track illustrates, the symbol systems present in rock art constitute a metaphorical description of the world which is esoteric and usually very different from our own, but one which is as meaningful and as all-encompassing as our scientific one. As anthropologists, archaeologists – scholars – of visual records from the past, it behoves us to be aware of this dimension of prehistoric imagery.

References

Benedict, R. 1935. *Zuni mythology*, Vol. 1. New York: Columbia University Press.

Brewer, T. 1978. Bahia Coyote rock art. In *Seven rock art sites in Baja California*, C. W. Meighan & V. L. Pontoni (eds), 215–36. Socorro, NM: Ballena Press Publications on North American Rock Art, no. 2.

Bunzel, R. L. 1932. *Zuni ritual poetry*. 47th Annual Report of the Bureau of American Ethnology, 1929–1930, 611–836. Washington, DC.

Davis, J. V. 1978. The occurrence of pecked figures at Hueco Tanks pictograph site. *American Indian rock art*, Vol. 4, 69–103. Papers of the 4th Annual ARARA Symposium, Tempe. El Toro, CA.

Di Peso, C., J. B. Rinaldo & G. Fenner 1974. *Casas Grandes: A folk trading center of the Gran Cichimeca*. Vol. 6, The Amerind Foundation Inc., Dragoon. Flagstaff: Northland Press.

Dumarest, Father N. 1919. Notes on Cochiti, New Mexico. *American Anthropological Association Memoirs*, no. 6. Lancaster, Pa.

Dutton, B. P. 1963. *Sun Father's way: the Kiva murals of Kuaua*. Albuquerque: University of New Mexico Press.

Fewkes, J. W. 1897. *Tusayan Katchinas*. 15th Annual Report of the Bureau of American Ethnology, 1893–94. Washington, DC.

Fewkes, J. W. 1898. *Archeological expedition to Arizona in 1895*. 17th Annual Report of the Bureau of American Ethnology, 1895–96. Washington, DC.

Flannery, K. V. 1982. The Golden Marshalltown: a parable for the archeology of the 1980s. *American Anthropologist* **84**(2), 265–78.

Frazer, Sir J. 1890. *The golden bough*, Vol. 1. London: Macmillan.

Grant, C. 1974. *Rock art of Baja California*. Los Angeles: Dawson's Book Shop.

Grant C., J. W. Baird & J. K. Pringle 1968. *Rock drawings of the Coso Range, Inyo County, California*. Maturango Museum, Publication no. 4. China Lake.

Green, J. W. 1967a. Rock art of the El Paso Southwest: Fusselman Canyon petroglyph site, EPAS-44. *The Artifact* **5**(1), 1–19.

Green, J. W. 1967b. Rock art of the El Paso Southwest: reinvestigation of the Fusselman Canyon petroglyph site, EPAS-44. *The Artifact* **5**(2), 35–44.

Hedges, K. 1983. Shamanic origins of rock art. In *Ancient images on stone: rock art of California*, J. A. Van Tilburg (ed.), 46–59. Los Angeles: The Rock Art Archive, The Institute of Archaeology, UCLA.

Heizer, R. F. & M. A. Baumhoff 1962. *Prehistoric rock art of Nevada and eastern California* Berkeley and Los Angeles: University of California Press.

Heizer, R. F. & T. R. Hester 1974. Two petroglyph sites in Lincoln County, Nevada. *Contributions of the University of California Archaeological Research Facility* **20**, 1–52.

Hibben, F. C. 1975. *Kiva art of the Anasazi at Pottery Mound.* Las Vegas: KC Publications.

Hudson, T. & G. Lee 1981. Function and symbolism in Chumash rock art. Paper read at the Annual Meetings of the Southwestern Anthropological Association, March 1981, Santa Barbara; and at the Annual Meetings of the Society for American Archaeology, 1981, San Diego.

King, T. J., Jr. 1978. A petroglyph assemblage from Cerrito de Cascabeles. In *Seven rock art sites in Baja California*, C. W. Meighan & V. C. Pontoni (eds), 124–77. Socorro, New Mexico: Ballena Press.

Kroeber, A. 1948. *Anthropology*, 2nd edn. New York: Harcourt, Brace.

Ladd, E. J. 1963. *Zuni ethno-ornithology*. MS thesis, Department of Anthropology, University of New Mexico.

Lange, C. 1959. *Cochiti: a New Mexico Pueblo, past and present.* Austin: University of Texas Press.

LeBlanc, S. A. 1980. The dating of Casas Grandes. *American Antiquity* **45**, 799–806.

Lewis-Williams, J. D. 1981. *Believing and seeing: symbolic meanings in southern San rock paintings.* New York: Academic Press.

Madsen, D. B. 1979. The Fremont and the Sevier: defining prehistoric agriculturalists north of the Anasazi. *American Antiquity* **44** (4), 711–22.

Meighan, C. W. 1966. Prehistoric rock paintings in Baja California. *American Antiquity* **31**, 37–92.

Meighan, C. W. 1969. *Indian art and history, the testimony of prehispanic rock paintings in Baja California.* Los Angeles: Dawson's Book Shop.

Nissen, K. M. 1982. *Images from the past: an analysis of six western Great Basin petroglyph sites.* Unpublished PhD dissertation, Department of Anthropology, University of California, Berkeley.

Parmentier, R. J. 1979. The mythological triangle: Poseyemu, Montezuma, and Jesus in the Pueblos. *Handbook of North American Indians*, Vol. 9: *Southwest*, A. Ortiz (ed.), 609–22. Washington: Smithsonian Institution.

Parsons, E. C. 1924. The Scalp Ceremony of Zuni. *American Anthropological Association Memoirs*, no. 31, Menasha.

Parsons, E. C. 1929. The social organization of the Tewa of New Mexico. *American Anthropological Association Memoirs*, no. 36, Menasha.

Parsons, E. C. 1932. *Isleta, New Mexico.* 47th Annual Report of the Bureau of American Ethnology, 1929–30. Washington, DC.

Parsons, E. C. 1939. *Pueblo Indian religion*, Vols. I & II. Chicago: University of Chicago Press.

Reagan, A. B. 1917. The Jemez Indians. *El Palacio* **4**(2), 24–72.

Rector, C. H. 1977. The function of east Mohave rock art. *American Indian Rock Art*, Vol. 3, A. J. Bock, F. Bock & J. Cawley (eds), 151–6. Whittier: American Rock Art Research Association.

Rector, C. H. 1981. Depictions in Baja California rock art. *Pacific Coast Archaeological Society Quarterly* **17**(1), 17–24.

Rector, C. H. & E. W. Ritter 1978. Turtle depictions in central Baja California rock art. *Pacific Coast Archaeological Society Quarterly* **14**(1), 21–4.

Reichel-Dolmatoff, G. 1967. Rock paintings of the Vaupes: an essay of interpretation. *Folklore Americas* **27** (2), 107–13. Center for Folklore and Mythology, UCLA.

Schaafsma, P. 1980. *Indian rock art of the southwest.* Albuquerque: University of New Mexico Press.

Smith, W. 1952. Kiva mural decorations at Awatovi and Kawaika–a. *Peabody Museum Papers*, Vol. 37. (Reports of the Awatovi Expedition, no. 5.) Harvard University, Cambridge, Mass.

Stephen, A. 1936. *Hopi Journal*, Parts I & II, E. C. Parsons (ed.). New York: Columbia University Press.

Stevenson, M. C. 1904. *The Zuni Indians: their mythology, esoteric fraternities and ceremonies.* 23rd Annual Report of the Bureau of American Ethnology, 1901–1902, Washington, DC.

Sutherland, K. 1976. A survey of 'Picture Cave' in the Hueco Mountains, Texas. *The Artifact* **14** (2), 1–32. El Paso Archaeological Society, El Paso.

Thomas, T. 1976. Petroglyph distribution and the hunting hypothesis in the central Great Basin. *Tebiwa* (Journal of the Idaho State University Museum) **18** (2), 65–74.

Tyler, H. A. 1979 *Pueblo birds and myths*. Norman: University of Oklahoma Press.

Von Werlhof, J. C. 1965. Rock art of the Owens Valley, California. *Reports of the University of California Archaeological Survey*, Vol. 65. Berkeley.

Whitley, D. S. 1982. Notes on the Coso petroglyphs, the etiological mythology of the western Shoshone, and the interpretation of rock art. *Journal of California and Great Basin Anthropology* **4** (2), 132–46.

Wright, B. 1977. *Hopi Kachinas: the complete guide to collecting Kachina dolls*. Flagstaff: Northland Press.

Young, M. J. 1982. *Images of power, images of beauty: contemporary Zuni perceptions of rock art*. Unpublished PhD dissertation, Department of Folklore and Folklife, University of Pennsylvania.

Young, M. J. 1985. Images of power and the power of images: the significance of rock art for contemporary Zunis. *Journal of American Folklore* **98**(387), 3–48.

12 *The bat in Tairona art: an under-recognized species*

ANNE LEGAST

In the beginning there was no sun. Rotten sticks were all that shone in the forest. Everything else was in darkness. At that time Mother Gualchovang had two sons, Mulkuexe and Sintana. They lived in Mulkuagakve.[1] Mulkuexe's wife was Namshaya,[2] and their son was Enduksama[3]. . .Mulkuexe was a 'Mama',[4] and was always fighting with Sintana. . .Mulkuexe was a bad man. He had a lot of gold and was like a sun, but he liked to burn the earth with his light. . .Sometimes he made everything go dark and nobody could find their way along the road. Sintana used to give him advice, but Mulkuexe would not listen.

And so Sintana thought: 'What will I do?' He went to Mulkuexe and said: 'They tell me that many men sleep with their daughters.' Mulkuexe got angry and said: 'That is very bad.' So Sintana took hold of Enduksama, Mulkuexe's son, and also his wife Namshaya and carried them off to his house. He changed Enduksama into a woman and gave him beautiful hair. But he dressed Namshaya in a simple carate shirt.[5] Then he said to Namshaya: 'Go back to Mulkuexe so that he will do it[6] with Enduksama'. So Namshaya and Enduksama went to Mulkuexe's place, but he did not recognize them. And Mulkuexe fell in love with Enduksama and said to Namshaya: 'I like your daughter very much. Give her to me.' Then Namshaya said: 'Very well.' Mulkuexe took a piece of gold, a round piece that he had on his chest, and gave it to Namshaya. . .Then Enduksama grew fat and after seven months gave birth to a son called Nurlitaba.[7] He was like a bird. Enduksama took hold of him and threw him into the bushes. But Namshaya found him and began to rear him. And so, when the child could speak, he met Mulkuexe and addressed him as 'Father Grandfather.' Then Mulkuexe realized what had happened, and he felt a great shame. He sent Enduksama far away so as never to see her again. Ever since then Enduksama comes out earlier than the sun. . .There already existed a sun on the earth, but it did not work well. Sintana now took Mulkuexe and sent him up to heaven as a sun. And Namshaya was sent as the moon. (Reichel-Dolmatoff, 1950–1, Vol. II, pp. 26–7)

Thus was born the bat, the first animal in creation according to the mythology of the Kogi Indians. Begotten in an incestuous and homosexual relationship between Mulkuexe, the solar lord, and his own son, the bat emerges from darkness and becomes responsible for the fertility of women.

'The bat symbolizes menstruation, since it "sucks blood". "Has the bat bitten you?"

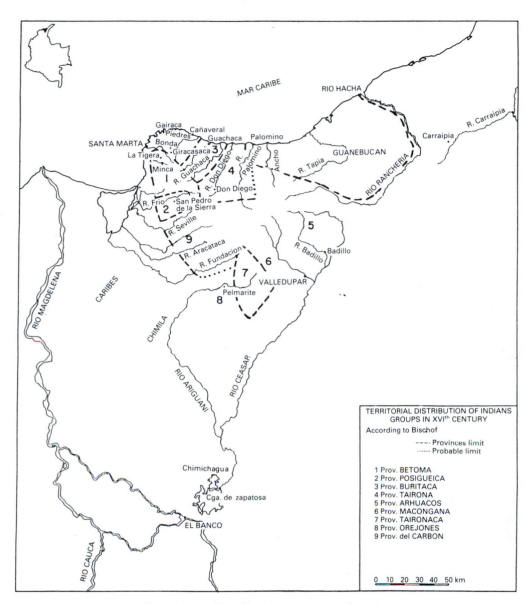

Figure 12.1 Distribution of zoomorphic pieces.

the Kogi women ask, by which they mean "Are you menstruating?" The young men say: "She is now a woman. The bat has bitten her", to indicate that a girl is now nubile. On the peak of the ceremonial houses and also in private dwellings, the Mama hangs a small object in the form of a woven cross that represents this bat and, at the same time, the female organ' (Reichel–Dolmatoff 1950–1, Vol. I, p. 270).

As a result of the Spanish conquest of northern Colombia, the Kogi, an indigenous group probably made up of the descendants of the Tairona, left their lands bordering on the Caribbean coast and retired to the higher slopes of the Sierra Nevada de Santa Marta. The Tairona left behind archaeological material rich in zoomorphic figures which bear witness to the close relationship that existed between this human group and their environment (Fig. 12.1).

A detailed study of approximately 4500 zoomorphic pieces in the Gold Museum of Bogotá reveals that numerous figures wrought in stone, ceramics, and gold represent the bat (Legast 1987) and demonstrates the essential role played in Tairona culture by that small nocturnal mammal.

Images of the bat are not only common, they are also found on objects such as the complex and eye-catching gold pectorals and pendants, where the bat is often depicted in combination with the human figure. Nevertheless, the bat has often not been recognized.

In Colombia alone some 145 species of bat have been identified. In the present Tairona National Park, once the home of Tairona Indians, Moreno (1981) captured 40 species belonging to seven different families, noteworthy for the wide variety of their facial characteristics (Figs 12.2 & 12.3). The perfect sense of orientation which allows the bat to fly in the dark and which is peculiar to this mammal is based on short-wave and high-frequency sound emitted and received by the animal by means of specialized organs often formed by folds in their skin.

The tragus (a membrane enclosed within the ear and situated at its base) occurs in different shapes and sizes – rounded, narrow, or elongated (Figs 12.2 & 12.3). The snout, either elongated or short and stubby, sometimes ends in a 'nose-leaf', a leaf-shaped membrane peculiar to the species of the Phyllostomidae family. This nasal membrane, either simple or trilobed, is sometimes extremely long relative to the rest of the face, as in the case of *Lonchorhina aurita*. Bats of the Noctolinidae family can be identified by their flat noses and harelips, and their large pointed ears; whereas those of the Molossidae family are recognizable by their rather short ears, the edges of which join at the front to form a membrane above the eyes, as a kind of visor (Fig. 12.3).

These characteristics give the bat a curious appearance, attractive in a way, and yet repulsive, enhanced by the teeth which, in the majority of the Microchiroptera, include fangs like those of flesh-eating mammals. In the Phyllostomidae family, the true vampire (*Desmodus rotundus*) is unmistakable for its long fangs in the upper jaw (Fig. 12.4).

The chiropteras have a life span of 15–20 years. Their diet varies according to species; they may be insect- or fruit-eaters, nectar-drinkers, blood-suckers, or omnivorous. During the day they rest in trees or rocks, or find shelters close to human habitation.

Without going into the features of each single species or genus, we must briefly enumerate the characteristics of the chiropteras of northern Colombia, especially the details of the head and face, since the body itself is rarely represented in Tairona art.

The ears are generally large and formed by folded membranes. The tragus is common to all the Microchiroptera of America. It occurs in different forms. The snout, in the Phyllostomidae family, ends in a nose-leaf, either simple or trilobed. In other families, it is flat or rather upturned, or has numerous folds of skin which

Figure 12.2 *Pyllostomus discolor* (Phyllostomidae). (Photograph by A. Cadena.)

Figure 12.3 Species of the Molossidae family. (Photograph by A. Cadena.)

Figure 12.4 Dentures of the authentic vampire, *Desmodus rotundus* (after Grzimek 1975, p. 94, Fig. 4b).

cover the face. In the Molossidae family, the strong auricular membranes unite at the front to form a type of visor over the eyes. In several species the lower lip is adorned by wart-like fleshy protuberances. Finally, strong canine teeth are common to many different species.

In the archaeological examples this last feature is often exaggerated. When the face is not immediately recognizable as that of a bat, the exaggerated teeth could lead one to mistake them for the fangs of felines or reptiles, such as crocodiles or serpents. However, in many instances the presence of a nose-leaf or a tragus dispels any doubt that we are, in fact, dealing with an artist's interpretation of a bat.

It is also important to remember that, in the representation of a feline head, the curve of the forehead would flow uninterrupted down to the nose; in contrast in the crocodile's skull there is a break below the eyes, and the long, flat nose cannot easily be confused with the snout of the bat. The serpent's head is not hard to identify, since it is generally depicted with a forked tongue.

Figure 12.5 Vessel in ceramic, 15.8 x 11.4 cm; MO CT1577, Gold Museum, Bogotá. (Photograph by J. M. Munera.)

In this chapter Tairona art is taken to be a single unit in time and space, with the assumption that all Tairona material is the expression of an inherent cultural unity and the continuous representation of symbols during different periods of time. Certain doubtful figures can only be identified by comparing them with the more realistic ones, ignoring, for the time being, any possible chronological differences.

The bat in Tairona art is represented either alone or associated with man, when the body is human and the head is bat-like; in some of these 'bat-men' features of other animals are also found.

The figures which depict bats alone are mainly made of clay or stone. The vessel in Figure 12.5 shows two bats apparently hanging upside-down, the posture adopted by these tiny mammals when they are at rest. On this piece, their heads are depicted with prominent snouts, and well-developed teeth are plainly visible; the snout seems to end in a rather underdeveloped nose-leaf. The ears are large. Despite the fact that these features are reminiscent of certain species of the subfamily Phyllostominae (such as *Vampyrum spectrum*), the figure is too stylized to permit a closer identification.

In the stone pendant (Fig. 12.6), the bat is depicted with its wings spread. The relief-work on the head, above the eyes, seems to imitate the prolonged ear membranes seen in the Molossidae family, such as those of the genus *Eumops*.

Figure 12.6 Stone pendant, 4.0 x 3.5 cm; MO LT799, Gold Museum, Bogotá. (Photograph by J. M. Munera.)

Figure 12.7 Stone pendant, 22.7 x 3.4 cm; unnumbered, Gold Museum, Bogotá. (Photograph by J. M. Munera.)

Figure 12.8 Ceramic fragment, 9.2 x 10.1 cm; MO CT3116, Gold Museum, Bogotá. (Photograph by J. M. Munera.)

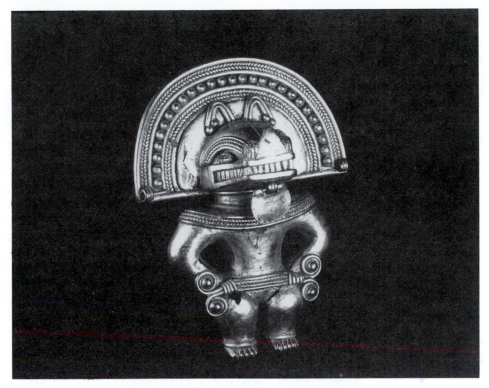

Figure 12.9   Gold pendant, 5.0 x 6.3 cm; MO 26173, Gold Museum, Bogotá. (Photograph by J. M. Munera.)

Much more stylized versions are found in the 'bat-winged' pendants common in both the Tairona area and in north-western Venezuela (Fig. 12.7).

On other pieces, such as pottery whistles, pendants, pectorals, and gold bells, the bat and human forms combine to produce figures typical of Tairona art.

Figure 12.8 shows a ceramic fragment representing a human body with a bat's head. The position of this hybrid being recalls that of Figure 12.5. The triangular nasal-leaf of the Phyllostomidae family is clearly recognizable, emphasized at its centre by a second triangle. The teeth with the prominent fangs are also characteristic of these small mammals. Modelled strips sprout from the nose and arch over the eyes, meeting behind the jaw: it seems likely that these adornments symbolize the two streaks of light-coloured hair which can be observed in this same area on several different genera, such as *Artibeus* and *Urodema* of the subfamily Stenoderminae, commonly found in northern Colombia.

These same features can be seen in the gold pendant in Figure 12.9: the ears (or possible the tragus) can be seen above the head. As in the previous figure, a decorated border at shoulder height probably indicates that the human being is wearing a mask with chiropteran features.

The Tairona evidently attempted to change facial features into bat-like form, as can be seen in Figure 12.10, which shows a half-human, half-animal figure with an extremely ornate double head-dress highly characteristic of Tairona art. On each side of the head, two bats hanging by their feet highlight the relationship between the human being and these tiny mammals. The bats have long, pointed ears like those of the fishing genus *Noctilio* of the Noctolionidae family.

On the head of this statuette, Tairona ear-rings dangle from human ears. There are also other noteworthy features: covering the eyes is a kind of visor, on either side of which are small mushroom-shaped plates which recall the bat's tragus, placed, in this case, at the base of the head-ornament, with two arches which perhaps symbolize the large ears diagnostic of many bats. The visor itself may represent the thick auricular membranes which meet above the eyes in several genera of the Molossidae family, such as *Molossus* sp. and *Eumops* sp., both of which are found in the Tairona area. The double-barred nose-ornament lifts up the wall of the nostrils and transforms them into an upturned nose or a nose-leaf. Finally, a lip-plug under the lower lip is reminiscent of the fleshy protuberances on the lower jaw of many bats. In this case, therefore, the visor with its tragus, the barred nose-ornaments, and the lip-plug, are all decorations which Tairona may have adopted in order to imitate the appearance of a bat. A great number of such pendants in museum collections have often been worn thin by much use.

Figure 12.10   Gold pendant, 6.4 x 6.2 cm; MO 12564, Gold Museum, Bogotá. (Photograph by J. M. Munera.)

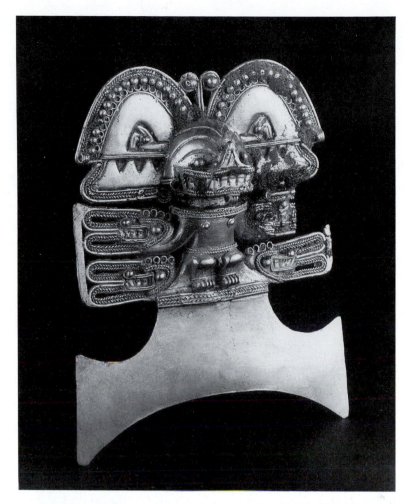

Figure 12.11 Gold pectoral, 9.5 x 11.9 cm; MO 24269, Gold Museum, Bogotá. (Photograph by J. M. Munera.)

As shown in Figure 12.11, the bat-men with features of the Stenoderminae subfamily may also be related to fork-tongued serpents belonging to the genus *Bothrops*, identified by its raised snout. The serpents appear at the figure's feet, or as a prolongation of its arms.

In Figure 12.12, the bat-man holds the two-headed serpent in his hands. On this pendant, the forked tongues are clearly recognizable, which suggests that the stick with a spiral design at each end, held in the hands of most bat-men, may represent two-headed serpents. If so, the two spirals might be a stylized representation of the forked tongues. This same relationship between a man with a bat-mask and serpents can be seen in a ceramic whistle (Fig. 12.13). The forked tongue is not depicted, but the zigzag symbol of the serpent (Legast 1987) confirms the presence of an ophidian figure.

Figure 12.12 Gold pendant, 5.9 x 7.2 cm; MO 11795, Gold Museum, Bogotá. (Photograph by J. M. Munera.)

Figure 12.13 Ceramic whistle, 9.1 x 8.9 cm; MO CT2306, Gold Museum, Bogotá. (Photograph by J. M. Munera.)

Figure 12.14   Ceramic statuette, 32.6 x 34.5 cm; MO CT736, Gold
Museum, Bogotá. (Photograph by J. M. Munera.)

The statuette Figure 12.14 shows a mask with bat-like features and also has serpents in its head-dress and on its shoulders. In this case there is a close relationship between the barred nose-ornament and the nose-leaf of the Phyllostomidae family. As in Figures 12.8 and 12.11, a triangular design has been cut into the centre of the nose-leaf.

Two kinds of bat-men – those that wear a mask with a prominent snout, strong jaws with fangs, and the nose-leaf of the Phyllostomidae family; and those with a tragus, visor, barred nose-ornament, and lip-plugs – are shown in Figures 12.15 and 12.16, respectively. In these examples both are also related to the bird world. The birds placed above the heads of the bat-men have features which bring to mind the condor (*Vultur gryphus*). The beak is strong and hooked, the comb is clearly visible, and the inflated neck may symbolize the gular dewlap protuberance

Figure 12.15   Gold pectoral, 11.9 x 9.5 cm; MO 16584, Gold Museum, Bogotá. (Photograph by J. M. Munera.)

which, in the male condor, is visible at the base of the neck. Despite the fact that the beaks are exaggeratedly large in relation to the head and are more like the beaks of Psittaciformes, if one compares them with larger and more naturalistic pieces, it becomes apparent that the birds on these pendants are condors (Legast 1987). Other figures forming part of the large head-dress seem to represent the heads of different birds with beaks that curve upwards.

One of the striking features of Tairona art is a tendency to combine the features of various bat families into a single figure (Legast 1987). On a ceramic fragment (Fig. 12.17) representing a seated bat-man, we find the high, tall, narrow nose-leaf reminiscent in its shape and proportions of the genus *Lonchorhina* of the Phyllostomidae family. At the same time, the jaws and heavy relief-work over the eyes are typical of members of the Molossidae family, such as *Eumops* sp. For this reason we cannot always be sure which family or species is being depicted. Figure 12.17 shows a representation which, like several others, is clearly male (and see Figs 12.11, 12.12, 12.15, & 12.16).

This chapter has illustrated the mythical importance of the bat for the Tairona who, in their representational art, show how the animal world and the human world are interrelated. 'For the Kogi, there is no strict dividing line between men and animals. Animals are considered as essentially gifted with all of man's features,

Figure 12.16 Gold pectoral, 14.7 x 12.6 cm; MO 16790, Gold Museum, Bogotá. (Photograph by J. M. Munera.)

excepting only his external appearance' (Reichel-Dolmatoff 1950–1, Vol. I, p. 261). Several mythical beings have the power to change from humans into animals:

Dikuijiname was the companion of Kashindukua and Noána-sé.[8] He was good and bad. They fought among themselves, but Dikuijiname always won. . .Dikuijiname went to his cansamaria (ceremonial dwelling) and Noána-sé and Kashindukua followed him there to eat him. But since he had a lot of 'spirit'[9] he saw this and changed into a human being. He was in his cansamaria, sitting there in human form, at nightfall, when he heard the others arrive. He swung into his hammock. Kashindukua turned into a tiger and Dikuijiname had prepared a big fire. Kashindukua sprang to grab Dikuijiname, but Dikuijiname turned into a bat and flew up to the roof. (Reichel-Dolmatoff 1950–1, Vol. II, p. 70)

Even though the bat is the son of Mulkuexe, the sun, the one who allows woman to begin her reproductive process, this tiny mammal does not seem to occupy the important place in Kogi mythology which the Tairona craftsmen have given it. The Tairona depict the bat not so much as a totemic emblem but more as an important deity. The Kogi identify themselves closely with the jaguar, which may explain the key position of this animal in their myth.

Figure 12.17 Ceramic fragment, 12.5 x 9.2 cm; unnumbered, Gold Museum, Bogotá. (Photograph by J. M. Munera.)

In speaking of their concept of death, Reichel-Dolmatoff affirms that:

The mask of Heiseí (death) represents a feline or, at least, the head of a feline; the lower jaw is protruding and both jaws have long fangs carved from the same wood and sometimes covered with caps of beaten gold. The brows are also somewhat protruding and lead to a rounded nose flattened on the sides. The eyes and mouth are perforated in all these masks. The Mulukú mask is similar to the Heiseí one;[10] however, while this last features a serpent carved in high relief above the forehead and cheeks, the Mulukú mask represents a human face with a prominent nose and a perforated nostril wall. The lower lip is decorated with a lip-plug, represented by a short, protruding cylinder. (Reichel-Dolmatoff 1950–1, Vol. II, pp. 146–7)

The description of these masks, especially that of Mulukú (Legast 1987, Figs 104 & 105) is remarkable in that it reminds us again of the bat-men: the nose ornaments which lift up the wall of the nostrils give to the mask-bearer the appearance of a bat, as can be seen in Figures 12.10, 12.12, 12.14, & 12.16.

The strong fangs, which are part of feline dentition, are also typical of bats and reptiles. It is possible that the mask of Heiseí, which is the symbol of death for the present-day Kogis, combines feline elements with those of other nocturnal animals, such as bats and serpents. The jaguar of Kogi mythology and the bat in Tairona archaeological material are both masculine and are associated with the serpent, symbol of evil.

On the other hand, as Reichel-Dolmatoff (1950–1, Vol. II, pp. 90–1) says: 'Heiseí has a remarkable sexual character and controls sexual life, especially that of the men. As a matter of fact, he has been occasionally described as the Father of Homosexuality. . .Heiseí is also closely associated with incest.' These characteristics of Heiseí remind us of the myth in which the bat, the first animal of the creation is the result of an incestuous and homosexual relationship between Mulkuexe and his own son.

Furthermore, for the Kogi the bat is associated with death: 'The owls and nocturnal birds in general form a category which sometimes includes bats and vampires. These animals are considered to be malignant and are associated with death and misfortune' (Reichel-Dolmatoff 1950–1, Vol. I, p. 262).

It is not yet possible to reach definitive conclusions as to the true symbolic significance of the bat in Tairona culture, but it is tempting to think that for these Indian groups bats may have enjoyed a role as important, or maybe equivalent to that of Heiseí for the Kogi.

Acknowledgements

This study has been possible thanks to the economic support of the Fundación de Investigaciones Arqueológicas Nacionales of the Banco de la República (Colombia). I am grateful to its director, Dr Luis Duque Gomez as well as to the director of the Gold Museum of Bogotá, Clemencia Plazas, and Ana Maria Falchetti for their constant encouragement and for having allowed me to study the archaeological material. I also wish to thank Dr Alberto Cadena, zoological bat specialist at the National University of Colombia, who helped in the task of identifying figures.

I wish to thank also Marianne Cardale Schrimpff for her important and very kind help in revising and correcting this text.

Notes

1   According to Reichel-Dolmatoff, a place near Hukumeiji. Others say that the place is called Mulkua-Kúngui, a synonym of Mulkuexe.
2   According to Reichel-Dolmatoff, from *nebbi* – jaguar.
3   According to Reichel-Dolmatoff, the planet Venus, also sometimes called *indèkana*.
4   Priest.
5   According to Reichel-Dolmatoff, *Túlbi* – Carate, a skin disease; *jákua* – shirt material. Now that Namshaya is a moon, this is a reference to her markings which, in other passages of these myths, are interpreted as 'a rag mask' or ashes which a zealous man throws in her face.
6   According to Reichel-Dolmatoff, ceremonial coitus, on the occasion of initiation.
7   According to Reichel-Dolmatoff, *Nurlita*; a bat, the first in creation.
8   Kashindukua and Noána-sé, sons of the Mother.
9   According to Reichel-Dolmatoff, in other words *alùna*.
10 See the illustrations in Preuss 1919.

References

Grzimek, B. 1975. *Le monde animal*, Vol. XI. Zürich: Editions Stauffacher.

Legast, A. 1980. *La fauna en la orfebrería sinú*. Fundación de Investigaciones Arqueológicas Nacionales, Banco de la República, Bogotá.

Legast, A. 1987. *La fauna en el mundo mítico Tairona*. Fundación de Investigaciones Arqueológicas Nacionales, Banco de la República, Bogotá.

Moreno Bejarano, L. M. 1981. *Distribución de los Chiróptera en el Parque Nacional Tairona*. Unpublished thesis. Universidad Nacional de Colombia, Facultad de Ciencias, Departamento de Biología, Bogotá.

Preuss, K. T. 1919. *Forschungsreise zu den Kagaba–indianern der Sierra Nevada de Santa Marta in Kolumbien*. Beobachtungen, Textaufnahmen und linguistische Studien. Vienna: Anthropos.

Reichel-Dolmatoff, G. 1950–1. *Los Kogí: Una Tribu Indígena de la Sierra Nevada de Santa Marta, Colombia*, 2 Vols. Bogotá: Vol. I, Instituto Etnológico Nacional, Imprenta Nacional; Vol. II, Editoria Iqueima.

13 Animals and zoomorphs in rock art of the Koolburra region, north Queensland

JOSEPHINE FLOOD

Zoomorphs are rare in Australian Aboriginal art, but form a principal subject of the rock paintings of the Koolburra region of Cape York Peninsula, north Queensland. This region (centred at latitude 15°33'S and longitude 144°03'E) lies about 50 km west-north-west of Laura, whose rock art has become well known through the research of Trezise (1969, 1971) and Rosenfeld (1981, 1982). The Koolburra area is a sandstone plateau surrounded by escarpments containing hundreds of rock shelters. A sample of 25 km² was surveyed for rock art on two expeditions in 1981 and 1982, totalling 11 weeks, and 163 sites were recorded. Seventy-four of these sites contained some 600 paintings, some of which were in association with stencils and/or engravings. A comprehensive description of this art body is in Flood (1987), so here only aspects of relevance to the issue of interpretation of animals in art will be discussed.

The art body is considered to belong to the last 8500 years, the period spanned by human occupation in the two excavated Koolburra sites, Green Ant and Echidna Shelters (Flood & Horsfall 1986, Flood 1987). Since some of the engravings are deeply patinated, some lie at or below present ground surface, and others have paintings or stencils superimposed on them, it is considered that the engravings generally pre-date the stencils and paintings. Among engraved motifs, non-figurative circular marks contribute 54 per cent and linear motifs 7 per cent; figurative motifs (motifs which resemble objects familiar to the observer) make up 38 per cent, 33 per cent being tracks – marks resembling traces on the ground left by fauna such as macropods (kangaroos, wallabies, etc.) and birds, and the other 5 per cent resembling actual artefacts or animals. Only four out of some 604 recorded engravings appear to depict animals; two are snake-like, one lizard-like, and one tortoise-like. However, if tracks are taken to be a *pars pro toto* representation of an animal, then a third of the engraved motifs are concerned with fauna. Of these there are some 73 individual marks resembling bird tracks (occasionally in pairs but usually found singly), 35 pairs of macropod tracks (always in pairs rather than singly), three single dingo tracks, and nine human footprints.

The subject matter of the Koolburra paintings is very different from that of the engravings. Naturalistic paintings of animals do not predominate at Koolburra, unlike much of Australian Aboriginal rock painting, and only 16 per cent of paintings resemble fauna (Fig. 13.1). Species in Koolburra paintings identified by

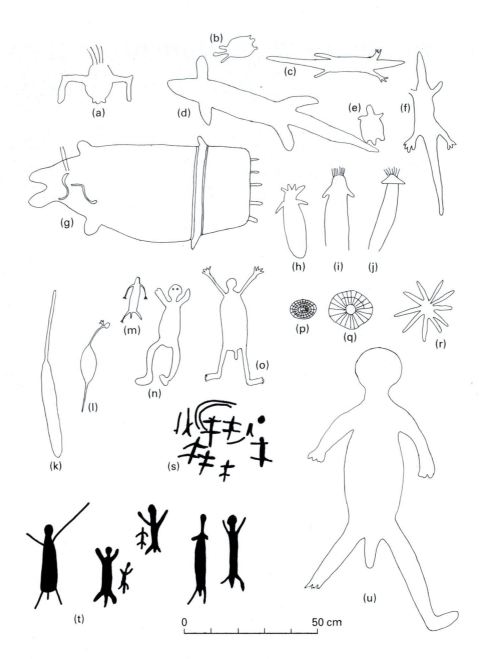

Figure 13.1 Painted figures from Koolburra sites: (a) bird-like figure in yellow outline (site K 80); (b) white-infilled 'tortoise' (K 163); (c) red-infilled 'crocodile' (SEK 1); (d), (e) large white-infilled 'crocodile' (BDC 5); (g) 'catfish', red with white outline and internal decoration (K 79); (h)–(j) 'catfish' (K 163) – (h) black outline with red infill, (i), (j) yellow infill; (k), (l) 'vegetable' motifs, red-infilled (BDC 14, K 163); (m)–(o) human figures, male, red-infilled (K 163, BDC 14, & K 163); (p), (q) spoked concentric circles in red outline (BDC 12); 'star-like' motif – white infilled, on ceiling of K 79; (s), (t) 'stick' figures, red-infilled, in the man-lizard stylization (K 101, SEK 2); (u) large male human figure, red-infilled (BDC 14).

Figure 13.2   The late Goobalathaldin (Dick Roughsey), an Aboriginal from the Lardil people in Mornington Island in the Gulf of Carpentaria, who identified animals and zoomorphs in the Koolburra rock art. (Photograph J. Flood.)

Aboriginal informants, such as Goobalathaldin (Fig. 13.2), are virtually confined to 'crocodiles', 'turtles', 'lizards', 'catfish', and 'snakes'. No painted 'macropods' or 'macropod tracks' were found, and 'bird tracks' were only numerous in one rock shelter. Motifs which appear in the paintings but not the engravings include sets of vertical stripes; wheel-like, star-like, feather-like, fan-like, fern-like, and yam-like marks; 'double arches'; fauna such as 'crocodile', 'catfish', and 'lizard'; 'human' figures; 'zoomorphs' and 'anthropomorphs'.

The fauna apparently portrayed in the Koolburra and Laura rock paintings are compared in Table 13.1, which demonstrates the more restricted range of fauna and absence of 'birds', 'macropods', and 'flying foxes' (Fig. 13.3) from the Koolburra paintings in contrast with their relative abundance in the Laura art. These differences are not explicable in terms of differences in local environment, for the environments of the Koolburra and Laura areas are very similar, the two regions being virtually identical in their flora and fauna. All the faunal species in Table 13.1 occur in both regions, but faunal subjects in rock paintings of the two areas are very different. Flying foxes, birds, dingoes, and macropods occur in the Koolburra and Laura regions now, and presumably also did so in the prehistoric past, yet paintings resembling them occur in the Laura paintings but not at Koolburra. Nor can these differences be explained by the lesser quantity of paintings at Koolburra; there is a

Table 13.1 Subject matter of Koolburra and Laura paintings.

Subject	Koolburra[a]		Laura[b]	
	No.	%**	No.	%**
Zoomorphs/anthropomorphs★	126	28	?	?
Human figures★	37	8	394	48
Stick figures man/lizard	62	14	?	?
Artefacts, tracks, etc.	133	29	71	9
bird tracks★	56		7	
macropod tracks	—		10	
footprints (human)	—		12	
circular motifs	13		19	
lines (single)	14			
sets of vertical stripes	7			
spoked concentric circles	7			
star-like	8			
comb-like	5			
double arches	5			
'feather-like'	5			
boomerang★	4		17	
basket	—		6	
other[c]	9			
Vegetable motifs	23	5	10	1
Fauna	71	16	334	41
'crocodiles'★	21		8	
'turtles'★	13		36	
'lizards'★	12			
'fish'★	8		85	
'snakes'★	2		19	
'macropods'	—		60	
'flying foxes'	—		48	
'birds'	—		64	
'echidna'	—		9	
'dingo'	—		5	
indeterminate fauna	15			
Motif marks	452	100%	822	99%
indeterminate marks	171		132	
Total paintings	623		954	
Hand stencils	1829=72% of total		93=9% of total	

(a) Data from 68 sites;   (b) data from Maynard 1976 (18 sites);   (c) 'other' comprises crosses (4), fan-like (3), shield-like (1), and trident-like (1).
★ Identified by Aboriginal informants;   ★★ percentage of total paintings excluding indeterminate marks.

real difference between the two bodies of art in terms of both subject matter and style of rock paintings. This difference appears to be culturally determined.

If the rationale for the Koolburra paintings had been 'hunting magic', animal, fish, or vegetable motifs would have been a far more frequent subject. For example, fish abound in the Kennedy River, but scarcely seem to feature in the art, in contrast with the art of Kakadu, where representations of fish are numerous both in the recent rock paintings and in the present environment of the region (Chaloupka 1984).

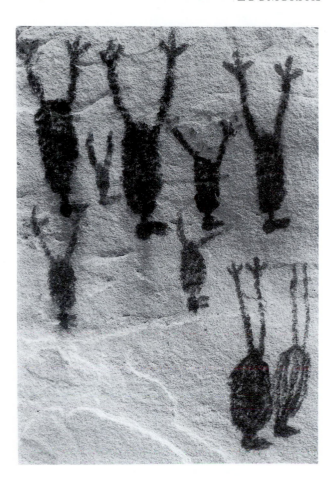

Figure 13.3 'Flying foxes' or fruit bats were depicted in red ochre hanging upside-down (as they do in trees at night) in paintings of the Laura region, but are not represented in the art of the Koolburra region, north of the Kennedy River (Site LK 3; photograph K. Huenecke).

Zoomorphs

Zoomorphic motifs are the most common subjects of the Koolburra paintings. 'Zoomorphic' is defined in the Macquarie Dictionary as 'ascribing animal form or attributes to beings or things not animal, representing a deity in the form of an animal'. Zoomorphs are figures which are primarily animals but with some human or 'supernatural' features, whereas anthropomorphs are basically human but with some 'supernatural' features. 'Anthropomorphic' is defined as 'ascribing human form or attributes to beings or things not human, especially to a deity'.

The term 'mythic being' could probably be used for all supernatural figures which appear in the Koolburra art, but it seems useful to make a distinction between zoomorphs and anthropomorphs. All the zoomorphs appear to represent the same beings, except for an engraved snake-like figure which has been interpreted by an Aboriginal informant as the Rainbow Serpent. The Rainbow Serpent is a fresh-looking line, about 170 cm long, engraved by pounding along a natural transverse rock ridge across the centre of the back wall of Green Ant Shelter, with a head bearing two 'horns' at its left-hand end, and two large roundish 'blobs' of paint on either side of the 'horns' which, although not attached to the head, gave me a strong visual impression of 'ears' (Fig. 13.4). The Aborigine who made the identification with the Rainbow Serpent was the late Dick Roughsey, or Goobalathaldin, of the Lardil people of Mornington Island in the Gulf of Carpentaria some 500 km west of Koolburra. Roughsey could therefore hardly be classed as a local informant, but was emphatic in his identification of this engraved figure.

The myth of the Rainbow Serpent or Snake is widespread in northern Australia, and in his autobiography, *Moon and rainbow* (1971, p. 86), Roughsey called it one of 'our biggest stories'. In the 1960s he and Tresize spent much time recording rock art in the Laura region with some old local Aborigines, who told stories of the Rainbow Serpent, whom they called Goorialla. In 1975 Roughsey published a children's book entitled *The Rainbow Serpent*, and the 'Rainbow Serpent' at Green Ant Shelter bears an uncanny resemblance to the pictures in his book. Yet he did not see the site until 1981, so cannot have based his depiction of the Rainbow Serpent on the Green Ant figure, but both have similar short 'horns', 'ears', v-shaped heads, and long rows of short lines decorating the 'serpent's' body.

The Rainbow Serpent plays an important role in the mythology of Cape York Peninsula among people such as the Wik on the west coast around Aurukun, some 330 km north-west of Koolburra (Von Sturmer 1978). In 1927 at Aurukun, Ursula McConnel recorded various myths, including one about 'Taipan, The Rainbow Serpent' (McConnel 1957, pp. 111–16). In the Laura-Koolburra region, traditional

Figure 13.4 Engraving of the head of the 'Rainbow Serpent' with 'horns' and ?'ears' and 170 cm long body stretching off to the right (Site K1: Green Ant Shelter 1; photograph J. K. Flood).

stories were told in the 1960s to Trezise and Roughsey by Aboriginal elders, such as George Pegus or Joogoomoo of the Gug-Yalanji from the Maytown–Palmer River area, and Harry Mole, last of the Gugu-Warra people, who had been a police tracker at Laura for 60 years. The Rainbow Snake saga recounted by these two men (Trezise 1969, pp. 66–9) told how Goorialla, the great Rainbow Serpent, travelled up from the south creating features of the landscape such as mountains and lakes. Later he stopped at Fairview 'where he made a lily lagoon called Minalinka. Goorialla turned his great body round and round but the ground was too hard to make it deep' (Roughsey 1975). Minalinka (now called Goose Lagoon) is set in hard soil and is large and shallow, and full of water-lilies. It lies about 20 km east of the Koolburra plateau and Green Ant Shelter 1 is probably about the closest rockshelter to it.

The long snake-like figure with horned head engraved at Green Ant Shelter 1 is a classic portrayal of a Rainbow Snake, as depicted in various parts of northern Australia. Roughsey also identified a long painted snake in one of the Deighton River shelters as a Rainbow Snake (Rosenfeld pers. comm.). The Rainbow Serpent or Snake plays a major role in the religion of much of Aboriginal Australia. This huge mythic being is sometimes male and sometimes female, and is generally associated with water-holes, rain, thunder, floods, seasonal fertility, and the shaping of the landscape. As in the Koolburra engraving, in bark paintings and rock art it is generally represented with 'horns' or antler-like projections on its head (cf. Isaacs 1980, pp. 60–9, Berndt & Berndt 1981, Pls 33 & 34).

There is no evidence as to the antiquity of the Green Ant Shelter 1 engraving, but Chaloupka (1984) has pointed out that the post-glacial sea rise (between about 9000 and 7000 years ago) and the change to estuarine conditions may have led to the Rainbow Serpent myth, which would make it probably the longest continuing religious belief in the world.

'Echidna People'

Some 191 other zoomorphs were recorded in 21 Koolburra painting sites. Morphologically, they seem to be echidnas, the spiny ant-eater of Australia which is an egg-laying monotreme, but they also have human characteristics such as a penis or breasts and a fringed skirt, and 'supernatural' features such as rays on their heads. The males generally have rays on their heads like a head-dress, and the females have a long split 'snout' or 'muzzle' and a fringed 'skirt' or pubic 'apron' (Figs 13.5–13.7).

The split 'muzzle' may be a sexual symbol as it only appears on female echidna figures, but the echidna (*Tachyglossus aculeatus*) does have a long, naked 'beak-like muzzle with a small mouth at the end which opens just wide enough to allow free movement of its long extensile tongue and unrestricted passage to the insect prey on which it feeds' (Ride 1970, pp. 191–3). The skull is high and bulbous and about ll cm long, and the jaws comprise two long, thin bones without any teeth, the food being pressed against the roof of the mouth by the tongue (Triggs 1985, p. 28). The heads of the female figures therefore resemble echidna skulls seen in side-view. The adult female echidna weighs about 5 kg, whereas the male weighs about 7 kg and usually

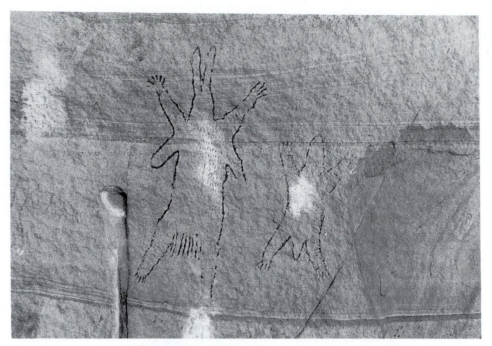

Figure 13.5 Zoomorphic 'Echidna People' in white outlined with red and with red 'spines'. The female has a split 'snout', breasts, and fringed skirt (Site K80; photograph J. Flood).

Figure 13.6 Left to right: two male zoomorphs with rayed heads and two female zoomorphs with breasts, in red outline with white or red infill (Site K80; photograph J. Flood).

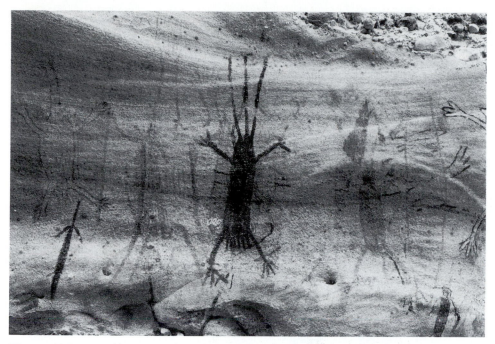

Figure 13.7 Female zoomorph with 'antennae-like' head painted in black pigment (Site K163; photograph J. Flood).

measures more than 30 cm. On the painted figures the body length (measured from shoulder to crutch) of male 'Echidna People' averages 35 cm and ranges from about 8 to 76 cm; the females' average body length is 36 cm, ranging from 13 to 66 cm. Thus, the actual bodies of the figures resemble echidnas' bodies in size. When the figures are measured from the tip of the head-dress to their toes, average height for males is 66 cm with a range from 25 to 120 cm, and average height for females 72 cm with a range from 32 to 116 cm. The zoomorphs' bodies tend to be pear-shaped or oval, the maximum width of the body averaging 42 per cent of body length in males and 36 per cent in females.

The identification of these figures as echidnas is supported by several other lines of evidence. Some of them have short spines painted all over their bodies, most have fairly bulbous bodies, and all are shown in plan-view with legs stretched out, in the same way that echidnas are depicted in galleries such as Giant Wallaroo near Laura (Fig. 13.8). Elsewhere in Australian rock art echidnas are sometimes shown in plan-view and sometimes in silhouette (cf. Berndt & Berndt 1981, Pl. 32). It might be thought that some of the figures resemble humans rather than echidnas or other animals, but the feet are not shown like human feet, which are quite distinctive, with the heel clearly shown (see Fig. 13.1).

Of the 191 zoomorphs recorded in 21 Koolburra art sites, 95 seem to be male, 24 female and the rest are indeterminate because parts of their bodies are missing. All figures are portrayed in frontal view rather than in profile, and they are consistently more carefully drawn than all other subjects. In contrast, in

Figure 13.8 A naturalistic picture of an echidna, in red ochre with white outline. Note the elongated toes on the back feet. (Giant Wallaroo site, Laura area; photograph J. Flood.)

the Laura paintings zoomorphs do not seem to be present, but anthropomorphs with head-dresses occur. Rosenfeld (pers. comm.) found that 'rayed head-dresses were exclusively male or unsexed, whereas antenna-like head-dresses could be either male or female.'

In the Koolburra art there are a few anthropomorphic figures, which are human figures with certain supernatural features. At Green Ant Shelter 1 such a figure is placed in the centre of the wall, with arms outstretched as if to protect the site. This is a male 'human' figure but with a curious form of head, ears, and body. The helmet-shaped head has large ears projecting low down on its sides – a head-form which has not been recorded elsewhere in the Koolburra paintings, but is common in the Laura art.

Ethnographic evidence concerning the echidna comes from the mythology of the Laura and Aurukun area on the west coast of Cape York Peninsula. A very similar type of head with split snout occurs on an Aboriginal carved wooden figure collected by Fred McCarthy in 1962 from Aurukun (Fig. 13.9). This carved echidna is painted in red and white bands, covered with spines, and has four short legs and a deeply split muzzle. Red and white are the colours used for most of the echidna figures in the Koolburra art, the bodies being white outlined with red. In the Echidna Dance at Aurukun the echidna died after he broke marriage rules by stealing the ancestral Taipan's wife (McCarthy pers. comm., Cooper *et al.* 1981). The echidna was one of the totems of the Wik-Munkan and featured in the myths recorded by McConnel at Aurukun (1930, p. 182, 1957, pp. 95–8). Kekuyang, the spiny ant-eater, was once a man, who stole the black snake, the wife of the carpet snake, kept others from the water-hole, and was speared for his greed, becoming the spiny ant-eater with his back all covered in quills, symbolizing spears. Joogoomoo from south of Laura recounted another story about the echidna (Trezise 1969, pp. 70–1), calling him 'Bulinmore' and telling how Bulinmore was very sacred, only a father's father could eat him and that he wears all those 'spears' as a reminder to the people that they must share the water and everything they have.

Certain other features of the zoomorphic figures are reminiscent of other aspects of the material culture of Aurukun. The rays on male figures' heads closely resemble and may represent the fan-shaped head-dresses of white cockatoo feathers worn in ceremonies at Aurukun by some of the men (cf. Morphy 1981, Pl. 5). Likewise, women, at least in the west of Cape York Peninsula, wore string aprons on ceremonial occasions, and in her book on *Myths of the Mungkan* (1957) McConnel included (as frontispiece) a photograph of women wearing such string pubic aprons and cer-

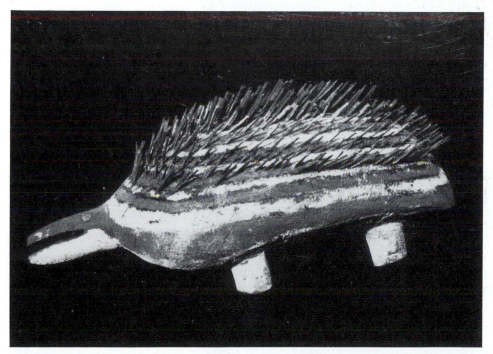

Figure 13.9 Carved wooden figure of an echidna from Aurukun, painted in red and white, and used in the Echidna Dance in which the echidna dies after breaking marriage rules by stealing the ancestral Taipan's wife. Figure collected by F. D. McCarthy in 1962, National Ethnographic Collection, National Museum of Australia, Canberra. (Photograph S. West.)

emonial body decorations closely resembling the 'spines' on the rock paintings.

Further evidence in support of the interpretation of these zoomorphic figures as 'ancestral beings' comes from their inter-site distribution. They occur at only 21 of the painted Koolburra sites, and two sites account for 46 per cent of them. Thus, although zoomorphs are numerically dominant, they are concentrated in a small number of sites and two large shelters, in particular, contain most of them. None of the zoomorph sites appear to contain human occupation deposits, but a few stone tools were found below Ancient Dreaming (K163). The distribution of these zoomorphic motifs therefore appears culturally determined, perhaps by clan boundaries or ancestral Dreaming tracks.

There is also a correlation between the presence of large, or very large, hand stencils high on shelter walls and the presence of zoomorphs. Eighteen of the 21 zoomorph sites contain hand stencils, which are mainly large or very large in size; children's stencilled hands are rare and babies' hands do not occur. High on the rock face at Echidna Dreaming (K80) very large hands (Fig. 13.10) are associated with zoomorphs. Children's hands are also present but confined to a small alcove below

Figure 13.10 Echidna Dreaming rock shelter with zoomorphs and large hand stencils high on the wall. (Photograph J. Flood.)

the zoomorphs at the base of the rock wall. The very large stencils may therefore have been made by clan elders in the course of ritual activities. The latter did not necessarily prevent the use of such shelters for camping, but Echidna Dreaming was certainly not an occupation site, since it has a rocky floor and is situated on the lip of the escarpment, high above the valley.

Conclusions

A horned 'snake-like' figure engraved along a natural transverse ridge or rock across the back wall of the Green Ant Shelter 1 has been interpreted as the Rainbow Serpent, on the basis of identification by an Aboriginal informant and local ethnography. Other Koolburra zoomorphs have been interpreted as representing ancestral mythic echidna beings from the Dreamtime or 'era of creation'. The echidna may have been a local totem, in view of its fairly important place in the mythology of Cape York Peninsula (cf. Roth 1897, 1901–10, Thomson 1933, 1972, McConnel 1939–40, Sharp 1939, Von Sturmer 1978). It may well be that the echidna was the totem of a Koolburra clan, and that increase ceremonies were held at totemic control centres, as described by Sharp (1939, p. 447). The 'echidna cult' was possibly a fairly recent development, although the absence of contact paintings, the heavy over-painting at sites such as Ancient Dreaming, and the high amount of paint-loss and flaking-off of most of the art argues for some antiquity.

The predominance of mythic beings in the Koolburra rock art indicates the all-pervasive nature of Aboriginal religion. This rock art was clearly more religious than secular, reflecting the Aboriginal belief in the interrelationship of all living things and in the shape-changing qualities of ancestral beings. The 'Rainbow Serpent' is well documented in the Aboriginal rock art and religion of northern Australia, but no parallels are yet known for the 'Echidna People' of the Koolburra plateau. Part-human, part-animal figures are rare in Aboriginal art, even though the concept of animal–human transformations is widespread, and this gives the Koolburra body of rock art a unique quality.

References

Berndt, R. M. & C. H. Berndt 1981. *Aboriginal Australian art: a visual perspective.* Sydney: Methuen.
Chaloupka, G. 1984. *From paleo art to casual paintings.* Monograph Series I, Northern Territory Museum of Arts and Sciences, Darwin.
Cooper, C., H. Morphy, D. J. Mulvaney & N. Peterson, 1981. *Aboriginal Australia.* Sydney: Australian Gallery Directors Council.
Flood, J. 1987. Rock art of the Koolburra Plateau, north Queensland. *Rock Art Research* **4**(2), 91–126.
Flood, J. & N. Horsfall 1986. Excavation of Green Ant and Echidna Shelters, Cape York Peninsula. *Queensland Archaeological Research* **3**, 4–64.
Isaacs, J. (ed.) 1980. *Australian Dreaming: 40,000 years of Aboriginal history.* Sydney: Landsdowne Press.

McConnel, U. H. 1930. The Wik-Munkun tribe, Part II. *Oceania* 1(2), 181–205.

McConnel, U. H. 1939–40. Social organisation of the tribes of Cape York Peninsula, north Queensland. *Oceania* **10**(1), 52–72, **10**(4), 434–55.

McConnel, U. H. 1957. *Myths of the Mungkan*. Melbourne: Melbourne University Press.

Maynard, L. 1976. *An archaeological approach to the study of Australian rock art*. Unpublished MA thesis, University of Sydney.

Morphy, H. 1981. The art of northern Australia. In *Aboriginal Australia*, C. Cooper, H. Morphy. D. J. Mulvaney & N. Peterson (eds), 52–65. Sydney: Australian Gallery Directors Council.

Ride, W. D. L. 1970. *A guide to the native mammals of Australia*. Melbourne: Oxford University Press.

Rosenfeld, A. 1981. In *Early man in north Queensland*, A. Rosenfeld, D. Horton & J. Winter (eds), 1–34, 50–88. Canberra: Australian National University.

Rosenfeld, A. 1982. Style and meaning in Laura art: a case study in the formal analysis of style in prehistoric art. *Mankind* **13**(3), 199–217.

Roth, W. E. 1897. *Ethnological studies among Queensland Aborigines*. Brisbane.

Roth, W. E. 1901–10. North Queensland ethnographic bulletins, 1–18. Sydney & Brisbane.

Roughsey, D. 1971. *Moon and rainbow*. Sydney: A. H. & A. W. Reed.

Roughsey, D. 1975. *The Rainbow Serpent*. Sydney: Collins.

Sharp, R. L. 1939. Tribes and totemism in north-east Australia. *Oceania* **9** (3), pp. 254–75, **9** (4), 439–61.

Thomson, D. F. 1933. The hero cult, initiation and totemism on Cape York. *Journal of the Royal Anthropological Institute* **63**, 453–537.

Thomson, D. F. 1972. *Kinship and behaviour in north Queensland. A preliminary account of kinship and social organisation on Cape York Peninsula*, H. W. Scheffler (ed.). Canberra: Australian Institute of Aboriginal Studies.

Trezise, P. J. 1969. *Quinkan country*. Sydney: Reed.

Trezise, P. J. 1971. *Rock art of south-east Cape York*. Canberra: Australian Institute of Aboriginal Studies.

Triggs, B. 1985. *Mammal tracks and signs. A field guide to south-eastern Australia*. Melbourne: Oxford University Press.

Von Sturmer, J. R. 1978. *The Wik region: economy, territoriality and totemism in western Cape York Peninsula, north Queensland*. Unpublished PhD thesis, University of Queensland, St Lucia.

14 Susquehannock animal art and iconography

W. FRED KINSEY, III

Introduction

Small and attractive animal and human images have been widely recognized and illustrated by numerous researchers of Susquehannock archaeology. These images occur as different avian, mammalian, and reptilian species incorporated into the design of pipes, ladles, and combs, and as free-standing ornaments. Human figures and faces are also an intrinsic part of the Susquehannock image-making tradition. In spite of the fact that these creations are not rare and they are conspicuous in any assemblage, the images have never been quantified nor systematically studied. As a topic with the potential to shed light upon human behaviour, cosmology, and belief systems, this art form has been largely ignored.

This chapter is an initial attempt to interpret the various zoomorphic and anthropomorphic images present in Susquehannock art, and to develop a working hypothesis about the role of this art in the culture. It focuses upon a sample size of 155 Susquehannock images, of which 110 are animal and 45 are human. For comparative purposes, 418 Seneca images are considered and of these 303 are animal and 115 are human.

Historical perspective

The Susquehannocks (Andaste and Minqua) were a large and populous offshoot of the Seneca and Cayuga-Iroquois Indians of western New York State (Fig. 14.1). They inhabited the lower Susquehanna Valley in south-central Pennsylvania from AD 1575 to 1680. For 100 years they were an important factor in the fur trade and a major force in controlling European settlement on the Pennsylvania frontier. The conventional model (Kinsey 1977, p. 102, Kent 1984) of Susquehannock culture history maintains that by 1680 the Susquehannock population was significantly diminished and their culture shattered as a result of prolonged warfare with the Iroquois on their northern boundary for control of the fur trade, incursions by Maryland settlers to the south, and the introduction of new diseases from which they had no natural immunity.

Around the year 1680, remnant Susquehannocks moved south to live among the Piscataway Indians of Maryland, near the confluence of the Piscataway Creek and the Potomac River. After a hiatus of about ten years, they returned to the Susquehanna Valley and became known as the Conestoga Indians. Living under the

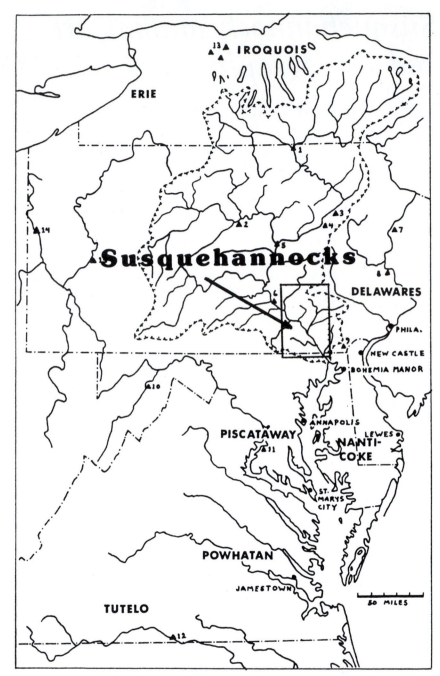

Figure 14.1 Map showing location of Susquehannock Indians (after Kent 1984).

protection of the Provincial Government in Philadelphia and the Seneca, who now played an influential role in the region, the Conestogas and other refugee groups survived under greatly reduced and impoverished circumstances. The last of the Conestoga-Susquehannock Indians were massacred in a raid on Lancaster in 1763 by the so-called 'Paxtang Boys'.

Much is known about the cultural history of the Susquehannock Indians from the archaeological record as well as from historic sources (Eshleman 1908), but the records reveal very little about social organization, and even less about beliefs and ceremonial practices. Over the past 50 years, five large and five smaller Susquehannock villages have been extensively excavated, studied, and reported. Kent's (1984) treatise is the most current and important work in a body of archaeological literature including Cadzow (1936), Witthoft & Kinsey (1959), Kinsey (1977), Webster (1983), and others. Susquehannock culture was similar to the better-known Iroquois culture, which featured extended matrilineal families residing in bark-covered longhouses in villages protected by a surrounding palisade wall.

Kent (1984, p. 18) provides a 10-stage or phase sequence for Susquehannock cultural history (Table 14.1). Population estimates made by Webster (1983, pp. 227–38) of the several villages range from 1250 to as many as 5000 persons at the large Strickler site, while Kent's more conservative estimates (1984, p. 364) are 1300–2900 for the same sites.

Although they were primarily agriculturalists (50–70 per cent of the diet) with corn (*Zea mays*) the single most important food, the Susquehannocks were also efficient hunters, trappers, gatherers, and fishers. The significance of protein derived from hunting activities generally has been underestimated. Studies by Guilday *et al.* (1962) and Webster (1983) of well-preserved archaeofauna from the Eschleman site testify that 72 different animal species, representing nearly 18 tons of consumable meat, were utilized by the Susquehannocks during their occupation of this site. Nevertheless, only three species were heavily exploited for food: white-tailed deer (52 per cent of meat consumed), elk (21 per cent), and bear (20 per cent).

Susquehannock material culture is represented by an abundance of utilitarian and non-utilitarian artefacts, including distinctive ceramic cooking and storage vessels, smoking pipes made of stone or ceramic, and a wide range of tools,

Table 14.1 Susquehannock cultural history (after Kent 1984).

Stages/phases	Dates (AD)
1 Common roots with the Iroquois, New York	−1450
2 Proto-Susquehannock, Bradford County	1450–1525
3 Early Schultz and Migration, Bradford & Tioga Counties	1525–1575
4 Schultz, Lancaster County	1575–1600
5 Washington Boro, Lancaster County	1600–1625
6 Transitional–Billmyer and Roberts, Lancaster County	1625–1645
7 Strickler, Lancaster County	1645–1665
8 Leibhart–Defeat and Turmoil, York County	1665–1680
9 The Void, Maryland	1680–1690
10 Conestoga and other Indians, Lancaster County	1690–1763

weapons, and personal ornaments fashioned from stone, bone, and antler. Only a few wooden artefacts have survived. As early as the last quarter of the 16th century, European trade items begin to occur on Susquehannock sites. European entrepreneurs quickly discovered that large profits could be made by exchanging cheaply produced Venetian glass beads, metal axes, knives, hoes, kettles, flintlock muskets, glazed earthen wares, pewter pipes, other mass produced goods along with alcoholic spirits, for valuable pelts. This expanding fur trade reached its peak by the middle of the 17th century, with beaver especially prized by those engaged in this lucrative enterprise.

Susquehannock and Seneca images

The Susquehannocks and Seneca were participants in a long indigenous artistic heritage found throughout the north-eastern woodlands that extends at least to the Late Archaic (4000–1000 BC) and probably even earlier, to the Paleo-Indian Period (10 000–8000 BC). Unfortunately, only a few examples of prehistoric native art manage to withstand the effects of weathering. A magnificent representation of a water-bird on an antler comb from Frontenac Island (3000–2000 BC) in central New York (Ritchie 1969, p. 116), is one of a few extant artistic creations which demonstrate that prehistoric native American art was much richer and more complex than is generally recognized from the surviving objects.

Seventeenth-century Susquehannock and Seneca art is at the recent end of this artistic heritage. The art, usually found in burial contexts, is associated with sociotechnic and ideotechnic objects. The former are described by Binford (1972, p. 24) as 'the material elements having their primary functional context in the social subsystems of the total cultural system.' Ideotechnic artefacts '. . .signify and symbolize the ideological rationalizations for the social system and further provide the symbolic milieu in which individuals are enculturated' (Binford 1972, p. 24). The objects are small and portable, and were created either by proficient carving or by skilful modelling. Some images appear as a decorative element incorporated into the design of pipes, ladles, and combs, but in other instances, ornaments, effigies, and pendants were made into three-dimensional free-standing representational images. All the art is naturalistic; it is not abstract. Decorative stylization (the incorporation of natural features within the medium into the design), colour, and line-markings, such as those made during the Upper Palaeolithic in Europe, were not utilized in Susquehannock and Seneca art.

Tables 14.2 and 14.3 compare Susquehannock and Seneca images and media. As expected, there is a high degree of similarity and a close correlation in the style and concept of image-making practices between Susquehannock and Seneca. Similar animals are used in similar ways on similar objects, and the media are the same. Nevertheless certain narrow differences in the distributions were observed. The Susquehannocks have a lower proportion of mammals and a higher proportion of reptiles (mostly turtles). Other proportions are nearly identical.

Most images show a keen sense of observation with respect to the pose of the animal and the internal relationships of forms. Thus, the relationships of

Table 14.2 Comparison of Susquehannock and Seneca animal and human images.

Animals	Susquehannock human and animal images							Seneca animal and human images					
	Native pipes	Trade pipes	Ornaments effigies	Ladles	Combs	Misc.	Totals	Native pipes	Trade pipes	Ornaments effigies	Ladles	Combs	Totals
birds	28	3	21	3	1		56	19	1	124	3	14	161
mammals	15	4	6	2	1		28	37	2	27	9	49	124
reptiles	5		17		1		23	6		6		3	15
other	1		1			1	3	1		2			3
Subtotal	49	7	45	5	3	1	110	63	3	159	12	66	303
Human	21		15		9		45	38	5	26	9	37	115
Total	70	7	60	5	12	1	155	101	8	185	21	103	418

Table 14.3 Comparison of media used to make Susquehannock and Seneca animal and human images.

Animals	Susquehannock media								Seneca media						
	Clay	Stone	Antler bone	Wood	Metal	Shell	Other	Totals	Clay	Stone	Antler bone	Wood	Metal	Shell	Totals
birds	22	6	6	4	4	13	1	56	15	2	16	3	6	119	161
mammals	8	9	2	2	4	3		28	32	2	56	10	3	21	124
reptiles	1	8	5		6	3		23	6	1	3		4	1	15
other	1			1	1			3	1					2	3
Subtotal	32	23	13	7	15	19	1	110	54	5	75	13	13	143	303
Human	13	20	11	1				45	40	2	51	12	8	2	115
Total	45	43	24	8	15	19	1	155	94	7	126	25	21	145	418

head to neck, neck to body, and eye to beak are strong. Proportions are carefully executed, and these artists made acute observations of the angles and directions of the subject's anatomy. Some images show a remarkable command of detail, with marks, patterns, and inlays used to achieve greater realism. An excellent sense of aesthetics appears to be revealed from what is included and what is omitted. It is evident that the native artists were studious observers of nature. Watching animals was a way of seeing order in their universe. It was a way of marking time, noting cycles and the changing of seasons; furthermore, their annual cycle was determined by these observations.

They excelled at manipulating clay, stone, shell, wood, bone, and antler as they embellished a variety of artefacts with naturalistic images. The Susquehannocks and Seneca also made small animal and human figurines, maskettes, and ornaments, while many artefacts were drilled for suspension.

By the mid 17th century, at the height of the fur trade when the Susquehannocks and Seneca had gained the greatest access to European trade goods, metal was sometimes used as a medium. Bird, reptile, and mammal images were fashioned from kettle brass, and a few were made of lead musket balls. As steel knives became commonplace, antler combs occurred with greater frequency, they were more elaborate and the teeth were more finely made. Multiple figures are depicted on Seneca combs of the 18th century and some combs are metaphors for stories, myths, and legends (Wray 1973, p. 11). Antler combs and maskettes made of catlinite or red pipestone were the major Seneca forms of artistic expression in the 18th century.

Although few perishable items of Susquehannock material culture have survived, Captain John Smith's description of his encounter with a party of 60 Susquehannock warriors in the Chesapeake Bay region in 1608 provides corroboration for the use of animal images on pipes, as adornments, and on personal attire (Eshleman 1909, p. 8):

> Those are the strangest peoples of all those countries, both in language and attire; for their language may well beseem their proportions, it sounding from them as a voice in the vault. Their attire is the skins of bears and wolfs, some have cassocks made of bear's head and skin that a man's head goes through, the skin's neck and ears of the bear fastened to his shoulders and the nose and teeth hanging down his breast; another bear's face split behind him and at the end of the nose hung a paw.
>
> The half sleeves coming to the elbows, were the necks of bears; and the arms through the mouth, with paws hanging at their noses. One had the head of a wolf hanging in a chain for a jewel; his tobacco pipe three-quarters of a yard long prettily carved with a bird, a deer or some such device, at a great end, sufficient enough to beat out one's brains; with bows and arrows and clubs suitable to their greatness. These are scarce known to Powhatan.

Susquehannock images

Birds

Birds represent half of the animal images in Susquehannock iconography and occur twice as frequently as mammals. They are often depicted on pipes, combs, and commonly occur as pendants or effigies (Figs 14.2b, c, e; 14.3d; 14.4a, b, d). Bird images and adornments are carved out of soft stone such as serpentine, and they are incorporated into pipe bowls. On clay pipes they are modelled in-the-round. Birds appear in a variety of positions and postures; they 'nest' so that the body forms the bowl of the pipe and the head either faces toward or away from the smoker. In some instances, the bird effigy perches on the rim of the bowl, and more rarely the bird's open mouth forms the bowl.

Waterfowl such as ducks, geese, herons, and loons are the most commonly illustrated birds with raptors (owls, hawks, and eagles) less frequently represented. One outstanding clay pipe came from a burial at the Strickler site in Washington Boro, Lancaster County, this image is an accurate rendition of the common loon (*Gavia immer*). Tiny pieces of kaolin are inlaid in parallel rows along the back and neck of the darker clay matrix to create a striking resemblance to the loon's distinctive speckled appearance.

A hawk-owl effigy (Fig. 14.5) from the previously mentioned site and collection, is exceptionally intriguing. Arthur Futer found this specimen in a burial where it had been attached to the bowl of a long-stem pewter trade pipe facing in the direction of the smoker. This wooden effigy (13.8 × 6.5 × 4.2 cm) is inlaid with pieces of brass arranged in patterns faithful to the plumage of the northern hawk-owl (*Surnia ulula*)

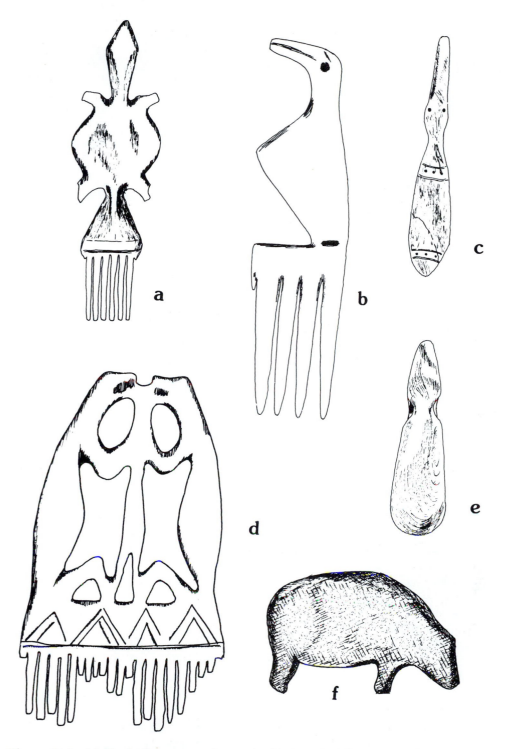

Figure 14.2 (a) Turtle figure on antler comb; (b) waterfowl figure on antler comb; (c) common loon, shell pendant; (d) mammal figures on antler comb; (e) waterfowl figure, shell pendant; (f) bear figure of catlinite.

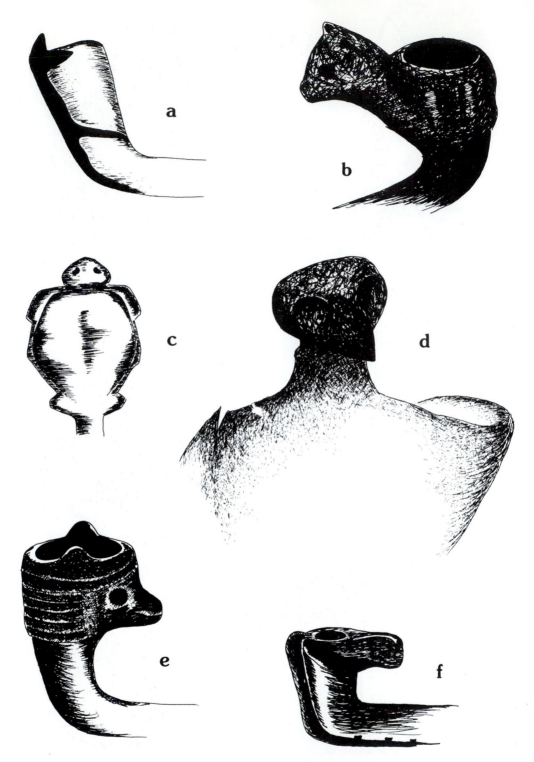

Figure 14.3 (a) Small mammal figure on stone pipe; (b) feline-like (cougar) figure on clay pipe; (c) turtle figure of stone; (d) bird of prey figure on handle of wooden ladle; (e) mammal (bear) figure on clay pipe; (f) horse-like figure on catlinite pipe.

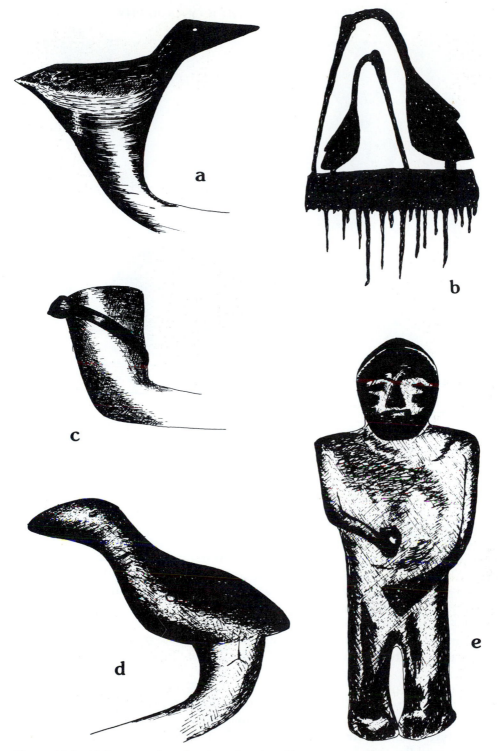

Figure 14.4 (a) Common loon figure on clay pipe; (b) heron or crane figures on antler comb; (c) snake figure on stone pipe; (d) duck-like figure on clay pipe; (e) human stone figure.

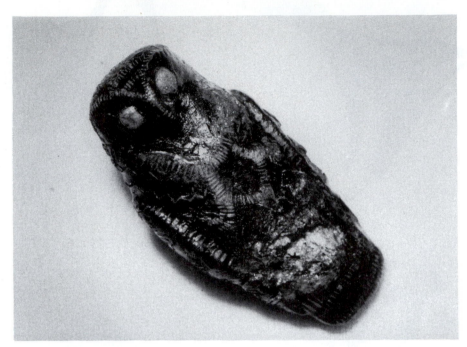

Figure 14.5 Susquehannock hawk-owl effigy from the Strickler site (wood with brass inlays).

whose breeding range and habitat extends from the Canadian Shield to the subarctic. Vagrants of this species are rarely observed south of their normal habitat. In fact, the hawk-owl has not been found in the archaeofauna of prehistoric or historic middens, nor has it been recorded in any ornithological records this far south of its range.

Patently, this striking effigy is the work of a highly skilled Indian craftsman. Wood and brass were used in combination to create a naturalistic image of an unusual raptor. There are a few other instances where Susquehannock and Iroquois wood carvings have been embellished by using pieces of brass as inlay, but none are as impressive as this one. In order to explain this unique representation, it may well be that either a Susquehannock craftsman created this piece following a sojourn in Huron territory where a hawk-owl was encountered, or else the pipe was secured through trade with the Huron.

Seven European trade pipes have bird or mammal effigies incorporated into the original design of the pipe. This rather curious occurrence of European goods patterned after native artistic and iconographic practices might be attributed to the fur trader and manufacturer seeking to match the product with the customer's preferences.

Although birds were not commonly depicted on Susquehannock combs, there is a magnificent example of a pair of waterfowl (cranes or herons) on an antler comb from the Byrd Leibhart site (Kent 1984, p. 178). The bodies are elongated and heavy around the middle, they have long necks, and the bills and legs are foreshortened.

Bird images appear more frequently on Seneca combs. Combs were made of flat sections of elk or deer antler with the animal shown in profile.

Small shell bird pendants, resembling waterfowl with folded wings, are especially common during the Strickler Phase, and for the Seneca they were popular at the Dann site (1660–75). These charming pendants were a favourite item and evidently were worn as pendants on necklaces or attached to clothing as decoration. They are about 3–4 cm long and are often decorated with finely incised lines and small circular drill-holes. Usually the markings are blackened to highlight the design elements. The general shape of the bird's body, and the relatively short beak and neck, suggest that the artists were depicting geese. Wray (1964, pp. 17–18) refers to them as possible geese or ducks. In addition to these 'geese' pendants, there are several small shell owl pendants from the Strickler site.

Bird figures were carved on the handle of wooden cooking and serving ladles. Unfortunately, due to generally poor preservation there are only five surviving Susquehannock ladles with carved images. A horned or eared owl is carved into the handle of one ladle from the Strickler site, and a bird of prey with a sharp hooked beak flanked by large, deep-set eyes is present on another. Wooden ladles are much more common among the Iroquois, and Prisch (1982) has made a detailed study of the morphology and symbolic possibilities of 701 Iroquois specimens.

Mammals

Mammal images (Figs. 14.2d, f; 14.3a, b, e, f) are about half as frequent as birds. In general, they tend to lack the sharp details associated with birds, and in most instances it is not possible to make species determinations with much confidence. The head and muzzle are the most frequently depicted body parts; however, unless the head is proportionally broad, the profile of a 'bear' can just as readily be interpreted as 'wolf', 'fox', or 'dog'. Size, colour and behaviour are distinguishing characteristics in the wild – attributes that are not present in this art form. Smaller mammals such as otters, martins, and fishers are equally difficult to identify. Cougars and other felines are more easily recognized by a relatively short muzzle and large eyes.

Unless form and proportions identify the species, or certain diagnostic details such as tail, paw, or general body profile are present, most of the mammal images in this study are recorded as generic mammal. Often mammal images are depicted on pipes, with the profile moulded on the bowl of a clay pipe or carved on a stone pipe. The image either faces the smoker or is turned in the opposite direction. The eyes on the bust of a cougar, on a clay pipe from the Strickler site, are accentuated by brass inlays. The full body of a small mammal is carved in low relief on the bowl of a stone pipe.

Several shell pendants resembling bear claws and at least one beaver pendant were found at the Strickler site; however, these were not preferred subjects for Susquehannock pendants. A catlinite pendant from the early 18th-century Conoy site in Lancaster County resembles a bear in full profile (Kent 1984, p. 168). Mammal images are a common theme on 18th-century Seneca antler combs.

Reptiles

Reptile images (Figs 14.2a, 14.3c & 14.4c) constitute 15 per cent of the Susquehannock sample of animal art and less than 4 per cent of the Seneca sample. They are limited to turtles and snakes, with the former the most common. It was not possible to make species identifications, and the 'snake' designation can just as easily be an 'eel'. One example from the Rochester Museum and Science Center is catalogued as eel by the late Charles Wray. Turtles and snakes appear as ornaments or pendants, as images on native-made pipes, but they are rarely present on antler combs.

One well-crafted stone pipe from the Strickler site has a serpent entwined around the stem and bowl. Turtle images usually occur as effigies or pendants pierced for suspension. Two small Susquehannock turtle images were fashioned from lead musket balls.

Human

Human face and figure images (Fig. 14.4e) are about equally popular for Susquehannock (29 per cent) and Seneca (28 per cent) where they occur on pipes, ornaments, ladles, and combs. Human art forms are executed differently than animal images. In the human portraiture, there is an exaggeration of proportions. Foreheads are small, heads and hands are large, and the eyes are often high on the face in proportion to the body. There are visual differences in the sense of weight between the 'heavy' animal images and the 'lighter' human depictions. Also, there is a general simplification of the human form with individual features achieved by simple abstract representations. Eyes, nose, and mouth are abstract and synthesized, such as the highly schematic figures on antler combs. The faces resemble masks, hands are oversized, and fingers are analogous to the teeth of the comb.

Other human depictions are equally stylized. There are three clay pipes from the Strickler site where the human form is very geometricized and highly integrated as part of the design concept. These pipes might have been crafted by a single individual, since they seem to be derived from the same mental template.

A majority of Susquehannock Washington Boro Phase burial ceramics depict two human faces beneath a notch on the lip at the castellation. Geometric and stylized images are incorporated on the pot by affixing a small piece of clay to the upper rim near the lip (Fig. 14.6). The nose was created by pinching and shaping, while short incised lines were used to portray eyes and mouth. These human faces and the occasional full-figure effigy are a diagnostic attribute and time marker for Washington Boro incised ceramics but they are not an intrinsic part of this study.

Effigy symbolism

Zoomorphic images have been interpreted by scholars in various ways. For the Iroquois and other north-eastern Indians, they have been identified as symbols of clan affiliation, as representations of myths, legends, folklore, and ceremonialism

Figure 14.6 Susquehannock full-figure human effigy on a pot from the Ibaugh site (clay).

(Fenton 1951, p. 49, Wray 1964, pp. 6–8). Speck (1945, p. 84) suggested that animal images pertain to magico-religious functions associated with renewal cults, such as the 17th-century Grand Medicine Society or Midewiwin of the Great Lakes area. Prisch (1982) believes the images on wooden ladles are multifunctional and that some are power symbols involving renewal and the triumph of life over death. Finally, Shimony (1961, p. 161) suggests that they served as the owners' identification mark.

Unlike certain native American groups such as Plains Indians and Eskimo, who depicted animals in their art which were of considerable economic importance, it was not the practice of the Susquehannocks or the Seneca to illustrate animals that were an important food resource. Deer and elk account for 73 per cent of the meat consumed by the Susquehannocks but these animals are *never* represented in Susquehannock and Seneca art! The bear constituted about 20 per cent of the Susquehannock meat supply and is only occasionally depicted. Squirrels, rabbits, and fish are other common archaeofauna *not* represented by the art.

None of the bird images are passerines; instead they are either flocking migratory birds or the more solitary raptors. Birds such as cranes, swans, herons, and other waterfowl, along with the raptors, may have been valued for plumage and body parts for use with ceremonial paraphernalia and dress. Carapace and plastron from box and musk turtles were made into rattles, cups, and small dishes. Moreover, it is probably significant that most of the species represented in Susquehannock animal art are a mere fraction of the total volume of the archaeofauna.

Animals favoured by the Susquehannocks in their art forms were not an important source of food, and this is also true for the Seneca. Migratory waterfowl (ducks, loons, herons, cranes, and geese); raptors (defined here as both nocturnal and diurnal birds of prey, including owls, hawks, and eagles); reptiles (turtles, snakes, and lizards); and small game animals (beaver and otter) were the animals most frequently depicted. In some instances the work of the artist is so life-like and the designs so accurate that the animal can be identified as to species. For example, the common loon is easily recognized as a favoured effigy on ceramic pipes.

Wray (1964) has shown that Seneca folklore, myth, and ritual was replete in the use of bird images. Furthermore, he has observed bird remains in human burials, including the intact skeleton of a great blue heron (Wray 1964, pp. 22–32).

The use of white shell as the principal medium for many of the bird pendants is not fortuitous but has symbolic significance. This concept has been developed by Hamell (1986) who postulates that there is a symbolic and metaphoric linkage between white shell and *daylight, brightness*, and *whiteness* which are qualities of *cognition, mind, knowledge*, and *being* for the northern Iroquois. Thus, I am suggesting that the small shell pendants resembling waterfowl were assigned a symbolically and metaphorically important role in Susquehannock cosmology.

Considering the image as a whole, and the amount of emphasis placed upon the execution of details such as eyes, ears, feet, and feathers, it is reasonable to hypothesize that the stylization of these details are measures of the importance assigned to the animal. Accordingly, there is a cosmological hierarchy within Susquehannock animal art. In this ranking, birds are at the top followed by mammals, reptiles, and humans. Images of human figures show the least amount of detail and are the most highly stylized. Clearly, the human images had a separate meaning and purpose in the Susquehannock belief system. Perhaps, human figures were assigned to other roles and were associated with Medicine Society rituals. These observations are not developed for the Seneca, but they may also be valid for their art.

The Susquehanna River Valley is a major eastern flyway for the semi-annual migration of huge numbers of waterfowl. In the early spring the birds pause to rest on the river flats and islands, and feed in nearby fields before continuing to their nesting grounds along the waterways and marshes of the Canadian arctic and subartic. This pattern is reversed each fall as they head toward southern latitudes for their winter residence. Western New York with its abundance of watercourses and proximity to the eastern Great Lakes is an equally inviting place for migrating water birds.

Other animals favoured in Susquehannock art are seasonal in nature and are scarce during certain times of the year. In the winter months the beaver and the otter are less active and keep to their lodges and dens, the bear hibernates, as do turtles and other reptiles. Table 14.4 is a comparison of Susquehannock and Seneca images by species, most of which are seasonal and migratory or hibernating species.

Table 14.4   Comparison of Susquehannock and Seneca animal images by species.

	Susquehannock	Seneca
birds	55 (50%)	161 (53%)
waterfowl	28 (51%)	136 (84%)
common loon	10	128
duck	1	
heron		4
goose		4
raptors	14 (25%)	9 (6%)
eagle		1
hawk		1
hawk-owl	1	
long-eared owl	1	
owl	9	3
generic	13 (24%)	16 (10%)
mammals	28 (26%)	124 (41%)
small	5 (18%)	12 (10%)
beaver	2	2
canine	1	
dog		1
otter	2	8
weasel		1
large	9 (32%)	59 (47%)
bear	7	52
cougar	1	5
horse	1	2
generic	14 (50%)	53 (43%)
reptiles	23 (21%)	15 (5%)
lizard	1	
snake	2	6 (40%)
turtle	17 (74%)	9 (60%)
generic	3	
other	3 (3%)	3 (1%)
beetle	1	
frog	2	
lion		1
monkey		2

Conclusions

Some of these animal forms may be secular clan symbols, but in view of the large number of non-clan animal species represented it seems unlikely that all the images are totemic in function. Instead, a majority of the representations are of species associated with the changing seasons. Nearly all of the animals depicted are either migratory visitors to the Susquehanna Valley or year-round residents who den in the winter.

The animals, especially the migratory waterfowl, are harbingers of change and renewal. It seems probable that the iconographic importance assigned to the animals by the Susquehannocks is associated with the seasonal cycle and a desire to propitiate them and, thereby, ensure the continuity of the life cycle. The Susquehannock animal representations were created for cosmological reasons and they were also endowed with ideological significance involving magico–religious practices. With the exception of the bear, none of these animals was an important source of food.

Until archival materials in the Pennsylvania Historical and Museum Commission and in other repositories are thoroughly mined for contributions to Susquehannock cosmology, ideology, and social customs, there is no way to determine the deeper meaning of Susquehannock animal art. As a working hypothesis, I am proposing that the animal effigies were used for ceremonial–religious purposes and that they were ideotechnic in purpose and in function. Therefore, effigy pipes were used as part of sacred rituals, ladles were used to serve consecrated food, while the small bird and other effigy pendants were worn as ceremonial paraphernalia. These sacred objects were used at grave site rituals performed by the shaman. The images were interred with the owner at his death and additional offerings were placed in the grave by close relatives and friends.

It appears, therefore, that seemingly minor and simple animal images may have the potential to provide insights into the poorly known and understood Susquehannock belief systems.

Acknowledgements

I extend thanks and appreciation to the following individuals: Arthur A. Futer, New Holland, for assistance in studying his extensive collection of the Strickler site; Kurt Carr, Pennsylvania State Museum; William Mangold, formerly of the Hershey Museum of American Life; Charles F. Hayes and Betty C. Prisch, Rochester Museum and Science Center; Jeanette Cole, Franklin and Marshall College, for her helpful insights; Karen Shaub for art work; and Jordan Marche, North Museum, for photography.

References

Binford, L. R. 1972. *An archaeological perspective*. New York: Seminar Press.

Cadzow, D. A. 1936. *Archaeological studies of the Susquehannock Indians of Pennsylvania*. Harrisburg: Pennsylvania Historical Commission.

Eshleman, H. F. 1908. *Lancaster County Indians: annals of the Susquehannocks and other Indian tribes of the Susquehanna Territory from about the year 1500 to 1763, the date of their extinction*. Lancaster.

Fenton, W. N. 1951. Locality as a basic factor in the development of the Iroquois social structure. *Bureau of American Ethnology Bulletin* **149**(3), 35–54. Washington, DC.

Guilday, J.E., P. W. Parmalee & D. P. Tanner 1962. Aboriginal butchering techniques at the Eschleman site (36La. 12), Lancaster County, Pennsylvania. *Pennsylvania Archaeologist* **32** (2), 59–83.

Hamell, G. R. 1986. *Life's immortal shell: Wampum among the northern Iroquoians*. Paper prepared for the Shell Bead Conference, Rochester Museum and Science Center, 15–16 November 1986.

Kent, B. C. 1984. *Susquehanna's Indians*. Harrisburg: Pennsylvania Historical and Museum Commission.

Kinsey, W. F. III, 1977. *Lower Susquehanna Valley: prehistoric Indians*. Ephrata: Science Press.

Prisch, B. C. 1982. *Aspects of change in Seneca Iroquois ladies*. Research Records no. 15. Rochester Museum and Science Center, Rochester.

Ritchie, W. A. 1969. *The archaeology of New York State* (rev. edn). Garden City: Natural History Press.

Shimony A. A. 1961. *Conservatism among the Iroquois at the Six Nations Reserve*. Yale University Publications In Anthropology 65. New Haven, Connecticut.

Speck, F. G. 1945. *The Iroquois, a study in cultural evolution*. Cranbrook Institute of Science Bulletin 23. Bloomfield Hills.

Webster, G. S. 1983. *Northern Iroquoian hunting: an optimization approach*. Unpublished PhD Dissertation, The Pennsylvania State University.

Witthoft, J. & W. F. Kinsey, III (eds) 1959. *Susquehannock miscellany*. Harrisburg: Pennsylvania Historical and Museum Commission.

Wray, C. F. 1964. The bird in Seneca archeology. *Proceedings of the Rochester Academy of Science* **11** (1), 1–32.

Wray, C. F. 1973. *Manual for Seneca Iroquois archeology*. Honeoye Falls, NY: Cultures Primitive.

15 *Animal metaphor in art from the Solomon Islands*

DEBORAH B. WAITE

This chapter considers the role of animals as visual and cultural metaphors among the people of the Solomon Islands. The Solomons, a principal group of Melanesian islands in the western Pacific Ocean, lie east of New Guinea and north of Vanuatu between 5° and 12° south of the equator (Fig. 15.1). The seven main islands are volcanic in origin, as are some of the small islands, but many of the latter are atolls.

Animal life in this tropical environment is one of extremes. Indigenous land animals are few. Mainly nocturnal, they include the opossum (cuscus), several varieties of phalanger (Australian marsupial) and bat, as well as bush rats and mice. Dogs and pigs, the latter a major source of meat, were introduced centuries ago, as were the Polynesian rat and roof rat (*Rattus exulans* and *R. rattus*, respectively). Horses, cows, cats, and chickens are recent introductions. Crocodiles occur on the larger islands and in the coastal waters; turtles, lizards, and snakes are common, but most snakes are non-poisonous and seldom reach significant size. Insects flourish and include magnificent butterflies and moths.

The air and sea abound with birds and fish of many types. Over 140 species of birds exist, including parrots, terns, herons, eagles, and frigate birds. Fish of many species occur and have long constituted the principal source of revenue for the people (British Solomon Islands, 1975, pp. 124–5).

Even the most cursory survey of art from the Solomon Islands reveals a strong preoccupation with animal imagery. Crocodiles are the major land/sea animal depicted in sculpture and painting from the western Solomon Islands. Images of sea birds also proliferate, and there are sporadic examples of butterfly images. In the eastern Solomons, from south Malaita to Santa Ana and Santa Catalina, birds and fish predominate in all categories of ritual art. Pigs, serpents, and the cuscus are infrequently represented. The significance of animals for Solomon Islanders emerges through analysis of the two inseparable channels of ritual and art within the pertinent cultural contexts.

Eastern Solomon Islands

Cultural contexts: bonito fishing and malaohu *initiation*

In the eastern Solomon Islands, annual fishing for species of bonito and tuna occurs between March and June during a period of calm and shifting winds. The appearance

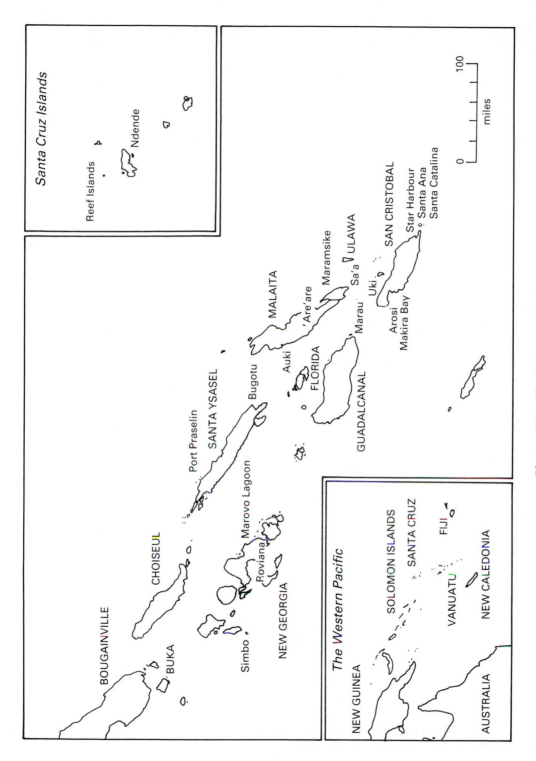

Figure 15.1 The Solomon Islands.

of the silvery blue bonito is an unforgettable phenomenon, judging from accounts taken from the 1880s to the 1960s, e.g.:

> A fully developed school [of bonito] is a frenzy of predation: thousands of thrashing and leaping bonito and dozens of diving swooping birds feeding on the bait; large groups of sharks closing in from the outside snapping at anything. The sea rolls with fish, parts of fish, and blood, true fishing birds plummet in for catches and dart out to contend with intimidations from the other species bent on robbing them. And there is the noise, a cacophonic blend of bird shrieks against the roar of a churning sea (Davenport 1981, p. 6).

Man and bonito have allegedly been thought to share two characteristics: both have an abundance of red blood, and the actions of both are controlled by supernatural spirits. It follows, then, within this culture, that initiation of young boys into adulthood has traditionally involved bonito fishing. One of the major objects of bonito fishing expeditions has been to secure fish required for the boys' initiation rituals.[1]

The initiatory process reveals cultural attitudes toward the bonito that further articulate resemblances between boys and the fish. A bonito fish is caught for each boy undergoing initiation, and the boy is required to hug the bonito to his body, thus performing the first ritual that brings him into close physical proximity to the fish. On Santa Catalina, the only island in the eastern Solomons where the initiation still survives,[2] the boy is taken out to sea in a bonito canoe, lying on his back and clasping the bonito to his chest; he is, in effect, being paddled out to sea 'as a fish' (Davenport 1981, p. 6).

The subsequent and most mystical part of the initiation is the process which, on one level, further substantiates the symbiotic identification of boy with bonito and, on another, initiates the transformation from boy to man. This may take three possible forms: having the initiate swallow a few drops of blood from the fish; touching the boy's body in several paces with the fish snout; or anointing him with salt water mixed with fish blood taken from inside the canoe. The immediate result of these acts is to put the boy into a weakened state from which he must gradually recover during a period of seclusion (from society and, in particular, from women):

> For the first few days, initiates are fed only liquids and soft foods, a process paralleled with the first days of life during which the infant is fed only coconut water until the mother's milk is flowing. (ibid. pp. 7–8)

This proscription and others, such as giving each boy a new sleeping mat, new food baskets, and special coconut scrapers, indicate the liminal phase of rebirth which will eventually culminate in the new status of manhood (cf. Turner 1964, pp. 5–6). It may be suggested that in this early period of the liminal transitory process, the boy is still conceived of as being like the bonito, absorption of which has facilitated this transition. The bonito themselves have been described as 'virgin born' and 'under the care of special ghosts and sharks' (Ivens 1927, p. 130), just as the boys in initiatory seclusion are treated as new-borns under the care of their guardians.

Following ritual transformation through the auspices of the bonito, the return of the newly initiated boys (men) to the community and secular life is further effected through animal metaphor. On Ulawa Island, fathers of the boys ceremonially paint-ed[3] a frigate bird image with white lime on the upper arms of the boys before they returned to the village; this allegedly protected them from evil forces (Ivens 1927, pp. 142–3). Wearing elaborate ornaments and carrying wooden plaques decorated with images of bonito and sea-birds (cf. Mead 1973b, Figs 13, 14), the boys return to the village and mount a large platform, *gea*, from which they are viewed by the villagers. The *gea* may take animal form so that the boys may mount and then climb down or emerge from a gigantic bird or fish as the culminating ritual act of their initiation.

Associated with the status of manhood is the physical stamina necessary for the new males to become fishermen of bonito and, ultimately, sponsors of initiations as well as the annual fishing quest (Davenport 1981, p. 5). The boy/bonito, thus, becomes the man/predator. As such, he is identifiable, metaphorically, with other predators: the fishing birds, sharks, and fish which, like men, exhibit the seemingly contradictory traits of predator and guardian/protector (revealed, for example, in the term guardian shark, or familiar shark used to describe certain of the sharks that surround schools of bonito). The former role may be seen as a necessary function of the latter in order to perpetuate transformation and, thus, the continuation of the life cycle.

Artefact clusters

Artefact clusters from the eastern Solomon Islands are indicated in Table 15.1 together with animals represented on the artefacts.

Table 15.1   Artefact clusters and associated animals, eastern Solomon Islands.

Canoe	Custom house	Initiation platform	Individual

prow:
  sea birds, fish
stern:
  dog
sides:
  birds, fish
paddles:
  fish
water containers:
  birds
	posts:
	  bonito, sharks, frigate
	  birds
	gable carvings:
	  fish, sea spirits
	tie beams:
	  bonito fishing
	  expeditions
	bowls:
	  sea birds, bonito,
	  dolphin, sharks
	caskets:
	  sharks, bonito canoes,
	  three-dimensional fish
	  images
		three-dimensional carvings:
		  sea birds, sharks, bonito,
		  bonito canoes
			personal ornaments:
			  birds, fish, sea spirits
			dance staffs:
			  birds, bonito, dolphin,
			  sharks
			lime spatulas:
			  sea spirits
			fishing floats:
			  sea spirits, birds, fish
			bowls:
			  birds, fish
			weapons:
			  birds, sea spirits
			tattooing, body painting:
			  birds, fish

Canoes

Canoes in the eastern Solomon Islands[4] belong to four main types: utility fishing canoes, small and large trading canoes, and bonito-fishing canoes. The two latter types are ornamented with carved, painted, and shell-inlaid images. Both spend a considerable time away from land and constitute portable extensions of segments of society and animal metaphor into the marine dimension. Trading canoes (Fig. 15.2) tend to be more elaborately decorated than the special ritual bonito-fishing canoes. Images of sea-birds, fish, and insects are carved in low relief and painted on both sides of the bow and stern (cf. De Tolna 1903, plate opposite p. 204, Ivens 1927, frontispiece). A fish, either generalized bonito, flying fish, or sailfish, is traditionally rendered on the top edge of the forward washboard. Highly schematized designs for schools of fish, or recognizably rendered frigate birds, terns, swordfish, or sailfish mark the inside positions of the five thwarts for the paddlers in the amidship field of the trading canoe (e.g. Davenport n.d., Pls 4, pp. 11, 12, Ivens, op. cit.). Animal designs on bow and stern may also be combined with geometric designs representing cumulus clouds, in order to signify cloud configurations that resemble the animals; discovering animal shapes in the clouds is a game played by crew members at sea (Davenport op. cit., Pl.7a–f, p. 13). Lastly, zigzag or connected lozenge designs rendered on the lower panels forward and aft have been called 'snakes' (*mwarogorogo*)

Figure 15.2 Trading canoe. San Cristobal (Museum für Völkerkunde, Basel (V) VG3473; photograph E. Paravicini, courtesy of the Museum Für Völkerdunde).

Figure 15.3 Bonito canoe, San Cristobal Island (Museum für Völkerkunde, Basel (F) VG3633; photograph E. Paravicini, courtesy of the Museum für Völkerkunde).

and apparently refer to the movement of the canoe through the water (Davenport n.d., p. 13). Designs chosen for representation are intended to depict, in a balanced and idyllic way, different aspects of the environment, the presence of which would signify a desired successful and safe, fine-weather voyage (Davenport ibid., p. 15).

Bonito canoes (Fig. 15.3) represent a special category utilized solely in fishing for bonito and tuna, a process that has always been surrounded with the ritual appropriate to fish believed to be governed by supernatural spirits. The canoes constitute votive offerings made by important men to their tutelary spirits (Davenport ibid., p. 5). Perfection of form is aimed for in construction and decoration, and there is generally little variation in the decorative scheme because of the desire to adhere strictly to ideal form. Upraised prows terminate in the head of a sea-bird with fish in beak; another bird is carved in high relief on the washboard of the prow section. The bottom plank of the forward section of the canoe displays three motifs: the eye of the canoe (a circular piece of conus shell), a bent-wing design representing 'bird's wing', and a rectangular pattern depicting part of a fish's tail. The entire forward section of the canoe is seen as the 'head' of both fish and bird, and the whole canoe is regarded as a composite bird–fish conceived of as a predator analogous to the sharks and birds that accompany and prey (or appear to prey) on the bonito (Davenport ibid., pp. 17–18).

A three-dimensional carving of a dog holding a bonito in its muzzle can be seen on the sterns of bonito canoes from Santa Ana/Catalina and Ulawa (Fig. 15.4). Apparently, its unlikely occurrence in this situation and the equally unlikely action of a dog catching a fish make it an appropriate sign of the supernatural nature of bonito fishing (Davenport ibid., p. 16).

Custom house

Custom houses have traditionally served as canoe-storage houses, meeting places, and foci for ritual in the eastern Solomon Islands. Recorded evidence from the mid-19th century to the present reveal them to be architectural structures richly embellished with relief carving (cf. Brenchley 1873, plate opposite p. 258). Tie beams at one time spanned the width of the interior of custom houses. Depicted on them in painting and low-relief carving were scenes of bonito fishing expeditions as well as individual images of bonito (Brenchley 1873, plate opposite p. 262, Waite 1987, Pl. 1, p. 17). Carvings attached to the gable fronts of canoe houses feature sharks (Fig. 15.5) or spirits of the sea, represented as anthropomorphs with fish appendages (see Fig. 15.10).

Custom-house posts were (and still are) carved with anthropomorphic images accompanied by images of bonito, sharks, and frigate birds. Older literature seldom identifies the anthropomorphic images, but according to Davenport (1968, pp. 9–11), they are regarded as spirits, many of whom controlled the schools of bonito as

Figure 15.4 Stern, bonito canoe (British Museum 1927–91; photograph courtesy of the British Museum).

Figure 15.5   Gable carving, height 53 cm, Santa Ana Island (Museum für Völker-kunde, Basel Vb 7115; collected by Paravicini, 1929; photograph courtesy of the Museum für Völkerkunde).

well as the sharks and birds that follow them. The images usually stand, holding fish in their arms and hands, while other fish may encircle their bodies or be represented above them together with frigate birds (e.g. Bernatzik 1936, illus. 112, 113, 115). Pairs of bonito fish occupy central positions on some posts (e.g. Davenport 1968, p. 10). The mythical shark–anthropomorph, Karemanua, a spirit frozen in a half-shark, half-anthropomorphic form while in process of transformation from man to shark, is also a fairly common subject for houseposts (e.g. Bernatzik op. cit., illus. 110), as are sharks with human figures standing in their jaws (e.g. Museum für Volkerkunde, Basel, UG7325), and figures standing within jaw-like triangular forms (Fig. 15.6).

Wooden caskets carved to represent sharks (*airi*) (Fig. 15.7) and bonito-fishing canoes (*againinunu*) have traditionally been kept in the rear of canoe houses to house the skulls and bones, respectively, of important men (Mead 1973a, pp. 16–18). A shark casket with the image of an anthropomorphic figure pierced by its jaws allegedly symbolizes the shark-man Karemanua (Fig. 15.7, Mead ibid., Fig. 2B & Pl. 4). Other three-dimensional carvings of a fish – in one recorded instance, a

Figure 15.6 Housepost, height 1.3 m, Santa Ana (Musée de l'Homme, Paris, Coll. Madeleine Rousseau; photograph courtesy of the Musée de l'Homme).

Figure 15.7 Casket, length 2.08 m, Santa Ana (Musée de l'Homme, Paris, 61.103.56; photograph courtesy of the Musée de l'Homme).

dolphin (Fig. 15.8) – could apparently be suspended in a custom house. No precise ritual function is recorded for the images.

Ceremonial bowls, some as long as 4.31 m, could be stored in custom houses (cf. Brenchley 1873, plate opposite p. 262). They were used to hold mashed taro pudding at feasts, especially initiation feasts, and were decorated with images of sharks and sea-birds (Fig. 15.9). An occasional bowl took the form of a bonito-fishing canoe (e.g. Bernatzik 1934, illus. 14).

Initiation platform

The initiation platform *gea* (Santa Ana/Catalina) or *tahe* (Malaita, Ulawa), consists of a large rectangular or triangular platform with paired or single flights of stairs on each side, so that boys walk up one side and down the other (cf. Fox 1925, p. 348). Shapes of the stage have been recorded as representing a hair comb, bonito fish, and fishhawk (Fox 1925, pp. 348, 349, Ivens 1927, p. 142, Davenport 1981, p. 13). Davenport reports that at an initiation held on Santa Catalina in 1966, the inspiration for a fishhawk stage came in a dream to one of the builders from a spirit, Wakio Ni Toro, Fishhawk of the Promontory. The resultant stage, 10 feet square and 15 feet high, constituted the bird's body, while ascending and descending ramps were the

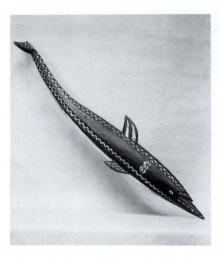

Figure 15.8 Dolphin, length 1.12 m Ulawa (British Museum 1944.Oc.2 1315).

Figure 15.9 Bowl, length 87.5 cm, Guadalcanal (Museum für Völkerkunde, Basel, VG 2668; photograph courtesy of the Museum für Völkerkunde).

wings. A bird's head and tail made of leaf panels were constructed at the front and back of the stage (Davenport, ibid.). In all recorded instances, three-dimensional carvings of sharks, sea-birds, bonito fish, and bonito fishing canoes were attached to the ramps, sides, and railings of the platforms, which varied in degree of elaboration depending upon the resources of the local community (Mead 1973b, p. 75, Davenport 1981, pp. 11–12).

Individual

The individual is the focal point and manipulator of a variety of art forms ranging from body decoration to weapons. All categories involve animal imagery. Patterns of facial tattooing include radial and V-shaped designs derived primarily from frigate-bird motifs (Mead 1973a, p. 30). Of the many shell ornaments worn in the eastern Solomons, one in particular, a flat disc serving as a pendant, head, or neck ornament, was (is) traditionally incised with bird and fish imagery (Fig.

Figure 15.10   Incised clam-shell disc, diameter 7.5 cm (Musée de l'Homme, Paris, 87.67.17).

15.10).[5] Typical designs evident on discs produced from the late 19th century to the present involve paired frigate birds with outspread wings, as well as sea-spirit images. The frigate birds are rendered, repeatedly, in a style which first appears on incised discs found archaeologically on Uki Island.[6] Site dates of AD 1480±90 and 1520±90 for deposits at the base, and AD 1510 and 1490 for the upper level give a chronological estimate for some of the earliest examples of frigate-bird imagery in the eastern Solomons (Newman 1975, pp. 17, 26a, Pl. 3).

Dance staffs and sticks also feature combinations of bird and fish imagery. One type of dance implement, a light weight staff with flat, curving blade, is known from Sa'a, Malaita, Ulawa, San Cristobal, and Santa Ana/Catalina (Waite 1987, pp. 41–2, Fig. 11). Designs lightly incised on the blades include frigate-bird-derived motifs. Blades may also comprise garfish, bonito, and frigate birds carved three-dimensionally and in open-work.

The blades of *qauata* (*pa'waa'ata*, *bwauata*), weapons, similar in shape to the dance staffs but larger and heavier, bear a stylized 'W' or frigate-bird wing pattern. These large clubs were used as shields to parry off spears (Guppy 1887, p. 87, Fox 1925, p. 310, Mead 1973a, p. 44).

Other privately utilized objects, such as small ritual bowls used on Santa Ana/Catalina in rituals held for a person's individual tutelary spirit (Fig. 15.11), lime sticks inserted into bamboo containers for powdered lime chewed in conjunction with betel nut, and floats employed in fishing for flying fish (Fig. 15.12), have also

Figure 15.11 Bowl, length 30 cm, Santa Catalina (Musée de l'Homme 62.1.9.1; photograph courtesy of the Musée de l'Homme).

Figure 15.12 Fishing float, length 73 cm (British Museum +2017; The Rev. R. B. Comins, 1883; photograph by D. B. Waite).

been decorated with different combinations of the same sea imagery displayed on personal ornaments, staffs, and other artefacts, such as the larger festival bowls (cf. Fig. 15.9). The latter, although cited under 'custom house' may also be considered as manifestations of the individual, since the ability to commission a carver for one of these bowls has traditionally been regarded as a major sign of status – especially for a candidate to the leadership role of big-man.

Combinations, such as a bird holding fish in beak and paired birds, as well as singly depicted birds, fish, and sea-spirits, thus recur with frequency within all categories of artefact clusters. It is this recurrence that makes interdependent the four clusters within the contexts of initiation and bonito fishing. The latter, in particular, has traditionally formed the contextual and symbolic fulcrum for animal symbolism in art from the eastern Solomons.

For the most part, creatures associated with the sea predominate in art and ritual among eastern Solomon Islanders. The dog carving on the stern of bonito canoes is a notable exception, chosen precisely for its exceptional character. Dogs appear also in the form of small ritual bowls, but these are few in number in comparison with the many bowls adorned with birds and fish (Fig. 15.13). Land animals appear infrequently in art, even though they may have served traditional social roles of some significance. Pigs constitute the primary meat desirable at all major feasts; they are rarely represented in art, although one or two pig-shaped bowls have been collected from San Cristobal (Fig. 15.14). Ritual offerings of pig meat to ancestral spirits have been recorded as aiding in averting illness and crop failures and in insuring victory before battle (e.g. Codrington 1891, pp. 129, 136–7, 139). The animal was, thus, consumed ritually, and as an object of consumption and sacrifice, it apparently did not serve as a metaphoric role model.

The cuscus appears to have been an insignificant animal socially, and appears seldom in the art. There are two or three existent cuscus carvings, all apparently once part of custom house posts (e.g. Bernatzik 1936, illus. 114).

Snakes have played a more prominent role in the mythology than in the visual arts. Beliefs in the existence of snake spirits have been recorded from most of the islands. Myths describe the existence of major creator spirits that assumed serpentine form (Codrington 1891, pp. 130–1, Fox 1925, pp. 92–8, 111). In the Arosi District of northern San Cristobal Island, a major centre of these beliefs, certain social groups were allegedly believed to descend from or relate to snakes. Ritual bowls belonging to members of these groups were identifiable by snakes carved in relief along the sides or on the tail (Fig. 15.15).

Figure 15.13 Bowl, length 43.3 cm, Santa Ana/Catalina (Bernatzik Collection, Vienna; photograph by D. B. Waite).

Figure 15.14 Bowl, San Cristobal (Museum für Völkerkunde, Basel, Vb 7182; photograph courtesy of the Museum für Völkerkunde).

Figure 15.15 Bowl, Florida Island (Museum of Archaeology and Anthropology, Cambridge University, Z10846; photograph courtesy of the Museum of Archaeology and Anthropology).

Western Solomon Islands

Cultural contexts: bonito fishing, net fishing, headhunting

In the western Solomon Islands (New Georgia Islands, Santa Isabel, Choiseul), traditional situations within which animal art appears include bonito fishing, fishing with nets for turtles and fish, and headhunting. Headhunting, which ceased near the end of the 19th century, constitutes the only cultural context that is non-existent today.[7] Bonito fishing has been surrounded by much of the same mystical allure that has pervaded it in the eastern Solomons, though initiations involving physical identity between initiate and fish were evidently absent.

Headhunting, once undertaken to procure heads for occasions such as the inauguration of new custom houses and canoes, and upon the death of a chief (Hocart 1931,

p. 383), involved ritual systems analogous to those of bonito fishing. A stone shrine on the beach was the focus of offerings and chants made to spirits prior to departure on either type of expedition, in order to guarantee safety of the crew and efficacy of the expedition. Payments of shell rings to spirits of the shrine and members of the expedition were made in both instances. A ritual termed *tita vagarata*, 'caulking to make bite', was performed on a bonito canoe during construction and on a headhunting canoe prior to departure. Insects were placed on prow and stern to the accompaniment of a chant which, in the case of a fishing canoe, urged:

> Caulk for biting, thou the canoe. . .thou the bonito shrine. . .make effective this canoe and make it catch bonito. (Hocart 1935, pp. 97–9)

The exhortation for the war canoe was comparable:

> Caulk to bite thou the war canoe here and do not rot, be the boards like stone. . .be strong ye boards, and be efficacious, thou. (Hocart 1931, 308–9)

Ngulu, or stroking, in which the sides of the canoe or its lead member were stroked with leaves four times to ward off potential disaster, was executed during construction and before departure; nets used in fishing and also in hunting pigs also received *ngulu* before use (Hocart 1931, pp. 308–10, 1937, p. 35, n.d., 19.3). Both canoes and nets were, in fact, addressed as though they were predatory animals.

Art clusters

Art clusters, distinct yet interrelated through shared rituals and animal motifs, include the bonito and war canoes, fishing nets, the custom house, and the individual. These are cited in Table 15.2.

Table 15.2 Artefact clusters and associated animals, western Solomon Islands.

Canoe	Custom house	Nets	Individual

bow:
    figurehead, bird
    carving
prow peak:
    bird/anthropo-
    morph, crocodile,
    bird, butterfly
sides:
    shell inlay patterns
paddles:
    birds,
    bird/anthropo-
    morph
water scoops:
    birds,
    bird/anthro-
    pomorph
	post:
	    crocodile &
	    anthropomorph
		net floats:
		    bird,
		    bird/anthropomorph
			staffs:
			    crocodiles &
			    anthropomorphs
			clubs:
			    crocodiles &
			    anthropomorphs
			personal ornaments:
			    frigate birds
			eating trough:
			    crocodile &
			    anthropomorphs
			mortuary huts:
			    tridacna plaques: birds
			    & anthropomorphs
			monument:
			    crocodiles &
			    anthropomorphs

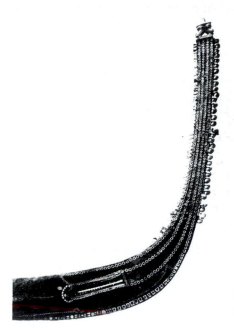

Figure 15.16 Canoe prow, detail, New Georgia Islands (Ulster Museum, Belfast, 963; presented to museum 1898; photograph courtesy of the Ulster Museum).

Canoes

The distinction between bonito and headhunting canoes and their respective decorative schemes is not precisely documented for the western Solomons. Both types of canoes were elaborately ornamented with small pieces of pearl shell inlaid along the bows and sides of the canoes. Of 18 named shapes of inlay pieces, three bear names referring to animals, although no visual similarity is apparent. They are: *Nole Paleo*, jawbone of *paleo* fish (Choiseul); *kuru*, 'bird in flight' (Choiseul), *pikupikutu*, 'to show part of its tail out of water' (New Georgia) (Canterbury Museum, accession files for canoe 5935; Waterhouse 1928, p. 81).

Images of crocodiles or crocodile heads were rendered on canoe prows with pieces of shell inlay on Santa Isabel Island and certain islands in the New Georgia group (Fig. 15.16; cf. Ribbe 1895, p. 314, Fig. 82). They recurred on other canoe ornaments from the same islands, including carvings attached to the prow peaks (e.g. Pitt Rivers Museum 1894.26.47. pp. 1–2; Gathercole *et al.* 1979, pp. 231, 19.12), and on the handles of canoe paddles. There is at least one recorded instance, from Simbo Island in the New Georgia group, of a canoe being given the name *Eavo*, or crocodile (Hocart 1931, p. 308). The presence of crocodile heads inlaid (and in some cases carved) on the prows of canoes suggests that they served as visual metaphors for the predatory powers of the canoe – powers invoked in the *tita vagarata* chants, although the chants never refer to crocodiles or any specific animals.

Information obtained in 1985–6 by archaeologists examining grave sites of the Kusage people on New Georgia Island suggests another role of the crocodile, at least for the Kusage. Two crocodile teeth discovered in a stone cist reportedly belonged to Leqegata, one of two crocodiles who once lived at the mouth of the Mase River. The people of the district encompassing the mouth of the Mase fed the animals and kept them as guardians who allegedly killed any strange crocodiles that ventured into the Mase. The crocodile named Leqegata died sometime near the end of the 19th century; the death of the other, called Saveni, was not remembered. The skull and two teeth of Leqegata were preserved at different sites; the skull was originally set on top of a stone at a place called Sogiana near the island coast; the teeth were taken up into the interior settlement of Maqala.[8] In at least this one instance, crocodiles assumed the role of protector as well as predator.

The frigate-bird prow-peak carving, whose presence denoted a bonito canoe in the eastern Solomon Islands, did not occur as a regular feature on canoes from the western islands. Paired frigate-bird heads, however, could be lashed to the bow just above the water-line (Fig. 15.17). Certain anthropomorphic figure-heads lashed immediately above the birds may have bird wings that project from the head (Fig. 15.18). The wings represent a comparatively minor feature (i.e. present on six of 50 examples) of an image whose presence was apparently mandatory on all canoes in the western Solomons. In the Marovo Lagoon district of New Georgia Island, a prow-peak carving commonly depicted an anthropomorphic image with a frigate bird replacing the head (Fig. 15.19); unlike the figure-head, the prow-peak carving had a limited regional distribution.

The bird anthropomorphs, paired bird carvings, and, in the Roviana district of New Georgia Island, the prow figure-heads, have been linked with a spirit being, called Kesoko, associated with both fishing and headhunting. Described

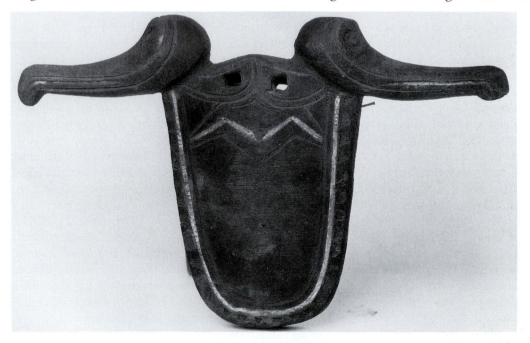

Figure 15.17 Canoe prow carving, height 22.8 cm, western Solomon Islands (British Museum 7905; ex-Wiseman Collection, 1865; photograph courtesy of the British Museum).

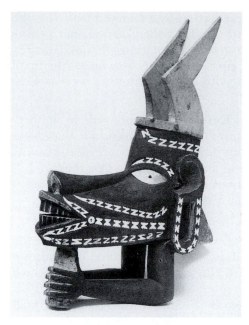

Figure 15.18 Canoe prow figure-head, height 39.8 cm, Choiseul (British Museum 1947. Oc.123; photograph by D. B. Waite).

Figure 15.19 Canoe prow-peak carving, height 74.8 cm, Ramada Island, New Georgia (Pitt Rivers Museum, Oxford University, D II 1895.22.160; photograph courtesy of the Pitt Rivers Museum).

as being crane-like in appearance (despite representation as a frigate bird), Kesoko was allegedly regarded as a spirit associated with (and invoked during) net fishing on Simbo and New Georgia islands, according to information obtained during the early years of this century (Hocart 1937, pp. 35, 38). A Roviana informant more recently described Kesoko in association with headhunting, as well as fishing, noting that he was:

> manlike in form but physically invisible. Kesoko was believed to have functioned as a pilot of the great *tomako* (canoe) through unknown waters, passages, reefs, and. . .to (have) look(ed) out for enemies to see that none escaped. . .the feet of Kesoko were short and his mouth was like that of a frigate bird or a seagull. . .Kesoko was an expert fisherman and. . .in the past he was the patron of fishing for the Vuraghare *mbutamutu* (clan) of Roviana. (Beti 1977, pp. 40, 47)

Frigate birds and bird/anthropomorphs were also painted on the blades of canoe paddles from Santa Isabel (Waite 1979, p. 261, Figs 13–15) and carved on bamboo scoops used in bonito fishing to make noises in the water that attracted the fish (Pitt Rivers Museum).

Butterfly prow ornaments were recorded by H. B. T. Somerville (1897) for small canoes from the Marovo Lagoon, New Georgia Island (Waite 1984, p. 49).

Custom house

Custom (canoe) houses were much less elaborately decorated than those in the eastern Solomon Islands. A single central housepost could be carved in the form of an anthropomorphic figure which might be accompanied by a crocodile (e.g. post carving, Museum für Volkerkunde, Basel, Vb 7682; collected by Paravicini in 1929).

Nets

Fishing for various species of small fish as well as turtles involved the use of large nets to which were attached floats carved of lightweight wood. These took the form of birds with anthropomorphic heads, seated anthropomorphs with bird heads (Fig. 15.20), and butterflies. The bird/anthropomorph combination allegedly represented spirits which protected and insured efficacy of the nets (Waite 1984, p. 44).[9]

Individual

As in the eastern Solomons, personally owned weapons and staffs could be adorned with animal images. The dominant species represented was the crocodile, rendered on the blade or tip of club handles with anthropomorphic figure or head in jaws (Figs 15.21 & 15.22). It should be noted that most clubs were not adorned at all, and the relative paucity of those which were decorated suggests that they were owned by individuals of considerable prestige. Curious, also, is the fact that animals were depicted on staffs and clubs but never on the shell-inlaid ceremonial shields which received solely anthropomorphic ornamentation.

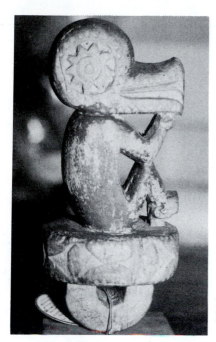

Figure 15.20 Net float, height 18 cm, New Georgia Island (Pitt Rivers Museum, Oxford University; Somerville Collection, 1895; photograph by D. B. Waite).

Figure 15.21 Club, Santa Isabel (British Museum 7065; photograph courtesy of the British Museum).

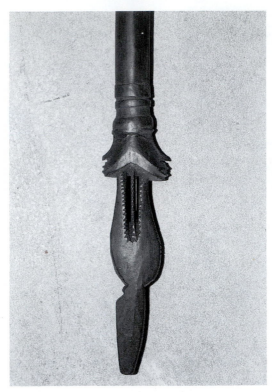

Figure 15.22 Detail of club handle, length 106 cm, western Solomon Islands (Pitt Rivers Museum, Oxford University; photograph courtesy of the Pitt Rivers Museum).

Personal ornaments of pearl shell from the New Georgia islands typically depicted paired frigate birds or bird-related designs (Fig. 15.23).

A single wooden eating-trough, approximately eight feet in length, was collected from New Georgia Island by C. M. Woodford near the end of the 19th century (Edge-Partington 1903, Pl. L, Figs 1–4). It took the form of a crocodile with an anthropomorphic figure standing in its jaws. Anthropomorphic heads were carved in relief along the sides. Information about the trough does not include data regarding its manufacture, but in all probability, just as in the eastern Solomon Islands, the right to commission the execution of such a vessel was the mark and prerequisite of an individual of significant status, that is, the big-man who would also have been the owner of decorated weapons and shields.

Mortuary huts erected to contain the skulls of deceased big-men, as well as skulls which they acquired in headhunting raids, received one major form of decoration. *Tridacna gigas* clam-shell plaques drilled with intricate open-work designs were placed on or inside the huts. Most contained anthropomorphic imagery, but several were ornamented with bird images (cf. Waite 1983).

A monument erected in front of the mortuary hut of Ingova, a prominent

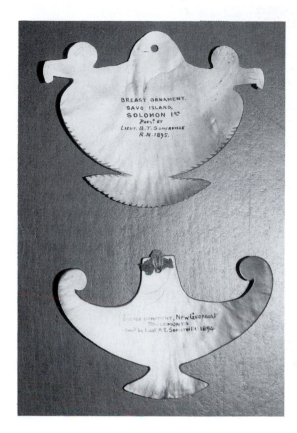

Figure 15.23 Pearl-shell breast ornaments, widths 11.6 cm, 11.2 cm, New Georgia Island (Pitt Rivers Museum, Oxford University; Somerville Collection; photograph by D. B. Waite).

leader (big-man) of the Roviana district, New Georgia Island (d. 1906), also reveals animal imagery: crocodiles with anthropomorphic heads in their jaws (De Tolna 1903, p. 331).

Comparison: conclusion

Animal art from the western and eastern Solomon Islands reveals choices of motif which reflect cultural preferences rather than differences in the physical presence or absence of animal species. The bonito is fished for in both regions, but whereas it is widely represented in art from the eastern Solomons, it rarely appears in art from the western Solomons. The same is true for sharks and dolphins.

Frigate birds are equally common in the art and environment of eastern and western islands. In both areas, the birds were regarded as heralds of the arrival of schools of bonito. Visual referents to the frigate and other sea-birds in art from the eastern Solomons seem to signify the bonito complex and sea-bird as predator, on the one hand, and, according to information furnished by Ivens (1927) and Fox (1925), affiliation with social groups identified with the different birds. In art from the western Solomons, bird imagery seems more specifically to refer to the afterlife

Table 15.3   Comparative roles of animals in the western and eastern Solomon Islands.

	Life	Afterlife
Eastern Solomons	boy: bonito man: shark: predator	man>shark (also serpent)
Western Solomons	man: crocodile: predator	man>bird

and, specifically, to spirits invoked in association with fishing, headhunting, and other enterprises. Bird-like behaviour was also signified by the presence of bird attributes (cf. Note 8).

The frigate bird as a predatory image, represented as a bird holding a fish on the prows of bonito canoes and on bowls in the eastern Solomons, was replaced by the crocodile as predator in the western Solomons. The crocodile, present in both regions, is almost non-existent in art from the eastern islands, but constitutes the major predator metaphor in the western islands. There, it seems to have developed in association with headhunting and related artefacts. Despite contextual differences, the crocodile of the western Solomons and the shark of the eastern Solomons appear to have served analogous metaphoric roles of protector/predator.

The ritual use of animal metaphor to assist in the process of transformation from one state of existence to another appears to have been a more obvious feature of the eastern Solomon Islands. The *malaohu* boys' initiation signified metaphoric transformation from the state of being like bonito to that of being like shark. Rituals associated with the deposition of a skull in a shark casket effected the transformation from human to shark in the afterlife.

Composite anthropomorphic/zoomorphic beings are equally common in art from the two areas. Half-bird, half-anthropomorphic images in art from the western Solomons apparently represented anthropomorphic spirits with avian behavioural and visual attributes. In the eastern Solomons, half-shark, half-anthropomorphic creatures, such as Karemanua, illustrated legendary acts of transformation from one state of existence to another. Other fish–anthropomorphs depicting sea-spirits were allegedly created from the blood of recently deceased people and simply represented a type of spirit being (non-ancestral) that coexisted with man in the universe. In the afterlife, seemingly, human spirits were reborn into the bodies of fish, especially sharks. The different roles are summarized in Table 15.3.

Notes

1   The name *malaohu*, or *maraufu*, given to the puberty initiation derived, according to Ivens, from *mala*, like, and *ohu*, to boil, referring to 'the boiling of the sea as the fish leap after their food' (Ivens 1927, p. 132). This information obtained from Sa'a, Malaita, and Ulawa, contrasts with that obtained by Davenport from Santa Catalina. There, the full name of the initiation is *maraufu ni waiau*, 'initiation to bonito'. This supposedly has connotations of transformation and change, one meaning of *mara* (Davenport 1981, p. 5).

2   The last full initiation on Santa Ana Island took place in 1943 (Mead 1973b).

3 Accounts of the *malaohu* initiation on Ulawa come from the 1920s, thus the use of tense must, of necessity, revert from present to past.

4 Canoes may be considered as an independent artefact cluster but could also be subsumed under the headings of 'custom house' and 'individual'. They are stored in custom houses located near the shore and used as canoe houses. Although communal from the standpoint of building and maintenance as well as occupancy, the leader of a crew and of the builders has special significance as initiator and is sometimes referred to as the canoe owner. On Santa Ana and Santa Catalina, organization of a canoe-building enterprise represents a major achievement of a recognized leader or 'big-man' (Davenport n.d., p. 3).

5 The disc was called *ulute* on Ulawa and at Sa'a and Malaita, *hitarai* on San Cristobal, *la'oniasi* by the Kwaio of Malaita, and *papafita* on Santa Ana (Monongai 1923, Fox 1925, p. 295, Bernatzik 1936, p. 54, Akin & Akin 1981, p. 34).

6 The site is called Su'ena site BB-2-7, a mound site apparently used primarily for the disposal of personal ornaments (see Newman 1975).

7 The cessation of headhunting was brought about by order of the British Colonial Government as well as by missionary influence and native initiative (see Zelenietz 1983).

8 The informant who provided this data was Simon Natu, chief of Paradise Village; he gave the information to Ian Willing. (R. Reeve (Office of Cultural Affairs, Western Province, Gizo, Solomon Islands), pers. comm. 1987).

9 Hocart collected from Simbo evidence of *mbelama meko*, a 'frigate bird of storms because it flies about when a storm is pending' and *Mbanara pu tatau* 'the chief that flies'. *Ave*, a sickness-causing spirit from Santa Isabel Island, allegedly resembled a man but flew like a bird. *Rokoveo*, an invisible spirit, lived at sea and could sit on the sea 'just like an *elekai* bird or a frigate bird. He eats small fish such as the *inambuku*; he walks on top of the water and catches them with his hand' (Hocart 1922, pp. 267, 280, 293, 1935, p. 105).

References

Akin, D. W. & K. G. Akin 1981. Traditional arts of East Kwaio, Malaita. *Pacific Arts Newsletter*, no. 13 (June) 31–4.

Bernatzik, H. A. 1934. *Sudsee*. Leipzig: Bibliographisches Institut Ag.

Bernatzik, H. A. 1936. *Owa Raha*. Vienna: Bernina Verlag.

Beti, G. O. 1977. Kesoko Pature. *The Journal of the Cultural Association of the Solomon Islands* **5**, 40–6.

Brenchley, J. L. 1873. *Jottings during the cruise of HMS 'Curacoa' in 1865*. London: Longmans.

British Solomon Islands 1975. *Report for the Year 1974*. Honiara, British Solomon Islands Protectorate.

Codrington, R. M. 1891. *The Melanesians. Studies in their anthropology and folklore*. Oxford: Clarendon Press.

Davenport, W. H. 1968. Sculpture of the Eastern Solomons. *Expedition* **10** (2), 4–25.

Davenport, W. H. 1981. Male initiation in Aoriki. *Expedition* **23** (2), 4–19.

Davenport, W. H. n.d. *The canoes of Santa Ana and Santa Catalina Islands, Eastern Solomon Islands*. Proceedings, Wright Symposium of Primitive & PreColumbian Art, Jerusalem, Israel, January, 1985.

De Tolna, R. Cte. Festetics 1903. *Chez les Cannibales. Huit Ans de Croisière dans l'Océan Pacifique a Bord du Yacht 'Le Tolna'*. Paris: Librairie Plon-Nourrit.

Edge-Partington, J. 1903. A food trough from Rubiana. *Man* **3**, 161–2.

Fox, C. E. 1925. *The threshold of the Pacific*. New York: Alfred A. Knopf.

Gathercole, P., A. L. Kaeppler & D. Newton 1979. *The art of the Pacific Islands*. Washington: National Gallery of Art.

Guppy, H. B. 1887. *The Solomon Islands and their natives*. London: Swan Sonnenschein.

Hocart, A. M. 1922. The cult of the dead in Eddystone of the Solomons. *Journal of the Royal Anthropological Institute* **52**, 71–112; 259–305.

Hocart, A. M. 1931. Warfare in Eddystone of the Solomon Islands. *Journal of the Royal Anthropological Institute* **61**, 301–24.

Hocart, A. M. 1935. The canoe and the bonito in Eddystone Island. *Journal of the Royal Anthropological Institute* **65**, 97–111.

Hocart, A. M. 1937. Fishing in Eddystone Island. *Journal of the Royal Anthropological Institute* **67**, 33–41.

Hocart, A. M. n.d. Unpublished manuscript. MS Papers 60. The Alexander Turnbull Library, Wellington, New Zealand.

Ivens, W. G. 1927. *Melanesians of the south-east Solomon Islands*. London: Kegan Paul.

Mead, S. M. 1973a. *Material culture and art in the Star Harbour Region, eastern Solomon Islands*. Royal Ontario Museum. Ethnography Monograph 1.

Mead, S. M. 1973b. The last initiation ceremony of Gupuna, Santa Ana, eastern Solomon Islands. *Records of the Auckland Institute and Museum* **10**, 69–95.

Monongai, B. 1923. *Material culture of San Cristobal* (trans. C. E. Fox). Manuscript in Otago Museum Library, Dunedin, New Zealand.

Newman, M. 1975. *Prehistoric and historic shell ornaments and decorative art in the southeast Solomons*. Unpublished Master's essay, Department of Anthropology, Auckland University, Auckland, New Zealand.

Ribbe, C. 1895. *Zwei Jahre unter den Kannibalen der Salomo-Inseln*. Dresden-Blasewicz: Beyer. Somerville, H. B. T. 1897. Ethnographical notes on New Georgia, Solomon Islands. *Journal of the Royal Anthropological Institute* **XXVI**, 357–413.

Turner, V. W. 1964. *Betwixt and between: the liminal period in rites de passage*. Symposium of New Approaches to the Study of Religion. Proceedings of the 1964 Annual Spring Meeting of the American Ethnological Society, 4–20.

Waite, D. B. 1979. Aspects of style and symbolism in the art of the Solomon Islands. In *Exploring the visual art of Oceania*, S. M. Mead (ed.) 238–64.

Waite, D. B. 1983. Form and function of Tridacna shell plaques from the western Solomon Islands. *Empirical Studies of the Arts* **1**, (1) 55–74.

Waite, D. B. 1984. The H. B. T. Somerville Collection of artefacts from the Solomon Islands. The general's gift, a celebration of the Pitt Rivers Museum centenary 1884–1984. *Journal of the Anthropological Society of Oxford*, Occasional Papers no. 3, 41–52.

Waite, D. B. 1987. Artefacts from the Solomon Islands in the Julius L. Brenchley Collection. London: British Museum Publications.

Waterhouse, J. H. L. 1928. *A Roulana and English dictionary with English–Roulana index and list of natural history objects*. Guadalcanal, Solomon Islands: Melanesian Mission Press.

Zelenietz, M. 1983. The end of headhunting in New Georgia. *The Pacification of Melanesia*, M. Rodman & M. Cooper (eds), 91–109. ASAO Monograph no. 7. London: University Press of America.

16 *The bestiary of rupestrian and literary origin in the Sahara and the Sahel: an essay in the investigation of correlations*

JEANNINE DROUIN

The disappearance of tropical mega-fauna in the Sahara and the Sahel is a fact, the mechanisms of which have been explained by specialists. The purpose of this chapter is to try to understand why and how certain species of this fauna, which have died out in sub-Saharan areas, are still preserved in the imagination of peoples of the area. We are concerned with the Tuareg people, on the one hand, and elephants (the only animals to be considered here), on the other. The scope of such an investigation is huge since my ambition is to compare the earliest rock art, i.e. that belonging to the stage of the big so-called 'Bubal' fauna, and perhaps to that of the 'Bovine' type in its first period, with the oral traditions of the 20th-century populations. This is why I will limit myself to connecting the data on rocks (according to prehistorians' generally accepted chronologies) to data provided by Tuareg culture, so as to suggest a certain number of hypotheses and cautious deductions.

A double question is immediately raised about both of these forms of cultural expression (which are separated by such a long period of time and each of which is endowed with well-structured signs, bearers of meaning). The first is 'What was the purpose of the rock carvings at the time when elephants existed in the region?' The second is 'Why is the elephant today associated with the oral tradition of the Tuareg, even though it is unknown physically?'

This double question about the 'archaeology of knowledge', is in fact a search for meaning which the correlations, once they are made explicit, are intended to reveal. It also involves the question of the validity of using anthropological data in the interpretation of prehistoric rock images, and the limits of its application.

Tuareg society and its precursors

The Tuareg, in whose society the myth we are concerned with is being transmitted, live a nomadic life in the Saharo-Sahelian area of the Niger, a southern region between the Adghagh of the Ifoghas and the chain of Air.

This section of the Tuareg community came to the south at a relatively recent date as the result of a large migration from the south of Libya down to the meander of the river Niger and the north of Nigeria. In fact, these Berbers of the south of the Sahara have a northern filiation whose main features are well known (Camps 1980). The Berber lineage composed of proto-mediterraneans of Oriental origin and other varied physical types (varying along parameters such as size, skeleton, pigmentation of the skin, eyes, hair) dates from approximately 9000 BC.

The substratum of today's population of the Maghreb, which dates from prehistoric times, is related to a period of continuous migratory movement from the Near East to the Atlantic, over several millenniums. In the Neolithic Age, the arrival of new populations was marked by the introduction of domestic animals and plants. As the Sahara was gradually drying up during the 3rd millennium BC part of the negroid population moved towards Tunisian Tell and Cyrenaica: they were going to become what the ancients called 'Ethiopians'. Other types with a clear complexion – horse-breeders and drivers of chariots – made their appearance during the 2nd millennium and reduced the 'Ethiopians' to slavery.

While the peopling of the Maghreb was becoming systematic in the 7th millennium, the Sahara was not yet a desert. A dynamic civilization had developed there, with Neolithic characteristics flourishing 2000 years earlier than in the Maghreb and in Europe. Between large barren zones there still existed profound lacustral expanses and rivers, and the humid climate of the mountain chains favoured shrub vegetation. Ceramics found in this region dating from the years 6700–6000 BC are not of a Mediterranean or an Egyptian origin, and represent a Saharan artistic tradition prior to the art of ancient Egypt and Europe. The population was negroid, of the Saharo-Sudanese Neolithic tradition. At that time, the Sahara was one of the four poles of Neolithic development, together with the Sudan of Khartoum, oriental Africa, and the Near East (Ki-Zerbo 1980, pp. 718–19).

In the Bovine period (3500 BC), rock paintings of Tassili give evidence of minority populations belonging to the white race. Their morphology seems to make them akin to the Fulani, a nomadic people who live presently in the Sahel. There is also evidence of distinctly mediterranean groups whose men had long hair and pointed beards and whose women wore long dresses made of cloth. It was, in fact, between the 4th and 2nd millenniums that these populations might have come from the east, passing round Tibesti or along the coasts of Cyrenaica (it is also possible that they were of Maghrebian origin).

In the Equine period, at the end of the Neolithic, the populations of mediterranean origin increased. This was the period when horses came from Egypt, where they were widely represented about 1600 BC, as were harnessed chariots. These Equine populations carried the lance and the javelin, and the men wore short tunics, while women wore long dresses. It seems that they imposed their authority on the negroid or melanoid populations who had preceded them: at any rate the latter were no longer represented in rock art. Historians of antiquity (Herodotus about 500 BC) called these horse-riders of mediterranean origin, the Getulae (from what is now south Tunisia) and the Garamantes (from Fezzan). The brown-skinned populations, driven away by the gradual dryness of the Sahara, moved southwards with their herds of cattle. Nowadays, they are supposedly represented by the Fulani of the Niger, Senegal, and Chad. Some of them settled in residual islands of vegetation and worked for the palaeo-Berber nomads who are pictured on rocks, in hunting scenes, with the attributes of warriors. They were the ancestors of the present Tuareg.

The various rock art sites throughout the Sahara, combined with anthropological research have now made it possible to locate negroid and mixed populations (crossed with white elements from the Mediterranean) in the north and centre of the Sahara, and negroid Sudanese populations in the south and west. Elements of white populations originating from the Mediterranean are testified in the Sahara (Tassili) during the Bovine period (3500 BC) as well as the Equine period (1700 BC).

Elephant imagery and prehistoric elephants

Elephants in Tuareg oral tradition

Wild and domestic animals have an important place in Tuareg oral literature, both prose and poetry. In poetry, cattle and camels are valorizing metaphors for the men and women of aristocracy. In prose, small domesticated animals – sheep and goats – are often associated with the representatives of wild fauna, either harmless or predatory, familiar to this population of nomadic pastoralists. Such wild animals, in partnership with domestic animals (whether or not they are associated with human beings), are often the victors in allegoric situations, which are themselves metaphors of social challenges and strategies.

The theme of the elephant is perplexing to the extent that it is an animal which no longer forms part of the familiar environment. Its name in Tuareg is *elu*, a word related to the Graeco-Latin and Semitic names; so are the terms for its characteristic features, that is to say its large size and its trunk which is called a 'hand' (*afus*). This conceptualization is identical to that in Latin (*manus, brachium*). The Tuareg living not far from the rock art sites have seen drawings of the pachyderm but probably no living example of it, in spite of the stories asserting that elephants still existed in the region a few decades ago.

Generally speaking, the elephant appears in oral tradition as the prototypical mastodon. In proverbs and riddles, it is the metaphor for that which is the biggest, the heaviest, the most cumbersome of all, the least easily hidden, and which creates irresolvable situations. The biggest of all animals, so much so – it is said – that the carnivorous animals themselves dare not attack it. It is sometimes named 'the king of animals' but, in this case, the term in Tuareg is differentiated from that attributed to the lion whose royal title is associated with the fear it inspires. In tales, the elephant is generally as stupid and naïve as it is big; it is abused now by the crafty jackal, now by the tiny squirrel. In a society where cleverness made up of trickery, skill, and subtlety, are highly praised, this latter conceptualization is not very flattering.

A completely different image of the elephant, and this is what interests us here, is reflected in a mythical narrative where the pachyderm is implicated in the adventures of a giant culture hero, who is reported to have invented all the major features of Tuareg society: writing, language, poetry, the one-stringed violin, and music. The two characteristics of this hero, giantism and intelligence, can neither be parted from each other, nor, apparently, matched together. His stature which placed him above human norms has as its corollary erotic demonstrations also above the norm: his giant-sized erotic impulses are disproportionate to the human condition of his partners, who burst at the beginning of their monstrous gestation. In order to have an offspring, he is compelled to mate with the biggest creature that ever existed – a female elephant. Yet even this elephant cannot withstand the weight of the giant foetus that eventually causes her to burst.

The libertine conduct of our hero with women, associated with sexual intercourse, is a social behaviour that complies with the ways of Tuareg society. Hence the passing from reality to supra-reality takes place smoothly, for imagery is anchored in a cultural context which makes it valid and genuine, gives it an internal logic, and regulates what will explain the world. This is the definition of myth (Aghali-Zakara & Drouin 1979, pp. 20–31).

Elephants in rock carvings

Different types of elephants have been known in the Maghreb and in the Sahara from the Tertiary period onwards. It is the elephant of average size, with developed ears and tusks, which is well attested from Somalia to the Atlantic, from the Mediterranean coasts to the sub-Saharan regions. Some were reported in Mauritania in 1935, as well as a few hypothetical cases in the Sahel about 1885 (Nicolas 1950, p.18). This residual fauna was similar to the elephants captured in large numbers by the Carthaginians in the Maghreb during the 1st millennium. They were domesticated for combat or killed for their ivory. They were represented on ancient coins of the Numidian kings – Masinissa, Jugurtha, Juba I, Bocchus, Juba II, and Ptolemy – between 220 BC and AD 40 (Camps & Esperandieu 1971) and are mentioned by the Graeco-Latin authors of antiquity.

But the most ancient representations in the region are those appearing on the rocks of the Saharan Atlas and in the mountains of Tassili and Fezzan in the Sahara. These large-sized representations have been classified by some as belonging to the period of the big wild fauna about 7000 BC, whereas other scholars trace them back to the Bovine period about 3500 BC. These pre- and protohistoric carvings are naturalistic, i.e. of great descriptive accuracy, yet with a minimum of means, since the carvers engraved only the essential lines (Fig. 16.1). This large-sized naturalistic art lasted a very long time and gave a place of prime importance to the elephant; however, one cannot assert whether these huge representations of the pachyderm preceded or followed, or were coeval with those of the great bubal – an animal of the big fauna which for a long time gave its name to this period of rock carving art.

The elephants, deeply carved in the rock and of big dimensions (up to 3 m, for the earliest period) are often associated with sexual demonstrations, which abound in Tassili (sites of the Djerat oued) and in the Fezzan (site of Akakous oued). From this period of the large fauna date large ithyphallic characters which either exceed 2 m or are of an average size (in the Djerat oued) (station VIII, XXV, etc.). In the later periods, Bovine and Equine, the characters became smaller and smaller (Fig. 16.2). Erotic scenes are dated from the archaic period: ithyphallic characters are often dressed or disguised as animals. They have enormous phalli and are in

Figure 16.1 Djado: elephant, height 2 m (Allard-Huard & Huard 1981, p. 25).

Figure 16.2 Oued Djerat: man running before an elephant (Allard-Huard & Huard 1981, p. 17).

Figure 16.3 Akakous: man and elephant marked by ithyphallism (Huard & Petit 1975, p. 164).

contact with women seated in the copulation position, coition scenes being rather frequent. Some carvings associate human character and elephant, each having a marked ithyphallism (Fig. 16.3).

Sexual intercourse between man and animal may be represented by a line which goes from the sex organs of a wild animal to a part of the body of the human character, most frequently to the eye. This type of carving is known in the central Sahara and in the Saharan Atlas (Huard & Allard 1973). In the southern Oran area, one example of a relationship between a man and a bubal has been discovered, to be compared with a similar case from the Djerat oued (Lhote 1975). These examples of sexual demonstrations form part of the correlation elements we are looking for, as will be seen below. Certain naturalistic frescos should also be noted, for example, in a large-sized fresco at Tassili (Fig. 16.4), belonging to the more recent phase of the hunters' art (Allard–Huard & Huard 1981), there is a row of 11 elephants, 1.2–0.5 m high. This fresco appears to illustrate the repetitive description of a mythical text showing the elephants going to the pond one behind the other. The theme echoes an episode in the myth of the Tuareg culture hero who selected his elephant spouse as she walked with others to a water-hole.

Further south, in Hoggar, the carvings are less significant than those of Tassili and Fezzan: they are the result of an expansion of the hunters' culture to the central Sahara (Huard & Petit 1975). One finds there, however, a carving of an elephant, 2 m high, and another, 1 m high (Fig. 16.5), among other smaller ones (Allard–Huard & Huard 1981). In the Air massif (Lhote 1972), the carvings have the schematization typical of the later carvings of the Bubal and Bovine periods in southern Oran area (see Fig. 16.5). It should be noted that no skeleton of an elephant has been found close to this mountain range. The carvings of the late Equine period (1700 BC) show a less marked interest in the manifestations of sexuality. The Tuareg consider that the authors of these rock carvings made 'at a time when the mountains were soft' were large people, an aetiological theme belonging to different African cultures in which the genesis of mountains and the deeds of giants are concomitant.

Figure 16.4 Tassili fresco of 11 elephants (from Allard–Huard & Huard 1981, p. 33).

Figure 16.5 Hoggar: small elephant 1 m long (Allard–Huard & Huard 1981, p. 29).

Figure 16.6 A group of very small elephants with butterfly-wing ears, from Borkou (from Allard-Huard & Huard 1981, p. 28).

The migration of the hunters towards the south, Djado and Tibesti as far as the Nigero-Chadian borders, is revealed by the treatment of the same subjects which shows evolved workmanship. Apart from a few examples of large-sized carvings (one ithyphallic giant, one elephant exceeding 2 m) the representations are generally of small size; similarly in Borkou where, except for an elephant of 3 m the other carvings are small and stylized (a group of elephants of 0.6 m, Fig. 16.6).

The elephant was salient from two points of view: its location and its characterizing features. The sites of Tassili and Fezzan are those which have probably been on the route of populations of mediterranean type from the 4th millennium (3500 BC) onwards, who came in contact with the local populations of dark complexion but non-negroid, themselves coming from pre-Neolithic populations, the possible authors of the carvings of the big fauna. These mediterranean populations, as we have seen, are those identified with the Garamantes rulers who continued to progress towards the south and were located in Air massif between the 8th and 9th centuries of our era, and whose presence in the Sahel dates from a few centuries ago.

The characteristics of the elephant carvings form part of the correlations which we seek to establish with the transmitted mythical tradition. The following commentary aims to argue hypotheses not certainties.

Correlations and hypotheses

To try to establish correlations between two cultural forms of expression – the ancient carvings and the present oral tradition – is to compare the archaeology of texts and that of the engravings as reciprocal means of interpretation. It is to try to elucidate some meaning and not *the* meaning.

The problem is twofold, namely: the function of the motif of the elephant in the myth of the culture hero, and the function of the representation of the elephant in pre- and protohistoric rock carvings.

I will not enter into the subtlety of the chronologically and spatially distinctive signs in the representation of elephants – such as one or two eyes, types of ears (Fig. 16.7) – for the questions I am confronted with are relatively general and relate to the central Sahara, i.e.:

(a) Who engraved the elephants of the Bubal period and those of the beginning of the Bovine period?
(b) What meaning do these sets of signs combined into pictures carry?
(c) Could the content have been transmitted, transposed, re-interpreted?

To the first question, prehistorians can reply with some certainty as follows: those who made the rock carvings are very likely negroid hunters, the first occupants before the arrival of the mediterranean populations who are identified as Libyco-Berbers. The latter were the ancestors of the Garamantes (mentioned by classical authors) who peopled the deserts during the millenniums preceding the dying of the Sahara, from the 4th millennium onwards (Mauny 1961, p. 456). The pastoralists with their herds of cattle moved gradually southwards. One might wonder why the Libyco-Berbers progressed through such regions (since the Roman pressure came much later), which were inhospitable except for the residual oases with relict vegetation. The present-day Berbers living in the desert and the sub-Saharan regions are their descendants (Mauny ibid.).

To try to answer the second question is to launch into the perilous exercise of interpreting signs which form systems carrying meaning both in text and carvings. Starting from this idea, prehistorians have taken into account the socio-economic situations of these societies of hunters who were submitted to the double necessity of striving for survival and protecting themselves from an abundant and more or less colossal fauna. That situation undoubtedly prompted them gradually to invent certain means of capture worked out while hunting, as well as a means of communication, a language of pictures whose final aim was at the same time to show and to say. In the rock art they show how they lived, what their ventures and huntsmanship were. Such representations could be understood as pedagogical and, at the same time, a kind of materialization and re-actualization of survival techniques (recollections of the group?). They express, in a magico-religious language, the relationships between the animal world and man, an expression that involves an address to the human group and perhaps to the animal one displayed there. Showing an animal is making it present; showing it in association with diverse traps (Fig. 16.8) may be a propitiatory step towards appropriation or neutralization (ethnographic studies of present-day traditional populations furnish many examples). Such an attempt is reinforced by establishing relationships between man and animal in many ways, such as the marking of magic symbols, and the representation of small unarmed people touching either the tail or the head of the large game. The latter is another propitiatory token of domination, and a variant of cultural features well attested in Maghrebian practices in particular (Allard-Huard & Huard 1981).

The attention is especially caught by the association of ithyphallic human figures and animals engaged in sexual intercourse: one possibility is that this represents sym-

Figure 16.7 Elephant (length 1.85 m) from Tilesti, with striped ears and trunk characteristic of tropical Africa (Allard-Huard & Huard 1981, p. 26).

Figure 16.8 Hunting scene with trap, from Hoggar (Allard-Huard & Huard 1981, p. 49).

pathetic magic, the associations pictured being apt to stimulate the fertilizing power of mastodons such as bubals and elephants. This stimulation could correspond to two objectives: to promote reproduction of an economic capital – the elephant itself – and, more generally, as a symbol of growth and fertility to enhance human fertility. Such belief in the prolific character of certain animals, as well as of certain plants, in relation to human fertility is still very much alive.

It is here that we can attempt to situate the articulation between the sign system of the engraved images and the sign system of the mythical text. The representations, in their complexity, are different, but analogies should be picked up: the mythical hero, who is a giant (consider the huge ithyphallic figures, mentioned above), copulates with a young female elephant that apparently is the only one able to endure, from her mate, the onslaughts which women of human size cannot survive. That is, the alliance of the giant with the mastodon could result, unlike its union with human beings, in the production of offspring. This is, so to speak, a last resort, but it is also a failure since the hero surpasses the largest of all animals from the physical point of view. Is this the expression of the domination of the animal world by humanity, embodied by another Prometheus, who was the origin of the most essential cultural features of society? This cultural theme is indissociable from that of sexuality whose objective is fertility, if only through water inseminated by the giant (as is said in another episode of the Tuareg mythic text). But his objective, thwarted by natural order, does not exclude libertinage of good form, a modernistic theme within the myth since it is actually a well-known Tuareg practice.

The myth is therefore dealing with the theme of sexuality, the treatment of which can be interpreted as the conceptualization of the animal world ruled by a physically and psychically super-real being.

The third enquiry is concerned with the possible modes of transmission for the assumed contents of the rock images. This is tantamount to examining, from a semiological point of view, the mythical text loaded with chronologically and spatially detectable borrowings, whose semantic fields have already been alluded to. Such examination presupposes the choice of certain hypotheses.

The name of the Tuareg hero and some of his libertine achievements, together with his poetical mind, are closely related to that of a pre-Islamic Arab poet. The invention of writing – which even now has not the utilitarian role which is the justification given for the birth of all writings – is accounted for as a direct means of opposition to the earliest Arab pressure: associated with the invention of language, it constitutes an ideological claim to an identity reaffirmed as pre-Koranic. Relatively modern literary motifs have also appeared expressing protest and claims for identity (involving culture and beliefs).

Furthermore, this culture hero is not only presented as pre-Islamic, but also as a witness of the dawn of humanity, because of his gigantic physique and contemporaneity with the genesis of the physical world: the time when giants accomplished great labours and carved history on rocks that were not yet solidified. It is the expression of the desire to assert the remotest ancestry.

Concerning the elephants, we have seen that those who engraved the big fauna were not the Libyco-Berber ancestors of the Tuareg, but that the latter had lived in contact with such representations, several millennia after their creation. They had also probably lived within, so to speak, the cultural 'bath' which explained them – it being understood that the cultural environment had most probably undergone great evolutions during such a long passage of time. It may be thought that the interpretations relating to the representation of sexual manifestations have been the most persistent, as far as one can judge from the place they have kept in present traditional populations.

At this stage in the enquiry one can raise the following question, concerning the prehistoric populations as well as the descendants of the Garamantes: why, of the two large mastodons represented in the archaic period, the bubal and the elephant, is it with the elephant that the largest number of ithyphallic characters are associated, and not with the bubal? The exception is a single representation of a man–bubal bestiality. The same question arises about the text in which that ancient Prometheus, an archetype of universal mythologies, whose cultural productivity is incompatible with natural fertility, is associated with the elephant – an archetype, besides, which is not in conformity with the metaphor of fertility and prosperity in Tuareg society.

Another chronological step in the relationship between man and animal is that of the social relationship established between elephants and the hero. In effect, in the Tuareg text, the young female elephant coveted by the hero 'among the elephants going in a row to the pond' (Aghali-Zakara & Drouin 1979, p. 25) represents (in his mind) sexual appropriation as a last resort after his failures with women. His purpose is notably different from that of the predatory hunters who used both traps and magic practices of neutralization or communication. We have additional evidence that this may signify a change in the conceptualization of elephants that occurred at an intermediary period between the prehistoric hunters and the present. The presence of elephants from Egypt to south Tunisia is well known, particularly in the country of the Getulae and Garamantes, thanks to the writings of Herodotus, Pliny, and Lucian, as early as the 5th century BC. In the Maghreb, at the same time, the capturing of elephants by the Carthaginians was no longer undertaken as an economic contribution to survival; its object had become domestication and barter of ivory. Elephants were used as fighting mounts during the Punic wars against Rome. The domestication of elephants in India and Mesopotamia is known as early as the 8th century before our era, and in Egypt in the 3rd century BC.

Relations between men and pachyderms have thus arguably become different since protohistory: a relationship of domination on the one hand, and of a certain intimacy and mutual understanding on the other. On coins, kings of Numidia combined their own effigies with the silhouette of an elephant. It is worth mentioning in this context that, in prehistoric times, a Nubian clan of Elephantine Island, facing Assouan on the Nile, seems to have had the elephant as an animal emblem, a symbol of prosperity for the region. This tradition, collected much later by Herodotus, asserts that the island controlled the source of the Nile which comes out of the womb of the Earth, at this very place, in order to fertilize the soil (*Dictionnaire de la Bible* 1930, pp. 960–1031). The elephant-hide, with its trunk curved like a crest, was the attribute of persons of rank such as Ptolemy IX and Cleopatra (2nd and 1st century BC). Another sign of the evolution of the concept of the elephant appears in what Pliny reports (*Histoires*, 1860, Vol. VIII, 1–12, pp. 318–24) concerning the psychology of elephants, details of which he heard from the Numidian king, Juba II (23 BC–AD 25). At that time elephants were supposed to have the same positive feelings as men, to whom it was thought they were the closest in intelligence: they understood language, were honest and pious, and worshipped their king; some were said to learn their lessons at night and write Greek characters; being cautious, wise, reserved, they could nevertheless be enamoured with human beings. Women are reported to have been loved by pachyderms, as well as a youngster; in the latter's case, the sex of his elephant partner was not made explicit. When they were suffering misfortune – in the Roman arenas, for example – they inspired feelings of pity and compassion. They knew how to thwart the guiles of hunters who got rich from the ivory of their tusks. This theme was resumed eight centuries later in the 'Seventh voyage of Sindbad the sailor' from the *Thousand and one nights*: an elephant tears up the tree in which Sindbad is hidden, busy shooting arrows at its companions; it carries him to the unknown location of the famous elephants' graveyard in order to make him understand that he will find a lot of ivory there from dead elephants and that he must avoid sacrificing the living. Among other positive characteristics noted were its long life which may reach 300 years, and the remedies that can be derived from it: blood, ivory scrapings, and contact with the trunk for curing rheumatisms, headaches, and liver pains, and as an aphrodisiac (Pliny 1860, Vol. II, p. 264).

What is interesting in these statements is obviously what they imply, and what they hide in the depths of the conceptualization. What can be seen is the evolution of the conceptualization of the elephant up to the Arab-Muslim period, whose literary themes are widely borrowed both from the Persian tradition and from the beliefs of classical authors. This attempt at drawing the inventory of significant data confirms, unsurprisingly, that time, especially long periods of time, reshapes conceptualizations while preserving a few kernels which comprise the universals already discussed.

Therefore it seems that, in our mythical text, the organization of the meaning is probably the result of a certain syncretism of cultural features carried by populations in contact, in the course of millenniums. After the physical disappearance of elephants, only the rock-carved images remained, and these were liable to reinterpretation, in relation to transmitted myths which had kept a part of their initial meaning. It should be noted that in the Maghreb the representations of prehistoric elephants do not reappear in the oral tradition of the Berbers, contrary to what happens with the Saharan Berbers.

In the Saharan regions, the Libyco-Berber written graffiti, dating probably from a later period (perhaps pre-Cameline), associated with or superimposed on prehistoric carvings of the large fauna and ithyphallic carvings, has very likely favoured the amalgam of concepts we have already seen – they were major themes in Tuareg cultural life and emblems of prosperity that had come from the mists of time. These ancient and new conceptualizations were then organized in accordance with the internal logic of Tuareg culture, strengthening it and perpetuating it: a text is authenticated and historicized because it is anchored in the society which continues to transmit it.

Conclusion

The object of this chapter has been to establish a conceptual link between carved images and oral tradition, as a system of signs, which are bearers of meaning.

The two types of representations correspond to systems of communication in a given cultural context, itself springing from the socio-economic and biological environment which generated it. These representations and the intermediate evidences which add to the picture show the evolution in the relationships that man has established with animals: over time antagonistic relations at the time of hunters, with slight differences in magico-religious practices tending both to establish a certain complicity with the animal world but also control over it. Then, in the domestication period, one comes across a symbolic representation of the animal as an image of prosperity, both propitiatory and emblematic, associated with royal effigies. The symbiotic life of man and animal brings about a process of mimesis whereby elephants then acquire the reputation of having human minds, this being in fact the ultimate integrating conceptualization of the imagination. The text of the Tuareg culture hero could correspond to the third step in which imagination apprehends complex chronological data, organized as sets of metaphors which are adapted to the cultural context of the Tuareg and are therefore in conformity with what is expected by the society that wishes to, and must, recognize itself in them.

According to Ki-Zerbo (1980, p. 724), art is both 'a mirror and a mainspring' (*l'art est reflet et moteur*). And yet a gap remains: in the society of the Tuareg, pastoralists of the 20th century, in the usual metaphors of poetic language, fertility and prosperity linked with feminine beauty are represented by the fertile young cow, whereas masculine beauty and energy are represented by the stud camel. The treatment of the elephant motif in the mythical text is therefore both odd (not typical of tales and other literary genres), and anachronistic. Such an anachronism cannot be accounted for, apparently, unless it is some residual conceptualization, which was handed down for milleniums until it went through transposition at the beginning of our era (the Arab-Muslim tradition has in fact resumed Pliny's relation); at this period elephants were initiators of heterosexual copulation. But, what do we know of the nature of the engraved demonstrations of sexuality as far as men and animals are concerned? Moreover, the conceptualization of the culture hero, a fertilizing spirit essential to human society, is not unrelated to that of the large ithyphallic beings associated with the large male proboscidea, whether they are ithyphallic or not.

We would then have the effect of a crossed relationship in which the dominant archaic elephant has, unquestionably, become a dominated effeminate animal; as far as the hero is concerned, he could be the man of the large fauna who sought to acquire pre-eminence over the animal world.

	Dominant	Dominated
Prehistory	elephant	man
History	man	elephant

Each of these representations (either engraved or textual) has one apparent meaning, and a hidden meaning – as it were the sign of something for someone, or 'a bridge between reality and abstraction' (*un pont entre le réel et l'idée*, Ki-Zerbo, 1980, p. 705). If we go no further than to hypothesize about the remote past, the myth of the culture hero, enlarged in the text by the elephant motif, awakens a distinctly ideological, ethnic, and cultural echo: it is both the reactualization of the recollections of the group, and the reassertion of its identity, strengthening its unity in facing pressures from without.

Dieterlen (1981) has sought to trace in the representations of the big fauna and Bovine periods obvious features belonging to present-day Fulani culture, and thus to establish a definitive filiation. The Fulani oral tradition, in this connection, should also be examined with the possibility in mind of crossed parameters: it would perhaps show that modes of thought have not been static through such long periods of time, and that the persistence of similarities that seem too great could be explained in some way other than in terms of plain linear filiation. The same signs have not necessarily the same content and may have very different authors, if only as a result of interplay of contacts and transmissions (Dieterlen 1981).

Let us mention another example of conceptual drift, starting from an initial datum: in the mountain massif of Air, in Niger, two large carved human figures have been regularly redrawn because the ritual drawing of their clothes favours the acquisition of new clothes during the year by the authors of the drawings. Moreover, these large-sized figures, who are designated by proper names, and also called 'giants', are supposed to be the creators of all petroglyphs. Late aetiological signifieds that have, undoubtedly, little to do with the initial intention. This shows how the contributions of oral tradition are at the same time fragile and revealing of mutation – but such statements demand much caution in their interpretation.

The search for correlations eventually provides a single certainty: the images, whether isolated or associated with elephants, whether they were engraved or orally transmitted, are metaphors whose efficacy depends on their degree of abstraction, it being intimately related to the socio-cultural context. One might dare to say, then, that the Saharan huntsmen of pre- and protohistory have spun out metaphors just as well as have the Tuareg, our present-day contemporaries.

References

Aghali-Zakhara, M. & J. Drouin 1979. *Traditions touarègues nigériennes*. Paris: L'Harmattan.

Allard-Huard, L. & P. Huard 1981. *Les gravures rupestres du Sahara et du Nil: I Les chasseurs*. Editions et Publications des Pères Jésuites en Egypt: Etudes scientifiques.

Camps, G. 1980. *Berbères aux marges de l'histoire*. Paris: Hespérides.

Camps, G. & G. Esperandieu 1971. Eléphant berbère. In *Encyclopédie berbère*, Vol. 2. Aix-en-Provence: LAPMO-CNRS.

Dictionnaire de la Bible 1930. Supplement II, 962–1031.

Dieterlen, G. 1981. Exposé de madame Germaine Dieterlen. In *La Nouvelle Revue d'Anthropologie*. Actes du Colloque franco-italien de la préhistoire saharienne, Paris, 3–4 December 1980, 77–79 Reims: Centre de Documentation Interculturelle, Département d'Anthropologie, Faculté des lettres et Sciences Humaines–Association de Coopération Culturelle et Technique (ACCT).

Huard, P. & L. Allard 1973. Les gravures anciennes de l'oued Djerat. *Libyca* **XXI**, 193–5. Algiers: CRAPE.

Huard, P. & J. Petit 1975. Les chasseurs graveurs du Hoggar. *Libyca* **XXIII**, 133–79. Algiers: CRAPE.

Ki-Zerbo, J. 1980. L'art préhistorique africain. in *Histoire Générale de l'Afrique*, Vol. I, 693–724. Paris: Jeune Afrique/Stock/Unesco.

Les Mille et Une Nuits 1871, (trans. Armel Guerne). Vol. 4, 1610–22.

Lhote, H. 1972. *Les gravures rupestres du nord-ouest de l'Aïr*. Paris: Arts et Métiers graphiques.

Lhote, H. 1975. *Les gravures rupestres de l'oued Djerat (Tassili-n-Ajjer)*. Algiers: CRAPE.

Mauny, R. 1961. *Tableau géographique de l'ouest africain au Moyen Age, d'après les sources écrites, la tradition et l'archéologie*. Dakar: IFAN.

Nicolas, F. 1950. *Tamesna: les Ioullemmeden de l'est ou Touareg Kel Dinnik*. Paris: Imprimerie Nationale.

Pliny the Elder 1860. *L'histoire naturelle*, Vols. I, V, VIII.

Thousand and One Nights (see *Les Mille et Une Nuits*).

17 *Dance in the rock art of central India*

SUDHA MALAIYA

It is not easy to pin-point when people first discovered the thrill of rhythm and its manifestation through dance. Dance may well have been present from the beginning of man's conscious development. In India, however, there is evidence from rock art that can help us to reconstruct some pathways in the evolution of Indian dance from prehistory to the present. The most significant shelters with paintings of dance have been found at Pachmarhi, Hoshangabad, Adamgarh, Bhopal, Bhimbetka, Kabrapahara (Singhanapura), Abchand (Sagar), Modi (Chambal), and Zhiri (Raisen). The aim of this chapter is to analyse the way in which dance is represented in Indian rock art and to consider what forms of dance can be identified and what information this provides about the development of dance in India.

There has been a great deal of controversy regarding the chronology of rock paintings in India. Wakankar & Brooks (1976) and Pandey (1969) have come forward with seemingly acceptable classifications based on superimposition, patination, art style, comparative study of subject matter, flora and fauna, excavation, and other such analytical tools. It is Pandey's classification that is more or less followed here (see Fig. 17.1). However, it must be clearly borne in mind that these classifications are based more on the animal figures than on the human ones, and the earliest examples of rock art lack human figures. Although the matter is still open to discussion, this is neither the purpose nor the scope of this chapter.

Although many of the paintings considered in this study date from as recently as 600 BC, nevertheless they have an ethos that links them to the Stone-Age paintings of other parts of India (Vatsyayana 1982). Indian examples are the primary source of information about the earliest form of dance for which we may be able to develop culturally continuous ethnographic parallels. The paintings reveal links between dances of the remote past and dance as practised today by folk and tribal peoples of central India.

The possible continuities of dance forms in central India seem quite remarkable. Many historians and archaeologists believe in the parallel existence of 'tribal' and 'complex' civilizations from 5000 years BC to the present time (Wakankar & Brooks 1976, p. 14). Groups such as the Bhils, Gonds, Koraku, Vega, Mudias, Oraons, Santhals, and Nagas are regarded as having descended from the earliest inhabitants of the land. It was ancestors of such groups who, until quite recently, maintained the tradition of painting on shelter walls and with whom continuities in dance between rock walls and present forms seem greatest.

It is possible to suggest two broad categories into which representations of dance can be classified. The first type consist of scenes, the main theme of which is the

Period		Probable date	Animal figures	Non-dancing human figures	Solo dance	Duet dance	Collective dance
I	Mesolithic	Lower Mesolithic	Bhopal	Sagar	Bhimbekta	Pachmarhi	Near TB Hospital, Bhopal
II		Upper Mesolithic	Bhopal	Raisen			
III	Chalcolithic	Lower Chalcolithic Neolithic	Raisen	Raisen	Bhimbekta	Shyamla Hills (Bhopal)	Kharwai
IV		Early Historic	Kharwai	Sagar			
V	Historic	Historic A.D.1–A.D. 500	Bhopal	Sagar	Pachmarhi	Bhimbekta	Abchand (Sagar)
VI		Late Historic A.D.500–A.D.1000	Kharwai	Sagar			

Figure 17.1 Classification of rock paintings in central India.

dance itself. Dance is a medium for the physical expression of psychological urges in an artistic manner. The principal motives behind dance could therefore vary from sheer entertainment of the participants themselves to celebration and expressive action on occasions such as birth, initiation, marriage, harvesting, success in the hunt, and victory in war.

The second type of scene consists of those which represent occasions including rituals, in which dancing is not performed for its own sake but for instrumental reasons, often considered magical, towards the realization of set objectives. These include themes such as the propitiation of natural forces, supremacy over animals, rites for fertility, protection from natural calamities, healings, death, and the like (see Seligman 1910, p. 154, Frazer 1922, Hambley 1926, p. 22, Frazer 1936).

The scenes in the first category are significant from the point of view of the gradual development of dance from simple, perhaps improvised, movements to complex and codified ones. They also provide examples of solo, duet, and group dances. The solo dancers portray a wide variety of dance movements and illustrate a range of frontal, lateral, and backward positions of the lower limbs, including flexions and extensions. These are perhaps the embryonic representations in art of poses which were later codified in technical language[1] as *nata jangha* (Fig. 17.2a) (Gupta 1967, pp. 247, 387), *parsvajanunatajanu* or *ardhamandali* (Fig. 17.2b), *alidha* or *pratyalidha sthanaka* (Figs. 17.2c,d), *urdhvajanu cari* (Fig. 17.2e) (Gupta 1967, p. 387, Fig. 1), and *vrscika pada* (Fig. 17.2f). The first two bear a close affinity with the basic stances of the *Manipuri* and *Bharatanatyam* classical dance styles, respectively. Solo dancers performing to the accompaniment of a drummer are also found at certain places. The dancers in many of the cases described above often have elaborate head-dresses, which may be purely for decoration or serve a ritual purpose.

Evidence of people dancing in pairs in prehistoric society is furnished by a number of rock paintings which display dancing couples in various attitudes. The legs are either bent forward (Fig. 17.2g) or are in a forked position. The latter is a movement rarely employed in Indian dancing (Fig. 17.2h). The arms are seen raised above the head or extended sideways (Gupta 1967, p. 246) as seen now in several folk dances, including the *Bhangra* of Punjab. Another common form of duet dancing is taking forward and backward steps alternatively, or moving briskly in rounds holding both the hands of the partners, as seen in certain examples (Figs. 17.2i, j). These constitute an important part of the *Rota* of Jammu and Kashmir, *Kikli* of Punjab and Madhya Pradesh, and *Fugdi* of Maharastra. Some scenes with multiple figures include isolated dancing pairs.

The overwhelming evidence of collective dance scenes from most of the rock shelters shows the prevalence of group dancing. Male performers and male and female performers together are common. Female figures alone are rare (Gupta 1967, p. 390). Scenes depicting families – enjoying dance and music after the day is done – are also found (Gupta 1967, p. 396, Wakankar & Brooks 1976, p. 50). The one from Lakhajwar is worth mentioning, where eight S-shaped dancers are dancing to two 5–6-stringed bow-shaped instruments[2] which may represent the precursors of the later highly developed 7–9-stringed *citra* and *vipanci vina*, mentioned by Bharata Muni. Its earliest sculptural representations are found at Rupara (1500 BC) and then at Bharhut (2nd century BC). In certain examples of group dancing, no known

Figure 17.2 (a) Solo dancer, Imlikhoh, Pachmarhi (Mesolithic) (Gupta 1967); (b) solo dancer, Zhiri, Raisen (Mesolithic) (courtesy S. K. Pandey); (c) solo dancer, Bhimbetka (Mesolithic) (courtesy S. K. Pandey); (d) solo dancer, Dharampuri, Bhopal (Chalcolithic) (courtesy S. K. Pandey); (e) solo dancer, Shyamla Hill, Bhopal (Chalcolithic) (courtesy S. K. Pandey); (f) solo dancer, Bhimbetka (Chalcolithic) (Gupta 1967); (g) dancing couple, Gufa Mandir, Bhopal (Chalcolithic) (courtesy S. K. Pandey); (h) duet dance, Bhimbetka (Historic) (courtesy S. K. Pandey); (i) dancing couple, Jambudwipa, Pachmarhi (Historic) (Gupta 1967); (j) dancing couple, Jambudwipa, Pachmarhi (Historic) (Gupta 1967); (k) family entertainment through dance and music, Lakhajwar, Bhopal (Mesolithic); (l) masked dancers, near TB hospital, Bhopal, Bhopal (Mesolithic) (courtesy S. K. Pandey).

choreographic pattern is discernible (Fig. 17.2k). There are also figures of masked dancers or 'wizards' (Wakankar & Brooks 1976, p. 80) in various attitudes and at times carrying certain objects (Fig. 17.2l). While the mask is essentially related to ritual, not all mask dances are ritualistic. In many classical and semi-classical dances, masks help in identifying the character represented and, by implication, the theme or story woven round it. In an example from Zhiri (Raisen) there are four figures dancing in almost similar attitudes, in a straight line, with extended arms and forked-leg position (Fig. 17.3a). The liveliest illustration, however, is from Bhimbetka in which a row of eight dancers, each with legs raised, is seen placed in two groups facing each other (Fig. 17.3b). This is a fine example of the representation of beauty in movement and space. The six dancers from Abchand (Fig. 17.3c) carrying something like a flower on a stem in a raised hand and with the other hanging low reminds one of a ritual dance of Ladakh, in which the *lamas* dance in similar fashion, as if plucking a flower from above and offering it to the Lord Buddha.

The multiplicity of scenes depicting hand-in-hand dancing may show early stages in the development of forms of dances that subsequently became more elaborate. The simple holding of hands (Fig. 17.3f) may have been a stage in the development of formal positions which included hands above the shoulders (Fig. 17.3d), on the shoulders (Gupta 1967, p. 390), or around the waist of the neighbouring dancer with the interlocking of arms (Fig. 17.3g) (Gupta 1967, pp. 30, 392). Such movements were the common form of Indian dancing and still constitute an important part of a number of folk dances, such as the *Zhumara* dance of Chattisgarh, the *Jabro* of Ladakh, and the *Desar*, among others (cf. Gurg 1967, pp. 11, 30). However, in certain cases the arms, while appearing to be interlocked, may actually be of individual dancers with their hands at the waists, and their elbows extended to the sides to touch those of the dancer on either side, as is the case with the *Bharatanatyam* and *Kathaka* dancers. This type of interlocking is also seen in hunt dances represented in a few examples from Bhimbetka and Modi (Vatsyayana 1982, Ch.1). One of the most significant in this series is an example in the rock shelter near the TB hospital, Bhopal, where eight figures of dancers are standing one behind the other in a row, each holding the waist of the dancer in front (Fig. 17.3h). This is very close to the *avaricha nacha* of Maharastra.

The interlocking of arms is an important feature of many of the collective dances of India. *Chai* of the Lushai tribe of Assam, *Dahikala* and *Dholacha* of Maharastra, *Rofa* of Jammu and Kashmir, *Santhal* dances of Bihar and Bengal, and a number of dances of central India freely utilize this formation (see also Khokar 1987). Analysis of the representations reveals that collective dances involving interlocking patterns, like the present-day folk dances, must have been characterized by variety in the floor patterns.

Scenes in which circular patterns of dance can be discerned are of great significance since Vatsyayana (1982) was puzzled by their supposed absence. These perhaps represent the precursors of the famous *Rasa* dances in which many dancers dance in a circle. The most striking amongst such scenes is one from Dharampuri, Bhopal (Fig. 17.3i), in which many stick-figures are seen jumping, running, and dancing around a central figure. The figure seems to be keeping time either by clapping hands or by beating cymbal-like objects, other figures are perhaps playing on a flute or

Figure 17.3 (a) Group dance, Zhiri, Raisen (Mesolithic) (courtesy G. S. Tyagi); (b) group dance, Bhimbetka (Mesolithic); (c) group dance, Abchand, Sagar (Chalcolithic) (courtesy S. K. Pandey); (d) hand-in-hand dancing, Kabra Pahara, Raigarh (Mesolithic); (e) hand-in-hand dancing, Zhiri, Raisen (Historic) (courtesy G. S. Tyagi); (f) hand-in-hand dancing, near TB hospital, Bhopal (Mesolithic) (courtesy S. K. Pandey); (g) collective dance with arms interlocked, Abchand, Sagar (Chalcolithic) (courtesy S. K. Pandey); (h) variation of collective dance, near TB hospital, Bhopal (Mesolithic); (i) dancing in a circle, Dharampuri, Bhopal (Mesolithic).

horn-shaped instrument called *singa*, while a few are portrayed in the half-kneeling position of *Natyasastra*. In some scenes from the Shyamla Hills, Bhopal, and from Bhimbetka the figures are shown in similar attitudes, but the circular pattern is not well defined. These scenes in which all the performers in the group dance and jump in a circle to a musical accompaniment, may represent dance forms that are close to the free and unregulated dances of the Saora tribe of Orissa.

Many paintings appear to represent hunting and others, possibly, dances associated with hunting, where armed and masked hunters dance around the prospective kill (Fig. 17.4a) or the hunted animal (Fig. 17.4b). These include both ritual and ceremonial dances to ensure and increase the supply of game or to celebrate success in hunting. Because of the problem of perspective in many paintings, it cannot be stated with certainty whether an animal shown in a painting is supposed to be alive or dead. Nor can it be established whether it represents the prospective kill or is merely a design to induce success through sympathetic magic. A fascinating scene from Lakhajwar shows eight stick-figures dancing in front of a bison, and adjacent to them is a team with bow and arrows involved in the preliminary preparations for a hunt. A few examples show post-hunt celebrations.

With the development of agricultural societies there came inter-tribal conflicts, and conflicts between the people of the valley and the shelter dwellers. There are many such scenes, showing mounted horsemen attacking people on foot (Wakankar & Brooks 1976). The shelter dwellers, during this period, must have been in constant danger of being attacked by either unfriendly tribes or enemies from the valleys. This must have required well-organized co-operation on the part of men, as would also have been the case for the capture of large game and animals. People had to be equipped with adequate training to keep them in readiness (see Agarkar 1950). It may be that dance was the medium through which training was imparted. Such war dances, especially when augmented by traditional ceremonies and cult objects, along with rousing music, were intended to arouse and develop psychological qualities needed for extraordinary feats of strength, courage, daring, endurance, discipline, leadership, organizational capacity, and group activity and solidarity. When there was no immediate danger of war, performances of these dances may have kept the members ready to meet any emergency and may have functioned to weld people into a group. Communal hunting reinforced by dancing survives today among the Boyas, Todas, Gonds, and others in forms strikingly similar to those shown in early rock paintings. The four jumping and dancing masked archers with bow and arrows from Adamgarh, Hoshangabad (Gupta 1967, pp. 281, 292), perhaps provide the best example. Another example is provided by the two shield- and sword-wielders from Abchand, Sagar. Their bison-horned masks are suggestive of some kind of sympathetic magic. The interlocked arms of the dancers in the scenes from Zhiri (Fig. 17.4d) are also of interest. On the one hand, these movements are common constituents of several combat and martial dances and, on the other, they may have developed into a whole series of stylized gaits and postures in the formal language of dance. The movements of *Chaddiya* dancers of Narendrapura district, Orissa; the *Gabar* hunt dance of *Madias* and the *Sala Rina* dance of the Gonds of central India; the sword and dagger dances of Rawai, Jaunpura, and the Rath region of Uttar Pradesh; *Pre-Vaisnava* dances of Manipur, *Phari Khanda* exercises

Figure 17.4 (a) Hunt dance, Lakhajwar (Mesolithic); (b) celebration after hunt, Shymla Hill, Bhopal (Historic); (c) processional dance, Bhimbetka (Mesolithic) (courtesy G. S. Tyagi); (d) warrior dance, Zhiri, Raisen (Historic); (e) magical dance, Kathotia Karad, Bhopal (Historic) (courtesy S. K. Pandey).

of *Seraikela* and *Mayurabhanja*; the *Chholia* sword dance of Kumaon; and the *Khukri Nuirilima* and *Khambalima* spear dances of Khasis of Assam are the closest survivals of such pre- and protohistoric dance forms, and each in turn anticipates later trends in art dances. Such war dances, both past and present, also provided the context for the development of sexual attraction.

Ritual dances based on beliefs in sympathetic magic were closely related to the hunt and war dances. Actions imitating the killing of enemies, such as the throwing of spears, were believed to help the dancers in killing, or warding off, real enemies. The activity of the hunt itself led to many rites and rituals. Animal sacrifice may have been part of the complex rituals. A beautiful example of such pre-sacrificial preparation comes from Bhimbetka (Fig. 17.4c). A figure holding a trident is preparing to sacrifice the animal in front of him. Below an archer prepares to shoot an arrow. The other archers represented could perhaps be performing an associated ritual dance. The circular structure in flames with a cross in-between is symbolic of the sacred fire, vaguely suggesting the concept of the *vedika*, the *yajna* of Vedic times (Vatsyayana 1982, Ch.1). Though the figures here are stick-figures, the presence of the trident suggests a later date. Another interesting scene is that from Kathotia Karad (Fig. 17.4e) which comprises two conspicuous groups, of six and seven dancers respectively, two shaman, and a buffalo. The dancers in the right-hand group are bending their legs, with arms interlocked, while the dancers in the group on the left are bowing to the front, with hands pointing downwards. This probably represents a dance of exorcism and trance known from all parts of India. The movements depicted here are strongly reminiscent of *Gabara, Karma*, and many other crop dances of central India, Bihar, and Orissa. The ritualistic practices can be traced to prehistoric times. One such scene comes from Kharwai (Fig. 17.5a). In it a group of four people are bowing in front of a figure probably symbolizing a fertility goddess. But unlike the previous example, the arms here are extended backwards. The motive for the dance may be connected with the fertility of the land or the growth of plants, as is suggested by the representations of vegetables which may be part of the scene.

Sickness was considered to be due to the influence of evil spirits, as is evident in an important scene from Bhimbetka in which a figure, probably of the shaman, brandishing a stick appears to be curing a sick person lying prostrate (Fig. 17.5b). The other figures are dancing in various attitudes. In order to interpret this scene we need to relate it to the varied ritualistic practices concerned with healing of the sick that were used in ancient times in India.

In many later paintings the developed concept of many Hindu gods and goddesses can be seen. Tribal myths and legends gave rise to many iconographical forms representing Hindu deities. One such significant scene, relating to the worship of sacred symbols such as the trident and cross, comes from Baniaberi, Pachmarhi, where this form of worship is still in practice. From Barkheda, Raisen, comes yet another interesting scene (Fig. 17.5c) depicting Ganesa, the son of Siva, dancing. A drummer on the left and a dancer on the lower right are offering worship through the dance. The scene from Zhiri, Raisen (Fig. 17.5d), may represent the idea of consecrated space. Five people are dancing in a defined bounded space while four are outside it. Such a movement pattern is suggestive of dance. The circles around

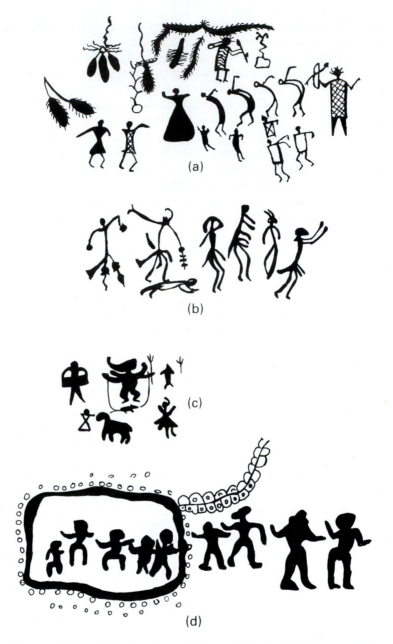

Figure 17.5 (a) Fertility dance, Kharwai (Chalcolithic) (courtesy S. K. Pandey); (b) healing dance, Bhimbetka (Chalcolithic) (courtesy S. K. Pandey); (c) sacred dance, Barkhera, Raisen (Historic); (d) sacred dance, Zhiri, Raisen (Historic).

the enclosed space, which may represent beads, make it clear that the area was something special or consecrated.

This study highlights that dance in India has a long and potentially traceable history. Dance served the dual purpose of fulfilling man's desire for self-expression and his aesthetic urge as well as serving a ritual function. There is no reason to conclude that traditional dancing was inspired merely for its utility or ritual value as is generally understood, though it appears on the basis of these scenes from Indian rock art that dance, like other forms of art, was often a component of ritual and religion from early on. It may be that in painting the dance forms the ritual potency of the dance was intensified and, at least, transferred to the paintings. It may be that the paintings were used as a teaching aid in the transmission of ritual dances. However, I think it unlikely and, indeed, there is no requirement that the paintings should have served a ritual purpose. Dance is a subject and could be painted like any other subject. The artists enjoyed dance, which was a very vital part of their life, and they found in painting a medium to give dance movements a tangible expression. The aesthetics of dances affected the aesthetic perception of human form, allowing the body to be represented in countless beautiful designs.

The collective dance scenes are significant from the point of view of tribal and folk dances of India. They may not be directly related to the contemporary classical traditions of dance, but they may well represent the seeds of the development of movements like *pindibandhas* (collective dance composition) of the *Natyasastra*. The artists are clearly representing a system of dance that involved the flexions and extensions of the limbs characteristic of later dance forms. The joints of the body have successfully been portrayed, and the use of knee and elbow joints in dance has been shown. Wrist and ankle joints must also have been used but it is difficult to judge from the paintings. The scenes of group dancing are numerous compared to solo and duet dancing. Mostly, the dances represented consist of simple movements, though a few are more stylized. The simplicity of technique and form perhaps accounts for the presence of similar dance patterns at Sagar and Raisen, on the one hand, and Raigarh and Chambal, on the other. Most of the movements found in the Mesolithic period are accompanied by music provided by percussion instruments, such as *dhola, dhapli*, etc., and wind instruments, like *singa, turhi*, flute, etc. A developed form of harp is also seen.

Indian rock paintings provide an excellent source of information about the development of dance in India, and show the possible way in which dance was integrated with other aspects of society at different periods of time. However, the paintings also reveal the key characteristics of an artistic tradition and the skill of the artists working within it, who, using an economy of line and a minimum of colour, were able to capture the kinetic rhythm of dance.

Notes

1 *Natyasastra* of Bharata Muni (c. 300 – 100 BC) is the earliest extant treatise on the art of theatre and dance. Chapters IV and VIII–XIII deal with dance and its technical language.
2 Few scholars believe that the bow and its sound are the inspiration behind the development of the stringed instruments (Deva 1978, p. 128).

References

Agarkar, A. G. 1950. *Folk dances of Maharastra*. Bombay: Rajabau Joshi.

Deva, B. C. 1978. *Musical instruments of India*. Calcutta: Firma KLM.

Frazer, J. 1922. *The Golden Bough* abridged edn. London: Macmillan.

Frazer, J. 1936. *Aftermath*. London: Macmillan.

Gupta, J. 1967. *Pragaitihasik Bharteeya Chitrakala*. Delhi: National Publishing House.

Gurg, L. 1967. *Bharata ke Loknrtya*. Hathras: Sangeet Karyalaya.

Hambley, W. D. 1926. *Tribal dancing and social development*. London: Witherby.

Khokar, M. 1987. *Dancing for themselves: tribal and ritual dance of India*. New Delhi: Himalayan Books.

Pandey, S. K. 1969. *Painted rock shelters of Madhya Pradesh with special reference to Mahakoshal*. Unpublished PhD dissertation, Sugor University, Sugor.

Seligman, C. G. 1910. *The Melanesians of British New Guinea*. Cambridge: Cambridge University Press.

Vatsyayana, K. 1982. *Dance in Indian painting*. New Delhi: Shakti Malik.

Wakankar, V. S. & R. R. R. Brooks 1976. *Stone Age painting in India*. Bombay: D. P. Taraporevala Sons.

INTERPRETING THE SYSTEM

18 Seeing the 'inside': Kunwinjku paintings and the symbol of the divided body

LUKE TAYLOR

This chapter examines how the Kunwinjku Aborigines of western Arnhem Land, north Australia, express their relationship with the world in X-ray paintings representing the human and animal forms of ancestral beings. The analysis focuses on the meanings of X-ray paintings in a number of different social contexts, and shows how the semantically productive quality of the images gradually becomes apparent to young Kunwinjku. The socialization of Kunwinjku to understand the symbolic potential of their art is one means of maintaining the coherence and vitality of the Kunwinjku belief system.

Kunwinjku describe the successive revelation of knowledge about the ancestral world as a progression from understanding the 'outside' meaning of things to understanding the 'inside' meaning. 'Outside' meanings are those considered to be comparatively obvious and are learned in the context of daily life in the public realm. On the other hand, 'inside' meanings relate to the actions of the ancestral beings who are understood to have created features of landscape and instituted the ceremonial practices of today's human groups. Access to 'inside' knowledge is restricted and revealed by older men to younger men as part of the initiatory structure of male ceremonial. The controlled transmission of such 'inside' or esoteric knowledge about the ancestral beings is a primary means of demonstrating power relations and maintaining social control amongst Aboriginal groups (Keen 1977, 1978, Myers 1980, Morphy 1985).

The meanings of X-ray paintings used in 'inside' contexts are built on the familiar meanings of X-ray paintings produced in public contexts. Kunwinjku are gradually taught to see the logical consistencies between 'outside' and 'inside' meanings and eventually learn to appreciate the metaphoric aspects of the artistic system. X-ray paintings develop a variety of meanings relating to the divided and systematically organized nature of human and animal bodies. Through their socialization to the many different meanings of these paintings, Kunwinjku are encouraged to see the symbolic potential of the image of the divided body. This key organic symbol provides a framework for encoding a complex array of relationships involving many different realms of Kunwinjku experience of their world. In learning to see, and eventually extend, the homology of relationships through this symbol, young Kunwinjku experience the value of knowledge relating to the ancestral beings. X-ray paintings help to create the meaningful texture of their religious understanding.

The X-ray style

The term X-ray art has been coined by researchers to describe the style of figure painting in which the internal organs and skeletal features of the subjects are represented, rather than the surface features such as fur, feathers, or scales. This style of painting is found over a wide area of Arnhem Land, although it is most prevalent in the west. The Kunwinjku painters with whom I worked do not have a word in their own language to describe this style (Carroll pers. comm.) but they do recognize this style of figure representation as being characteristic of their language group and a number of neighbouring language groups. They describe it simply as 'our way of painting' and occasionally point to the way such infill of figures distinguishes their own political and cultural identity from that of language groups who usually paint in a different way.

Kunwinjku employ a relatively limited set of motifs to indicate the internal organs and bones of a figure. By their characteristic shape and general position within the figure Kunwinjku can readily identify which organs or bones are denoted by the motif. The same motif can occur in the same position within different figure types to indicate the internal organs or bones that are considered to be analogous in the two distinct species (Fig. 18.1, Colour Section 3).

In some cases the X-ray motifs used may be specific to a particular figure type.[1] While the denotative meaning of an X-ray motif as a particular body part is relatively unambiguous, the body parts themselves often have a variety of meaningful associations in Kunwinjku thought. These second-order meanings could be described as the connotative meaning of the X-ray motifs (Barthes 1978, pp. 89–94). Such connotations derive from the way the figure itself, as an ancestral being, is understood to be integrated with the wider order of the world. Ancestral beings are often said to have created certain features of landscape by leaving behind parts of their bodies, or on other occasions they are said to have made sacred objects in the same manner. These extended associations comprise the 'inside' knowledge of the actions of the specific ancestral being that are usually revealed in ceremonies, through the telling of myths, or through songs and dances.

A single being may be associated with the introduction of a number of ceremonies and have traversed the lands of many clans. This results in an extensive range of potential connotations for any painting of that figure. However, the artists employ a variety of means to ensure that from this wide potential range of meanings a restricted meaning is produced. We must examine the particular arrangement of figures and motifs within any one painting to see how they 'mutually condition' the possible meaning of the painting as a whole (Morphy 1977, p. 180, Saussure 1978, pp. 127–34). The scope of this chapter will be confined to an examination of one distinctive means by which Kunwinjku artists influence the way their paintings are interpreted by elaborating the internal infill of the figures. Elsewhere (Taylor 1984, 1987) I have analysed other stylistic features of Kunwinjku paintings that condition their meaning. Kunwinjku artists can employ different types of X-ray motif to orient the interpretation of their paintings in particular ways. The most common variation is between what is considered by Kunwinjku a relatively naturalistic type of X-ray infill (Fig. 18.2, Colour Section 3), and a geometric type which they say relates to the patterns used in paintings for the Mardayin ceremony (Fig. 18.3, Colour Section 3). The naturalistic type of infill is characterized by X-ray motifs organized within the body of the figure in a manner that closely follows the natural model of the species. The geometric type of infill is characterized by X-ray motifs that have very simplified form, and by lines that divide the body of the figure into shapes which are not intended to closely relate to the natural model.[2] Both types of X-ray infill are said to show the internal features of the figure in question. However, the meanings of figures infilled with the naturalistic type of X-ray tend to be restricted to the pragmatic realm of food and food division. The use of geometric X-ray or naturalistic motifs decorated with dotted line and cross-hatched line patterns of infill associate the figure with shades of meaning which are developed within the Mardayin ceremony.

The distinctions between naturalistic and geometric X-ray features should not be viewed as absolute categories so much as poles in a continuum of variation. Kunwinjku bark painters can creatively mix elements of both types in a single painting, or produce subtle variations in the shape of individual X-ray motifs which results in a range of intermediary forms. Often the visual references to designs employed in a ceremonial context are quite subtle, since the paintings are only intended to be correctly interpreted by other Kunwinjku who are familiar with the ceremonies in question. In addition to these primary X-ray types, senior Kunwinjku artists can also create other variations on the X-ray theme. They can modify familiar X-ray motifs to suggest particular and possibly new readings of certain subjects. Such visual interpretations accord with what is generally understood of these subjects from ancestral myths, songs, dances, and other paintings that relate to them.

In what follows, a number of different paintings will be closely examined to show variations in the type of X-ray used in different social contexts and the specific meanings encoded by the paintings in each case. This analysis shows that, for Kunwinjku who have been fully socialized into the meanings of paintings, the image of the divided body comes to exist for them as a symbol which is productive of meaning. Senior artists, who experience this productivity in a more complete way, can convert their understanding to innovations in the form of the paintings.

X-ray paintings of food animals

Previous analyses of the meaning of X-ray art have focused attention on the way this style is used to depict the preferred edible parts of animals. The association of X-ray motifs with important food parts is certainly a significant part of their meaning and one that Kunwinjku frequently articulate (Carroll 1977). The divisions of animal bodies created by using X-ray infill correspond to the standard cuts of meat into which Kunwinjku traditionally divide their game. Kunwinjku today follow relatively strict rules for dividing and sharing large animals (Altman 1982a, pp. 222–65, 1982b). Some paintings explicitly relate to this activity of dividing animals (Aboriginal Arts Board 1979, p. 107, Berndt & Berndt 1982, Pl. 28. p. 53). In such paintings the motifs representing the body organs of the animal may become detached from the figure to show the disassociation of the animal's body. As Carroll (1977, pp. 123–4) has shown, Kunwinjku relate their rules for the division of game to the myth which describes how the *mimi* spirits first showed humans the correct way to cut and cook their animals. This myth is told to children in the open context of the camp, and children readily interpret paintings like this in terms of the *mimi* myth. In this secular context, children first learn to associate the motifs of X-ray paintings with their experience of the division and sharing of game which also occurs in the public arena of the camp.

A number of writers have seized on the fact that X-ray art is used to show important food parts, and they have gone on to suggest that the primary function of X-ray paintings was for the magical increase in the numbers of food animals. For example, Lommel proposes that the X-ray style of art 'is based on the conviction that a whole animal can be brought back to life by the depiction of certain vitally important parts, the skeleton, the heart, the lungs and so on' (1967, p. 132). This theory would find little support amongst the Kunwinjku. Kunwinjku do not have simple magical practices which relate to the resuscitation of game animals in the manner suggested. They do have increase sites associated with paintings, but these paintings do not exhibit an elaborate X-ray style of infill in the same way as paintings in public rock shelters.

Hypotheses which relate the meaning of X-ray paintings to simple magical practices fail to do justice to the importance of X-ray art as a metaphoric system for Kunwinjku. Magical hypotheses represent a limited interpretation of totemic ritual as being simply concerned with food and they neglect the general philosophical and religious nature of totemic thought. The primary function of X-ray paintings is the communication of knowledge about the ancestral beings. Kunwinjku use paintings to pass this knowledge on to their children. In this sense, the association of X-ray motifs with food parts is seen by Kunwinjku as the most 'outside' or public and literal level of interpretation of these paintings.

X-ray paintings and the Kunwinjku view of death

An important set of connotations that are conveyed by some Kunwinjku X-ray paintings are those associated with death and decay. These connotations are not activated in all cases, since many X-ray animals are shown in lively poses such as fleeing a hunter or dancing in ceremonies. However, in some paintings the representation of internal organs, and particularly the skeletal features of animal and human figures, are explicitly intended to signify the decomposed state of the subject. For Kunwinjku, such physical decay also implies a transformation to the spiritual state of existence and such paintings are interpreted to show the essentially immortal spirit of the subject, not simply a 'dead' figure. To fully understand the range of connotations of such paintings would require a more extensive analysis than is possible to present here,[3] so this discussion is restricted to paintings which relate to the Kunwinjku Lorrkun or hollow-log burial ceremony.

The Kunwinjku Lorrkun ceremony was instituted by *kandakidj*, the antilopine kangaroo, and bark paintings of this ancestral being have connotations which relate to the themes of final reburial of human remains and spiritual regeneration of human souls expressed in this ceremony. The senior Kunwinjku artist, Yirawala,

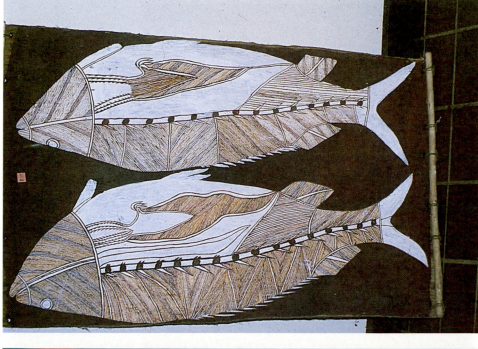

Figure 18.2 Bark painting of two ox-eye herrings by the artist Nguleingulei from western Arnhem Land, Australia, which shows the naturalistic type of X-ray infill. The gill rakers, stomach, gut, and backbone of the fish are shown in a detailed way which is considered to be relatively life-like by Kunwinjku.

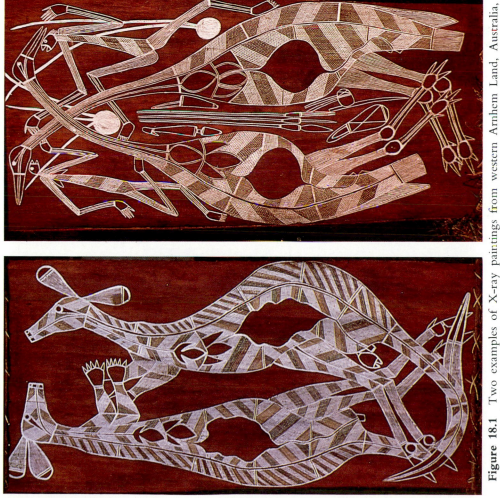

Figure 18.1 Two examples of X-ray paintings from western Arnhem Land, Australia, showing the similar shape and positioning of the X-ray motifs in each case. The painting on the left shows two antilopine kangaroos and the right-hand painting shows two brolgas (bark paintings by Robin Nganjmira).

Figure 18.7 Bark painting by Yirawala of Lumaluma, the leader of the Mardayin. This painting indicates the bones of Lumaluma that subsequently became sacred objects used in the Mardayin ceremony. The motifs used to indicate these bones are similar to those used in X-ray paintings of less important beings, but here they are additionally decorated with dotted line and cross-hatching patterns also used on sacred objects in the Mardayin. (Photo courtesy the Australian National Gallery, copyright Aboriginal Artists Agency.)

Figure 18.6 Bark painting by Yirawala showing Lumaluma, the original creator of the Mardayin ceremony. The sacred objects created by this being are shown as dilly bags, pointed wooden poles, and circular stones inside Lumaluma's body. The motifs that represent these objects are positioned where the internal organs of the figure should normally be shown, thus stressing the way Lumaluma's organs became sacred objects for the Kunwinjku. (Photo courtesy the Australian National Gallery, copyright Aboriginal Artists Agency.)

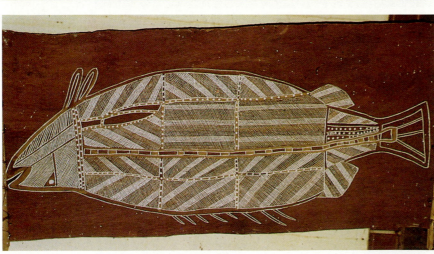

Figure 18.3 Bark painting of a silver barramundi by the artist Karwulku which shows the geometric type of X-ray infill. Here the gill rakers, stomach, gut, and backbone of the fish are also shown, but in a simplified, geometric form. Such X-ray infill, in combination with dotted dividing lines and multi-coloured cross-hatching motifs, is seen to relate the bark painting with a style of painting used in the Mardayin ceremony. Accordingly this bark painting has connotations which derive from the incorporation of the silver barramundi as a major ancestral being of the Mardayin ceremony.

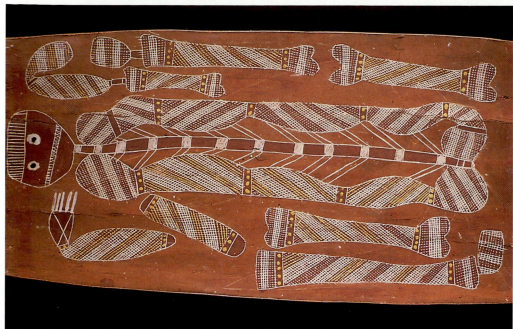

Figure 18.9 Bark painting by Yirawala which shows the truncated torso and bones of Lumaluma, the leader of the Mardayin ceremony. Here Lumaluma is shown to be dissected to reveal his sacred body parts. The decorative patterns on these bones are closely related to the designs painted on the sacred objects used in the Mardayin ceremony. (Photo courtesy the Australian National Gallery, copyright Aboriginal Artists Agency.)

Figure 18.8 Bark painting by Yirawala showing Lumaluma, the leader of the Mardayin ceremony. In this painting human beings are shown removing Lumaluma's limbs to obtain the sacred objects that are his bones. The bones are shown inside the limbs using familiar X-ray motifs. However, they are decorated with bright patterns of dots that indicate their sacred status. (Photo courtesy the Australian National Gallery, copyright Aboriginal Artists Agency.)

Figure 19.4 Panels X and XI from Taira, northern Chile, showing typical dark-red painted and engraved figures; each segment of the scale is equivalent to 10 cm (photograph by F. Maldonado).

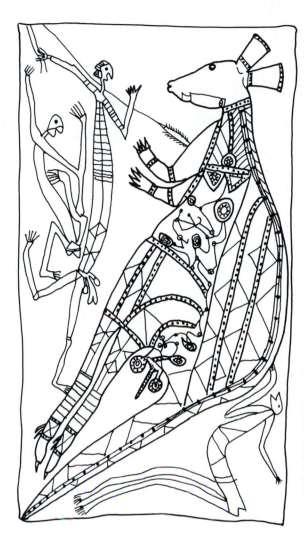

Figure 18.4 Bark painting by Yirawala which shows the *mimi* spirits spearing *kandakij*, the antilopine kangaroo, the ancestral being responsible for instituting the Kunwinjku Lorrkun reburial ceremony. The bright patterns of dots on the X-ray motifs and dividing lines of this figure identify the subject as an ancestral being. The internal organs are likened to sacred objects which are also painted in this way. (Drawing from a painting published in Holmes 1972, p. 69, painting copyright Aboriginal Artists Agency.)

has produced a number of paintings of this subject (see Figs 18.4 & 18.5, also Holmes 1972, pp. 69, 88–9). In many respects these paintings resemble the previous X-ray paintings of *mimi* figures and kangaroos that were interpreted to show the correct way of dividing game. However, the X-ray motifs used by Yirawala in his paintings of Lorrkun subjects suggest the 'inside' ceremonial meanings of his paintings.

In the first example (Fig. 18.4), the ancestral nature of the subject is signified by the way the X-ray elements and joint dividing lines of the figure are decorated with bright dotted patterns. In Kunwinjku ceremonial paintings dotted patterns such as these are used to decorate sacred objects which represent the internal organs of animal species (Kupka 1972, pp. cv–cx). In this context the visual brilliance of the design is used to highlight the ancestral power of the objects. The use of these same dotted patterns on the X-ray motifs of this kangaroo identify the figure as an ancestrally powerful being, with internal organs that are like sacred objects.

Yirawala uses these patterns to distinguish his representation from paintings which show just food animals.

Yirawala described this painting as a representation of a particular ancestral scene associated with the Lorrkun ceremony. The ceremony includes one dance sequence where an actor, decorated with a body design that indicates the ribs and backbone of the kangaroo, is speared and killed by another actor. The action sequence represented in this painting denotes this 'inside' ritual sequence, and not a simple hunting scene, although this is one possible 'outside' interpretation of the painting for those young children who have not seen the ceremony.

For those Kunwinjku initiated into the Lorrkun ceremony and who are familiar with the themes developed in it, this bark painting has additional connotations. Yirawala has provided the myth which relates to this ceremony to elucidate the further meanings of his painting (Holmes 1972, pp. 69, 87).

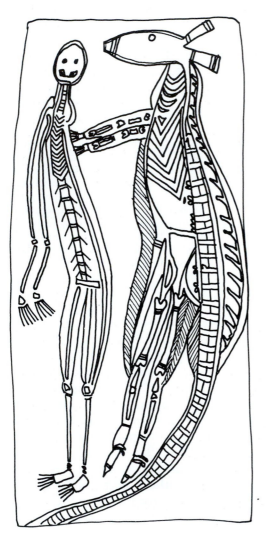

Figure 18.5 Bark painting by Yirawala which shows a human being and *kandakidj*, the antilopine kangaroo, in skeletal form. The skeletal features of these figures associated them with connotations of death and decay and spiritual reincarnation developed in the Lorrkun ceremony. Kunwinjku see the spirits of humans and ancestral beings as dwelling in their bones after their death. The relative permanence of bone is an analogue of the immortal aspect of these spirits. (Drawing of painting held in the Australian National Gallery, copyright Aboriginal Artists Agency.)

Briefly, this myth describes how the antilopine kangaroo was killed and eaten by the *mimi* spirits and his bones left scattered on the ground. The mother of this kangaroo eventually found these bones, sung over them and placed them in a hollow-log coffin so that the soul of the kangaroo, which still resided in the bones, could eventually be reborn in another body. This myth is described as the ancestral precedent for the performance of this ceremony by humans in the present day. In the Lorrkun ceremony, the bones of the human dead are placed in a hollow-log coffin and songs and dances are performed and paintings made on the log to ensure that the clan soul of the deceased is released from the bones and guided back to sites in that clan's estate lands. This soul may be reincarnated in a child born to the clan at a later stage.

Yirawala has explicitly intended that his painting should be associated with the themes of death, decay, and spiritual reincarnation that are developed in the songs, dances, and ritual practices of the Lorrkun ceremony. The painting is a metaphor of the nature of the human condition and not simply a representation of an ancestral event.

In another painting by Yirawala which refers to the same ceremony (Fig. 18.5) this analogy between the myth of the antilopine kangaroo and the fate of human spirits is made explicit. The equivalence between the human figure in skeletal form and the figure of the antilopine kangaroo in skeletal form is highlighted by their juxtaposition in the one painting. The X-ray motifs used to represent the bones of each figure are very similar and emphasize the identity between them. This equivalence is accentuated by the manner in which the legs of the kangaroo are depicted as straightened beneath its body to give the impression that it is 'standing'. Usually Kunwinjku paint kangaroos with the lower limbs of the hind legs bent away from the tail to suggest the normal posture of this animal.

The lack of X-ray motifs for the internal organs of these figures in favour of skeletal motifs signifies the decomposed and spiritual aspect of the figures, since Kunwinjku generally identify bones as the locus of spiritual being rather than flesh. The relative permanence of bone is seen to embody the permanent, enduring, spiritual side of being.

In the Lorrkun ceremony this association is reinforced by practices that stress the identity between the bones of the deceased, the clan spirit contained within them, and the enduring spiritual aspect of the ancestral beings from whom the clan is descended. The ancestral beings are held to be responsible for the creation of sites in the landscape which are imbued with their powerful and fertilizing spiritual essence. This is often described as resulting from the ancestral being leaving a part of his body at the site. In addition these beings created the original human ancestors of today's clan groups. According to the Kunwinjku ideology of patrilineal inheritance, a clan is conceived as the group of individuals who have inherited their spiritual identity from these original beings through their father's line. The clan maintains the custody of the sites created by these beings through time by virtue of their intrinsic spiritual connection with them. As one facet of this series of associations, the clan sites are conceived as repositories of the spirits of deceased clan members. These spirits may leave the sites to cause the wives of clan members to conceive children born to the clan. The Lorrkun ceremony constitutes the occasion when the spirit is finally released from the bones of the clan member to return to these sites. Often the Lorrkun hollow-log coffin is placed near one of the sites owned by the deceased and the bones of the deceased are likened to the bones of the ancestral beings who created the site. In this way, the ancestral power of the site is continually enhanced by the sentimental attachments of the living to their dead relatives placed near the site.

The emphasis on the bones of the figures in Yirawala's painting is a direct reference to this nexus of spiritual connections. The juxtaposition of the two skeletal figures articulates the metaphor of similarity between the spiritual essence of the human and ancestral being. This association of identity lies at the heart of Kunwinjku totemic belief.

The combination of an obviously dead human figure with a skeletal X-ray representation of an animal figure is a common compositional form in Kunwinjku bark paintings. The variation in the animal figure used suggests the different ancestral affiliations of the dead human. Kunwinjku do not use X-ray paintings on the coffin of the deceased in the Lorrkun ceremony itself. These paintings consist of simple silhouette figures in white paint, although the figures do represent ancestral beings associated with the deceased. However, body paintings of different animal figures infilled with skeletal X-ray motifs are employed in Kunwinjku Wubarr and Mardayin ceremonies, and Mardayin at least has a mortuary component.[4] Such paintings signify particular totemic groups and identify the spiritual affiliations of the deceased individuals for whom the ceremony is held. Bark paintings composed in the way described above, exhibit an analogous use of X-ray designs to identify the ancestral affiliations of the dead.

Apart from these explicit totemic references, X-ray paintings of ancestral beings also relate to the wider human, natural, and ancestral life cycles. They show the interrelationships between these cycles. X-ray bark paintings are often described to represent 'cooked' animals and at the most 'outside' level this can be interpreted in terms of food preparation. However, in some ceremonies the description of X-ray paintings as 'cooked' has more general reference. The Wubarr ceremony involved dances where certain actors wear skeletal X-ray body paintings which identify 'cooked' ancestral beings, in direct contrast to other dances where the actors wear simple silhouette body paintings, with no X-ray motifs, that are described to identify the same ancestral beings in their 'raw' state (Long 1964). The dances of the 'cooked' beings are staged *after* the dances of the 'raw' beings and signify the change of state of the being after it has been burned by grass fires. The ceremony as a whole is concerned with the cycle of seasonal fertility instigated by Ngalyod, the Rainbow Serpent (Berndt & Berndt 1951, pp. 114–38). This is signified by dances which represent the characteristic behaviour of certain species at different times of the year, and other signs of the passage of time, such as the motif of fire which represents the hunting fires lit by Aboriginal groups in the dry season (Berndt & Berndt 1951, p. 115, Taylor 1987). The dances of the 'cooked' ancestral beings refer both to the way these fires are intended for the capture of food and to the change of seasons. Kunwinjku see the change of seasons, and the resulting changes from scarcity to plentiful supply of food species, to be a result of the agency of Ngalyod, the Rainbow Serpent, who 'swallows' and 'regurgitates' the natural species at different times of the year. Hiatt (1975) has shown how these images of 'swallowing' and 'regurgitation' by the Rainbow Serpent are a common way of expressing themes of death, rebirth, and natural, social, and spiritual fertility in Arnhem Land and over a wide area of Australia. In the Kunwinjku Lorrkun ceremony the bones and spirit of the deceased are considered to be 'swallowed' by the Rainbow Serpent, since the hollow-log coffin itself is described as one transformation of this original creator being. Major Kunwinjku ceremonies, such as Wubarr, are not simply concerned with calling on Ngalyod to ensure the fertility of the natural species but also with ensuring the fertility of the world at the social and spiritual levels.

From this perspective the representation of the death, cooking, eating, or 'swallowing' of ancestral species has a potentially extensive set of reverberations for those Kunwinjku who are initiated to the meanings of Kunwinjku ceremonies. X-ray paintings are described to show 'cooked' figures in a number of different cultural realms, yet the meanings which are highlighted in each case may be different. However, Kunwinjku artists who understand the essential relationships between meanings developed in these 'outside' and 'inside' realms can create paintings which articulate the analogies between them. Yirawala's paintings overtly represent the death of the antilopine kangaroo who became food for the *mimi* spirits, yet the paintings also express general metaphors of bodily decay and spiritual transformation, and suggest that both ancestral beings and human spirits are the 'food' of the original creator, Ngalyod. Yirawala's paintings, in turn, help younger Kunwinjku to understand aspects of their ceremonial experience.

X-ray paintings and the ancestral body

In previous examples it was described how Kunwinjku view the bones of their dead as the sacred embodiment of the ancestral clan spirit of the deceased. Generally, Kunwinjku see their most powerful sacred objects and places to consist of the transformed body parts, especially the bones, of the ancestral beings. In possessing these objects, and tending these sites, present-day humans maintain their communion with the actual bodily substance and power of these beings (Berndt & Berndt 1951, p. 133). In one of Yirawala's paintings (Fig. 18.4) the sacred quality of the internal organs of the being were signified by the bright dotted patterns on the X-ray motifs of the figure. In the following set of paintings, Yirawala has highlighted the metaphoric qualities of his paintings in a similar way, yet, through a number of important variations he develops the meanings of the works along different lines.

In this set of paintings (Figs 18.6–18.9, Colour Section 3), Yirawala has represented Lumaluma, a major ceremonial figure who introduced the Mardayin ceremony to western Arnhem Land. Lumaluma is also said to be responsible for the creation of all the sacred objects used in the Mardayin ceremony. He did this by taking the objects out of his own body. In this series of paintings Yirawala depicts various stages of this process of creation, and uses the X-ray technique to show the sacred objects inside Lumaluma's body.

In Figure 18.6 these objects are shown as dilly bags and pointed wooden poles inside the chest of the figure, and as circular stones in the place of his testes. In this painting Yirawala plays on the expectation that the internal organs of the figure will be situated in these positions. Such expectation is built through the viewer's familiarity with the conventions of previous X-ray paintings. However, by the shape of these motifs, and by their characteristic decoration, the viewer can interpret these motifs as sacred objects. By this means Yirawala indicates that Lumaluma's internal organs are really sacred objects, a reading which accords with the mythology for this being and is known by individuals initiated to the Mardayin ceremony. In addition, the limbs of the figure are infilled with bright patterns of multicoloured cross-hatching and dotted bands, a design characteristic of the paintings on sacred objects used in the Mardayin ceremony. Kunwinjku view the brightness and visual activity produced by such designs as aesthetic qualities that contribute to the representation of the ancestral power of the figure. A good artist can enliven the figure with bright colours and variations in cross-hatching patterns and dotted dividing line motifs which achieve a striking, yet balanced, effect. He can also attempt a more vital treatment of the figure outline itself. Kunwinjku experience the visual boldness of such paintings as a direct exposure to the power of the ancestral beings.

In Figures 18.7–18.9 Yirawala has shown the bones of Lumaluma as the sacred objects secreted within his body. The motifs used to identify the backbone and bones of the limbs have the same outline shape as the motifs used in his previous paintings of the antilopine kangaroo (Fig. 18.5). Accordingly, the Lumaluma paintings encode a similar set of meanings regarding the permanent spiritual aspect of the figure as these other skeletal X-ray paintings. However, Yirawala decorated the skeletal motifs in the Lumaluma paintings with dotted line and cross-hatching motifs that signify their identity with sacred objects used in the Mardayin ceremony. Yirawala has produced these paintings as a sequence which shows how the body of Lumaluma was gradually taken apart and the sacred objects collected. In Figure 18.7 (Colour Section 3) the legs and penis have been cut off from the body. In Figure 18.8 (Colour Section 3) human beings are shown taking these limbs from Lumaluma. The hands, feet, and genitals have already been removed. In Figure 18.9 (Colour Section 3) Lumaluma is shown as a dissected figure with the bones of his limbs, decorated as sacred objects, scattered around his truncated body. Kupka (1972, pp. lxxv–lxxxvii) records sacred objects used in the Mardayin ceremony that are identified as Lumaluma's bones, and some of these were made by Yirawala. Yirawala's bark paintings of these bones show many basic similarities with the actual painted objects. By means of the particular combination of X-ray motifs with Mardayin patterns, Yirawala has articulated a metaphor associating the dissolution and decay of the body with the themes of spiritual and social regeneration expressed in the Mardayin ceremony.

The Lumaluma myth is told to the initiates of the Mardayin ceremony. Briefly, the myth describes how all the Mardayin sacred objects, the body paintings used in the ceremony as well as the human ancestors of today's clan groups, were released from Lumaluma's body when he died. In Yirawala's version of the myth these sacred objects of the different clans are identified as the organs and bones of Lumaluma. An excerpt from the myth explains this:

> the giant instructed the people to cut up his body and take it to the mainland, but his huge size made this impossible, so the people compromised. They took

sections of the bones and vital organs. Dua [Duwa patrimoiety] took the heart, lungs, kidneys and all the round bones. Jiritja [Yirridja patrimoiety] took all the long bones and long organs. In the Maraian [Mardayin] ceremony, painted designs and symbols of wood and stone represent those bones and organs of Lumah-lumah [Lumaluma] (Holmes 1972, pp. 66–71).

While the paintings of Lumaluma show him in human form, this form is better seen as a visual framework for a more abstract conception. Lumaluma is a major creator being, and his body is imagined to incorporate all the sacred objects and all the ancestors of the clan groups of the present day. He is the major being celebrated by the many clan groups that gather to help perform Mardayin ceremonies. The Lumaluma myth provides the rationale for these many groups to see themselves as having a commonality of interests. While each clan performs with their own sacred objects, the myth of Lumaluma describes how all these sacred objects belonged to the one original body, as did the ancestors of each different clan group. Lumaluma is a symbol of the overall unity of these groups despite their totemic and political differences at another level. The body of Lumaluma is a metaphor of the regional body of clan groups who must stress the conception that they are all one people if the performance of the ceremony is to proceed at all. The body form of Lumaluma is conceived in this abstract way as an expression of the idea that human social groups are potentially distinct yet organically related, like the limbs, bones, and organs of the human body. The image of the divided body of Lumaluma provides a metaphor whereby people can express their clan autonomy and their interdependence at the same time.

Yirawala's paintings relate explicitly to these themes and the paintings are intended to encode these sociological connotations. In previous examples using skeletal X-ray motifs, Yirawala used the motifs to show the bones of a single human being. However, in the paintings of Lumaluma, Yirawala has reworked the motifs by the addition of patterns which show the bones to be the sacred objects owned by individual clan groups.

X-ray paintings and landscape

The final set of paintings to be analysed here consist of X-ray paintings which encode 'inside' meanings relating to the spatial relationships between topographic features of clan lands. At an 'outside' level these paintings are also interpreted to show the body parts and internal organs and bones of ancestral beings. The metaphors of these paintings express the way Kunwinjku conceive of the spatial organization of sites in their lands in terms of an abstract model of the divided yet organically related body parts of the ancestral being that created those lands. Such sites are described as transformations of the actual body parts of the ancestral being, and all the sites thus created are considered to be intrinsically connected. The association between body parts and landscape is developed principally within the Mardayin ceremony and in the X-ray paintings used in the Mardayin. Paintings interpreted to show X-ray features occur in a number of contexts in this ceremony.

In the most public phases of the ceremony actors wear figurative body paintings which are infilled with either the naturalistic type of X-ray infill (Fig. 18.2) or the geometric type (Fig. 18.3). Often the geometric motif used to indicate the internal organs of these figures consists of a simple 'x'-shaped motif or a series of these motifs joined end to end (xxx). Both these types of X-ray infill are described as representing the internal organs or bones of the figure, and the two types of infill appear to be interchangeable in the context of the public dances where such designs are used. Different actors dancing together in the one dance for the same species may employ either of the two types of infill in their respective body paintings. A single dancer may wear a pair of such paintings, each of which shows a different type of X-ray infill. These body paintings are not characterized by the dotted patterning of the motifs, or by the patterns of multicoloured cross-hatching which characterize designs considered to be ancestrally powerful. These relatively public designs do not encode meanings which refer to specific clan lands.

The more important and ancestrally powerful paintings used in the Mardayin ceremony are painted on sacred objects used in the ceremony and on the chests of initiates when they are brought to see the objects for the first time. These paintings generally have a geometric form. The sacred objects painted with these designs consist of highly simplified figurative forms (Spencer 1928, pp. 832–43, Mountford 1956, pp. 460–6) and the body paintings are usually produced within a square frame (Berndt & Berndt 1970, between pp. 102 & 103, Kupka 1972, p. 78). The X-ray motifs used in these paintings are predominantly geometric. These paintings are additionally infilled with cross-hatching, and the X-ray motifs and dividing lines are decorated with coloured dots. It is these paintings that are interpreted both as X-ray designs and as schematic maps of ancestral lands.

While these geometric paintings can be interpreted as X-ray designs by men who have been initiated to the Mardayin ceremony, this reading of the paintings is not immediately obvious to the uninitiated. Young Kunwinjku are taught how to interpret these geometric designs as part of their initiatory experience. The juxtaposition of familiar naturalistic X-ray paintings with the geometric types is one important means by which this is achieved. In learning that naturalistic and geometric types of infill are interchangeable in the public body paintings of the Mardayin, the initiate learns to see the way they encode similar meanings. This experience prepares him for understanding the meanings of geometric paintings which are revealed as he is initiated to the 'inside' aspects of the ceremony.

Mountford (1956, Pl. 148 F & G, pp. 461, 463; see Fig. 18.10) has recorded the meanings of a sacred object, used in the Mardayin ceremony, which also shows this juxtaposition of the two different types of X-ray. Both sides of this object are painted with designs that represent the silver barramundi ancestor. On one side of the object the figure of the ancestor has been painted and the vertebrae and the internal organs have been represented using naturalistic X-ray motifs. A smaller representation of the mullet ancestor, the food of the silver barramundi, has also been shown using naturalistic X-ray infill. This painting is interpreted to show just the body and internal organs of the ancestral being. On the other side of the object the design is painted in a geometric way. However, this design is interpreted to show both the body parts of the ancestral being and the features of landscape created by

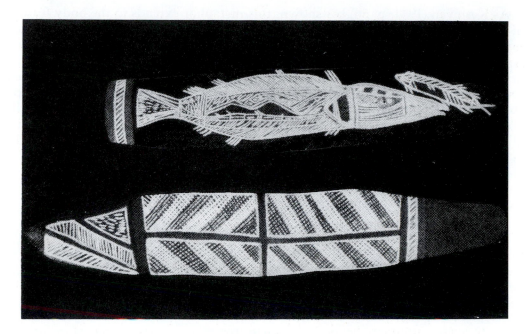

Figure 18.10 The designs painted on two sides of a sacred object used in the Mardayin ceremony recorded by Mountford (1956, p. 461, Pl. 148 F & G). The top painting shows the silver barramundi ancestor with the stomach, gut, and backbone represented by naturalistic X-ray motifs. The bottom painting is on the other side of the same object and shows the body parts of the silver barramundi ancestor and the sacred sites created by him using more geometric motifs. (Reproduced by permission of the publishers.)

it. The analogy between the two types of X-ray painting is made very clear by the way the two designs are painted on either side of the object.

The initiate seeing this object for the first time will recognize the 'outside' meanings of the naturalistic X-ray painting. This is because he will have already gained a familiarity with the conventions of this kind of representation in bark paintings produced in the public camp. However, he must be told that the more geometric design also represents body parts of the silver barramundi, and that the design can also be interpreted to show geographic features made by the ancestor. In order for him to understand the relationships between the two designs the analogies between them may be pointed out. For example, the mid-line of the geometric design is analogous to the motif that represents the backbone in the more naturalistic design. In addition, the lines that divide the head from the body and the tail from the body in the naturalistic X-ray design are also echoed in the geometric design. Once the initiate can identify these equivalences he can go on to look for further similarities himself, working from what he knows of the relationships between body parts that he has learned from his experience with naturalistic X-ray paintings in public contexts. He can compare the relationships between the different meanings of each painting and test the way that the image of the divided body of the ancestral being serves as a metaphor for the relationships between features of his clan lands.

As Kesteven (1984, p. 56) has shown, this metaphor extends to the body features of clan members themselves. They learn to see their own body as a metaphor of the topographic organization of their clan lands, features such as birthmarks on their body being seen as equivalent to sacred sites within their clan lands. This extension of the metaphor is advanced in the Mardayin ceremony when initiates have the geometric design for their clan lands painted onto their own body. In this way the more abstract metaphors of the organization of clan lands and the creative transformative powers of the ancestral beings are linked with the initiates' intuitive understanding of their own body. The metaphors of sacred Mardayin paintings are thus grounded in the initiates' personal, sensible, understanding of the world.

Conclusion

The common element of all X-ray paintings is the way they stress the organic nature of human and animal bodies. Kunwinjku paint the anatomical elements of these figures to show them as the organized parts of an ordered system. The figure is not just a 'shell' (Berndt & Berndt 1982, p. 57) but is composed of divided and separate, though ultimately articulated, parts. This basic understanding is the key that unlocks a multitude of different metaphors expressed in Kunwinjku art.

By focusing attention beyond the overt representational aspect of paintings, beyond the surface to the inside of the figure, X-ray infill helps Kunwinjku to see the esoteric and 'inside' meanings of these paintings. Young Kunwinjku are progressively introduced to the multiplicity of ways that the internal elaboration of a figure can influence the meaning of the painting as a whole. Through this experience they learn to abstract the basic structural similarities between the different forms of these paintings and the more general structural analogies between the meanings encoded by them. In this way they are socialized into understanding the symbolic potential of the image of the divided body and how this symbol encodes relationships between many realms of their experience of the world.

Kunwinjku children first learn to interpret the 'outside' meanings of X-ray bark paintings in the context of everyday camp life. Later, they see that X-ray paintings are also incorporated in the most public phases of Kunwinjku ceremonies and they are taught to interpret these paintings in terms of the general themes of these ceremonies. With their initiation to the restricted and 'inside' phases of ceremony they are taught to interpret geometric types of paintings as if they were X-ray designs, and they learn the extended metaphors of these paintings. With the decline in the performance of some ceremonies, particularly Wubarr and Mardayin, bark paintings depicting the ancestral figures of these ceremonies are becoming an increasingly important medium for the transmission of knowledge of these subjects.

Before Kunwinjku came into contact with Europeans, and the development of the market for bark paintings, rock paintings provided another important medium for the transmission of knowledge about the ancestral beings. Kunwinjku say they stopped painting on rock once they stopped living in rock shelters and went to live in the mission and government towns, or made corrugated iron houses at locations in their own lands. However, they do say that rock art was important

Figure 18.11 Bark painting by Yirawala which shows two initiates painted with Mardayin ceremonial body paintings. (Drawing of painting held in the Australian National Gallery, copyright Aboriginal Artists Agency).

for the illustration of stories for their children. Mountford (1956, pp. 223–4) also records the use of X-ray paintings of the antilopine kangaroo to instruct initiates to the Wubarr ceremony. Different rock paintings exhibit the same variation between naturalistic X-ray infill and the more geometric type identified in this analysis of bark paintings and ceremonial designs. Brandl (1973, pp. 168–9) has labelled this variation in the infill of rock paintings as a change from 'standard' to 'complex' X-ray and Chaloupka (1985, p. 277) uses the terms 'descriptive' and 'decorative' to identify the same variation. Brandl (1973, p. 176) investigated the possibility that the geometric type of X-ray infill was associated with ceremonial paintings but found that his informants identified these patterns as anatomical features, justifying their inclusion as a type of X-ray. The analysis presented here suggests that this 'outside' interpretation of these paintings may conceal meanings that relate to ceremonial themes. The similarity between such 'complex' or 'decorative' X-ray rock paintings and Kunwinjku bark paintings of figures wearing Mardayin body paintings suggests

Figure 18.12   Rock painting at Deaf Adder Creek recorded by Brandl (1973, p. 30, Fig. 60). The painting shows a woman infilled with geometric X-ray patterns. The cross between the breasts appears to represent a breast girdle of the type still worn by women and young male initiates in ceremonies in Arnhem Land today. The fact that the geometric X-ray patterns are shown on the torso and thigh of the woman highlights the similarity between this figure and the initiates in Fig. 18.11. Mardayin body paintings are painted only on the torso and thigh of participants in the same way (Berndt & Berndt 1970: between pp. 102 and 103). (Drawing reproduced by permission of the publishers, Australian Institute of Aboriginal Studies, Canberra.)

that the relationship between rock art and ceremonial themes deserves further analysis (Figs 18.11 & 18.12).[5]

Kunwinjku learn to see how such diverse realms of experience as that of food division and sharing, human mortality, the relationships between social groups, and the topographic relations of the sites in their clan land can all be structured in terms of images of bodily disintegration and reintegration. The controlled revelation of knowledge, which is an aspect of the artistic system, is integrated with the child's socialization to other realms of cultural knowledge. Thus, for example, the knowledge of the meanings of songs or dances performed in ceremony or the understanding of the ancestral associations of features of clan landscape may condition the child's ability to fully understand the logical consistency of metaphors developed in the art.

Variations in the forms of individual paintings may highlight specific meanings in different contexts. However, on ceremonial occasions initiates are encouraged to see what Munn (1973, p. 212) has called the 'connective' function of the paintings. Initiates are prompted to see the extensive metaphors of connection between the many X-ray paintings they have seen in their lifetime and to treat the X-ray paintings of ceremony as symbolic forms. The socialization of Kunwinjku to the many meanings of paintings in 'outside' and 'inside' contexts is organized in a way that helps to create this symbolic potential of the paintings. Once initiates have learned the basic form of the metaphors expressed in the paintings, they can extend the analogies of the divided body to the ever-widening stock of their personal experiences. The symbol helps to encode relationships between the different realms of their experience.

In the changing circumstances of Kunwinjku life, brought about partly through their incorporation within the modern Australian nation state, X-ray paintings continue to maintain the relevance and semantic productivity of the symbol of the divided body. Artists in the modern period have created paintings which relate to their experience of the changing environment in X-ray paintings of motor vehicles, guns, ships, or introduced animal species. Such subjects are painted alongside inno-vative variations of familiar cultural themes. While the meanings of the divided body symbol may be expanded in this way, the core metaphors of this symbol remain little changed. X-ray paintings help Kunwinjku to understand the fundamental spiritual connections between individuals and the social and ancestral order. In doing this, X-ray paintings, like the Warlbiri *guruwari* designs described by Munn, maintain a view of the world that is *persuasive*. Following Munn (1973, p. 211) and Myers (1980, p. 198) we can see that the symbols produced by the operation of systems of signi-fication, such as art, help to create a logically consistent, encompassing, and above all, *convincing* view of the world order. For Kunwinjku the experience of seeing the 'inside' meanings of X-ray paintings takes the form of revelations of the truth of knowledge relating to the ancestral beings, a revelation of the truth of their belief.

Acknowledgements

This chapter is a revised version of a paper delivered at the Australian Archaeological Conference at Valla in 1986. The fieldwork upon which this study is based was carried out in 1981–3 with the support of a Commonwealth Department of Education Scholarship and an Australian Institute of Aboriginal Studies research grant. I wish to thank Dr Howard Morphy, Dr Jon Altman, Maureen MacKenzie, and Robyn Lincoln for their helpful comments on the presentation of this material.

Notes

1   A full analysis of the range of X-ray motifs employed in Kunwinjku paintings is beyond the scope of this chapter. A detailed analysis is included in Taylor 1987.

2   In distinguishing between 'naturalistic' and 'geometric' X-ray motifs I employ the same basic distinction identified by Munn (1966, pp. 940–1) between artistic motifs that have 'continuous' and 'discontinuous' meaning ranges. The term 'naturalistic' is used rather than 'continuous' because Kunwinjku say that these motifs 'look like' the internal features they signify. Iconicity is an important factor in the production of these motifs (Morphy 1980). The 'geometric' X-ray motifs incorporate a more heterogeneous class

of meanings which are metaphorically related (Munn 1966, p. 940). Iconicity is not so important in the production of these motifs, although it is relatively important in the positioning of these motifs within the body of the figure. The different degree of iconicity is related to the different ways the producer intends the work to be interpreted (Morphy 1980, p. 30).

3   See Taylor 1987 for an extended discussion.

4   Wubarr and Mardayin are now only infrequently performed by Kunwinjku. I have not seen them, although their subjects are often represented in bark paintings. My own analysis relies on film records of these ceremonies (Australian Institute of Aboriginal Studies 1964, 1968) and the documentation for them (Long 1964, Peterson 1968) as well as published accounts (Berndt & Berndt 1951, 1970, Elkin 1961). See Taylor 1987 for an extended analysis of the use of body paintings in these ceremonies.

5   In the rock paintings at Deaf Adder Creek recorded by Brandl (1973) it is women who are most often shown infilled with patterns that suggest Mardayin body paintings. This may be considered to conflict with the fact that women are excluded from wearing such designs in the present day. However, in this most western region of Arnhem Land women are said to be the original creator beings responsible for the introduction of these ceremonies. The rock paintings may represent these mythical creators.

References

Aboriginal Arts Board 1979. *Oenpelli bark paintings*. Sydney: Ure Smith.

Altman, J. C. 1982a. *Hunter-gatherers and the state: the economic anthropology of the Gunwinggu of north Australia*. Unpublished PhD thesis, The Australian National University.

Altman, J. C. 1982b. Hunting buffalo in north-central Arnhem Land: a case of rapid adaption among Aborigines. *Oceania* **52** (4), 274–85.

Australian Institute of Aboriginal Studies 1964. *Uwar at Goulburn Island*. 16mm film.

Australian Institute of Aboriginal Studies 1968. *Maraian at Croker Island*. 16mm film.

Barthes, R. 1978. *Elements of semiology*. New York: Hill & Wang.

Berndt, R. M. & C. H. Berndt 1951. *Sexual behaviour in western Arnhem Land*. New York: The Viking Fund.

Berndt, R. M. & C. H. Berndt 1970. *Man, land and myth in north Australia: the Gunwinggu people*. Sydney: Ure Smith.

Berndt, R. M. & C. H. Berndt 1982. *Aboriginal Australian art: a visual perspective*. Sydney: Methuen.

Brandl, E. J. 1973. *Australian Aboriginal paintings in western and central Arnhem Land*. Canberra: The Australian Institute of Aboriginal Studies.

Carroll, P. J. 1977. Mimi from western Arnhem Land. In *Form in indigenous art*, P. J. Ucko (ed.). Canberra: The Australian Institute of Aboriginal Studies.

Chaloupka, G. 1985. Chronological sequence of Arnhem Land plateau rock art. In *Archaeological research in Kakadu National Park*, R. Jones (ed.). Canberra: Australian National Parks and Wildlife Service.

Elkin, A. P. 1961. Maraiin at Mainoru, 1949. *Oceania* **31** (4), 259–93; **32** (1), 1–15.

Hiatt, L. R. 1975. Swallowing and regurgitation in Australian myth and rite. In *Australian Aboriginal mythology: essays in honour of W. E. H. Stanner*, L. R. Hiatt (ed.). Canberra: The Australian Institute of Aboriginal Studies.

Holmes, S. 1972. *Yirawala: artist and man*. Sydney: Jacaranda Press.

Keen, I. 1977. Ambiguity in Yolngu religious language. *Canberra Anthropology* **1** (1), 33–49.

Keen, I. 1978. *One ceremony, one song: an economy of religious knowledge among the Yolngu of north-east Arnhem Land.* Unpublished PhD thesis, The Australian National University.

Kesteven, S. 1984. Linguistic considerations of land tenure in western Arnhem Land. In *Further applications of linguistics to Australian Aboriginal contexts,* G. R. McKay & B. A. Sommer (eds). Applied Linguistics Association of Australia Occasional Papers no. 8, 47–64.

Kupka, K. 1972. *Peintres Aborigines d'Australie.* Paris: Société des Océanistes, Musée de l'Homme.

Lommel, A. 1967. *Shamanism: the beginnings of art.* New York: McGraw-Hill.

Long, J. 1964. Documentation to the film *Uwar at Goulburn Island.* Canberra: Australian Institute of Aboriginal Studies.

Morphy, H. 1977. *'Too many meanings': an analysis of the artistic system of the Yolngu of northeast Arnhem Land.* Unpublished PhD thesis, The Australian National University.

Morphy, H. 1980. What circles look like. *Canberra Anthropology,* **3** (1), 17–36.

Morphy, H. 1985. Inside and outside: the Yolngu system of knowledge. Unpublished paper delivered at the Department of Prehistory and Anthropology, Arts Faculty, The Australian National University.

Mountford, C. P. 1956. *Art, myth and symbolism: records of the American-Australian expedition to Arnhem Land, 1948,* Vol.1. Melbourne: Melbourne University Press.

Munn, N. D. 1966. Visual categories: an approach to the study of representational systems. *American Anthropologist* **68**, 936–50.

Munn, N. D. 1973. *Warlbiri iconography.* Ithaca: Cornell University Press.

Myers, F. R. 1980. The cultural basis of politics in Pintupi life. *Mankind* **12** (3), 197–214.

Peterson, N. 1968. Documentation to the film *Maraian at Croker Island.* Canberra: Australian Institute of Aboriginal Studies.

Saussure, F. de 1978. *Course in general linguistics.* London: Fontana/Collins.

Spencer, B. 1928. *Wanderings in wild Australia.* London: Macmillan.

Taylor, L. 1984. *Dreaming transformations in Kunwinjku bark paintings.* Paper delivered at the Australian Institute of Aboriginal Studies Biennial Conference 'Aboriginal arts in contemporary Australia'. Forthcoming in Conference Proceedings.

Taylor, L. 1987. *'The same but different': social reproduction and innovation in the art of the Kunwinjku of western Arnhem Land.* Unpublished PhD thesis, The Australian National University.

Warner, W. L. 1937. *A black civilisation.* New York: Harper & Brothers.

19 *Camelids in the Andes: rock art environment and myths*

JOSE BERENGUER & JOSE LUIS MARTINEZ

Introduction

In 1938 when the Americanist Stig Rydén passed through the Atacama Desert (northern Chile) on his way to Bolivia, he stayed for one week at the Loa River, surveying various places of archaeological importance. Possibly due to the fact that Rydén (1944) was guided by a person who knew the place well, he found two interesting rock art sites at Taira where images of the South American camelid predominated.[1] Half a century after the discovery, the Taira style has been found in a broad area of the Loa River and its tributaries.

Although our long-range objective is to determine the role played by rock art in the prehispanic societies of the region, our immediate objective in this chapter is a more modest one: to look into the connotative aspects of two or three Taira panels. There are no direct accounts of the prehispanic rock art of the Andes. Apparently, this art disappeared a short while after the arrival of the Conquistadors in the 16th century. Therefore, any attempt to discover its meaning is a difficult task for which methodologies have only recently been developed. In this respect the works of Lewis-Williams (1982, 1983), that link rock art with other expressions of the cognitive system of the San hunter-gatherers from South Africa, have been illuminating. However, in our case we are dealing with a type of rock art that was produced by very different societies.

In the past, Taira rock art was looked at from a typically empirical perspective (Lewis-Williams 1983) and the representations were interpreted in an almost literal form. Rydén (1944, pp. 80–1) held that, 'it appears to have been the artist's intention to depict a definite episode, viz. a herd of llamas being driven along by a number of men' carrying slings in their hands. Mostny (1969, p. 139) observed, 'camelid hunting scenes with naked hunters carrying bows, and groups of dressed persons who possibly had to enclose the animals'. And Niemeyer (1972, p. 83) saw, 'hunting scenes . . . with men evidently armed with bows'. These three authors were referring to basically the same group of figures, and many other figures from these same panels were left without any interpretation. Although both Niemeyer and Rydén saw the possibilities for a more complex explanation, perhaps associated with hunting (Rydén 1944, pp. 84–8) or the breeding of camelids (Niemeyer 1967, p. 161),[2] the interpretations in the main were descriptive. However, we know from elsewhere in the Andean world that visual communication systems were often associated with mythological subjects. On a priori grounds it would seem productive to explore the potential of Andean myths to interpret the Taira rock art. By this we do not simply mean looking for direct visual representations of mythical events. It may be necessary to go to a deeper level of analysis before correspondences become apparent. In this chapter, therefore, we first analyse the structure of certain camelid myths, and from this identify the categories and oppositions that underlie the mythic discourse. After this we try to determine if these categories are also present in Taira rock art. Only by starting with this structural analysis is it possible to discover internal links that relate myths to rock art. Based on this analysis we suggest an interpretation of the meaning of the panels which, we argue, is more valid than those proposed by Rydén, Mostny, and Niemeyer. The chapter concludes with a very preliminary discussion of the implications that come out of this stage of the research.

Taira and its environment

From its origin at the Miño volcano (Fig. 19.1a), at 3900 m above sea-level, to its mouth in the Pacific Ocean, the Loa River is about 440 km long. It is the only river which crosses the Atacama Desert, the most arid desert in the world (Weischet 1975). Its river basin has a surface area of 33 570 km², but in spite of being so extensive its water resources basically come from the upper basin, which only covers around 20 per cent of the total surface (Niemeyer 1979). Thus, this high area of the river basin is decisive in the supply of water, the most critical resource of the desert.

The Upper Loa River

Between its origin at Miño and its end at the oasis of the Chiuchiu, the upper course of the river, or Upper Loa, has as its eastern tributaries the waters of the Chela River, San Pedro River, and Salado River. It flows for almost 150 km from north to south, flanked by two Andean mountain chains.

The Upper Loa River can be divided into three zones. In the first zone the river is fed by the water from the melting ice of the mountains and by the summer rain. During the dry season the region forms an ideal habitat for the herding of camelids. The river then flows through an intermediate zone in which the surface supplies of water diminish and underground ones get bigger. Within the canyon herding conditions are favourable and small-scale agriculture is possible. Finally, the river enters a desert zone, leaving behind its canyon, with large pampas on either side devoid of vegetation. With the exception of the last stretch, where there are two Indian villages, the area today has a scarce and dispersed population. In contrast, the prehispanic population of the Upper Loa River is thought to have been much larger (Berenguer *et al.* 1985).

The locality of Taira

Taira is on the middle stretch of the Upper Loa (Fig. 19.1b). Here the canyon reaches its greatest majesty, with cliffs of 40 m to 60 m high formed by an almost vertical rocky wall and a talus of debris which descends with a pronounced slope until the end of the ravine (Fig. 19.2). The location of Taira is very special since it is situated

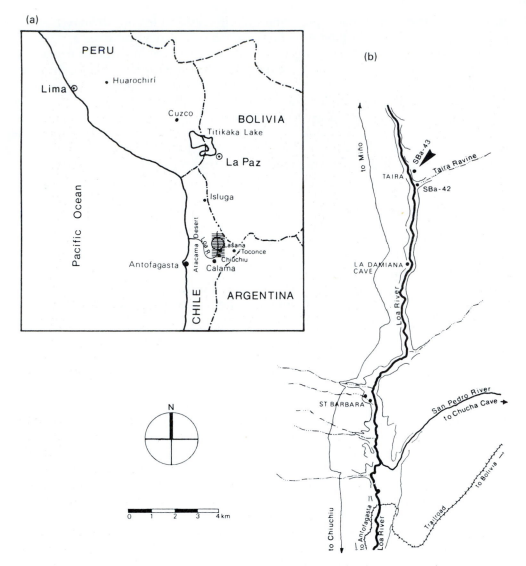

Figure 19.1 Principal places mentioned in this chapter: (a) map of the south-central Andes and part of the central Andes; the shaded area corresponds to the Upper Loa River and the circle represents the 'intermediate stretch'; (b) map of the 'intermediate stretch' of the Upper Loa River. (Drawing by C. Sinclaire.)

Figure 19.2 Panoramic view of the locality of Taira at the point where the canyon begins to open. At the left the rock shelter of SBa–43 may be observed and at the centre the Loa River with some of the springs which rise there. (Photograph by J. Berenguer.)

exactly at the point where the width of canyon undergoes a major change. Down the river it broadens, permitting the development of riverine *vegas*; whereas upstream the canyon narrows and big blocks of stone cover the floor of the valley and partially cover the river bed, leaving only two visible narrow strips of grass. Because of the narrowness and height of the canyon, even in summer Taira has only a few hours of sunshine. As a result, at certain hours of the day there is a sharp contrast between the shade of valley and the light of the upper pampas.

Just before the narrow part ends, many springs of underground water, which are slightly salty to the taste, appear on the eastern side. Their temperature (28° C) is probably related to the neighbouring volcanic system.[3] There are 16 known springs, but undoubtedly more of them must exist. Apart from these, there are 19 other springs divided between 13 different places in the rest of the valley (Niemeyer 1979). The concentration of springs found at Taira is unusual. Almost all of them are covered with grass and their existence is recognized by the dark green colour of the grass. They sometimes show a cut at the centre forming a tiny stream of water which flows towards the river. Two of them, Ampahuasi or Baños de Taira, are pools which are occasionally used today as thermal baths. The river flows rapidly, its flow greatly increased by the underground waters of the east. In conclusion, Taira is one of the most humid places in the valley, with an important supply of waters that springs up from the depths and that visibly comes from the east where the volcanoes are found.

On the pampas that open up at both sides of the canyon a poor shrub-like vegetation grows. Its principal species are the *tara* (*Fabiana densa*), the *pesco-tola* (*Baccharis boliviensis*), and the *rica-rica* (*Acantolippia punensis*). Tinamous (*Nothoprocta petlandii*) and rhea (*Rhea americana*) are often found on the pampas which, indeed, are named after these birds. On the river terraces many hydrophilous plants grow, such as the *brea* (*Tessaria absinthioides*), the *grama* (*Distilchlis humilis* Phil., *Muhlenbergia asperifolia*), juncos (*Juncus depauperatus* Phil.), the *cortadera* (*Cortaderia atacamensis*), and the *cola de zorro* (*Hordeum comosum*). It is common to observe in this sector different species of ducks and of small birds, and it is not unusual to see big vultures such as the condor (*Vultur gryphus*), especially towards the beginning of the summer. Two mammals that still survive in the area are the fox (*Dusicyon* sp.) and the vizcacha (*Lagidium* sp.), a semi-gregarious rodent that lives on the rocks. The chinchilla, another rodent, is virtually extinct, and the name of the locality, Taira, could refer to the tayra, an aquatic carnivore of the Mustelidae family (Gilmore 1950, p. 375) whose presence has not yet been detected in the zone.

In the past, the wild camelids, such as the *vicuña* (*Vicugna vicugna*) and the guanaco (*Lama guanicoe*), probably descended from the mountain range to graze on the *vegas* of Taira and at other points in the valley. Judging by their remains in archaeological contexts, these animals played an important role in the nomadic hunters' diet. Today, they rarely come down into the area. The *vegas* today maintain a much smaller herding group than the one that existed in prehispanic times. During the rainy season (from December to March) the llamas (*Lama glama*), sheep, and goats are taken to graze at the pampas, which at that time are covered by tender green grass generically called *pelillos* (*Artistida adscencionis* L., *Boutelova simplex* Lag.).

Rock art at Taira

The two groups of rock art described by Rydén are on the eastern side of the canyon near where the springs lie. Both of them occur at the line of rupture between the canyon's wall and the talus of debris, as indeed does most of the rock art of the region. 'Group 2' which we have labelled as SBa–42 (Berenguer *et al.* 1975) is found at that part of the Taira ravine where there are many springs. 'Group 1', or SBa–43, is around 300 m north of this place. In this chapter we present an analytical description of the most important aspects of this last group. The investigation of these sites is continuing and this analysis must be considered as a preliminary one. For a more complete description of SBa–42 and 43 we refer the reader to Rydén's work (1944, pp. 65–93).

SBa–43 is 30 m above river-level (Fig. 19.2). Partially hidden from view, a structure consisting of five enclosures may be seen on the opposite side of the river, but its relation with the site has not been demonstrated. The site is on a terraced surface, 8.5 m wide by 20 m long, protected by the canyon's wall, which at that place extends over the terrace as a corbel (Fig. 19.3). At this small rock shelter there are three architectural structures and 20 panels of rock art. The structures are found attached to the rock shelter and they comprise two low semi-circular platforms (A and C) and one semi-cupola (B), all of them made of stone and built in a very rudi-

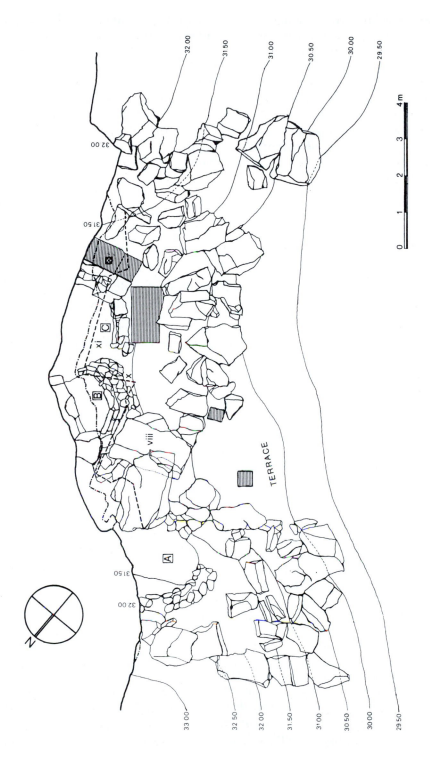

Figure 19.3 Plan of the SBa–43 site. The segmented line corresponds to the wall where rock art is found, the Roman numerals show the studied panels, the letters show the architectural structures, and the shadowed areas correspond to archaeological excavations. (Drawing by F. Maldonado.)

mentary way. The last one has a narrow, square cavity entrance which only allows one person through. Inside there is a semi-circular hole carved on the shelter's wall, which Rydén (1944, p. 88 & Map 6) wrongly described as a 'cave'.

The representations of dark-red painted figures are typical of Taira art. The majority of outlines have been executed by a deep engraving made by percussion and probably finished by scraping (Fig. 19.4, Colour Section 3). We will use the term 'pictoengraving' to refer to this technique. A few figures which have been only painted may be seen, as well as a larger number of figures which are only engraved. Apparently, the red colours were made with a substance known in the area as *almagre* (Niemeyer 1967, p. 160) which is undoubtedly a kind of ochre (Rydén 1944, p. 80).

The components

The rock art is primarily naturalistic and practically all the figures in the panels represent elements of the surrounding environment.

Prevalence   Figures of camelids are the most frequent. Next in importance are figures of human beings, birds, and certain elements that will be interpreted later.

Realism   The camelid is reproduced with great fidelity and in a great variety of positions. This contrasts with the human figures which are more stylized although no less dynamic, and with some birds that are as realistic as the camelids but more rigid.

Identification of species   There is no evidence from the representations which allows us to establish whether they are wild or domesticated camelids but, as we will argue later, there are good reasons for supposing they are domesticated ones. In the case of the birds, at least one is definitely a tinamou, another seems to be a flamingo, although it has features that make it similar to a rhea. Nevertheless, the most abundant group corresponds to a type of bird that we could call 'fabulous' since, apparently, one like it does not exist in nature[4] (Fig. 19.5).

Sex   In the case of the human figures and birds there are no features which permit us to identify sex. In the case of camelids, on the other hand, the general weight of evidence leans in many cases to the likelihood that they are female. The emphasis on the abdomen is striking, with it being marked in some cases by wider engraved lines than those in the rest of the figure. In other cases, there are representations of large camelids with smaller camelids between their legs in a suckling position. Moreover, there are certain signs which could be interpreted as representing sexual characteristics, for example vulva-shaped features (Fig. 19.6) and, more speculatively, the U-shaped signs and orifices that occur in certain of the pictoengravings.

Form   The body and the head of the camelid are always represented in profile; its ears are represented in a vertical position or inclined slightly backwards, and its tail is turned downwards. Usually, four legs are shown. In the bigger camelids the artist shows its characteristic cloven hooves. Humans are represented in front view and in semi-profile, frequently with a large body and with their four extremities clearly shown. They are often shown wearing clothes or holding certain large or oval objects. The birds are always represented in profile, with folded wings and with both legs visible. The margin of variation of the camelids is very broad. This does not occur with the birds, since they are represented with very little variation in the position of the legs. On the other hand, the range of variation in the humans is closer to that of the camelids.

Size The literature frequently refers to the great size of the Taira camelids (Niemeyer 1967, p. 161, 1972, p. 83, Mostny & Niemeyer 1983, p. 52), which in some cases may be over 80 cm tall. But what is not mentioned is that the great majority are of a small size, including figures of up to 10 cm. Humans never reach the size of the big camelids and they are generally of the same scale as the middle-sized ones. However, there is a group which is so small that they fit in the space between the legs and the abdomen of one of the camelids. In contrast to the camelids and the humans, the birds have a uniform size in proportion to their species; their scale would correspond to that of the middle-sized camelids.

Figure 19.5 Panel VIII; each segment of the scale is equivalent to 10 cm. Notice the representation of birds on the upper-left part and at the centre of the panel. (Photograph by F. Maldonado.)

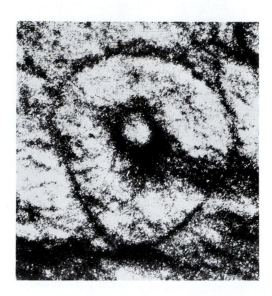

Figure 19.6 Detail of panel XI in which the representation of a possible vulva is shown. (Photograph by F. Maldonado.)

Depth of field   In order to obtain the illusion of perspective, the Taira artists seem to have used superpositioning and juxtaposition of figures of different size.

The composition

We will begin with the analysis of panels X and XI as a set (Fig. 19.4). In order to make the description easier, the panels have been divided into quadrants defined by the intersection between the vertical edge which separates both panels and a more or less horizontal crack which crosses the complete set. These quadrants have been labelled with numbers. In this way number '1' corresponds to the bottom-right quadrant, number '2' to the bottom-left quadrant, number '3' to the upper-right quadrant, and number '4' to the upper-left quadrant (Fig. 19.7).

Within the composition the camelid figures follow a definite direction of movement going alternately from right to left and from left to right in an ascending sequence. At the bottom of quadrant 1 the animals move towards the left and the camelid which is alone in quadrant 2 represents the last one of that row. Entering once again into quadrant 1, it is no longer a row, but a 'herd' of camelids going towards the right, as if it were penetrating the cavity which is at the end. It should be noted that the animals that lead the group bend their heads forward in order to enter the cavity. In this same quadrant, but a little further up, another row of camelids moves from right to left, ending their track at an angle formed by two converging cracks. In quadrant 3 the direction of the animals changes again, moving once again as a 'herd' from left to right, but this time they intermingle with a row of camelids which do the same but in the opposite direction. The composition seems to end in quadrant 4 where the sequence apparently repeats itself in a reduced way (one camelid at a time), as well as descending in such a way that the camelid which is at

Figure 19.7 Panels X and XI; the numbers indicate the quadrants into which the compostion has been divided. (Drawing by F. Maldonado.)

the base of this quadrant would correspond to the last one of the series.[5] Therefore, there is an apparent way of 'reading' these two panels.

This was precisely what made us centre our attention on these two panels and look into the possibility of decoding them. On the basis of the heuristic principle of starting from the best-known aspects to the least-known ones, we incorporated panel VIII (Fig. 19.5) and we plan to do the same in the future with the rest of the panels. Thus, of the 20 known panels recognized in SBa–43 we will examine only three here, that is panels VIII, X, and XI. None of them will be analysed completely, since they have areas that still present many problems of interpretation. In any case, the three of them occupy a central position at the site, that is they are next to the enclosure with the semi-cupola shape, or structure B (Fig. 19.3).

In general terms, the size of the camelids in panels X–XI becomes larger as they go up the wall and they reach quadrant 4. They only begin to get smaller in the last one when they go down through the quadrant. We also notice that the depth, the thickness, and the number of lines of the figures' outlines increase as they go up the wall. A change parallel to this one is produced with the superpositioning. In spite of the variable quality of quadrants 1 and 2 the figures are seldom superimposed, but in quadrants 3 and 4 there is less variety and greater superpositioning. The camelid is the only component which is present in all the compostions. Other motifs have a more localized distribution which amounts to the following order: the 'fantastic' birds, vulvas, 'U', and orifices are only found in quadrants 1 and 2, but more so in quadrant 1; human beings, artefacts, camelids with enlarged abdomens, and camelids shown breast-feeding others, are all found only in quadrants 3 and 4, but mainly in quadrant 3.

Therefore, there is a lower plane (quadrants 1 & 2) and an upper one (quadrants 3 & 4) defined by marked differences in the size of the camelids, in the characteristic of the outlines of the figures, in the degree of the superpositioning and of the variability, and in the components present in each quadrant.

If we compare these panels with panel VIII we find differences and similarities (Figs. 19.7 & 19.5). Among the differences we may note the form of the 'readings' which in panel VIII is from left to right, since practically all the figures take that direction. Size is another difference, since in panel VIII the tendency is to increase the dimensions of the figures as they advance vertically and horizontally towards the centre. This same pattern is observed in relation to the depth, the thickness, and the number of lines of the figures' outlines. Among the similarities it is interesting to note that the camelids go around in groups, from left to right, which is the same direction that the 'herds' take in panels X and XI. The ubiquity of the camelid as a figure may also be mentioned in contrast to the markedly localized distribution of the other components. Humans are situated only at the upper-left corner, and birds occupy only the upper-left half of the left part of this panel. Another noticeable similarity is the division of the panel into a lower plane that is varied, and an upper, less varied one separated by a natural line of the rock which meanders through its width. It is clear that in both the elaboration of the figures and the structuring of the composition the artists of Taira were governed by precise rules.

Camelids in the Andean myths

In the introduction we made clear that our basic assumption about Andean rock art is that its theme had to do with myth. In the previous section we saw that the only figure which is omnipresent in Taira rock art is the camelid. On this basis we began a review of Andean myths in which the camelid was also prominent. The search was guided by some images which have a central position in the panels. In quadrant 3 of panel XI a large camelid apparently suckles a younger one. Underneath it there are six human beings in large tunics, on either side there are two marauding figures carrying large objects in their hands (Figs. 19.4 & 19.7). Certain superficial similarities between this scene and some passages of the Yakana myth drew our attention to an account gathered by the priest Francisco de Avila in Huarochirí (near Lima) towards the end of the 16th century. Starting from this we also used other Andean mythical accounts from various regions and from different periods which, as a whole, have permitted us to clarify and deepen some aspects of our analysis. We refer to the colonial myths, such as the one obtained by Polo de Ondegardo at Cuzco, in the 16th century, as well as to present-day myths like those studied by Martínez (1976) among the Aymaras of Isluga (north of Chile) and by Gow & Gow (1975) from the same region of Cuzco (Fig. 19.1a).

The version of the Huarochirano myth we use here is the one recorded by Urioste (1983). The text is found in Chapter 29 under the following epigraph: 'How the so called Yakana comes down from the upper firmament to drink water. We shall also talk about the other stars and include their names':[6]

They say that the one we have called Yakana is the creator of the llamas and it moves in the middle of the sky. We humans have also seen her come as something black. Yakana has her orbit within the Milky Way. She is very big and she moves through the sky appearing as a dark place with two eyes and with a very large neck. People call her Yakana.

Yakana used to drink water from the springs and if someone's destiny was richness she would fall over him. This person was crushed by a great quantity of wool while another one pulled out Yakana's wool.

This occurred at night. In this way, the next day at dawn the man would discover the wool that had been pulled. He discovered it was of different colours: blue, white, black and mottled, and it was well matted down. Since he didn't have llamas he immediately went to exchange the wool and he worshipped Yakana at the place where he had seen it and where he had pulled the wool. After worshipping Yakana he bought a male and female llama. As a consequence of this transaction he eventually had two or three thousand llamas. It has been told that in the old times Yakana appeared in a similar way to many people of this province.

And they tell that Yakana drinks sea water at midnight and without anyone knowing it. If she did not drink it the ocean could cover the whole world in an instant.

There is a black place which moves in front of Yakana. They call it Tinamou. It is also said that Yakana has a son and it seems as if she were suckling him.

We know that there are also three stars that march in a straight line. They are called Cóndor, Gallinazo and Halcón. (Urioste 1983, pp. 217, 219)

Yakana is a llama which suckles its young. It was precisely the similarity between the representation of the suckling camelids in Taira (quadrants 3 & 4) and this description of Yakana with her son which, for the first time, suggested a homology to us. Apparently this was a widely diffused theme, since the description of Yakana is similar to the one that Polo de Ondegardo picked up in the south of Peru, this time under the names of Urcuchillay and Catachillay. This is the case of the stars 'that understand about the conservation of herds' and that 'pretend to be a sheep with its lamb' (Polo 1961 (1554), p. 3).[7]

But, both in the myth and the panel, formal resemblance and narrative order seems to be secondary. The categories expressed in the myth (and in the typical language of these kinds of accounts) are the ones that really provide a way of 'reading' the rock art of SBa–43.

Yakana

In the text Yakana is referred to as *llamap camaquin*, which has been translated in several ways: as the 'double' of the llamas (Arguedas 1975, p. 124), or as the *cámac* of them (Taylor 1976, p. 214, 1980, p. 189), or as their 'creator' (Urioste 1983, p. 217). The idea is quite clear, despite the varieties of translation. Yakana is linked in a direct way to aspects such as the reproduction of herds, their increase, and also the existence itself of the llamas as animals (Taylor 1976). *Camaquin*, a derivative of *cámac* has been translated as 'vital force' (Taylor 1976, p. 235) and it applied in the Andes to those who had the capacity to transmit to others of their same species this animating force which permitted them to live (Duviols 1978).

The relationship to procreation seems to be implied not only by the term *llamap camaquin* but also by the conceptualization of Yakana as female. She is suckling her young, which relates her to other attributes associated with *camaquin*, such as the capacity of maintaining, of nurturing, and even more of breeding. She is also the one who provided the possibility for the fortunate ones to have 2000 or 3000 animals. In this way she is responsible for the increase and growth of herds.

Probably because Yakana refers to a black constellation (Urton 1981a, p. 477 *et seq.*), the idea of 'darkness' is repeated many times in the text.[8] We see Yakana 'as coming as something black', it appears as a 'dark place', and her principal acts (giving fortune to people and drinking the water) were done at night when no one saw her. This emphasis on 'darkness' contrasts with the absence of signifiers that have to do with 'light', its opposite. This antithesis may also be sensed in the observation at first hand of this black constellation. In fact, when we personally saw Yakana, on one occasion in a very dark and clear sky (7 May 1985), she disappeared an hour later when the moon came out and it lightened the sky. It was as if Yakana and the light were incompatible.

This constellation is found in the Milky Way, which in Andean perception was seen as Mayu, the River (Urton 1981a). Yakana lies in the middle of this celestial river, occupying a prominent position (Zuidema & Urton 1976, p. 66). In addition, one of its most important activities was to drink 'the water from the springs and from the sea' at midnight, thus protecting the world from a possible inundation. The association between the llamas and the water is a frequent theme. Zuidema & Urton (1976, p. 73) point out that 'the waters always relate to llamas and to salt', in this way they refer to the many myths and rituals in which the association of the water and the llamas was explicit, and where salty objects were mentioned or used. Avila's book contains the many myths of llamas which are announcers of the deluge and the inundation of the world. In them the protective character of these camelids is pointed out, since with their actions they succeed in saving humanity (Ortiz 1980).

Lastly, Yakana is clearly a female since she not only has a child but is also suckling it. The 'feminine' aspect of this image is explicit and it emphasizes the absence of signifiers that denote its opposite, that is the 'masculine'.

In conclusion, Yakana expresses various categories that have a heavy symbolic load: the capacity to procreate or to reproduce; her responsibility in nursing and maintaining herds; her influence in the increase of the llamas; the idea of being something dark; the link to the water; and her female sexuality.

The springs

The celestial llama 'used to drink water from the springs'. This idea is also found in the prehispanic myth of the origin of llamas from the Urcococha, Chinchaycocha, and Choccllococha lakes (in Chinchaicocha, Peru), where they are responsible for the creation of three *puquios* or springs (Zuidema & Urton 1976, p. 70). The phrase 'drink water from the springs', both introduces the spring as signifier and simultaneously establishes a relationship between Yakana and these water sources.

We need to refer briefly here to some concepts and ideas which appear associated with springs. Some springs are considered as having especially significant associations. When this occurs they are conceptualized in Aymara as *juturi* (origin places).[9] Consistent with this they appear as 'creational holes' for herds in many regions of the Andes (Martínez 1976, 1983, p. 95 *et seq.*) and as such, like Yakana, they are directly related to the existence and reproduction of the llamas and alpacas. The *juturi* or *puquio* thus appear full of significance and are, in one way or another, articulators of the same categories that are associated with Yakana: 'fertility' (procreation); 'increase' (multiplication); 'breeding' (maintaining, conservation); 'humidity' (water); 'darkness' (night, dark), and 'femininity'.

The idea of 'fertility', of the procreation of herds is expressed in the Aymara conception of *juturi* as well as in some Quechua myths of which ethnographic versions are known. One of them which refers to herds was recorded in the Ocongate region (Cuzco) and contributes to a better understanding of the relationship between springs, llamas, and Yakana:

> A long time ago there were *alpacas*. At dawn they had hidden under the ground where there are springs. When the sun came out again all the animals came out of the spring. This is why we are making a *despacho* [offerings] for a spring and for the lakes at the foot of the Ausangate [a volcano]. If the underground spring

did not exist we would not have had animals. This is why we make offerings (Gow & Gow 1975, p. 142).[10]

The springs then have a role in the breeding or maintaining of herds. Even when the animals are in other places far away from their place of origin their owner must try to go the 'natal' *juturi* to perform the appropriate ceremonies. If this is impossible then he must at least perform the ceremony at a distance, but always facing towards the 'natal' *juturi*, since the herds belong to that spring and not to another because 'it has created them and it has bred them' (Martínez 1976, p. 285).

The idea of 'darkness' is also associated powerfully with the springs and is expressed through certain events that happen at night. In fact one of the most important signs of a *juturi* in today's Indian community of Isluga (northern Chile) is the presence of certain birds associated with darkness. These are the *ch'ullumpi*, small ducks that emerge from the springs preceding the mythical exit of the llamas (Martínez 1976, p. 284). It is said that these birds go out at night 'in the days of darkness . . .' (Martínez 1976, p. 284). The reference to 'darkness', marked by the absence of the moon, is reaffirmed by the fact that ritual payments to *juturi* are likewise made at night when it is very dark (Martínez 1976, p. 285).

Lastly, the idea of 'femininity' is expressed through the spring water itself. The springs are 'very deep holes' from the interior of which animals come out (Martínez 1976, p. 281). The generative quality of femininity is seen here because of the similarity of this image with childbirth and with the uterus. In both cases they are cavities that expel the being they give birth to into the light (from the inside towards the outside). The properties are absolutely consistent with this feminine conception of the springs and at the same time it helps to better understand the use of the concepts 'humidity' and 'darkness' to signify female fertility.[11]

An axis of signification

Our review of the mythical accounts has concentrated on those most relevant to camelids and the key categories and oppositions that emerge relate to this focus. However, Yakana as well as the *juturi* form part of wider semiological systems that could throw more light on the underlying conceptual system.[12] This is one of the directions we will follow in the next stage of our research.

Briefly outlining what has been said until now we can state that in the myth a number of categories are significant and their significance is emphasized by the absence or omission of their opposites. In Table 19.1 the terms have been ordered according to the sequence in which they have been mentioned in this section, and a plus sign (+) has been used to show the presences and a minus sign (−) to show the absences.

The categories are identical for Yakana and *juturi* or springs. Both mythical accounts express the same with greater or less intensity. It is possible to reduce Table 19.1 even more by seeking order within it. According to ethnographic accounts of the springs, 'humidity' and 'darkness' are complementary to 'femininity' and to 'fertility', all of these point to a more comprehensive category which can be reduced to creation, the 'moment of giving life':

Table 19.1 Significant categories in Andean myth.

Categories	Yakana	Water-springs (*juturi*)
fertility/	+	+
sterility	−	−
breeding/	+	+
non-breeding	−	−
increase/	+	+
decrease	−	−
darkness/	+	+
clarity	−	−
humidity/	+	+
dryness	−	−
feminine/	+	+
masculine	−	−

fertility + humidity + darkness + femininity = creation (giving life)

On the one hand, 'breeding' refers to a later moment, while 'suckling' and 'growing' refer to what has been already created. Similar considerations apply to the concept of 'increase'. Breeding and increase taken together result in the conservation or maintenance of the species:

breeding + increase = conservation (maintaining life)

Therefore it is possible to state that the categories articulate with one another within the semiological system along an axis that extends from creation at the one end to conservation at the other.

Other signifiers

In both accounts we find other elements which seem important to us because of the meaning they may have, but whose place in the overall system of signification is still not fully understood.

One of these is the means by which men obtain their fortune in llama herds both in the case of Yakana and *juturi*. Yakana appeared to people at night and when she came down the men pulled out her wool. On the following day they discovered that it was different colours. In the account of the *juturi* something similar happens. During the night the men try to take possession of the animals that have come out of the springs but they generally only obtain tufts of wool.

The Yakana myth then shows that the wool obtained in this way enabled the purchase of a couple of animals that subsequently multiplied. In the case of the *juturi* myth the night hunt also resulted in an abundance of llamas. Why was wool given instead of animals? What does the colour of those wools mean in the case of Yakana? We know that the colour of the wool is important in camelids' classification (Flores Ochoa 1981), but in the Yakana myth they also talk about dyed colours and about matted-down wool, which implies the processing of wool further after shearing. Why is this important and why is this wool the one that Yakana gives? These questions remain to be answered.[13]

The reference to birds also stands out. The Huarochirano myth refers to the presence of a tinamou, or Yutu, which precedes Yakana and her offspring. Curiously enough, this is represented by another dark constellation described as 'a dark place that moves in front of Yakana' (Urioste 1983, p. 219). In this way the 'birds–camelids' association is present in the Yakana myth (Yakana and Yutu) as well as in the mythical accounts of the springs of Isluga (llamas and *ch'ullumpis*). The meaning of this relationship is not yet clear to us, but it seems to be important since it is integrated within the everyday life of the llama herders of some Andean communities. In them it is common to name the camelids after the wild birds in an affectionate manner, something that is not done in the case of other herded or domesticated species.[14]

Decoding Taira

In this section we try to establish if the categories that are present in the myths are present in SBa-43 and in what ways they are represented. We also try to demonstrate whether or not the paintings reveal a similar axis of signification.

The axis of signification: creation–conservation

In order to express the idea of 'creation' in the myths, signifiers that relate to 'fertility', 'humidity', 'darkness', and 'femininity' were used.

In the Taira panels we find at least two elements that could mean 'fertility'. On the one hand, we find the abdomens of the camelids in quadrant 3 are outlined in a thicker line than the rest of their bodies and one that is thicker than that used on other camelids (Fig. 19.7). In one of these cases the camelid has a double line or double abdomen. This could represent either the increase or the decrease of the size of the abdomen. The significance of this is that the enlargement of the abdomen is used by herders as one of the first signs of pregnancy (Palacios 1981, p. 221). In addition, in quadrant 1 a vulva is represented which not only expresses a specific sex, but also emphasizes fertility (almost by definition).

Dampness was expressed in the myths through the relationship between Yakana, water, and the springs. In the case of the rock art we enter a dimension of representation which was entirely unknown to us at the beginning of this research: the use of certain features of the environment as elements that could also be used as signifiers. In order to express dampness in Taira it would not have been necessary to resort to rock art. The site itself is the wettest one in the area. In addition, the river in this place has a more abundant flow and the springs are physically present in greater quantity than is the case elsewhere along the river's course. There is no other place where there are 16 springs in such a small area. They are the same signifiers as in the myth but this time they are physically present (Figs 19.2 & 19.8).

With 'darkness' there is a similar situation, but of a more subtle kind. We suggest

Figure 19.8   One of the Taira springs; in the background is the Loa
River. (Photograph by J. Berenguer.)

that it was expressed in the choice of the site where the panels were produced. Any
visitor who arrives at the place, even on a summer's day at three or four in the
afternoon, will immediately perceive the sharp contrast between the dazzling light
of pampa, through which one enters the canyon, and the penumbra of the canyon
itself. Taira is one of the darkest places in the valley and a place which receives only
a few hours of sunlight.[15]

We think it is significant that of all the places available for painting, the chosen
place for these specific panels was a rock shelter; that is the representations were
done at a place that was doubly dark: a rock shelter within a canyon (Fig. 19.9) We
do not know if in different topographical conditions they would have used other
elements to signify darkness, but it is clear that at Taira the physical features of the
place were fully utilized.

The general composition of panels X and XI signifies 'femininity'. The representation of the llamas suckling or with their abdomens modified contributes to this.
And, in an even more explicit way, the vulva of quadrant 1 admits no ambiguity.
Neither do the orifices and the inverted 'U' to which we have already referred,
assuming we have correctly interpreted them as female signs (Fig. 19.4). Evidence
from two other caves supports our interpretation of these as symbols of female
sexuality. In the first cave, the cave of the Damiana further down the river, there are
many engraved orifices on the walls, and an inspection revealed abundant evidences
of herding activities. More directly in the cave of the Chuchas at Incaliri (less than
30 km away), similar orifices next to the vulvas (now made by modern Indians) are
recognized by the herders as *chuchas* (Chilean expression which means 'vulvas').[16]

We have shown so far how all the signifieds associated with creation are encoded

Figure 19.9 General view of the SBa–43 rock shelter showing, from left to right, panels VIII, IX (not studied), X, and XI. At the bottom are archaeological remains of structures.

in the panels and in their environmental setting. The components of our conservation pole, breeding and increase, are equally represented in the panels.

Breeding is expressed in a number of ways within the panels. A simple look at the panels is enough to make one realize that as the camelids go up they gradually 'grow' (Fig. 19.7). This gradual increase in their size is a major sign of breeding. However, the concept in Taira art seems often to be reinforced by other signs. In this case 'breeding' is also signified by the representation of suckling llamas, all of which are located in an upper line of quadrants 3 and 4, that is at the top of the line of growth.

It seems that the artists followed a procedure similar to the previous one in order to signify the notion of 'increase'. The composition begins with very few small camelids in one single row on the lower plane and as they go up so superpositioning increases. In quadrant 3, indeed, a sensation of perspective of various planes of depth

Table 19.2 Categories represented in the rock art of SBa-43.

Categories	Yakana and water-springs (*juturi*) myths	Taira SBa-43
fertility/	+	+
sterility	–	–
breeding/	+	+
non-breeding	–	–
increase/	+	+
decrease	–	–
darkness/	+	+
clarity	–	–
humidity/	+	+
dryness	–	–
feminine/	+	+
masculine	–	–

is achieved. This is created by a particular combination of superpositioning and variations in the sizes of adjoining figures. We think that the general order of the representation in a zigzag line makes sense from this point of view. Of course, the ascending zigzag line of the camelids permits this game of planes but we think that it also contributes to the idea of 'increase' starting with the opposition between the quantity of animals present in each of the lines. If we observe closely we will see that the llamas that go from right to left do it in a row, while the ones that go from left to right seem to advance in 'herds', not in any order and covering a bigger space on the panels (Fig. 19.7).

In one way or another, through one signifier or another, it is possible to find in panels X and XI the set of categories. The same categories are represented in the rock art of SBa–43 as were expressed in the myths of Yakana and of the springs (see Table 19.2).

Therefore, it is possible to state that in the panels from site SBa–43 there is the same axis of signification as is found in the Yakana and in the *juturi* mythical accounts. Essentially all three belong to the same signifying set: *that of the beliefs relating to the creation and conservation of herds.*

More signifying relations

Of the elements of the Yakana and *juturi*, at least one is present in the Tairan art. As stated previously camelids that came out from the springs and from the 'creational holes', or *juturi*, are associated with the *ch'ullumpi*. We do not know if the ducks that swarm through the river's canyon during the summer time are really the same as these *ch'ullumpi*, but their presence could be linked with the association previously seen between birds and camelids.[17]

Therefore it is very suggestive that the same association should be found in the panels. In panels VIII and X for example, small 'fantastic' birds are pictoengraved at the upper-right corner of quadrant 1 (Fig. 19.10). They are 'fantastic' birds and

Figure 19.10 Detail of panel VIII where the flamingo or rhea may be observed, as well as four 'fantastic' birds. Representations of these birds are also found at the extreme right of quadrant 1 of panel XI (see Fig. 19.4). (Photograph by F. Maldonado.)

Figure 19.11 Detail of panel VIII which shows the figure of a *tinamou*. (Photograph by F. Maldonado.)

not real ones (see note 4). One possible interpretation of this departure from the realism which seems to characterize the rest of the representations may be found in some ethnographic versions which clearly identify the *ch'ullumpi* as mythical beings. This makes it likely that what would have been represented in Taira would be an association between some mythical bird and the camelids, as is the case today with the herders of Isluga.

The association is also present in panel VIII, the flat slab of stone on the terrace. At the centre of this, a tinamou (Yutu) is pictoengraved and is followed by other birds grouped within a well-defined space (Fig. 19.11).

Overall, in spite of the limitation of our study, the search in SBa–43 for correlations of the representations with the myths has been shown to be an enriching one. The insight from the site with respect to the mythical categories goes beyond the level of the axis of signification, for example to confirm the association between birds–camelids. A better understanding of this relationship needs further research.

Summary and conclusions

It is clear that in Taira rock art and its environment there are several features which strongly suggested to us some Andean myths about domesticated camelids. We argued, however, that it is not possible to discover the internal links between myths and rock art by basing them on apparent relations and visible similarities. These are useful to initiate research but a deeper analysis is then required. We first of all reduced the content of the myths to a number of basic categories. Once this reduction had been achieved, and after an ordering process, we arrived at an 'axis of signification', its poles being *creation* and *conservation*. The same operation was made with the Taira site, and it was found that rock art and its environment complement each other to represent the same categories and therefore the same 'axis of signification' present in the myths.

The conclusion is that there are systematic relations that link the environment of the Loa River, the Taira rock art, and certain Andean myths within a 'signifying set', associated with beliefs about the creation and conservation of herds. Instead of illustrating merely hunting or herding scenes, as had been argued in the past, the panels represent concepts concerning the origin and maintenance of the llamas and alpacas.

In our opinion the nature of Taira rock art as a 'text' has been made clear. Of course, we are aware that as such it presents different possibilities of reading and various levels of signifying. What we have done has been to get close to one of those readings and to one of those levels. Already in describing the panels we have observed an order – from the bottom to the top – which could correspond to a nature–culture axis. This ordering seems to be parallel and probably complementary to that of *creation* and *conservation*.

On the other hand we have seen that we are not dealing with just any rock art of any place. If something has been achieved with this 'contextual approach' to Taira rock art, it has been to show how the physical features of the place selected as the location of the art, are an important part of the 'texts'. Let us remember that Taira is at an intermediate stretch of the Upper Loa, it is essentially a place of mediation: between a natural hydraulic net (ravines) and another artificial one (watering channels), between a rainy zone and other zones without any rain at all, between a herding culture and an agricultural one, between a zone with vegetation and another one without any vegetation, between a high place and a low one. In sum, between a *peneño* bioma and a desert one. Taira itself is a dark and humid place which is at the same time, due to its springs, connected to the earth's depths and the volcanoes of the area. In Andean perception both of these are places where herd animals are 'born'. Therefore, it could be assumed that Taira rock art was done there and only at the place where the 'numinous' was present. It was then a sacred space, rich in reference and full of mythical content within which the rock art was integrated to complement a previous meaning. The rock art of Taira is integrated within this environment. Indeed, we suggest that there is such 'dialogue' between them that it is difficult not to think about the geography as a basic ingredient in this system of visual communication.

Obviously we are still only half-way in the task of explaining the meaning of these panels, and much farther away from establishing their role in the prehispanic communities of the Atacama Desert. Lewis-Williams (1983) assigns an important role to ritual as another of the expressions of the cognitive system of a culture in which it is necessary to find the kind of links here observed between myth and rock art. Only then is it possible to begin a detailed exegesis of the problem of meaning that may lead to a more complete explanation. As a consequence, we have extensive work ahead, looking for ethnographic data about Andean herding rites. Already, we know that when herds were put together for mating some herding cultures performed rites to ensure the fertility of the camelids. These rites were associated with springs and involved caking the animals in red ochre (Mariscotti 1978, pp. 101, 168 *et seq.*). We also know that in ceremonies like these ones, known as *empadres* or 'sowing of herds', both men and women used to carry ropes and, accompanied by drums, they used to invoke the springs or ponds where the herds had come out (Duviols 1974 *apud* Mariscotti 1978, p. 324, note 102, Palacios 1981, pp. 221–2). These ropes and drums could well correspond to the enlarged oval objects that the human figures of Taira handle (Figs 19.4 & 19.7). But rather than just looking for analogous representations in the rock art, when we analyse ritual we should look at the underlying structure of categories to see to what exent the same signifying axis is present.

Finally, let us say that to the degree to which ritual appears as a point of articulation between the belief system and the economic and social base (cf. Rappaport 1971, Drennan 1976), the study of ritual will not only permit a more complete explanation of the meaning of the Taira panels, but it will also be possible to understand their role and that of rock art better in the reproduction of the herding society of the Atacama Desert.

Acknowledgements

We thank Carlos Aldunate, Luis Cornejo, and Francisco Gallardo of the Museo Chileno de Arte Precolombino for their useful comments on an earlier version of this chapter. We also thank Gabriel Martínez and Verónica Cereceda of the Asociación de Antropólogos Sur-Andionos, who made very important suggestions about myths, rock art, and other systems of visual communication. Our thanks also to Victoria Castro of the Department of Anthropology (Universidad de Chile) for the data she has given us about Incaliri, and to Jürgen Rothman of the Silviculture Department (Universidad de Chile) for help in identifying the species of birds. We would also like to acknowledge Carolina Botto, Luis Cornejo, Fernando Maldonado, Carole Sinclaire, and Varinia Varela for their great collaboration in fieldwork.

Notes

1 Rydén (1944, pp. 91, 93) thought that its authors were the same as those that occupied a habitation site located about 500 m to the south, and suggested that they would have corresponded to the 'atacameña' population that was buried down the valley at the cemetery 'Los Antiguos' of Lasana. In today's terms this population is equivalent to phase II of the Lasana complex which has been tentatively dated between AD 800 and 1535 (Pollard 1970). There is still insufficient evidence to demonstrate this hypothesis. In any case, we share Rydèn's opinion that the panels were in use for a long period. Our excavation and thermoluminescence dates suggest that one of these rock art sites was in use around AD 500 and that at least one of its panels was made earlier than that date.

2 Without doubt the problem is caused in part by the difficulty in identifying the distinct species of camelids in the rock art. It is often impossible to discriminate between representations of wild camelids (guanaco and *vicuñas*) and domesticated ones (llamas and alpacas).

3 The oriental chain is of volcanic origin which makes it different from the occidental chain. At the height of Taira stands the San Pedro volcano (6159 m above sea-level) and a small volcanic cone called La Poruña, whos lavas ran, in the past, on the upper pampa, stopping a few hundred metres from the canyon. The Indians of the region say 'the volcano lives here'.

4 We consulted the onithologis Jürgen Rothman for this part of the research.

5 The conventionalized sequence with one figure under another and alternatively facing towards the left and the right is very frequent in Wari, Tiwanaku, and Parakas fabrics (e.g. Dockstader 1967, Fig. 99). On the other hand, the ordering of the whole composition reminds us of the *bustrofedon*, a primitive form of writing of the Old World already noted by Kroeber and others in Andean fabrics (e.g. Dockstader 1967, Fig. 130, cf. Moche ceramics in Fonan 1978, Figs 54 & 123).

6 The second part of the epigraph makes reference to other constellations which are mentioned in the last part of the text and that have been omitted here as not being directly relevant to the problem we are dealing with, at least for the time being.

7 In the Spanish language of the 16th and 17th centuries, the name of the camelids was assimilated to the Spanish sheep-herding vocabulary. Thus, there were two types of sheep and their lambs, from 'Castilla' (sheep) and 'from the land' (llamas). In this myth Polo de Ondegardo refers to the 'sheep of the land'.

8 In the Southern Hemisphere, the constellations of dark clouds, also called Yana Phuyu (Urton 1981b, p. 170) or black constellations, 'are located in that portion of the Milky

Way where the denser group of stars may be seen and the surface of luminous intensity is largest. This is why the clouds of interstellar dust (the black constellations) which cross the Milky Way appear clearer by contrast. From the Earth these black spots look like giant shadows or silhouettes set against the luminosity of the Milky Way. In contrast with the constellations which are composed of stars, which I have characterized as inanimate, geometric, or architectural, the black constellations represent animals or plants and genrally animals' (Urton 1981a, p. 479)

9   *Juturi* is 'origin and beginning; a burrow from where things come out' (Bertonio 1984 (1612), p. 170). In Quechua they are called *puquio*.

10 This conception is also present today in the Indian locality of Toconce in the basin of the Salado River no more than 60 km to the south-east of Taira.

11 Martínez (1983, p. 98) when analysing the 'gods of the mountains' states that one of the configurations of these *wak'a* that is related to the production of herds and minerals could be called 'uterine configuration'. It is characterized as being associated with inside, below, chthonic, hollow, interior light, water, ejection, and production. As can be seen from this there is a lot of similarity between this configuration and what we have called *creation*.

12 The *juturi* form part of another signifier set, that of ordering the productive space; while Yakana is part of the ordering of celestial space and its constellations.

13 It is possible that the reference to the variety of colours of the wool in Yakana does not necessarily have any relation with this myth but rather with the possible play on structural oppositions that is part of the account of the set of constellations. Urton (1981b, p. 178) points out that the black constellations that represent some animals (Mach'acuay, the serpent; Yutu, the tinamou; and Yakana, the llama) are assimilated to night, to darkness, and to the celestial in apparent contradiction with their mundane coloured earthly reality.

14 We thank Verónica Cereceda for this fact which contributed to a better understanding of the bird's role in Taira.

15 The day of greatest sunlight (summer solstice), the sun shines directly over the panels for 5 h 50 min and over the valley for 8 h 22 min, but the day of the least sunlight (winter solstice), it shines 2 h 40 min and 4 h 35 min respectively. This fact acquires relevance when one considers that Taira is 1°26' to the north of the Tropic of Capricorn.

16 We thank Victoria Castro and Carlos Aldunate for this information gathered in Incaliri in 1985.

17 It seems that for the Indians of Isluga the *ch'ullumpis* are mythical birds with a great similarity to some ducks, but without corresponding to any speific species. However, among the neighbouring Uru-Chipaya Indians of Coipasa the *ch'ullumpi* are a specific type of duck that may be seen on the streams of the Lauca River. This is the reason for the possible ambiguity of the interpretation. We thank Gabriel Martínez and Verónica Cereceda for this information which we hope to have understood correctly. On the other hand, Flores Ochoa (1981, p. 200) points out that the male camelids used as stallion animals in the Cuzco region are called *ch'ullumpi*. Thus, once again this bird is associated with the reproduction and fertility of herds (recurring themes in Taira), albeit this time with an inverse (male) sign.

References

Arguedas, J. M. 1975. *Dioses y hombres de Huarochirí*. Mexico: Siglo XXI Editores.

Berenguer, J., F. Plaza, L. Rodriguez & V. Castro 1975. Reconocimiento arqueológico del río Loa Superior, sector Santa Bárbara. *Boletín de Prehistoria de Chile* **7–8**, 49–97, Santiago.

Berenguer, J., C. Aldunate, V. Castro, C. Sinclaire & L. Cornejo 1985. Secuencia del arte rupestre en el Alto Loa: una hipótesis de trabajo. In *Estudios en arte rupestre*, C. Aldunate, J. Berenguer & V. Castro (eds). Santiago: Museo Chileno de Arte Precolombino.

Bertonio, L. 1984 (1612). *Volcabulario de la lengua Aymara*. Cochabama: Ediciones CERES.

Dockstader, F. 1967. *Indian art in South America*. Greenwich, Conn.: New York Graphic Society.

Donnan, C. B. 1978. *Moche art of Peru*. University of California, Los Angeles: Museum of Cultural History.

Drennan, R. D. 1976. Religion and social evolution in formative Mesoamerica. In *The early Mesoamerican village*, K. V. Flannery (ed.), 345–68, New York: Academic Press.

Duvios, P. 1978. Camaquen, Upani: un concept animiste des anciens péruviens. *Amerikanistiche Studien* **20**, 1, 132–44.

Flores Ochoa, J. 1981. Clasificación y nominación de camélidos sudamericanos. In *La tecnología en el mundo andino*, H. Letchman & A. M. Soldi (eds), 195–215, Mexico: Universidad Autónoma de México.

Gilmore, R. M. 1950. Fauna and ethnology of South America. In *Handbook of South American Indians*, J. H. Steward (ed.), Vol. 6, 345–464. Washington, DC: Smithsonian Institute.

Gow, D. & R. Gow 1975. La alpaca en el mito y el ritual. *Allpanchis* **8**, 141–64. Cuzco.

Lewis-Williams, J. D. 1982. The economic and social context of Southern San rock art. *Current Anthropology* **23** (4), 429–49.

Lewis-Williams, J. D. 1983. Introductory essay: science and rock art. *Southern African Archaeology Society Goodwin Ser.* **4**, 3–13.

Mariscotti, A. M. 1978. Pachamama Santa Tierra. In *Indiana*, Supplement 8. Berlin: Gebr. Mann Verlag.

Martínez, G. 1976. El sistema de los Uywiris en Isluga. In *Homenaje al Dr. Gustavo Le Paige SJ*, L. Núñez (ed.), 255–327. Anales de la Universidad del Norte: Antofagasta.

Martínez, G. 1983. Los dioses de los cerros en los andes. *Journal de la Société des Américanistes* **LXIX**, 85–116.

Mostny, G. 1969. Ideas mágico-religiosas de los Atacamas. *Boletín del Museo Nacional de Historia Natural* **30**, 129–45.

Mostny, G. & H. Niemeyer. 1983. *Arte rupestre chileno*, Serie el Patrimonio Cultural Chileno, Depto de Extensión Cultural del Ministerio de Educación, Santiago.

Niemeyer, H. 1967. Un nuevo sitio de art rupestre en Taira. *Revista Universitaria* **LII**, 159–64.

Niemeyer, H. 1972. *Las pinturas rupestres de la sierra de Arica*. Santiago: Editorial Jerónimo de Vivar.

Niemeyer, H. 1979. *Estudio de recionalización del área de riego del río Loa*. Santiago: Ministerio de Obras Públicas.

Ortiz, A. 1908. *Huarochirí, 400 años después*, Fondo Editorial, Universidad Católica del Perú, Lima.

Palacios, F. 1981. Tecnología del pastoreo. In *La tecnología en el mundo andino*, H. Letchman & A. M. Soldi (eds), 217–32, Mexico: Universidad Autónoma de México.

Pollard, G. C. 1970. *The cultural ecology of ceramic-stage settlement of the Atacama Desert*. Doctoral thesis. Columbia University, published on demand by University Microfilm International, Ann Arbor, Michigan.

Polo de Ondegardo, J. 1961. (1554). Errores y superticiones de los indios . . . In *Colección de libros y documentos referentes a la historia del Perú*, Lima.

Rappaport, R. A. 1971. Ritual, sanctity and cybernetics. *American Anthropologist* **73**, 59–76.

Rydén, S. 1944. *Contributions to the archaeology of the Rio Loa Region*. Göteborg: Elanders Boktryckeri Aktiebolag.

Taylor, G. 1976. Camay, camac et camasca dans le manuscrit quechua de Huarochirí. *Journal de la Société des Américanistes* **LXIII**, 231–44.

Taylor, G. 1980. *Rites et traditions de Huarochirí*. Paris: L'Harmattan.

Urioste, J. 1983. *Hijos de Pariya Qaqa: la tradición oral de Waru Chiri*, 2 vols. New York: Syracuse University.

Urton, G. 1981a. La orientación en la astronomía Quechua e Inca. In *La tecnología en el mundo andino*, H. Letchman & A. M. Soldi (eds), Vol. 1, 475–90. Mexico: Universidad Autónoma de México.

Urton, G. 1981b. *At the crossroads of the earth and the sky: an Andean cosmology*. Austin: University of Texas Press.

Weischet, W. 1975. Las condiciones climáticas del desierto de Atacama como desierto extremo de la tierra. *Norte Grande* **3–4**, 363–73.

Zuidema, T. & G. Urton 1976. La constelación de la Llama en los Andes peruanos. *Allpanchis* **9**, 59–119.

20 *Social roles of animal iconography: implications for archaeology from Hopi and Zuni ethnographic sources*

NANCY H. OLSEN

This chapter is about culture change and cultural continuity using data from western Pueblo people who live in villages at the southern tip of Black Mesa, Arizona, and on the Mogollon Rim between New Mexico and Arizona. It has two underlying premises. The first is that Hopi and Zuni people have successfully resisted acculturation efforts by the dominant society of the United States (Brew 1979, p. 522). The second is that Pueblo people are descendants of prehistoric Anasazi who built towns and settlements at Mesa Verde, Colorado, Chaco Canyon, New Mexico, on the Pajarito Plateau, New Mexico, and on Black Mesa, Arizona.

Culture change, as advanced by Steward (1955) provided American archaeology with a paradigm which could be used to explain and order differences observed in archaeological assemblages and data sets from the field. Change is a uniformitarian law. However, while culture changes, it also contains elements which continue through change. I like to call those elements 'common denominators'. They act as integrative agents for culture, creating limits of tolerance for change.

The purpose of this study is to focus on one cultural component or 'common denominator' that may account, at least in part, for Hopi and Zuni continuity of culture from prehistoric times to the present.

Graphic images, documented by ethnographers of the western Pueblos provide evidence of an iconographic system in operation for over 100 years. Continuities are formal and semantic, such that, when records are consolidated, a 'vocabulary' of graphic images emerges which can be traced historically and culturally to reveal a complex iconography in use in a variety of contexts over time.

It is proposed here that the imagery is an externalization of an unseen, but necessary, component of culture – shared knowledge (cf. Geertz 1973, p. 89). Recognition of those visual elements and meanings in their specific combinations constitutes and maintains boundaries between social subgroups (Cohen 1985, p. 74) within Hopi and Zuni culture, such as clan identification, village residence, *kiva* affiliation, and society statuses.

Iconographic continuity, then, is expressed by traditional use of certain images in particular contexts on a continuing basis. The significance of continuities differ according to Hopi, Zuni, or social scientist perspectives. While social scientists are interested in the social meanings communicated by the iconography, or the degree to which it is embedded in the culture, the native Americans consider their past and present joined by means of it. A 'lexicon' of shapes, images, and colours form basic group identities which link them with the past (Stevenson 1904, p. 1104, Stephen & Parsons 1936, p. 110, Young 1985, p. 6). 'The People' searched for their prophesied home or 'centre of the world', travelling north, south, east, and west. As the ancestors travelled, they stopped from time to time and built pueblos, planted corn, beans and squash, cotton, tobacco, and performed their ceremonies. Now clans relate stories of their oral traditions which link them with one or another direction of migration, and dances contributed to the good of the whole (Fewkes 1896, p. 151, Sekaquaptewa & Udall 1969, p. 82, Lomatewama 1983, Cordell & Jones 1985, p. 60). By tracing the development of western Pueblo iconography in its various media, following it back into prehistory as far as possible, the cognitive use of art and developmental stages of that cognitive system may be unravelled.

To do this in a manner satisfactory to both Pueblo people and science, a cross-cultural perspective will be used that recognizes differences between an insider's 'emic' perception of their iconography and the outsider's 'etic' view. In doing so, oral tradition is separated from scientific analysis in order to appreciate the value of each.

The emic perception of Pueblo images maintains that the knowledge and information contained in the forms and context combinations is a reminder of group identity, social roles, obligations to each other, and to the Earth (Ortiz 1979). Etically, graphic images document economic values, contain calendrical notations, history, legal decisions, and enumerations, validate political office, and bank religious knowledge. The point is argued at length in an earlier analysis (Olsen 1985, p. 43) that Zuni and Hopi iconographies function mnemonically, acting as the device which allows retrieval of cultural information in the collective, long-term cultural memory.

Cultural attitudes of Indians and non-Indians differ towards the iconographic 'lexicon' (Highwater 1976, p. 8, Sturtevant 1986, p. 23). While mainstream society perceives non-alphabetic forms as art and therefore describes and analyses Pueblo iconography in terms customarily reserved for art, such as style or composition, members of the western Pueblos perceive the same images as direct communication. In order to bridge those difference this chapter follows ideational theories of culture established in semiotics (Sebeok 1977, Eco 1984) and by Lévi-Strauss (1963, 1982), Goodenough (1968), and Geertz (1973). Forms and meanings are separated temporarily in order to examine relationships of form with contexts. Later, indigenous meanings are added in order to illustrate distributions of meaning with form.

Now it is possible to construct a paradigm for archaeology based on the linguistic and cognitive anthropological studies. Since such studies have found that ideographic and logographic writing develops and changes slowly (Voegelin & Voegelin 1961, Wang 1973), we can ask whether pictographic elements of Hopi and Zuni might display similar evolutionary principles. Identical elements located in corresponding contexts of the archaeological record which are expected to have been authored by Hopi and Zuni predecessors, the western Anasazi, might contain analogous features. A range of elements might be expected to represent, through use on various media, the graphic 'lexicon' of those ancestors. Comparisons between 'lexicons' may show changes or continuities, and give present-day scholars some insight into the developmental processes which have taken place between the past and the present.

Representational categories in the present-day 'lexicon'

Hopi and Zuni people date their present towns on the southern tip of Black Mesa, Arizona, and on the Zuni River in New Mexico to *c.* AD 1100 (Brew 1979, p. 514, Woodbury 1979, p. 468), but claim ancestry with prehistoric sites in south-western Colorado, southern Utah, and northern Arizona, down to and including Black Mesa (Fewkes 1894, p. 394, 1896, p. 151). Individuals studying the basketry fragments of the Walpi Project (Adovasio & Andrews 1981) remarked upon the similarity of the items to those found at Mesa Verde (Fig. 20.1). If the culture is unbroken from at least AD 1100 to the present, we may logically conclude that present visual vocabularies (and each element in them) are the products of centuries of repetition and gradual modification. We can ask questions which will define and describe the 'lexicon'.

When Fewkes (1892, 1894, 1896, 1897, 1898, 1900, 1903), Mallory (1893), Stevenson (1904), Cushing (1920, 1972), and Stephen (Stephen & Parsons 1936) were recording Hopi and Zuni cultures in the last decades of the 1800s and the early years of the present century, interest ran high about ceremonial aspects of native American life. Thus ethnographies reported much about the religious life of the community and sacrificed other aspects. Later ethnographers such as Colton & Colton (1931), Forde (1931, 1949), Beaglehole (1937), Colton (1937), Titiev (1937, 1944), Hack (1942) and Eggan (1950) focused on social and economic aspects to fill in the etic picture of western Pueblo life.

More recently, Pueblo individuals such as Edward Dozier (1966, 1970), Alfonso Ortiz (1969), and Emory Sekaquaptewa (1976) have provided science with literature about the emic view. Autobiographies of Hopi people (Talayesva & Simmons 1942, Qoyawayma 1964, Sekaquaptewa & Udall 1969), poetry by Ramson Lomatewama (1983), paintings by Hopi artists of Second Mesa, including Delbridge Honanie, Terrance Talaswaima, Milland Lomakema, Michael Kabotie, and Neil David Sr., or older artists like Fred Kabotie or Otis Polelonema have expressed emic views of Pueblo. Since those presentations of traditional elements are in formats which the outside world recognizes, the artistic and literary expressions are understood better than the elements found incised in rock faces around the Hopi Mesas and Zuni shrines.

Elements abstracted through years of use appeared to early documentarians as 'simple', but can now be appreciated by Pueblo art *aficionados* as components of a complex system used in very particular ways, holding layers of contextual meanings together with historical significance, like a toothpick might hold together layers of a club sandwich.

Collection of graphic representations from early and recent sources provides a representative sample of images (or forms) along with contexts and meanings. The motifs are sometimes thought to have 'translatable' meanings, in the same way that

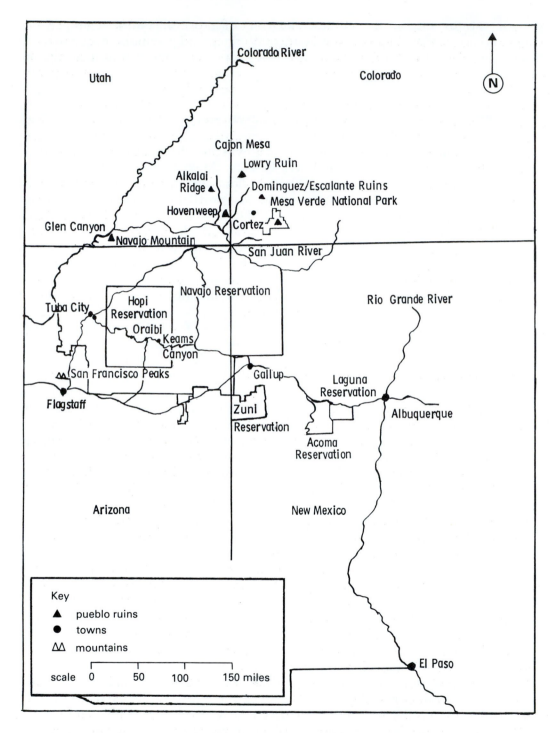

Figure 20.1 Hopi and Zuni Pueblos in relation to the Mesa Verde-Hovenweep region.

Romance languages have one-to-one meanings, generally speaking. However, a Zuni exhibit of their rock art (Hopi Cultural Centre 1981), specifically states that there is no one meaning for a motif; often the meanings change every time contexts change. It is at this point in this study, that meanings are separated from elements of form for the sake of discovering relationships between forms and contexts.

Separation of meaning from elements shows that identical forms appear in different contexts. Further, motif repetitions were relatively common between Hopi and Zuni visual vocabularies. Enough similarity of elements exists to argue that Hopi and Zuni iconographies represent an overlapping communication system (Olsen 1985, p. 32).

When contextual meanings were combined with the sign form, the information transmitted could be categorized by subject matter. Clan identification, history, origin and migration stories, affirmation of political office, political status, land allotment decisions, communication with ancestors, counts of years, people, irrigation tallies, and deities who are seasonally important, all could be determined from the settings in the emic view. It is anticipated that further investigation will show links with other Pueblo groups of western Pueblo designation, such as Acoma and Laguna. Relationships with eastern Pueblo iconography are expected to exist as well, but with some major divisions in contextual use, differences of meaning and/or seasonal and ceremonial intent.

Quantitative analysis of forms from ethnographies

Elements and their variations taken from their ethnographic sources separate into 236 discrete classifications of sign form. Those sources include *Hopi journal of Alexander Stephen* (Stephen & Parsons 1936), Stevenson's *The Zuni Indians, their mythology, esoteric fraternities and ceremonies* (1904), Fewkes' *Hopi kachinas drawn by native artists* (1903), Cushing's *Zuni fetishes* (1972) and *Zuni breadstuffs* (1920), Colton's *Hopi kachina dolls* (1949) and *Black sand* (1937), and Titiev's 'A Hopi salt expedition' (1937), *Old Oraibi, a study of the Hopi Indians of Third Mesa* (1944), Wright's *Hopi silver; the history and hallmarks of Hopi silversmithing* (1982), and the Hopi Arts and Crafts – Silvercrafts Cooperative Guild brochure (n.d.). Every entry which contained a picture, native meaning, and context was recorded and counted.

This data-set could have been larger but would only have become redundant. Although the type of sampling was dependent upon authors' choices and is something of a 'grab sample', it is hoped that by combining ethnographic information from several different sources, whatever bias exists will be balanced out. The number of times that each element appeared in a given context was counted, then contexts and motifs were numbered and entered into a statistics package (Statpak) created for the IBM Personal Computer.

Descriptive statistics allows investigation of the data-set to understand what characteristics it contains. Using the inference of statistics, the degree to which the data-set contains enough variation to represent a 'normal' population can be estimated. It allows comparison between variables, it measures frequency distributions in order to demonstrate users' preferences and cultural choices based on tradition.

Ultimately, the information about the data-set will be used to make interpretations about the sample populations for theory development.

The 236 discrete classifications of sign form which were identified were grouped into general classifications such as: anthropomorphic, zoomorphic, biomorphic, geometric, land and weather, Sun/Moon/stars, colours, and man-made artefacts (such as bows). A secondary classification refined the categories into whole figures, head/parts, paws/hands/feet, paw/hand/footprint, skin/bone/horns, straight lines, squares, curves, circles, triangles, cloth, feathers, stairsteps, diamond, combination curves/lines, feathers and colours (red, blue, yellow, green, and a black and white combination). Contexts counted were grouped as *kiva* hatchway, *kiva* floor/altar, *kiva* floor/sand painting, *kiva* wall, *kiva* altar/backdrop or background, *kiva* altar/figures or objects, irrigation, farm fields, granary, springs or seeps, next to trail, on the trail, runner body paint, shrine, *kachina* outfits, *kachina* body paint, *kachina* mask, priest body paint, priest head-dress and paraphernalia, society initiate's body paint, ceremonial kilts/belts/cloaks (woven), house rooms, cliffs and boulders, governor's petition, and silversmith's hallmark. Contexts which are less self-evident, but culturally important, such as seasons in which a motif appears and *kiva* affiliation of motif use, were available from the ethnographies and included in the list.

Descriptive statistics confirmed that the population of sign forms is normal and representative in so far as the population contained enough repetitions in each category to show a bell-shaped curve with a mean of 2.676, a variance of 3.221, and a standard deviation of 1.795. Within the normal parameters, however, the statistics programme showed that the curve was skewed to the left in contexts of *kiva* walls, *kiva* hatchway, shrine, *kachina* masks, priest head-dresses and paraphernalia, society initiate's body paint motifs, ceremonial kilts/belts/cloaks, and cliffs, boulders, *kiva* backdrops and *kiva* altar figures. Two other populations, *kiva* sand paintings and *kachina* outfits contexts showed bi-modality, or two curves instead of one per context. Intensive preference for certain elements (such as feathers) causes such repetition of a single element in a particular context that skewness may occur as a result. Additionally, the focus of the ethnographer recording data may also cause skewness, particularly in an era when unbiased random samples were unknown. A larger data-set might correct the skewness and bi-modalities; or the categories may need further dividing to correct the problem since skewness and bi-modality usually indicate that more than one event is present within the classification.

Relative frequency distributions of the entire sample show that anthropomorphic figures occupy 36.4 per cent of the sample, biomorphic (plants/insects) images represent 30.2 per cent, zoomorphic motifs take up 11.4 per cent of the sample, geometric elements are 10.8 per cent, celestial bodies occupy 4.2 per cent, and man-made artefacts are 3.1 per cent. Motifs used habitually in black and white combinations represent 1.8 per cent of the total sample population.

Categories containing homogeneous ranks of distribution were slightly different from the above distribution. While geometric motifs, for example, ranked fourth in the total sample percentage, it is the most homogeneously distributed category, appearing in every context, season, and *kiva*. It is so prevalent throughout Pueblo representation that it could be considered one component of Pueblo 'style'. Ranking second in homogeneous distribution and pervading nearly every context with connotations specific to time, place, and event, are the representations of mammals, birds, reptiles, and amphibians. However, certain of the classifications dominated specific categories of time and/or *kiva*; usually the association went together (for example, a chevron shape in Horn Kiva).

There are two different kinds of zoomorphic representations, man-made and man-modified ones. The latter consists of the animal itself or parts of the animal used as a sign. The former condition includes two-dimensional (flat) illustrations of animals drawn, painted, or incised on flat, permanent surfaces such as *kiva* walls, rock faces, *kiva* altar backdrops and curtains, shrines, and farm-field boulders. The three-dimensional reproductions consist of animal, bird, and reptile stone carvings which are placed on *kiva* altars, or around sand paintings. In either case, the man-made representations are abstractions of the true creature, using only significant features of the species as identifying shapes. Proportions, characteristic ways of carrying tail feathers, wings, horns or antlers, or movement, potentially represent, or stand for, the whole, real creature.

Similarities which can be found in a bear's paw-print and badger's paw-print are not confused because of the relative proportions of pad to claws. The hook of the eagle's beak can be distinguished from a parrot's beak by the relative proportions in body shape and tail feathers. In three-dimensional carvings, the abstracted use of two or three features is continued, but the colour of the stone used may have more symbolic value than representational value. The same animal or bird, such as those symbolizing the guardians of the six directions (Cushing 1972), may be represented in several colours of stone, each representing a different 'brother' or assistant to the direction guardian.

When meanings are restored to form and context, documented evidence of social categories emerges such that animals, birds, reptiles, and amphibians are used exclusively to refer to man-made situations; such as clan symbols, as representatives of power for curing, as assistants to spirits and *kachinas*, and as messengers for The People. In the emic view, animals have power to travel between men and spirits/*kachinas* to mediate between them. The natural abilities of an animal or bird are interwoven with their powers in myths and histories. Thus, the shrike on *kiva* walls recalls in ceremonial context the shrike's assistance to The People when they were searching for the opening into this world from the previous one. The shrike was the only bird who could fly high enough to find the opening, yet be small enough to fly through it (Nequatewa 1936, p. 21). The shrike is therefore honoured by remembrance.

The man-made representations have a symbolic referent in that the represented image does not refer to itself, but something *other*. The representation is transformed meaning with intrinsic significance for a social group of Hopi or Zuni – a clan or society. However, the man-modified representations designate the animal itself in its capacity as assistant to man, implying its spiritual power. In this group the actual parts of the animal are used. The whole bodies of a skunk, weasel, and raccoon, attached to a strung bow, with eagle feathers attached gives notice at the *kiva* hatchway of a ceremonial event, and keeps away bad spirits. Bear claws, badger claws, or porcupine claws are worn as necklaces by Snake Society men to indicate status as good warriors (Stephen & Parsons 1936, p. 709).

The capacities of the animal, bird, or living reptile are many, and while their presence adds power or brings efficacy to the religious event, the animal's parts also signify the economic side of Pueblo life, since they represent procurement and earned status.

A third category of representation is difficult to pigeon hole neatly. It is made up of animals which are larger than life, or are part animal, part deity or spirit, or part man. Water serpents belong to this classification. Their presence is central to ceremonies which occur at the spring equinox at Hopi and Zuni. Although the names are different in Hopi and Zuni languages, appearances are enough alike to leave no doubt in either emic or etic views as to whom the representations refer in the oral traditions. Further, the appearances never change from year to year, thus the finished appearance, as well as all the individual motifs on the water serpents, become associated with that representation and that personification.

'Ogre' *kachinas* appear with animal-like heads containing a wide snout with many sharp teeth. While the rest of the figure is a man's body, the overall image is ferocious. The emic view of the Nata'shka Father *kachina* mask is fear. This *kachina* is particularly responsible for enforcing correct Hopi behaviour on children (Hartman Lomawaima pers. comm.). The etic view of the *kachina* and his helpers is that of an agent of social control. Depending on how traditional or progressive the Hopi village is, the *kachina* has the duty of frightening the children into wanting to follow the correct Hopi ways of life.

Horns, antlers, and feathers are used to construct 240 different *kachina* masks, which are not necessarily animal in appearance. Some of the *kachina* spirits represent animals or birds such as the Eagle Kachina, or the Tcub Kachina (pronghorn antelope) whose herds existed in Hopi and Zuni areas 100 years ago. Other *kachina* masks are representations of abstract concepts whose identification comes about through combinations of geometric motifs and horn, antler, or feather additions and combinations. The composite whole mask appears fantastic (in the art historical sense of the word), but stands for some Hopi or Zuni value, concept, or deity which has earned a place of honour in the society.

In some cultural systems, animals represent primarily totemic figures. Native American groups such as the north-west coast Kwakiutl, Haida, Tlingit, or Tsminshin have oral traditions which link a family lineage to a particular animal or bird, due to a pact, marriage, gifts of special knowledge, or rights to hunt or fish in a given territory bestowed upon an ancestor of the lineage by that animal (Burland 1965, p. 24, Malin 1978, p. 46, Levi-Strauss 1982, p. 14). Lineages and inheritance are expressed in carved totem poles and family crest masks which can contain as many as three animal/bird/fish/ancestor faces in one mask.

In contrast, 73 Hopi and Zuni clan symbol categories make up the representative sample's portion of clan identifications, but only 31 per cent of them are animal, bird, reptile, or amphibian (Olsen 1986, pp. 7–9). The remaining 69 per cent are distributed among other classifications, such as Earth, Sun, Cloud, Tobacco, Corn, Bow, Flute, or *Kachina*. Therefore, animal clan symbols make up the largest number in the clan symbol category, but do not dominate.

Zoomorphic elements appear outside the clan symbol category in sodality contexts as well, such as the Snake Society or as a custodian of curing powers such as the Mountain Lion or Badger. Often the zoomorphic elements appear to have a significant relationship with their contexts, but a chi-square test of probability can provide mathematical corroboration. In this test, the null hypothesis states that there is no symbolic relationship between animal, bird, reptile, and amphibian representations and their context. The alternative hypothesis states that a significant relationship exists. At the 95 per cent confidence level and higher, significant relationships appeared in *kiva* altar backdrops, shrines, *kachina* masks, priest head-dresses and ceremonial paraphernalia, seasons, *kiva* classifications, governor's petition, and hallmark contexts. At a little less than 95 per cent confidence level, the *kiva* altar category showed a correlation of animals and contexts, which might be considered a trend rather than a confirmed association.

In the shrine, governor's petition, and hallmark contexts, where animal and non-animal clan symbols are used as a means of self-identification, the relationship between contexts and animals' images remained the most constant. Further, clan symbols represent the most public, egalitarian type of information to which everyone in the Pueblo society has access, and are the most stable, unchanging motifs in the 100 years of Hopi and Zuni ethnographic documentation. The images do not change diachronically or synchronically from either the emic or etic perspective. Traditionally, each person makes a version of their clan symbol which identifies the individual. Usually the range of variation is narrow, representing variations on a conceptual theme.

Individual motifs were documented by Mallory in 1886, by Colton & Colton in 1931, by Titiev in 1937 and identified, in all cases, by contemporary Hopi. Recently the range of variation has changed from a limited number to a broader range of variation, since Hopi and Zuni silversmiths recently adopted the use of clan symbols as hallmarks in their work (Hopi Arts and Crafts Guild n.d., Wright 1982). In such a context, full animal shapes are often too large for the media, hence a large variety of paw-print marks differentiate members of the Bear Clan, or the Badger Clan, the Rabbit Clan, and so on. Others chose highly abstracted silhouettes to signify the Parrot Clan, Snake Clan, or Turkey Clan.

Clan symbols also designate boundaries of ownership on farm-field boulders. They contain information regarding resolutions over boundary disputes (Forde 1931, p. 367). The hypothesis is that the clan symbols appeared in the farm fields during the turn of the century when arroyo down-cutting was making farm fields of Third Mesa unusable and overpopulation was creating a greater demand (Titiev 1944, Bradfield 1971).

A second chi-square test of probability was done in order to investigate the degree to which animal symbols appearing on permanent surfaces, such as *kiva* walls, *kiva* floor, seeps and springs, next to a trail, in a shrine, house room walls, cliffs, and boulders, are clan symbols. The null hypothesis states that there will be no significant relationship between elements found in those places and clan symbols. The alternative hypothesis declares a significant relationship.

In all variables but one, no significant relationship could be established at the 95 per cent confidence level. That means that the null hypothesis could not be rejected. The single exception was the shrine context where a strong relationship could be demonstrated at a 98.7 confidence level. In other settings, such as the irrigation/farm field/granary, and boulders next to the trail, the appearance of clan symbols was sufficiently random for the statistical package to be unable to establish the clan symbol presence as habitual or intentional with the context. The fact that the chi-square test could not reject the null hypothesis for the farm fields seems to confirm more strongly the speculation that their appearance on the boulders was due to an episode in Hopi history rather than a cultural habit. However, the focus on boundaries as recipients of information may not be an occasional behaviour, if one considers Whorf's analysis of the Hopi language (Whorf 1956). In his discussion on the Hopi perception of space, Whorf notes that there are 19 words for walls, edges, boundaries, but only two for designating enclosed space (Whorf 1956, p. 200). The implication here is that the cultural affinity to use space and boundary terms as 'locator' parts of speech (ibid., pp. 201–2) may account for clan symbols and other graphic elements' presence along the trails, on cliffs as well as farm fields. More investigation is required on this topic.

Finally, the patterning of motif appearance in and around the towns shows the manner in which the cultural matrix of shared knowledge extends from the living areas into the landscape to special use locations. The ethnographies make it quite clear that seeps, shrines, and boulders which hold clan history are visited on a regular basis and are part of the invisible body of information which makes up the world-view of traditional Hopi and Zuni people.

Inferences for archaeology

The custom of cutting clan symbols into lithic surfaces in shrine contexts is not recent. The tradition was old in the 1880s when Mallory (1886, p. 29) recorded the information from a Hopi at Willow Springs. Comparing historical patterns of cognitive organization with ones from the archaeological record brings questions to mind regarding the antiquity of the iconographic system.

In the American Southwest, rock art studies have gone in two directions. One is the characterization of the technique and form of the elements in stylistic terms, as would be appropriate if the rock art was 'art' in the Western European sense of the word. Since rock art can not be dated directly, but only indirectly by association with the archaeological sites where it is found or nearby, the style of the 'art' is dated by the association with the surface indications of the site's time period (Turner 1963, Grant 1967, Schaafsma 1971, 1980). Since assemblages are usually dated by their stratigraphic provenances, with stylistic assignments made from the dated association, to date rock art by style is reversing the process and is in danger of becoming circular logic and self-perpetuating.

The other direction is toward seeking ethnographic information about rock art of an ethnic group in order to build explanations for the images appearing on canyon walls and boulders in the archaeological record (Grant 1978, Hopi Cultural Centre 1981, Young 1985).

In the Four Corners region of the American Southwest, the same art could be evidence of Desert Archaic Indians who occupied the region beginning c. 2000 BC, Basketmaker or Anasazi who farmed in the area c. 200 BC to AD 1300, Navajo who appeared in the region after AD 1500, or southern Ute whose ancestors may have occupied the area side-by-side with the Anasazi (Winter 1985, p. 24). Therefore, strategies for discovering which ethnic hand may have created images are an important consideration in building theory.

Binford has stated that it is necessary to start theory-building with definitions (1977, p. 29). He specifies that a definition declares 'a relationship between a concept, word or phrase, and a class of empirical or observable experience'. Descriptive definitions of rock art systematize possible chronological sequences of style development, but as yet no analytical definition which is compatible with information reported by ethnographic sources or an emic perception has been considered for the American Southwest.

Since non-verbal communication systems have come under scrutiny by anthropologists, the examination of graphic systems have produced very interesting results (Taylor 1975, Marcus 1980, Geertz 1983, Kubik 1986). It is evident that visual communication systems exist as a condition of human life in many parts of the world where oral traditions maintain cultural information. Further, ethnographies provide evidence of the strategies used by cultures for organizing their images and giving them meanings; strategies which can be applied to the archaeological record, first toward developing theory useful for explanation of the rock art and, second, toward discovery of the ethnicity of the creator.

A working definition, developed from the above discussion, may be expressed in the following manner: rock art is that portion of a culture's visual communication system which is painted and incised onto rock surfaces. The system will consist of a 'lexicon' of elements particular to the culture, will have affinities for certain contexts, and will show organizational principles at work indicating cognitive structure.

In 1974–77 an opportunity to test the new definition of rock art presented itself. A research project designed to study the adaptation of Anasazi to Cajon Mesa offered a chance to investigate the relationships between the reconstructed regional economic system and the rock art found associated with the sites (Fig. 20.2). A field school of San Jose State University under the direction of Dr J. C. Winter (1975, 1976, 1977) set up camp at Hovenweep National Monument on Cajon Mesa. The project was one of the first in the Mesa Verde area to focus on environmental adaptation as a research design, specifically looking for evidence of prehistoric farming methods developed for the semi-arid country. In three summers' work 1 per cent of the total Cajon Mesa acreage was surveyed in sections of 40 square metre-grids located in a non-stratified, random sampling strategy.

Since Anasazi are known to have planted corn, beans and squash in the Four Corners area since AD 500, the Hovenweep Archaeological Project used a systems theory model of culture as the basis for designing research questions. The test questions for rock art, therefore, could be formulated on the basis of appearance, form, repetition, archaeological contexts identified independently of the elements, and clustering, and be treated as another subsystem (Olsen 1980).

As the farming complex began to emerge from the data, a group of graphic images began to emerge also. Formal characteristics of the graphic elements repeated in the same place, in several places, in pairs, and with similar site features, was consistent

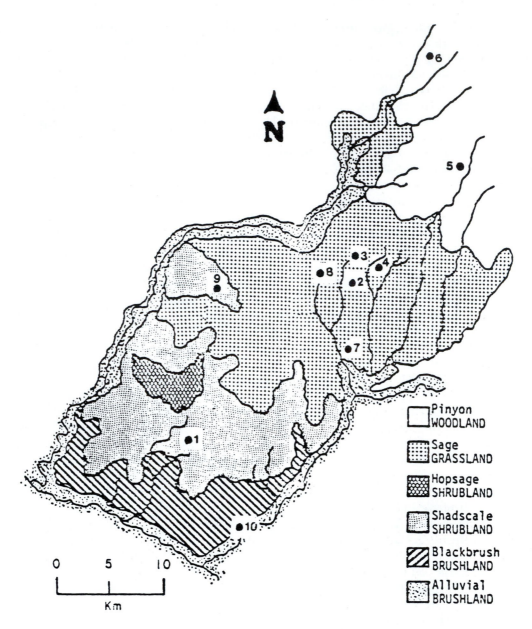

Figure 20.2 Rock art sites associated with Hovenweep/Cajon Mesa environmental zones (from Winter 1976): (1) Hov. 51–52; (2) Hov. 430; (3) Hov. 57–58; (4) Hov. 64–67; (5) Hov. 600; (6) Hov. 664, 665; (7) Hov. 536; (8) Hov. 4, 8, 15, 366; (9) Hov. 480; (10) Hov. 608, 612.

with Anasazi limited and multiple use sites, making Anasazi authorship a strong possibility (Olsen 1986, pp. 7–9).

The Anasazi graphic repertoire assembled from Hovenweep sites and Mesa Verde sites and artefacts was more complex and non-random than expected. While portable items such as pottery, bone beads, and twined sandals contained predominantly abstract (geometric) elements, non-portable locations such as rock walls, boulders, *kiva* plasters, room plasters, and building stones contained predominantly two-dimensional zoomorphic and anthropomorphic images (Figs 20.3, 20.4, & 20.5). A separate category of three-dimensional objects (carved) contained nearly 100 per cent zoomorphic elements. Images and contexts analogous to the ethnographic ones suggest symbolic semantic intent on the part of the creators, hence the investigation of the prehistoric motifs took the standpoint that they could also assemble into a 'lexicon'.

Comparison of ethnographic Hopi and Zuni elements with motifs thought to be produced by Anasazi showed that 25 per cent are identical in form and potentially overlap. However, while 60 per cent of contemporary rock art symbols are clan symbols (animal and non-animal), only 38 per cent of images from the prehistoric 'lexicon' which are identical in form may stand for early clan/sodality or totemic affiliation. Most of the potential clan motifs which can be compared with the historic images are zoomorphic, either whole images or hoof and bird tracks.

Three hypotheses are suggested which might explain the percentage difference in

Figure 20.3   Hovenweep Castle ruins showing the 'keyhole'-shaped doorway.

Figure 20.4   Hovenweep no. 8 showing 'keyhole' sign, bird, and spiral.

symbolic use of clan images. First, some of the Anasazi motifs may be clan symbols which are not recognized because they have disappeared from the oral traditions or have transferred their attribution to a different category, such as mythology. Second, the difference in percentage may signify that more information than ownership, identity, or 'locater' information was included in the prehistoric record. A third hypothesis explaining the larger clan symbol population now, argues that Hopi and Zuni populations are known to be aggregations of people from different places. Oral histories tell of migrations to Hopi and Zuni from four directions. The Mesa Verde–Hovenweep area is only one of those directions and would therefore not represent the same breadth of clan variability which the present Hopi mesas now do.

Storage/granary sites having associated features of ceremonial use contained non-random appearances of mountain sheep, elk, and/or deer hoof-prints or whole figures (Fig. 20.6). Since the mesa environment proved to be unable to support herds of large game animals in the past (White 1977, p. 337), the probability that the appearance of these animals in rock art represents a social rather than a hunting intent is strong. A present thin population of mule deer (*Odocoileus hemionus*) continue to live in the northern pinyon–juniper zone of the mesa, but prehistorically the only evidence of deer in the middens was as a shaped tool. Faunal food-sources at Hovenweep were identified as rabbit, turkey, and other small game (ibid.). In fact, garden hunting is proposed as a possible explanation for the character of faunal assemblages in the archaeological records of the Mesa Verde–Hovenweep area (Neusius 1984).

Figure 20.5 Possible Anasazi shrine near Canon Ball Mesa, showing mountain lion paw-prints, human hand, and an anthropomorphic figure.

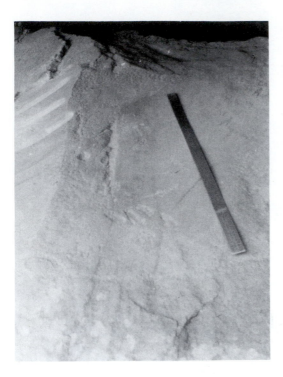

Figure 20.6 Site of granary/storage and of a possible *kiva*/special case site. Shows animal prints and grinding grooves.

More recently the Dolores Archaeological Project (1978–85) included a rock art study of the Dolores River Valley, using the research questions already in place with interesting results (Ives 1986). The Dolores River Valley is about 112 km east of Hovenweep, and contains many elements identical with Hovenweep ones. Ives found that the greatest diversity of rock art motifs appeared during periods when population began moving into the valley during Ceramic period 1. The next period showing the second greatest motif diversity was Ceramic period 4, when climatic conditions for agriculture deteriorated and the population was decreasing (Ives 1986, p. 252).

A contingency table was developed to test the dependence of motifs from Hovenweep–Mesa Verde on seven general host media, such as cliffs/boulders/rock shelters, *kiva* plasters, room walls, building stones, ceramics, weaving, carved stone, and incised bone (Olsen 1986, p. 23). The analysis of degree of dependency of motifs on the locations, using chi-squared values and Cramer's V-test showed strong intentional association. Linking statistical data from ethnographic contexts with archaeological quantitative analysis, the probability that Hovenweep Anasazi identified and organized themselves in lineages using totemic signs is a strong one (Olsen 1986, p. 10).

In contemporary western Pueblos, religious granary/storage locations under the mesa top are no longer used. Corn is stored inside homes, seeds are kept in the *kivas*, but shrines around the edges of the mesas are still in use for storing ceremonial gear and for extended seclusion by certain priests at prescribed times of the year. If these Anasazi granary/ceremonial–single habitation sites, such as Hovenweep 15 (Fig. 20.7), with mountain sheep/antelope/elk/deer symbols, are the predecessors of those contemporary special-use sites around the mesas, then it is not inconsistent to propose that the motifs' identity specifies a clan or sodality; and that they function in a socially symbolic manner. Remnant tradition in present-day social organization of Hopi indicates that may be so. Inheritance of certain chief priest offices within a

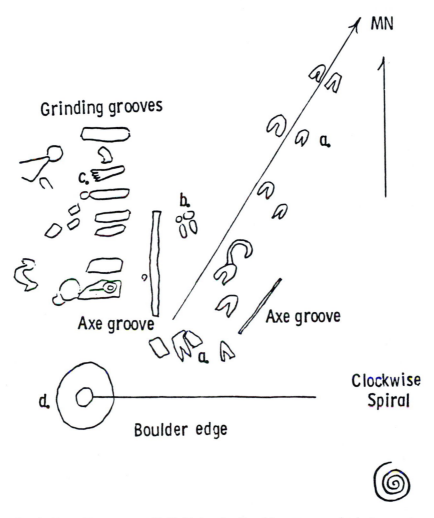

Figure 20.7 Hovenweep 15. Field sketch of boulder top petroglyphs in association with granary and *kiva*-like features: (a) mountain sheep/antelope hoof-prints aligned in a north-east–south-west pattern; (b) deer/elk hoof-prints; (c) grinding grooves with human left footprint incised; (d) abstract circle within circle and line which points toward the mesa top. Clockwise spirals are the most prevalent element in Hovenweep rock art.

lineage ties some clans to certain societies. For example, within the Bear Clan, the Chief Priest of the Soyal Priesthood is inherited, the Snake Clan holds the office of Chief Priest of the Snake Society, and the Antelope Clan maintains the Chief Priest office of the Antelope Society (Stephen & Parsons 1936).

The last phases of Anasazi occupation in the Hovenweep–Mesa Verde area showed development of water-control devices, such as check dams, rim dams, terracing, channels for irrigation made from enlarged seeps, and reservoirs as strategies for farming maintenance under increasingly difficult, drought conditions. Symbolic use of lineage/sodality motifs is thought to have been added to agricultural features during the period of AD 1100–1300.

Other clan-like symbols, including a bear paw-print and bird tracks incised on a reservoir impound wall parallels the agricultural contexts of rock art observed in the ethnographies. Boundary demarcation using totemic symbols may have been the intent of those elements, particularly as Cajon Mesa was experiencing drought conditions during late Pueblo phases (Weir 1977). Use of clan symbols to declare ownership, establish boundaries and/or define 'locater' functions may have served as a strategy to manage stress then, as now.

Conclusions

That art communicates is a generally accepted fact. That art can be considered a cultural system has been argued eloquently by Geertz (1983, p. 94), and that semiotic inquiry can be applied to the iconographic systems of contemporary and prehistoric cultures in a useful manner has been noted in the archaeological contexts. If archaeology can also be anthropology, then the advantages of the systems theory application to the archaeological data can be appreciated. For example, contexts for all of the rock art could be provided by the research project's focus on the economic systems of adaptation. Without the recognition of farm fields, reservoirs, and granary–special-use sites, the rock art would appear to be located, as some earlier descriptions have noted, 'in the middle of nowhere'.

Relationships to the nearby occupation sites could be established through the types of farming features, which bore such similarity with present Hopi and Zuni farming techniques noted by Cushing (1920), Hack (1942), and Forde (1931, 1949) that similar Anasazi cultural systems are hypothesized for Hovenweep (Winter 1978, p. 97). Comparison of motifs in different contexts affirms that a visual communication system was probably present among the Anasazi of the Mesa Verde region. Correspondences of identical motifs with contemporary Hopi and Zuni strongly suggest historical linkages which the oral traditions and archaeology already acknowledged. To unravel the intricate relationships of images would be to describe and define developmental cognitive processes of the western Pueblo culture.

For example, while clan symbols may not be present in as great a percentage as in the archaeological record, the ratio of animal representation to human representation has decreased in the historic sample. Twenty-one per cent of the Anasazi 'lexicon' is zoomorphic, but 11.4 per cent of the present 'lexicon' is zoomorphic today. On the other hand, the presence of human figures has doubled from 15.7 per cent to

36.4 per cent. It is now the largest category of the sample. Furthermore, a 'common denominator' of host media can be seen in the use of permanent surfaces to sustain zoomorphic images. Animal shapes which are known ethnographic clan symbols may be a means of understanding the early representation of social organization. If the cognitive system is a development from the Anasazi, one can see the trend towards anthropomorphism as a process of self-recognition or awareness. On the other hand, the role of animals as spiritual 'assistants' appears to have changed less from prehistoric times.

Apart from the symbolic development of animal and human relationships in the visual vocabulary, an evolutionary use of colour is quite apparent. In the Anasazi repertoire, black and white as a combination common in ceramics and some rock art, becomes embedded in the colour repertoire of the ethnographic reports. Red was the exceptional colour used in rock art contexts at Hovenweep and Mesa Verde, but is presently an important ceremonial and seasonal colour.

The value of ethnographic information for understanding cognitive processes in contemporary Pueblo iconography which is demonstrated here for the Southwest has already proved to be of great value in other regions such as Australia (Munn 1973, Vinnicombe 1986) and South Africa (Lewis-Williams 1983, 1986). In keeping with Native American philosophy, which regards life as a whole and does not separate parts of it in order to understand it, animal motifs occupy a sizeable portion of the historic and prehistoric 'lexicons', but share importance with motifs of other categories, such as earth, weather, or plants. We can see that there is much more to the visual vocabularies than just animal images. We can see a complex world-view expressed by a complicated system of image combinations in particular contexts.

The application of 'art' as a cultural system for archaeological investigation is useful as a paradigm for research and theory-building and allows us some understanding of the human phenomenon called 'art' outside the Western European frame of reference.

From the etic perspective, increased recognition that oral traditions can be supported by a non-alphabetic communication system of graphic images is a step towards understanding alternative strategies which humans devise to record and document their world-view, cosmology, and history. Further, it provides a link with the past which has escaped attention until now.

From the emic perspective, recognition from the outside society of the historical value of the iconography in the traditional artistic processes may create one more bridge of understanding between the two worlds and in the words of one Hopi poet:

> There is no need
> For us to speak
>
> Silence
> Will speak
> for us.

From *After the rains* by Ramson Lomatewama 1983.

References

Adovasio, J. M. & R. L. Andrews 1981. Basketry and miscellaneous perishable artefacts from Walpi: a summary. Paper prepared for the symposium: 'Walpi: 285 years of culture change at a historic Hopi village,' 46th Annual Meeting of Society for American Archaeology, San Diego, CA, 29 April–2 May.

Beaglehole, E. 1937. *Notes on Hopi economic life.* Yale University Publications in Anthropology, no. 15. New Haven: Yale University Press.

Binford, L. R. 1977. General introduction. In *For theory building in archaeology*, L. Binford (ed.), 1–10. New York: Academic Press.

Bradfield, M. 1971. The changing pattern of Hopi agriculture. *Royal Anthropological Institute of Great Britain and Ireland Occasional Paper* **30**.

Brew, O. J. 1979. Hopi prehistory and history to 1850. In *Handbook of North American Indians* A. Ortiz (ed.), 514–23. Smithsonian Institution, Washington, DC.

Burland, C. A. 1965. *North American Indian mythology.* London: Hamlyn.

Cohen, A. P. 1985. *The symbolic construction of community.* London: Tavistock.

Colton, H. S. 1937. *Black sand – prehistory in northern Arizona.* Albuquerque: University of New Mexico Press.

Colton, H. S. 1949. *Kachina dolls, with a key to their identification.* Albuquerque: University of New Mexico Press.

Colton, H. S. & M. R. F. Colton 1931. Petroglyphs, the record of a great adventure. *American Anthropologist* **33**, 32–7.

Cordell, L. S. & D. Jones 1985. *Anasazi world.* Portland: Graphic Arts Centre.

Cushing, F. H. 1920. *Zuni breadstuffs.* Heye Foundation, Indian Notes and Monographs 8. Museum of the American Indian, New York.

Cushing, F. H. 1972. *Zuni Fetishes*, facsimile edn. Las Vegas: K. C. Publications.

Dozier, E. P. 1966. *Hano, a Tewa Indian community in Arizona.* New York: Holt, Rinehart & Winston.

Dozier, E. P. 1970. *The Pueblo Indians of North America.* New York: Holt, Rinehart & Winston.

Eco, U. 1984. *Semiotics and the philosophy of language.* Bloomington: Indiana University Press.

Eggan, F. 1950. *Social organization of the western Pueblos.* Chicago: University of Chicago Press.

Fewkes, J. W. 1892. A few Tusayan pictographs. *American Anthropologist* **5**, 9–26.

Fewkes, J. W. 1894. Kinship of Tusayan villages. *American Anthropologist* **7**, 394–417.

Fewkes, J. W. 1896. Prehistoric culture of Tusayan. *American Anthropologist* **9**, 151–74.

Fewkes, J. W. 1897. Tusayan totemic signatures. *American Anthropologist* **10**, 1–11.

Fewkes, J. W. 1898. The winter solstice ceremony at Walpi. *American Anthropologist* **11**, 101–15.

Fewkes, J. W. 1900. *Tusayan flute and snake ceremonies.* Annual Report of 1897–1898, Bureau of American Ethnology.

Fewkes, J. W. 1903. *Hopi kachinas drawn by native artists.* Annual Report of 1903, Bureau of American Ethnology. Reprint 1969. Glorieta, NM: Rio Grande Press.

Forde, C. D. 1931. Hopi agriculture and land ownership. *Journal of the Royal Anthropological Institute of Great Britain and Ireland.* **61**, 357–407.

Forde, C. D. 1963 (1949 5th edition). *Habitat, economy and society. A geographical introduction to ethnology.* New York: E. P. Dutton.

Geertz, C. 1973. *The interpretation of cultures, selected essays.* New York: Basic Books, Harper Colophon Books.

Geertz, C. 1983. *Local knowledge. Further esssays in interpretive anthropology.* New York: Basic Books.

Goodenough, W. H. 1968. *Description and comparison in cultural anthropology*. The Lewis Henry Morgan lectures presented by the University of Rochester, Rochester, New York. Chicago: Aldine.

Grant, C. 1967. *Rock art of the American Indian*. New York: Thomas Y. Crowell.

Grant, C. 1978. *Canyon de Chelly, its people and its rock art*. Tucson: University of Arizona Press.

Hack, J. T. 1942. *The changing physical environment of the Hopi Indians of Arizona*. Papers of the Peabody Museum of American Archaeology and Ethnology. Harvard 35.1.

Highwater, J. 1976. *Song from the Earth: American Indian painting*. Boston: New York Graphic Society.

Hopi Arts and Crafts – Silversmiths Cooperative Guild, Second Mesa n.d. Arizona.

Hopi Cultural Centre 1981. *Zuni rock art*. Exhibit brochure, sponsored by Pueblo of Zuni from Youthgrants in the Humanities and Special Programs Division of the National Endowment of the Humanities and New Mexico Humanities Council (1980).

Ives, G. A. 1986. Rock art of the Dolores River Valley. In *Dolores Archaeological Program: research designs and initial survey results*, compiled by A. E. Kane, W. D. Lipe, T. A. Kohler & C. K. Robinson. Prepared under the supervision of Dr D. A. Breternitz, Principal Investigator. United States Department of the Interior, Bureau of Reclamation, Engineering and Research Center, Denver, June, 235–52.

Kubik, G. 1986. African graphic systems with particular reference to the Benue-Congo or 'Bantu' languages zone. In *Muntu*. Libreville (Gabon).

Lévi-Strauss, C. 1963. *Totemism*, (trans. R. Needham). Boston: Beacon Press.

Lévi-Strauss, C. 1982. *The way of the masks*, (trans. S. Modelski). Seattle: University of Washington Press.

Lewis-Williams, J. D. 1983. The rock art of southern Africa. In *The imprint of man*, E. Anate (ed.). Cambridge: Cambridge University Press.

Lewis-Williams, J. D. 1986. Seeing and construing: a neurological constant in San rock art. Paper presented at 'The longest record: the human career in Africa', a conference in honour of J. Desmond Clark, Berkeley, 12 April.

Lomatewama, R. 1983. *Silent winds, the poetry of one Hopi*. Cortez, Colorado: La Plata Printing.

Malin, E. 1978. *A world of faces, masks of the northwest coast Indians*. Portland: Timber Press.

Mallory, G. 1886. *A preliminary paper*. Fourth Annual Report of the Bureau of Ethnology to the Secretary of the Smithsonian Institution, 1882–1883. Washington, DC.

Mallory, G. 1893. *Picture writing of the American Indians*. Tenth Annual Report of the Bureau of Ethnology to the Secretary of the Smithsonian Institution 1888–1889. J. W. Powell, Director, Washington, DC. Reprint, 1972. Vols 1 & 2. New York: Dover Publications.

Marcus, J. 1980. Zapotec writing. *Scientific American*, February, **242**(2), 50–64.

Munn, N. 1973. *Walbiri iconography, graphic representation and cultural symbolism in a central Australian society*. Ithaca: Cornell University Press.

Nequatewa, E. 1936. *Truth of a Hopi, stories relating to the origin, myths and clan histories of the Hopi*. Museum of Northern Arizona, Bull. No. 8, Flagstaff. Sixth printing 1985.

Neusius, S. W. 1984. Garden hunting and Anasazi game procurement: perspectives from Dolores. Paper presented at the 49th Annual Meeting of the Society of American Archaeology, Portland, 11–14 April.

Olsen, N. H. 1980. *Hovenweep rock art: an Anasazi visual communication system*. Unpublished Master's thesis, Department of Anthropology, San Jose State University, San Jose.

Olsen, N. H. 1985. *Hovenweep rock art: an Anasazi visual communication system*. Institute of Archaeology Occasional Papers no. 14, University of California at Los Angeles, LA.

Olsen, N. H. 1986. The role of rock art redefined: implications for archaeology from Hopi and Zuni ethnography. In *Cultural attitudes to animals including birds, fish and invertebrates*. World Archaeological Congress, vol. 3 (mimeo).

Ortiz, A. 1969. *The Tewa world: space, time, being and becoming in a Pueblo society*. Chicago: University of Chicago Press.

Ortiz, S. 1979. Native American art. Lecture delivered at De Anza College, Cupertino, California, 21 February.

Qoyawayma, P. (E. Q. White) 1964. *No turning back, a Hopi Indian woman's struggle to live in two worlds*. Albuquerque: University of New Mexico Press.

Schaafsma, P. 1971. *The rock art of Utah*. Papers of the Peabody Museum of Archaeology and Ethnology, Harvard 65.

Schaafsma, P. 1980. *Indian rock art of the Southwest*. Albuquerque: University of New Mexico Press.

Sebeok, T. A. (ed.) 1977. *A perfusion of signs*. Bloomington: Indiana University Press.

Sekaquaptewa, E. 1976. Hopi Indian ceremonies. In *Seeing with a native eye; essays on native American religion*, W. H. Capps (ed.). New York: Harper Forum Books.

Sekaquaptewa, H. & L. Udall 1969. *Me and mine, the life story of Helen Sekaquaptewa as told to Louise Udall*. Tucson: University of Arizona Press.

Stephen, A. & E. C. Parsons 1936. *Hopi journal of Alexander M. Stephen*, Vols 1 & 2. Columbia University Contributions to Anthropology XXIII. Reprint 1969, New York: AMS Press.

Stevenson, M. C. 1904. *The Zuni Indians, their mythology, esoteric fraternities and ceremonies*. The 23rd Annual Report of the Bureau of American Ethnology to the Secretary of the Smithsonian Institution, J. W. Powell, Director. Reprint 1970, New York: Johnson Reprint.

Steward, J. H. 1955. *The theory of culture change; the methodology of multilinear evolution*. Chicago: University of Illinois Press.

Sturtevant, W. C. 1986. The meaning of native American art. In *The arts of the North American Indian: native traditions in evolution*, E. L. Wade (ed.). New York: Hudson Hills Press, in association with the Philbrook Art Center, Tulsa.

Talayesva, D. & L. Simmons 1942. *Sun Chief, the autobiography of a Hopi Indian*. New Haven: Yale University Press.

Taylor, A. R. 1975. Nonverbal communications systems in native North America. *Semiotica* **13**(4), 329–74.

Titiev, M. 1937. A Hopi salt expedition. *American Anthropology* **39**, 244–58.

Titiev, M. 1944. *Old Oraibi: a study of the Hopi Indians of Third Mesa*. Papers of the Peabody Museum of American Archaeology and Ethnology, Harvard 22.

Turner, C. 1963. *Petroglyphs of the Glen Canyon region*. Bulletin no. 38, Glenn Canyon Series No. 4, Northern Arizona Society of Science and Art, Flagstaff.

Vinnicombe, P. 1986. Rock art: material property and spiritual reality. Paper presented at 'The longest record: the human career in Africa', a conference in honour of J. Desmond Clark, University of California, Berkeley, 12 April.

Voegelin, C. F. & F. M. Voegelin 1961. Typological classification of systems with included, excluded, and self-sufficient alphabets. *Anthropological Linguistics* **3**(1), 55–96.

Wang, W. S.-Y. 1973. The Chinese language. *Scientific American* **228** (2), 50–63.

Weir, G. H. 1977. Pollen evidence for environmental change at Hovenweep National Monument AD900–AD1300. In *Hovenweep 1976*, J. C. Winter (ed.), Archaeological Report no. 3, Department of Anthropology, San Jose State University, San Jose.

White, T. E. 1977. Further studies of the potential faunal resources on Cajon Mesa. In *Hovenweep 1976*, J. C. Winter (ed.). Archaeological Report no. 3, Department of Anthropology, San Jose State University, San Jose.

Whorf, B. L. 1956. Linguistic factors in the terminology of Hopi architecture. In *Language, thought and reality, selected writings of Benjamin Lee Whorf*, J. B. Carroll (ed.), 199–206. Cambridge, Mass.: MIT Press.

Winter, J.C. 1975. *Hovenweep 1974*. Archaeological Report no. 1, Department of Anthropology, San Jose State University, San Jose.

Winter, J. C. 1976. *Hovenweep 1975*. Archaeological Report no. 2, Department of Anthropology, San Jose State University, San Jose.

Winter, J. C. 1977. *Hovenweep 1976*. Archaeological Report no. 3, Department of Anthropology, San Jose State University, San Jose.

Winter, J. C. 1978. Anasazi agriculture at Hovenweep, 1: Field systems. In *Limited activity and occupation sites, a collection of conference papers*, A. E. Ward (ed.), Contributions to Anthropological Studies no. 1, Centre for Anthropological Studies, Albuquerque.

Winter, J.C. 1985. Hovenweep through time. *Exploration*, 22–8. Annual Bulletin of the School of American Research, Santa Fe.

Woodbury, R. B. 1979. Zuni prehistory and history to 1850. In *Handbook of North American Indians*. Vol. 9: *Southwest*, A. Ortiz, (ed.). Smithsonian Institution, Washington, DC.

Wright, M. N. 1982. *Hopi silver; the history and hallmarks of Hopi silversmithing*, 3rd edn. Flagstaff: Northland Press.

Young, M. J. 1985. Images of power and the power of images: the significance of rock art for contemporary Zunis. *Journal of American Folklore* **98**(387), 1–48. American Folklore Society. Washington DC.

21 *Freedom of information: aspects of art and society in western Europe during the last Ice Age*

IAIN DAVIDSON

Introduction

The Upper Palaeolithic art of Europe is best known for some of its sculptures (e.g. Venus figurines) and for its painted caves (e.g. Lascaux and Altamira). There are many other categories of art within the general class of phenomena in the same time period, roughly 35 000 to 10 000 years ago, and same geographic distribution, from the Iberian peninsula to the Urals, with notable absence in south-east Europe, Greece, and the east Mediterranean. Upper Palaeolithic art was not a unitary phenomenon, although some of the themes were repeated in more than one category. Amongst the less famous categories are pictures made on stone plaquettes[1] by painting or engraving or a combination of the two. Sites with these decorated stone plaquettes are not evenly distributed across the whole space nor the whole time in which one or other category of art is found. The sites are rather scarce and seem to be widely spaced through western Europe. Although some of the sites are confined to the later part of the period, the art on stone plaquettes seems to have been made in the period between 22 000 and 10 000 years ago. In this chapter I argue that this category of art can be related to the economic use of space and resources in that region and time period and, hence, that we can infer something of the social context in which the art was created.

Art and fisher–gatherer–hunter society

While it would be possible to attempt to specify the economic and social relations by appeal to a relationship between social relations and the behaviour associated with pictures in some group of existing people, I prefer not to do this as it is clear that the specific form of such social relations is determined by ideologies which are not linked in any simple manner with the material objects through which they may, at times, have been expressed.

  Macintosh (1977) recorded how even his experienced zoological eye was responsible for mistaken identification of up to 90 per cent of the taxa represented in some

Australian art sites. He even failed to identify correctly the sex of human figures. Macintosh's conclusion was that there was a:

> total dependence upon revelation from a local informed Aboriginal for the correct assemblage and integration of the individual items (even after informed identification) to express the purpose and thought context of the paintings. (Macintosh 1977, p. 197)

In the cave art of southern Africa, Vinnicombe (1976) was able to relate depictions to the mythology known for the same region, and Lewis-Williams (e.g. Lewis-Williams & Loubser 1986) has demonstrated that the depiction may record very specific detail of such mythology. But there is reason to believe that the mythological stories, associated with a set of images, may change. Layton (1985), for example, has discussed two sets of images in north-western Australia. One set was created by the present Aboriginal people of the region, while the other was created prehistorically, in a quite different style. The modern people do not claim to have been those responsible for the execution of the prehistoric images but they incorporated them into their mythology. Moreover, for both sets of images, the associated stories varied, sometimes strongly from individual to individual.

These examples from southern Africa and Australia serve to illustrate that art may be associated with meaning beyond the nature of its images. The identification of images may itself be determined by understanding of the conventions by which things were depicted (see also Morphy 1977, 1980). In all of these studies the mythology enables us to understand the relations between people, and to see that the relations were expressed through art. But the mythology itself may change, as, indeed, did the relations between people. In interpreting prehistoric art, we cannot use any more than these general principles as rules about meaning in art. Upper Palaeolithic art may have been closely related to mythology in some similar way but we cannot specify how.

If we wish to interpret the art in terms of relations between people, then we need to do it by some other means than through an understanding of the mythology associated with artistic creation.

The divisibility of art

I recognize as 'art' a whole series of objects, including cave walls, which have intentional marks or modifications on them. Some of these objects may be functional, and in this case the marks or modifications which constitute the 'art' do not form a necessary part of the functional form of the object. Other objects do not seem to have any function other than as supports for the intentional marks or modifications. I ignore, for the moment, the importance of depiction as a function in itself. A spear-thrower may be designed, but undecorated – which would not be 'art' because we cannot separate form and function – or it may include a three-dimensional sculpture of a bison, where the form is clearly more than functional. Often these objects would not be recognized as art by any people other than archaeologists. Other definitions by art historians, by art appreciators, or by the general public are not relevant for my purposes here. In this chapter I am only concerned with the category of Upper Palaeolithic 'art' called mobile 'art', and more particularly with the category of plaquette art, which appears to have had no other functions than depiction and the communication of meaning associated with depiction.

The surviving mobile 'art' may be divided into:

(a)   objects in which the whole object may be regarded as 'art', like the *contour découpé* horse's head pendants of Isturitz, Arudy, and La Viña (Fortea 1981), or some of the Venus figurines;

(b)   carved objects which may have been functional, like the spear-throwers and some of the harpoons;

(c)   objects on which were composed artistic designs, such as the palettes, and some of the *bâtons de commandement*;

(d)   the scratched and marked stone and bone objects in which Marshack (1972) discerns lunar calendars;

(e)   engravings on bones, such as the scapulae from Altamira and Castillo, or the first Upper Palaeolithic art find at Le Chaffaud; and

(f)   a group of portable engravings and paintings on stone which appears to have no immediate function.

This chapter concentrates on the portable engravings and paintings, which include the remarkable assemblage from Parpalló, which was the focus for my own recent study of the prehistoric economy of the southern Valencia province of Spain (Davidson 1980, 1983, 1986).

All objects in this category may be dated by their discovery in stratified archaeological deposits. Indeed, Leroi-Gourhan (1965, pp. 97–102) used comparison between the plaquette 'art' and wall 'art' as a basis for his chronological scheme. Leroi-Gourhan, however, included all plaques and plaquettes, large and small, and of whatever material, including bone. Moreover, many of them contain engravings or paintings of animals, just as in parietal 'art', and the species representation in the pictures may be compared with the contemporary species representation in the bones at the site, and the animal-based subsistence of the site system.

In studying only this one category of 'art' it is important to make an observation about the divisibility of 'art'. In modern societies there are many things which archaeologists, using the broad definition I have outlined, would recognize as 'art' if they had to treat them as archaeological materials. In Australia, for example, these include sand paintings, body paintings, bark paintings, decorated burial poles, shields, boomerangs, message sticks, and sacred boards, as well as paintings and engravings on rock surfaces in caves or open air. The different material contexts, in which things which could be called 'art' are produced, have different social contexts of their production. These social contexts have different associations of ideology and function.

To give a simple example from Australia. Message sticks were wooden objects marked with a variety of incised designs (see, for example, Howitt 1889, Mathews 1897, 1898, Roth 1906, Hamlyn-Harris 1918). These were carried by messengers from one group to invite people of another group to a ceremony or to ask people to bring *pituri* (a widely traded narcotic plant) (Watson 1983). It is generally agreed that the designs themselves carried no 'message', but for the device to be effective, there must have been some recognition of what was and what was not a 'valid' token of the status of the messenger. The rules of this design system were not communicated to the ethnographers who collected the message sticks.

In contrast to this, we may consider shields (see, for example Davidson 1937). These were used by men and had a role in hand-to-hand combat as parrying shields. Many of these had bold, brightly coloured designs, which made them objects of display as well as defensive tools. In this case we may notice the excluding nature of the message which was communicated by the designs. Again the rules by which these messages could be understood are unrecorded by ethnographers.

So, there were two classes of objects which conveyed messages across boundaries between groups of people, but one set of messages (on sticks) had the function of connecting the groups, while the other (on shields) had the effect of separating the groups. Put another way, message sticks were used in the context of open communication between people, and shields defined a context where communication was closed.

The sacred boards, the *churingas* of central Australia, were objects which could only be seen in limited contexts within a group of people. These were contexts of restricted ceremony associated with initiation. Here, the boundaries existed within a group of people. This association needs to be understood clearly before prehistoric European objects, such as the mammoth tooth from Tata (Schwarcz & Skoflek 1982), are called by this name.

In the case of all of these objects, if they survived archaeologically, the intentional marks would be recognized as 'art' in the broad terms defined here. The particular classes of object do not matter for the point that I wish to make here. I have selected the object classes because they illustrate the point clearly, but I could have made the same point about cave paintings, bark paintings, or body decoration: *'art' is not a unitary phenomenon. Different categories of 'art' may have different social contexts of production with different associated ideologies and functions.* This fundamental general principle is applicable across the range of contexts in which 'art' is found in archaeological sites.

It seems that there is a language of communication, whereby the validity of a message may be given meaning by the context of the conveying of it (see, for example, Morphy 1977, 1980). There must be a grammar appropriate to particular situations and particular 'divisions' of 'art'. If this follows, it would also seem reasonable to consider single categories as separate entities. I will be considering plaquette 'art' as one such entity.

The conclusions I reach will not necessarily be the same as the conclusions others might reach in considering the contexts and implications of other categories of prehistoric art, such as cave art, Venus figurines, or *contour découpé* horse's heads; different categories of 'art' have different contexts and meanings. Some analyses of 'art' may indicate a context of open communication between groups, other analyses may reveal closure between groups, while it might also be possible to discover 'art' which derived from restrictions within social organizations. A single group of people may have restrictions within it without destroying group solidarity, and it may be open to communication with other groups for some purposes and yet closed to the same groups for other purposes. Any conclusions from the study of one division of the whole phenomenon of 'art' will be complementary to those from the study of other divisions, within the same geographic and chronological limits, as together they constitute a single system of communication of a single social system.

Parpalló and plaquette 'art'

Parpalló (Pericot 1942, Davidson 1983), in south-eastern Spain, had over 6000 pieces of stone, each about the size of a human hand, decorated with engraved, painted, and engraved and painted designs, many of which included animal figures. These pieces were stratified in archaeological deposits which can be dated to between 20 000 and 12 000 years BP (Bofinger & Davidson 1977). Only Les Mallaetes, 3 km away on the same mountain, has 'art' in the same style and, of 24 plaquettes, only one has a picture of an animal. That depiction is in a deposit dated earlier than the first use of Parpalló (Fortea 1978). Three other sites in eastern Spain, San Gregorí (Fortea 1973), Matutano (Olaria et al. 1981), and Tossal de la Roca (Cacho pers. comm.) have small numbers of engraved stones. There is only one each at San Gregorí (a plaquette) and Matutano (a pebble). Those at San Gregorí and Tossal de la Roca (pebbles) are in a different style, and appear to be much later. The absence or scarcity at other sites in the region suggests that there may have been a deliberate restriction to one site of importance.

During the analysis of the animal bones from Parpalló, I discovered one bone engraved with a design in the same 'artistic' tradition as the plaquette art (Aparicio 1981). The importance of this bone is that bone was a raw material commonly available as the medium for the execution of 'art' but that the use of bone as a support was extremely rare. My characterization of 'art' is that it is divisible into separate categories. The apparently general choice of stone plaquettes rather than the readily available bone as a support for 'art' suggests that it is legitimate to consider the 'art' on stone plaquettes as a separate category.

Arguments that these sketches are 'trailers for the big picture' in the cave 'art' (see Hadingham 1979, pp. 239–46 for discussion) are denied by the absence of significant quantities of cave 'art' in eastern Spain. The suggestion that these are 'doodles' or 'craft activities' of the sort recorded at hunting stands by modern hunters (Binford 1978) is denied by the scarcity of plaquette 'art' sites. Hunting stands might have been expected to be a common site type, and boredom a frequent occurrence, so on this interpretation plaquette 'art' sites should be common.

The limited evidence from Les Mallaetes tends to support the argument. Unfortunately, there are no figures from Les Mallaetes yet available for the rate of discard of flaked stone or retouched tools, and the bone tools are generally acknowledged to be very few (Fortea & Jordá 1976). Nevertheless, my analysis of the mammal bones from the recent excavations (Davidson 1976) suggests that the density of unworked bone finds was about 0.9 per year (allowing for the size of the excavated area as about one-fifteenth of the site), of which rather more than two-thirds were unidentifiable fragments. This estimate includes rabbit bones which were not available (though abundant) at Parpalló. Nevertheless, for the incomplete collections from Parpalló the density of bone finds, in the surviving collections, was about 2.5 per year, or about (at least) 25 times the density of Les Mallaetes.

When we turn to the 'art' at Les Mallaetes we find that in the original excavations there was a total of 16 plaquettes in five different stratigraphic contexts which might generously (including ochre stains) be said to contain 'art' (Fletcher 1956), and four more pieces from the 1970 excavations. Even allowing that these were partial excavations, the absolute numbers were very much less than for Parpalló, perhaps 300 in the whole site. Moreover, only one plaquette, of the 20, contained an animal figure. This was from a layer said to be contemporary with the earliest layers at Parpalló (Fortea 1978). Allowance for the size of the excavated area would suggest no more than a total of 15 animal pictures at Les Mallaetes. The rate of production of 'art' at Les Mallaetes suggests that this was not just a poorer version of Parpalló, with Parpalló occupied 25 times more frequently than Les Mallaetes. In addition, there is no record of 'art' at the other sites of the immediate vicinity, and only a few ochre-stained plaquettes at Volcán.

The amount of material discarded in any one visit to a cave seems to have been very small, and that includes 'art'. Nevertheless, there are differences between sites in the relative abundance of different discarded materials, and in particular, for this argument, 'art' seems to have been concentrated at Parpalló, and hardly practised, if at all, at the other sites which formed part of the same local exploitation system. If 'art' was part of a behaviour which had no particular importance then we should expect 'art' to be more widely distributed. Even if Parpalló gives the scale of production of 'art', as one or two representations each year, there is no reason why 'art' should be confined to particular sites. Moreover, given that there may have been some reason why it should have been confined to particular sites, is it not then surprising that there are so few of these? Perhaps we may generalize that there were a few sites of particular importance for the production of this particular 'art', and that most of the individual pieces found at sites such as La Madeleine, Abri Pataud, Laugerie-Haute, and Les Mallaetes may be considered as exceptional within the contexts within which 'art' was usually produced. It is also possible, at least for the situation between Parpalló and Les Mallaetes, that these scarce finds are related to the changing relationships between the sites. Specifically, the use of Les Mallaetes became far more closely associated with summer after the layer in which the only animal artistic representation was found. Parpalló, used mostly after the layer in which the animal picture was left at Les Mallaetes, has evidence throughout of red deer antlers, either shed or from massacred animals, indicating a winter to spring use. Estévez (1981) has indicated the range of possibilities of the significance of the association between 'art' and particular seasons of occupation of Parpalló, in eastern Spain, and Gönnersdorf, another plaquette site in western Germany.

At first sight, then, this seems to be another case of aggregation, by an argument similar to that of Conkey (1980), 'art' being practised primarily at the aggregation site. Some such argument is necessary if we are to argue that any sort of information was communicated through the 'art', unless we envisage the occupants of Parpalló as a community entire unto themselves. In Conkey's argument, however, the information was widespread, and the different elements came together at one site. In this case, the information is almost entirely restricted to one site in the whole of eastern Spain.

I choose to emphasize the restriction because the capacity to restrict access to information is an important part of the power relations of social groups. Such relations might be associated with hierarchies of some sort. It is difficult to see how or why the information was not communicated at other sites or places unless the ideology of restriction was enforced or reinforced in some way.

My argument is supported by the spatial distribution of other sites with large numbers of pieces of 'art' executed on portable stone plaquettes.

Other sites with stone plaquettes

Inspection of the distribution of other sites with large quantities of plaquette 'art' shows that a similar phenomenon exists in the western Pyrenees, central Pyrenees, the confluence of the Dordogne and Vézère rivers, and Cantabria. Late in the Upper Palaeolithic the tradition may have spread to northern France and Germany.

When we examine the distribution, in western Europe, of sites with engraved stone plaquettes we find a remarkable distribution. A few early sites like La Ferrassie, in the Dordogne, have a few plaquettes or blocks, some of which do have animal representations, but many of which only have vulvas engraved on them (but see Bahn 1986). These examples are all distributed within 20 or 30 km of each other (Delluc & Delluc 1978, 1981).

There are many sites with one or two representations, but very few with large numbers. Hadingham (1979, pp. 229–46) identified five sites (Labastide, Gönnersdorf, Parpalló, Limeuil, and La Marche) as 'centres of intense and peculiar artistic activity, concentrated on small pieces of stone'. I would add to these, sites with abundant engraved and painted plaquettes: Isturitz in the Basque Country, Badegoule in Dordogne, Enlène in the central Pyrenees, and Tito Bustillo in Cantabria.

Labastide has parietal as well as mobile 'art' (Bégouen 1938, Omnès 1982, 1983), and a radio-carbon date of 14 260±440 BP (Ly-1405). Hadingham (1979, p. 245) mentions 'nearly 1000 engraved plaques', but Omnès (1982, p. 164) only mentions 51, published by three different authors. Labastide does, however, have a remarkable description of the context of the engraved plaquettes:

> At the end of the cavern, on an earthy path more than 1300 feet in, are two large circles made of stones touching one another in the manner of cromlechs. Within the circles are charcoal, charred bones, horses' jaws and teeth, and chipped flints. There are also reindeer-horn javelin-points, and several lime-stone slabs with fine engravings of horses, reindeer, bison, mammoths, and a bear's head. All these slabs were lying on the ground face down. This is undoubtedly part of some rite, for the same thing has been noticed in other caverns. (Casteret 1939, p. 35)

The cave of Enlène is said to have 574 engraved plaques (Bahn 1983, p. 243). It is clear that plaquettes occur in large numbers at very few of the sites, despite the fact that many sites have a few of them.

Isturitz (Saint-Périer 1930, 1936, Saint-Périer & Saint-Périer 1950) has a sequence of industries from the Mousterian through to the Late Magdalenian, that is, through-out the last Glacial period, with extremely rich 'art' of many forms, especially the carved bone rods, and the magnificent horse's head pendants. In addition, there are engravings on limestone and schist plaquettes in Gravettian, Solutrean, and Magdalenian layers.

Badegoule, in Dordogne, also contains one of the 'classic' sequences (Cheynier 1949), with abundant engravings on limestone and occasional schist plaquettes through the stratified Solutrean sequence. Badegoule seems to have been unoccupied at the period when Limeuil was rich in plaquette 'art'. Limeuil (Capitan & Bouyssonie 1924), in Dordogne, is basically a single-period site with rich later Magdalenian layers and abundant engravings on limestone. Limeuil is remarkable for the repetitive detail of the reindeer and horse representations.

Tito Bustillo in Cantabria (Moure 1985) has 83 plaquettes in layers dated to 14 930±70 BP (GrN-12753). It also contains a horse's head pendant similar to many from the Pyrenees. Plaquettes are only found at three sites in northern Spain, and there are four fragments from Urtiaga (dated 10 280±190 BP), and seven fragments making a single plaquette at Ekain (dated 12 050±190 BP) (Moure 1982, 1985, p. 121).

Gönnersdorf, in western Germany near Koblenz, is an open site dated to 10 430±230 (Ly -768) with many hundreds of engraved plaquettes. About 300 plaquettes have female figures (Bosinski 1973, Bosinski & Fischer 1974, Rosenfeld 1977) and many others have animal figures, including horses (which are abundant among the animal bones from the site) and mammoths.

La Marche, in western France in the *département* of Vienne, and rather north of the classic Dordogne region, is chiefly remarkable for its plaquettes, about 1500 of them (Hadingham 1979, p. 230). Many of these had complex patterns of overlaid engravings which required painstaking decipherment (Pales & Tassin de Saint-Péreuse 1969, 1981, Pales 1976). The major groups of figures are carnivores (including bears and felines), humans, and equids and bovids. The site is dated to the Late Magdalenian.

Enlène, in the complex of sites in the central Pyrenees which includes the famous caves of Tuc d'Audoubert and Les Trois Frères, contains an accumulation of numerous plaquettes for which ingenious explanations have been advanced (from lamps to plates or magic menus) (Bégouën & Clottes 1981). Many of these plaquettes were engraved, and recent excavations have recovered fragments which join others previously known (Bégouën *et al.* 1982, 1984). The new fragments were found at the base of a layer dated at 12 900±140 BP (Gif-5321) and on the surface of a layer dated at 13 400±120 BP (Gif-5770). The fact of accumulation of plaquettes reinforces the impression from the Pyrenean sites of the reality of the concept of centres of abundance of plaquette 'art'.

There are doubtless other sites with abundant plaquette 'art', but the literature is not always easy to interpret. There are several reasons for this. Many of the sites were excavated a long time ago, and the collections dispersed into different private collections. If, as is the case with much of the plaquette 'art', the objects are not of great beauty (in the sense of the great cave paintings or the sculpted spear-throwers) they may remain unpublished. Moreover, there is often an uncertainty in the literature because verbal reference does not always distinguish plaquettes of stone which have been decorated from those which have not. Indeed the excavators, in some cases, may not have noticed. In addition, distinction is sometimes not made between work done on stone and work executed on bone. Sometimes no division at all is made between different categories of mobile 'art'.

An example of the difficulty is provided by the site of Fontalès in the Quercy region of France. Three recent papers discuss 20 plaquettes and an engraved pebble (Pajot & Plenier 1976, Dams & Dams 1978, Welté 1985). The site was emptied in 1865 and the collections dispersed. It may be a site which should be included in the group we are discussing here, but it is probably impossible to tell now.

The relations of people with plaquette 'art'

Parpalló is one of a group of cave sites in the mountains in the southern part of Valencia province which have been studied in varying degrees of detail. All have some similarities of artefacts which would suggest their contemporary use between about 20 000 and 15 000 years BP. Parpalló was excavated between 1929 and 1931 (Pericot 1942) and it contained a richness and a sequence of stone and bone artefact types similar to the expectations derived from knowledge of French cave sites.

Parpalló was used from before 22 000 years BP to at least 13 000 years BP (see Bofinger & Davidson 1977). The sequence should be regarded as continuing until more recent dates, and we do not know when the 'art' stopped (e.g. Fullola 1979).

The fauna consists primarily of Spanish ibex and red deer with small quantities of equids of two sizes, and smaller quantities of *Bos primigenius*, wild cattle, which, appropriately in the land of bullfights, are the largest ever recorded. Pericot (1942, 1968) recorded that the bones of rabbits were extremely abundant in all parts of the site, but did not keep them, so I cannot comment in detail. There is a slight change in the fauna in the 'Magdalenian' levels of the site, where the bones of deer increase in abundance, so that they may even have provided more meat than the ibex (Davidson 1980, 1983).

The animals represented in the pictures are rather difficult to quantify, because there are three separate estimates which are not consistent with each other (Table 21.1). Nevertheless, the three estimates agree that deer are the most commonly represented animals, and that although ibex are next in abundance, horses are relatively more abundant in the pictures than would be expected in a simplistic interpretation of the relation between the pictures and the animals brought to the site. Cattle are a comfortable last in abundance, as in the bones. Some other species are represented even less frequently, e.g. lynx and suids. Rabbits are unrepresented in the pictures. A new detailed study of the original plaquettes is being undertaken by Valentín Villaverde and his students at the University of Valencia, but even the impressions from Pericot's work suggest that a simplistic interpretation is not adequate. There is also no indication of change in relative abundance of depicted species which corresponds with changes in relative abundance of bones of the same species through the sequence of use of the site.

I have shown elsewhere (Davidson 1980, 1983) that the local economy of the prehistoric sites in the south of Valencia province may be understood by studying them in conjunction with one another. The various sites were excavated at different times,

Table 21.1 Species represented in Parpalló art according to Pericot (1942), Dominguez (1972) from Pericot, and my conservative identifications from Pericot.

	Pericot 1942					Dominguez 1972					Davidson				
	Deer	Capra	Horse	Bovid	$\frac{Capra}{Deer}$	Deer	Capra	Horse	Bovid	$\frac{Capra}{Deer}$	Deer	Capra	Horse	Bovid	$\frac{Capra}{Deer}$
11.893–12.959	11	5	3	1	0.45	9	7	4	1	0.78	4	2	3	1	0.50
12.959–15.223	14	7	7	7	0.5	13	10	6	6	0.77	1	3	1	3	3.0
15.223–16.555	6	7	2	2	1.17	6	4	2	2	0.67	4	3	0	1	0.75
16.555–17.221	2	2	4	0	1.0	1	2	4	0	2.0	1	2	2	0	2.0
17.221–17.887	10	10	5	2	1.0	4	9	6	2	2.25	5	5	4	1	1.0
17.887–18.886	14	4	11	1	0.29	9	4	13	1	0.44	5	2	6	1	0.40
18.886–20.218	10	10	8	7	1.0	9	11	7	7	1.22	2	5	4	0	2.5
20.218–21.550	9	7	2	2	0.78	9	6	2	3	0.67	5	5	2	2	1.0
21.550	0	2	2	1	—	0	2	2	1	—	0	0	1	1	—

by different excavators and with different objectives, but some of the attendant difficulties can be overcome because of the good radio–carbon chronology (Bofinger & Davidson 1977), and the consequently satisfactory typological chronology, based on distinctive artefacts rather than assemblage composition.

In the initial phases of use of the region, say around 30 000 years ago, there were rather few sites, with hunting camps and no particular integration of activities between the sites which have survived. This pattern could be said to be typical of that which would be expected in a foraging economy, with encounter hunting of animals by small groups of hunters. By 25 000 years ago there is some evidence of the tactical use of sites in a seasonal round, and perhaps, therefore, of more logistical organization of activities. This pattern of organization was extended, so that about 20 000 years ago there were extensive visits to a distant shore, and a greater number of sites in use. This period may also be one when dispersion into the hills and tablelands to the west took place seasonally, producing sporadic sites such as Niño (see Bailey & Davidson 1983, Davidson 1983).

This pattern continued through the following five millenniums, but the frequency of visits to the shore began to decline and eventually almost ceased, despite the fact that this was a period in which the shore was itself moving closer to the caves as a result of eustatic rise in sea-level. The apparent reduction of numbers of sites which were used corresponds to the period of reduction in size of the site catchments, and to the intensification of use of the antlers of deer as raw material for the manufacture of increasingly important artefacts. Other changes in patterns of exploitation are also indicated, particularly at Volcán, where ibex became less abundant in the faunal remains.

After 15 000 years BP the evidence is more equivocal, and only Parpalló and Volcán were certainly occupied. There is no certain evidence of intensification or specialization, despite this reduction of known sites. There is some indication of an increasing abundance of deer at Parpalló (Davidson 1980, 1983).

Implicit in this interpretation is that Les Mallaetes was generally used in summer, but there is also evidence that Volcán, close to the present coast, was also used in summer (Eastham pers. comm.).

I have argued that the advantage in a hunting economy of using Les Mallaetes, close to the top of the mountain on which it is situated, was at best marginal to the prehistoric hunters, and that it is necessary to postulate that other sites were used during the same season, and that the group which may have aggregated (cf. Conkey 1980) at a site such as Parpalló, in cooler months, dispersed during the summer. The extent of this dispersion may be indicated by the changing relations with the shore, and would suggest that the years of maximum dispersion were before, (?during), and after the period of maximum cold. At this period seasonal variability of resource availability would have been reduced. These are conditions which might be expected to increase both the dispersion of human groups and seasonal and local mobility of individuals.

Freedom of information and restricting freedom

Some other recent work has emphasized the importance of the information contained in 'art' (Leroi-Gourhan 1965, 1981, Marshack 1972, Vinnicombe 1972a, 1976, Conkey 1980, 1983, 1985, Gamble 1980, 1982, 1983, 1986). And others have stressed increasing social complexity during the Upper Palaeolithic (White 1982).

I have suggested that there are grounds for treating 'art' on stone plaquettes as a separate category. The sites with abundance of this 'art' are rather few, although stone plaquettes as a support for the art must have been rather abundant. Detailed study of the site of Parpalló, where such 'art' occurs abundantly, suggests that we may consider the implications of the restriction of access to the information contained in the art.

If we treat the 'art' painted and/or engraved on plaquettes as a separate category of 'art', with its own special information content, then we must conclude, either that 'art' sites were aggregation sites (cf. Conkey 1980), or that information was not only imparted through the 'art' but also restricted, or both. The evidence from the study of the prehistoric economy suggests that it was both.

If it was otherwise, then we would expect a more random distribution of this 'art' in space and time. The few sites with abundant plaquette 'art' are far from random. Mostly the sites are widely spaced across western Europe. Some are evidently preferred sites themselves, which may have had key roles in the economic systems of regions which were themselves preferred regions during the Upper Palaeolithic. If we inspect this pattern of locations, then the sites must be interpreted as central to some level of territoriality. The question is: at what level of territoriality?

In recent suggestive though hardly conclusive studies, Wobst (1974, 1976) made a useful distinction between local family groups and larger maximum bands. Local family groups would normally be of 18–25 people who generally associated with each other. The larger maximum bands would be composed of about ten such family groups, which would normally need to maintain at least occasional contact for long-term breeding survival. I suggest that the successful maintenance of long-term relations and identity among such groups would require also the maintenance of a body of shared information. Moreover, restriction of access to information would ensure the identification of individual family groups with the maximum band, and increase the probability of contact between individual family groups on occasions when restricted information might be shared.

If you consider my interpretation of settlement patterns derived from a consideration of faunal exploitation, site exploitation territories, and site characteristics and distributions (Davidson 1983), I suggested that foraging for grasses and rapidly breeding animals was an activity of small groups which were seasonally dispersed. I suggest that there was some greater aggregation, and more complex logistical organization in winter. The pattern, of course, changed through time.

Dwyer & Minnegal (1985), recently revised Horn's model for the 'optimal' pattern of distribution for foragers in terms of resource patchiness. In fact, aggregation sites or preferred sites emerge as most profitable when resources are patchily distributed. Dispersal is optimum for exploiting fine-grained environments.

Optimal foraging models tend to consider only food resources, and the costs and benefits in terms of energy. It is, of course, true that other members of the foraging species are also resources necessary to the continued survival of that species, and the costs of access to these resources must often be measured in some currency other than energy. Thus, in a situation in which the foraging species is dispersed, because food resources are not patchy, the members of the species themselves are patchily distributed. The optimal situation for mating is therefore to aggregate. Human groups which dispersed seasonally for the exploitation of particular resources having a short period of availability might have needed some mechanism to ensure the aggregation of the group at other seasons. Is it possible that the few sites with abundant engraved and painted plaquettes played a key role in ensuring the aggregation of locally dispersed foraging groups?

Plaquette 'art' sites were clearly exceptional within a group of related sites, and activities at them clearly included both domestic and ritual. At such sites, regularly visited over long periods, and through 'cultural' changes, information and genes may have been shared. In this way the rights and rites of the territorial group would be reproduced.

Even supposing that the number of surviving sites with plaquette art is a small sample of the sites which originally existed, and even supposing that they were also not the only sites at which necessary but restricted information was shared, their number is very small, and could be taken to indicate a rather small number of maximum bands in Europe during the last Glacial period, and low population density.

If there were only nine such sites, at the core of nine maximum band territories, then we can make some calculations about population densities. If Spain and France have a combined area of just over 640 000 km^2, each maximum band territory would have an area of about 71 000 km^2 and each family group about 7100 km^2. If the family group size was between 18 and 25 then each individual would hypothetically have exclusive access to 284–395 km^2, a radius of 9.5–11 km, or a population density of 0.0025–0.0035 people per square kilometre. Figures for recent fisher–gatherer–hunter (FGH) population densities suggest that this estimate is very low. Wobst's (1974, 1976) estimate was 0.05 per square kilometre.

I would suggest that local densities probably varied considerably, with areas like the *mesetas* of Spain effectively unoccupied through much of the period of the Upper Palaeolithic, and with low densities or rare visits in the north of France and Germany, as Gamble (1983) has shown. Halving the available area in this way would double the population density. Supposing that one in every ten such core sites has been identified would further increase the population density to 0.05–0.07 people per square kilometre, still low in comparison with modern fisher–gatherer–hunters. Clearly, many assumptions are implied in this estimate, but it may represent a satisfactory order of magnitude.

The conclusions of Bahn (1982) and Jochim (1983) can be cast in a similar light. Bahn (1982), studying the evidence from the French Pyrenees, suggested that there were 'super sites' of which Isturitz was one and Mas d'Azil was another, corresponding to the foci in the western and central Pyrenees respectively. The movement of materials and the common presence of characteristic 'art' objects (cf. Sieveking 1976) suggested occasional contacts between these sites, or centres, and Périgord.

Jochim (1983), by analysing the spatial distribution of caves with art, of the four different styles identified by Leroi-Gourhan, showed that there was a remarkably resilient pattern which could be interpreted as indicating four separate interaction networks. These had their centres in the Cantabrian region, in the western Pyrenees, in the central Pyrenees, and in the Périgord heartland. We could add to this analysis that they might correspond with Conkey's Altamira, and my suggestion for Isturitz, Enlène, and the combined centre of Limeuil and Badegoule. Eastern Spain would not emerge as a centre from such an analysis because of the paucity of cave 'art' sites in this region. There is some suggestion in Jochim's analysis of a northward expansion in the latest phase of the 'art', the Late Magdalenian. This tendency is also indicated by the expansion to the north represented by the plaquette sites of La Marche and Gönnersdorf, and the proliferation of plaquette sites of this period in the Pyrenees.

If we choose to take these few central tendencies as indications of the general location of centres of association of groups of people, then we are also left with rather few of what might be called territories in western Europe during the Upper Palaeolithic. Moreover, my argument suggests that these territories were the domain of social hierarchies which retained their control over these centres of association.

Dennell (1983, pp. 92–7) suggested that improved communication was an important part of the increasingly complex conceptualization which contributed to the economic success of European Upper Palaeolithic technology. Gamble (1983), indeed, emphasized that the need for an efficient means of encoding information was greatest in the harsher environments of northern latitudes. We may argue that, by restricting access to information, a hierarchy controlled the economy and potential for survival of the groups concerned. I would suggest that, whatever the productivity of the economic system, this control was part of the reason why there seems to have been little economic change within the Upper Palaeolithic in some regions (e.g. eastern Spain, see Davidson 1983), through the failure to convert productivity into production. Gilman (1984, p. 123) argues that increased 'production security [?productivity?] . . . made social cooperation more unstable' so that social solidarity needed to be reinforced through ritual expressed in the 'art'. My suggestion that information related to the relationship with nature, expressed in the 'art', might be restricted suggests that the link between production and social control was even more tightly maintained.

The different aspects of the interpretation of the information content of Palaeolithic 'art' each offer slightly different aspects of the relations between people and ideas. One suggests the community of ideas held in common by the whole society (Gamble 1982), another that ideas may have been differentially distributed within a wide group, but that there was a common sharing of ideas when the group aggregated (Conkey 1980). The third aspect, offered here, is that ideas may have been available only in conditions of restricted access. These three aspects should be seen as complementary parts of a single information system.

Acknowledgements

A version of this chapter was originally presented at the Theoretical Archaeology Group Conference in Southampton in 1980, and in the ensuing period I have had the privilege to discuss it with a large number of distinguished scholars. These include J. Clegg, J. Clottes, R. Dennell, A. Eastham, M. Eastham, J. Estévez, C. Gamble, R. Layton, M. Lorblanchet, H. Morphy, M. Morwood, A. Rosenfeld, V. Villaverde, P. Vinnicombe and, especially, P. Ucko. They have been responsible for helping me to remove infelicities which are not here, and for giving me some confidence that the ideas were worth publishing, but any remaining errors or stupidities are still mine.

Note

1 I use the word plaquette as a direct transcription of the word used in Spain and France. Bégouën et al. (1982, p. 15) define this as a 'mobile object on a lithic support, even when it is a piece of limestone or a pebble which is not necessarily flat'.

References

Aparicio, J. 1981. Nueva pieza de arte mobiliar Parpallense. *Archivo de Prehistoria Levantina* **16**, 39–58.

Bahn, P. G. 1982. Inter-site and inter-regional links during the Upper Palaeolithic. The Pyrenean evidence. *Oxford Journal of Archaeology* **1**(3), 247–68.

Bahn, P. G. 1983. *Pyrenean prehistory.* Warminster: Aris & Phillips.

Bahn, P. G. 1986. No sex, please, we're Aurignacians. *Rock Art Research* **3** (2), 99–120.

Bailey, G. N. & I. Davidson 1983. Site exploitation territories and topography: two case studies from Palaeolithic Spain. *Journal of Archaeological Science* **10**(2), 87–115.

Bégouën, H. 1938. Les plaquettes de pierre gravés de la Grotte de Labastide (Hautes-Pyrénées). *IPEK. Jahrbuch für Prähistorische un Ethnmographische Kunst* **13**, 1–10.

Bégouën, R. & J. Clottes 1981. Nouvelles fouilles dans la Salle des Morts de la Caverne d'Enlène à Montesquieu-Avantès (Ariège). *Congrès Préhistorique de France* **21**, 33–70.

Bégouën, R., J. Clottes, J.-P. Giraud & F. Rouzand 1982. Plaquette gravée d'Enlène, Montesquieu-Avantès (Ariège). *Bulletin de la Société Préhistorique Française* **79**, Comptes Rendus des Séances Mensuelles, (4), 103–9.

Bégouën, R., J. Clottes, J.-P. Giraud & F. Rouzand 1984. Compléments à la grande plaquette gravée d'Enlène. *Bulletin de la Société Préhistorique Française* **81**, Comptes Rendus des Séances Mensuelles, (5), 1–7.

Binford, L. R. 1978. Dimensional analysis of behavior and site structure: learning from an Eskimo hunting stand. *American Antiquity* **43** (3), 330–61.

Bofinger, E. & I. Davidson 1977. Radiocarbon age and depth: a statistical treatment of two sequences of dates from Spain. *Journal of Archaeological Science* **4**, 231–43.

Bosinski, G. 1973. Le site magdalénien de Gönnersdorf (Commune de Nuewied, vallée de Rhin moyen, R. F. A.). *Bulletin de la Société Préhistorique de l'Ariège* **28**, 25–48.

Bosinski, G. & G. Fischer 1974. Die Menschdarstellungen von Gönnersdorf der Ausgrabung von 1968. Wiesbaden: Franz Steiner.

Capitan, L. & J. Bouyssonie 1924. *Limeuil. Son gisement à gravures sur pierres de l'age du renne.* Paris: Librairies Emil Nourry.

Casteret, N. 1939. *Ten years under the Earth.* Harmondsworth: Penguin Books.

Cheynier, A. 1949. Badegoule. Station solutréenne et proto-magdalénienne. *Archives de l'Institut de Paléontologie Humaine* **23**.

Conkey, M. W. 1980. The identification of prehistoric hunter-gatherer aggregation sites: the case of Altamira. *Current Anthropology* **21** (5), 609–30.

Conkey, M. W. 1983. On the origins of Paleolithic art: a review and some critical thoughts. *The Mousterian legacy*, E. Trinkaus (ed.), 201–27. Oxford: BAR International Series 164.

Conkey, M. W. 1985. Ritual communication, social elaboration, and the variable trajectories of Paleolithic material culture. In *Prehistoric hunter–gatherers. The emergence of cultural complexity*. T. D. Price & J. A. Brown (eds), 299–323. Orlando: Academic Press.

Dams, L. & M. Dams 1978. Les plaquettes gravées de Fontalès (Tarn-et-Garonne) conservées au Musée de Saint-Antonin-Noble-Val. *Bulletin de la Société Préhistorique de l'Ariège* **33**, 77–89.

Davidson, D. S. 1937. *A preliminary consideration of Aboriginal Australian decorative art.* Philadelphia: American Philosophical Society.

Davidson, I. 1976. Les Mallaetes and Mondúver: the economy of a human group in prehistoric Spain. In *Problems in economic and social archaeology*, G. de G. Sieveking, I. K. Longworth & K. E. Wilson (eds), 483–99. London: Duckworth.

Davidson, I. 1980. *Late Pleistocene economy in eastern Spain.* Unpublished PhD thesis, University of Cambridge.

Davidson, I. 1983. Site variability and prehistoric economy in Levante. In *Hunter–gatherer economy in prehistory. A European perspective*, G. N. Bailey (ed.), 79–95. Cambridge: Cambridge University Press.

Davidson, I. 1986. The geographical study of late Palaeolithic stages in eastern Spain. In *Stone Age prehistory*, G. N. Bailey & P. Callow (eds), 95–118. Cambridge: Cambridge University Press.

Delluc, B. & G. Delluc 1978. Les manifestations graphiques Aurignaciennes sur support rocheux des environs des Eyzies (Dordogne). *Gallia Préhistoire* **21** (1), 213–438.

Delluc, B. & G. Delluc 1981. Les plus anciens dessins de l'homme. *La Recherche* **118** (12), 14–22.

Dennell, R. W. 1983. *European economic prehistory.* London: Academic Press.

Dominguez, A. 1972. Notas para un estudio sobre la fauna representada en las placas de piedra del paleolítico superior español. *Estudios (Zaragoza)* **1**, 37–47.

Dwyer, P. & M. Minnegal 1985. Andaman islanders, pygmies, and an extension of Horn's model. *Human Ecology* **13** (1), 111–19.

Estévez, J. 1981. Paleoeconomía y arte prehistórico. In *Altamira Symposium*, P. Lopez & C. Cacho (eds), 197–204. Madrid: Ministerio de Cultura.

Fletcher, D. 1956. Problèmes et progrès du Paléolithique et du Mésolithique de la région de Valencia (Espagne). *Quärtär* **7–8**, 66–90.

Fortea, J. 1973. *Los complejos microlaminares y geométricos del Epipaleolítico Mediterraneo español.* Facultad de Filosofia y Letras, Universidad de Salamanca.

Fortea, J. 1978. Arte paleolítico del Mediterraneo español. *Trabajos de Prehistoria* **35**, 99–149.

Fortea, J. 1981. Investigaciones en la cuenca media del Nalón, Asturias (España). Noticia y primeros resultados. *Zephyrus* **32–3**, 5–16.

Fortea, J. & F. Jordá 1976. La cueve de Les Mallaetes y los problemas del Paleolítico Superior del Mediterraneo español. *Zephyrus* **26–7**, 129–66.

Fullola, J. M. 1979. *Las industrias líticas del Paleolítico Superior ibarico*. Valencia: Trabajos Varios del Servicio de Investigacíon Prehistórica.

Gamble, C. S. 1980. Information exchange in the Palaeolithic. *Nature* **283**, 522–3.

Gamble, C. S. 1982. Interaction and alliance in Palaeolithic society. *Man* **17**, 92–107.

Gamble, C. S. 1983. Culture and society in the Upper Palaeolithic of Europe. In *Hunter–gatherer economy in prehistory. A European perspective*, G. N. Bailey (ed.), 201–11. Cambridge: Cambridge University Press.

Gamble, C. S. 1986. *The Palaeolithic settlement of Europe*. Cambridge: Cambridge University Press.

Gilman, A. 1984. Explaining the Upper Palaeolithic revolution. In *Marxist perspectives in archaeology*, M. Spriggs (ed.), 115–26. Cambridge: Cambridge University Press.

Hadingham, E. 1979. *Secrets of the Ice Age. The world of the cave artists*. London: Heinemann.

Hamlyn-Harris, R. 1918. On messages and message sticks employed among the Queensland Aborigines. *Memoirs of the Queensland Museum* **5**, 1–22.

Howitt, A. W. 1889. Notes on Australian message sticks and messengers. *Journal of the Royal Anthropological Institute* **18**, 314–32.

Jochim, M. A. 1983. Palaeolithic cave art in ecological perspective. In *Hunter–gatherer economy in prehistory: a European perspective*, G. N. Bailey (ed.), 212–19. Cambridge: Cambridge University Press.

Layton, R. 1985. The cultural context of hunter–gatherer rock art. *Man* **20** (3), 434–53.

Leroi-Gourhan, A. 1965. Préhistoire de l'art occidental. Paris: Mazenod.

Leroi-Gourhan, A. 1981. Les signes parietaux comme marqueurs ethniques. *Altamira Symposium*, P. Lopez & C. Cacho (eds), 289–94. Madrid: Ministerio de Cultura.

Lewis-Williams, J. D. & J. H. N. Loubser 1986. Deceptive appearances: a critique of southern African rock art studies. *Advances in World Archaeology* **5**, 253–89.

Macintosh, N. W. G. 1977. Beswick Creek cave two decades later: a reappraisal. In *Form in indigenous art: schematisation in the art of Aboriginal Australia and Prehistoric Europe*, pp. 191–7. Canberra: Australian Institute of Aboriginal Studies.

Marshack, A. 1972. *The roots of civilization*. New York: McGraw-Hill.

Mathews, R. H. 1897. Message sticks used by the Aborigines of Australia. *American Anthropologist* **10**, 288–98.

Mathews, R. H. 1898. Message sticks. *Science of Man* **1** (6), 141–2.

Morphy, H. 1977. Schematisation, meaning and communication in toas. In *Form in indigenous art: schematisation in the art of Aboriginal Australia and prehistoric Europe*, P. J. Ucko (ed.), 77–89. Canberra: Australian Institute of Aboriginal Studies.

Morphy, H. 1980. What circles look like. *Canberra Anthropology* **3** (1), 17–36.

Moure, J. A. 1982. *Placas grabadas de la cueva de Tito Bustillo*. Departmento de Prehistoria y Arqueologia, Universidad de Valladolid.

Moure Romanillo, J. A. 1985. Nouveautés dans l'art mobilier figuratif du Paléolithique cantabrique. *Bulletin de la Société Préhistorique de l'Ariège* **40**, 99–129.

Olaria, C., F. Gusi, J. Estévcz, J. Casbo & M. L. Rovira 1981. El yacimiento magdaleniense superior de Cova Matutano (Villafamés, Castellón). Estudio del sondeo estratigráfico. 1979. *Cuadernos de Prehistoria y Arqueología Castellonenses* **8**, 21–100.

Omnès, J. 1982. La grotte ornée de Labastide (Hautes-Pyrénées). Lourdes: J. Omnès.

Omnès, J. 1983. The Magdalenian sanctuary of the cave of Labastide (Hautes-Pyrénées, France). *Oxford Journal of Archaeology* **2** (3), 253–63.

Pajot, B. & A. Plenier 1976. Quelques gravures Magdaléniennes enédites de l'abri Fontalès (St-Antonin-Noble-Val, Tarn-et-Garonne). *Bulletin de la Société Préhistorique de l'Ariège* **31**, 21–9.

Pales, L. 1976. *Les gravures de la Marche. II. Les Humains*. Bordeaux: L'Institut de Préhistoire de Bordeaux.

Pales, L. & M. Tassin de Saint-Péreuse 1969. *Les gravures de la Marche. I. Félins et Ours* Bordeaux: L'Institut de Préhistoire de Bordeaux.

Pales, L. & M. Tassin de Saint-Péreuse 1981. *Les gravures de la Marche. III. Equidés et Bovidés*. Paris: Ophrys.

Pericot, L. 1942. *La cueva del Parpalló*. Madrid: CSIC.

Pericot, L. 1968. La vida económica de España durante el Paleolítico Superior. In *Estudios de economía antigua de la Peninsula Ibérica*, M. Tarradell (ed.), 19–31. Barcelona: Editorial Vicens-Vives.

Rosenfeld, A. 1977. Profile figures: schematisation of the human figure in the Magdalenian culture of Europe. In *Form in indigenous art: schematisation in the art of Aboriginal Australia and prehistoric Europe*, P. J. Ucko (ed.), 90–109. Canberra: Australian Institute of Aboriginal Studies.

Roth, W. E. 1906. Notes on government morals and crime. *North Queensland Ethnography Bulletin* **8**.

Saint-Périer, R. de 1930. La grotte d'Isturitz. I. Le Magdalénien de la salle de Saint-Martin. *Archives de l'Institut de Paléontologie Humaine* **7**.

Saint-Périer, R. de 1936. La grotte d'Isturitz. II. Le Magdalénien de la grande salle. *Archives de l'Institut de Paléontologie Humaine* **17**.

Saint-Périer, R. de & S. de Saint-Périer 1950. La grotte d'Isturitz. III. Les Solutréens, les Aurignaciens et les Moustériens. *Archives de l'Institut de Paléontologie Humaine* **25**.

Schwarcz, H. P. & I. Skoflek 1982. New dates for the Tata, Hungary archaeological site. *Nature* **295**, 590–1.

Sieveking, A. 1976. Settlement patterns of the later Magdalenian in the central Pyrenees. In *Problems in economic and social archaeology*, G. de G. Sieveking, I. H. Longworth & K. E. Wilson (eds), 583–603. London: Duckworth.

Vinnicombe, P. 1972a. Motivation in African rock art. *Antiquity* **46**, 124–33.

Vinnicombe, P. 1972b. Myth, motive and selection in southern African rock art. *Africa* **42**, 192–204.

Vinnicombe, P. 1976. *People of the Eland*. Pietermaritzburg: University of Natal Press.

Watson, P. L. 1983. *This precious foliage: a study of the Aboriginal psycho-active drug pituri*. Sydney: Oceania Publications.

Welté, A.-C. 1985. Approche technique de trois profils d'équidés de l'Abri de Fontalès (Tarn-et-Garonne). *Bulletin de la Société Préhistorique de l'Ariège* **40**, 195–210.

White, R. 1982. Rethinking the Middle/Upper Palaeolithic transition. *Current Anthropology* **23** (2), 169–92.

Wobst, H. M. 1974. Boundary conditions for Palaeolithic social systems: a simulation approach. *American Antiquity* **39**, 147–78.

Wobst, H. M. 1976. Locational relationships in Palaeolithic society. *Journal of Human Evolution* **5**, 49–58.

Index

Note that references to figures are printed in italic type.